Dictionary of British Portraiture

IN FOUR VOLUMES

EDITED BY RICHARD ORMOND AND MALCOLM ROGERS

WITH A FOREWORD BY JOHN HAYES
DIRECTOR OF THE NATIONAL PORTRAIT GALLERY

VOLUME

1

The Middle Ages to the Early Georgians · Historical figures born before 1700

COMPILED BY DR ADRIANA DAVIES

B.T.BATSFORD LIMITED · *LONDON*
IN ASSOCIATION WITH
THE NATIONAL PORTRAIT GALLERY · *LONDON*

© National Portrait Gallery 1979
ISBN 07134 1468 5

Filmset in 'Monophoto' Bembo by
Servis Filmsetting Ltd, Manchester
Printed in Great Britain by
The Anchor Press Ltd,
Tiptree, Essex
for the publishers
B.T. Batsford Ltd,
4 Fitzhardinge Street
London W1H 0AH

DICTIONARY OF
BRITISH PORTRAITURE

Volume 1

Foreword

This four-volume *Dictionary of British Portraiture*, of which the first two volumes are now published, was the idea of Sam Carr, Director of Batsford. He was correct in his view that there exists no comprehensive handbook to the portraits of famous British men and women. Specialized surveys and studies there are, but no compact work to which the researcher or layman can turn easily for information about the likeness of this or that individual. The present dictionary cannot claim to be a complete or exhaustive study; inevitably there has to be a degree of selection in the people represented, and the portraits that have been listed. This is explained in the introduction. But within these limitations it does offer a reliable guide to the portraiture of a wide range of eminent British men and women from the Medieval period to the present day.

The dictionary relates directly to the purposes for which the National Portrait Gallery was founded in 1856: the collection, preservation and study of historical portraits. It has been compiled mainly from the Gallery's own immense archive, and I am delighted that its resources should be made available in this way. The information in the archive has been gathered slowly over the course of the last century or so by many devoted scholars and members of staff, and I think it is only right that I should first record our debt to them. Without their labours such a dictionary could never have been compiled. I would also like to pay a special tribute to the staff of the Guthrie Room, who maintain the archive, add to its holdings, and answer so many questions so patiently and efficiently. The work of editorial supervision has been handled most competently by my colleagues, Richard Ormond and Malcolm Rogers, who originally discussed the project with Sam Carr, and have now guided the first two volumes through the press. To Sam Carr himself we are grateful for his continuing enthusiasm and support, without which the project would never have materialised. Mrs Underwood undertook the task of typing the entries with her usual thoroughness and accuracy. Finally, I must thank our two hard-working and dedicated compilers, who took on the daunting job of recording and researching the thousands of portraits listed here. It is a tribute both to their enthusiasm and to their composure in the face of sometimes inadequate, sometimes confusing records, that the work has been completed so expeditiously. We are deeply grateful to them for the skill and accuracy with which they have carried out their task.

JOHN HAYES

Introduction

The aim of the present dictionary is to provide a listing of the portraits of famous figures in British history that are either in galleries and institutions, or in collections accessible to the public. It is intended for the general researcher and student who needs a reliable guide to portraits on public view of which illustrations can be obtained relatively easily. It is not concerned with the intricacies of iconography, though decisions have had to be taken about the likely authenticity of particular images, nor is it comprehensive. The decision to exclude portraits in private collections was dictated by the need to limit the scope of the work, by the difficulty of obtaining permission from owners to use their names, and by the impossibility of directing readers to the specific location of privately-owned works. In a few entries it has been indicated that a privately-owned portrait is the only known likeness, or the most significant likeness, of a particular person.

The series of detailed National Portrait Gallery catalogues have provided invaluable information for those sitters included in them. They are as follows:

Roy Strong *Tudor and Jacobean Portraits* (2 vols), 1969
David Piper *Seventeenth Century Portraits*, 1963
John Kerslake *Early Georgian Portraits* (2 vols), 1977
Richard Ormond *Early Victorian Portraits* (2 vols), 1973
Richard Walker *Regency Portraits*, forthcoming

Extensive use has also been made of Freeman O'Donoghue and Henry Hake, *Catalogue of Engraved British Portraits . . . in the British Museum* (6 vols), 1908–25.

Each volume of this dictionary covers a different historical period. Though there were arguments in favour of dividing the dictionary alphabetically, it was decided on balance that it would be more useful to make each volume self-contained. The chronological dividing-lines are inevitably arbitrary, and will mean that certain figures, whose contemporaries appear in one volume, are by accident of birth in another. But provided that the reader knows the birth date of his or her chosen subject, there should be no problem in turning to the correct volume.

The question of selection was a thorny one. We have relied heavily, though not exclusively, on the *Dictionary of National Biography*. A number of minor figures listed there are omitted in this work, and others who are excluded, but whom we felt to be important, appear in this dictionary. Readers will no doubt be disappointed by some omissions, but it is important to remember that the non-appearance of a particular figure may simply reflect the fact that no authentic portrait of him or her is known.

This is especially true of the earlier periods from which so few portraits survive.

The entries themselves are cast in a condensed form, but we hope they will be comprehensible once the format has been mastered.

The arrangement of the entries is as follows:

Surname of the sitter, with Christian names (peers are listed under their titles)
Birth and death dates, where known
Profession or occupation
Known portraits, recorded under:

P	Paintings	SC	Sculpture
D	Drawings	T	Tapestry
M	Miniatures	W	Stained-glass windows
MS	Manuscripts	PR	Prints
SL	Silhouettes	C	Caricatures
G	Groups	PH	Photographs

Within each category portraits are listed chronologically, and then alphabetically by name of artist where known.

Information on individual portraits is arranged as follows:

name of artist
date of portrait where known
size (ie half length, whole length, etc)
other distinguishing features (with Garter, in a landscape, etc)
medium, in the case of drawings, groups, prints and caricatures
location, with accession number in the case of national galleries and museums

For further details see abbreviations opposite.

The absence of illustrations will be a cause of complaint. But the only possible solution would have been to illustrate everything (a selection would have satisfied few), and that would have made the series prohibitively large and expensive. In any case the dictionary has been conceived as a reference work and not a picture book, and it is as such that it must stand or fall.

RICHARD ORMOND

MALCOLM ROGERS

Abbreviations

A

ABBOT, George (1562-1633) archbishop of Canterbury.
P Attrib ROWLAND LOCKEY, after 1609, tql, University College, Cambridge. UNKNOWN, 1623, tql in robes, Abbot's Hospital, Guildford; copy, NPG 2160. UNKNOWN, c1623, Fulham Palace, London.
SC CHRISTMAS BROTHERS, 1635, tomb effigy, Holy Trinity, Guildford.
PR S.PASSE, 1616, hl in cap, line, NPG.

ABBOT, Robert (1560-1617) bishop of Salisbury.
PR W. and M.VAN DE PASSE, 1622, hl with book, line, for *Herwologia*, BM. F.DELARAM, c1618, hl with book, line, BM, NPG.

ABELL, William (fl 1640) alderman of London.
PR W.HOLLAR, hl with barrel, etch, BM. UNKNOWN, hl, oval, with another of R.Kilvert, facsimile of *The Copie of a Letter sent from the Roaring Boyes in Elizium*, 1641, BM, NPG. UNKNOWN, hl with Kilvert, woodcut, NPG.

ABERCORN, James Hamilton, 6th Earl of (1656-1734) privy councillor.
PR HARDING, hl in peer's robes, stipple, for Adolphus, *British Cabinet*, 1800, BM, NPG.

ABERDEEN, George Gordon, 1st Earl of (1637-1720) statesman.
P UNKNOWN, hl, oval, Haddo House, Grampian region, Scotland.

ABERGAVENNY, George Nevill(e), 3rd or 5th Baron (1461?-1535?) warden of the Cinque ports.
D HANS HOLBEIN, jun, hs, chalks, Wilton House, Wilts.
M H.HOLBEIN, after 1534, hs, oval, w/c, Buccleuch Estates, Selkirk, Scotland.

ABNEY, Sir Thomas (1640-1722) lord mayor of London.
P UNKNOWN, hl as young man, Bank of England, London. UNKNOWN, hs with chain of office, Bank of England.

ACONTIUS, Jacobus (1500?-1566?) philosopher and engineer.
PR UNKNOWN, hl in skull-cap, line, BM.

ADAM, William (1688-1748) architect and father of Robert and John.
SC Attrib L.F.ROUBILIAC, marble bust, SNPG 1033.

ADAMSON, Patrick (1537-1592) Scottish prelate.
P UNKNOWN, 1569, hs, SNPG 757.

ADDISON, Joseph (1672-1719) essayist, poet and statesman.
P SIR GODFREY KNELLER, c1710, hl, 'Kit-cat Club' portrait, NPG 3193; version, hl, Bodleian Library, Oxford. CHARLES JERVAS, 1714, tql, Knole (NT), Kent. SIR G.KNELLER, 1716, tql, Yale University Library, New Haven, USA. MICHAEL DAHL, 1719, hl, NPG 714. JONATHAN RICHARDSON, hl, Althorp, Northants.

ADDISON, Lancelot (1632-1703) divine.
PR UNKNOWN, wl, line, NPG.

ADDY, William (fl 1685) author of a system of shorthand.
PR J.STURT, after Barker, 1695, hs, oval, line, NPG. J.STURT, after Barker, hs, oval, line, NPG.

AELFGIFU, Queen, see Emma.

AETHELBERT, see Ethelbert.

AETHELRED, see Ethelred.

AETHELSTAN, see Ethelstan.

AIRLIE, James Ogilvy, 1st Earl of (1586-1664) royalist.
P UNKNOWN, hl in armour, Airlie Castle, Tayside region, Scotland.

AIRLIE, James Ogilvy, 2nd Earl of (1615?-1703?) royalist.
P Attrib WILLIAM DOBSON, hl in armour, Airlie Castle, Tayside region, Scotland.

AIKMAN, William (1682-1731) portrait painter.
P Self-portrait, hs, SNPG 309; version, Penicuik House, Lothian region, Scotland. Self-portrait, c1710, hl in turban, Uffizi, Florence, engr P.A.Pazzi, line, BM.

AILESBURY, Robert Bruce, 2nd Earl of Elgin and 1st Earl of (d1685) lord chamberlain.
P Attrib SIR PETER LELY, wl in robes, Deene Park, Northants.
PR W.FAITHORNE, hl, line, BM. R.WHITE, after Sir P.Lely, tql in peer's robes, line, BM, NPG.

AILESBURY, Sir Thomas (1576-1657) patron of mathematical learning.
P UNKNOWN, c1650, tql, Clarendon Coll on loan to Plymouth Art Gallery.

AILESBURY, Thomas Bruce, 3rd Earl of Elgin and 2nd Earl of (1655-1741) Jacobite.
PR F.HARREWIJN, tql seated in peer's robes, line, BM, NPG.

AILESBURY, William (1615-1656) translator.
P UNKNOWN, c1649-50, hl, Clarendon Coll on loan to Plymouth Art Gallery.

AIRAY, Henry (1560?-1616) puritan divine.
P UNKNOWN, tql, Queen's College, Oxford.
SC UNKNOWN, 1616, brass effigy, Queen's College Chapel, line engr, BM, NPG.

ALABASTER, William (1567-1640) Latin poet and divine.
PR J.PAYNE, after Cornelius Johnson, hs, line, BM.

ALASCO, John, see LASKI.

ALBANY, John Stewart, Duke of (1481-1536) regent of Scotland.
D Studio of JEAN CLOUET, jun, c1525, hs, black pencil, Chantilly Museum, France.

ALBEMARLE, Arnold Joost van Keppel, 1st Earl of (1669-1718) courtier and general.
P SIR GODFREY KNELLER, c1700, hs in armour, NPG 1625. SIR G.KNELLER, 1702, tql, Chatsworth, Derbys. By or after SIR G.KNELLER, tql in armour, Woburn Abbey, Beds, engr J.Smith, mezz, BM.

ALBEMARLE, Christopher Monck, 2nd Duke of (1653-1688) soldier and governor of Jamaica.
P By or after THOMAS MURRAY, c1682, hl in breastplate, Old Schools, Cambridge.
SC GEORGE BOWER, silver medal, BM.
PR I.BECKETT, after T.Murray, hl in breastplate, oval, mezz, BM, NPG.

ALBEMARLE, George Monck, 1st Duke of (1608-1670)

soldier and statesman.

P SIR PETER LELY, c1660, wl in armour with Garter George, Chatsworth, Derbys. SIR P.LELY, c1665–66, tql, NMM, Greenwich; version, NPG 423. Studio of SIR P.LELY, wl in Garter robes, SNPG 900. J.M.WRIGHT, 1668, tql in armour with Garter insignia, Longleat, Wilts. UNKNOWN, wl in Garter robes, Guildhall, Exeter.

M SAMUEL COOPER, c1660, hs in armour, oval, w/c, Buccleuch Estates, Selkirk, Scotland; unfinished version, Royal Coll.

SC THOMAS SIMON, 1660, electrotype of medal, BM.

PR R.GAYWOOD, hl in private dress, etch, BM, NPG. R.GAYWOOD, after F.Barlow, hl when General Monck, etch, BM, NPG. D.LOGGAN, 1661, hl in armour, ad vivum, BM, NPG 833.

ALCOCK, John (1430–1500) Bishop of Rochester, Worcester and Ely.

P UNKNOWN, wl kneeling in robes, Jesus College, Cambridge.

ALCUIN, or Albinus or Ealwhine or Eadwine (735–804) theologian, man of letters, and educational reformer.

MS UNKNOWN, 12th cent, wl seated with book, the Eadwine Psalter, Trinity College, Cambridge.

ALDRICH, Henry (1647–1710) divine and scholar.

P SIR GODFREY KNELLER, hl, Christ Church, Oxford, engr John Smith, 1696, mezz, BM, NPG. UNKNOWN, hl as young man, Christ Church.

SC UNKNOWN, three marble busts, different types, Christ Church.

ALEXANDER, William, see 1st Earl of Stirling.

ALEYN, Charles (d1640) poet.

PR UNKNOWN, after W.Marshall, line, for The Historie of the Wise and Fortunate Prince Henrie, 1638, NPG.

ALFRED (849–901) king of the West-Saxons.

SC UNKNOWN, c887, silver penny, NPG 4269 and BM.

ALLEN, John (1660?–1741) physician and inventor.

P THOMAS FRYE, 1739, tql seated, Royal College of Physicians, London.

ALLEN, Ralph (1694–1764) philanthropist.

P WILLIAM HOARE, c1715, tql with manuscript, Devon and County Hospital, Exeter. JOHN VAN DIEST, c1728, tql, Guildhall, Bath. THOMAS HUDSON, c1740–54, tql seated with letter, Hurd Episcopal Library, Hartlebury. ARTHUR POND, c1757, tql seated, Hurd Episcopal Library.

SC ISAAC GOSSET, sen, wax profile, Hurd Episcopal Library. PRINCE HOARE, c1757, marble bust, Royal National Hospital for Rheumatic Diseases. PRINCE HOARE, c1757, marble bust on pedestal, City of Bath.

PR W.HOARE, profile head, etch, 1764, BM, NPG.

ALLEN, Thomas (1542–1632) mathematician.

P UNKNOWN, 1633, hl, Trinity College, Oxford.

D UNKNOWN, hl, pastel, Bodleian Library, Oxford.

ALLEN, Thomas (1681–1755) divine.

PR UNKNOWN, wl seated, line, NPG.

ALLEN, William (1532–1594) cardinal.

PR E. DE BOULONOIS, hl, line, for Bullar Académie des Sciences et des Artes, 1682, BM, NPG. T.A.DEAN, after Moysten, hl, stipple, NPG.

ALLESTREE, Richard (1619–1681) royalist divine.

P UNKNOWN, hl, Eton College, Berks.

G SIR PETER LELY, tql seated with John Fell and John Dolben, oil, Christ Church, Oxford.

PR D.LOGGAN, hl, line, BM, NPG.

ALLEYN, Edward (1566–1626) actor and founder of Dulwich College.

P UNKNOWN, wl, Dulwich College Gallery, London.

ALLIN, Sir Thomas (1612–1685) naval commander.

P SIR PETER LELY, c1666, tql, NMM, Greenwich. SIR GODFREY KNELLER, c1680, hl in armour, NMM.

ALLIX, Peter (1641–1717) protestant preacher.

P JOSEPH FREEMAN, after unknown artist, Emmanuel College, Cambridge.

ALSOP, Vincent (d1703) nonconformist divine.

P UNKNOWN, hl, Dr Williams's Library, London.

AMBROSE, Isaac (1604–1663) puritan divine.

PR UNKNOWN, hl, line, for Works, 1674, BM, NPG.

AMES, Joseph (1689–1759) bibliographer and antiquary.

PR ROBERT LAURIE, tql seated, mezz, NPG. T.HODGETTS, after Laurie, mezz, for Typographical Antiquities, 1810, BM, NPG.

AMES, William (1576–1633) puritan divine.

PR W.MARSHALL, hl, line, for Fresh Suit Against Ceremonies, 1633, BM, NPG. UNKNOWN, hs, oval, line, BM, NPG.

AMHURST, Nicholas (1697–1742) poet and political writer.

PR J.SIMON, after Sir G.Kneller, tql, mezz, BM. UNKNOWN, hs, oval, line, for The Craftsman, vol VIII, 1737, BM, NPG.

ANCRAM or ANCRUM, Robert Ker, 1st Earl of (1578–1654) royalist.

P JAN LIEVENS, c1652, hs, SNPG L210.

ANDERSON, Sir Edmund (1530–1605) judge.

P UNKNOWN, c1590–1600, tql, NPG 2148; version, Inner Temple, London.

G UNKNOWN, 'Lord Burghley presiding over Court of Wards and Liveries', oil, Goodwood, W Sussex.

PR W.FAITHORNE, hs, line, for Reports, 1664, BM, NPG.

ANDREWES, Lancelot (1555–1626) bishop of Winchester.

P UNKNOWN, hs, Longleat, Wilts. UNKNOWN, hs, Bodleian Library, Oxford. UNKNOWN, tql, Jesus College, Oxford.

PR S.PASSE, 1618, hl with book, line, BM, NPG.

SC UNKNOWN, 1636, tomb effigy, Southwark Cathedral, London.

ANGLESEY, Arthur Annesley, 1st Earl of (1614–1686) lord privy seal.

P After J.M.WRIGHT, (type of 1676), tql seated in robes, NPG 3805; versions, hs, Emmanuel College, Cambridge; tql, Ashmolean Museum, Oxford.

ANGLESEY, Christopher Villiers, 1st Earl of (1593?–1630) courtier.

G UNKNOWN, 'The Family of the Duke of Buckingham', oil, 1628, Royal Coll.

ANNANDALE, William Johnston(e), 1st Marquess of (d1721) lord privy seal of Scotland.

P ANDREA PROCACCINI, c1718, wl seated with antiquities, Hopetoun House, Lothian region, Scotland.

PR JOHN SMITH, after Sir G.Kneller, 1703, hs in robes, oval, mezz and line, BM.

ANNE of Bohemia (1366–1394) first queen of Richard II.

MS UNKNOWN, c1382, Queen kneeling before Virgin in miniature Book of Hours, Bodleian Library, Oxford.

SC NICHOLAS BROKER and GODFREY PREST, c1395–97, gilt-bronze effigy, Westminster Abbey, London; electrotype, NPG 331. UNKNOWN, wooden funeral effigy, Westminster Abbey.

ANNE (1456–1485) queen of Richard III.

MS UNKNOWN, wl with Richard III, Salisbury Roll, Buccleuch Estates, Selkirk, Scotland. UNKNOWN, wl with small bear, Rous Roll, English version, BL Add Ms 48976 and Latin version, College of Arms.

PR GRIGNION, after Vertue, wl copy of Salisbury Roll figure, line, NPG.

ANNE Boleyn (1507-1536) second queen of Henry VIII.
P UNKNOWN, late 16th cent, hs with B-shaped jewel, NPG 668; versions, NPG 4980 (15), and Royal Coll.
PR R.ELSTRACKE, hs, for *Baziliwlogia*, 1618, BM.

ANNE of Cleves (1515-1557) fourth queen of Henry VIII.
P HANS HOLBEIN, jun, tql, Louvre, Paris; version, hs, oval, V & A. UNKNOWN, hl, Royal Coll.

ANNE (1665-1714) queen of Great Britain and Ireland.
P WILLIAM WISSING, 1685-6, wl with small dog, SNPG 939. JOHN RILEY, tql seated when princess, Althorp, Northants. SIR GODFREY KNELLER, 1689, wl when princess, Blenheim, Oxon. Attrib MICHAEL DAHL, c1690, wl with robes, NPG 1616. After SIR G.KNELLER, c1694, tql with Duke of Gloucester, NPG 325. Studio of JOHN CLOSTERMAN, c1702, tql with robes and crown, NPG 215. SIR G.KNELLER, c1702, wl crowned with sceptre, Inner Temple, London. E.LILLEY, 1703, wl with robes and sceptre, Blenheim. M.DAHL, c1712, wl in robes and crown, NMM, Greenwich.
M LAWRENCE CROSS, c1700, hs, oval, Royal Coll. C.BOIT, 1706, wl seated with George of Denmark, Royal Coll.
SC FRANCIS BIRD, 1712, statue, St Paul's Cathedral, London, modern replica. J.M.RYSBRACK, 1738, statue, Blenheim. JOHN CROKER, medal, BM.
PR I.BECKETT, after W.Wissing, tql seated with pearls, mezz, BM, NPG.

ANNE of Denmark (1574-1619) queen of James I.
P UNKNOWN, before 1603, hs, Embassy (DoE), Copenhagen. MARCUS GHEERAERTS, c1610-15, wl with fan, Woburn Abbey, Beds; version, 1614, tql, Royal Coll. Attrib WILLIAM LARKIN, c1612, hl in mourning, NPG 4656. PAUL VAN SOMER, c1617, wl, Royal Coll. After VAN SOMER, hl, NPG 127.
M ISAAC OLIVER, hs, w/c, NPG 4010; version, V & A.
SC WILLIAM CURE, c1614-15, statue, Trinity College, Cambridge.

ANNESLEY, Arthur, see 1st Earl of Anglesey.

ANNESLEY, Sir Francis, see 1st Baron Mountnorris.

ANNESLEY, Samuel (1620?-1696) puritan nonconformist.
P UNKNOWN, c1692, hl, Dr Williams's Library, London.
PR A.FOGG, hl, stipple, for Calamy, *Nonconformists' Memorial*, 1802, BM, NPG.

ANNET, Peter (1693-1769) deistical writer.
PR UNKNOWN, hs, line, for *Lectures*, 1768, BM, NPG.

ANSON, George Anson, 1st Baron (1697-1762) admiral.
P THOMAS HUDSON, c1747, tql in peer's robes, Shugborough (NT), Staffs. JAN WANDELAAR, 1751, tql in uniform, Goodwood, W Sussex. SIR JOSHUA REYNOLDS, tql in uniform, 1755, Shugborough.
SC T.PINGO, 1747, brass medal, BM. Attrib L.F.ROUBILIAC, marble bust, Shugborough. After JAMES TASSIE, plaster medallion, SNPG 503.

ANSTIS, John (1669-1744) Garter king of arms.
PR T.MILTON, after T.Maynard, hl in robes, line, pub 1803, NPG.

ANSTRUTHER, Sir William, Lord (d1711) Scottish judge.
PR JOHN SMITH, after Sir J.B.Medina, 1694, hl, oval, mezz, BM.

ANTHONY, John (1585-1655) physician.
PR T.CROSS, tql, line, for *Lucas Redivivus*, 1656, BM, NPG.

APSLEY, Sir Allen (1616-1683) royalist leader.
D T.ATHOW, (type of 1648), hl in armour, wash, Sutherland Coll, Ashmolean Museum, Oxford.

ARBUTHNOT, John (1667-1735) physician and wit.
P SIR GODFREY KNELLER, hl, University of Glasgow; version, Ickworth (NT), Suffolk. WILLIAM ROBINSON, hl, SNPG 92.

ARCHER, John (fl 1660-1684) physician.
PR UNKNOWN, hl, oval, etch, NPG.

ARGYLL, Archibald Campbell, 7th Earl of (1576?-1638) soldier and statesman.
P UNKNOWN, hs in armour, Drummond Castle, Tayside region, Scotland.

ARGYLL, Archibald Campbell, 8th Earl and 1st Marquess of (1607?-1661) soldier and statesman.
P L.SCHUNEMAN, c1632, wl, Buccleuch Estates, Selkirk, Scotland. DAVID SCOUGAL, c1650, hs, oval, SNPG 1408; version, NPG 3109.

ARGYLL, Archibald Campbell, 9th Earl of (1629-1685) royalist.
P UNKNOWN, c1660-70, tql seated with wife, NPG 3902. Attrib L.SCHUNEMAN, c1670, tql with staff, SNPG 1611. UNKNOWN, hl in armour, oval, Bowhill (Buccleuch Estates), Selkirk, Scotland.
M Attrib DAVID LOGGAN, c1680, hs, oil, SNPG 1197.

ARGYLL, Archibald Campbell, 1st Duke of (d1703) statesman.
P Attrib WILLIAM AIKMAN, hl, oval, Inveraray Castle, Strathclyde region, Scotland. MARY BEALE, hl, oval, Bowhill (Buccleuch Estates), Selkirk, Scotland. NICHOLAS MAES, hl, Inveraray Castle. N.MAES, hl in Roman armour, Inveraray Castle.
G SIR J.B.MEDINA, wl in Roman armour, with two sons, Inveraray.

ARGYLL, Archibald Campbell, 3rd Duke of (1682-1761) statesman.
P WILLIAM AIKMAN, c1715, wl in robes, as Earl of Ilay, Royal Coll. ALLAN RAMSAY, hl with wig, Inveraray Castle, Strathclyde region, Scotland, engr J.Faber, jun, 1749, mezz, BM, NPG. A.RAMSAY, wl seated in robes, City Art Gallery, Glasgow. Attrib A.RAMSAY, c1758, hs in robes, SNPG 908.
PR J.FABER, jun, after A.Ramsay, 1744, hl in wig, mezz, BM, NPG.

ARGYLL, John Campbell, Duke of Greenwich and 2nd Duke of (1680-1743) politician.
P J.B.CLOSTERMAN, 1704, tql in robes of Knight of Thistle, Melbourne Hall, Derbys. WILLIAM AIKMAN, c1720-5, hl with ribbon and star of Garter, NPG 737; version, wl, Royal Coll. THOMAS BARDWELL, 1740, tql with map, NPG 3110. ALLAN RAMSAY, 1740, wl in peer's robes, Inveraray Castle, Strathclyde region, Scotland.
SC L.F.ROUBILIAC, 1748, monument, Westminster Abbey, London; terracotta model, V & A.

ARLINGTON, Henry Bennet, 1st Earl of (1618-1685) member of Cabal ministry.
P Studio of SIR PETER LELY, c1665-70, tql seated, NPG 1853; version, Longleat, Wilts. Studio of LELY, 1676, wl in Garter robes, Christ Church, Oxford, engr, tql, line, for Guillim, *Heraldry*, 1679, BM, NPG.
G After G.NETSCHER, 'The Earl and Countess of Arlington with their daughter', tql seated in Garter robes, Euston Hall.

ARMIN, Robert (fl 1610) actor and dramatist.
PR UNKNOWN, wl in facsimile title page for *History of the two Maids of More-clake*, 1609, woodcut, for Harding, *Shakespeare Illustrated*, 1790, BM, NPG.

ARMINE or **Armyne, Mary, Lady (1589-1676)** philanthropist.
PR F.H. VAN HOVE, hs, oval, line, for S.Clarke, *Lives*, 1683, BM, NPG.

ARMINE or **Armyne, Sir William** (1593-1651) parliamentarian.
D UNKNOWN, hl in armour, wash, Sutherland Coll, Ashmolean Museum, Oxford.

ARMSTRONG, Archibald (*d*1672) jester to James I and Charles I.
PR T.CECILL, wl, line, for *Jests*, 1630, BM. R.GAYWOOD, wl, etch, for *Jests*, 1660, BM.

ARMSTRONG, John (1674?-1742) major-general and chief engineer of England.
PR J.McARDELL, hl in armour, oval, mezz, BM.

ARMSTRONG, Sir Thomas (1624?-1684) royalist.
PR UNKNOWN, hs, line, pub 1801, NPG.

ARMSTRONG, William (1602?-1658?) known as Christie's Will, border freebooter.
PR UNKNOWN, hl on horseback, line, NPG.

ARMYNE, see Armine.

ARRAN, James Hamilton, 3rd Earl of (1530-1609) suitor of Mary Queen of Scots.
PR P. VAN GUNST, after A. van der Werff, hs in armour, oval, line, for Larrey, *Hist d'Angleterre*, 1707, BM, NPG.

ARRAN, James Hamilton, Duke of Châtelherault and 2nd Earl of (*d*1575) governor of Scotland.
P Attrib ARNOLD VAN BROUNCKHORST, 1578, tql, SNPG L 1.

ARRAN, James Hamilton, 4th Earl of (1589-1625), see 2nd Marquess of Hamilton.

ARROWSMITH, Edmund (1585-1628) Jesuit.
PR UNKNOWN, hl with dagger in breast, line, NPG.

ARUNDEL, Henry Fitzalan, 12th Earl of (1511?-1580) soldier and courtier.
P Attrib JOHN BELKAMP, hl with Garter George, oval, Knole (NT), Kent. Attrib HANS EWORTH, 1581, wl in armour on horseback, Chatsworth, Derbys. Attrib STEVEN VAN DER MEULEN, *c*1570, hs with Garter George, NPG 4693. UNKNOWN, 1558, hl with Garter George, Longleat, Wilts.
G M.GHEERAERTS, sen, 'Procession of Garter Knights, 1576', etch, BM.

ARUNDEL, Henry Frederick Howard, 3rd Earl of (1608-1652) royalist.
P SIR ANTHONY VANDYCK, hl, Arundel Castle, W Sussex. SIR A.VANDYCK, tql in armour, Arundel Castle.

ARUNDEL, John Fitzalan, 7th Earl of (1408-1435) soldier.
SC UNKNOWN, tomb effigy, St Nicholas Church, Arundel, W Sussex.

ARUNDEL, Philip Howard, 1st Earl of (1557-1595) Roman Catholic courtier.
P UNKNOWN, hs as boy, oval, Arundel Castle, W Sussex. UNKNOWN, hs, aged 18, Arundel Castle. UNKNOWN, hs, oval, Arundel Castle.

ARUNDEL or **FITZALAN, Thomas** (1353-1414) son of Earl of Arundel and archbishop of Canterbury.
P LUCAS DE HEERE, tql with rose, Penshurst, Kent. UNKNOWN, hl oval, Lambeth Palace, London.
MS UNKNOWN, early 15th cent French, 'Archbishop Arundel preaching in cause of Henry', BL Harley Ms 1319, fol 12.

ARUNDEL and SURREY, Thomas Fitzalan, 5th Earl of (1381-1415) lord treasurer and warden of the Cinque ports.
SC UNKNOWN, alabaster tomb effigy, St Nicholas Church, Arundel, W Sussex.

ARUNDEL and SURREY, Thomas Howard, 2nd Earl of (1585-1646) art collector and patron.
P UNKNOWN, *c*1612, tql with Garter George, Buccleuch Estates, Selkirk, Scotland, engr S.Passe, as after 'M.Miereveldt', hl, aged 30, oval, line, BM. DANIEL MYTENS, *c*1618, wl seated, Arundel Castle, W.Sussex. D.MYTENS, *c*1618, hl with wife, Arundel Castle. SIR P.P.RUBENS, 1629, hs in armour, NPG 2391. SIR P.P.RUBENS, 1629, tql in armour, Isabella Stewart Gardner Museum, Boston, USA. SIR ANTHONY VANDYCK, *c*1635, tql in armour with grandson, later 6th Duke of Norfolk, Arundel Castle.
G SIR A.VANDYCK, the 'Madagascar Portrait', tql seated with wife, secretary and globe, oil *c*1639, Kunsthistorisches Museum, Vienna. After PHILIP FRUYTIERS, family group, (type of *c*1642), Arundel Castle.
PR W.HOLLAR, 1639, wl on horseback, etch, BM.

ARUNDELL, Blanche, née Somerset, Lady (1583-1649) defender of Wardour Castle.
PR G.NOBLE, after Sir P.Lely, hs, oval, line, for Seward, *Anecdotes*, 1795, BM, NPG. E.SCRIVEN, after Sir P.Lely, tql with book, stipple, for Lodge, *Portraits*, 1820, BM, NPG.

ARUNDELL of Wardour, Henry, 3rd Baron (1606?-1694) royalist.
PR R.COOPER, after miniature, hs, oval, line, NPG.

ARUNDELL of Wardour, Thomas, 1st Baron (1560-1639) soldier of fortune.
PR R.COOPER, after miniature, hs, oval, stipple, NPG.

ARUNDELL of Wardour, Thomas, 2nd Baron (1584-1643) royalist.
PR R.COOPER, after miniature, hs, oval, stipple, NPG.

ASHBURNHAM, John (1603-1671) royalist.
PR E.HARDING, hl in armour, stipple, for Harding, *Biographical Mirror*, 1799, BM, NPG. R.GRAVES, after Daniel Mytens, tql, line, BM, NPG.

ASHE, Simeon (*d*1662) nonconformist divine.
PR UNKNOWN, hs, line, NPG.

ASHLEY-COOPER, Anthony (1621-1683), see 1st Earl of Shaftesbury.

ASHLEY-COOPER, Anthony (1671-1713), see 3rd Earl of Shaftesbury.

ASHMOLE, Elias (1617-1692) antiquarian.
P JOHN RILEY, tql, 1683, Ashmolean Museum, Oxford. J.RILEY, 1689, hs, Ashmolean Museum; copy, NPG 1602.
PR W.FAITHORNE, hs, line, for *Theatrum Chemicum*, 1652, BM, NPG.

ASHTON, Charles (1665-1752) divine.
P Attrib R.PYLE, tql in robes, Jesus College, Cambridge, engr J.McARDELL, mezz, BM, NPG.

ASHTON, Hugh (*d*1522) archdeacon of York.
SC UNKNOWN, 1522, tomb effigy, St John's College Chapel, Cambridge.

ASHTON, John (*d*1691) Jacobite conspirator.
PR R.WHITE, after J.Riley, hl, line, BM, NPG.

ASTLEY, Sir Jacob Astley, Baron (1579-1652) royalist.
PR T.WORLIDGE, hl in cuirass, etch, pub 1757, BM, NPG.

ASTON, Sir Thomas (1600-1645) royalist.
G JOHN SOUCH of Chester, 'Sir Thomas Aston at the Deathbed of his Wife', oil, *c*1635, Manchester City Art Gallery.

ASTON of Forfar, Walter Aston, Baron (1584-1639) ambassador.
D T.ATHOW, hl, wash, Sutherland Coll, Ashmolean Museum,

Oxford.
PR R.COOPER, tql, stipple, for Lodge, *Portraits*, 1815, BM, NPG.

ATHELSTAN or **AETHELSTAN (895-940)** king of West-Saxons and Mercians.
MS UNKNOWN, hl with book, for Bede, *Life of St Cuthbert*, c930, Corpus Christi College, Cambridge.

ATHLONE, Frederick Christian Ginkel, 2nd Earl of (1668-1719) general.
P THEODOR NETSCHER, wl in armour, Castle Amerongen, The Netherlands. UNKNOWN, hl in armour, oval, Castle Amerongen.

ATHLONE, Godert de Ginkel, 1st Earl of (1644-1703) general.
P Attrib JAN DE BAEN, tql in armour as young man, Castle Amerongen, The Netherlands. SIR GODFREY KNELLER, 1692, tql in armour, NGI 486. JUIRIAAN OVENS, c1665, wl in armour, Castle Amerongen. UNKNOWN, tql in armour, Castle Amerongen. UNKNOWN, wl in armour with valet, Castle Amerongen.
PR J.HOUBRAKEN, after Countess of Athlone, hs in armour, oval, line, BM, NPG. P.SCHENK, 1703, hl in armour, oval, mezz, BM, NPG. R.WHITE, 1691, hl in armour, oval, line, BM, NPG.

ATHOLL, James Murray, 2nd Duke of (1690?-1764) lord privy seal.
P JEREMIAH DAVISON, c1738, hl with Thistle ribbon and star, oval, Blair Castle, Tayside region, Scotland (two types). ALLAN RAMSAY, 1743, hl, oval, SNPG 925.
SC JOHN CHEERE, 1748, gilded bust, Blair Castle.

ATHOLL, John Murray, 1st Marquess of (1635?-1703) royalist.
P L.SCHUNEMAN, tql in breastplate, Dunvegan Castle, Isle of Skye, Scotland. JACOB DE WITT, wl in classical dress, Blair Castle, Tayside region, Scotland.
PR R.COOPER, after Sir P.Lely, hs, stipple, NPG.

ATHOLL, John Murray, 1st Duke of (1659/60-1724) soldier and statesman.
P THOMAS MURRAY, 1705, wl, Blair Castle, Tayside region, Scotland. T.MURRAY, hs in Thistle robes, oval, Blair Castle.

ATKINSON, Paul (1656-1729) Franciscan friar.
PR R.GRAVE, hl, line, for Caulfield, *Remarkable Persons*, 1819, BM, NPG.

ATKYNS, Sir Edward (1587-1669) judge.
P J.M.WRIGHT, c1650-60, wl with robes, wrongly called Robert Atkyns, Lincoln's Inn, London.

ATKYNS, Richard (1615-1677) writer on typography.
PR W.SHERWIN, hs with cuirass, line, BM, NPG.

ATKYNS, Sir Robert (1647-1711) topographer.
PR UNKNOWN, hs, line, pub 1812, BM, NPG.

ATTERBURY, Francis (1662-1732) bishop of Rochester.
P SIR GODFREY KNELLER, hl, Christ Church, Oxford, engr G.Vertue, line, for *Sermons*, 1735, BM, NPG.

ATTERBURY, Lewis (1656-1731) divine.
PR G.VERTUE, after T.Gibson, 1727, hl, line, for *Sermons*, 1743, BM.

AUBREY, John (1626-1697) antiquary.
M WILLIAM FAITHORNE, 1666, hs, black lead and indian ink,

Ashmolean Museum, Oxford.
PR M. VAN DER GUCHT, after W.Faithorne, hs, line, for *Natural History of Surrey*, 1719, BM, NPG.

AUBREY, William (1529-1595) master in chancery.
PR W.HOLLAR, after monument in Old St Paul's, hl with skull, etch, NPG. UNKNOWN, hl, stipple, pub 1797, BM, NPG.

AUDLEY of Walden, Thomas Audley, Baron (1488-1544) lord chancellor and founder of Magdalene College, Cambridge.
P BIAGIO REBECCA, after Hans Holbein, jun, wl seated, Audley End (DoE), Essex. UNKNOWN, after H.Holbein, tql, Audley End; version, Magdelene College.

AUSTIN, William (1587-1634) barrister and writer.
PR G.GLOVER, hs, oval, line, for *Meditations*, 1635, BM, NPG.

AUSTIN, William (fl 1662) classical scholar and verse writer.
PR A.HERTOCHS, hl, line, for *Anatomy of the Pestilence*, 1666, BM, NPG.

AUVERQUERQUE, Henry Nassau, Count of (1641-1708) master of the horse to William III.
P By or after SIR GODFREY KNELLER, tql in armour, Orange-Nassau Museum, The Hague.
PR J.SMITH, after Sir G.Kneller, hl in armour, oval, mezz, BM, NPG.

AVERY, Benjamin (d1764) physician and trustee of Dr Williams's Library.
P SAMUEL WEBSTER, tql seated, Dr Williams's Library, London.

AVERY, John (fl 1695) pirate.
G W.PRITCHARD, after W.Jett, 'Capt Avery and his crew taking one of the Great Mogul's ships', wl, line engr, BM.

AXTEL(L), Daniel (d1660) parliamentarian.
G UNKNOWN, 'The Regicides Executed in 1660', hs, oval, line engr, 1660, BM.
PR UNKNOWN, after Regicides engr, hs, etch, NPG.

AYLESBURY, see Ailesbury.

AYLESFORD, Heneage Finch, 1st Earl of (1647?-1719) privy councillor and statesman.
G R.WHITE, 'The Bishops' Council', seven ovals, line engr, 1688, BM, NPG.

AYLETT, Robert (1583-1655?) religious poet and master in chancery.
PR T.CROSS, 1635, hl, line, for *Divine and Moral Speculations*, 1654, BM, NPG.

AYLMER, John (1521-1594) bishop of London.
PR R.WHITE, hl, line, for Strype, *Life*, 1701, BM, NPG.

AYLMER, Matthew Aylmer, Baron (1655-1720) naval commander.
P After SIR PETER LELY, tql as young man, NMM, Greenwich. JONATHAN RICHARDSON, c1692-3, tql, NMM.

AYMER de Valence, see 1st Earl of Pembroke.

AYRES, John (fl 1680-1700) writing master.
PR R.WHITE, hs, oval, line, for *Arithmetick*, 1693, BM, NPG. J.STURT, hl with scroll, line, for *Tutor to Penmanship*, 1695, BM.

AYSCUE, Sir George (fl 1646-1671) admiral.
PR UNKNOWN, hl, oval, line, no 708 of an Italian set, BM, NPG.

AYTON or **AYTOUN, Sir Robert (1570-1638)** poet.
SC UNKNOWN, bust on monument, Westminster Abbey, London.

B

BABINGTON, Gervase (1550?-1610) bishop of Worcester.
PR R.ELSTRACK, tql with book, line, for *Works*, 1615, BM, NPG. PASSE, hl with book, line, for Holland, *Herwologia*, 1620, BM, NPG.

BABINGTON, John (fl 1635) mathematician and gunner.
PR JOHN DROESHOUT, hs, oval, line, for *Pyrotechnic*, 1635, BM, NPG.

BACKWELL, Edward (d 1683) London goldsmith and banker.
PR UNKNOWN, tql with ship, line, a Dutch plate, BM, NPG.

BACON, Anne, née Cooke, Lady (1528-1610) wife of Sir Nicholas and mother of Francis.
P G.H.GOWER, 1580, tql with book, Gorhambury, Herts. UNKNOWN, hl, Gorhambury.
M Attrib ISAAC OLIVER, c1600, hs, w/c, The Walters Art Gallery, Baltimore, USA.
SC UNKNOWN, terracotta, Gorhambury.

BACON, Francis, see Viscount St Alban.

BACON, Sir Nathaniel (1585-1627) painter.
P Self-portrait, c1618-20, wl seated, Gorhambury, Herts. Self-portrait, c1625, hs, NPG 2142.
SC UNKNOWN, bust effigy, Culford Church, Suffolk.

BACON, Sir Nicholas (1509-1579) lord-keeper.
P UNKNOWN, 1562, hl, Corpus Christi College, Cambridge. UNKNOWN, 1578-79, hl with jewelled dragon whistle pendant, NPG 164; versions, Petworth (NT), W Sussex; Christ Church, Oxford.
SC UNKNOWN, terracotta bust, Gorhambury, Herts.
PR E.PASSE, after NPG 164 type, line, for Holland, *Herwologia*, 1620, BM, NPG.

BAGFORD, John (1650-1716) shoemaker and book collector.
PR G.VERTUE, after H.Howard, 1728, hl, line, BM, NPG.

BAGWELL, William (fl 1655) merchant and writer on astronomy.
PR W.FAITHORNE, 1659, hs, oval, line, for *Wit's Extraction*, 1664, BM, NPG.

BAILEY, Nathan or Nathaniel (d 1742) lexicographer.
PR UNKNOWN, hl, line, BM, NPG.

BAILLIE, Lady Grizel (1665-1746) poet.
P MARIA VERELST, 1725, tql with veil, Mellerstain, Borders region, Scotland.

BAILLIE, Robert (d 1684) patriot.
PR J.SHURY, hs in armour, line and stipple, for Chambers, *Dictionary of Eminent Scotsmen*, BM, NPG.

BAINBRIDGE, Christopher (1464?-1514) archbishop of York and cardinal.
PR N.PARR, hl, line, NPG.

BAINES, Sir Thomas (1622-1680) physician.
P CARLO DOLCI, hl with book, Fitzwilliam Museum, Cambridge. ISAAC FULLER, hl, Christ's College, Cambridge.
SC JOSEPH CATTERNS, 1684, relief medallion for monument, Christ's College Chapel.

BAKER, Charles, see David Lewis.

BAKER, David or in religion, **Augustine (1575-1641)** Benedictine monk.
PR W.HOLL, hs in habit, oval, stipple, pub 1835, BM, NPG.

BAKER, George (1540-1600) surgeon.
PR UNKNOWN, wl, woodcut, for *Book of Distillations*, 1599, NPG. UNKNOWN, several woodcuts with medical scenes, NPG.

BAKER, Henry (1698-1774) naturalist and poet.
PR W.NUTTER, after Thomson, hl with microscope, stipple, for Nichols, *Literary Anecdotes*, 1812, BM, NPG. MISS TURNER, hl, oval, lith, BM, NPG.

BAKER, John (1661-1716) admiral.
PR G.WHITE, after T.Gibson, hl, oval, mezz, BM, NPG.

BAKER, Sir Richard (1568-1645) religious and historical writer.
PR W.MARSHALL, hl, oval, line, for *Chronicle*, 1643, BM, NPG.

BAKER, Thomas (1656-1740) antiquary.
P Attrib CHARLES BRIDGES, hl, Bodleian Library, Oxford; version, Somerset House, London; engr J.Simon, mezz, BM, NPG.

BAKER, William (1668-1732) bishop of Norwich.
P UNKNOWN, tql, Wadham College, Oxford.

BALCARRES, Colin Lindsay, 3rd Earl of (1654?-1722) statesman.
P JOHN RILEY, tql in peer's robes, Traquair House, Borders region, Scotland.

BALCHEN, Sir John (1670-1744) admiral.
P JONATHAN RICHARDSON, tql, NMM, Greenwich.

BALE, John (1495-1563) bishop of Ossory.
PR PASSE, hl with book, line, for Holland, *Herwologia*, 1620, BM.

BALFOUR, Sir James (1600-1657) Scottish historian and herald.
P UNKNOWN, hl with book, SNPG 1551.

BALFOUR, Sir William (d 1660) parliamentary general.
PR UNKNOWN, hl, line, NPG. UNKNOWN, wl on horseback, line, NPG.

BALMERINO, Arthur Elphinstone, 6th Baron (1688-1746) Jacobite, executed for treason.
PR UNKNOWN, hl, mezz, BM. UNKNOWN, hl with Lord Kilmarnock, two ovals with vignette of execution, line, BM.

BALTIMORE, George Calvert, 1st Baron (1580?-1632) statesman.
M PETER OLIVER, hs, Fink Coll, Walters Art Gallery, Baltimore, USA.
PR J.CALDWALL, after unknown artist, hl, line, for Pennant, *Journey from Chester*, 1782, BM, NPG.

BALVAIRD, Andrew Murray, 1st Baron (1597?-1644) minister of Abdie.
P Attrib GEORGE SCOUGAL, hl, Scone Palace, Perth, Scotland.

BAMBRIDGE, Thomas (d 1741) warden of the Fleet Prison.
G Studio of WILLIAM HOGARTH, 'Committy of the house of Commons (the Gaols Committee)', oil, c1729, NPG 926.
PR R.GRAVE, wl, profile, line, for Caulfield, *Remarkable Persons*, 1819, BM, NPG.

BANBURY, William Knollys, 1st Earl of (1547-1632) soldier and statesman.
P DANIEL MYTENS, wl in Garter robes, Ranger's House (GLC), Blackheath, London.
SC UNKNOWN, alabaster and marble effigy with wife, Rotherfield Greys Church, Oxon.
PR S.PASSE?, hl, oval, line, BM, NPG.

BANCROFT, John (1574-1640) seventh bishop of Oxford.
P UNKNOWN, hl with cap, Christ Church, Oxford. UNKNOWN, tql with skull, University College, Oxford.

BANCROFT, Richard (1544-1610) archbishop of Canterbury.
P UNKNOWN, c1604, hl, NPG 945.

BANISTER, Richard (d1626) oculist.
P UNKNOWN, 1620, tql, Royal College of Surgeons, London.

BANKES, Sir John (1589-1644) chief justice of common pleas.
P After GILBERT JACKSON, (type of c1641), tql seated in robes, NPG 1069. UNKNOWN, 1643, Sudbury Hall (NT), Derbys.

BARBON or BAREBONE(S), Praise God (1596?-1679) anabaptist and politician.
PR UNKNOWN, hs, line, BM, NPG.

BARCLAY, John or Jean (1582-1621) author.
P UNKNOWN, hs, The University, Amsterdam, Holland.
SC FRANCOIS DUQUESNOY, 1627-28, marble bust, Convento di sant'Onofrio, Rome, Italy; version, Museo Tassiano, Rome.
PR C.MELLAN, after D. du Monstier, hs, line, for *Argenis*, 1623, BM, NPG.

BARCLAY, William (1546/7-1608) Scottish jurist.
PR C. DE MALLERY, hs, oval, line, for *De Regno* 1600, BM, NPG.

BAREBONE(S), Praise God, see Barbon.

BARGENY, John Hamilton, 1st Baron (d1658) royalist.
P By or after CORNELIUS JOHNSON, (type of 1647), hl, Airlie Castle, Tayside region, Scotland.

BARGRAVE, Isaac (1586-1643) dean of Canterbury.
P CORNELIUS JOHNSON, hl, The Deanery, Canterbury; version, Clare College, Cambridge.
SC UNKNOWN, after C.Johnson, relief medallion on monument, Canterbury Cathedral, engr J.Cole, line for Dart, *Canterbury Cathedral*, 1726, BM, NPG.

BARHAM, Henry (1670?-1726) naturalist.
PR G.VERTUE, 1721, hl, oval, BM, NPG.

BARKER, Hugh (d1632) lawyer.
SC NICHOLAS STONE, 1632, relief bust, New College Chapel, Oxford.

BARKSTEAD, John (d1662) regicide.
P UNKNOWN, hl with musket, Dr Williams's Library, London.
D T.ATHOW, hl, wash, Sutherland Coll, Ashmolean Museum, Oxford.
PR UNKNOWN, hs, line, pub 1810, BM, NPG.

BARLOW, Thomas (1607-1691) bishop of Lincoln.
P SIR PETER LELY, tql seated, Bodleian Library, Oxford. UNKNOWN, hl with hat, Queen's College, Oxford.
PR D.LOGGAN, hs, oval, line, BM, NPG. R.WHITE, after Henne, hs, oval, line, BM, NPG.

BARNARD, Sir John (1685-1764) merchant and politician.
SC J.A.DASSIER, copper medal, BM. JOHN KIRK, medal, BM. PETER SCHEEMAKERS, 1737, marble statue, Royal Exchange, London.
PR J.FABER, jun, after A.Ramsay, tql, mezz, pub 1739, BM, NPG.

J.MCARDELL, after A.Ramsay, hs, oval, mezz, pub 1754, BM, NPG.

BARNARDISTON, Sir Nathaniel (1588-1653) puritan.
PR F.H. VAN HOVE, hs, oval, line, for S.Clarke, *Lives*, 1683, BM, NPG.

BARNARDISTON, Sir Samuel (1620-1707) Whig politician.
PR R.WHITE, 1700, hs, oval, line, BM, NPG.

BARNARDISTON, Sir Thomas (d1669) parliamentarian.
PR R.PAGE, hs in armour, stipple, for *Essex, Suffolk and Norfolk Characters*, 1820, BM, NPG.

BARNES, Joshua (1654-1712) Greek scholar and antiquary.
P UNKNOWN, hs in robes, oval, Emmanuel College, Cambridge.
PR G.WHITE, hs, oval, line, for *Anacreon*, 1705, BM, NPG.

BARNETT, Curtis (d1746) commodore.
P JOHN ELLYS, 1743-44, tql, NMM, Greenwich.

BARON, Bartholomew, in religion Bonaventura (d1696) Irish Franciscan and writer.
PR W.KILIAN, after B.Schramann, hl in habit, line, for *Works*, 1668, BM, NPG.

BARON, Bernard (1696-1762) engraver.
G GAWEN HAMILTON, 'A Conversation of Virtuosis . . . at the Kings Armes', oil, 1735, NPG 1384.

BARON, Robert (fl 1645) poet and dramatist.
PR W.MARSHALL, hl, line, for *Cyprian Academy*, 1648, BM, NPG.

BARRINGTON, John Shute Barrington, 1st Viscount (1678-1734) lawyer.
PR UNKNOWN, after J.Richardson, hl, stipple, pub 1802, NPG.

BARROW, Isaac (1630-1677) mathematician and divine.
P UNKNOWN, hs, Trinity College, Cambridge, engr B.Holl, line, NPG.
D DAVID LOGGAN, 1676, hs, oval, plumbago, NPG 1876.
SC UNKNOWN, 1677, bust on monument, Westminster Abbey. L.F.ROUBILIAC, 1756, marble bust, Trinity College, Cambridge; model for bust, terra cotta, British Museum.

BARROWBY, William (1682-1751) physician.
PR J.S.MÜLLER, after F.Hayman, hl, mezz, BM, NPG.

BARRY, Elizabeth (1658-1713) actress.
PR C.KNIGHT, after Sir G.Kneller, hs, oval, stipple, for Harding, *Biographical Mirror*, 1792, BM, NPG.

BARWICK, John (1612-1664) divine.
PR G.VERTUE, hs, oval, line, for P.Barwick, *Life*, 1721, BM, NPG.

BARWICK, Peter (1619-1705) physician.
PR G.VERTUE, hs, oval, line, for *Life of John Barwick*, 1721, BM, NPG.

BASSEVI, Giacomo, see Cervetto.

BASTWICK, John (1593-1654) physician and controversialist.
PR UNKNOWN, hs, oval, line, for *New Discovery of the Prelates' Tyranny*, 1641, BM, NPG. T.CROSS, wl in armour, line, for *Routing of Independents and Sectaries*, 1646, BM, NPG. W.HOLLAR, hs, oval, etch, BM, NPG.

BATES, William (1625-1699) presbyterian divine.
P Attrib SIR GODFREY KNELLER, hs, Dr Williams's Library, London, engr R.White, line, for *Works*, 1700, BM, NPG.
PR W.FAITHORNE, hs, oval, line, for *Harmony of the Divine Attributes*, 1675, BM, NPG. J.STURT, hs, oval, line, for *Sermons*, 1687, BM, NPG.

BATH, John Grenville, 7th Earl of (1628-1701) lord-lieutenant of Cornwall and Devon and privy councillor.
P J.M.WRIGHT, tql, Dunrobin Castle, Highland region, Scotland.

BATH, Sir William Pulteney, 1st Earl of (1684-1764) statesman.
P SIR GODFREY KNELLER, 1717, hl, the 'Kit-cat Club' portrait, NPG 3194. UNKNOWN, c1750, tql seated, Raby Castle, Durham. After SIR JOSHUA REYNOLDS, c1755–57, tql seated in robes, NPG 35. SIR J.REYNOLDS, 1761, tql seated in robes, NPG 337.
G CHARLES PHILIPS, 'Tea-party at Lord Harrington's House', oil, 1739, Yale Center for British Art, New Haven, USA.
SC JOSEPH WILTON, portrait medallion, profile bust, Westminster Abbey, London. J.A.DASSIER, copper medal, BM.
PR D.MARTIN, after A.Ramsay, 1763, hl in peer's robes, line, BM, NPG. W.H.MOTE, after C.Jervas, tql seated, line and stipple, NPG.

BATHURST, Allen Bathurst, 1st Earl of (1684-1775) statesman.
SC JOSEPH NOLLEKENS, marble bust on monument, St John the Baptist Church, Cirencester, Glos.
PR C.BESTLAND, hs, aged 25, oval, stipple, pub 1803, BM, NPG.

BATHURST, Ralph (1620-1704) dean of Wells.
P SIR GODFREY KNELLER, 1694, hs, oval, Trinity College, Oxford. WILLIAM SONMAN, after D.Loggan, 1698, hs, oval, Trinity College, Oxford.
SC UNKNOWN, plaster bust taken from death mask, Trinity College, Oxford.
PR D.LOGGAN, 1676, hs, from life, oval, line, BM, NPG.

BATTELEY, John (1646-1708) divine.
P Attrib J.B.BUCKSHORN, tql, Trinity College, Cambridge. UNKNOWN, hl, oval, Trinity College, Cambridge.

BATTELL, Ralph (1649-1713) divine.
PR J.SIMON, after M.Dahl, hl, oval, mezz, E.Cooper exc, BM, NPG.

BATTEN, Sir William (d1667) admiral.
D T.ATHOW, tql in breastplate, wash, Sutherland Coll, Ashmolean Museum, Oxford.

BAXTER, Richard (1615-1691) puritan divine.
P Attrib JOHN RILEY, hs, oval, Dr Williams's Library, London, engr, T.Trotter, line, 1783, for Middleton, *Biographica Evangelica*, BM, NPG. UNKNOWN, after R.White, 1670, hs, oval, NPG 521.
M UNKNOWN, after R.White, 1670, hs, NPG 875.
PR ROBERT WHITE, hl with book, oval, line, for *Life of Faith*, 1670, BM, NPG.

BAXTER, William (1650-1723) scholar.
PR G.VERTUE, after J.Highmore, hs, line, for *Glossarium Antiquitatum*, 2nd ed, 1733, BM, NPG.

BAYES, Joshua (1671-1746) nonconformist divine.
P UNKNOWN, hs, Dr Williams's Library, London.
PR HOPWOOD, hs, stipple, NPG.

BAYFIELD, Robert (fl 1668) physician of Norwich.
PR W.FAITHORNE, hs, oval, line, for *Enchiridion Medicum*, 1655, BM, NPG.

BAYLY, Benjamin (1671-1720) divine.
PR G.VERTUE, hl, oval, line, BM, NPG.

BEALE, Charles, sen (1631-1705) painter, husband of Mary.
P Attrib MARY BEALE, c1660–70, hs, NPG 1279.
M T.FLATMAN, 1664, hs, oval, V & A.

BEALE, Charles, jun (1660-1774) portrait painter, son of Charles, sen, and Mary.
PR T.CHAMBERS, after Mary Beale, hs with mother, oval, line, for Walpole, *Anecdotes*, 1762, BM, NPG. UNKNOWN, after Mary Beale, c1680, hs, line, NPG.

BEALE, Mary (1633-1699) portrait painter.
P Self-portrait, c1665, tql seated with canvas, NPG 1687.

PR T.CHAMBERS, after Mary Beale, hs with son Charles, oval, line, for Walpole, *Anecdotes*, 1762, BM, NPG.

BEALE, William (d1651) royalist divine.
P UNKNOWN, hl, St John's College, Cambridge.

BEARD, Thomas (d1632) puritan divine and teacher of Oliver Cromwell.
PR UNKNOWN, wl, line, copy from print for *Pedantius*, 1631, pub 1801, BM, NPG.

BEATON or BETHUNE, David (1494-1546) Cardinal archbishop of St Andrews.
P UNKNOWN, hs with biretta, SNPG L 121; version, Blairs College, Aberdeen.

BEAUCHAMP, Edward Seymour, Baron (1561-1612) son of Edward, Earl of Hertford.
P Attrib HANS EWORTH, wl as infant with mother, oval, Petworth (NT), W Sussex.

BEAUCHAMP, Richard de (d1388), see Baron Kidderminster.

BEAUCHAMP, Richard de (1381/2-1439), see 13th Earl of Warwick.

BEAUCHAMP, Thomas de, see 12th Earl of Warwick.

BEAUCLERK, Charles, see 1st Duke of St Albans.

BEAUFORT, Henry (d1447) bishop of Winchester and cardinal.
SC UNKNOWN, tomb effigy, Winchester Cathedral, engr J.Basire, line, for *Vetusta Monumenta*, vol II, 1789, BM, NPG.

BEAUFORT, Henry Somerset, 1st Duke of (1629-1700) statesman.
P SIR PETER LELY, c1660-62, tql with breastplate, Badminton House, Avon. SIR P.LELY, tql, Badminton. Attrib SIR GODFREY KNELLER, wl in Garter robes, Badminton. UNKNOWN, tql in Garter robes, Badminton.
G STEPHEN BROWNE, family group, oil, 1685, Badminton.
SC Attrib GRINLING GIBBONS, tomb effigy on monument, St Michael's Church, Badminton. JOHN ROETTIER, silver medal, BM.
PR W.FAITHORNE, hl in armour, *ad vivum*, oval, line, BM. R.WHITE, after Sir G.Kneller, tql in Garter robes, line, for Guillim, *Heraldry*, 1679, BM, NPG.

BEAUFORT, Henry Somerset, 2nd Duke of (1684-1714) Tory politician.
P Attrib MICHAEL DAHL, tql seated in peer's robes, Badminton House, Avon. M.DAHL, c1712–14, hs in Garter robes, oval, Badminton, engr G.Vertue, line, BM. M.DAHL, c1712–14, wl in Garter robes, Badminton.
G PETER ANGELIS, 'Queen Anne and the Knights of the Garter', oil, 1713, NPG 624.

BEAUFORT, John (1403-1444), see 1st Duke of Somerset.

BEAUFORT, John (1373?-1410), see 1st Earl of Somerset.

BEAUFORT, Margaret, see Countess of Richmond and Derby.

BEAUMONT, Basil (1669-1703) rear-admiral.
P MICHAEL DAHL, tql, NMM, Greenwich.

BEAUMONT, Francis (1584-1616) dramatist.
P UNKNOWN, hl, Knole (NT), Kent, engr G.Vertue, 1729, hs, oval, line, BM, NPG.

BEAUMONT, John (d1701) royalist colonel.
G R.WHITE, 'The Portsmouth Captains', line engr, 1688, BM, NPG.

BEAUMONT, Joseph (1616-1699) master of Peterhouse.
P UNKNOWN, hs, oval, Peterhouse College, Cambridge, engr R.White, hs, oval, line, for *Psyche*, 1702, BM, NPG.

BECK, Cave (1623-1706?) writer on pasigraphy.
G UNKNOWN, 'seated with an Asiatic, an African and an American', wl, line engr, for *Universal Character*, 1657, BM.

BECKETT, Thomas à (1118?-1170) archbishop of Canterbury.
G UNKNOWN, 'Murder of Thomas à Beckett', wl kneeling, oil, Lambeth Palace, London.
MS UNKNOWN, *c*1200, 'Martyrdom of St Thomas Becket', wl kneeling, full-page miniature in Latin psalter, BL Harley MS 5102, fol 32. Other scenes, BL Harley MS 900, fol 566; BL Kings MS 9, fol 386.

BECKET, William (1684-1738) surgeon and antiquary.
PR R.PAN, hl, line, NPG.

BECKETT, Isaac (1653-1719) mezzotint engraver.
PR JOHN SMITH, hl, mezz, BM. W.H.WATT, hs, line, for Walpole, *Anecdotes*, 1849 ed, BM, NPG.

BECKINGTON, Thomas (1390?-1465) bishop and statesman.
MS UNKNOWN, wl seated in robes, full-page illumination in MS, New College, Oxford.
SC UNKNOWN, tomb effigy, Wells Cathedral.

BECON, Thomas (1512-1567) protestant divine.
PR UNKNOWN, hl with book, aged 49, woodcut, for *Bookes*, 1563, BM, NPG. UNKNOWN, hs profile, aged 41, woodcut, for *Principles of Christian Religion*, 1576, BM, NPG.

BEDELL, William (1571-1642) bishop of Kilmore and Armagh.
PR UNKNOWN, hs, line, Trinity College, Dublin.

BEDFORD, Francis Russell, 2nd Earl of (1527?-1585) statesman.
P UNKNOWN, hl with Garter George, Woburn Abbey, Beds.
D HANS HOLBEIN, jun, *c*1540–42, hs as boy, chalks, Royal Coll.
PR M.GHEERAERTS, sen, 'Procession of Garter Knights, 1576', etch, BM.

BEDFORD, Francis Russell, 4th Earl of (1593-1641) statesman.
P Attrib ROBERT PEAKE, *c*1600, wl with falcon and dogs, Woburn Abbey, Beds. Attrib CORNELIUS JOHNSON, hs as young man, oval, Woburn Abbey. SIR ANTHONY VANDYCK, 1636, wl with spaniel, Woburn Abbey.
SC UNKNOWN, alabaster tomb effigy with wife, Bedford Chapel, St Michael's Church, Chenies, Bucks.

BEDFORD, John, Duke of (1389-1435) see JOHN of Lancaster.

BEDFORD, John Russell, 1st Earl of (1486?-1555) gentleman of the privy chamber.
P After HANS HOLBEIN, jun, (type of *c*1540), hs, semi-profile, Woburn Abbey, Beds. UNKNOWN, *c*1555, tql, Woburn Abbey.
D H.HOLBEIN, *c*1540, hs, semi-profile, chalks, Royal Coll.
G UNKNOWN, 'Edward VI and the Pope', oil, *c*1548–49, NPG 4165.
SC UNKNOWN, alabaster tomb effigy with wife, Bedford Chapel, St Michael's Church, Chenies, Bucks.

BEDFORD, Lucy Russell, née Harington, Countess of (d1627) patroness of poets.
P Attrib JOHN DE CRITZ, 1606, wl, Woburn Abbey, Beds. Attrib WILLIAM LARKIN, *c*1615, wl, Gripsholm Castle, Sweden. UNKNOWN, (called Countess of Bedford), *c*1620, tql seated, Woburn Abbey.
PR S.PASSE, hl, oval, line, BM, NPG.

BEDFORD, William Russell, 1st Duke of (1613-1700) soldier and statesman.

P JOHN PRIWITZER, 1627, wl with page?, Woburn Abbey, Beds. SIR ANTHONY VANDYCK, *c*1633, wl with 2nd Earl of Bristol, Althorp, Northants. SIR A.VANDYCK, *c*1637, tql seated with wife, Wilton House, Wilts. SIR PETER LELY, 1676, wl in Garter robes, Woburn. JOHANN KERSEBOOM, *c*1685, wl with dog, Hardwick Hall (NT), Derbys. SIR GODFREY KNELLER, *c*1692, wl in Garter robes, NPG 298.
M EDWARD LUTTEREL, 1698, hs, chalks, NPG 1824.
SC Attrib FRANCIS BIRD, *c*1701, seated effigy with wife, Bedford chapel, St Michael's Church, Chenies, Bucks.

BEDINGFIELD, Sir Henry (1511-1583) knight and supporter of Queen Mary.
P UNKNOWN, inscr 1573, hl, Oxburgh Hall (NT), Norfolk, engr J.Swaine, line, BM.

BEDINGFIELD, Sir Henry (1633-1687) chief justice.
P R.WHITE, wl in robes, Lincoln's Inn, London, engr White, 1685, hs, oval, line, BM; version, Oxburgh Hall (NT), Norfolk.

BEDLOE, William (1650-1680) adventurer.
PR R.WHITE, hl, oval, line, for *Life*, 1681, BM, NPG.

BEHN, Aphra (1640-1689) dramatist and novelist.
PR R.WHITE, after J.Riley, hs, oval, line, for *Plays*, 1716, BM, NPG.

BELASYSE, Thomas, see 1st Earl of Fauconberg.

BELASYSE of Worlaby, John Belasyse, Baron (1614-1689) royalist general.
PR R.WHITE, after Sir A.Vandyck, tql as young man, line, BM, NPG.

BELHAVEN, John Hamilton, 2nd Baron (1656-1708) statesman.
P SIR J.B.MEDINA, after Sir G.Kneller, SNPG 1553. After SIR G.KNELLER, hs in robes, oval, SNPG 907. UNKNOWN, hs in robes, oval, Lennoxlove, Lothian region, Scotland.

BELHAVEN, Robert Douglas, Viscount (1574?-1639) master of the household to Charles I.
SC JOHN SCHURMAN, effigy on wall monument, Abbey Church, Holyrood House, Edinburgh.

BELL, Francis (1590-1643) Franciscan friar.
PR UNKNOWN, hs with knife in breast, oval, for Mason, *Certamen Seraphicum*, 1649, BM.

BELL, Sir Robert (d1577) judge.
PR W.C.EDWARDS, after crayon drawing, hs in robes, line, BM, NPG.

BELLASYS, John, see Belasyse.

BENBOW, John (1653-1702) admiral.
P SIR GODFREY KNELLER, 1701, tql with breastplate, NMM, Greenwich.
G UNKNOWN, tql with Ralph Delavall and unidentified seated man, oil, *c*1692–3, NMM.

BENDLOWES, William (1516-1584) lawyer and serjeant-at-law.
P UNKNOWN, 1564, hl, St John's College, Cambridge.
SC UNKNOWN, brass, Great Bradfield Church, Essex.

BENLOWES, Edward (1603?-1676) poet.
P S.WALTER, 1650, hl seated, St John's College, Cambridge.
PR F.BARLOW, hs, oval, etch, for *Theophila*, 1652, BM, NPG.

BENN, William (1600-1680) divine.
PR J.CALDWALL, hl, line, NPG.

BENNET, Benjamin (1674-1726) nonconformist divine.
PR J.PINE, hs, line, NPG.

BENNET, Christopher (1617-1655) physician.
PR P.LOMBART, hs, oval, line, BM, NPG.

BENNET, Henry, see 1st Earl of Arlington.

BENSON, George (1699-1762) divine.
P UNKNOWN, hs, Dr Williams's Library, London, engr J.McArdell, mezz, for *Life of Christ*, 1764, BM, NPG.

BENSON, Martin (1689-1752) bishop of Gloucester.
P JONATHAN RICHARDSON, tql, Christ Church, Oxford, engr George Vertue, 1739, line, BM, NPG. UNKNOWN, c1740, tql holding college cap, Christ Church.
SC After W.WHITLEY, 1891, plaster replica medallion, SNPG 302.

BENSON, Robert, see Baron Bingley.

BENTHAM, Thomas (1513-1578) bishop.
SC UNKNOWN, bas relief effigy on table tomb, wl, Eccleshall Church, Staffs.

BENTINCK, William, see 1st Earl of Portland.

BENTLEY, Richard (1662-1742) scholar and critic.
P SIR JAMES THORNHILL, 1710, tql seated, Trinity College, Cambridge; copy, NPG 851. T.HUDSON, after J.Thornhill, 1749, wl, Trinity College, Cambridge.
SC L.F.ROUBILIAC, 1756, marble bust, Trinity College, Cambridge; terra cotta model, BM; plaster cast, Lambeth Palace, London.

BENTLEY, Thomas (1693?-1742) classical scholar.
C P.L.GHEZZI, etch, wl standing, BM, NPG.

BERENGARIA (d after 1230) queen of Richard I.
SC UNKNOWN, 13th cent, stone tomb effigy, Le Mans, France; plaster cast, V & A.

BERKELEY, George Berkeley, 1st Earl of (1628-1698) statesman.
P UNKNOWN, tql in peer's robes, Berkeley Castle, Glos.
D T.ATHOW, hs, wash, Sutherland Coll, Ashmolean Museum, Oxford.
M N.DIXON, hs, oval, monogram, Berkeley Castle.
SC JEAN BAPTISTE DU FOUR, silver medal, BM.

BERKELEY, George (1685-1753) bishop of Cloyne.
P JOHN SMIBERT, c1732, hl seated with book, NPG 653. UNKNOWN, c1734, tql, Lambeth Palace, London. JAMES LATHAM, c1734-38, hs, Trinity College, Dublin. UNKNOWN, tql seated with book, Trinity College, Dublin.
G JOHN SMIBERT, 1730, 'Bermuda Group', Yale University Art Gallery, New Haven, USA; version, Trinity College, Dublin.
PR W.SKELTON, after Vanderbank, 1800, tql seated with fountain in background, line, NPG. UNKNOWN, hl in civil dress, line, NPG.

BERKELEY, James Berkeley, 3rd Earl of (1680-1736) admiral.
P SIR GODFREY KNELLER, c1710?, 'Kit-cat Club' portrait, NPG 3195, mezz, J.Faber jun, 1731, BM, NPG; versions, Berkeley Castle, Glos; NMM, Greenwich. Attrib ENOCH SEEMAN, tql with Garter star, Berkeley Castle. UNKNOWN, tql, Melbourne Hall, Derby.

BERKELEY of Stratton, John Berkeley, 1st Baron (d1678) soldier.
P UNKNOWN, tql in armour, Berkeley Castle, Glos.
G G.NETSCHER, 1676, tql seated with wife and son, Berkeley Castle.

BERKELEY of Stratton, John Berkeley, 3rd Baron (1663-1697) admiral.
P MICHAEL DAHL, tql in armour, Berkeley Castle, Glos.

BERKELEY, Sir Robert (1584-1656) judge.
PR G.POWLE, hs, oval, etch, BM, NPG.

BERKELEY, Sir William (1639-1666) vice-admiral.
P SIR PETER LELY, c1666, tql with breastplate, NMM, Greenwich.

BERNARD, Sir Charles (1650-1711) surgeon.
P T.MURRAY, c1711, Worshipful Company of Barbers, London.

BERNARD, Francis (1627-1698) physician.
PR W.ANGUS, hs, line, pub 1817, NPG. UNKNOWN, hs, oval, line, BM.

BERNARD, Richard (1568-1641) puritan divine.
PR W.HOLLAR, hl with book, etch, for *Thesaurus Biblicus*, BM, NPG.

BERNARDI, John (1657-1736) major.
PR G.VAN DER GUCHT, after W.Cooper, hs with armour, oval, line, for *History*, 1729, BM, NPG.

BERNERS, John Bourchier, 2nd Baron (1467-1533) statesman and author.
P UNKNOWN Flemish artist, c1520-26, hl with orange, NPG 4953.

BERRIMAN, William (1688-1750) divine.
PR S.RAVENET, after Philips, hs, oval, line, BM, NPG.

BERTIE, Montague, see 2nd Earl of Lindsey.

BERTIE, Peregrine, see Lord Willoughby de Eresby.

BERTIE, Robert, see 1st Earl of Lindsey.

BERWICK, James Fitzjames, 1st Duke of (1670-1734) natural son of James II and Arabella Churchill.
P NICCOLO CASSANA, hs in armour, oval, Althorp, Northants. N.CASSANA, tql in armour, Blenheim Palace, Oxon. NICOLAS DE LARGILLIÈRE, hs, Musée de Nîmes, France.

BETHEL, Slingsby (1617-1697) sheriff of London.
PR W.SHERWIN, wl with scroll, line, BM.

BETHUNE, David, see Beaton.

BETTERTON, Thomas (1635-1710) actor.
P Studio of SIR GODFREY KNELLER, c1690-1700, hs, NPG 752; versions, Garrick Club, London; Knole (NT), Kent.

BEVERIDGE, William (1637-1708) bishop of St Asaph.
P BENJAMIN FERRERS, c1708, hl, Bodleian Library, Oxford, engr M. van der Gucht, line, for *Sermons*, 1709, BM, NPG.

BICKHAM, George (d1769) writing master and engraver.
PR GEORGE BICKHAM, hs, oval, line, for *Universal Penman*, 1741, BM.

BICKLEY, Thomas (1518-1596) bishop of Chichester.
P UNKNOWN, hs, Magdalen College, Oxford; versions, Magdalen; Merton College, Oxford.

BILL, William (d1561) dean of Westminster.
SC UNKNOWN, brass bas relief on monument, wl, Westminster Abbey, London.

BILLINGSLEY, Martin (fl 1618-1637) writing-master.
PR W.HOLE, hl with quill pen, aged 27, oval, line, for *Pens Excellencie*, 1618, BM, NPG.

BILSON, Thomas (1547-1616) bishop of Winchester.
P UNKNOWN, hs, Lambeth Palace, London.

BINGHAM, Sir Richard (1528-1599) governor of Connaught.
P UNKNOWN, 1564, hl with sword, NPG 3793.

BINGLEY, Robert Benson, Baron (1676-1731) politician.
M ANDREAS VON BEHN, 1704, hl, vellum, V & A.

BINNING, Charles Hamilton, Lord (1697-1733) poet.
PR I.GERIMIA, hl, oval, stipple, pub 1806, NPG. UNKNOWN, hl, oval, stipple, for Walpole, *Royal and Noble Authors*, 1805, BM, NPG.

BISHOP, William (1554-1624) Catholic divine.
PR UNKNOWN, hs, oval, stipple, pub 1810, NPG.

BISSE, Philip (1667-1721) bishop of Hereford.
P UNKNOWN, tql seated, New College, Oxford, engr G.Vertue, after T.Hill, 1719, hs, oval, line, BM, NPG.

BLACKADDER, John (1664-1729) lieutenant-colonel.
P UNKNOWN, tql with breastplate, SNPG 1534.

BLACKALL, Offspring (1654-1716) bishop of Exeter.
P MICHAEL DAHL, tql, Bishop's Palace, Exeter, engr J.Sturt, hs, oval, line, for *Sermons*, 1706, BM, NPG.

BLACKBURNE, Lancelot (1658-1743) archbishop of York.
P ISAAC SEEMAN, 1726, tql seated, Bishopthorpe Palace, York, engr G.Vertue, 1727, line, BM, NPG; versions, Bishop's Palace, Exeter; Christ Church, Oxford, attrib J.Highmore.

BLACKERBY, Richard (1574-1648) puritan divine.
PR F.H.VAN HOVE, hs, oval, line, for S.Clarke, *Lives*, 1683, BM, NPG.

BLACKMORE, Sir Richard (d1729) physician and writer.
P Attrib JOHN CLOSTERMAN, c1700, hs, oval, Royal College of Physicians, London.

BLACKWALL, Anthony (1674-1730) classical scholar.
PR G.VERTUE, hs, oval, line, for *Sacred Classics*, 1727, BM, NPG.

BLACKWOOD, Adam (1539-1613) Scottish writer.
PR JOHN PICART, hl, line, for *Works*, 1644, BM, NPG.

BLAGRAVE, John (d1611) mathematician.
PR UNKNOWN, hl with mathematical instruments, line, NPG. 'D.L.', hs, oval, line, for *Mathematical Jewel*, NPG.

BLAGRAVE, Joseph (1610-1682) astrologer.
PR UNKNOWN, hl, aged 72, line, for *Introduction to Astrology*, 1682, BM, NPG.

BLAGRAVE, Thomas (d1688) musician.
P UNKNOWN, hs, Faculty of Music, Oxford.

BLAIR, James (1656-1743) Scottish Episcopalian divine and founder of a Virginia college.
P JAMES HARGREAVES, 1705, hs, College of William and Mary, Williamsburg, USA.

BLAKE, Robert (1599-1657) admiral.
P UNKNOWN, hl, NMM, Greenwich. UNKNOWN, hs, Wadham College, Oxford.

BLAKENEY, William Blakeney, Lord (1672-1761) defender of Minorca.
P SIR GEORGE CHALMERS, hl with baton, SNPG 315, mezz, J.MCARDELL, 1756, BM, NPG.

BLANDFORD, Walter (1619-1675) bishop.
P UNKNOWN, hl, Wadham College, Oxford; version, Hartlebury Castle, Worcs.

BLANTYRE, Alexander Stewart, 5th Lord (d1704) Scottish statesman.
P UNKNOWN, hs in peer's robes, oval, Winton House, Pencaitland, Lothian region, Scotland. UNKNOWN, hs in armour, oval, Lennoxlove, Lothian region, Scotland.

BLATHWAYT, William (1649?-1717) politician.
P MICHAEL DAHL, tql, Dyrham Park (NT), Avon.

BLENCOWE, Sir John (1642-1726) judge.
PR G.VERTUE, after A.Russell, 1713, hs, line, BM, NPG.

BLIGH, Thomas (1685-1775) lieutenant-general and Irish MP.
P THOMAS GAINSBOROUGH, hs in uniform, Metropolitan Museum of Art, New York, USA.

BLITH, Walter (fl 1649) agricultural writer.
PR UNKNOWN, wl with gardening tools, line, for *Survey of Husbandry*, 1653, BM.

BLOME, Richard (d 1705) publisher and compiler.
PR UNKNOWN, hs, oval, mezz, NPG.

BLOOD, Thomas (1618?-1680) adventurer.
D UNKNOWN, hs, wash, Pepys Library, Magdalene College, Cambridge. UNKNOWN, hs with armour, oval, wash, Pepys Library, Magdalene College.
PR R.WHITE, hs, oval, mezz, BM, NPG.

BLOUNT, Charles, see Earl of Devonshire.

BLOUNT, Sir Henry (1602-1682) traveller.
PR D.LOGGAN, 1679, hs, oval, line, BM, NPG.

BLOUNT, Martha (1690-1762) friend of Pope.
P 'J.J.', 1713, hl, Mapledurham House, Oxon. CHARLES JERVAS, tql with sister Teresa, Mapledurham House; version, Fitzwilliam Museum, Cambridge.

BLOUNT, Mountjoy, see Earl of Newport.

BLOW, John (1648-1708) composer.
PR R.WHITE, hs, oval, line, for *Amphion Anglicus*, 1700, BM, NPG. UNKNOWN, after J.Closterman, hs, oval, process block, BM, NPG.

BOBART, Jacob, sen (1599-1680) botanist.
PR M.BURGHERS, after D.Loggan, hs, oval, line, BM. UNKNOWN, wl with gardening tools, line, NPG.

BOBART, Jacob, jun (1641-1719) botanist.
P UNKNOWN, hs, Library, Botanic Garden, Oxford.

BODLEY, Sir Thomas (1545-1613) founder of the Bodleian Library.
P UNKNOWN, 1634–35, tql with sword, Bodleian Library, Oxford. UNKNOWN, 1636–37, hs, Bodleian.
M School of NICHOLAS HILLIARD, 1598, hs, w/c, Bodleian Library.
SC UNKNOWN, 1605, marble bust in niche, Bodleian Library. NICHOLAS STONE, 1615, alabaster bust on monument, Merton College Chapel. JEAN VARIN, medal, BM.

BOHEMIA, Sophia, Princess of, see SOPHIA.

BOIT, Charles (d1726?) enamel painter.
PR A.BANNERMAN, hs with turban, oval, line, with J.Baker for Walpole, *Anecdotes*, 1762, BM, NPG.

BOLEYN, Thomas, see Earl of Wiltshire.

BOLINGBROKE, Henry St John, 1st Viscount (1678-1751) statesman and writer.
P Attrib A.S.BELLE, c1712?, tql in peer's robes, NPG 593. SIR GODFREY KNELLER, 1715, tql in robes, Petworth (NT), W Sussex. Attrib CHARLES JERVAS, after c1723, hs, DoE, 10 Downing St, London. Attrib JONATHAN RICHARDSON c1730?, hs with turban, NPG 1493. UNKNOWN, c1730-40, hl, Lydiard Mansion, Borough of Thamesdown, Wilts.
M UNKNOWN, c1740-50, hl, enamel, NPG 3067.
SC J.M.RYSBRACK, 1737, marble bust, Lydiard Mansion. J.M.RYSBRACK, 1737, marble bust, Petworth. L.F.ROUBILIAC, relief portrait medallion, profile, Parish Church of St Mary, Battersea, London.
PR G.WHITE, after T.Murray, c1705, hl, oval, mezz, BM NPG.

BOLINGBROKE, Oliver St John, 1st Earl of (1580?-1646) parliamentarian.
PR W.HOLLAR, hs, oval, etch, BM, NPG.

BOLTON, Charles Paulet, 6th Marquess of Winchester and 1st Duke of (1625?-1699) statesman.
PR R.WHITE, tql in peer's robes, line, for Guillim, *Heraldry*, 1679, BM, NPG.

BOLTON, Robert (1572-1631) puritan.
PR J.PAYNE, 1632, hs, line, for *Four Last Things*, 1632, BM, NPG.

BOLTON, Samuel (1606-1654) divine.
P UNKNOWN, Christ's College, Cambridge.
PR W.FAITHORNE, hs, oval, line, for *Dead Saint Speaking to Saints*, 1657, BM, NPG.

BONAVENTURA, Bartholomew, see Baron.

BOND, Martin (1558-1643) merchant adventurer.
P UNKNOWN, tql with stick, St Bartholomew's Hospital, London.

BONNELL, James (1653-1699) accountant-general of Ireland.
SC UNKNOWN, bas relief bust, St John's Church, Dublin, line engr, BM, NPG.
PR R.WHITE, hs, oval, line, NPG.

BONNER, Edmund (1500?-1569) bishop of London.
PR UNKNOWN, wl seated burning Thomas Tomkins's hand with a candle, woodcut, for Foxe, *Acts and Monuments*, 1563, BM, NPG.

BOOKER, John (1603-1667) astrologer.
PR W.HOLLAR, hl with book, etch, BM. UNKNOWN, hs, line, NPG.

BOORDE, Andrew (1490?-1549) physician and traveller.
PR UNKNOWN, wl seated, woodcut, NPG.

BOOTH, Barton (1681-1733) actor.
P JOHN VANDERBANK, hs, oval, Garrick Club, London, engr G. van der Gucht, line, for *Life and Poems*, 1733, BM, NPG.

BOOTH, George (1622-1684), see 1st Baron Delamere.

BOOTH, George (1675-1758), see 2nd Earl of Warrington.

BOOTH, Henry (1652-1694), see 1st Earl of Warrington.

BORGUIGNON, Hubert François, see Gravelot.

BORLASE, Sir John (1576-1648) soldier, master of ordinance in Ireland.
P M.J.VAN MIEREVELDT, 1625, tql in armour, NPG 4933.

BOSCAWEN, Hugh, see 1st Viscount Falmouth.

BOSTON, Thomas (1677-1732) Scottish divine.
PR R.SCOTT, hs, oval, stipple, NPG.

BOTHWELL, James Hepburn, 4th Earl of (1535?-1578) third husband of Mary, Queen of Scots.
P OTTO BACHE, study of mummified head, SNPG L 106.
M UNKNOWN, 1566, head, oval, SNPG 869.

BOTLEY, Samuel (1642-1696?) writer on stenography.
PR UNKNOWN, hs, oval, line, for *Rich's Shorthand*, 1674, NPG.

BOULTER, Hugh (1672-1742) archbishop of Armagh.
P By or after FRANCIS BINDON, tql seated, NPG 502; versions, Christ Church, Oxford; Magdalen College, Oxford.
G F.BINDON, 1742, wl with afflicted people, Trinity College, Dublin, engr J.Brooks, BM, NPG.
SC SIR HENRY CHEERE, 1742, monument, Westminster Abbey, London. UNKNOWN, marble bust, Christ Church, Oxford.
PR T.BEARD, after M.Ashton, 1728, tql seated, mezz, BM, NPG.

BOURCHIER, Henry, see 1st Earl of Essex.

BOURCHIER, John, see 2nd Baron Berners.

BOURCHIER, Thomas (1404?-1486) archbishop of Canterbury and cardinal.
SC UNKNOWN, monument, Canterbury Cathedral.

BOURN, Samuel (1648-1719) dissenting minister.
PR M.VAN DER GUCHT, hs, oval, line, for *Sermons*, 1722, NPG.

BOWER, Archibald (1686-1766) historian.
PR J.FABER, jun, after Sir J.Reynolds, 1755, hl with book, mezz, BM.

J.McARDELL, after G.Knapton, tql seated, mezz, BM, NPG.

BOWES, Sir George (1527-1580) soldier.
PR R.EASTON, hs, mezz, NPG.

BOWES, Sir Jerome (d1616) ambassador.
P UNKNOWN, late 16th cent, wl with sword, Ranger's House (GLC), Blackheath, London.

BOWES, John Bowes, Baron (1690-1767) lord chancellor of Ireland.
P NATHANIEL DANCE, NGI 504.
SC JOHN VAN NOST, relief medallion on monument, Christ Church Cathedral, Dublin, engr John Lodge, 1779, NPG.
PR J.BROOKS, tql seated in robes, mezz, BM, NPG.

BOWES, Sir Martin (1500?-1566) lord mayor of London.
P UNKNOWN, tql in robes, Goldsmiths' Hall, London.

BOWES, Sir Robert (1495?-1554) commander and lawyer.
G UNKNOWN, 'Edward VI Granting the Charter to Bridewell Hospital in 1553', wl with scroll, Bridewell Hospital, Surrey, engr G.Vertue, 1750, line, BM, NPG.
PR UNKNOWN, hs, oval, etch, NPG.

BOWYER, William, sen (1663-1737) printer.
P UNKNOWN, hs, Stationer's Hall, London, erigr J.Basire, line, pub 1812, BM, NPG.

BOWYER, William, jun (1699-1777) printer and author.
PR J.BASIRE, hs, oval, line, for *Conjectural Emendations*, 1812, BM, NPG.

BOYD, Mark Alexander (1563-1601) Scottish Latin scholar.
PR T.DE LEU, hs in profile, oval, line, for Sir R.Sibbald, *Scotia Illustrata*, 1683, BM.

BOYD of Trochrig, Robert (1578-1627) divine.
PR RIVERS, hs, stipple, pub 1795, NPG.

BOYD, Zachary (1585?-1653) Scottish divine.
P UNKNOWN, hl, Glasgow University, engr Trotter, line, 1795, NPG.

BOYER, Abel (1667-1729) miscellaneous writer.
PR J.BASIRE, hl with quill pen, oval, line, for *French and English Dictionary*, 1783, BM, NPG.

BOYLE, Charles, see 4th Earl of Orrery.

BOYLE, Henry (d1725), see Baron Carleton.

BOYLE, Henry (1682-1764), see 1st Earl of Shannon.

BOYLE, Michael (1609?-1702) archbishop of Armagh and chancellor of Ireland.
PR R.PURCELL, after G.Soest, hl with lord chancellor's purse, oval, mezz, BM. D.LOGGAN, hs, oval, line, BM, NPG.

BOYLE, Richard (1566-1643), see 1st Earl of Cork.

BOYLE, Richard (1612-1697), see 1st Earl of Burlington.

BOYLE, Richard (1695-1753), see 3rd Earl of Burlington.

BOYLE, Hon Robert (1627-1691) natural philosopher and chemist.
P Attrib JOHN RILEY, 1682, tql seated, The Royal Society, London. JOHANN KERSEBOOM, c1689-90, tql seated with book, The Royal Society; copies, NPG 3930 and Hardwick Hall (NT), Derbys, engr John Smith, 1689, hs, oval, mezz, BM, NPG. JOHN SMITH, 1689, hs, oval, mezz, BM, NPG.
SC J.M.RYSBRACK, 1733, marble bust, Royal Coll.
PR W.FAITHORNE, c1659, hs with air pump, oval, line, BM, NPG.

BOYLE, Roger, see 1st Earl of Orrery.

BOLEYN, Anne, see ANNE Boleyn.

BOYS, Edward (1599-1667) divine.
PR W.FAITHORNE, hs, oval, line, for *Sermons*, 1672, BM, NPG.

BOYS, John (1571-1625) dean of Canterbury.
P UNKNOWN, hl in robes, The Deanery, Canterbury.
SC UNKNOWN, marble monument effigy, Canterbury Cathedral, engr J.Cole, line, NPG.
PR J.PAYNE, 4 small portraits, shown praying, writing, meditating and preaching, line, for *Workes*, 1622, BM, NPG.

BRACEGIRDLE, Anne (1663?-1748) actress.
PR J.STOW, after Harding, hl, oval, line, pub 1811, BM, NPG.
W.VINCENT, wl with boy, mezz, for Howard and Dryden, *The Indian Queen*, BM, NPG.

BRACKLEY, Sir Thomas Egerton, 1st Baron Ellesmere and 1st Viscount (1540?-1617) lord chancellor.
P UNKNOWN, (type of *c*1596), tql in civil dress, NPG 3783.
UNKNOWN, (type of *c*1603), tql seated in peer's robes, Clarendon Coll on loan to Buckland Abbey (NT), Devon; version, Bodleian Library, Oxford.

BRADBURY, Thomas (1677-1759) congragational minister.
PR G.WHITE, after T.Gibson, hl, oval, mezz, BM, NPG. G.VERTUE, after Gibson, 1725, line, BM. J.FABER, jun, after M.Grace, 1749, tql seated, mezz, BM, NPG.

BRADFORD, Francis Newport, 1st Earl of (1620-1708) royalist.
P SIR GODFREY KNELLER, hs, oval, Weston Park, Salop. SIR G.KNELLER, hs in armour, oval, Weston Park. MICHAEL DAHL, hs, oval, Weston Park.

BRADFORD, John (1510?-1555) protestant martyr.
PR PASSE, hl, line, for Holland, *Herwologia*, 1620, BM, NPG.

BRADFORD, Samuel (1652-1731) bishop of Rochester.
P UNKNOWN, hs, oval, The Deanery, Westminster, London.

BRADLEY, James (1693-1762) divine and astronomer.
P THOMAS HUDSON, *c*1742–47, hl, oval, Royal Society, London; copy, NPG 1073.

BRADSHAW, John (1602-1659) regicide.
PR M.VAN DER GUCHT, hs, oval, line for Ward, *History of the Rebellion*, 1713, BM, NPG.

BRADSHAW, William (1671-1732) bishop of Bristol.
P ENOCH SEEMAN, *c*1718, hs, Christ Church, Oxford.

BRADY, Nicholas (1659-1726) divine and poet.
P Attrib HUGH HOWARD, hs, NGI 613.

BRADY, Robert (*d*1700) historian and physician.
P UNKNOWN, Gonville and Caius College, Cambridge.
PR E.HARDING, 1799, hs, oval, stipple, BM, NPG.

BRAITHWAITE, Richard, see Brathwaite.

BRAMHALL, John (1594-1663) archbishop of Armagh.
P UNKNOWN, hs, oval, Sidney Sussex College, Cambridge, engr E.Harding, 1796, stipple, NPG.

BRAMSTON, Sir John (1577-1654) judge.
P UNKNOWN, wl in robes, Colchester Museum; version, hl, NPG 462.

BRANDON, Charles (*d*1545), see 1st Duke of Suffolk.

BRANDON, Charles (1537?-1551), see 3rd Duke of Suffolk.

BRANDON, Henry, see 2nd Duke of Suffolk.

BRANTHWAITE, William (*d*1620) translator of the Bible.
P UNKNOWN, Emmanuel College, Cambridge; version, Gonville and Caius College, Cambridge.

BRATHWAITE, Richard (1588?-1673) poet.
PR R.VAUGHAN, wl, line, in title to *English Gentleman*, 1630, BM. W.MARSHALL, hs, oval, line, for *Survey of History*, 1638, BM, NPG.

BRAY, Sir Reginald (*d*1503) statesman and architect.
D UNKNOWN, after window in Priory Church, Malvern, Worcs, wl in armour, w/c, Stanford Hall, Leics, engr J.Carter, etch, for *Specimens of Ancient Sculpture and Painting*, 1790, BM.

BREADALBANE, John Campbell, 1st Earl of (1635-1716) soldier and statesman.
P SIR J.B.MEDINA, hl in robes, SNPG 996.

BREADALBANE, John Campbell, 3rd Earl of (1696-1782) statesman and diplomat.
P JEREMIAH DAVISON, 1730, tql seated with documents, SNPG 993. After ALLAN RAMSAY, hl, Dunrobin Castle, Highland region, Scotland.

BRENTFORD, Patrick Ruthven, Earl of (1573?-1651) royalist general.
PR P.PAUL (S. de Wilde), hs, in armour, etch, BM, NPG.

BRERETON, Sir William (1604-1661) parliamentary commander.
PR UNKNOWN, hs in armour, oval, line, for Vicar, *Englands Worthies*, 1647, BM. G.GLOVER, wl on horseback, line, BM.

BRETTERG, Katherine (1579-1601) puritan.
PR UNKNOWN, hs, oval, line, for S.Clarke, *Marrow of Ecclesiastical History*, BM, NPG.

BRETTINGHAM, Matthew (1699-1769) architect.
P J.T.HEINZ, sen, hl, Royal Institute of British Architects, London.

BRIANT, Alexander (1553-1581) Jesuit.
PR UNKNOWN, tql with knife in breast, no 78 in a sheet of heads of Jesuits, line, BM, NPG.

BRICE, Andrew (1690-1773) printer.
PR R.WOODMAN, after Mrs Jackson, hl seated, line, BM.

BRIDEOAKE, Ralph (1613-1678) bishop of Chichester.
SC WILLIAM BIRD, 1678, marble monumental effigy, wl, St George's Chapel, Windsor.

BRIDGE, William (1600?-1670) puritan divine.
PR J.CALDWALL, hs, oval, line, NPG. W.SHERWIN, hs, line, BM, NPG.

BRIDGEMAN, Charles, see Bridgman.

BRIDGEMAN, John (1577-1652) bishop of Chester.
P Attrib CORNELIUS JOHNSON, hl, Weston Park, Salop. PAUL VAN SOMER, hl, Weston Park. UNKNOWN, tql with book, Bishop's House, Chester.

BRIDGEMAN, Sir Orlando, 1st Bart (1606?-1674) lord keeper.
P PIETER BORSSELER, hs with purse of Great Seal, oval, Weston Park, Salop; version, tql, Chirk Castle, Clwyd, Wales. J.M.WRIGHT, 1671, wl in robes with purse, Inner Temple, London.
PR W.FAITHORNE, hl in robes, line, for Dugdale, *Origines*, 1671, BM.

BRIDGES, John (1666-1724) topographer.
PR G.VERTUE, after G.Kneller, 1726, hl, line, BM, NPG.

BRIDGES, Noah (fl 1661) stenographer and mathematician.
M SAMUEL COOPER, 1666, hs, w/c, Fondation Custodia, Institut Néerlandais, Paris.
PR W.FAITHORNE, hs, line, for *Vulgar Arithmetique*, 1653, BM.

BRIDGEWATER, John Egerton, 1st Earl of (1579-1649) lord-lieutenant of Wales.
P UNKNOWN, hl, oval, Tatton Park (NT), Cheshire.

BRIDGEWATER, John Egerton, 2nd Earl of (1622-1686) privy councillor.
P Attrib WILLIAM CLARET, hl, oval, Tatton Park (NT), Cheshire, engr A.Blooteling?, 1680, mezz, BM.

BRIDGEWATER, John Egerton, 3rd Earl of (1646-1701) first lord of admiralty.
P UNKNOWN, c1675, hl in peer's robes, on loan to Marlborough House (DoE), London.
PR JOHN SMITH, after Sir G.Kneller, 1661, hl in armour, oval, mezz, BM, NPG.

BRIDGMAN, Charles (d1738) gardener.
G GAWEN HAMILTON, 'A Conversation of Virtuosis . . . at the Kings Armes', oil, 1735, NPG 1384. W.HOGARTH, 'An Assembly of Artists', oil, c1735, Ashmolean Museum, Oxford. W.HOGARTH, 'A Rake's Progress', Third State, plate 2d, engr, BL Sat 2173.

BRIGGS, William (1642-1704) physician and oculist.
PR J.FABER, jun, after R.White, tql seated, mezz, BM, NPG.

BRIGHTMAN, Thomas (1562-1607) puritan divine.
PR UNKNOWN, hl, line, for *Revelation of the Revelations*, 1644, BM, NPG.

BRISTOL, George Digby, 2nd Earl of (1612-1677) politician and royalist commander.
P SIR ANTHONY VANDYCK, c1633, wl with 1st Duke of Bedford, Althorp, Northants; version, Sherborne Castle, Dorset.
D SIR A.VANDYCK, head, sketch for Althorp portrait, Sherborne Castle.
PR W.HOLLAR, after H.van der Borcht, tql in armour, etch, BM. UNKNOWN, hs, oval, line, for J.Heath, *Chronicle*, 1663, BM, NPG.

BRISTOL, John Digby, 1st Earl of (1580-1653) diplomat and statesman.
P CORNELIUS JOHNSON, 1628, hs, oval, NGI.
PR R.ELSTRACK, hl, oval, line, BM, NPG, V & A.

BRISTOL, John Hervey, 1st Earl of (1665-1751) Whig politician.
P J.B.VAN LOO, 1742, hl, oval, Ickworth (NT), Suffolk. UNKNOWN, hl, Ickworth. UNKNOWN, tql with coronet on table, Ickworth. UNKNOWN, wl in peer's robes, Ickworth.

BRITTON, Thomas (1654?-1714) the 'musical small-coal man'.
P JOHN WOLLASTON, 1703, hl with coal measure, NPG 523.
PR THOMAS JOHNSON, after J.Wollaston, hl tuning harpsichord, oval, mezz, BM, NPG.

BROCAS, Sir Bernard (1330?-1395) warrior.
SC UNKNOWN, tomb effigy, Westminster Abbey, London, engr C.A.Stothard, 1810, line, NPG.

BROGHILL, Roger Boyle, Baron, see 1st Earl of Orrery.

BROME, Alexander (1620-1666) attorney and poet.
PR D.LOGGAN, hs, oval, line, for *Songs and Poems*, 1664, BM, NPG.

BROME, Richard (d1652?) dramatist.
PR T.CROSS, hl with laurel wreath, line, for *Five New Plays*, 1653, BM, NPG.

BROMLEY, Sir Thomas (1530-1587) lord chancellor.
P UNKNOWN, hl in robes, Capesthorne, Cheshire.

BROMLEY, William, sen (1664-1732) secretary of state.
P Attrib JOHN CLOSTERMAN, 1710, tql, Christ Church, Oxford. MICHAEL DAHL, c1712, tql with robes and scroll, Examination Schools, Oxford, engr John Smith, 1712, hs, oval, mezz, BM, NPG.

BROMLEY, William, jun (1699?-1737) politician.
P UNKNOWN, hs, oval, Bodleian Library, Oxford.

BROOK, Sir Basil (1576-1646?) royalist.
PR UNKNOWN, hs, oval, etch, NPG.

BROOKE, Elizabeth, née Colepepper, Lady (1601-1683) religious writer.
PR UNKNOWN, hl, oval, line, for N.Parkhurst, *Funeral Sermon*, 1684, BM, NPG.

BROOKE, Ralph (1553-1625) herald.
PR UNKNOWN, hs, oval, line, BM, NPG.

BROOKE, Robert Greville, 2nd Baron (1608-1643) parliamentary general.
PR UNKNOWN, hs with cuirass, etch, NPG.

BROOME, William (1689-1745) divine and poet.
PR G.VERTUE, after D.Heins, hl, oval, line, for *Poems*, 1727, BM.

BROUGHTON, Hugh (1549-1612) divine and rabbinical scholar.
P UNKNOWN, 1588, tql, Christ's College, Cambridge, engr J.Payne, line, BM, NPG.

BROUNCKER, Henry Brouncker, 3rd Viscount (d1688) courtier.
P After SIR PETER LELY, c1675, tql, NPG 1590.

BROUNCKER, William Brouncker, 2nd Viscount (1620?-1684) first president of the Royal Society.
P Studio of SIR PETER LELY, c1674, tql seated, Royal Society, London; versions, NPG 1567; Althorp, Northants.
PR W.HOLLAR, after John Evelyn, wl pointing to bust of Charles II, etch, for Sprat, *History of the Royal Society*, 1667, NPG.

BROWN, Charles (d1753) naval officer.
P UNKNOWN, 1740, tql, NMM, Greenwich, engr J.Faber, jun, 1740, mezz, BM, NPG.
SC UNKNOWN, medals, tql and wl, BM.

BROWN, George (1650-1730) arithmetician.
PR G.VERTUE, after E.Wright, hs, oval, line, for *Arithmetica Infinita*, 1718, BM, NPG.

BROWN, John (d1532) sergeant painter to Henry VIII.
P UNKNOWN, hs, Painters' Hall, London.

BROWN, Sir Robert (d1760) merchant.
P Attrib JONATHAN RICHARDSON, 1730s, hs, Hatfield House, Herts.

BROWN, Thomas (1663-1704) satirist.
PR J.TUCK, hs, line, for Caulfield, *Remarkable Persons*, 1819, BM. UNKNOWN, hs, etch, BM.
C 'E.K.', hs, with allegorical figures, line, NPG.

BROWNE, Alexander (fl 1660) miniature painter.
PR A.DE JODE, after J.Huysmans, hl, oval, line, BM, NPG, V & A.

BROWNE, Sir Anthony (d1548) politician.
P UNKNOWN, after 1540, hs, NPG 5186.
SC UNKNOWN, monumental effigy, Battle Church, Sussex, line engr, pub 1777, BM.

BROWNE, Anthony (1526-1592), see 1st Viscount Montague.

BROWNE, Edward (1644-1708) physician and traveller.
P UNKNOWN, hl, Royal College of Physicians, London.

BROWNE, John (1642-1700?) surgeon.
PR R.WHITE, hs, oval, line, for *Discourse of Wounds*, 1678, BM, NPG. UNKNOWN, head, etch, in title to *Myographia Nova*, 1694, BM.

BROWNE, Peter (d1735) bishop of Cork and Ross.
P HUGH HOWARD, tql, Trinity College, Dublin.

BROWNE, Sir Richard (d 1669) parliamentary general.
P UNKNOWN, 1648, hl, one of set of five portraits of members imprisoned after Pride's Purge, 1648, NPG 2109.
D UNKNOWN, hl, wash, Sutherland Coll, Ashmolean Museum, Oxford.
SC UNKNOWN, silver medal, BM.
PR UNKNOWN, hl in armour, line, for Ricraft, *Survey of England's Champions*, 1649, BM, NPG.

BROWNE, Sir Richard (1605-1683) ambassador to France.
PR PHILIP AUDINET, after R.Nanteuil, hl, line, for Bray, *Memoirs of Evelyn*, 1818, BM, NPG.

BROWNE, Samuel (d 1668) judge.
P J.M.WRIGHT, wl in robes, Lincoln's Inn, London.

BROWNE, Sir Thomas (1605-1682) physician and author.
P Attrib JOAN CARLILE, c 1641–50, hs with his wife, NPG 2062. UNKNOWN, after J.Carlile, hl, Royal College of Physicians, London.
M UNKNOWN, after Robert White, hs, plumbago, NPG 1969.
PR F.H.VAN HOVE, hl, oval, line, for *Pseudodoxia*, 1672, BM. P.VANDERBANK, hs, oval, line, for *Miscellaneous Tracts*, 1683, BM, NPG. ROBERT WHITE, hs, oval, line, for *Works*, 1686, BM, NPG.

BROWNE, Sir William (1692-1774) physician.
P THOMAS HUDSON, 1767, wl in president's gown, Royal College of Physicians, London.
PR J.DIXON, after T.Hudson, tql in gown, mezz, BM, NPG.
C UNKNOWN, 1771, wl with wig and stick, etch, NPG.

BROWNLOW, Richard (1553-1638) chief prothonotary of the court of common pleas.
P UNKNOWN, tql seated in robes, Belton House, Lincs, engr T.Cross, line, for *Declarations and Pleadings*, 1653, BM, NPG, V & A.
SC JOSHUA MARSHALL, 1638?, bust on monument, Belton House.

BROWNRIG, Ralph (1592-1659) bishop of Exeter.
P UNKNOWN, hl, Pembroke College, Cambridge.
PR W.FAITHORNE, hl, oval, line, for *Sermons*, 1661, BM, NPG.

BRUCE of Kinloss, Edward Bruce, 1st Baron (1549?-1611) judge.
D G.P.HARDING, after painting of 1604, tql, NPG 2401.
SC UNKNOWN, wl tomb effigy, Public Record Office Museum, London, engr Barrett, line, NPG.

BRUCE, Robert, see 1st Earl of Ailesbury.

BRUCE, Thomas, see 2nd Earl of Ailesbury.

BRUCE, Sir William (d 1710) architect.
P J.M.WRIGHT, 1665, hl as young man, SNPG 894. SIR J.B.MEDINA, hl as older man, SNPG 957.
D UNKNOWN, after Sir J.B.Medina, hl, wash, SNPG 109.

BRUDENELL, Sir Robert (1461-1531) judge.
P UNKNOWN, 1527, wl in robes of chief justice of Common Pleas, Deene Park, Northants.
SC UNKNOWN, alabaster effigies of him and two wives, Deene Church, Northants.

BRUEN, John (1560-1625) puritan.
PR UNKNOWN, hs, oval, line, NPG.

BRUGIS, Thomas (fl 1640?) army surgeon.
PR T.CROSS, hs, oval, with four subjects illustrating his profession, line, for *Vade Mecum*, 1657, BM, NPG, V & A.

BRYDGES, Giles, see 3rd Baron Chandos.

BRYDGES, James, see 1st Duke of Chandos.

BUCCLEUCH, Ann Scott, Countess of (1651-1731/2) wife of Duke of Monmouth and Buccleuch.

P Studio of SIR PETER LELY, tql seated, Buccleuch Estates, Selkirk, Scotland; version, hs, oval, Buccleuch Estates, WILLEM WISSING, hl, oval, Buccleuch Estates. Attrib W.WISSING, tql seated with black page, Buccleuch Estates. W.WISSING, wl in robes, Buccleuch Estates.
G SIR GODFREY KNELLER, family group with sons, Earls of Dalkeith and Deloraine, oil, Buccleuch Estates.

BUCER, Martin (1491-1551) protestant reformer.
PR UNKNOWN, hl, oval, woodcut, for French ed of Beza, *Icones*, 1581, BM, NPG. UNKNOWN, hl with book, woodcut, NPG.

BUCHAN, James Erskine, 6th Earl of (d 1640) lord of bedchamber to Charles I.
P Attrib Adam de Colone, 1626, hl, SNPG L234.
D 11th EARL OF BUCHAN, after George Jamesone, 1795, chalk, SNPG 1635.
PR TROTTER, hs, line and stipple, pub 1798, NPG.

BUCHANAN, George (1506-1582) historian and scholar.
P After ARNOLD VAN BROUNCKHORST, c 1581, tql with book, NPG 524; versions, SNPG 1148, and St Andrew's University.

BUCK, Samuel (1696-1779) draughtsman and engraver.
PR R.HOUSTON, after J.Highmore, hl with his brother Nathaniel, mezz, for Buck, *Views*, 1774, BM, NPG.

BUCKERIDGE, John (1562?-1631) bishop of Rochester and Ely.
P UNKNOWN, hs, oval, St John's College, Oxford; version, tql, St John's College.

BUCKINGHAM, Edward Stafford, 3rd Duke of (1478-1521) soldier and statesman.
P UNKNOWN, hl, Magdalene College, Cambridge. UNKNOWN, hl, Longleat, Wilts.

BUCKINGHAM, George Villiers, 1st Duke of (1592-1628) courtier and favourite of James I.
P Attrib WILLIAM LARKIN, c 1616, wl in Garter robes, NPG 3840. DANIEL MYTENS, c 1620–22, hs in armour with Garter ribbon, Royal Coll. After SIR BALTHASAR GERBIER?, c 1623, wl, Clarendon Coll on loan to Palace of Westminster, London. Attrib SIR B.GERBIER?, wl in armour, NMM, Greenwich. SIR P.P.RUBENS, c 1625, hs, Pitti Palace, Florence. M.J.VAN MIEREVELDT, c 1625, hl, Lamport Hall, Northants. D.MYTENS, 1626, wl with Garter George, Euston Hall, Suffolk. After D.MYTENS, hs in Garter robes, Royal Coll.
D SIR P.P.RUBENS, 1625, hs, Albertina, Vienna.
M SIR B.GERBIER, 1618, wl on horseback, oval, Syon House, Brentford, Middx.
G UNKNOWN, 'Family of the Duke of Buckingham', oil, 1628, Royal Coll; version, NPG 711.
PR S.PASSE, 1617, hl, oval, line, BM.

BUCKINGHAM, George Villiers, 2nd Duke of (1628-1687) statesman and dramatist.
P SIR ANTHONY VANDYCK, 1635, wl with brother, Francis, Royal Coll. Attrib HENRI GASCAR, c 1665, tql in breastplate, Longleat, Wilts. SIR PETER LELY, c 1675, hl in Garter robes, NPG 279.
G UNKNOWN, 'Family of the Duke of Buckingham', oil, 1628, Royal Coll; version, NPG 711.
PR I.BECKETT, after S.Verelst, hl in Garter robes, oval, mezz, BM, NPG.

BUCKINGHAM and NORMANBY, John Sheffield, 1st Duke of (1648-1721) statesman and author.
P SIR GODFREY KNELLER, c 1685–88, tql in armour, NMM, Greenwich; version, NPG 1779. SIMON DUBOIS, 1696, Hughenden Manor (NT), Bucks. JONATHAN RICHARDSON, c 1703–05, wl seated in robes with Seal bag, Examination Schools, Oxford.

SC LAURENT DELVAUX, DENIS PLUMIER and PETER SCHEEMAKERS, *c*1721, effigy on monument, Westminster Abbey, London.
PR J.SMITH, after Sir G.Kneller, tql in Garter robes, mezz, BM, NPG. G.VERTUE, after Sir Godfrey Kneller, 1722, hs with Garter George, oval, line, BM, NPG.

BUCKINGHAMSHIRE, John Hobart, 1st Earl (1694?-1756) politician.
P J.T.HEINS, wl, Blackfriar's Hall, Norwich.
PR J.FABER, jun, after T.Hudson, wl in robes, mezz, BM.

BUDGELL, Eustace (1686-1737) writer.
PR J.FABER, jun, after D.Firmin, 1720, hl, oval, mezz, BM,

BUGG, Francis (1640-1724?) writer against Quakerism.
PR F.H.VAN HOVE, hl with gloves, oval, line, BM, NPG.

BUISSIÈRE, Paul (*d*1739) anatomical writer and surgeon.
P UNKNOWN, hl, Royal Society, London.

BULKELEY, Lady Sophia (fl 1688) lady of the bedchamber to queen of James II.
PR H.GASCAR, tql with vase, mezz, BM.

BULKLEY, Peter (1583-1659) puritan divine, rector of Odell.
P UNKNOWN, hl, Odell Church, Beds.

BULL, George (1634-1710) bishop of St David's.
P UNKNOWN, 1700, hl, Exeter College, Oxford, engr M. van der Gucht, oval, line, BM, NPG.

BULL, John (1563?-1628) composer.
P UNKNOWN, 1589, hl with skull and sand-glass, Faculty of Music, Oxford.

BULL, John (*d*1642) London weaver.
PR T.HEYWOOD, wl seated weaving, woodcut, for 'A True Discourse of the Two infamous upstart Prophets, Richard Farnham, Weaver of White-Chapell, and John Bull, Weaver of Saint Butolphs . . .', 1636, Bodleian Library, Oxford, and BM.

BULLAKER, Thomas, in religion, John Baptist (1604?-1642) Catholic martyr.
PR UNKNOWN, hs with knife in breast, line, for Mason, *Certamen Seraphicum*, 1649, BM.

BULLEIN, William (*d*1576) physician.
PR UNKNOWN, hs, oval, line, copy from woodcut for *Government of Healthe*, 1559, pub 1805, BM, NPG.

BULLINGHAM, Nicholas (1512?-1576) bishop of Lincoln and Worcester.
SC UNKNOWN, tomb effigy, Worcester Cathedral.

BULLOCK, William (1657?-1740?) comedian.
D Attrib SYLVESTER HARDING, after Thomas Johnson, hl, w/c, NPG 2540; copy, Garrick Club, London.
PR C.HALL, after W.Hogarth, hl, oval, mezz, pub 1781, BM, THOMAS JOHNSON, *c*1710-20, hl mezz, BM.

BULSTRODE, Sir Richard (1610-1711) diplomat.
PR S.HARDING, after unknown artist, hs in armour, oval, stipple, pub 1795, BM, NPG.

BULSTRODE, Whitelocke (1650-1724) essayist.
PR T.COLE, after Sir G.Kneller, hl, line, NPG.

BULWER, John (fl 1654) physician.
PR W.FAITHORNE, hl, oval, line, for *Anthropometamorphosis*, 1653, BM, NPG.

BUNYAN, John (1628-1688) author of *Pilgrim's Progress*.
P THOMAS SADLER, 1684-5, hl with book, NPG 1311, engr J.Sturt, hl without book, line, for *Works*, 1692, BM, NPG.
D ROBERT WHITE, hl, pencil on vellum, BM.

PR R.WHITE, hl leaning on bank, asleep, with vision, line for *Pilgrim's Progress*, 1679, 12°, BL.

BURBAGE, Richard (1567?-1619) actor.
P UNKNOWN, hs, Dulwich College Gallery, London.

BURCHETT, Josiah (1666?-1746) secretary to the admiralty.
P JACQUES MAUBERT, wl, The Admiralty, on loan to Concourse Hall, Ministry of Defence, London, engr G.Vertue, hl, oval, line, for Burchett, *Naval History*, 1720, BM, NPG.

BURGESS, Daniel (1645-1713) nonconformist minister.
PR J.DRAPENTIER, hl, oval, line, for *Character of a Godly Man*, 1691, BM. J.FABER, sen, 1707, hl, oval, mezz, BM, NPG. G.VERTUE, hs, oval, line, for *Psalms*, 1714, BM. UNKNOWN, hl preaching, line, copy from a contemporary satirical print, in Caulfield, *Remarkable Persons*, 1819, BM, NPG.

BURGH, Sir John (1587-1627) commander in the Netherlands.
PR T.CECIL, hl with armour, oval, line, for R.Markham, *Description of . . . Sir John Burgh*, 1628, BM, NPG.

BURGHERSH, Bartholomew Burghersh, Baron (*d*1355) statesman.
SC UNKNOWN, tomb effigy, Lincoln Cathedral.

BURGHERSH, Henry (1292-1340) bishop of Lincoln.
SC UNKNOWN, tomb effigy, Lincoln Cathedral.

BURGHLEY, William Cecil, 2nd Baron (1542-1623) soldier and statesman.
P Attrib HANS EWORTH, *c*1565, tql seated with book and hour glasses, Hatfield House, Herts. By or after ARNOLD VAN BROUNCKHORST, *c*1560-70, tql with staff, NPG 2184. Attrib MARCUS GHEERAERTS, after *c*1585, tql in Garter robes with staff, NPG 362. Attrib JOHN DE CRITZ, *c*1596-97, wl seated, Hatfield House. UNKNOWN, wl seated on donkey, Bodleian Library, Oxford.
SC UNKNOWN, tomb effigy, St Martin's Church, Stamford, Northants.

BURGUNDY, Margaret of York, Duchess of, see MARGARET.

BURKITT, William (1650-1703) vicar of Dedham.
PR R.WHITE, 1703, hs, oval, line, for *Expository Notes on the New Testament*, BM, NPG.

BURLEY, Sir Simon (1336-1388) soldier and courtier.
PR W.HOLLAR, tomb in old St Paul's, etch, for W.Dugdale, *The History of St Paul's Cathedral*, 1658, NPG, V & A.

BURLINGTON, Richard Boyle, 1st Earl of (1612-1697) statesman.
P After SIR ANTHONY VANDYCK, hs, oval, Chatsworth, Derbys; versions, NPG 893; Knole (NT), Kent. SIR PETER LELY, *c*1670, hs as older man, Buccleuch Estates, Selkirk, Scotland.

BURLINGTON, Richard Boyle, 3rd Earl of (1695-1753) statesman.
P SIR GODFREY KNELLER, 1716, tql, Chatsworth, Derbys, engr John Faber, jun, 1734, for 'Kit-cat Club' series, mezz, BM, NPG. Attrib JONATHAN RICHARDSON, *c*1717-19, tql with architectural background, NPG 4818. GEORGE KNAPTON, 1743, tql seated with bust of Inigo Jones, Chatsworth.
G SIR G.KNELLER, *c*1700, Lord Burlington and his sisters, Chatsworth; copy of right hand part of portrait with greyhound, NPG 2495, possibly based on engr John Smith, after Kneller, 1701, mezz, BM, NPG.
PR UNKNOWN, 1731-33, hl as captain of Gentlemen Pensioners, mezz, BM, NPG.

BURNET, Elizabeth (1661-1709) author.
PR M.VAN DER GUCHT, after Sir G.Kneller, hs with veil, line, for *Some Account of her Life*, 1709, BM, NPG.

BURNET, Gilbert (1643-1715) bishop of Salisbury.
P UNKNOWN, 1681, hl with book, SNPG L27. By or after JOHN RILEY, *c*1689–91, tql seated with Garter robes, SNPG L252; versions, tql, Crathes Castle (NT of Scotland), Grampian; hl, oval, NPG 159. UNKNOWN, tql seated with Garter robes, cathedral in background, Lambeth Palace, London.
M UNKNOWN, hs, oil, Crathes Castle.
PR G.VERTUE, after Mrs S.Hoadly, 1723, hl, oval, line, BM, NPG. R.WHITE, hl aged 44, oval, line, BM.
C UNKNOWN, wl standing half each in pulpit and barrel, line, NPG.

BURNET, Thomas (*c*1635-1715) divine, master of Charterhouse.
P Attrib FERDINAND VOET, 1675, hl, oval, NPG 526. SIR GODFREY KNELLER, *c*1693, tql, Charterhouse School, Surrey.
PR R.WHITE, hs, oval, line, for *Theory of Earth*, 1697, BM, NPG.

BURNET, Sir Thomas (1694-1753) judge.
PR J.FABER, jun, after A.Ramsay, tql seated in robes, mezz, BM, NPG.

BURNET, William (*d*1729) colonial governor.
P JOHN WATSON, hl, Colby College, Waterville, Maine, USA.

BURROUGH, Sir James (1691-1764) amateur architect.
P D.HEINS, Gonville and Caius College, Cambridge.

BURROUGHES, Jeremiah (1599-1646) puritan divine.
PR T.CROSS, 1646, hl with book, oval, line, for *Gospel Worship*, 1648, BM, NPG.

BURROUGHS, Joseph (1685-1761) baptist minister.
P UNKNOWN, hl, oval, Dr Williams's Library, London.

BURTON, Henry (1578-1648) divine.
PR UNKNOWN, hs, oval, woodcut, for *Divine Tragedie lately acted*, 1641, BM. G.GLOVER, hl with book, oval, line, for *Life*, 1648, BM, NPG.

BURTON, Hezekiah (*d*1681) divine.
D Attrib MARY BEALE, hs, red chalk, BM.
PR R.WHITE, after M.Beale, hs, oval, line, for *Discourses*, 1684, BM, NPG.

BURTON, John (1696-1771) classical scholar, vice-provost of Eton.
PR UNKNOWN, after Cosins, sen, hs, oval, stipple, BM, NPG.

BURTON, Robert (1577-1640) author of 'Anatomy of Melancholy'.
P GILBERT JACKSON, 1635, hl with book, Brasenose College, Oxford.
SC UNKNOWN, marble bust in niche, Christ Church Cathedral, Oxford.

BURTON, William (1575-1645) antiquary.
P UNKNOWN, 1604, hl, Society of Antiquaries, London.
PR F.DELARAM, tql aged 47, oval, line, for *Leicestershire*, 1622, BM, NPG, V & A.

BURTON, William (1609-1657) schoolmaster and author.
PR W.HOLLAR, hl with book, oval, etch, for *Commentary on Antoninus*, 1658, BM, NPG.

BURY, Mrs Elizabeth (1644-1720) religious diarist.
PR G.BURDER, hs, oval, line, pub 1777, BM, NPG.

BURY, Thomas (1655-1722) chief baron of exchequer.
P JONATHAN RICHARDSON, 1719, tql seated in robes, Gray's Inn, London, engr John Smith, 1720, hl, oval, mezz, BM, NPG.

BUSBY, Richard (1606-1695) headmaster of Westminster school.
P After ROBERT WHITE, hl, NPG 419; versions, Christ Church, Oxford; Westminster School, London.
SC FRANCIS BIRD, after death mask, 1695, monumental effigy, Westminster Abbey, London. Attrib J.M.RYSBRACK, marble bust, Christ Church, Oxford.
PR R.WHITE, after H.Tilson, hl, oval, line, BM.

BUSHELL, Thomas (1594-1674) mining engineer and master of mint.
SC UNKNOWN, various medals, BM.

BUTCHER, Richard (1583-1665?) antiquary.
PR R.CLAMP, hl with book, stipple, for Harding, *Biographical Mirror*, 1795, BM, NPG.

BUTLER, James (1610-1688), see 1st Duke of Ormonde.

BUTLER, James (1665-1745), see 2nd Duke of Ormonde.

BUTLER, Joseph (1692-1752) bishop of Durham.
P UNKNOWN, hs as young man, oval, Magdalen College, Oxford. UNKNOWN, tql with scroll, Bishop Auckland Palace, Durham.

BUTLER, Piers, see 8th Earl of Ormonde.

BUTLER, Richard, see 1st Viscount Mountgarret.

BUTLER, Samuel (1612-1680) satirist.
P GERARD SOEST, *c*1670–80, tql, NPG 2468; copy, Bodleian Library, Oxford.
D EDWARD LUTTEREL, *c*1680, hs, gouache and pastel, NPG 248.
SC Attrib J.M.RYSBRACK, bust on monument, Westminster Abbey, London.

BUTLER, Thomas, see Earl of Ossory.

BUTLER, William (1535-1618) physician to James I.
PR S.PASSE, hl with book, oval, line, BM, NPG.

BUTTS, Sir William (*d*1545) physician to Henry VIII.
P HANS HOLBEIN, jun, *c*1540–43, hs, Isabella Stewart Gardner Museum, Boston, USA. After H.HOLBEIN, hs, NPG 210.
G H.HOLBEIN, 'Henry VIII and the Barber Surgeons', oil, *c*1540–43, Barbers' Company, London.

BYFIELD, Adoniram (*d*1660) puritan.
PR R.COOPER, after earlier engr, hl with demon, stipple, NPG.

BYFIELD, Nicholas (1579-1622) puritan.
P UNKNOWN, 1620, hs, Dr Williams's Library, London.

BYRD, William (1538?-1623) composer.
PR UNKNOWN, from an earlier engr, hs, circle, with another of T.Tallis, reproduction, BM.

BYROM, John (1692-1763) teacher of shorthand.
PR TOPHAM, after D.Rasbotham, hl with papers, line, pub 1814, NPG.

BYRON, John Byron, 1st Baron (*d*1652) statesman.
PR S.DE WILDE, hl in armour, etch, BM.

BYRON, Sir Thomas (*d*1644) commander of the Prince of Wales' regiment.
D W.N.GARDINER, hl in armour, wash, Sutherland Coll, Ashmolean Museum, Oxford.

C

CADOGAN, William Cadogan, 1st Earl of (1675-1726) general.
P HANS HYSING, tql with armour, Goodwood, W Sussex. Attrib L.LAGUERRE, c1716, tql with armour, NPG 18, engr J.Simon, hl, mezz, BM, NPG.

CAESAR, Adelmare (d1559) physician to Queens Mary and Elizabeth.
P Attrib GERLACH FLICKE, 1558, tql, Rousham House, Oxon.

CAESAR, Sir Charles (1590-1642) judge.
D G.P.HARDING, after unknown artist, hl, oval, w/c, NPG 2402; version, Sutherland Coll, Ashmolean Museum, Oxford.

CAESAR, Henry (1562-1636) dean of Ely.
PR UNKNOWN, hs, oval, stipple, NPG.

CAESAR, Sir Julius (1558-1636) judge, master of the rolls.
P UNKNOWN, 1597, wl, Rousham House, Oxon.
PR R.ELSTRACK, hl with scroll, line, BM, NPG.

CAESAR, Sir Thomas (1561-1621) baron of the exchequer.
PR UNKNOWN, after a miniature, hs, oval, stipple, NPG.

CAIUS, John (1510-1573) scholar and physician, co-founder of Gonville and Caius College.
P UNKNOWN, hl, Gonville and Caius College, Cambridge. UNKNOWN, hs, profile, Gonville and Caius College.
PR PASSE, hl, profile, line, for Holland, *Herwologia*, 1620, BM.

CALAMY, Benjamin (1642-1686) divine.
P UNKNOWN, hl, oval, St Catherine's College, Cambridge, engr M. van der Gucht, line, for *Sermons*, 1690, BM, NPG.

CALAMY, Edmund (1600-1666) puritan divine.
PR R.WHITE, hs, oval, line, BM, NPG.

CALAMY, Edmund (1671-1732) nonconformist biographer.
PR G.VERTUE, hs, oval, line, for *Sermons*, 1722, BM, NPG.

CALDERWOOD, Sir William, see Lord Polton.

CALDWELL, John, see Fenwick.

CALLANDER, James Livingstone, 1st Earl of (1674) general.
PR UNKNOWN, hl in armour, line, for Ricraft, *Survey of England's Champions*, 1647, BM.

CALVELEY, Sir Hugh (d1393) soldier.
SC UNKNOWN, tomb effigy, Bunbury Church, Cheshire, drawing Charles A.Stothard, indian ink, BM.

CALVER, Edward (fl 1649) puritan and author of Wilbie, Suffolk.
PR W.HOLLAR, hl, oval, etch, BM.

CALVERLEY, Henry (1604-1661) royalist.
P UNKNOWN, 1638, hs, oval, Wallington Hall (NT), Northd.

CALVERT, George, see 1st Baron Baltimore.

CAMBELL, Sir James (1570-1642) lord mayor of London.
PR G.GLOVER, tql, line, for E.Browne, *A Rare Paterne of Justice and Mercy*, 1642, BM.

CAMDEN, William (1551-1623) antiquary and historian.
P MARCUS GHEERAERTS, 1609, hs, Bodleian Library, Oxford;

version, NPG 528. UNKNOWN, 1622, hl with book, Worcester College, Oxford.
PR R.GAYWOOD, hl in herald's coat, etch, for Morgan, *Sphere of Gentry*, 1661, BM, NPG.

CAMERON, Sir Ewen (1629-1719) of Lochiel, Jacobite.
P UNKNOWN, hl in armour, SNPG L138.

CAMPBELL, Alexander Hume, see 2nd Earl of Marchmont.

CAMPBELL, Archibald (1576?-1638), see 7th Earl of Argyll.

CAMPBELL, Archibald (1607?-1661), see 1st Marquess of Argyll.

CAMPBELL, Archibald (1629-1685), see 9th Earl of Argyll.

CAMPBELL, Archibald (d1703), see 1st Duke of Argyll.

CAMPBELL, Archibald (1682-1761), see 3rd Duke of Argyll.

CAMPBELL, Duncan (1680-1730) deaf and dumb fortuneteller.
PR PRICE, after T.Hill, hl, oval, line, for *Life and Adventures*, 1720, BM. M.VAN DER GUCHT, hs, oval, line, for *Life*, 1720, BM, NPG.

CAMPBELL, John (1598-1663), see 1st Earl of Loudon.

CAMPBELL, John (1635-1716), see 1st Earl of Breadalbane.

CAMPBELL, John (1680-1743), see 2nd Duke of Argyll.

CAMPBELL, John (1696-1782), see 3rd Earl of Breadalbane.

CAMPEGGIO, Lorenzo (1472-1539) papal legate.
PR E.HARDING, from a medal, bust, profile, stipple, pub 1793, NPG.

CAMPION, Edmund (1540-1581) Jesuit.
PR J.NEEFS, hl with knife in breast, line, BM, NPG.

CANT, Andrew (1590?-1663) Scottish preacher.
PR S.FREEMAN, after unknown artist, hl, stipple, for Chambers, *Dict of Eminent Scotsmen*, BM, NPG.

CANUTE (994?-1035) king of the English, Danes and Norwegians.
MS UNKNOWN, c1016–20, wl with his wife, placing cross on altar of Newminster, BL Stowe Ms 944, fol 6.

CANYNGE, William (1399?-1474) merchant and monk.
SC UNKNOWN, tomb effigy, St Mary Redcliffe, Bristol.
PR H.ENGLEFIELD, hl profile from effigy, etch, BM, NPG.

CAPELL of Hadham, Arthur Capell, 1st Baron (1610-1649) royalist.
P After HENRY PAERT, c1680–1700, tql in armour, NPG 1520.
M After JOHN HOSKINS, 19th cent, hs, oval, NPG L 152 (13).
G CORNELIUS JOHNSON, c1640, tql seated with wife and family, NPG 4759.

CAPELL, Arthur (1631-1683), see 1st Earl of Essex.

CARBERY, John Vaughan, 3rd Earl of (1640?-1713) politician and courtier.
P SIR GODFREY KNELLER, c1700-10, hl, the 'Kit-cat Club' portrait, NPG 3196, engr J.Faber, jun, 1733, mezz, BM, NPG.

CARDMAKER, John (d 1555) protestant martyr.
PR UNKNOWN, wl with John Warne about to be burned at stake, wood cut, NPG.

CARDROSS, David Erskine, 2nd Baron (1616-1671) royalist.
P UNKNOWN, hl in armour, The Binns (NT), central region, Scotland.
D 11th EARL OF BUCHAN, pencil and chalk, SNPG 1636.
PR TROTTER, hs, line, pub 1798, NPG.

CARDROSS, Henry Erskine, 3rd Baron (1649?-1693) privy councillor and general of the Mint.
P Attrib L.SCHUNEMAN, hl in robes, SNPG 2206.

CAREW, Sir Alexander, 2nd Bart (1609-1644) politician.
P UNKNOWN, wl, Antony House (NT), Cornwall.

CAREW, Bamfylde Moore (1693-1770?) king of the gypsies.
PR J.FABER, jun, after R.Phelps, 1750, hl with dog, mezz, BM, NPG.

CAREW, George Carew, Baron, see Earl of Totnes.

CAREW, Sir John (d 1660) regicide.
M SAMUEL COOPER, hs in armour, oval, w/c, Antony House (NT), Cornwall; version, V & A.
G UNKNOWN, 'The Regicides Executed in 1660', hs, oval, line engr, one of ten small portraits surrounding Oliver Cromwell, BM.

CAREW, Sir Nicholas (d 1539) courtier of Henry VIII.
P HANS HOLBEIN, jun, hl in armour, Buccleuch Estates, Selkirk, Scotland. UNKNOWN, hs, Antony House (NT), Cornwall.
D HANS HOLBEIN, jun, hs, chalk, Basle Gallery, Switzerland.

CAREW, Sir Peter (1514-1575) soldier.
P GERLACH FLICKE, hl with hat, NGS 1934.

CAREW, Richard (1555-1620) antiquary.
P UNKNOWN, 1586, hl with book, Antony House (NT), Cornwall.

CAREW, Thomas (1595?-1639?) poet.
PR UNKNOWN, after a medal, hs, profile, oval, line, NPG.

CAREY, George, see 2nd Baron Hunsdon.

CAREY, Henry (1524?-1596), see 1st Baron Hunsdon.

CAREY, Henry (1596-1661), see 2nd Earl of Monmouth.

CAREY, Henry (d 1743) musician and poet.
PR J.FABER, jun, after J.Worsdale, hs, oval, mezz, for *Poems*, 1729, BM, NPG.

CAREY, Robert, see 1st Earl of Monmouth.

CARLEILL, Christopher (1551?-1593) naval and military commander.
PR PASSE, hs, oval, line, for Holland, *Herwologia*, 1620, BM, NPG. ROBERT BOISSARD, hl with baton, line, NPG.

CARLETON, Dudley, see 1st Viscount Dorchester.

CARLETON, George (1559-1628) bishop of Chichester.
PR F.HULSIUS, hl, oval, line, for *Thankfull Remembrance of God's Mercie*, 1630, BM, NPG.

CARLETON, Henry Boyle, Baron (d 1725) politician.
P SIR GODFREY KNELLER, tql, Hardwick Hall (NT), Derbys, engr J.Houbraken, oval, line, for Birch, *Heads*, 1741, BM, NPG.

CARLETON, Mary (1642?-1673) adventuress and criminal.
PR J.CHANTRY, hl, octagon, line, for *Memoirs*, 1673, BM.

CARLISLE, Charles Howard, 1st Earl of (1629-1685) general and diplomat.
P SIR GODFREY KNELLER, tql in peer's robes (lengthened to wl by W.Aikman, 1729), Castle Howard, N Yorks.
PR A.BLOOTELING, tql in armour, line, for Guillim, *Heraldry*, 1679,

BM, NPG. W.FAITHORNE, hl in cuirass, octagon, line, for *Relation of his Three Embassies*, 1669, BM, NPG.

CARLISLE, Charles Howard, 3rd Earl of (1669-1738) statesman.
P SIR GODFREY KNELLER, c1700–10, hl, 'Kit-cat Club' portrait, NPG 3197. WILLIAM AIKMAN, c1728–29, wl in peer's robes, Castle Howard, N Yorks.

CARLISLE, James Hay, 1st Viscount Doncaster and 1st Earl of (d 1636) courtier.
P UNKNOWN, 1628, wl, NPG 5210.
PR F.ALIAMET, after 'A.Vandyck', hl, oval, line, BM, NPG. S.PASSE, hl with gloves, oval, line, BM, NPG.

CARLISLE, Lucy Hay, née Percy, Countess of (1599-1660) beauty and wit.
P SIR ANTHONY VANDYCK, tql with fountain, Petworth (NT), W Sussex.
PR P.DE BAILLIEU, after Sir A.Vandyck, tql seated, line, for Vandyck, *Iconographie*, BM, NPG. G.VERTUE, after Sir A.Vandyck, hs, oval, line, BM, NPG.

CARLOS, Major William (d 1689) royalist.
M UNKNOWN, c1656, hs, oval, V & A.

CARMICHAEL, Sir James Carmichael, 1st Baron (1578?-1672) Scottish judge.
P UNKNOWN, hs in robes, Parliament Hall, Edinburgh.

CARNARVON, Robert Dormer, 1st Earl of (1607?-1643) royalist.
P After SIR ANTHONY VANDYCK, wl with wife and negro page, Longleat, Wilts.
D SIR A.VANDYCK, wl, black and white chalk, study for 'Pembroke family picture', BM.
G SIR A.VANDYCK, 4th Earl of Pembroke and his family, oil, 1634–35, Wilton House, Wilts.
PR B.BARON, after Sir A.Vandyck, life-size head after Wilton picture, line, pub Boydell, 1770, BM, NPG.

CARNWATH, Robert Dalyell or Dalzell, 6th Earl of (d 1737) Jacobite.
D SIR J.B.MEDINA, hs in armour, oval, indian ink and wash, BM.

CAROLINE (1683-1737) Queen of George II.
P SIR GODFREY KNELLER, 1716, wl in state robes with crown on table, Royal Coll; copy, NPG 529. Studio of CHARLES JERVAS, c1727, wl version of coronation portrait, NPG 369. JACOPO AMIGONI, 1735, wl seated with cherubs, NPG 4332. JOSEPH HIGHMORE, c1735, hs, profile, oval, Royal Coll. JOHN VANDERBANK, 1736, wl with sceptre, Goodwood, W Sussex.
SC J.M.RYSBRACK, 1739, terracotta bust, Royal Coll.

CARPENTER, George Carpenter, Baron (1657-1732) lieutenant-general.
PR J.FABER, jun, hl, mezz, NPG.

CARPENTER, Richard (d 1670?) theological mountebank.
PR T.CROSS, hl with 4 scenes of men with monsters, line, NPG. W.MARSHALL, 1641, hl with book, line, NPG. W.FAITHORNE, hs with man vomiting demon, oval, line, for *Two Sermons*, 1657, BM, NPG.

CARR, Robert, see Earl of Somerset.

CARRINGTON, Sir Archibald Primrose, Lord (1616-1679) Scottish judge.
P JOHN SCOUGALL, tql seated in robes, Penicuik House, Lothian region, Scotland; versions, hl, Parliament Hall, Edinburgh, and SNPG 1607.

CARSTARES, William (1649-1715) Scottish divine and politician.

P WILLIAM AIKMAN, c1712, tql seated with book, Edinburgh University. UNKNOWN, hs, SNPG 933.

CARTER, John (1554-1635) puritan, rector of Belstead, Suffolk.
PR J.DUNSTALL, hl with hour-glass, oval, etch, for S.Clarke, *Lives*, 1683, BM, NPG.

CARTER, Lawrence (1672-1745) judge, baron of exchequer.
PR G.VERTUE, after J.Richardson, hl in robes, line, BM, NPG.

CARTERET, John, see 2nd Earl Granville.

CARTWRIGHT, Thomas (1535-1603) puritan divine.
PR UNKNOWN, hl, line, for S.Clarke, *Lives*, 1683, BM, NPG.

CARTWRIGHT, Thomas (1634-1689) bishop of Chester.
P After GERARD SOEST, c1680, hl, NPG 1090; version, Queen's College, Oxford. UNKNOWN, c1686-9, hl with doctor's cap, NPG 1613; version, Queen's College, Oxford.

CARTWRIGHT, William (1611-1643) divine and dramatist.
PR P.LOMBART, hl, line, for *Poems and Plays*, 1651, BM.

CARTWRIGHT, William (d1687) actor.
P JOHN GREENHILL, c1680, hl with dog, Dulwich College Gallery, London.

CARUE, Thomas, see Carve.

CARVE or **Carue, Thomas (1590-1672)** traveller and historian.
PR M.VLIZMÄYR, hl with book, oval, line, for *Anacephalaeosis Hibernica*, 1651, BM.

CARY, Elizabeth, see Viscountess Falkland.

CARY, Henry, see 1st Viscount Falkland.

CARY, Lucius, see 2nd Viscount Falkland.

CARYL, Joseph (1602-1673) independent divine.
P UNKNOWN, tql seated, Dr Williams's Library, London, engr R.White, hs, oval, line, for *Commentary on Job*, 1676, BM, NPG.

CASAUBON, Isaac (1559-1614) classical scholar.
P UNKNOWN, late 16th or early 17th cent, hs, NPG 1776.
PR R.van GUNST, after A.van der Werff, hl, oval, line, for *Epistolae*, 1709, BM, NPG.

CASAUBON, Meric (1599-1671) classical scholar, son of Isaac.
PR P.van GUNST, after A.van der Werff, hl, oval, line, for *Epistolae*, 1709, BM.

CASE, John (d1600) Aristotelian commentator.
P UNKNOWN, hl with skeleton, St John's College, Oxford.
SC UNKNOWN, monumental effigy, wl kneeling figure, St John's College Chapel, Oxford.

CASE, Thomas (1598-1682) presbyterian divine.
P UNKNOWN, hl, Dr Williams's Library, London.

CASLON, William (1692-1766) type-founder.
PR J.FABER, jun, after F.Kyte, tql with scroll, mezz, BM.

CASS, Sir John (1666-1718) merchant and benefactor of city of London.
SC L.F.ROUBILIAC, 1751, lead statue, wl, Cass Institute, London.

CASTELL, Edmund (1606-1685) Semitic scholar.
PR W.FAITHORNE, hl, oval, line, for *Lexicon Heptaglotton*, 1669, BM, NPG.

CASTLEMAINE, Barbara Palmer, Countess of, see Duchess of Cleveland.

CASTLEMAINE, Roger Palmer, Earl of (1634-1705) diplomat and author.
P UNKNOWN, 1664, wl with secretary, Powis Castle (NT), Powys, Wales.
PR W.FAITHORNE, hs, oval, line, for *War between the Venetians and Turks*, 1666, BM, NPG.

CATESBY, Robert (1573-1605) conspirator.
G CRISPIN VAN DE PASSE, 'The Gunpowder Plot Conspirators, 1605', line engr, NPG 334A.
PR UNKNOWN, after C.Passe, hl, profile, line, pub 1794, NPG.

CATESBY, William (d1485) squire of the body to Richard III.
SC UNKNOWN, brass tomb effigy, Ashby St Ledgers Church, Northants.

CATHERINE of Valois (1401-1437) queen of Henry V.
SC UNKNOWN, funeral effigy, wl, wood, Westminster Abbey, London.

CATHERINE of Aragon (1485-1536) first queen of Henry VIII.
P UNKNOWN, c1530, hl with Spanish hood, NPG 163; version, Museum of Fine Arts, Boston, USA.
M Attrib LUCAS HORNEBOLTE, hs with cross pendant, oval, NPG 4682. UNKNOWN, hs with Spanish hood, oval, Buccleuch Estates, Selkirk, Scotland. UNKNOWN, hl with monkey, Buccleuch Estates.
W UNKNOWN, c1518-28, wl kneeling, The Vyne chapel (NT), Hants.

CATHERINE Parr (1512-1548) sixth queen of Henry VIII.
P Attrib WILLIAM SCROTS, c1545-50, hl with pendant, NPG 4618.

CATHERINE of Braganza (1638-1705) queen of Charles II.
P UNKNOWN, mid 17th cent, wl as child of ten, Museu Regional de Evora, Portugal. After DIRK STOOP, c1660-1, tql as Infanta, NPG 2563; version, hs, NPG 353. SIR PETER LELY, c1663-65, tql seated, Royal Coll. JACOB HUYSMANS, c1664, wl as shepherdess with sheep, Royal Coll. J.HUYSMANS, c1664, wl as St Catherine, Royal Coll. Attrib Studio of J.HUYSMANS, c1670, hs with ringlet on shoulder, oval, NPG 597. BENEDETTO GENNARI, c1675-85, wl with sheep, Goodwood, W Sussex.
M SAMUEL COOPER, hs, oval, Royal Coll.
SC GEORGE BOWER, various medals, BM. JAN ROETTIER, various medals and badges, BM.
PR W.HOLLAR, 1661, hl as Infanta, etch, BM. N.MUNIER, tql as Infanta, etch, pub D.Stoop, Lisbon, 1662, BM.

CAVE, Sir Ambrose (d1568) knight.
P Attrib SIR ANTONIO MOR, tql with garter, Stanford Hall, Leics.

CAVE, Edward (1691-1754) printer.
PR T.WORLIDGE, after F.Kyte, tql with turban, etch, for *Gentleman's Magazine*, 1754, BM, NPG.

CAVENDISH, Sir Charles (1591-1654) mathematician.
D G.P.HARDING, hl, wash, Sutherland Coll, Ashmolean Museum, Oxford.

CAVENDISH, Charles (1620-1643) royalist general.
P Attrib ADRIAEN HANNEMAN, hl, Hardwick Hall (NT), Derbys.

CAVENDISH, Christian, see Countess of Devonshire.

CAVENDISH, George (1500-1561?) biographer of Wolsey.
P UNKNOWN, 16th cent, hs, Hardwick Hall (NT), Derbys.

CAVENDISH, Henry (d1616) soldier and politician.
P UNKNOWN, 16th cent, hs with cap, Hardwick Hall (NT), Derbys.

CAVENDISH, Margaret, see Duchess of Newcastle.

CAVENDISH, Thomas (1560-1592) circumnavigator.
P MARCUS GHEERAERTS, hl with earring, Berkeley Castle, Glos. UNKNOWN, hl, Longleat, Wilts.
PR C.PASSE, hl with map, line, for *Effigies Regum . . . in re nautica,*

1598, BM. PASSE, hs with compass, oval, line, for Holland, *Herwologia*, 1620, BM, NPG.

CAVENDISH, Sir William (1505?-1557) statesman.
P Attrib JOHN BETTES, *c*1545, hl, on loan to Hardwick Hall (NT), Derbys.

CAVENDISH, William (d1626), see 1st Earl of Devonshire.

CAVENDISH, William (1591?-1628), see 2nd Earl of Devonshire.

CAVENDISH, William (1592-1676), see Duke of Newcastle.

CAVENDISH, William (1617-1684), see 3rd Earl of Devonshire.

CAVENDISH, William (1640-1707), see 1st Duke of Devonshire.

CAWLEY, William (1602-1667) regicide.
P UNKNOWN, 1620, hl, Chichester City Council.

CAWTON, Thomas (1605-1659) divine.
PR UNKNOWN, hl, aged 54, line, for *Life*, 1662, BM, NPG.

CAXTON, William (1422?-1491) the first English printer.
MS UNKNOWN, Flemish, *c*1475, wl presenting book to Margaret of York, Ms in Huntington Library and Art Gallery, San Marino, USA.

CECIL, Sir Edward, see Viscount Wimbledon.

CECIL, James (d1683), see 3rd Earl of Salisbury.

CECIL, James (d1693), see 4th Earl of Salisbury.

CECIL, Robert, see 1st Earl of Salisbury.

CECIL, Thomas, see 2nd Baron Burghley.

CENTLIVRE, Susannah (1667?-1723) dramatist and actress.
PR P.PELHAM, after D.Firmin, 1720, hl, oval, mezz, BM, NPG.

CERVETTO or **Bassevi, Giacomo (1682?-1783)** violoncellist.
PR M.A.PICOT, after J.Zoffany, hl with cello, oval, mezz, pub 1771, BM.

CHADERTON, William (1540?-1608) bishop of Chester and Lincoln.
P UNKNOWN, 1602, hl, Manchester City Art Gallery.

CHALLONER, Richard (1691-1781) Roman Catholic bishop of Debra.
PR UNKNOWN, hl in profile, oval, stipple, BM, NPG. UNKNOWN, wl, line, pub 1784, NPG.

CHALONER, Sir Thomas (1521-1565) diplomat.
P UNKNOWN, 1559, hl with balances, NPG 2445.
PR W.HOLLAR, tql, line, BM, NPG. UNKNOWN, hs, oval, woodcut, for *De Rep Anglorum Instawranda*, 1579, BM, NPG.

CHAMBERLAIN, Robert (fl 1678) arithmetician.
PR W.BINNEMAN, hl, oval line, for *Accomptant's Guide*, 1679, BM, NPG.

CHAMBERLAYNE, William (1619-1689) physician and poet.
PR A.HERTOCHS, hl, oval, line, for *Pharonnida*, 1659, BM, NPG.

CHAMBERLEN, Hugh (1664-1728) physician.
SC PETER SCHEEMAKERS, *c*1730, tomb effigy, Westminster Abbey, London; terracotta model, V & A.

CHAMBERLEN, Paul (1635-1717) physician.
PR T.TROTTER, after R.White, hl, oval, line, pub 1794, BM, NPG.

CHAMBERS, John, see Chambre.

CHAMBRE or **Chambers, John (1470-1549)** physician to Henry VIII.

P HANS HOLBEIN, jun, *c*1541-3, hl, Kunsthistorisches Museum, Vienna.
M Attrib PETER OLIVER, after H.Holbein, hs, oval, Royal College of Physicians, London.

CHANDLER, Edward (1668?-1750) bishop of Durham.
P UNKNOWN, hl, oval, Durham Cathedral Library. UNKNOWN, tql, Bishop Auckland Palace, Durham, engr G.Vertue, 1738, line, BM, NPG.

CHANDLER, Samuel (1693-1766) theologian.
P MASON CHAMBERLIN, tql seated, Royal Society, London. UNKNOWN, hs, oval, Dr Williams's Library, London.

CHANDOS, Giles Brydges, 3rd Baron (1547-1594) MP for Gloucestershire.
P HEIRONIMO CUSTODIS, hl, Woburn Abbey, Beds.

CHANDOS, James Brydges, 1st Duke of (1673-1744) MP for Hereford.
P HERMAN VAN DER MYN, *c*1725, wl seated in robes, NPG 530.
M C.F.ZINCKE, hs, oval, enamel, Buccleuch Estates, Selkirk, Scotland.
G SIR GODFREY KNELLER, family group, oil, 1713, National Gallery of Canada, Ottawa. JOHN WOOTTON, group riding with Prince of Wales, oil, 1737, Royal Coll.
SC GRINLING GIBBONS, 1717, marble statue on monument, St Lawrence's Church, Whitchurch, Middx.
PR B.READING, after M.Dahl, hl in robes, line, pub 1820, BM.

CHAPMAN, George (1559?-1634) poet.
PR W.HOLE, hs, oval, line, for *Homer*, 1616, BM. W.PASSE, hl, line, for *Homer's Battle of the Frogs and Mice*, *c*1624, BM.

CHARDIN, Sir John (1643-1713) jeweller and traveller.
P Attrib MICHAEL DAHL, hs, Royal Society, London. UNKNOWN, *c*1711, tql seated with map and black page, NPG 5161.
M JEAN PETITOT, hs, oval, enamel, Louvre, Paris.
PR D.LOGGAN, hl, oval, line, for *Travels*, 1686, BM, NPG.

CHARLES I (1600-1649) king of Great Britain and Ireland.
P By or after ROBERT PEAKE, sen, *c*1610, wl in long gown as Prince of Wales, SNPG 2212. UNKNOWN, *c*1612, wl with Garter robes, NPG 2562. PAUL VAN SOMER, *c*1617-20, wl seated with small dog, Statens Museum For Kunst, Copenhagen. Attrib ABRAHAM VAN BLIJENBERCH, *c*1617-20, wl, NPG 1112. GERARD HONTHORST, *c*1628, hl with letter, NPG 4444. DANIEL MYTENS, 1628, wl with Garter ribbon, Royal Coll. Studio of D.MYTENS, 1631, wl with crown, sceptre and orb on table, NPG 1246. D.MYTENS, *c*1630-2, hl with Henrietta Maria, Royal Coll. SIR ANTHONY VANDYCK, 1633, wl in armour on horseback with M. de St Antoine beside, Royal Coll. SIR A.VANDYCK, *c*1635-36, wl with armour on horseback, NG 1172. SIR A.VANDYCK, wl with Duke of Hamilton tending horse, Louvre, Paris. SIR A.VANDYCK, 1636, wl in robes, Royal Coll. SIR A.VANDYCK, 1636, hl seen from three different positions, Royal Coll. UNKNOWN, *c*1645, tql, with Sir Edward Walker, NPG 1961. SIR PETER LELY, 1647, hl, with son, James, Duke of York, Syon House, Brentford, Middx. EDWARD BOWER, 1648, tql seated with Garter star and ribbon at his trial, Royal Coll.
G SIR A.VANDYCK, wl seated with wife and two eldest children, oil, 1632, Royal Coll.
M Studio of ISAAC OLIVER, *c*1612, hs, oval, w/c, NPG 3064. I. OLIVER, *c*1616, hs, oval, Royal Coll. PETER OLIVER, 1621, hs, oval, Royal Coll. JOHN HOSKINS, *c*1645, hs, tree trunk behind, Royal Coll.
SC NICHOLAS BRIOT, 1633, silver medal, SNPG 916. N.BRIOT, 1639, medal commemorating dominion of seas, profile, BM. JEAN ROETTIER, memorial medal, hs, Ashmolean Museum, Oxford.

After HUBERT LE SUEUR, bronze bust, hs in armour, NPG 297; version, *c*1635, with helmet, Stourhead (NT), Wilts. After H.LE SUEUR, *c*1610–51, bronze equestrian statue, Royal Coll.

CHARLES II (1630-1685) king of Great Britain and Ireland.
P Studio of SIR ANTHONY VANDYCK, *c*1638, wl in armour, Royal Coll. CORNELIUS JOHNSON, 1639, wl when Prince of Wales, NPG 5103. WILLIAM DOBSON, *c*1644, tql in armour with page, SNPG 1244; version, 1644, without page, Royal Coll. After ADRIAEN HANNEMAN, *c*1648, tql with breastplate, Knole (NT), Kent; version, hl, NPG 1499. J.M.WRIGHT, *c*1661, wl seated in regalia, Royal Coll. Studio of J.M.WRIGHT, *c*1660–5, tql seated in Garter robes, NPG 531. SIMON LUTTICHUYS, *c*1660, wl in armour, on loan to DoE, British Embassy, The Hague, Netherlands. Attrib JACOB HUYSMANS, *c*1665–70, hl with queen, Syon, Brentford, Middx. HENRI GASCAR, 1670s, hs, Antony House (NT), Cornwall. SIR PETER LELY, *c*1675, wl seated in state robes, Euston Hall, Suffolk. After SIR P.LELY, *c*1675, hl with breastplate, oval, NPG 153. SIR G.KNELLER, 1670s, hl in coronation robes, Saltram House (NT), Devon, engr R.White, 1679, hs, line, BM. Studio of JOHN RILEY, *c*1680–5, hl in armour, NPG 3798. WILLEM WISSING, *c*1683, tql in armour, Royal Coll. UNKNOWN, wl 'pineapple portrait', Royal Coll.
D SAMUEL COOPER, head, profile, red and black chalk, Royal Coll.
M DAVID DES GRANGES, *c*1648, hs, oval, NPG L152 (14). S.COOPER, 1665, hl, w/c, Goodwood, W Sussex. By or after S.COOPER, hs in armour, oval, Euston Hall, Suffolk.
G SIR A.VANDYCK, three eldest children of Charles I, oil, 1635, Royal Coll. SIR A.VANDYCK, five eldest children of Charles I, wl with dog, oil, 1637, Royal Coll; copy, tql, NPG 267. HIERONYMUS JANSSENS, 'The Ball at the Hague', oil, *c*1660, Royal Coll. ANTONIO VERRIO, 'The Sea Triumph of Charles II', oil, *c*1674, Royal Coll.
SC JOHN BUSHNELL, 1667, statue, Old Bailey, London. J.BUSHNELL, terracotta bust, Fitzwilliam Museum, Cambridge. GRINLING GIBBONS, *c*1682, bronze statue, Royal Hospital, Chelsea, London. JOHN ROETTIER, 1660, medal, BM. THOMAS SIMON, 1661, coronation medal, BM. UNKNOWN, terracotta bust, Royal Coll. UNKNOWN, wax funeral effigy, Westminster Abbey.
PR FRED. BOUTTATS, after J.van der Hoecke, *c*1650, hl, oval, line, BM, NPG. C.VISSCHER, after G.Honthorst, *c*1650, hs, oval, line, BM. C.VAN DALEN, after P.Nason, 1650s, tql, line, BM.

CHARLETON, Walter (1619-1707) physician.
P SIR GODFREY KNELLER, hl with turban, Hunterian Coll, Glasgow University.
PR P.LOMBART, hl, oval, line, for *Immortality of the Soul*, 1657, BM, NPG. D.LOGGAN, 1679, hs, oval, line, for *Inquiries into Human Nature*, 1680, BM, NPG.

CHARLTON, Sir Job, Bart (1614-1697) judge.
P UNKNOWN, hs in robes, oval, Royal Courts of Justice (DoE), London; copy, John Bridge, 1886, Palace of Westminster, London.

CHARNOCK, Stephen (1628-1680) puritan theologian.
P Attrib JOHN RILEY, hl, oval, Dr Williams's Library, London.
PR R.WHITE, hs, oval, for *Discourses*, 1684, BM, NPG.

CHARTERIS, Francis (1675-1732) styled 'Colonel', gambler and criminal.
PR G.WHITE, hl profile with thumbs tied together, mezz, BM.

CHAUCER, Geoffrey (1340?-1400) poet.
P UNKNOWN, after T.Occleve, wl, NPG 532.
MS THOMAS OCCLEVE, *c*1412, for *De Regimine Principis*, BL Harley Ms 4866, fol 88. Versions, wl on horseback, *Ellesmere Chaucer*, Huntington Library, San Marino, USA; wl to right, BL Royal Ms 17 D IV; wl to left, BL Add Ms 5141; wl, BL

Lansdowne Ms 851.

CHAUCER, Thomas (1367?-1434) speaker of the House of Commons.
SC UNKNOWN, brass effigy, wl, Ewelme Church, Oxon, engr G.Fisher, lith, NPG.

CHAUNCY, Sir Henry (1632-1719) topographer.
PR J.SAVAGE, tql seated, line, for *Hist of Hertfordshire, 1700*, BM,

CHEKE, Sir John (1514-1557) Greek scholar.
SC Attrib LODOVICO LEONI, *c*1555, medal, profile bust, BM; bronze copy, NPG 1988.
PR PASSE, hs, oval, line, for Holland, *Herwologia*, 1620, BM, NPG.

CHENEVIX, Richard (1698-1779) bishop of Waterford and Lismore.
PR J.HALL, hs, oval, line, for Maty, *Memoirs of Lord Chesterfield*, 1777, BM, NPG.

CHÉRON, Louis (1655-1725) painter and engraver.
PR AUBERT, hs, oval, line, NPG. G.B.CECCHI, after L.Chéron, hl, line, BM.

CHESELDEN, William (1688-1752) surgeon.
P JONATHAN RICHARDSON, hl with turban, oval, Royal College of Surgeons, London, engr J.Faber, jun, 1753, mezz, BM.
D J.RICHARDSON, head, pencil, NPG 4995. Attrib GERARD VAN DER GUCHT, head, profile, pencil, Royal College of Surgeons.
SC Attrib J.M.RYSBRACK, terracotta bust, Royal College of Surgeons.

CHESTER, Sir William (1509?-1595?) lord mayor of London.
P UNKNOWN, hl, Drapers' Company, London.

CHESTERFIELD, Catherine Kirkhoven, Countess of (*d*1667) governess of Mary, princess royal, daughter of Charles I.
P SIR ANTHONY VANDYCK, tql with Lucy, Countess of Huntingdon, Yale Center for British Art, New Haven, USA.

CHESTERFIELD, Philip Stanhope, 2nd Earl (1633-1713) soldier and statesman.
P SIR PETER LELY, tql seated with wife, Melbourne Hall, Derbys.

CHESTERFIELD, Philip Stanhope, 4th Earl of (1694-1773) politician and author.
P After WILLIAM HOARE, *c*1742, hl with Garter star and book, NPG 158. BENJAMIN WILSON, 1752, hl, Temple Newsam, Leeds. ALLAN RAMSAY, 1765, hl with Garter star, NPG 533.
D W.HOARE, *c*1742, hs with Garter star, pastel, V & A.
SC L.F.ROUBILIAC, *c*1745, plaster bust, BM. JOSEPH WILTON, 1757, marble bust, BM.
PR E.BELL, after T.Gainsborough, 1769, hl with book, oval, mezz, pub 1826, BM, NPG. J.COLLYER, after I.Gosset, hl, profile, oval, line, BM, NPG. UNKNOWN, after O.Humphry, hs, oval, stipple, for Walpole, *Royal and Noble Authors*, 1806, BM, NPG.

CHETHAM, Humphrey (1580-1653) founder of Chetham Hospital and Library.
P UNKNOWN, hl, Chetham Hospital and Library, Manchester.

CHETWYND, Walter (*d*1693) antiquary.
PR R.WHITE, 1691, hl, oval, line BM, NPG. H.MEYER, after Sir P.Lely, hl, mezz, BM.

CHEYNE, George (1671-1743) physician.
PR J.FABER, jun, after J.Van Diest, hl, oval, mezz, BM.

CHEYNE, William, see 2nd Viscount Newhaven.

CHICHELE, Henry (1362?-1443) archbishop of Canterbury.
P SAMPSON STRONG, 1609, tql in robes, All Souls College, Oxford.
SC UNKNOWN, 1443, tomb effigy, Canterbury Cathedral.
W UNKNOWN, *c*1440–50, wl in robes, All Souls College Chapel.

CHICHELEY, Sir John (c1640-1691) rear-admiral.
P Attrib JACOB HUYSMANS, c1664, tql, NMM, Greenwich.

CHICHELEY, Sir Thomas (1618-1699) master general of the ordinance.
P UNKNOWN, wl in robes, Grocers' Company, London.

CHIFFINCH, Thomas (1600-1666) closet-keeper to Charles II.
P SEBASTIEN BOURDON, c1650-60, hl with bust, NPG 816.

CHIFFINCH, William (1602?-1688) closet-keeper to Charles II.
P After JOHN RILEY, c1670-80, hl, Dulwich College Gallery, London; version, hs, oval, NPG 1091.

CHILD, Sir Francis, sen (1642-1713) banker.
P UNKNOWN, wl in lord mayor's robes, Christ's Hospital, Horsham, Sussex.

CHILD, Sir Francis, jun (1684?-1740) banker.
P UNKNOWN, wl in lord mayor's robes, Christ's Hospital, Horsham, Sussex.

CHILD, Sir Josiah, Bart (1630-1699) chairman of East India Company.
P Attrib JOHN RILEY, tql, Woburn Abbey, Beds.
SC JOHN NOST, marble effigy with son, St Mary and Christchurch, Wanstead, London.

CHILD, William (1606?-1697) musician.
P UNKNOWN, 1663, wl in robes, Faculty of Music, Oxford.

CHILLINGWORTH, William (1602-1644) theologian.
PR UNKNOWN, hl, oval, mezz, NPG.

CHISENHALE, Edward (d1654) historian.
PR UNKNOWN, wl kneeling, line, for *Catholike History*, 1653, BM, NPG.

CHUBB, Thomas (1679-1747) religious writer.
P GEORGE BEARE, 1747, hl, NPG 1122.

CHURCHILL, Anne, see Countess of Sunderland.

CHURCHILL, Arabella, later Mrs Godfrey (1648-1730) mistress of James II.
P After SIR PETER LELY, tql seated with dog, Althorp, Northants. Studio of SIR P.LELY, tql seated, Althorp. Attrib J.M.WRIGHT, hl as child with brother Winston, Blenheim, Oxon.

CHURCHILL, George (1654-1710) admiral.
P SIR GODFREY KNELLER, 1704, hl, NMM, Greenwich; chalk drawing for portrait, NMM.

CHURCHILL, John (1650-1722), see 1st Duke of Marlborough.

CHURCHILL, Sarah, see Duchess of Marlborough.

CHUTE, Chaloner (d1659) speaker of the House of Commons.
P UNKNOWN, wl, The Vyne (NT), Basingstoke, Hants.

CIBBER, Caius Gabriel (1630-1700) sculptor.
PR A.BANNERMAN, hl, oval, line, NPG.

CIBBER, Colley (1671-1757) actor, poet and dramatist.
P GIUSEPPE GRISONI, tql as 'Lord Foppington', Garrick Club, London.
SC Attrib CHEERE workshop, painted plaster bust, NPG 1045.
PR G.VAN DER GUCHT, after J.B.Vanloo, hl, oval, line, for *Apology*, 1740, BM.

CLARE, John Holles, 1st earl of (1564?-1637) soldier and politician.
PR R.CLAMP, tql, stipple, for Harding, *Biographical Mirrour*, 1792, BM, NPG.

CLARENCE, Lionel, Duke of, see LIONEL of Antwerp.

CLARENCE, Thomas, Duke of, see THOMAS.

CLARENDON, Edward Hyde, 1st Earl of (1609-1674) statesman.
P After ADRIAEN HANNEMAN, c1648-55, hl, hexagonal, NPG 773. After SIR PETER LELY, (type of c1660-65), tql in Lord Chancellor's robes, Clarendon Coll on loan to Palace of Westminster, London. SIR P.LELY, c1660-65, hl in robes, Bodleian Library, Oxford, engr M.Burghers, hs, oval, line, BM, NPG and R.White, BM.
SC THOMAS SIMON, 1662, silver medal, profile, NPG 4361.
PR D.LOGGAN, 1666, hs in robes, *ad vivum*, line, BM, NPG.

CLARENDON, Henry Hyde, 2nd Earl of (1638-1709) statesman.
P SIR PETER LELY, 1661, tql seated with 1st wife, Thedosia Capel, Badminton House, Avon.

CLARENDON, Jane Hyde, née Leveson-Gower, Countess of (d1725) wife of 4th Earl of Clarendon and celebrated beauty.
PR J.FABER, jun, after Sir G.Kneller, wl, one of set of Hampton Court Beauties, mezz, BM; same plate, tql, mezz, NPG.

CLARK, John (1688-1736) writing-master and accountant.
PR G.BICKHAM, hl, oval, line, for *Penman's Diversion*, 1708, BM, NPG.

CLARKE, Alured (1696-1742) dean of Exeter.
P JAMES WILLS, tql seated, Royal Devon and Exeter Hospital, Exeter.

CLARKE, Sir Charles (d1750) judge, baron of the exchequer.
P GEORGE BEARE, tql, Corpus Christi College, Cambridge.

CLARKE, George (1661-1736) politician.
P Attrib SIR GODFREY KNELLER, tql, Worcester College, Oxford. After SIR G.KNELLER, hs, All Souls College, Oxford. SIR G.KNELLER, tql with Prince George of Denmark, All Souls College.
M THOMAS FORSTER, Holburne of Menstrie Museum, Bath.
SC SIR HENRY CHEERE, c1756, bronze bust, All Souls College.

CLARKE, John (1582-1653) physician.
P UNKNOWN, c1645-50, hl, Royal College of Physicians, London.

CLARKE, Matthew (1664-1726) independent minister.
PR G.WHITE, hl, oval, mezz, BM.

CLARKE, Samuel (1599-1683) minister of St Benet Fink, biographer.
PR T.CROSS, hl, line, for *Marrow of Ecclesiastical History*, 1650, BM, NPG. R.GAYWOOD, hl, oval, etch, for *Looking Glass for Saints and Sinners*, 1654, BM, NPG. R.WHITE, hl, oval, line, for *Lives*, 1683, BM, NPG.

CLARKE, Samuel (1625-1669) orientalist and biblical commentator.
P UNKNOWN, hl, Bodleian Library, Oxford.

CLARKE, Samuel (1626-1701) biblical commentator.
PR R.WHITE, hl, oval, line, BM, NPG.

CLARKE, Samuel (1675-1729) metaphysician.
P After CHARLES JERVAS, tql seated with bust of Newton, Royal Coll. UNKNOWN, wl seated, NPG 266.
SC JOHN CHEERE, bronzed plaster bust, Castle Museum, York. G.A.GUELFI, c1733, marble bust, Royal Coll. JAMÈ VERHYCH, 1719, platinated lead bust, NPG 4838.

CLARKSON, David (1622-1686) nonconformist minister.
PR R.WHITE, after M.Beale, hs, oval, line, for *Sermons*, 1696, BM, NPG.

CLAVEL, John (1603-1642) reformed criminal.
PR W.MARSHALL, hl, oval, line, for *Recantation of an ill led Life*, 1628, BM.

CLAVERING, Robert (1671-1747) bishop of Peterborough.
P By or after THOMAS GIBSON, tql seated, Christ Church, Oxford.

CLAYPOLE, Elizabeth, née Cromwell (1629-1658) second daughter of Oliver Cromwell.
P J.M.WRIGHT, 1658, tql, NPG 952.
M SAMUEL COOPER, 1652, hs, oval, Buccleuch Estates, Selkirk, Scotland.
SC THOMAS and ABRAHAM SIMON, silver medal, BM.

CLAYPOLE, John (d 1688) parliamentarian, married Cromwell's daughter Elizabeth.
P UNKNOWN, hl in armour, NPG 4673.
SC ABRAHAM SIMON, silver medal, BM.

CLAYTON, Charlotte, see Lady Sundon.

CLAYTON, Sir Robert (1629-1707) politician, lord mayor of London.
P LORENZO DA CASTRO, c1680, wl seated, Bank of England, London. UNKNOWN, c1680, hl, Bank of England. JONATHAN RICHARDSON, 1706, wl seated, Drapers' Company, London. JOHN RILEY, tql seated, Guildhall, London.
SC RICHARD CRUTCHER, 1705, statue on monument with wife, Bletchingley Church, Surrey.

CLEIN or Cleyn, Francis (1590?-1658) painter.
PR T.CHAMBARS, hs, oval, line, for Walpole, *Anecdotes*, 1762, BM, NPG.

CLEMENT, Gregory (d 1660) regicide.
G UNKNOWN, 'The Regicides Executed in 1660', hs, oval, line engr, BM.
PR UNKNOWN, hs, oval, line, NPG.

CLENCH, Sir John (d 1607) judge, baron of the exchequer.
M ISAAC OLIVER, 1583, hs, Buccleuch Estates, Selkirk, Scotland.
PR W.HOLLAR, hs, etch, for Dugdale, *Origines*, 1666, BM.

CLERK, Sir John, 2nd Bart (1676-1755) of Penicuik, judge and antiquary.
P WILLIAM AIKMAN, hl, oval, Penicuik House, Lothian region, Scotland. W.AIKMAN, tql in robes, Penicuik; copy, SNPG 1355. SIR J.B.MEDINA, hl with book, Penicuik.
D WILLIAM VAN MIERIS, hs, oval, aged 19, pencil, Penicuik.

CLERK, Josiah (1639-1714) physician.
P UNKNOWN, c1690, tql seated, Royal College of Physicians, London.

CLERKE, Henry (d 1687) physician.
P UNKNOWN, hs in doctor's robes, Magdalen College, Oxford.

CLEVELAND, Barbara Palmer, née Villiers, Countess of Castlemaine and Duchess of (1640-1709) mistress of Charles II.
P Numerous portraits were painted by SIR PETER LELY and studio, c1660-75, among them: wl seated head on hand, Knole (NT), Kent; tql as St Barbara, NPG 387; tql seated as Madonna and child, NPG 2564; tql in Turkish dress?, Euston Hall, Suffolk; tql seated, National Gallery of Art, Washington, USA; tql seated with putti behind, Euston Hall; tql, Uffizi, Florence; tql as Minerva, Royal Coll; tql as shepherdess, Althorp, Northants; wl with Diana Fountain, Goodwood, W Sussex. SIR GODFREY KNELLER, wl in peer's robes, Bank of England, London, engr I.Beckett, hl, oval, mezz, BM, NPG. After SIR G.KNELLER, c1705, tql seated in mourning, NPG 427.
M SAMUEL COOPER, 166?, hl, oval, Althorp. S.COOPER, head, Royal Coll. NICHOLAS DIXON, hl with child, oval, Althorp.

PR R.WILLIAMS, after W.Wissing, hl, oval, mezz, BM, NPG.

CLEVELAND, Charles Fitzroy, 1st Duke of (1662-1730) natural son of Charles II by Barbara Villiers, Duchess of Cleveland.
P MICHAEL DAHL, wl in Garter robes, Raby Castle, Durham.

CLEVELAND, John (1613-1658) cavalier poet.
PR UNKNOWN, hl with book, oval, line, for *Poems*, 1661, BM, NPG. UNKNOWN, bust on pedestal, line, NPG.

CLEVELAND, Sir Thomas Wentworth, 4th Baron Wentworth of Nettlestead and 1st Earl of (1591-1667) soldier and statesman.
P After SIR ANTHONY VANDYCK, 1636, wl, Gorhambury, Herts.

CLEYN, Francis, see Clein.

CLIFFORD, Anne, see Countess of Pembroke and Montgomery.

CLIFFORD, George, see 3rd Earl of Cumberland.

CLIFFORD, Henry, see 5th Earl of Cumberland.

CLIFFORD, Margaret, see Countess of Cumberland.

CLIFFORD, Martin (d 1677) author.
PR M.VAN DER GUCHT, hl, oval, line, for Cowley, *Works*, 1710, BM, NPG.

CLIFFORD, Thomas, see 1st Baron Clifford of Chudleigh.

CLIFFORD of Chudleigh, Thomas Clifford, 1st Baron (1630-1673) statesman.
P SIR PETER LELY, c1672, tql in peer's robes, Ugbroke Park, Devon; version, hl, NPG 204.
M SAMUEL COOPER, hs, oval, w/c, Ugbroke Park.

CLINTON, Edward Fiennes de, see 1st Earl of Lincoln.

CLITHEROW, Sir Christopher (d 1641) merchant.
P UNKNOWN, Christ's Hospital, Horsham, Sussex.

CLOTWORTHY, Sir John, see 1st Viscount Massereene.

CLOUGH, Richard (d 1570) merchant.
PR J.BASIRE, after M.Griffith, tql, line, for Pennant, *London*, BM, NPG.

COBBE, Charles (1687-1765) archbishop of Dublin.
PR A.MILLER, after F.Bindon, tql seated, mezz, BM.

COBHAM, Sir Richard Temple, 1st Viscount (1675-1749) general and politician.
P SIR GODFREY KNELLER, c1710, hl, the 'Kit-cat Club' portrait, NPG 3198. After J.B.VANLOO, (type of c1740), hl, oval, NPG 286, engr G.Bickham, 1751, line, BM, NPG.
SC PETER SCHEEMAKERS, c1740, marble bust, V & A.

COCKBURN, Archibald (fl 1722) clergyman and author.
PR G.VAN DER GUCHT, hs, oval, line, BM, NPG.

COCKBURN, Catharine (1679-1749) dramatist and philosophical writer.
PR UNKNOWN, hl, oval, line, BM, NPG.

COCKER, Edward (1631-1675) arithmetician and writing-master.
P After RICHARD GAYWOOD, hl, oval, NPG 274.
PR R.GAYWOOD, hs, oval, etch, for *Pen's Triumph*, 1658, BM. R.GAYWOOD, hl with pen, oval, etch, BM.

CODRINGTON, Christopher (1668-1710) governor of Leeward Isles.
P SIR JAMES THORNHILL, wl, All Souls' College, Oxford.
SC SIR HENRY CHEERE, 1734, marble statue, All Souls' College.

COGAN, William (d 1774) philanthropist.
P UNKNOWN, Wilberforce House, Hull. UNKNOWN, Guildhall.

Hull.

COKAYNE, Sir Aston (1608-1684) poet.
PR UNKNOWN, bust, stipple, modern copy of engr for *Poems*, 1669, BM.

COKE, Sir Edward (1552-1634) lord chief justice of England.
P UNKNOWN, wl in robes, Holkham Hall, Norfolk. Attrib PAUL VAN SOMER, wl in robes, Inner Temple, London. UNKNOWN, tql, Palace of Westminster, London.
SC L.F.ROUBILIAC, 1757, marble bust, Trinity College, Cambridge. NICHOLAS STONE, 1638, relief effigy on monument, St Mary's Church, Tittleshall, Norfolk.
PR J.PAYNE, hs, oval, line, for *Institutes*, 1629, BM, NPG. D.LOGGAN, hl in robes, line, for *Juridiciales*, 1666, BM, NPG.

COKE, George (d 1646) bishop of Hereford.
P UNKNOWN, hl, Bishop's Palace, Hereford.

COKE, Sir John (1563-1644) secretary of state to Charles I.
P UNKNOWN, tql in robes, Melbourne Hall, Derbys. UNKNOWN, hl, NMM, Greenwich.

COLDEN, Cadwallader (1688-1776) botanist and American loyalist.
P MATTHEW PRATT, tql, Metropolitan Museum of Art, New York. JOHN WOLLASTON, hl, Metropolitan Museum of Art.

COLE, Abdiah (1610?-1670?) physician.
PR T.CROSS, hs, line, for *Practice of Physick*, 1655, V & A.

COLE, Sir Ralph, 2nd Bart (1625?-1704) amateur artist.
PR F.PLACE, after Sir P.Lely, hl, mezz, BM.

COLE, William (1635-1716) physician.
PR R.WHITE, hs, oval, line, for *Treatise on Apoplexies*, 1689, BM, NPG.

COLEPEPPER, William (d 1726) poet and politician.
G R.WHITE, the Kentish petitioners, hs, oval, line engr, 1701, BM.

COLERAINE, Henry Hare, 2nd Baron (1636-1708) antiquary and author.
PR W.FAITHORNE and G.VERTUE, tql in robes, line, BM, NPG. W.FAITHORNE, after Lord Coleraine, wl as pilgrim with emblems, line, for trans of Lauredanus, *Ascent of the Soul*, 1681, BM, NPG. UNKNOWN, 1703, hl in robes, oval, mezz, BM, NPG.

COLERAINE, Henry Hare, 3rd Baron (1693-1749) antiquary.
P JONATHAN RICHARDSON, hl as young man, Society of Antiquaries, London.
D GEORGE VERTUE, 1740, hs, oval, w/c, BM.

COLET, John (1467?-1519) dean of St Paul's and founder of St Paul's School.
MS PETER MEGHEN, 1506–9, wl kneeling before St Matthew, *New Testament*, Ms Dd 7.3, University Library, Cambridge.
SC Attrib PIETRO TORRIGIANO, bust, St Paul's School, London; plaster cast, NPG 4823.
PR UNKNOWN, monument St Paul's Cathedral, London, line engr for Dugdale, *St Paul*, 1658, BM.

COLEY, Henry (1633-1695?) astrologer and mathematician.
PR R.WHITE, hs oval, line, BM, NPG. UNKNOWN, hs, oval, line, BM, NPG. UNKNOWN, hs within horoscope, line, BM, NPG.

COLLEGE, Stephen (1635?-1681) 'the protestant joiner', executed for treason.
PR UNKNOWN, hs, oval, line, BM, NPG.

COLLIER, Jeremy (1650-1726) non-juring divine.
PR R.WHITE, hl, oval, line, for *Dictionary*, 1701, BM, NPG.

COLLINGES, John (1623-1690) presbyterian divine.
PR R.WHITE, hl, oval, line, for *Discourses*, 1678, BM, NPG.

COLLINGWOOD, George (d 1716) Jacobite, executed for treason.
PR UNKNOWN, wl, line, BM, NPG.

COLLINS, Samuel (1576-1651) divine, provost of King's College, Cambridge.
P UNKNOWN, hl, King's College.

COLLINS, Samuel (1618-1710) anatomist.
PR W.FAITHORNE, hl, oval, line, for *Anatomy*, 1685, BM, NPG.

COLLINSON, Peter (1694-1768) antiquary and botanist.
P UNKNOWN, tql seated, Mill Hill School, London.
M NATHANIEL HONE, 1765, hs, oval, NPG L152 (21).

COLMAN, Walter, Christopher in religion (d 1645) Franciscan friar and poet.
PR UNKNOWN, hl in habit, oval, line, for Mason, *Certamen Seraphicum*, 1649, BM, NPG.

COLSON, John (1680-1760) mathematician.
P JOHN WOLLASTON, 1741, hl, Old Schools, Cambridge.

COLSON, Lancelot (fl 1668) physician and astrologer.
PR J.DUNSTALL, tql seated, etch, for *Poor Man's Physician*, 1633, BM, NPG.

COLSTON, Edward (1636-1721) philanthropist.
P JONATHAN RICHARDSON, tql, City Council, Bristol, engr G.Vertue, 1722, BM, NPG.
SC J.M.RYSBRACK, 1728, marble tomb effigy, All Saints' Church, Bristol.

COLWALL, Daniel (d 1690) treasurer of Royal Society.
P UNKNOWN, hs, oval, Royal Society, London.
PR R.WHITE, 1681, hl, oval, line, BM, NPG.

COMBER, Thomas (1575-1654) dean of Carlisle.
P UNKNOWN, hl, Trinity College, Cambridge.

COMBER, Thomas (1645-1699) dean of Durham.
PR G.LUMLEY, hl, oval, mezz, BM, NPG.

COMPTON, Henry (1632-1713) bishop of London.
P SIR GODFREY KNELLER, c1700, hl, NPG 2952. SIR G.KNELLER, wl, Christ Church, Oxford. JOHN RILEY, tql, Queen's College, Oxford.
SC GEORGE BOWER, 1688, silver medal, NPG 152A.
PR D.LOGGAN, 1679, hs, oval, line, BM, NPG.

COMPTON, Spencer (1601-1643), see 2nd Earl of Northampton.

COMPTON, Spencer (1673?-1743), see 1st Earl of Wilmington.

COMPTON, Sir William (1625-1663) royalist.
P SIR PETER LELY, c1655, tql in breastplate, Ham House (NT), London. HENRY PAERT, after Sir P.Lely, tql, NPG 1522.

COMYNS, Sir John (d 1740) judge.
P UNKNOWN, tql in robes, Lincoln's Inn, London.
PR G.VERTUE, hl, oval, line, for *Reports*, 1744, BM, NPG.

CONANT, John (1608-1694) theologian.
PR UNKNOWN, hl, oval, line, BM, NPG.

CONDUITT, John (1688-1737) master of the mint.
SC J.S.TANNER, silver medals, BM.

CONGREVE, William (1670-1729) dramatist.
P SIR GODFREY KNELLER, 1709, hl, 'Kit-cat Club' portrait, NPG 3199. Studio of SIR G.KNELLER, c1709, hs, oval, NPG 67.
SC FRANCIS BIRD, after Sir G.Kneller, 1729, memorial relief effigy, Westminster Abbey, London. JOHN CHEERE, bronze bust, Castle Museum, York.

CONINGSBY, Sir Thomas (1551-1625) soldier.
P Attrib GEORGE GOWER, 1572, hl with birds, NPG 4348.

CONINGSBY, Thomas Coningsby, Earl of (1656?-1729) Whig politician.
P THOMAS BALE, wl, Yale Center for British Art, New Haven, USA.
G SIR GODFREY KNELLER, wl seated with two daughters, oil, 1722, Tower of London.
SC L.F.ROUBILIAC, marble statue on family monument, Hope Church, Hereford.

CONNY, Robert (1645?-1723) physician.
P ALEXANDER VANDERHAGEN, tql seated, Bodleian Library, Oxford, engr John Faber, jun, 1722, mezz, BM. UNKNOWN, tql in doctor's gown, Magdalen College, Oxford.

CONOLLY, William (1662-1729) speaker of Irish House of Commons.
SC THOMAS CARTER, sen, monument with wife, Celbridge Church, County Kildare, Eire.
PR P.FOURDRINIER, tql in robes, line, BM.

CONYBEARE, John (1692-1755) bishop of Bristol.
P UNKNOWN, hl, Exeter College, Oxford; version, hs, Christ Church, Oxford.

COOK, John (d1660) judge and regicide.
G UNKNOWN, 'The Regicides Executed in 1660', hs, oval, line engr, BM.
SC THOMAS SIMON, silver medal, BM.
PR UNKNOWN, hl with book, German line engr, BM. UNKNOWN, hs, oval, line, NPG.

COOKE, Sir Anthony (1504-1576) politician.
SC UNKNOWN, 1576, marble and alabaster effigy on family monument, St Andrew's Church, Romford, Essex.

COOKES, Sir Thomas, 2nd Bart (d1701) founder of Worcester College, Oxford.
P MICHAEL DAHL, tql, Bodleian Library, Oxford. UNKNOWN, wl with bust of King Alfred, Worcester College, Oxford.
SC Attrib JOHN NOST, hl monumental effigy with wife, Tardebrigge Church, Worcs.

COOLING, Richard (d1697) clerk of the privy council.
PR UNKNOWN, hl, mezz, BM.

COOPER, Anthony Ashley (1621-1683), see 1st Earl of Shaftesbury.

COOPER, Anthony Ashley (1671-1713), see 3rd Earl of Shaftesbury.

COOPER, Samuel (1609-1672) miniature painter.
D Self-portrait, hs, pastel, V & A. After S.COOPER, hl, w/c, NPG 2891.

COPLEY, Sir Godfrey, 2nd Bart (d1709) politician.
PR JOHN SMITH, after Sir G.Kneller, hs, oval, mezz, BM.

CORAM, Thomas (1668?-1751) philanthropist.
P WILLIAM HOGARTH, 1740, wl seated, Thomas Coram Foundation for Children, London. B.NEBOT, 1741, wl with foundling, Thomas Coram Foundation.
D After W.HOGARTH, 1740, hs, wash, NPG 2427.

CORBET, Miles (d1662) lawyer and regicide.
PR R.COOPER, hl, oval, line, BM, NPG.

CORBET, Richard (1582-1635) bishop of Oxford.
P UNKNOWN, wl in robes, Christ Church, Oxford.

CORBETT, William (d1748) violinist and composer.
PR J.SIMON, after J.Austen, hl, oval, mezz, BM.

CORDELL, Sir William (d1580) master of the rolls.
P UNKNOWN, tql, Melford Hall (NT), Suffolk.
SC CORNELIUS CURE, tomb effigy, Holy Trinity Church, Long Melford, Suffolk.

CORK, Richard Boyle, 1st Earl of (1566-1643) Irish statesman.
M ISAAC OLIVER, c1610-15, hs, oval, w/c, NPG 2494.
SC UNKNOWN, tomb effigy on monument, Youghal, Cork, Eire.

CORK, Richard Boyle, 2nd Earl of (1612-1697), see 1st Earl of Burlington.

CORK, Richard Boyle, 4th Earl of (1695-1753), see 3rd Earl of Burlington.

CORNELIUS, John (1557-1594) Jesuit.
PR UNKNOWN, hl, profile, line, NPG.

CORN(E)WALL, James (1699-1744) navy captain.
SC UNKNOWN, relief medallion on monument, Westminster Abbey, London, line engr, NPG.

CORNISH, Henry (d1685) alderman of London.
G J.SAVAGE, 'Anti-Papists', eight ovals around Duke of Monmouth, line engr, BM.
PR UNKNOWN, hl, line, NPG.

CORNWALL, John, Earl of, see JOHN of Eltham.

CORNWALLIS, Sir Charles (d1629) diplomat.
P UNKNOWN, tql, NPG 4867.

CORNWALLIS, Sir Thomas (1519-1604) diplomat.
P Attrib GEORGE GOWER, hl, Audley End (DoE), Essex.
SC UNKNOWN, monument, Broome Church, Suffolk.

CORYATE, Thomas (1577?-1617) traveller.
PR UNKNOWN, hl, oval, line, for *Crudities*, 1611, BM. NPG. UNKNOWN, wl with courtesan, line, for *Crudities*, BL. UNKNOWN, wl on elephant, woodcut, for *Letters from Asmere*, 1616, NPG.

COSIN, John (1594-1672) bishop of Durham.
P UNKNOWN, hs, oval, Durham Cathedral.
PR W.DOLLE, hs, oval, line, for I.Basire, *Funeral Sermon*, 1673, BM, NPG.

COTTAM, Thomas (1549-1582) Jesuit.
PR UNKNOWN, hl, line, NPG.

COTTERELL, Sir Charles (1612?-1702) courtier.
P WILLIAM DOBSON, hs, octagonal, Rousham House, Oxon. SIR GODFREY KNELLER, tql seated, Rousham. SIR PETER LELY, hs, oval, BM. JOHN RILEY, 1687, hs, Rousham.
M W.DOBSON, hs, oval, Rousham.
G W.DOBSON, hl with the artist and Nicholas Lanier, oil, Alnwick Castle, Northd.

COTTERELL, Sir Charles Lodowick (1654-1710) courtier.
P Attrib MICHAEL DAHL, c1690, hs, oval, Rousham House, Oxon. Attrib JOHN GREENHILL, hs, Rousham. SIR GODFREY KNELLER, tql, Rousham.

COTTINGTON, Francis Cottington, 1st Baron (1578-1652) diplomat.
P UNKNOWN, 1634?, hs, NPG 605; version, wl, Clarendon Coll on loan to Council House, Plymouth.

COTTON, Charles (1630-1687) poet.
PR W.W.RYLAND, after Sir P.Lely, hl, oval, line, for Walton, *Compleat Angler*, 1760, BM, NPG.

COTTON, Sir John, 3rd Bart (1621-1701) scholar.
PR R.WHITE, after Sir G.Kneller, hl, oval, line, BM.

COTTON, Sir Robert Bruce, 1st Bart (1571-1631)

antiquary.
P UNKNOWN, 1629, hs, oval, BM; version, hl, NPG 534.
PR G.VERTUE, after P.van Somer, hl with Ms, line, for *Vetusta Monumenta*, BM.

COTTRELL, Sir Charles, see Cotterell.

COTTRELL, Sir Charles Lodowick, see Cotterell.

COURAYER, Pierre François le (1681-1776) French divine.
P UNKNOWN, hl, oval, Bodleian Library, Oxford; version, hs, NPG 5177.
PR ELIZA B.GULSTON, after Hamilton, hl, oval, etch, NPG.

COURTEN, William (1642-1702) naturalist.
P UNKNOWN, hl, BM.

COURTENAY, Edward, see Earl of Devon.

COURTENAY, William (1342?-1396) archbishop of Canterbury.
SC UNKNOWN, alabaster tomb effigy, Canterbury Cathedral.

COUTTS, John (1699-1751) merchant.
PR J.McARDELL, after A.Ramsay, hl, oval, mezz, BM, NPG.

COVELL, John (1638-1722) traveller.
P UNKNOWN, Christ's College, Cambridge.

COVENTRY, Henry (1619-1686) secretary of State.
P MARY BEALE, tql in robes, Longleat, Wilts.

COVENTRY, Sir John (d 1682) politician.
P WILLIAM DOBSON, c1650, hl, oval, Longleat, Wilts.

COVENTRY, Thomas Coventry, 1st Baron (1578-1640) lord keeper.
P CORNELIUS JOHNSON, 1634, hl in lord keeper's gown, Longleat, Wilts. C.JOHNSON, 1639, tql in peer's robes, NPG 4815; version, Clarendon Coll, on loan to House of Lords.

COVENTRY, Sir William (1628?-1686) politician.
P JOHN RILEY, c1670, tql seated, Longleat, Wilts.

COWARD, William (d 1738) London merchant.
P UNKNOWN, tql, New College, London.

COWLEY, Abraham (1618-1667) poet.
P After SIR PETER LELY, c1660, hs, NPG 74, engr W.Faithorne, line, for *Poemata Latina*, 1668, BM, NPG and *Works*, 1668, BM, NPG. SIR P.LELY, c1666-67, tql seated, NPG 4215.
PR R.VAUGHAN, hl, aged 13, line, for *Poetical Blossoms*, 1633, BM, NPG.

COWPER, Mary Cowper, 1st Countess of (1685-1724) lady of bedchamber to Princess of Wales.
PR UNKNOWN, hl, oval, stipple, NPG.

COWPER, Spencer (1669-1728) judge.
P SIR GODFREY KNELLER, hl, Oriel College, Oxford.
SC L.F.ROUBILIAC, marble relief effigy on monument, St Mary's Church, Hertingfordbury, Herts.

COWPER, William Cowper, 1st Earl of (1665?-1723) lawyer and lord chancellor.
P By or after JONATHAN RICHARDSON, c1710?, wl in chancellor's robes, NPG 736. SIR GODFREY KNELLER, 1722, hl in peer's robes, NPG 1228.

COWPER, William (1666-1709) surgeon.
P JOHN CLOSTERMAN, hl, oval, Royal College of Surgeons, London, engr John Smith, mezz, for *Anatomy*, 1698, BM, NPG.

COX, Richard (1500-1581) bishop of Ely.
P UNKNOWN, hl in robes, Trinity Hall, Cambridge; version, Trinity College, Cambridge.

COX, Sir Richard (1650-1733) Irish judge.

P UNKNOWN, hl in robes, NGI.

CRAB, Roger (1621?-1680) ascetic.
PR UNKNOWN, wl, woodcut, for *Life*, 1655, BM, NPG.

CRACKENTHORPE, Richard (1567-1624) divine.
P UNKNOWN, tql seated, Queen's College, Oxford.

CRADOCK, Samuel (1621?-1706) congregational divine.
P UNKNOWN, hl, Dr Williams's Library, London, engr R.White, hs, line, for *Knowledge and Practice of Salvation*, 1702, BM, NPG.

CRADOCK, Zachary (1633-1695) provost of Eton.
P Attrib JOHN GREENHILL, hl, oval, Eton College, Berks.

CRAGGS, James, sen (1657-1721) postmaster-general.
P Attrib JOHN CLOSTERMAN, c1710, tql seated, NPG 1733. MICHAEL DAHL, c1719-21, hl, General Post Office, London.
PR G.VERTUE, after Sir G.Kneller, 1728, tql, line, BM, NPG.

CRAGGS, James, jun (1686-1721) secretary of state.
P Studio of SIR GODFREY KNELLER, c1708, tql, NPG 1134, engr G.Vertue, 1720, line, NPG; J.Simon, mezz, 1720, NPG.
SC G.B.GUELFI, 1727, marble statue on monument, Westminster Abbey, London.
PR C.KNIGHT, after Sir G.Kneller, hl with turban, stipple, NPG.

CRAIG, John (d 1655) Scottish physician.
P UNKNOWN, hl, SNPG 2143.

CRAIG, Sir Thomas (1538-1608) Scottish lawyer.
PR G.VERTUE, 1731, hl, oval, line, BM, NPG.

CRAIGHALL, Sir John Hope, Lord (1605?-1654) judge.
P GEORGE JAMESONE, hl, SNPG L94.

CRANBOURNE, Robert Cecil, 1st Viscount, see 1st Earl of Salisbury.

CRANE, Sir Francis (d 1636) director of tapestry works at Mortlake.
D LUCAS VORSTERMAN, hs, oval, chalk, BM.

CRANFIELD, Lionel, see 1st Earl of Middlesex.

CRANLEY, Thomas (1337?-1417) archbishop of Dublin.
SC UNKNOWN, brass, effigy, New College, Oxford.

CRANMER, Thomas (1489-1556) archbishop of Canterbury.
P GERLACH FLICKE, 1546, tql seated, NPG 535. UNKNOWN, hl, Trinity College, Cambridge. Attrib JOHN BELKAMP, Knole (NT), Kent.
G UNKNOWN, 'Edward VI and the Pope', oil, c1548-49, NPG 4165. UNKNOWN, wl being tested by crowd, woodcut, for Foxe, *Actes and Monuments*, 1563, NPG.
PR T.BEZA, hs, oval, for *Icones*, 1589, NPG.

CRAVEN of Ryton, John Craven, Baron (1610-1648) founder of scholarships at Oxford and Cambridge.
P Attrib GERARD HONTHORST, 1647, hl in armour, oval, Powis Castle (NT), Powys, Wales.

CRAVEN, William Craven, 1st Earl of (1606-1697) soldier and courtier.
P UNKNOWN, tql in armour, NPG 270. Attrib PRINCESS LOUISE, 1647, hl, NPG 4517.
D G.P.HARDING, after unknown artist, hs in armour, ink and wash, NPG 3018.
PR UNKNOWN, wl on horseback, line, BM, NPG.

CRAWFORD, John Lindsay, 17th Earl of (1596-1678) statesman.
P UNKNOWN, 1663, hs, oval, SNPG 817.

CREECH, Thomas (1659-1700) translator.
P WILLIAM SONMANS, hs, oval, Bodleian Library, Oxford.

CREIGHTON, Robert (1593-1672) bishop of Bath and Wells.
P UNKNOWN, hl in robes, Corporation, Wells, Somerset; copy, Bishop's Palace, Wells.

CRESSWELL, Madam (fl 1670-1684) procuress.
PR UNKNOWN, after M.Laroon, wl, line, for Tempest, *Cries of London*, BM.

CREW of Stene, John Crew, 1st Baron (1598-1679) politician.
D UNKNOWN, tql in robes, wash, Sutherland Coll, Ashmolean Museum, Oxford.

CREW of Stene, Nathaniel Crew, 3rd Baron (1633-1721) bishop of Durham.
P UNKNOWN, c1675-85, tql with book, Bishop's Palace, Chichester; version, hl, NPG 656, engr Francis Place, hs, oval, mezz, BM, NPG. SIR GODFREY KNELLER, tql in bishop's robes, Lincoln College, Oxford, engr David Loggan, c1676-88, hs, oval, line, BM, NPG. SIR G.KNELLER, 1698, tql in peer's robes, Bodleian Library, Oxford.

CREW(E), Sir Randolph (1558-1646) judge.
P UNKNOWN, tql in robes of lord chief justice, Palace of Westminster, London.

CREW(E), Sir Thomas (1565-1634) speaker of the House of Commons.
P UNKNOWN, hs in robes of sergeant-at-law, Palace of Westminster, London.

CRICHTON, James, 'the Admirable' (1560-1585?) scholar.
P UNKNOWN, hl, Royal Coll; version, attrib John Medina, jun, Lennoxlove, Lothian region, Scotland.

CRISP(E), Sir Nicholas (1599?-1666) royalist.
P CORNELIUS JOHNSON, c1635, tql, Parham Park, W Sussex.
M C.JOHNSON, hs, Fondation Custodia, Institut Néerlandais, Paris.
PR R.H.CROMEK, wl, line, BM, NPG.

CRISP(E), Tobias (1600-1643) antinomian.
PR A.SOLY, hl, oval, line, for *Sermons*, 1690, BM, NPG.

CROFT, Herbert (1603-1691) bishop of Hereford.
P UNKNOWN, hs, Croft Castle (NT), Hereford. UNKNOWN, hl, Croft Castle.

CROFT, Sir James (d1590) lord deputy of Ireland.
P UNKNOWN, hs, Croft Castle (NT), Hereford.

CROFT, William (1677?-1727) musician.
P THOMAS MURRAY, c1720, hl, oval, Faculty of Music, Oxford. UNKNOWN, c1690?, tql with book, NPG 1192.
SC UNKNOWN, marble bust on monument, Westminster Abbey, London.
PR G.VERTUE, after T.Murray, hl, oval, line, for *Musica Sacra*, 1724, BM, NPG.

CROKE, Sir George (1560-1642) judge.
P UNKNOWN, 1626, tql in robes, Inner Temple, London; version, hs, Royal Coll.

CROKE, Sir John (1553-1620) judge and speaker of House of Commons.
P UNKNOWN, hs in robes, Palace of Westminster, London.

CROMARTIE or CROMARTY, George Mackenzie, 1st Earl of (1630-1714) statesman.
P Attrib MICHAEL DAHL, c1708, tql in peer's robes, Parliament Hall, Edinburgh. Attrib SIR J.B.MEDINA, hs, oval, SNPG 304, engr P.Vanderbank, as after J.B.Medina, line, BM.

PR J.SMITH, hl, oval, mezz, BM.

CROMPTON, Hugh (fl 1657) poet.
PR A.HERTOCHS, tql, aged 18, line, BM. UNKNOWN, hs, oval, line, for *Pierides*, 1658, BM.

CROMWELL, Elizabeth, see Claypole.

CROMWELL, Henry (1628-1674) son of Oliver Cromwell, statesman.
D T.ATHOW, after miniature, hs in armour, wash, Sutherland Coll, Ashmolean Museum, Oxford. G.P.HARDING, tql in armour, wash, Sutherland Coll, Ashmolean.

CROMWELL, Oliver (1599-1658) soldier and statesman.
P ROBERT WALKER, 1649, tql in armour with page, Leeds Art Gallery; version, NPG 536. SIR PETER LELY, 1653-4, hs in armour, oval, City Museum and Art Gallery, Birmingham. Attrib SIR P.LELY, c1654, tql in armour, Uffizi, Florence.
M SAMUEL COOPER, c1653, hs, oval, unfinished, Buccleuch Estates, Selkirk, Scotland; version, 1656, NPG 3065. By or after S.COOPER, c1655, hs, profile, Chatsworth, Derbys.
SC EDWARD PIERCE, c1654-8, marble bust, Ashmolean Museum, Oxford; bronze cast, NPG 438. UNKNOWN, 1658, plaster death-mask, Ashmolean; version, 'the Frankland mask', NPG 4025. Attrib THOMAS or ABRAHAM SIMON, funeral effigy, tinted plaster with glass eyes, Bargello, Florence. T.SIMON, 1650, 'the Dunbar Medal', silver, hs profile, NPG 4365. T.SIMON, c1651, 'the Lord General medal', silver, hs, BM; electrotype, NPG 1486. T.SIMON, 'the Lord Protector medal', hs, profile, NPG 4366. T.SIMON, 1654, 'Inauguration medal', hs, profile, BM.

CROMWELL, Richard (1626-1712) lord protector.
P Attrib SIR PETER LELY, hl in armour, Claydon House (NT), Bucks.
M UNKNOWN, hs, oval, NPG 4350.
PR W.HAYNESWORTH, hl, line, BM, NPG. W.HOLLAR, hl, etch, BM, NPG.

CROMWELL, Thomas, see Earl of Essex.

CROONE, William (1633-1684) physician.
P MARY BEALE, hl, Royal College of Physicians, London.

CROSBY, Sir John (d1475) alderman of London.
SC UNKNOWN, tomb effigy with wife, St Helen, Bishopsgate, London, line engr, 1794, NPG.

CROSSRIG, David Hume, Lord (1643-1707) Scottish judge.
P UNKNOWN, hl, oval, Edinburgh University.

'CROUCHBACK', Edmund, see Earl of Lancaster.

CROWE, Mitford (d1719) governor of Barbados.
PR J.SMITH, after T.Murray, hl in armour, oval, mezz, BM, NPG.

CRUSO, Timothy (1656?-1697) presbyterian minister.
PR R.WHITE, after T.Forster, hl, oval, line, NPG.

CUDWORTH, Ralph (1617-1688) divine, leader of Cambridge neo-Platonists.
P UNKNOWN, hs, Emmanuel College, Cambridge.
PR G.VERTUE, after D.Loggan, 1684, hs, oval, line, for *Morality*, 1731, BM, NPG.

CULLEN, Sir Francis Grant, Lord (1658-1726) Scottish judge.
P JOHN SMIBERT, c1720-26, hs in robes, oval, SNPG 1521.

CULLUM, Sir Thomas, Bart (1587?-1664) alderman and sheriff of London.
PR J.BASIRE, tql, line, for Cullum, *Hist of Hawsted and Hardwick*, 1813, BM.

CULPEPER, Nicholas (1616-1654) writer on astrology and herbalist.

PR T.CROSS, hl, line, for *Physical Directory*, 1649, BM, NPG.

CUMBERLAND, George Clifford, 3rd Earl of (1558-1605) naval commander.

P After NICHOLAS HILLIARD, hs, NPG 277; version, Bodleian Library, Oxford.

M N.HILLIARD, c1585, hs, oval, Nelson Gallery, Kansas City, USA. N.HILLIARD, c1580–94, hs, oval, NPG L152 (11). N.HILLIARD, c1590, **wl in** tournament dress, NMM, Greenwich.

G UNKNOWN, posthumous wl with family, 1649, on loan to Carlisle Record Office. UNKNOWN, Queen Elizabeth and Garter Knights, oil, c1600, wl, Sherborne Castle, Dorset.

PR W.ROGERS, hs, oval, line, BM. R.VAUGHAN, hl in armour, oval, line, BM, NPG.

CUMBERLAND, Henry Clifford, 5th Earl (1591-1643) royalist.

P UNKNOWN, hs in armour, oval, Holkham Hall, Norfolk. UNKNOWN, hl in armour, oval, Chatsworth, Derbys.

CUMBERLAND, Margaret Clifford, Countess of (1560?-1616) youngest daughter of Francis Russell, Earl of Bedford.

P UNKNOWN, 1585, hs, Gorhambury, Herts; version, NPG 415.

M LAWRENCE HILLIARD, hs, oval, V & A.

SC UNKNOWN, tomb effigy, Appleby Church, Westmorland.

CUMBERLAND, Richard (1631-1718) bishop of Peterborough.

P Attrib THOMAS MURRAY, c1706, hs, Bishop's Palace, Peterborough, engr J.Smith, mezz, BM, NPG.

CUNINGHAM, William (fl 1586) physician and astrologer.

PR UNKNOWN, hl with book, oval, woodcut, from *Cosmographical Glasse*, 1559, BM.

CUNNINGHAM, William, see 9th Earl of Glencairn.

CURLE or **CURLL, Walter (1575-1647)** bishop of Winchester.

P UNKNOWN, 1635, hl in robes, Winchester College, Hants. UNKNOWN, Peterhouse College, Cambridge.

PR THOMAS CECILL, hl, oval, line, BM, NPG.

CUTLER, Sir John (1608?-1693) London merchant and philanthropist.

P UNKNOWN, hl, oval, Grocers' Company, London, engr, unknown, stipple, pub 1815, NPG.

SC ARNOLD QUELLIN, 1681–2, marble statue, Grocer's Company. A.QUELLIN, 1683, statue, Guildhall Museum, London.

CUTPURSE, Moll, see Mary Frith.

CUTTS, John Cutts, Baron (1661-1707) soldier.

P Attrib THOMAS MURRAY, hs, oval St Catherine's College, Cambridge. Studio of WILLIAM WISSING, c1685, hl in armour, oval, NPG 515.

PR J.SIMON, after Sir G.Kneller, tql in armour, mezz, BM, NPG.

D

DACRE, Gregory Fiennes, 10th Baron (1539-1594) statesman.
PR UNKNOWN, monumental effigy of himself and wife in Chelsea Church, etch, pub 1815, BM.

DACRE, Thomas Fiennes, 9th Baron (1517?-1541) courtier.
P HANS EWORTH, after H.Holbein, jun, c1555, hs, small portrait in corner of portrait of wife, Mary Nevill, Baroness Dacre, National Gallery of Canada, Ottawa.

DAHL, Michael (1659?-1743) portrait painter.
P Self-portrait, 1691, tql with bust, NPG 3822.
G GAWEN HAMILTON, 'A Conversation of Virtuosis . . . at the King's Arms', oil, 1735, NPG 1384.
PR T.CHAMBARS, after M.Dahl, hs, oval, line, for Walpole, *Anecdotes*, ed 1762, BM.

DALE, Samuel (1659?-1739) physician.
P UNKNOWN, hl, Apothecaries' Hall, London.
PR GEORGE VERTUE, hl, oval, line, for *Pharmacologia*, 1737, BM, NPG.

DALRYMPLE, Sir Hew, Bart (1652-1737) lord president of court of session.
P WILLIAM AIKMAN, 1722, tql seated in robes of lord president, Parliament Hall, Edinburgh. Attrib SIR J.B.MEDINA, hl, SNPG 621.

DALRYMPLE, James, see 1st Viscount Stair.

DALRYMPLE, John, see 2nd Earl of Stair.

DALTON, Michael (d1648?) legal writer.
PR MICHAEL TYSON, after C.Neve, 1623, hs, oval, etch, BM, NPG. W.MARSHALL, hs, octagon, line, for *Manuall or Analecta*, 1648, BM.

DALYELL or **DALZELL, Robert,** see 6th Earl of Carnwath.

DALYELL or **DALZELL of Binns, Thomas (1599?-1685)** general.
P Attrib DAVID PATTON, hl in armour, The Binns (NT), central region, Scotland. Attrib L.SCHUNEMAN, tql in armour, SNPG 2129; version, The Binns.
PR P.VANDERBANK, after D.Patton, hl, oval, line, BM, NPG.

DALZELL or **DALZIELL, Robert (1662-1758)** general.
PR PETIT FILIUS, after C.Alexander, hl, line, NPG.

DAMPIER, William (1651-1715) circumnavigator.
P THOMAS MURRAY, c1697-8, hl with book, NPG 538.

DANBY, Henry Danvers, Earl of (1573-1644) statesman.
P SIR ANTHONY VANDYCK, wl in Garter robes, The Hermitage, Leningrad.
D SIR A.VANDYCK, tql, black chalk study for Hermitage picture, BM.
PR V.GREEN, after Sir A.Vandyck, wl in robes, mezz, for *Houghton Gallery*, 1775, BM. E.SCRIVEN, after M.Miereveldt, tql, stipple, for Lodge, *Portraits*, BM.

DANIEL, Samuel (1562-1619) poet.
G UNKNOWN, 'Appleby Castle triptych', oil, c1646, hs, small portrait in left-hand panel, Record Office, The Castle, Carlisle.

PR THOMAS COCKSON, hl, oval, line, for *Civile Wares*, 1609, BM, NPG.

DANIEL, Sir William (d1610) judge.
P UNKNOWN, c1604, tql in robes, NPG 717.

DANVERS, Henry, see Earl of Danby.

DANVERS, Sir John (1588?-1655) regicide.
PR UNKNOWN, hs, oval, line, for Thane, *Autography*, BM, NPG.

DARCIE, Abraham (fl 1625) translator and author.
PR F.DELARAM, hl, line, for trans of Camden, *Annales*, 1625, BM, NPG.

DARNLEY, Henry Stewart or **Stuart, Lord (1545-1567)** husband of Mary Queen of Scots.
P UNKNOWN, hs as a boy, Hardwick Hall (NT), Derbys. Attrib HANS EWORTH, 1562, wl with brother, Holyroodhouse, Edinburgh; version, H.Eworth, 1563, wl, Royal Coll. UNKNOWN, c1565, tql with Mary, Hardwick Hall.
M UNKNOWN, hs, oval, Mauritshuis, The Hague, Netherlands.
G LIVINUS DE VOGELAARE, 'The Memorial of Lord Darnley', oil, 1568, Holyroodhouse.
SC UNKNOWN, alabaster kneeling effigy on the tomb of his mother, the Countess of Lennox, Westminster Abbey, London; electrotype, NPG 359.
PR R.ELSTRACK, hl, oval, line, BM, NPG.

DARSSIE, Abraham, see Darcie.

DART, John (d1730) antiquary.
PR J.FABER, hl with book, mezz, for *Westmonasterium*, 1742, BM, NPG.

DARTIQUENAVE, Charles (1664-1737) epicure and wit.
P SIR GODFREY KNELLER, 1702, hl, NPG 3239. After SIR G.KNELLER, hl, 'Kit-cat Club' portrait, NPG 3201.

DARTMOUTH, George Legge, 1st Baron (1648-1691) admiral.
P By or after JOHN RILEY, c1685-90, tql in armour, NPG 664. UNKNOWN, hl in armour, oval, NMM, Greenwich.

DARTMOUTH, William Legge, 1st Earl of (1672-1750) lord keeper of the privy seal.
PR JAMES FITLER, tql in robes, line, NPG.

DAVENANT, John (1576-1641) bishop of Salisbury.
P UNKNOWN, hl, Queen's College, Cambridge, engr T.Trotter, line, for Middleton, *Biographia Evangelica*, 1783, BM, NPG.

DAVENANT, Sir William (1606-1668) poet and dramatist.
PR W.FAITHORNE, after J.Greenhill, hs, oval, line, for *Works*, 1672, BM, NPG.

DAVENPORT, Sir Humphrey (1566-1645) judge.
P UNKNOWN, Capesthorne Hall, Cheshire.

DAVENPORT, John (1597-1670) puritan divine, founder of colony of New Haven.
P UNKNOWN, hs, Yale University, New Haven, USA.

DAVIES or **DAVIS, Christian (1667-1739)** known as 'Mother Ross', female soldier.
PR UNKNOWN, wl in uniform on horseback, line, for Caulfield, *Remarkable Persons*, 1819 (copy from *Life*, 1740), BM, NPG.

DAVIES, John (1565?-1618) poet and writing master.
PR UNKNOWN, hl, oval, line, copy from *Writing Schoolmaster*, 1631, BM, NPG.

DAVIES, John (1679-1732) president of Queen's College, Cambridge.
P UNKNOWN, Queen's College.

DAVIES, Robert (1648-1728) Welsh antiquary and collector of Welsh manuscripts.
SC SIR HENRY CHEERE, 1728, statue, Mold, Clywd, Wales.

DAVIS, Mary or Moll (fl 1663-1669) actress and mistress of Charles II.
P SIR PETER LELY, *c*1670, tql with guitar, Weston Park, Salop, engr R.Tompson, mezz, BM, NPG.
PR G.VALCK, after Sir P.Lely, 1678, hs, oval, mezz, BM, NPG.

DAVISON, William (fl 1635-1660) chemist and physician.
PR P.LOMBART, after D.Schultz, hs, oval, line, BM.

DAWES, Sir William, 3rd Bart (1671-1724) archbishop of York.
P SIR GODFREY KNELLER, 1717?, tql seated, Bishopthorpe Palace, York.
PR G.GRIBELIN, after J.Closterman, hs, oval, line, for *Sermons*, 1707, BM, NPG. G.VERTUE, after T.Murray, hl, oval, line, BM, NPG.

DAY, John (1522-1584) printer.
PR UNKNOWN, 1562, hl, oval, woodcut, BM, NPG. UNKNOWN, hl, oval, woodcut, for Foxe, *Acts and Monuments*, 1563, BM.

DAY, William (1529-1596) bishop of Winchester.
PR M.GHEERAERTS, sen, 'Procession of Garter Knights, 1576', etch, BM.

DEANE, Sir Anthony (1638?-1721) shipbuilder.
P SIR GODFREY KNELLER, 1690, hl with sketch, NPG 2124. Attrib JOHN GREENHILL, hs, oval, NMM, Greenwich.

DEANE, Richard (1610-1653) admiral and general at sea.
P ROBERT WALKER, 1653, hl in armour, NMM, Greenwich.

DEE, John (1527-1608) mathematician and astrologer.
P UNKNOWN, hs, oval, Ashmolean Museum, Oxford, engr W.P.Sherlock, stipple, BM, NPG.

DEFOE, Daniel (1661?-1731) journalist and novelist.
G GEORGE BICKHAM, 'The Whigs Medly', line engr, 1711, caricature of Defoe's head in pillory and Defoe sitting between the pope and the devil, BL, satirical prints 1570A.
PR M.VAN DER GUCHT, after J.Taverner, hs, oval, line, for *Coll of Writings of Author of True Born Englishman*, 1703, NPG. M.VAN DER GUCHT, after J.Taverner, hs, oval, line, for *Jure Divino*, 1706, BM, NPG 3960.

DEKKER, Thomas (1570?-1641?) dramatist and pamphleteer.
PR UNKNOWN, hl, woodcut, for *Dreams*, 1629, BL; copy, line, NPG.

DELAMERE, George Booth, 1st Baron (1622-1684) royalist.
D W.N.GARDINER, hl, wash, Sutherland Coll, Ashmolean Museum, Oxford.

DELAMERE, Henry Booth, 2nd Baron, see 1st Earl of Warrington.

DELANY, Patrick (1685?-1768) divine and friend of Swift.
M UNKNOWN, hs, oval, NGI 3728.
SC Attrib JOHN VAN NOST, *c*1768, marble bust, Trinity College, Dublin.

DELAUNE, Gideon (1565?-1659?) apothecary.
P Attrib CORNELIUS JOHNSON, 1640, hl, Apothecaries' Hall, London.

SC NICHOLAS YOUNG, *c*1676, alabaster bust, Apothecaries' Hall.

DELAVALL, Sir Ralph (1645?-1707) admiral.
P MICHAEL DAHL, wl, Seaton Delaval Hall, Northd.
G UNKNOWN, tql with Captain Benbow and Thomas Phillips?, oil, *c*1692-3, NMM, Greenwich.

DE LA WARR, John West, 1st Earl (1693-1766) soldier and statesman.
D 4th LORD BYRON, 1719, wl in shooting dress, ink and wash, BM, engr H.Roberts, line, BM, NPG.

DE LA WARR, Thomas West, 3rd Baron (1577-1618) governor of Virginia.
P W.L.SHEPHARD, after contemporary portrait, hs, Virginia State Library, Richmond, USA.

DE LA WARR, William West, 1st Baron (1519?-1595) courtier.
P Follower of HANS HOLBEIN, jun, (called De la Warr), *c*1550, tql, TATE 4252.

DELORAINE, Henry Scott, 1st Earl of (1676-1730) gentleman of bedchamber to George I.
P SIR GODFREY KNELLER, wl as boy with brother, Earl of Dalkeith, Buccleuch Estates, Selkirk, Scotland. UNKNOWN, wl as boy with dog, Buccleuch Estates.
G SIR G.KNELLER, family group with mother and brother, oil, Buccleuch Estates.
PR W.FAITHORNE, jun, after J.Closterman, tql with servant and horse, mezz, BM.

DELVAUX, Laurent (1695-1778) sculptor.
PR A.VAN HAECKEN, after I.Whood, 1735, hl with bust, mezz, BM, NPG. W.HIBBART, after I.Whood, hl with bust, etch, for Walpole, *Anecdotes*, 1762, BM, NPG.

DENBIGH, Basil Feilding, 2nd Earl of (d 1674) parliamentary general.
PR W.HOLLAR, 1631, hs, oval, BM, NPG.

DENBIGH, William Feilding, 1st Earl of (d 1643) royalist.
P SIR ANTHONY VANDYCK, wl with Indian boy, NG 5633.

DENHAM, Sir John (1615-1669) poet.
PR J.COLLYER, after unknown artist, hs, oval, line, for Johnson, *Poets*, 1779, BM, NPG. L.LEGOUX, hl, stipple, for *Memories of Count Grammont*, 1808, BM, NPG.

DENISON, John (d 1629) divine.
PR UNKNOWN, hs, line, BM, NPG. R.SAWYER, hs, line, pub 1820, BM, NPG.

DENNIS, John (1657-1734) critic.
PR J.VAN DER GUCHT, hl, oval, line, for *Life*, 1734, BM, NPG. S.IRELAND, after W.Hogarth, hl, etch, facsimile of pen sketch, 1799, BM, NPG.

DERBY, Charlotte Stanley, née de la Trémoille or Trémouille, Countess of (1599-1664) royalist.
P Attrib BALTHASAR FLESSIERS, (called Countess of Derby), hl as young woman, Althorp, Northants. UNKNOWN, after *c*1651, tql seated in widow's dress, NPG 4296.
G SIR ANTHONY VANDYCK, family group, oil, *c*1636, Frick Collection, New York.

DERBY, Edward Stanley, 3rd Earl of (1509-1572) statesman.
D HANS HOLBEIN, jun, head, chalks, Royal Coll.

DERBY, Henry, 4th Earl of Derby (1531-1593) statesman.
M ISAAC OLIVER, hs, oval, NPG L152 (40).
G M.GHEERAERTS, sen, 'Procession of Garter Knights, 1576', etch, BM.

PR H.R.COOK, hl with Garter George, stipple, for Harding, *Biographical Mirror*, 1810, BM, NPG.

DERBY, James Stanley, 7th Earl of (1607-1651) royalist.
P After SIR ANTHONY VANDYCK, c1636–37, hs, oval, NPG 90. After SIR A.VANDYCK, tql in armour, Manx Museum, Douglas, Isle of Man.
G SIR A.VANDYCK, family group, oil, c1636, Frick Collection, New York.

DERBY, Margaret Beaufort, see Countess of Richmond and Derby.

DERHAM, William (1657-1735) theologian and naturalist.
P GEORGE WHITE, hl, oval, Royal Society, London.
PR J.GREEN, hs, oval, line, BM, NPG.

DERING, Edward (1540?-1576) puritan divine.
PR PASSE, hl, line, for Holland, *Herwologia*, 1620, BM, NPG.

DERING, Sir Edward, 1st Bart (1598-1644) politician.
P CORNELIUS JOHNSON, hl, Parham, W Sussex, engr G.Clover, line, for *Speeches in Matters of Religion,* 1640, BM, NPG.

DERWENTWATER, Sir James Radcliffe, 3rd Earl of (1689-1716) Jacobite.
P W.SYKES, 1715, wl in robes with spaniel, Ingatestone Hall, Essex.
PR G.VERTUE, after Sir G.Kneller, tql in robes, line, BM, NPG.

DESAGULIERS, John Theophilus (1683-1744) scientist.
P UNKNOWN, hl, NMM, Greenwich.
PR P.PELHAM, after H.Hysing, hl with magnifying glass, mezz, BM. J.TOOKEY, after H.Hysing, line, BM, NPG.

DESBOROUGH, John (1608-1680) general.
SC UNKNOWN, silver medal, BM.
PR UNKNOWN, wl on horseback, line, NPG.

D'ESPAGNE, Jean (1591-1659) French protestant pastor and theologian.
PR J.C.BÖCKLIN, hl, oval, line, BM. UNKNOWN, hl, line, NPG.

DESPENSER, Edward le (d1375) warrior.
SC UNKNOWN, wl kneeling effigy, Tewkesbury Abbey, Glos.

DETHICK, Sir Gilbert (1519?-1584) Garter king-of-arms.
PR M.GHEERAERTS, sen, 'Procession of Knights of Garter, 1576', etch, BM.

DE VERE, Diana, see Duchess of St Albans.

DEVEREUX, Robert (1566-1601), see 2nd Earl of Essex.

DEVEREUX, Robert (1591-1646), see 3rd Earl of Essex.

DEVEREUX, Walter, see 1st Earl of Essex.

DEVON, Edward Courtenay, Earl of (1526?-1556) courtier.
P Attrib STEPHEN VAN DER MEULEN, tql, Woburn Abbey, Beds.

DEVONSHIRE, Charles Blount, 8th Baron Mountjoy and Earl of (1563-1606) lord deputy of Ireland.
P UNKNOWN, c1597, hs, Mapledurham House, Oxon; version, wl in robes, Mapledurham House.
M NICHOLAS HILLIARD, 1587, hs, oval, w/c, Antony House (NT), Cornwall.
G UNKNOWN, 'The Somerset House Conference', oil, 1604, NPG 665.
PR T.COCKSON, wl on horseback, BM.

DEVONSHIRE, Christian Cavendish, Duchess of (d1675) royalist.
P Attrib PAUL VAN SOMER, 1619, tql with daughter, North Carolina Museum of Art, Raleigh, USA.
G Attrib GERARD HONTHORST, wl with daughter and two sons, Chatsworth, Derbys.

SC UNKNOWN, monument with her husband and four children, All Saints' Church, Derby.

DEVONSHIRE, William Cavendish, 1st Earl of (d1626) courtier.
P UNKNOWN, hl, Hardwick Hall (NT), Derbys.

DEVONSHIRE, William Cavendish, 2nd Earl of (1591?-1628) courtier.
P UNKNOWN, 1625, hl with armour, Hardwick Hall (NT), Derbys. Attrib DANIEL MYTENS, hl in peer's robes, Hardwick Hall. Attrib PAUL VAN SOMER, tql with son, North Carolina Museum of Art, Raleigh, USA.
SC UNKNOWN, monument with wife and four children, All Saints' Church, Derby.

DEVONSHIRE, William Cavendish, 3rd Earl of (1617-1684) royalist.
P UNKNOWN, 1638, hl, Hardwick Hall (NT), Derbys. Attrib SIR PETER LELY, hl, Burghley House, Northants; version, Hardwick Hall. SIR ANTHONY VANDYCK, wl, Chatsworth, Derbys.

DEVONSHIRE, William Cavendish, 1st Duke of (1640-1707) statesman.
P Attrib SIR GODFREY KNELLER, hs, oval, Hardwick Hall (NT), Derbys. After SIR G.KNELLER, tql in armour, Chatsworth, Derbys. SIR G.KNELLER, wl in Garter robes, Chatsworth. A.F.VAN DER MEULEN, wl on horseback, Chatsworth. J.M.WRIGHT, hs, oval, Hardwick Hall.
M JOHN HOSKINS, 1644, hl with dog, w/c, Burghley House, Northants.

DICK, Sir William, Bart (1580?-1655) provost of Edinburgh, sufferer in cause of Charles I.
PR R.VAUGHAN, 3 line engr, 'prosperous', 'in prison', 'dead', for *The Lamentable Estate and Distressed Case of Sir William Dick,* 1657, BM.

DIGBY, George, see 2nd Earl of Bristol.

DIGBY, John, see 1st Earl of Bristol.

DIGBY, Sir Kenelm (1603-1665) author, sea captain, diplomat and scientist.
P CORNELIUS JOHNSON, c1629, tql, Althorp, Northants. SIR ANTHONY VANDYCK, 1632, tql seated with armillary sphere (fragment cut from group portrait), Royal Coll. After SIR A.VANDYCK, (type of c1636), hl with sunflower, Antony House (NT), Cornwall; version, hl with armillary sphere, Weston Park, Salop. After SIR A.VANDYCK, c1640, hl in armour, NPG 486.
M PETER OLIVER, 1627, hs, oval, NPG L152 (12). SIR A.VANDYCK, 1632, hl double miniature with wife, Sherborne Castle, Dorset.
G After SIR A.VANDYCK, tql seated with wife and two sons, oil, 1632, Sherborne Castle.
PR R.GAYWOOD, 1654, head, etch, BM, NPG. T.CROSS, hs, line for *Receipts in Physick,* 1668, BM, NPG. UNKNOWN, hl, line, for *Immortality of Reasonable Souls,* 1645, BM.

DIGBY, Lettice, Lady, see Baroness Offaley.

DIGBY, Venetia, Lady (1600-1633) celebrated beauty, wife of Sir Kenelm Digby.
P SIR ANTHONY VANDYCK, 1633, hl on her death-bed, Dulwich College Gallery, London. SIR A.VANDYCK, c1633, wl as 'Prudence', Palazzo Reale, Milan; version, Royal Coll.
M PETER OLIVER, hs, oval, Burghley House, Northants. After SIR A.VANDYCK, 1632, hl, double miniature with husband, Sherborne Castle, Dorset.
G After SIR A.VANDYCK, tql seated with husband and two sons, oil, 1632, Sherborne Castle.

PR J.BASIRE, sculptured bust, line, for Pennant, *Tour from Chester to London*, 1786, BM, NPG.

DIGGES, Sir Dudley (1583-1639) judge and diplomat.
P CORNELIUS JOHNSON, 1636, hs, oval, Gray's Inn, London.

DILKES, Sir Thomas (1667?-1707) admiral.
P SIR GODFREY KNELLER, *c*1704-5, tql, NMM, Greenwich.

DILLENIUS, John James (1687-1747) professor of botany at Oxford.
P UNKNOWN, hl with drawing, Bodleian Library, Oxford.

DILLON, Wentworth, see 4th Earl of Roscommon.

DINGLEY, Robert (1619-1660) puritan divine.
PR T.CROSS, hl, line, BM.

DISBROWE, John, see Desborough.

DISNEY, John (1677-1730) divine.
PR R.WHITE, hs, oval, line, for *Essay upon the execution of the Laws*, 1710, BM, NPG.

DIXIE, Sir Wolstan (1525-1594) lord mayor of London.
P UNKNOWN, 1593, hl in robes, Christ's Hospital, Horsham, Sussex; copy, Emmanuel College, Cambridge.

DIXON, Robert (*d*1688) royalist divine.
PR J.COLLINS, after W.Reader, hl, oval, line, BM.

DOBSON, William (1610-1646) portrait painter.
P After self-portrait, *c*1642-46, hs, NPG 302.
G Self-portrait, hl with Sir C.Cotterell, and N.Lanier, oil, Alnwick Castle, Northd.
PR J.ENGLISH, after W.Dobson, hs, oval, etch, BM, NPG.

DOCWRA, Sir Thomas (*d*1527) prior of Knights of St John.
PR W.ROGERS, wl in armour, line, for Segar, *Honour Military and Civil*, 1602, BM, NPG.

DOD, John (1549?-1645) puritan divine.
PR T.CROSS, hs, oval, line, BM, NPG.

DODDRIDGE or DODERIDGE, Sir John (1555-1628) judge.
P UNKNOWN, hs in robes, oval, NPG 539; versions, Society of Antiquaries, London; Exeter College, Oxford.

DODINGTON, George Bubb, see Baron Melcombe.

DODWELL, Henry (1641-1711) scholar and theologian.
P UNKNOWN, *c*1697, tql, Bodleian Library, Oxford.
PR M.VAN DER GUCHT, hl, oval, line, NPG.

DOGGETT, Thomas (*d*1721) actor.
P THOMAS MURRAY, *c*1691, wl as 'Nincompoop' in *Love for Money*, Sherborne Castle, Dorset. UNKNOWN, hs, Garrick Club, London.

DOLBEN, Sir Gilbert (1658-1722) judge.
P SIR GODFREY KNELLER, tql in robes, Christ Church, Oxford. UNKNOWN, wl in robes, Bodleian Library, Oxford.

DOLBEN, John (1625-1686) archbishop of York.
P UNKNOWN, tql seated, Christ Church Oxford; version, Bishopthorpe, York.
G SIR PETER LELY, tql seated with R.Allestree and J.Fell, oil, *c*1660, Christ Church.
SC Attrib JASPER LATHAM, wl tomb effigy, York Minster.
PR R.THOMPSON, after J.Huysmans, tql, mezz, BM, NPG.

DOLBEN, John (1662-1710) politician.
P JOHN RILEY, 1680s, Waddesdon Manor (NT), Bucks.

DOLBEN, Sir John (1684-1756) divine, prebendary of Durham.
P Attrib R.TAYLOR, hs, Christ Church, Oxford. Attrib

R.TAYLOR, wl, Balliol College, Oxford, engr J.Faber jun, *c*1750, tql, mezz, BM, NPG. UNKNOWN, hs as young man, Balliol College.

DOLBEN, Sir William (1627?-1694) judge.
P UNKNOWN, hs in robes, Lincoln College, Oxford.

DOMINIS, Marco Antonio de (1566-1624) dean of Windsor.
P UNKNOWN, tql seated, Chatsworth, Derbys.
PR W.J.DELFF, after M.Miereveldt, hs, oval, line, BM, NPG. R.ELSTRACK, after M.Miereveldt, 1617, hl, oval, line, NPG. JOHN BILL, 1617, tql seated, line, NPG.

DONNE, John (1572?-1631) poet and divine.
P After ISAAC OLIVER, hs, NPG 1849. UNKNOWN, 1620, hs, oval, Deanery, St Paul's Cathedral, London; version, V & A, engr P.Lombart, line, for *Poems*, 1633, BM, NPG.
M I.OLIVER, 1616, hs, Royal Coll, engr M.Merian, jun, line, for *Sermons*, 1640, BM, NPG.
SC NICHOLAS STONE, 1631, white marble effigy, wl, St Paul's, engr W.Hollar, etch, for Dugdale, *St Paul's*, 1658, BM.
PR M.DROESHOUT, hl in shroud, oval, line, for *Death's Duell*, 1633, BM. W.MARSHALL, hl, aged 18, oval, line, for *Poems*, 1635 and 1639, BM, NPG.
Note – the celebrated portrait of Donne as a melancholic lover in a black hat by an unknown artist, *c*1595, hl, oval, is in a private collection.

DOOLITTLE, Thomas (1632?-1707) nonconformist divine.
PR J.STURT, hs, 'aged 51', oval, line, BM, NPG. R.WHITE, hs, oval, line, BM, NPG. UNKNOWN, hl when young, line, BM, NPG.

DOPPING, Anthony (1643-1697) bishop of Kildare and Meath.
P UNKNOWN, hs, oval, Trinity College, Dublin.

DORCHESTER, Catherine Sedley, Countess of (1657-1717) mistress of James II.
P Studio of SIR PETER LELY, *c*1675, tql seated, NPG 36, engr R.Tompson, mezz, BM, NPG. Attrib SIR GODFREY KNELLER, *c*1676-77, tql seated, Althorp, Northants. Studio of SIR G.KNELLER, 1684, tql seated, Ranger's House (GLC), Blackheath, London.
M LAWRENCE CROSS, *c*1685-90, hs, oval, w/c, NPG 1696.
PR I.BECKETT, after Sir G.Kneller, tql seated, mezz, BM, NPG. R.WILLIAMS, after W.Wissing, hl, oval, mezz, BM, NPG.

DORCHESTER, Dudley Carleton, 1st Viscount (1573-1632) diplomat.
P MICHAEL VAN MIEREVELDT, *c*1620, hl, NPG 3684. Studio of M.VAN MIEREVELDT, 1625, hs, NPG 110.

DORCHESTER, Henry Pierrepoint, 1st Marquess of (1606-1680) royalist who studied medicine and law.
P UNKNOWN, 1691, hs, oval, Royal College of Physicians, London.

DORIGNY, Sir Nicholas (1658-1746) painter and engraver.
PR BARRETT, hs, line for Walpole, *Catalogue of Engravers*, 1794, BM, NPG.

DORISLAUS, Isaac (1595-1649) diplomat.
PR I.BUYS, hs, oval, line, NPG. UNKNOWN, hl, oval, line, pub 1792, BM, NPG.

DORMER, James (1679-1741) general.
P J.B.VAN LOO, tql seated, Rousham House, Oxon.

DORMER, Jane, see Duchess of Feria.

DORMER, John (1669-1719) country gentleman.
P SIR GODFREY KNELLER, 1706, hl, Rousham House, Oxon. SIR G.KNELLER, *c*1710, hl, 'Kit-cat Club' portrait, NPG 3203.

DORMER, Robert (1607?-1643), see 1st Earl of Carnarvon.

DORMER, Sir Robert (1649-1726) judge.
SC UNKNOWN, wl effigy on monument, St Mary and Holy Cross Church, Bucks.

DORRINGTON, Theophilus (d1715) divine and controversialist.
PR G.BOUTTATS, after C.Franck, hs, oval, line, for *Family Devotions*, 1703, BM, NPG.

DORSET, Anne Clifford, Countess of, see Countess of Pembroke and Montgomery.

DORSET, Charles Sackville, 1st Earl of Middlesex and 6th Earl of (1638-1706) courtier and poet.
P SIR GODFREY KNELLER, 1694, wl in Garter robes, Knole (NT), Kent; version, hl, NPG 250. SIR G.KNELLER, c1697, hl, the 'Kit-cat Club' portrait, NPG 3204. Attrib SIR G.KNELLER, tql seated in turban, Knole.

DORSET, Sir Edward Sackville, 4th Earl of (1591-1652) soldier and statesman.
P Attrib WILLIAM LARKIN, 1613, wl, Ranger's House (GLC), Blackheath, London. Studio of SIR ANTHONY VANDYCK, c1635, wl with breastplate, Knole (NT), Kent.

DORSET, Lionel Cranfield Sackville, 1st Duke of (1688-1765) courtier.
P SIR GODFREY KNELLER, c1695, wl with sister and a fawn, Knole (NT), Kent. SIR G.KNELLER, c1710, hl, the 'Kit-cat Club' portrait, NPG 3205. SIR G.KNELLER, 1717, wl in Garter robes, Knole. JOHN WOOTTON, 1727, wl on horseback, Knole. Studio of SIR JOSHUA REYNOLDS, c1756, hs in Garter robes, Privy Council Office (DoE), London.
D Attrib ROSALBA CARRIERA, hs with Garter star, pastel, Knole.
G J.WOOTTON, 1727, 'View of Dover Castle', oil, 1727, Knole.

DORSET, Richard Sackville, 3rd Earl of (1589-1624) joint lord-lieutenant of Sussex.
P Attrib WILLIAM LARKIN, 1613, wl, Ranger's House (GLC), Blackheath, London. Attrib W.LARKIN, c1615, wl, Knole (NT), Kent.
M ISAAC OLIVER, 1616, wl, V & A.
SC SIMON PASSE, silver medal, hl, BM.

DORSET, Richard Sackville, 5th Earl of (1622-1677) courtier.
P CORNELIUS DE NEVE, 1637, wl with brother Edward, Knole (NT), Kent. UNKNOWN, hl, Knole.
SC C.G.CIBBER, 1677, kneeling effigy with wife on son's tomb, Sackville Chapel, St Michael's Church, Withyham, Sussex.

DORSET, Robert Sackville, 2nd Earl of (1561-1609) statesman.
P UNKNOWN, 1608, tql, Knole (NT), Kent.

DORSET, Thomas Sackville, 1st Earl of (1536-1608) statesman and poet.
P Attrib MARCUS GHEERAERTS, 1601, tql with staff of office, Knole (NT), Kent; version, attrib John de Critz, NPG 4024.
G UNKNOWN, 'The Somerset House Conference', oil, 1604, NPG 665.

DOUGLAS, Charles, see 3rd Duke of Queensberry.

DOUGLAS, George, see Earl of Dumbarton.

DOUGLAS, James (d1581), see 4th Earl of Morton.

DOUGLAS, James (1658-1712), see 4th Duke of Hamilton.

DOUGLAS, James (1662-1711), see 2nd Duke of Queensberry.

DOUGLAS, Margaret, see Countess of Lennox.

DOUGLAS, Robert, see Viscount Belhaven.

DOUGLAS, William (1582?-1648?), see 7th Earl of Morton.

DOUGLAS, William (1635-1694), see 3rd Duke of Hamilton.

DOUGLAS, William (1637-1695), see 1st Duke of Queensberry.

DOVE, Thomas (1555-1630) bishop of Peterborough.
P UNKNOWN, hs, Bishop's Palace, Peterborough.

DOVER, Henry Jermyn, 1st Baron (1636-1708) follower of James II.
P UNKNOWN, tql in armour, Ickworth (NT), Suffolk.

DOVER, Robert (1575?-1641) founder of the Cotswold games.
PR UNKNOWN, wl on horseback, line, copy from woodcut for *Annalia Dubrensia*, 1636, for Caulfield, *Remarkable Persons*, 1794, BM, NPG.

DOWNING, Sir George, 1st Bart (1623?-1684) soldier and politician.
P UNKNOWN, tql, Harvard University, New Haven, USA.

DOWNING, Sir George, 3rd Bart (1684?-1749) founder of Downing College.
P UNKNOWN, tql, Downing College, Cambridge.

DRAKE, Sir Francis (1540?-1596) circumnavigator and admiral.
P UNKNOWN, (type of c1580-85), wl, NPG 4032. After WILLIAM SEGAR?, (type of c1590), hl, City Art Gallery, Plymouth. After MARCUS GHEERAERTS, (type of c1594), tql with globe, NMM, Greenwich; version, 1616, Plymouth Art Gallery.
M Studio of NICHOLAS HILLIARD, 1581, hs, oval, NPG 4851.
PR Attrib JODOCUS HONDIUS, c1583, tql, line, BM, NPG 3905. C.VAN DE PASSE, sen, hl, line, for *Effigies Regum ac Principum*, 1598, BM.

DRAKE, Francis (1696-1771) surgeon and antiquary.
P PHILIP MERCIER, 1743, hl with books, Mansion House, York. NATHAN DRAKE, 1756, hl, oval, City Art Gallery, York.
PR V.GREEN, after N.Drake, 1771, hl, oval, mezz, BM, NPG.

DRAKE, James (1667-1707) physician and political writer.
PR M.VAN DER GUCHT, after T.Forster, hl, oval, line, for *Anatomy*, 1707, BM, NPG.

DRAKE, Samuel (1623-1673) royalist divine.
PR A.BIRRELL, hl, line, BM, NPG.

DRAYTON, Michael (1563-1631) poet.
P UNKNOWN, 1628, hs, oval, Dulwich College Gallery, London.
SC Attrib EDWARD MARSHALL, c1631, marble bust on tomb, Westminster Abbey, London.
PR W.HOLE, 1613, hl, oval, line, for *Poems*, 1619, BL; facsimile, 1796, BM, NPG.

DRUMMOND, George (1687-1766) lord provost of Edinburgh.
P SIR GEORGE CHALMERS, 1764, tql seated, SNPG 829.
PR A.BELL, after J.Alexander, 1752, tql in robes, mezz, BM, NPG.

DRUMMOND, James (1648-1716), see 1st titular Duke of Perth.

DRUMMOND, James (1675-1720), see 2nd titular Duke of Perth.

DRUMMOND, John, see 1st Earl and titular Duke of Melfort.

DRUMMOND of Hawthornden, William (1585-1649) poet.
P UNKNOWN, 1612, hs, SNPG 1096.

PR R.GAYWOOD, 1654, hl, oval, etch, for *History of Scotland,* 1654–55, BM, NPG.

DRUMMOND, William (1617?-1688), see 1st Viscount Strathallan.

DRURY, Sir Dru or **Drue (1531?-1617)** courtier.
P ROBERT PEAKE, hl, Courteenhall, Northants.
MS UNKNOWN, from Drury family pedigree, Delapré Abbey, Northamptonshire Records Office.

DRURY, Sir Robert (d 1536) speaker of the House of Commons.
P UNKNOWN, c1550–1600, wl, Courteenhall, Northants.

DRURY, Sir William (1527-1579) marshal of Berwick and lord-justice of Irish council.
P UNKNOWN, c1570–75, hl in armour, Guildhall, Thetford; versions, attrib George Gower, Buccleuch Estates, Selkirk, Scotland; Courteenhall, Northants; and NPG 1911.

DRYDEN, John (1631-1700) poet and dramatist.
P UNKNOWN, c1664, hs, Bodleian Library, Oxford. JOHN RILEY, c1685, tql seated with book, Traquair House, Borders region, Scotland, engr P.van Gunst, hs, oval, line, for *Virgil,* 1709, NPG. SIR GODFREY KNELLER, 1693, tql, NPG 2083, engr, unknown, hl, line, for *Luctus Britannici,* 1700, BM. SIR G.KNELLER, 1697, hl without wig, Trinity College, Cambridge; copy, NPG 57. JAMES MAUBERT, wl seated with dog, NPG 1133.
SC PETER SCHEEMAKERS, 1731, marble bust, Westminster Abbey, London.
PR W.FAITHORNE, after J.Closterman, c1690, hl, oval, mezz, BM, NPG.

DUBOIS, Simon (d 1708) painter.
PR A.BANNERMAN, hl, holding portrait, line, for Walpole, *Anecdotes,* 1762, BM, NPG.

DUBOURDIEU, Isaac (1597?-1692?) French protestant minister in London.
PR P.VAN SOMER, hs, mezz, BM.

DUBOURDIEU, Jean-Armand (1642?-1726) controversialist.
PR P.PELHAM, after D.Firmin, 1723, hl, oval, mezz, BM, NPG. UNKNOWN, hl, oval, line, NPG.

DUDLEY, Alice Dudley, Duchess of (d 1669) wife of Sir Robert Dudley.
SC EDWARD MARSHALL, c1668, marble tomb effigies of herself and daughter, Stoneleigh Church, Warwicks.

DUDLEY, Ambrose, see Earl of Warwick.

DUDLEY, Edmund (1462?-1510) statesman and lawyer.
G UNKNOWN, wl with Henry VII and Sir R.Empson, oil, Belvoir Castle, Leics.

DUDLEY, Lady Jane, née Grey (1537-1554) scholar and humanist, proclaimed Queen 1553.
P Attrib MASTER JOHN, c1545, wl, NPG 4451; version, tql, Seaton Delaval Hall, Northants.
PR W. and M.PASSE, hl, line, for Holland, *Herwologia,* 1620, BM, NPG.

DUDLEY, Lettice, see Countess of Leicester.

DUDLEY, Robert (1532?-1588), see Earl of Leicester.

DUDLEY, Sir Robert (1574-1649) naval commander and inventor.
M NICHOLAS HILLIARD, wl, National Museum, Stockholm, engr J.Brown, wl, line, for G.P.Harding, *Illustrious Persons,* BM, NPG.

DUGDALE, Sir John (1628-1700) Norroy king-of-arms.
P UNKNOWN, hl, Society of Antiquaries, London, engr J.Burché,

stipple, with erroneous title 'Sir William Dugdale Knt.', for Dallaway, *Heraldic Inquirer,* 1793, BM, NPG.

DUGDALE, Richard (fl 1680-97) Surey, Lancs, demoniac.
PR UNKNOWN, wl, woodcut, for Z.Taylor, *Popery and Knavery proved on the Surey Dissenters,* 1699, BM; facsimile, 1798, NPG.

DUGDALE, Stephen (1640?-1683) informer against the Catholics.
PR R.WHITE, hs, oval, line, BM, NPG.

DUGDALE, Sir William (1605-1686) Garter king-of-arms and antiquary.
P UNKNOWN, c1675, hs, NPG 540; version, hs with Garter badge, oval, Bodleian Library, Oxford.
PR W.HOLLAR, tql seated, etch, for *Warwickshire,* 1656, BM, NPG. H.ROBINSON after P.Borsseler, tql seated with book, for *Life,* 1827, BM, NPG.

DUJON, Francis, see Junius.

DUMBARTON, George Douglas, Earl of (1636?-1692) colonel.
P HENRI GASCARS, tql in armour, Lennoxlove, Lothian region, Scotland.

DUNBAR, Gavin (1455?-1532) bishop of Aberdeen.
SC UNKNOWN, tomb effigy, St Machan's Cathedral, Aberdeen.

DUNBAR, George Home, Earl of (d 1611) lord high treasurer of Scotland.
P UNKNOWN, tql with Garter George, SNPG 816.
D G.P.HARDING, (after type of c1610), tql, wash, Sutherland Coll, Ashmolean Museum, Oxford.

DUNCH, Edmund (1657-1719) politician and bonvivant.
P SIR GODFREY KNELLER, c1700–10, hl 'Kit-cat Club' portrait, NPG 3206, engr J.Faber, jun, 1733, mezz, BM, NPG.

DUNCOMBE, William (1690-1769) miscellaneous writer.
P JOSEPH HIGHMORE, 1721, tql seated, Corpus Christi College, Cambridge, engr T.Cook, hs, oval, line, for J.Nichols, *Select Collection of Poems,* 1780, BM, NPG.

DUNDAS of Arniston, Sir James (d 1679) politician.
P UNKNOWN, hl in armour, Arniston House, Lothian region, Scotland.

DUNDAS of Arniston, Robert, Lord (1685-1753) president of Scottish court of session.
P Attrib SIR J.B.MEDINA, hl, oval, Arniston House, Lothian region, Scotland.

DUNDAS of Arniston, Robert, Lord (d 1727) ordinary lord of session.
P UNKNOWN, hs in armour, oval, Arniston House, Lothian region, Scotland.

DUNDEE, John Graham of Claverhouse, 1st Viscount (1649?-1689) Jacobite.
P UNKNOWN, hs, SNPG 2183.
D UNKNOWN, hs in armour, oval, ink, SNPG 588.
PR J.S.AGAR, after Sir P.Lely, hl with stick, stipple, for Lodge, *Portraits,* BM, NPG.

DUNFERMLINE, Sir Alexander Seton, 1st Earl (1555-1622) lord chancellor of Scotland.
P MARCUS GHEERAERTS, 1610, tql, SNPG 2176.

DUNFERMLINE, Charles Seton, 2nd Earl of (1608-1672?) lord privy seal.
P Attrib SIR ANTHONY VANDYCK, wl in robes, SNPG 2222.
SC ABRAHAM SIMON, 1646, silver and lead medal, BM; plaster cast, SNPG 50.

DUNSTAN, Saint (924-988) archbishop of Canterbury.
MS UNKNOWN, wl seated with book. BL Royal MS 10 A XIII.

DUNSTER, Samuel (1675-1754) translator of Horace.
PR M.VAN DER GUCHT, hs, oval, line, NPG.

DUNTON, John (1659-1733) bookseller.
PR M.VAN DER GUCHT, after F.Knight, hs, oval, line, NPG.

DUPPA, Brian (1588-1662) bishop of Winchester.
P UNKNOWN, tql seated with Garter mantle, Christ Church, Oxford.

DURAS, Louis, see Earl of Feversham.

D'URFEY, Thomas (1653-1723) poet and dramatist.
P J.VAN DER GUCHT, hl, Knole (NT), Kent.
PR G.VERTUE, after E.Gouge, hl, oval, line for *Wit and Mirth*, 1719, BM, NPG.

DURIE, Alexander Gibson, Lord (d 1644) Scottish judge.
PR R.WHITE, after D.Paton, hs in robes, oval, line, for *Decisions of the Lords of Council*, 1690, BM, NPG.

DYCHE, Thomas (fl 1719) schoolmaster.
PR UNKNOWN, hs, oval, line, NPG.

DYER, Sir James (1512-1582) judge.
P UNKNOWN, *c*1575, hs in robes, NPG 1294.
PR J.DRAPENTIER, 1675, hs, oval, line, for *Reports*, BM, NPG.

DYER, William (1636?-1696) nonconformist divine.
PR UNKNOWN, hs, oval, line, for *Sermons*, 1668, BM, NPG.

DYSART, Elizabeth Murray, Countess of, see Duchess of Lauderdale.

DYSART, William Murray, 1st Earl of (1600?-1651) royalist.
P CORNELIUS JOHNSON, hl in armour, Ham House (NT), London.
M DAVID PATON, hs, plumbago, Ham House.

DYVE, Sir Lewis (1599-1669) royalist.
PR P.AUDINET, hs, line, BM.

E

EARLE, John (1601?-1665) bishop of Salisbury and author.
P UNKNOWN, c1660, hl, oval, NPG 1531.

EASTON, Adam (d1397) cardinal.
SC UNKNOWN, tomb effigy, St Cecilia Church, Rome.

ECHARD, Laurence (1670?-1730) historian and archdeacon of Stow.
P SIR GODFREY KNELLER, hl, Christ's College, Cambridge, engr G.Vertue, 1719, line, for *Hist of England*, 1720, BM, NPG.

EDES or EEDES, Richard (1555-1604) dean of Worcester.
SC UNKNOWN, monument, Worcester Cathedral, Worcs.
PR E.HARDING, hl, stipple, for Harding, *Biographical Mirrour*, 1796, BM, NPG.

EDGAR (944-975), king of the English.
MS UNKNOWN, wl seated, BL Cotton Ms Tiberius, A III, fol 2b. UNKNOWN, 966, wl, Charter of Edgar to the New Minster, Winchester, BL.
SC UNKNOWN, silver penny, BM.

EDGCUMBE, Richard Edgcumbe, 1st Baron (1680-1758) politician.
PR S.W.REYNOLDS, after J.Reynolds, tql with dog, mezz, pub 1825, BM.

EDMONDS, Sir Clement (1564?-1622) clerk of the council and author.
PR UNKNOWN, head, oval, line, for *Observations upon Caesar's Commentaries*, 1604, BM.

EDMONDES, Sir Thomas (1563?-1639) diplomat and treasurer of the household.
P DANIEL MYTENS, c1620, tql with staff, NPG 4652.

EDMUND (841-870) king of the East Angles, martyr and saint.
G UNKNOWN, Wilton Diptych, oil, c1389-98, NG 4451.

EDMUND (922?-946) king of the English.
SC UNKNOWN, silver penny, BM.

EDMUND of Langley, 1st Duke of York (1341-1402) fifth son of Edward III.
SC UNKNOWN, c1377-80, effigy on tomb chest of Edward III, Westminster Abbey, London.

EDRED (d955) king of the English.
SC UNKNOWN, silver penny, BM.

EDWARD, 'the Elder' (d924) king of the Angles and Saxons.
SC UNKNOWN, silver penny, BM.

EDWARD, 'the Martyr' (963?-978) king of the English.
SC UNKNOWN, silver penny, BM.

EDWARD. 'the Confessor' (d1066) king of the English.
MS UNKNOWN, wl, BL Royal Ms 20A, II, fol 5. UNKNOWN, BL Additional Ms 33241, fol IV.
SC UNKNOWN, polychrome carving in the triforium, south transept, Westminster Abbey, London. UNKNOWN, statue, Canterbury Cathedral. Attrib THEODORIC, c1065, silver pennies, NPG 4048 and NPG 4049. UNKNOWN, wax seal, BM.
W UNKNOWN, wl in robes, All Souls College, Oxford.

EDWARD I (1239-1307) king of England.
MS UNKNOWN, 1297-98, hs and wl, Memoranda Roll E 368, Public Record Office, London.
SC UNKNOWN, mid-13th century, head as prince, corbel in Westminster Abbey, London. UNKNOWN, statue, choir screen, York Minster. UNKNOWN, wax seals, BM and King's College, Cambridge. UNKNOWN, silver groat, BM.

EDWARD II of Caernavon (1284-1327) king of England.
MS UNKNOWN, wl seated with Queen Isabella, Christ Church Ms 92, fol 4V, Bodleian Library. UNKNOWN, wl seated being offered crown, BL Royal Ms 20 A, II, fol 10.
SC UNKNOWN, 1330s, alabaster tomb effigy, Gloucester Cathedral; electrotype, NPG 439. UNKNOWN, statue, choir screen, Canterbury Cathedral. UNKNOWN, silver penny, BM.
W UNKNOWN, wl in robes, All Souls College, Oxford.
PR J.BASIRE, after great seal, wl seated and on horseback, line, NPG. UNKNOWN, his great seal, line, for Sandford, *Genealogical History*, 1677, BM.

EDWARD III (1312-1377) king of England.
P UNKNOWN, 17th century, hs, one of set of 16 early English kings and queens, NPG 4980(7).
MS Illuminations in various Mss: Cambridge University Muniments 174861 (Charter of 19 Sept, 1343); Ms A7, St John's College, Cambridge; BL Cotton Ms Nero D VI, fol 4 and fol 31; BL Cotton Ms Claudius D II, fol 136; BL Cotton Ms Nero E II; BL Royal Ms 20 C VII.
SC STEPHEN HADLEY, 1377, funeral effigy, Westminster Abbey, London. UNKNOWN, c1377-80, gilt copper tomb effigy, Westminster Abbey; electrotype, NPG 332. UNKNOWN, statue, choir screen, York Minster. UNKNOWN, wax seal, BM.

EDWARD IV (1442-1483) king of England.
P UNKNOWN, hl, Royal Coll. UNKNOWN, hl, NPG 3542. UNKNOWN, 17th century, hs, one of set of 16 early English kings and queens, NPG 4890(10).
MS Illuminations in various Mss: *The Dictes and Sayings of the Philosophers*, Ms 265, Lambeth Palace, London; parchment roll of his pedigree, BL Harleian Ms 7353; *Novelles croniques dangleterre*, BL Royal Ms 15, EIV, fol 14; BL Royal Ms 18 D ii.
W WILLIAM NEVE, c1482, hl, north transept, Canterbury Cathedral.
PR UNKNOWN, his great seal, line, for Sandford, *Genealogical History*, 1677, BM.

EDWARD V (1470-1483) king of England.
MS UNKNOWN, wl at left of Edward IV, *The Dictes and Sayings of the Philosophers*, Ms 265, Lambeth Palace, London.
W UNKNOWN, c1482, wl kneeling, Canterbury Cathedral. UNKNOWN, c1482, wl kneeling, St Giles Church, Little Malvern, Worcs.

EDWARD VI (1537-1553) king of England.
P HANS HOLBEIN, jun, c1539-40, hl with rattle, Mellon Coll, National Gallery, Washington, USA. After H.HOLBEIN, c1542, hl, NPG 1132. UNKNOWN, c1545, hl with rose, Buckland Abbey (NT), Devon. UNKNOWN, c1546-47, tql with Prince of Wales' feathers, Royal Coll; version, 1547, wl, Petworth (NT), W Sussex. After H.HOLBEIN, c1543-46, hs, profile, oval, Metropolitan Museum, New York, USA. UNKNOWN, c1546, hl with flower, profile, NPG 442; version, Jones Coll. V & A. WILLIAM SCROTS, 1546, hs, profile, 'anamorphosis', NPG 1299. W.SCROTS, after c1550, wl, Louvre, Paris; version, Royal Coll.

D H.HOLBEIN, *c*1539–40, hl with rattle, Royal Coll. H.HOLBEIN?, *c*1542, hl, Royal Coll.

G UNKNOWN, 'Family of Henry VIII', as prince, oil, *c*1547, Royal Coll. UNKNOWN, 'Edward VI and the Pope', oil, *c*1548–49, NPG 4165. UNKNOWN, 'Family of Henry VIII', as king, oil, *c*1570, Sudeley Castle, Glos. UNKNOWN, 'Granting Bridewell Hospital Charter', oil, 17th century, King Edward's School, Witley, Surrey. UNKNOWN, 'Granting Christ's Hospital Charter', oil, 17th century, Christ's Hospital, Horsham, Sussex.

SC UNKNOWN, marble bust, NPG L118. UNKNOWN, 1547, gold coronation medal, BM. UNKNOWN, wax seals, BM.

EDWARD, Prince of Wales, 'the Black Prince' (1330-1376) son of Edward III.

SC UNKNOWN, *c*1377–80, gilt copper tomb effigy, Canterbury Cathedral; electrotype, NPG 396. UNKNOWN, various coins, BM.

EDWARD, Prince of Wales (1453-1471) only son of Henry VI.

MS UNKNOWN, falling from horse at battle of Tewkesbury, Ms 236, Ghent University Library, The Netherlands. JOHN ROUS, wl, The Rous Roll, College of Arms, London.

EDWARDS, George (1694-1773) naturalist.

SC ISAAC GOSSET, Wedgwood jasper medallion, Wedgwood Museum, Barlaston, Staffs.

PR J.S.MÜLLER, after B.Dandridge, hl, oval, line, BM, NPG. J.S.MÜLLER, after I.Gosset, hs, profile, oval, line, for *Essays on Natural History*, 1770, BM, NPG.

EDWARDS, John (1637-1716) Calvinist divine.

PR G.VERTUE, hl, oval, line, for *Theologia Reformata*, 1713, BM, NPG. R.WHITE, hs, oval, line, for *Sermons*, 1698, BM, NPG.

EDWARDS, Thomas (1652-1721) divine and orientalist.

P THOMAS MURRAY, 1712, tql, St John's College, Cambridge.

EDWARDS, Thomas (1699-1757) author and critic.

PR W.HOLL, hs, stipple, pub 1828, BM. NPG.

EGERTON, John (1579-1649), see 1st Earl of Bridgewater.

EGERTON, John (1622-1686), see 2nd Earl of Bridgewater.

EGERTON, John (1646-1701), see 3rd Earl of Bridgewater.

EGERTON, Sir Thomas, see Viscount Brackley.

EGMONT, Sir John Perceval, 1st Earl of (1683-1748) politician.

G WILLIAM VERELST, 'The Georgia Council of 1734', oil, Henry Francis du Pont Winterthur Museum, USA.

SC VINCENZO FELICI, 1707, marble bust, NPG 1956.

PR J.SMITH, after Sir G.Kneller, 1704, wl as young man, mezz, BM, NPG. J.FABER, jun, after H.Hysing, 1734, tql in peer's robes, mezz, BM, NPG.

ELCHIES, Patrick Grant, Lord (1690-1754) Scottish judge.

P ALLAN RAMSAY, 1749, hl, oval, SNPG 152.

ELDER, William (fl 1680-1700) engraver.

PR J.NUTTING, hl, oval, line, BM, NPG.

ELDRED, John (1552-1632) traveller.

SC UNKNOWN, relief bust in medallion, Great Saxham Church, Suffolk. UNKNOWN, brass effigy, Great Saxham Church, engr J.Besire, line, NPG.

ELDRED, William (fl 1646) master gunner of Dover Castle.

PR UNKNOWN, hl with match and rule, oval, woodcut, for *Gunner's Glasse*, 1646, BM.

ELEANOR of Aquitaine (1122?-1204?) queen of France and England, wife of Henry II.

SC UNKNOWN, tomb effigy, Fontevrault Abbey, France.

ELEANOR of Castile (d1290) queen of Edward I.

SC WILLIAM TOREL, 1291–93, gilt-bronze tomb effigy, Westminster Abbey, London; electrotype, NPG 345. UNKNOWN, wax seal, BM.

ELEANOR of Provence (d1291) queen of Henry III.

PR UNKNOWN, from a window formerly in Bexhill Church, tql with Henry III, line, BM, NPG.

ELERS, John Philip (fl 1690-1730) potter.

SC WILLIAM HACKWOOD, wedgwood medallion, The Emily Winthrop Miles Coll, Brooklyn Museum, New York.

ELGIN, Robert Bruce, 2nd Earl of, see 1st Earl of Ailesbury.

ELGIN, Thomas Bruce, 3rd Earl of, see 2nd Earl of Ailesbury.

ELIOT, Sir John (1592-1632) statesman.

P After PAUL VAN SOMER, (type of 1628), hs, oval, Palace of Westminster, London.

PR F.HOLL, tql, stipple, copy of earlier engr, NPG.

ELIOT, John (1604-1690) 'apostle to the Indians'.

P UNKNOWN, hl, Museum of Fine Arts, Boston, USA.

ELIZABETH Woodville (1437?-1492) queen of Edward IV.

P UNKNOWN, hl, Royal Coll; versions, Queen's College, Cambridge; Ashmolean Museum, Oxford.

MS UNKNOWN, *The Dictes and Sayings of the Philosophers*, Ms 265, Lambeth Palace, London.

ELIZABETH of York (1465-1503) queen of Henry VII.

P UNKNOWN, *c*1502, hs with rose, Royal Coll; version, NPG 311.

G REMIGIUS VAN LEEMPUT, after H.Holbein, jun, 'Privy Chamber Group', oil 1667, Royal Coll.

MS UNKNOWN, *Book of the Fraternity of Corpus Christi*, Skinners' Company London.

SC LAURENCE, 1503, wood funeral effigy, Westminster Abbey, London. PIETRO TORRIGIANO, *c*1512–18, bronze tomb effigy, Westminster Abbey; electrotype, NPG 291.

W UNKNOWN, wl with three sisters, St Giles' Church, Little Malvern, Worcs.

ELIZABETH (1533-1603) queen of England and Ireland.

P UNKNOWN, *c*1542–47, tql as princess, Royal Coll. UNKNOWN, *c*1559, 'Coronation' portrait, tql, NPG 5175. UNKNOWN, *c*1558–60, the 'Northwick Park' pattern, hs, NPG 4449. UNKNOWN, *c*1563, the 'Barrington Park' pattern, tql, Badminton House, Avon. Attrib NICHOLAS HILLIARD, *c*1575–80, 'Phoenix' portrait, tql, NPG 190. Attrib N.HILLIARD, 'Pelican' portrait, tql, Walker Art Gallery, Liverpool. UNKNOWN, from *c*1575, the 'Darnley' pattern, tql, NPG 2082. All the following portraits use the 'Darnley' face mask. UNKNOWN, *c*1575–80, the 'Garter' portrait, hl, Royal Coll; version, NPG 200. UNKNOWN, from *c*1575, 'Raveningham' portrait, tql, Yale University Art Gallery, New Haven, USA. UNKNOWN, from *c*1575, 'Penshurst' portrait, tql, Penshurst, Kent. UNKNOWN, *c*1580, 'Siena sieve' portrait, tql, Pinacoteca di Siena, Italy. UNKNOWN, *c*1580–85, 'Hampton Court' portrait, hl, Royal Coll. UNKNOWN, *c*1585–90, 'Arbury' portrait, tql, Arbury Hall, Warwicks; version, attrib John Bettes, jun, NPG 2471. UNKNOWN, from *c*1595, 'Weavers' Company' portrait, tql, Guildhall Art Gallery, London. UNKNOWN, *c*1590–1600, 'Brocket' portrait, hs, St John's College, Cambridge. Attrib GEORGE GOWER, from *c*1588, the 'Armada' pattern, tql, Woburn Abbey, Beds; version, NPG 541. MARCUS GHEERAERTS,

from c1592, the 'Ditchley' pattern, wl, NPG 2561.
UNKNOWN, c1594–95, the 'Buccleuch' pattern, tql, Buccleuch
Estates, Selkirk, Scotland. Other paintings not conforming to
above types: attrib WILLIAM SEGAR, 1585, 'Ermine' portrait, tql
Hatfield House, Herts; attrib M.GHEERAERTS, c1600, 'Rainbow'
portrait, tql, Hatfield.
D FEDERIGO ZUCCARO, 1575, wl, BM.
M N.HILLIARD, 1572, hs, oval, NPG 108. N.HILLIARD, c1580, tql
with lute, oval, Berkeley Castle, Glos. N.HILLIARD, c1580–84,
hs, oval, Royal Coll. N.HILLIARD, c1588, hs, Buccleuch Estates.
N.HILLIARD, from c1590, 'Mask of Youth' pattern, hs, oval,
V & A. ISAAC OLIVER, hl, oval, unfinished, V & A.
G UNKNOWN. 'Family of Henry VIII', as princess, oil, c1547,
Royal Coll. Attrib HANS EWORTH, 'Elizabeth and the Three
Goddesses', oil, 1569, Royal Coll. Attrib ROBERT PEAKE, sen,
'Procession to Blackfriars', oil, c1600, Sherborne Castle, Dorset.
M.GHEERAERTS, sen, 'Procession of Garter Knights, 1576', etch,
BM.
SC S.VAN HERWIJCK, 1565, lead medal, hs, profile, NPG 4294. Attrib
CHARLES ANTHONY, 1601, gold medal, NPG L155. UNKNOWN,
various medals and coins, BM. UNKNOWN, various seals, BM.
UNKNOWN, c1570–75, marble bust, NPG L120. Attrib WILLIAM
KERWIN, c1586, statue, St Dunstan's-in-the-West, London.
UNKNOWN, 1597, statue, seated, Trinity College, Cambridge.
MAXIMILIAN COLTE, c1605–07, white marble tomb effigy,
Westminster Abbey, London; electrotype, NPG 357.
PR Numerous engravings, BM, NPG.

ELIZABETH, Queen of Bohemia (1596-1662) daughter of
James I.
P DANIEL MYTENS, c1626–27, wl with feather fan, Royal Coll.
Studio of M.J.VAN MIEREVELDT, c1625–30, hl, NPG 71. After
GERARD HONTHORST, 1628, wl, on loan to DoE; version,
Woburn Abbey, Beds. After G.HONTHORST, (type of c1630), wl
with fringe, Clarendon Coll on loan to Plymouth Art Gallery,
engr W.J.Delff, 1630, hl, oval, line, BM, NPG. G.HONTHORST,
c1632, hl as widow, Buccleuch Estates, Selkirk, Scotland. Studio
of G.HONTHORST, 1642, wl with dog, NPG L123. Studio of
G.HONTHORST, (type of 1642), hl, oval, NPG 511.
G.HONTHORST, 1650, hl with veil, Ashdown House (NT), Oxon.
M ISAAC OLIVER, c1610, hs, oval, Royal Coll. NICHOLAS
HILLIARD, c1610, hl, oval, V & A.
G G.HONTHORST, allegorical family group, Landes Museum,
Hannover, W.Germany. C.VAN DE PASSE, after a medal, hs with
husband and son, oval, line engr, NPG. ADRIAN VAN DE VENNE,
procession on horseback, oil, 1626, Rijksmuseum, Amsterdam.
SC Attrib FRANCOIS DIEUSSART, 1641, marble bust, V & A.
UNKNOWN, various medals, BM.
PR C.VAN DE PASSE, c1612, hl, oval, BM, NPG. R.ELSTRACK, c1612,
wl with husband, line, BM. B.BOLSWERT, after M.J. Van
Miereveldt, 1615, tql, aged 16, line, BM, NPG.

ELIZABETH, Princess (1635-1650) second daughter of
Charles I.
P SIR PETER LELY, c1647–50, hs, Syon house, Brentford, Middx.
G SIR ANTHONY VANDYCK, 'The Five Eldest Children of Charles
I', oil, 1637, Royal Coll. SIR P.LELY, 'The Youngest children of
Charles I', oil, 1647, Petworth (NT) W Sussex.
PR R.GAYWOOD?, hl, oval, etch, for Wase, Electra of Sophocles, 1649,
BM, NPG. W.HOLLAR, 1650, hl, oval, etch, BM.

ELLESMERE, Sir Thomas Egerton, Baron, see Viscount
Brackley.

ELLIS, Clement (1630-1700) religious writer.
PR UNKNOWN, hl, oval, line, for Discourses on the Parables, 1704, BM,
NPG.

ELLIS, John (1698-1791) scrivener and political writer, deputy
for Broad Street ward.
PR W.PETHER, after T.Frye, 1781, hl, mezz, NPG. B.READING, after
T.Frye, hl, oval, line, for European Mag, 1792, BM, NPG.

ELLIS, Philip, in religion Michael (1652-1726) Catholic
bishop in partibus.
PR H.MEYER, hl, stipple, for Ellis Correspondence, 1828, BM, NPG.

ELLIS, Welbore (1651?-1734) bishop of Meath.
P WILLIAM SONMANS, before 1721, wl seated, Christ Church,
Oxford.

ELLIS or ELLYS, Sir William (1609-1680) judge.
P J.M.WRIGHT, c1650–60, wl in robes, Guildhall Library, London.

ELPHINSTONE, Arthur, see 6th Baron Balmerino.

ELPHINSTONE, William (1431-1514) bishop of Aberdeen
and founder of Aberdeen University.
P UNKNOWN, hl in robes, Aberdeen University, Scotland.

ELSTOB, Elizabeth (1683-1756) Anglo-Saxon scholar.
PR S.GRIBELIN, head in initial letter G, in trans of Aelfric's English-
Saxon Homily, 1709, line, BM. B.READING, hs, line, facsimile,
from English-Saxon Grammar, 1715, NPG.

ELTON, Richard (fl 1650) military writer.
PR J.DROESHOUT, hl in armour, oval, line, for Compleat Body of the
Art Military, 1650, BM, NPG.

ELYOT, Sir Thomas (d1546) diplomat and author.
D HANS HOLBEIN, jun, hs, chalks, Royal Coll.

ELYS, Edmund (fl 1707) divine and poet.
PR W.FAITHORNE, hs, octagon, line, for Miscellanea, 2nd ed 1662,
BM, NPG.

EMLYN, Thomas (1663-1741) first Unitarian minister in
England.
PR G.VAN DER GUCHT, after J.Highmore, hs, oval, line, for Sermons,
1742, BM, NPG. J.HOPWOOD, after J.Highmore, hs, oval, stipple,
BM, NPG.

EMMA, called AELFGIFU (d1052) queen, wife of King
Ethelred II and King Canute.
MS UNKNOWN, c1016–20, wl with King Canute presenting cross to
Newminster, BL Stowe Ms 944, fol 6.

EMPSON, Sir Richard (d1510) statesman and lawyer.
G UNKNOWN, wl with Henry VII and Edmund Dudley, oil,
Belvoir Castle, Leics.

ENDECOTT, John (1588?-1665) governor of New England.
PR D.L.GLOVER, hl, stipple, NPG.

ENT, Sir George (1604-1689) physician.
PR R.WHITE, hl, oval, line, for Animadversiones in M.Thrustoni,
1679, BM, NPG.

ERDESWICKE, Sampson (d1603) historian of Staffordshire.
SC UNKNOWN, 1601, monumental effigy, Sandon Church, Sandon,
Staffs.

ERLE, Thomas (1650?-1720) general.
PR J.SIMON, after Sir G.Kneller, tql in armour, mezz, BM, NPG.

ERNEST AUGUSTUS, see Duke of York and Albany.

ERPINGHAM, Sir Thomas (1357-1428) soldier.
PR UNKNOWN, from window formerly in Norwich Cathedral, wl
kneeling, line, pub 1793, BM, NPG. UNKNOWN, tql, oval, line, for
Harding, Shakspeare Illustrated, 1793, BM, NPG.

ERSKINE, David, see 2nd Baron Cardross.

ERSKINE, Ebenezer (1680-1754) founder of Scottish secession church.
P UNKNOWN, hl, SNPG 1238.

ERSKINE, Henry, see 3rd Baron Cardross.

ERSKINE, James (d1640), see 6th Earl of Buchan.

ERSKINE, James (1679-1754), see Lord Grange.

ERSKINE, John (d1572), see 1st Earl of Mar.

ERSKINE, John (1562?-1634), see 2nd Earl of Mar.

ERSKINE, John (1675-1732), see 6th Earl of Mar.

ERSKINE, John (1695-1768) Scottish lawyer.
P Attrib H.SMITH, hl, oval, Parliament Hall, Edinburgh.
PR D.LIZARS, after Sir J.B.Medina, hl, octagon, line, NPG.

ERSKINE, Ralph (1685-1752) Scottish seceding divine and poet.
P RICHARD WAITT, 1712, SNPG 1239.
PR BUCK, hl, oval, line NPG. T.CHAMBERS, hl, oval, line, NPG.

ESSEX, Arthur Capell, 1st Earl of (1631-1683) statesman.
P SIR PETER LELY, hs as young man, oval, Badminton House, Avon. SIR P.LELY, hl, Syon House, Middx, engr B.Picart, 1724, hs, oval, line, NPG.
G SIR P.LELY, tql with wife, oil, Yale Center for British Art, New Haven, USA.
SC GEORGE BOWER, silver medal, BM.

ESSEX, Henry Bourchier, 1st Earl of (d1483) treasurer of England.
SC UNKNOWN, statue on monument, Little Easton Church, Essex, engr J.Basire, line, NPG.

ESSEX, Robert Devereux, 2nd Earl of (1566-1601) soldier and favourite of Queen Elizabeth I.
P WILLIAM SEGAR, 1590, tql, NGI 283. Attrib W.SEGAR, c1590–92, hl with Garter George, Museum of Fine Arts, Boston, USA. MARCUS GHEERAERTS, c1596, wl, Woburn Abbey, Beds; version, tql, Trinity College, Cambridge. M.GHEERAERTS, c1597, wl with Garter robes, NPG 4985. After M.GHEERAERTS, hl, NPG 180.
M NICHOLAS HILLIARD, c1593–95, wl, Wrest Park (DoE), Beds. ISAAC OLIVER, c1596, hs, oval, NPG 4966; version, Royal Coll.

ESSEX, Robert Devereux, 3rd Earl of (1591-1646) parliamentary general.
P Attrib DANIEL MYTENS, wl, NPG L115.
M SAMUEL COOPER, hs, oval, Royal Coll.
SC THOMAS SIMON, gold and silver medal, BM. UNKNOWN, various medals and badges, BM.
PR R.ELSTRACK, hl with armour, line, BM, NPG. W.HOLLAR, wl on horseback, etch, BM, NPG. W.HOLLAR, 1644, wl, etch, BM, NPG. W.MARSHALL, hl with truncheon, oval, line, for *Manor & Forme of his Funeral*, 1646, BM, NPG.

ESSEX, Thomas Cromwell, Earl of (1485?-1540) statesman.
P HANS HOLBEIN, jun, tql seated, The Frick Coll, New York, USA; version, NPG 1727.
SC UNKNOWN, 1538, silver-gilt medal, hs, profile, BM.

ESSEX, Walter Devereux, 1st Earl of Essex (1541?-1576) military commander, earl-marshal of Ireland.
P UNKNOWN, 1572, tql in armour, NPG 4984.
PR M.GHEERAERTS, sen, 'Procession of Knights of Garter, 1576',

etch, BM. PASSE, hl, oval, line, for Holland, *Herwologia*, 1620, BM, NPG.

ESTE, Charles (1696-1745) bishop of Waterford.
P Attrib J.B.VAN LOO, tql seated in robes, Christ Church, Oxford.

ETHELBERT, (d866) king of the West-Saxons and Kentishmen.
SC UNKNOWN, statue, Canterbury Cathedral.

ETHELRED I (d871) king of the West-Saxons and Kentishmen.
SC UNKNOWN, brass effigy, hl, Wimborne Minster, Dorset.

ETHELRED, 'the Unready' (968?-1016) king of England.
SC UNKNOWN, silver penny, BM.

ETHELSTAN (893?-950) king of the West-Saxons and Mercians.
MS UNKNOWN, wl presenting book to St Cuthbert, in Bede, *Life of St Cuthbert*, c930, Corpus Christi College, Cambridge.
SC UNKNOWN, silver penny, BM.

EUSDEN, Laurence (1688-1730) poet laureate.
D JONATHAN RICHARDSON, hl, black chalk, BM.

EVANS, John (d1724) bishop of Meath.
P Attrib MICHAEL DAHL, tql seated, Lambeth Palace, London.

EVANS, John (1678-1730) divine.
P UNKNOWN, hl, oval, Dr Williams's Library, London.

EVANS, Philip (1645-1679) Jesuit executed for treason.
G UNKNOWN, 'Titus Oates and Jesuits', Oates in pillory surrounded by heads of seven Jesuits, line engr, BM.
PR ALEX VOET, hs with knife in breast, oval, line, NPG.

EVELYN, John (1620-1705) writer and virtuoso.
P HENDRICK VAN DER BORCHT, 1641, hl, NPG L148. ROBERT WALKER, 1648, hl, NPG L166.
PR R.NANTEUIL, 1650, hl, oval, line, BM, NPG 3258. R.GAYWOOD, 1654, hl, oval, etch, BM. T.BRAGG, after Sir G.Kneller, hl, line, for *Memoirs*, 1818, BM, NPG.

EVERARD, John (1575?-1650?) divine and mystic.
PR T.CROSS, hl, line, for *Gospel Treasury Opened*, 1659, BM, NPG.

EXETER, John Holland, Duke of (1352?-1400) follower of Richard II executed by Henry IV.
MS UNKNOWN, early 15th century French, wl on horseback with Duke of Surrey riding to meet Henry IV, BL Harley Ms 1319, fol 25; and meeting Henry IV at Chester, BL Harley Ms 1319, fol 30b.

EXETER, Thomas Cecil, 1st Earl, see 2nd Baron Burghley.

EYRE, Sir Robert (1666-1735) judge and chancellor to the Prince of Wales.
P UNKNOWN, hl in robes, oval, Lincoln's Inn, London. UNKNOWN, tql in robes, Guildhall, Salisbury, Wilts.

EYRE, Sir Samuel (1633-1698) judge.
P UNKNOWN, hl in robes, oval, Guildhall, Salisbury, Wilts.
SC UNKNOWN, 1698, bust on monument, St Mary's Church, Lancaster, Lancs.

F

FAGIUS, Paul (1504-1549) German protestant divine, reader of Hebrew at Cambridge.
PR UNKNOWN, hl, profile, oval, woodcut for Beza, *Icones*, 1580, NPG. H.HONDIUS, jun, hl, line, for Verheiden, *Effigies*, 1602, BM, NPG.

FAIRBORNE, Sir Stafford (d 1742) admiral.
P SIR GODFREY KNELLER, c 1703–08, tql, NMM, Greenwich.

FAIRCHILD, Thomas (1667?-1729) gardener.
P RICHARD? VAN BLEECK, hl, School of Botany, Oxford University.

FAIRCLOUGH, Daniel, see Featley.

FAIRCLOUGH, John, see Featley.

FAIRCLOUGH, Samuel (1594-1677) nonconformist divine.
PR F.H.VAN HOVE, hl, oval, line, for S.Clarke, *Lives*, 1683, BM, NPG, V & A.

FAIRFAX of Cameron, Ferdinando Fairfax, 2nd Baron (1584-1648) general for the parliament.
P EDWARD BOWER, 1646, tql seated, City Art Gallery, York.
PR UNKNOWN, hl, oval, line for Vicar, *England's Worthies*, 1647, BM. R.S.[AWYER], hl, line, for modern reprint of Ricraft, *Survey of England's Champions*, 1647, BM, NPG.
SC UNKNOWN, silver badges, BM.

FAIRFAX, Robert (1666-1725) rear-admiral.
P MARY BEALE, 1685, hl in armour, Gorhambury, Herts.

FAIRFAX of Cameron, Thomas Fairfax, 1st Baron (1560-1640) diplomat.
P UNKNOWN, hs, Aynho Park, Northants.

FAIRFAX of Cameron, Thomas Fairfax, 3rd Baron (1612-1671) general for the parliament.
P Attrib EDWARD BOWER, tql in armour, Althorp, Northants.
SC THOMAS SIMON, 1645, gold medal, NPG 4624. UNKNOWN, various medals and badges, BM.
PR W.FAITHORNE, after R.Walker, hl in armour, oval, line, BM, NPG 3624. W.MARSHALL, after E.Bower, wl on horseback, line, for *England's Recovery*, 1647, BM, NPG.

FAITHORNE, William (1616?-1691) draughtsman and engraver.
PR J.FILLIAN, after W.Faithorne, hs, oval, line, BM, NPG.

FALKLAND, Elizabeth Cary, Viscountess (1585-1639) linguist who adopted Roman Catholicism.
D T.ATHOW, wl, wash, Sutherland Coll, Ashmolean Museum, Oxford.

FALKLAND, Henry Cary, 1st Viscount (1576-1633) lord deputy of Ireland.
PR J.BARRA, after Paul van Somer, hl with truncheon, oval, line, BM. J.BROWN, after P.van Somer, wl with hat, line and stipple, for Harding, *Ancient Historical Pictures*, 1844, BM, NPG.

FALKLAND, Lucius Cary, 2nd Viscount (1610?-1643) soldier and politician.
P Attrib SIR ANTHONY VANDYCK, c 1638, hl, Chatsworth, Derbys; versions, Holkham Hall, Norfolk; Longleat, Wilts.
M Attrib JOHNS HOSKINS, hs, oval, NPG L 152(42).

FALKNER, William (d 1682) divine.
PR J.STURT, hl, oval, line, for *Two Treatises*, 1684, BM, NPG.

FALMOUTH, Hugh Boscawen, 1st Viscount (c 1680-1734) MP for Tregony.
P MICHAEL DAHL, hl, Badminton, Avon.

FANE, John, see 7th Earl of Westmorland.

FANE, Mildmay, see 2nd Earl of Westmorland.

FANSHAWE, Anne, née Harrison (1625-1680) wife of Sir Richard Fanshawe.
P After C.DOWSON, hl, Valence House, Dagenham, Essex.
PR C.M.FANSHAWE, hs, etch, NPG.

FANSHAWE, Henry (1506-1568) remembrancer of the exchequer.
P UNKNOWN, hs, Valence House, Dagenham, Essex.

FANSHAWE, Sir Richard (1608-1666) diplomat and author.
P WILLIAM DOBSON, tql with dog, Valence House, Dagenham, Essex.
PR W.FAITHORNE, hl, oval, line, BM, NPG.

FANSHAWE, Thomas (1533-1601) remembrancer of the exchequer.
P Attrib MARCUS GHEERAERTS, hl, Valence House, Dagenham, Essex.

FANSHAWE, Sir Thomas Fanshawe, 1st Viscount (1596-1665) remembrancer of the exchequer.
P After SIR PETER LELY, hl, Valence House, Dagenham, Essex.

FANSHAWE, Sir Thomas Fanshawe, 2nd Viscount (1639-1674) remembrancer of the exchequer.
P School of SIR PETER LELY, hs, oval, Valence House, Dagenham, Essex.

FARNHAM, Richard (d 1642) fanatic.
PR UNKNOWN, from a broadsheet, wl with John Bull, woodcut, for *A True Discourse of the two Infamous Upstart Prophets*, 1636, reprint J.Caulfield, 1795, NPG.

FARQUAR, George (1678-1707) dramatist.
G M.VAN DER GUCHT, wl in allegorical scene, line engr, for *Works*, 1711, NPG.
PR R.CLAMP, hs, oval, stipple, BM. FREEMAN, hs, stipple, NPG.

FAUCONBERG, Thomas, the Bastard of (d 1471) rebel.
MS UNKNOWN, wl attacking London, Ghent Ms 236, Ghent University, The Netherlands.

FAUCONBERG, Thomas Belasyse, 1st Earl (1627-1700) son-in-law of Oliver Cromwell.
PR A.BLOOTELING, 1676, after Mary Beale, hl in armour, oval, line, BM, NPG. R.WHITE, tql in robes, line, for Guillim, *Heraldry*, 1679, BM, NPG.

FAULKNER, George (1699?-1775) bookseller and alderman of Dublin.
PR W.SHARP, hs, oval, line, for *Works of Lord Chesterfield*, 1777, BM, NPG.

FAWKENER, Sir Everard (1694-1758) merchant and diplomat.
D UNKNOWN, head, profile, oval, pastel, V & A.

FAWKES, Guy (1570-1606) conspirator.
G G.VAN DE PASSE, 'Gunpowder Plot Conspirators, 1605', line engr, NPG 334A.

FAZACKERLEY or FAZAKERLEY, Nicholas (d 1767) lawyer and politician.
P ARTHUR DAVIS, 1763, wl, Harris Art Gallery, Preston.

FEATLEY or FAIRCLOUGH, Daniel (1582-1645) controversialist.
PR W.MARSHALL, hl, oval, line, for *Dippers Dipt*, 1646, BM, NPG. UNKNOWN, wl in graveclothes on tomb, line, for W.Leo, *Funeral Sermon*, 1645, BM, NPG.

FEATLEY or FAIRCLOUGH, John (1605?-1666) divine, chaplain to Charles I.
PR F.H.VAN HOVE, hl in allegorical scene, line, in title to *Fountaine of Tears*, 1646, BM, NPG.

FEILDING, Basil, see 2nd Earl of Denbigh.

FEILDING, Robert, called Beau (1651?-1712) soldier and rake.
PR I.BECKETT, after Sir G.Kneller, tql in armour, mezz, BM. NPG. I.BECKETT, after W.Wissing, tql with dog, mezz, BM, NPG. R.TOMPSON, after Sir P.Lely, tql in fancy dress, mezz, 'J.van der Vaart fecit', BM, NPG.

FEILDING, William, see 1st Earl of Denbigh.

FELL, John (1625-1686) bishop of Oxford.
P After SIR PETER LELY, tql with book, Christ Church, Oxford. UNKNOWN, hs, Christ Church.
G SIR P.LELY, tql with J.Dolben and R.Allestree, oil, Christ Church.

FELL, Samuel (1584-1649) dean of Christ Church.
P UNKNOWN, hl with book, oval, Christ Church, Oxford. UNKNOWN, hs, Christ Church.

FELTON, John (1595?-1628) assassin of the Duke of Buckingham.
PR R.SAWYER, wl with dagger, line, facsimile of rare print, pub 1830, BM, NPG.

FELTON, Nicholas (1556-1626) bishop of Ely.
P UNKNOWN, hl in robes, Pembroke College, Cambridge.

FENNER, Sir Edward (d 1612) judge.
P UNKNOWN, 1608, hs, NPG 4958.
SC UNKNOWN, marble monumental effigy, Hayes Church, Middx.

FENNER, William (1600-1640) puritan divine.
PR W.HOLLAR, hl, etch, for *Divine Message*, 1647, BM; same plate, date altered to 1651, BM, NPG. J.STAFFORD, after Hollar, 1656, hl, etch, BM, NPG.

FENTON, Elijah (1683-1730) poet.
PR H.R.COOKE, after S.Harding, hl with turban, stipple, NPG.

FENWICK or CALDWELL, John (1628-1679) Jesuit, executed for treason.
PR M.BOUCHE, hs with knife in breast, oval, line, for M.Tanner, *Brevis Relatio*, 1683, BM, NPG.

FENWICK, Sir John, Bart (1645?-1697) conspirator, executed for treason.
PR R.WHITE, after W.Wissing, hl, oval, line, BM, NPG.

FERG, Francis de Paula (1689-1740) landscape painter.
PR J.F.BAUSE, after F.Ferg, hs, oval, line, for *Neuen Bibliotek der Schönen Wissenschaften*, BM, NPG.

FERIA, Jane Dormer, Duchess of (1538-1612) companion of Queen Mary.
P Attrib SANCHEZ COELLO, tql aged 25, Rousham House, Oxon.

FERRAR, Nicholas (1592-1637) theologian.
P Attrib CORNELIUS JOHNSON, tql, Magdalene College, Cambridge.

FEVERSHAM, Louis Duras, Earl of (1640?-1709) general.
PR I.BECKETT, after J.Riley, hl, oval, mezz, BM, NPG.

FIDDES, Richard (1671-1725) historian.
PR N.PIGNÉ, hl, oval, line, for *Theologia Speculativa*, 1718, BM, NPG. G.VERTUE, hl, oval, line, for *Life of Wolsey*, 1724, BM, NPG.

FIELD, Nathaniel (1587-1633) actor and dramatist.
P UNKNOWN, hs, Dulwich College Gallery, London.

FIENNES or FIENES, Gregory, see 10th Baron Dacre.

FIENNES, Nathaniel (1608?-1669) parliamentarian.
P M.J.VAN MIEREVELDT, tql in armour, Broughton Castle, Oxon.
PR W.HOLLAR, 1644, hl, oval, etch, BM, NPG.

FIENNES or FIENES, Thomas, see 9th Baron Dacre.

FIENNES, William, see 1st Viscount Saye and Sele.

FIGG, James (d 1734) pugilist.
PR J.FABER, jun, after J.Ellys, hl with shaved head, oval, mezz, BM, NPG.

FINCH, Anne, see Countess of Winchilsea.

FINCH, Daniel, see 7th Earl of Winchilsea.

FINCH, Edward (1664-1737?) composer and divine.
SC J.M.RYSBRACK, 1728, terracotta bust, V & A. J.M.RYSBRACK, marble bust on monument, York Minster.

FINCH, Sir Heneage (1580-1631) speaker of the House of Commons.
P UNKNOWN, hs in robes of sergeant-at-law, NPG 4552.
SC NICHOLAS STONE, 1632, bust on monument, V & A, formerly St Mary's Church, Eastwell, Kent.

FINCH, Heneage (1621-1682) see 1st Earl of Nottingham.

FINCH, Heneage (1647?-1719), see 1st Earl of Aylesford.

FINCH, John Finch, 1st Baron (1584-1660) speaker of House of Commons.
P After SIR ANTHONY VANDYCK, (type of c 1640), tql seated in robes, NPG 2125.
PR G.GLOVER, hl with wings on shoulders, oval, line, BM, NPG. W.HOLLAR, after E.Bower, hs, oval, etch, BM, NPG. G.VERTUE, after C.Johnson, hs, oval, line, for Ward, *Hist of the Rebellion*, 1713, BM, NPG.

FINCH, Sir John (1626-1682) physician.
P CARLO DOLCI, hl, Fitzwilliam Museum, Cambridge, SIR PETER LELY, hs, Christ's College, Cambridge.
SC JOSEPH CATTERNS, 1684, relief portrait medallion, Christ's College Chapel.

FINET(T), Sir John (1571-1641) master of the ceremonies.
D G.P.HARDING, after an original portrait, tql seated, w/c, NPG 2404.

FINGER, Gottfried (fl 1685-1717) composer.
PR S.GRIBELIN, bust in allegorical setting, line, for *Sonatae XII*, 1688, BM, NPG.

FISHER, James (1697-1775) a founder of the Scottish secession church.
G UNKNOWN, 'Founders of Scottish Secession Church', lith, NPG.

FISHER, Jane, née Lane, Lady (d 1689) Stuart loyalist.
P UNKNOWN, c 1660, hl with crown, NPG 1798.

FISHER, John (1459-1535) bishop of Rochester.
D HANS HOLBEIN, jun, c 1528, hs, chalks, Royal Coll. After H.HOLBEIN, head, NPG 2821.

FITTON, Mary (fl 1600) maid of honour to Queen Elizabeth.
P UNKNOWN, c1595, tql, Arbury Hall, Warwicks.

FITZALAN, Henry, see 12th Earl of Arundel.

FITZALAN, John, see 7th Earl of Arundel.

FITZALAN, Thomas (1353-1414), see Arundel.

FITZALAN, Thomas (1381-1415), see 5th Earl of Arundel and Surrey.

FITZEUSTACE, Roland, see Baron Portlester.

FITZGERALD, Gerald (1487-1534), see 9th Earl of Kildare.

FITZJAMES, James, see 1st Duke of Berwick.

FITZROY, Charles, see 1st Duke of Cleveland.

FITZROY, George, see 2nd Duke of Northumberland.

FITZROY, Henry (1519-1536), see 1st Duke of Richmond.

FITZROY, Henry (1663-1690), see 1st Duke of Grafton.

FITZWILLIAM, John (1651-1699) nonjuror.
P UNKNOWN, 1662, hl, Magdalen College, Oxford.

FITZWILLIAM, William, see Earl of Southampton.

FLAMSTEED, John (1646-1719) first astronomer royal.
P UNKNOWN, c1680?, hl, oval, NPG 1855. THOMAS GIBSON, 1712, tql seated, Royal Society, London.

FLATMAN, Thomas (1637-1688) poet and miniature painter.
P Attrib self-portrait, c1660, hs, NPG 1051. Self-portrait, hl, Knole (NT), Kent.
D Attrib J.HAYLS, hs, Antony House (NT), Cornwall, engr A.Walker, hs, oval, line, for Walpole, *Anecdotes of Painting*, 1763, BM, NPG.
PR W.FAITHORNE, jun, tql seated with print, mezz, BM.

FLAVEL, John (1630?-1691) presbyterian divine.
P UNKNOWN, hl, oval, Dr Williams's Library, London.
PR M.VAN DER GUCHT, hs, oval, line, NPG. R.WHITE, hs, oval, line, BM, NPG.

FLEETWOOD, Charles (d1692) parliamentary general.
P ROBERT WALKER, hl in armour, Society of Antiquaries, London, engr J.Houbraken, hl, oval, line, for Birch, *Heads*, 1740, BM, NPG.
PR UNKNOWN, wl in armour, line, contemporary engr, BM.

FLEETWOOD, George (1622?-after 1664) regicide.
M SAMUEL COOPER, 1647, hs in armour, oval, NPG 1925.

FLEETWOOD, William (1656-1723) bishop of Ely.
P Attrib JONATHAN RICHARDSON, tql seated, Lambeth Palace, London; version, Bishop's Palace, Ely, engr J.Simon, mezz, BM.
M BERNARD LENS, hs, oval, NPG 5118. B.LENS, hs, oval, NPG 5119.
PR R.WHITE, hs, when 'Mr Fleetwood M.A.', oval, line, BM, NPG.

FLEMING, Caleb (1698-1779) dissenting minister.
P Attrib MASON CHAMBERLIN, 1772, hs, Dr Williams's Library, London.

FLEMING, Sir George, Bart (1667-1747) bishop of Carlisle.
PR J.FABER, jun, after J.Vanderbank, tql seated, mezz, BM, NPG.

FLEMING, James (1682-1751) major-general and colonel.
SC L.F.ROUBILIAC, 1751, relief portrait medallion on monument, Westminster Abbey, London.

FLEMING, Richard (d1431) bishop of Lincoln and founder of Lincoln College, Oxford.
P UNKNOWN, c1638, hl in robes, Lincoln College.
SC UNKNOWN, tomb effigy, Lincoln Cathedral.

FLEMING, Robert (1660?-1716) presbyterian minister.

P Attrib JOHN CLOSTERMAN, hs, oval, Bodleian Library, Oxford.
PR R.WHITE, after C.D.Gard, 1701, hs, oval, line, NPG.

FLEMING, Sir Thomas (1544-1613) chief-justice of the king's bench.
P UNKNOWN, 1596, hl, NPG 1799.
SC UNKNOWN, tomb effigy, with wife, St Michael's Church, North Stoneham, Hants.

FLETCHER of Saltoun, Andrew (1655-1716) Scottish patriot.
P After WILLIAM AIKMAN, hs, oval, SNPG 890. After W.AIKMAN, hs, oval, SNPG L262.
D 11th EARL OF BUCHAN, 1794, pencil and chalk, SNPG 1642.

FLETCHER, Andrew (1692-1766), see Lord Milton.

FLETCHER, John (1579-1625) dramatist.
P UNKNOWN, c1620, tql, Clarendon Coll on loan to Plymouth Art Gallery, engr W.Marshall, hs, oval, line, for Beaumont, *Comedies and Tragedies*, 1647, BM, NPG. UNKNOWN, hl, oval, Knole (NT), Kent; copy, NPG 420.

FLITCROFT, Henry (1697-1769) architect.
P Attrib BARTHOLOMEW DANDRIDGE, hl in turban, RIBA, London.

FLORIO, John (1553?-1625) author, compiler of an Italian-English dictionary.
PR W.HOLE, hl, aged 58, oval, line, for *Dictionary*, 1611, BM, NPG.

FLUDD, Robert (1574-1637) physician and Rosicrucian.
PR M.MERIAN, tql, etch and line, for *Philosophia Sacra*, 1626, BM. UNKNOWN, tql, oval, line, for Boissard, *Bibliotheca Chalcographica*, 1650, BM, NPG.

FOGG, Laurence (1623-1718) dean of Chester.
P UNKNOWN, tql, St John's College, Cambridge.

FOLKES, Martin (1690-1754) antiquary.
P WILLIAM HOGARTH, 1741, hl, Royal Society, London.
D UNKNOWN, head, Fitzwilliam Museum, Cambridge.
M BERNARD LENS, c1720, hl with quadrant, w/c, NPG 1926.
SC L.F.ROUBILIAC, 1749, marble bust, Wilton House, Wilts; plaster model, BM. ANTOINE DASSIER, 1740, medal, BM.
PR JOHN SMITH, after J.Richardson, 1719, hl in turban, oval, mezz, BM. J.FABER, jun, after J.Vanderbank, 1737, tql with bust of Newton, mezz, BM, NPG. J.MCARDELL, after T.Hudson, c1748-50, tql seated, mezz, BM, NPG.

FORBES of Culloden, Duncan (1685-1747) president of the Scottish court of session.
P JEREMIAH DAVISON, c1737, tql seated, Advocates Hall, Edinburgh, engr J.Faber, jun, 1748, mezz, BM, NPG. After J.DAVISON, hs, oval, NPG 61.
SC L.F.ROUBILIAC, 1752, statue, Advocates Hall.

FORBES, John (1571-1606) Capuchin friar, 'Father Archangel'.
PR J.PICART, tql with crucifix, line, for *Father Angel of Joyeuse*, etc, Douay, 1623, BM. AUDRAN, hl with crucifix, line, NPG.

FORBES, Patrick (1564-1635) bishop of Aberdeen.
PR R.G., hs, oval, line, for *Funeral of Patrick Forbes*, 1635, BM, NPG.

FORBES, William (1585-1634) first protestant bishop of Edinburgh.
P UNKNOWN, hs, SNPG 773.
D 11th EARL OF BUCHAN, after G.Jamesone, pencil and chalk, SNPG 1629.

FORMAN, Simon (1552-1611) astrologer and quack doctor.
PR R.GODFREY, after Bullfinch, hs, line, pub 1776, BM, NPG.

FORSTER, Thomas (fl 1690-1710) miniaturist.
PR G.WALKER, after T.Forster, hl, oval, etch, from a drawing, pub 1803, BM.

FORSTER, Thomas (1675?-1738) politician and general.
PR J.T.WEDGWOOD, after C.Rosalba, hs, line, for Rodd, *Portraits*, BM, NPG.

FORTESCUE, Sir Edmund (1610-1647) royalist.
PR H.DANCKERTS, 1647, hs in armour, oval, line, NPG.

FORTESCUE, Sir John (1394?-1476?) lord chief justice of the king's bench.
SC UNKNOWN, painted stone tomb effigy, St Eadburga Church, Ebrington, Glos.
PR W.FAITHORNE, hl, octagonal, line for *Fortescutus Illustratus*, 1663, BM, NPG.

FORTESCUE, Sir John (1531?-1607) chancellor of the exchequer.
P SIDNEY HUNT, after contemporary portrait, 1879, tql, Bodleian Library, Oxford.

FORTESCUE, William (1687-1749) master of the rolls.
PR J.FABER, jun, after T.Hudson, 1741, tql in robes, mezz, BM, NPG.

FORTESCUE of Credan, John Fortescue-Aland, Baron (1670-1746) judge.
PR J.FABER, jun, 1733, after Sir G.Kneller, tql seated in robes, mezz, BM, NPG. G.VERTUE, 1750, after Sir G.Kneller, hs in robes, oval, line, BM, NPG.

FOSTER, James (1697-1753) nonconformist divine.
PR J.N.BERNIGEROTH, after J.Wills, 1750, tql, line, NPG. P.VAN BLEECK, after J.Wills, tql, mezz, BM, NPG. S.F.RAVENET, after W.Smith, 1752, hs, oval, line, BM, NPG.

FOSTER, Sir Michael (1689-1763) judge.
PR J.FABER, jun, after J.Wills, tql in robes, mezz, BM, NPG. J.NEAGLE, after J.Wills, 1792, tql, line, BM, NPG.

FOSTER, Robert (1589-1663) chief justice of the king's bench.
SC UNKNOWN, marble bust on monument, St John the Baptist Church, Egham, Surrey.

FOTHERBY, Martin (1549?-1619) bishop of Salisbury.
P UNKNOWN, hl, The Deanery, Canterbury Cathedral.

FOUNTAINE, Sir Andrew (1676-1753) warden of the mint and collector.
SC J.A.DASSIER, copper medal, BM. L.F.ROUBILIAC, 1747, marble bust, Wilton House, Wilts. ANTONIO SELVI, copper medal, BM.
PR W.C.EDWARDS, after Armstrong, hl, line, BM, NPG.

FOWKE, John (d 1662) lord mayor of London.
D T.ATHOW, after contemporary portrait, hl, wash, Sutherland Coll, Ashmolean Museum, Oxford.

FOWLER, Edward (1632-1714) bishop of Gloucester.
PR JOHN SMITH, after Sir G.Kneller, 1717, tql seated, mezz, BM, NPG.

FOX, George (1624-1691) founder of the Society of Friends.
PR THOMAS FAIRLAND, hl, lith, NPG. J.HOLMES, after G.Honthorst, hs, stipple, pub 1699, BM, NPG.

FOX, Sir Stephen (1627-1716) lord commissioner of the treasury and paymaster-general.
P J.BAKER, tql, Chelsea Hospital, London, engr J.Simon, hl, oval, mezz, BM, NPG. SIR PETER LELY, c1670, tql seated, NPG 2077.

FOXE, John (1516-1587) martyrologist.
P UNKNOWN, hl, NPG 24.
PR WILLEM and MAGDALENA VAN DE PASSE, hl, line, for Holland, *Herwologia*, 1620, BM, NPG. G.GLOVER, hl, line, for Foxe, *Actes and Monuments*, 1641, BM.

FOXE, Richard (1448?-1528) bishop of Winchester.
P JOHANNES CORVUS, hl, Corpus Christi College, Oxford; copy, NPG 874.
SC UNKNOWN, tomb effigy, Winchester Cathedral.

FRAMPTON, Robert (1622-1708) bishop of Gloucester.
P UNKNOWN, hs, Bishop's Palace, Gloucester.

FRAMPTON, Tregonwell (1641-1727) keeper of the king's horses at Newmarket.
P By or after JOHN WOOTTON, tql seated, NPG 4312, engr J.Faber, jun, mezz, BM, NPG.

FRANCK, Mark (1613-1664) theologian.
PR W.DOLLE, hl, oval, line, BM, NPG.

FRANKLAND, Joyce (1531-1587) benefactor of Caius and Emmanuel Colleges, Cambridge, and of Lincoln and Brasenose Colleges, Oxford.
P UNKNOWN, 1586, tql, Gonville and Caius College, Cambridge; version, Brasenose College, Oxford.

FRANKLAND, Richard (1630-1698) nonconformist tutor.
P UNKNOWN, hs, Dr Williams's Library, London.

FRASER, Sir Alexander (1537?-1623) founder of Fraserburgh.
P UNKNOWN, hl, Craigston Castle, Grampian region, Scotland.

FRASER, Simon, see 11th Baron Lovat.

FREDERICK V (1596-1632) king of Bohemia, husband of Elizabeth, daughter of James I.
P After GERARD HONTHORST, (type of c1625), hl, profile, oval, Longleat, Wilts. After M.J.VAN MIEREVELDT, 1628, wl, on loan to DoE. G.HONTHORST, c1630, hl in classical dress, NPG 1973. G.HONTHORST, c1634, hl in armour, Buccleuch Estates, Selkirk, Scotland.
M ISAAC OLIVER, c1612, hl, oval, Royal Coll. PETER OLIVER, 1624, hs, oval, Buccleuch Estates; version, Maruitshuis, The Hague, Netherlands.
G G.HONTHORST, allegorical family group, Landes Museum, Hannover, W.Germany. C.VAN DE PASSE, after a medal, hs with wife and son, oval, line, NPG.
PR R.ELSTRACK, c1612, wl with wife, line, BM. C.VAN DE PASSE, hl, line, NPG.

FREIND, John (1675-1728) physician to Queen Caroline.
P MICHAEL DAHL, tql seated with bust of Hippocrates, Bodleian Library, Oxford; version, Royal College of Physicians, London, engr George Vertue, 1730, line, BM, NPG.
SC FERDINAND ST URBAIN, copper medal, BM.

FREIND, Robert (1667-1751) headmaster of Westminster school.
P MICHAEL DAHL, hs, oval, Christ Church, Oxford. UNKNOWN, c1729, hs, Christ Church.
SC J.M.RYSBRACK, marble bust, Christ Church.

FREKE, John (1688-1756) surgeon.
D UNKNOWN, hs, oval, red chalk, NPG.

FREWEN, Accepted (1588-1664) archbishop of York.
P UNKNOWN, tql seated, Bishopthorpe Palace, York.
SC UNKNOWN, tomb effigy, York Minster.

FREWEN, John (1558-1628) puritan divine.
PR E.SCRIVEN, after M.Garrard, tql with skull, stipple and line, NPG.

FREWEN or FREWIN, Richard (1677?-1761) physician of Westminster and Christ Church, Oxford.
P MICHAEL DAHL, hs, oval, Christ Church, Oxford. UNKNOWN, hs, Christ Church.
SC L.F.ROUBILIAC, 1757, marble bust, Christ Church.

FRITH, Mary or **'Moll Cutpurse' (1584?-1659)** thief.
PR UNKNOWN, wl with sword, woodcut for T.Middleton and
T.Dekkar, *The Roaring Girle; or Moll Cut-Purse*, 1611, NPG
UNKNOWN, tql dressed as a man, etch, for *Life*, 1662, BM, NPG.

FROBISHER, Sir Martin (1535?-1594) navigator.
P. CORNELIUS KETEL, 1577, wl, Bodleian Library, Oxford.
PR PASSE, hs, oval, line, for Holland, *Herwologia*, 1620, BM, NPG.

FROST, John (1626?-1656) nonconformist divine.
PR R.VAUGHAN, hl, octagon, line, for *Sermons*, 1657, BM, NPH.

FROWDE, Philip (d 1738) poet, friend of Addison.
PR J.FABER, jun, after T.Murray, 1738, hl, oval, mezz, BM, NPG,
V & A.

FRYER, John (d 1733) traveller.
PR R.WHITE, hs, oval, line, for *Travels*, 1698, NPG.

FULKE, William (1538-1589) puritan divine.
PR W.MARSHALL, hl, oval, line, for *New Testament*, 1633, BM, NPG.

W.MARSHALL, wl in niche, line, for *New Testament*, BM.
UNKNOWN, hs, line, BM, NPG.

FULLER, Isaac (1606?-1672) painter.
P Self-portrait, 1670, tql with sketch, Bodleian Library, Oxford.
Self-portrait, tql with bust, and boy, NPG 2104; version, Queen's
College, Oxford.

FULLER, Thomas (1608-1661) divine and historian.
PR D.LOGGAN, hl, oval, for *Worthies of England*, 1662, BM, NPG.

FULLER, Thomas (1654-1734) physician.
PR G.VERTUE, after D.Timewell, hs, oval, line, for *Pharmacopoeia
Domestica*, 1739, BM, NPG.

FULLER, William (1608-1675) bishop of Lincoln.
P UNKNOWN, hs, oval, Christ Church, Oxford.

FULLER, William (1670-1717?) imposter, pilloried for libel.
PR F.H.VAN HOVE, hl, oval, line, for *Life*, 1703, BM, NPG.
UNKNOWN, hl, line, NPG.

G

GADBURY, John (1627-1704) astrologer.
PR T.CROSS, hl with celestial globe, line, for *Doctrine of Nativities*, 1658, BM. UNKNOWN, hl, oval, line, for *Collection of Nativities*, 1663, BM, NPG.

GAGE, Sir Henry (1597-1645) royalist.
P Perhaps after WILLIAM DOBSON, tql, NPG 2279.

GAGE, Sir John (1479-1556) statesman and military commander.
P UNKNOWN, *c*1620-30, wl in Garter robes, Royal Coll; version, Firle Place, E Sussex.
D HANS HOLBEIN, jun, hs, chalk and ink, Royal Coll.
SC GERARD JOHNSON, 1595, alabaster tomb effigy with wife, St Peter's Church, Firle, E Sussex.

GALE, John (1680-1721) Baptist minister.
P Attrib JOSEPH HIGHMORE, hl, Dr Williams's Library, engr G.Vertue, hl, oval, line, for *Sermons*, 1726, BM, NPG.

GALE, Roger (1672-1744) antiquary.
P Attrib JOHN VANDERBANK, hl, Society of Antiquaries, London. ISAAC WHOOD, 1738, hl, oval, Trinity College, Cambridge. UNKNOWN, hs, oval, Old Schools, Cambridge, engr J.J. van den Berghe, stipple, for J.Adolphus, *British Cabinet*, 1799, BM, NPG.

GALE, Samuel (1682-1754) antiquary.
P Attrib ISAAC WHOOD, hl, Society of Antiquaries, London. School of SIR GODFREY KNELLER, tql, Society of Antiquaries.

GALE, Thomas (1507-1587) surgeon.
PR UNKNOWN, hs, oval, woodcut, for *Institution of a Chirurgion*, 1563, BM, NPG.

GALE, Thomas (1635?-1702) dean of York, antiquary.
P SIR GODFREY KNELLER, 1689, hl, City Art Gallery, York. Attrib JOHN RILEY, hs, Royal Society, London. UNKNOWN, hs, oval, Trinity College, Cambridge.

GALWAY, Henri de Massue, 2nd Marquess of Ruvigny, and 1st Earl of (1648-1720) general.
P UNKNOWN, tql in breastplate, Corsham Court, Wilts.
PR J.SIMON, after P.de Graves, hs in armour, oval, mezz, BM, NPG.

GAMBLE, John (d1687) musician in chapel royal and composer.
PR T.CROSS, hl, oval, line, for *Ayres and Dialogues*, 1656, NPG.

GARANCIERES, Theophilus (1610-1680) physician.
PR W.DOLLE, wl seated, line, for *Prophecies of Nostradamus*, 1672, BM, NPG.

GARDINER, James, sen (1637-1705) bishop of Lincoln.
P Attrib MARY BEALE, tql seated, Lambeth Palace, London. UNKNOWN, Emmanuel College, Cambridge.

GARDINER, James, jun (1679?-1732) sub-dean of Lincoln.
PR G.VERTUE, after J.Verelst, hl, oval, line, for trans of *Rapin on Gardens*, 1718, BM, NPG.

GARDINER, James (1688-1745) colonel of dragoons.
PR T.KITCHIN, after Van Deest, hs, oval, line, NPG. J.T.WEDGWOOD, hl, line, pub 1815, BM, NPG.

GARDINER, Stephen (1483?-1555) bishop of Winchester and lord chancellor.

P UNKNOWN, hl, Trinity Hall, Cambridge; version, Plas Newydd (NT), Isle of Anglesey, Wales.

GARGRAVE, Sir Thomas (1495-1579) speaker and vice-president of the council of the North.
P UNKNOWN, (type of *c*1570), hs, NPG 1928.

GARNETT, Henry (1555-1606) Jesuit, executed for complicity in Gunpowder Plot.
PR A.LOMMELIN, hl, with corn-straw above, line, NPG. J.WIERIX, hs, oval, line, BM. UNKNOWN, hl, line, Dutch inscription, BM, NPG. UNKNOWN, corn-straw, with his face in centre, oval, line, for Endamon-Joannes, *Apologia*, 1619, BM, NPG.

GARRARD, Marcus, see Gheeraerts.

GARRARD, Sir Samuel (1650-1724) lord mayor of London.
P SIR JAMES THORNHILL, hl, oval, Guildhall Art Gallery, London.
D T.ATHOW, after school of Sir G.Kneller, wl in robes, wash, Sutherland Coll, Ashmolean Museum, Oxford.

GARTH, Sir Samuel (1661-1719) physician and poet.
P UNKNOWN, *c*1705-10, hl, oval, NPG 1076. SIR GODFREY KNELLER, *c*1710, hl, the 'Kit-cat Club' portrait, NPG 3208. UNKNOWN, *c*1705-10, hs, oval, Knole (NT), Kent.

GASCOIGNE, George (1525?-1577) poet.
MS UNKNOWN, poet offering tale of 'Hemetes the Hermyte' to Queen, 1575, BL Royal Ms 18, A 49.
PR UNKNOWN, hs in armour, oval, woodcut, for *Steele Glas*, 1576, NPG.

GASCOIGNE, Richard (d1716) Jacobite, executed at Tyburn.
PR UNKNOWN, hs, oval, line, NPG. UNKNOWN, hl, line, for Caulfield, *Remarkable Persons*, 1819, BM, NPG.

GASCOIGNE, Sir William (1350?-1419) judge.
SC UNKNOWN, tomb effigy with wife, All Saints' Church, Harewood, Yorks.

GASTRELL, Francis (1662-1725) bishop of Chester.
P After MICHAEL DAHL, hs, oval, Christ Church, Oxford.
PR G.VERTUE, after M.Dahl, 1728, tql, line, BM. NPG.

GATES, Bernard (1685?-1773) musician, master of choristers of the Chapel Royal.
P Attrib JOHN RUSSELL, hl, Faculty of Music, Oxford.
PR UNKNOWN, hl, oval, stipple, for *Selection of Biography*, pub 1784, BM.

GAUDEN, John (1605-1662) bishop of Worcester.
P UNKNOWN, hl, Lambeth Palace, London; copy, Fulham Palace, London.
SC UNKNOWN, relief bust on monument, Worcester Cathedral.
PR T.CROSS, wl standing with Charles I, for *Hieraspistes*, 1653, BM.

GAULTIER, James (1600-1670?) French lutenist.
PR J.LIVENS, hl with lute, etch, BM.

GAY, John (1685-1732) poet and dramatist.
P MICHAEL DAHL, hl with turban, Knole (NT), Kent.
SC J.M.RYSBRACK, 1736, relief medallion on monument, Westminster Abbey, London. UNKNOWN, head carved on frame of 'Beggars' Opera', Tate, London.

PR G.BICKHAM, after W.Aikman, hl, oval, line, pub 1729, BM.
F.KYTE, after W.Aikman, hl, oval, mezz, BM.

GEE, Sir Orlando (d1705) registrar of court of admiralty.

SC FRANCIS BIRD, 1705, marble bust on monument, Isleworth
Church, Middx.

GEFFREY or **GEFFRYE, Sir Robert (1613-1703?)** lord
mayor of London.

P UNKNOWN, wl in robes, Bridewell Royal Hospital, Witley,
Surrey.

SC JOHN VAN NOST, 1723, lead statue, replaced by copy 1912,
Geffrye Museum, London.

GELDORP, George (fl 1611-1660) portrait-painter.

PR A.BANNERMAN, hs with J.van Belcamp, two ovals, line, for
Walpole, *Anecdotes*, 1765, NPG.

GELL, Sir John, Bart (1593-1671) parliamentary
commander.

PR R.GRAVES, hl, line, BM.

GENINGES, Edmund (1567-1591) Catholic priest executed
for treason.

PR M.BAS, hl, line, for *Life*, 1614, BM, NPG.

GENINGES, John (1570?-1660) Franciscan friar.

PR M.BAS, wl kneeling, line, for *Life and Death of E.Geninges*, 1614,
BM.

GENT, Thomas (1693-1778) printer and topographer at York.

P NATHAN DRAKE, hl, Yorkshire Archaeological Society, Leeds,
engr V.Green, mezz, pub 1771, BM, NPG.

GENTILESCHI, Artemisia (1590?-1642?) painter.

P Self-portrait, tql, almost profile, Royal Coll. Self-portrait, tql
seated, Althorp, Northants.

GENTILESCHI, Orazio (1563-1647) painter.

D SIR ANTHONY VANDYCK, c1632, hl, chalk, pen and sepia, BM,
engr L.Vosterman, line, for Vandyck, *Iconographie*, BM.

GEORGE I, George Lewis (1660-1727) king of Great
Britain and Ireland and Elector of Hanover.

P H.H.QUITER, 1705, tql in armour, Blenheim Palace, Oxon.
Studio of SIR GODFREY KNELLER, c1714, wl in state robes,
Houghton Hall, Norfolk. After SIR G.KNELLER, c1714, hl in
robes, oval, NPG 488. Studio of SIR G.KNELLER, c1714, hs in
armour, profile, NPG 4223. Studio of SIR G.KNELLER, c1714-18,
wl seated in Garter robes, NPG 544; version, Royal Coll. Attrib
MICHAEL DAHL, c1714-27, wl in state robes, Burghley House,
Northants. ENOCH SEEMAN, 1717, wl in coronation robes,
Middle Temple, London. JOHN VANDERBANK, 1726, wl on
horseback, Royal Coll. G.W.FOUNTAINE or LAFONTAINE, tql
with Garter ribbon, Royal Coll, engr G.W.Monguibert, 1733,
line, BM.

SC JOHN CROKER, various medals, BM. Attrib ISAAC GOSSET, wax
profile medallion, V & A. E.HANNIBAL, gold medal, BM. DAVID LE
MARCHAND, ivory bust, V & A. J.M.RYSBRACK, terracotta bust,
NPG 4156. J.M.RYSBRACK, marble bust, Christ Church, Oxford.
UNKNOWN, bronze equestrian statuette, V & A.

PR J.FABER, jun, after D.Stevens, 1722, hl in robes, mezz, BM.
B.LENS, after Seaghley, (type of c1702), hl in armour, mezz, BM.
JOHN SMITH, after J.Hirseman, hl in armour, mezz, BM.
R.TOMPSON, after Sir G.Kneller, (type of c1680-82) tql in
cuirass, mezz, BM, NPG.

GEORGE II (1683-1760) king of Great Britain and Ireland.

P Attrib SIR GODFREY KNELLER, before 1714, hl in armour,
Niedersächsiche Landesgalerie, Hannover, W Germany. SIR
JAMES THORNHILL, c1714-15, hs, oval, Royal Coll; version, NPG
205. Studio of CHARLES JERVAS, c1727, wl in state robes, NPG

368. ENOCH SEEMAN, c1730, wl in state robes, Royal Coll.
JOSEPH HIGHMORE, 1730s, wl in state robes, Walker Art
Gallery, Liverpool. THOMAS HUDSON, 1744, wl seated in state
robes, NPG 670. By or after THOMAS WORLIDGE, c1753, tql in
profile, NPG 256. SIR JOSHUA REYNOLDS, c1756, hl,
Bishopthorpe, York. JOHN SHACKLETON, c1755, wl in state
robes, SNPG 221. ROBERT EDGE PINE, 1759, Audley End (DoE),
Essex. Attrib CHARLES PHILIPS, wl with small dogs as old man,
Marble Hill House (GLC), London. There are a number of
equestrian portraits by various artists: J.HIGHMORE, Goodwood
House, W Sussex; C.JERVAS and JOHN WOOTTON, Blickling
Hall (NT), Norfolk; DAVID MORIER, c1743, Royal Coll;
J.WOOTTON, c1754, with Duke of Cumberland, National Army
Museum, London.

G WILLIAM HOGARTH, The Family of George II, oil, c1733, Royal
Coll. Attrib J.V.HAIDT, Group associated with Moravian
Church, oil, c1752-54, NPG 1356.

SC ISAAC GOSSET, wax profile medallion, Royal Coll. E.HANNIBAL,
medal, BM. LUDWIG VON LÜCKE, 1760, ivory bust, V & A.
L.F.ROUBILIAC, marble bust, Royal Coll. J.M.RYSBRACK, 1738,
marble bust, Royal Coll.

PR W.FAITHORNE, after L.Fontaine, (type of c1701), hl in armour,
oval, mezz, BM, NPG. JOHN SMITH, after J.Hirseman, 1706, hl in
armour, oval, mezz, BM, NPG.

GEORGE of Denmark, Prince (1653-1708) consort of
Queen Anne.

P K.VAN MANDER, boy in armour, Nationalhistorishe Museum,
Frederiksborg Castle, Denmark. G.GALTON, 1680, hl in armour,
oval, National Portrait Gallery, Gripsholm Castle, Sweden.
WILLIAM WISSING, 1684, tql in armour, Reedtz-Thot Coll,
Gaunø Castle, Denmark, engr I.Beckett, mezz, BM, NPG. JOHN
RILEY, c1687, tql in classical dress, Royal Coll; version, NPG 326.
MICHAEL DAHL, c1690, hs in armour, oval, Royal Coll.
M.DAHL, 1704, wl on horseback, Royal Coll. By or after
M.DAHL, c1705, tql in armour, NPG 4163. SIR
GODFREY KNELLER, c1704, wl with Garter George, NMM,
Greenwich. SIR G.KNELLER, 1705, tql with George Clarke, All
Souls College, Oxford.

M CHARLES BOIT, 1706, wl seated with Queen Anne, enamel on
copper, Royal Coll.

SC GEORGE BOWER, medal, BM. JOHN CROKER, medal, BM.
MICHAEL ROEG, medal, BM.

GERARD, Charles, see 1st Earl of Macclesfield.

GERARD, John (1545-1612) herbalist.

PR W.ROGERS, hl with flower, oval, line, for *Herball*, 1598, NPG.
J.PAYNE, hl, line, for 1633 ed, BM.

GERBIER, Sir Balthasar (1591?-1667) painter, architect and
courtier.

G SIR PETER PAUL RUBENS and followers, family group, oil,
c1629-38, Royal Coll.

PR P.PONTIUS, after 'A.Vandyck', hl, line, for *Iconographie*, BM, NPG.

GERMAIN(E), Lady Betty (1680-1769) wife of Sir John
Germain, friend of Swift.

P CHARLES PHILIPS, 1731, wl seated, Knole (NT), Kent.

D WILLIAM HOARE, hl, pastel, Knole.

GETHIN, Lady Grace, née Norton (1676-1697) learned
lady.

SC UNKNOWN, marble kneeling figure on monument, Westminster
Abbey, London.

PR W.FAITHORNE, after A.Dickson, hl, oval, for *Reliquiae
Gethinianae*, 1699, BM, NPG.

GETHING(E), Richard (1585?-1652?) calligrapher.

PR J.CHANTRY, hl, oval, line, for *Calligraphotechnia*, 1652, BM, NPG.

GHEERAERTS, Marcus, sen (1510?-1590?) painter and engraver.
PR W.HOLLAR, after M.Gheeraerts, hs, oval, etch, Royal Coll. A.BANNERMAN, after W.Hollar, line, NPG.

GIBBONS, Christopher (1615-1676) organist.
P 'A.V.DYCK', hl with scroll, oval, Faculty of Music, Oxford.

GIBBONS, Grinling (1648-1720) wood-carver and statuary.
P SIR GODFREY KNELLER, c1690, tql with bust, Hermitage, Leningrad; copy, NPG 2925.
D SIR J.B.MEDINA, hs, red chalk, BM. After J.CLOSTERMAN, tql seated with wife, chalk, SNPG 358.
SC Self-portrait, wood medallion, Chartsworth, Derbys.
PR JOHN SMITH, after J.Closterman, tql with wife, mezz, BM, NPG.

GIBBONS, Orlando (1583-1625) musical composer.
P UNKNOWN, hs, oval, Faculty of Music, Oxford.
SC NICHOLAS STONE, relief medallion on monument, Canterbury Cathedral.

GIBBONS, William (1649-1728) physician.
P UNKNOWN, before 1729, tql, St John's College, Oxford.

GIBBS, James (1682-1754) architect.
P Attrib ANDREA SOLDI, c1746, tql seated, St Martin-in-the-Fields, London. UNKNOWN, 1749, tql, Oriel College, Oxford. J.M.WILLIAMS, 1752, hl with book, Bodleian Library, Oxford; version, NPG 504.
G GAWEN HAMILTON, 'A Conversation of Virtuosis . . . at the King's Armes', oil, 1735, NPG 1384.
SC J.M.RYSBRACK, 1726, marble bust, St Martin-in-the-Fields; version, Bodleian Library, J.M.RYSBRACK, marble bust as older man, Radcliffe Camera, Oxford.
PR B.BARON, 1736, profile head in medallion, line, bookplate, Bodleian Library, BM. B.BARON, after W.Hogarth, (type of c1747), hl, octagon, line, for *Description of the Radcliffe Library*, BM, NPG. P.PELHAM, after H.Hysing, tql as young man, mezz, BM, NPG.

GIBSON, Sir Alexander, see Lord Durie.

GIBSON, Edmund (1669-1748) bishop of London.
P JOHN VANDERBANK, c1735, tql seated, Queen's College, Oxford; version, Bodleian Library, Oxford. UNKNOWN, hl with book, Bodleian Library.

GIBSON, Edward (1668-1701) portrait painter.
D Self-portrait, c1690, hs, chalk, NPG 1880.

GIBSON, Richard (1615-1690) miniature painter.
P After SIR PETER LELY, (type of c1658), tql with bust, NPG 1975. SIR P.LELY, c1650-60, wl with wife, Kimbell Art Museum, Forth Worth, USA.
D Self-portrait, hs, chalks, BM.

GIFFARD, Bonaventure (1642-1734) Catholic bishop.
P JAMES RUSSELL, after unknown artist, hl in robes, Magdalen College, Oxford.
PR T.BURFORD, after H.Hysing, tql seated, mezz, BM, NPG.

GILBERT, Claudius (1670-1743) ecclesiastic, fellow of Trinity College, Dublin.
SC SIMON VIERPYL, marble bust, Trinity College, Dublin.

GILBERT, Sir Geoffrey (1674-1726) judge.
P MICHAEL DAHL, c1723, tql in robes, Lincoln's Inn, London, engr J.Faber, jun, 1725, mezz, BM, NPG.

GILBERT, Sir Humphrey (1539?-1583) navigator.
PR WILLEM and MAGDALENA VAN DE PASSE, hl with armillary sphere, oval, line, for Holland, *Herwologia*, 1620, BM, NPG.

GILBERT, John (1693-1761) archbishop of York.

P JAMES WILLS, 1740s, tql seated, Christ Church, Oxford; version, Bishopthorpe, York.

GILBERT, Samuel (d1692?) rector and floriculturist.
PR R.WHITE, hs, oval, line, for *Florist's Vademecum*, 1683, BM, NPG.

GILBERT, William (1540-1603) physician to Queen Elizabeth and James I and scientist.
PR R.CLAMP, after Harding, hl with globe, stipple, for Harding, *Biographical Mirrour*, NPG.

GILL, John (1697-1771) Baptist minister and author.
PR J.WRIGHT, after M.Chamberlin, tql seated, mezz, pub 1770, BM. G.VERTUE, after J.Highmore, jun, 1748, hl, oval, BM, NPG.

GILMOUR, Sir John (d1671) Scottish judge.
P Attrib L.SCHUNEMAN, tql in robes, Parliament Hall, Edinburgh.

GILPIN, Edward (1517-1583) archdeacon of Durham.
P UNKNOWN, hl, Queen's College, Oxford.

GINKEL, Frederick Christian, see 2nd Earl of Athlone.

GINKEL, Godert, see 1st Earl of Athlone.

GIPPS, Sir Richard (1659-1708) master of the revels to Charles II.
PR JOHN SMITH, after J.Closterman, hl, oval, mezz, BM, NPG.

GLANVILL, Joseph (1636-1680) divine.
PR W.FAITHORNE, hl, oval, line, for *Discourses*, 1681, BM, NPG.

GLANVILLE, Sir John, sen (1542-1600) judge.
P UNKNOWN, 1600, tql in robes, Lincoln's Inn, London.

GLANVILLE, Sir John, jun (1586-1661) serjeant, speaker of the House of Commons.
P UNKNOWN, 1643, hl in robes with mace, Lincoln's Inn, London; version, NPG 876.

GLAS, John (1695-1773) founder of Glasites, sect of independent presbyterians.
PR J.MCARDELL, after W.Millar, hl, oval, mezz, NPG.

GLENCAIRN, William Cunningham, 9th Earl of (1610?-1664) lord chancellor of Scotland.
P J.M.WRIGHT, hl in robes, SNPG 661.

GLISSON, Francis (1597-1677) physician.
P UNKNOWN, c1670, hs, Royal College of Physicians, London, engr W.Faithorne, hl, oval, line, for *Tractatus de Natura* etc, 1672, BM, NPG.

GLOUCESTER, Henry, Duke of (1640-1660) third son of Charles I.
P Attrib ADRIAEN HANNEMAN, c1653-54, tql in cuirass, National Gallery of Art, Washington, USA. JOHANN BOECKHORST, c1659, tql in armour, Groothuis, Bruges, Belgium; copy, NPG 1932. PIETER THYSSENS, c1660, tql in cuirass, Knole (NT), Kent. Studio of SIR PETER LELY, probably posthumous, wl in Garter robes, Euston Hall, Suffolk.
G SIR P.LELY, three children of Charles I, oil, 1647, Petworth (NT), W Sussex.
PR C.VAN DALEN, after S.Luttichuys, c1660, hl in armour, oval, line, BM, NPG. UNKNOWN, wl as infant, line, BM, NPG.

GLOUCESTER, Humphrey Plantagenet, Duke of, see HUMPHREY.

GLOUCESTER, William, Duke of (1689-1700) son of Queen Anne and Prince George of Denmark.
P SIR GODFREY KNELLER, c1691, wl seated with dog, Royal Coll, engr J.Smith, mezz, BM, NPG. After SIR G.KNELLER, (type of c1694), tql with mother, NPG 325. EDMUND LILLY, c1698, wl in Garter robes, Royal Coll. SIR G.KNELLER, 1699, hl in breastplate, oval, Royal Coll. WILLIAM CLARET, c1699, wl in

Garter robes, Royal Coll.
PR J.SMITH, after Sir G.Kneller, wl in Roman dress, aged 4, mezz, BM, NPG. J.SMITH, after T.Murray, wl in Garter robes with Benjamin Bathhurst, mezz, BM.

GLYNNE, Sir John (1603-1666) judge.
G UNKNOWN, family group, oil, Lincoln's Inn, London.
PR P.CALDWALL, tql seated in robes, line, NPG. UNKNOWN, hs, oval, NPG.

GOAD, John (1616-1689) headmaster of Merchant Taylors' School and astrologer.
PR R.WHITE, hl aged 62, oval, line for *Astro-meteorologica*, 1686, BM, NPG.

GODFREY or **GODFREY-HANCKWITZ, Ambrose, sen (d1741)** chemist.
PR G.VERTUE, after R.Schmutz, 1718, hs with chemical appliances, line, BM, NPG.

GODFREY, Ambrose, jun (d1756) chemist.
PR G.VAN DER GUCHT, hs, oval, line, BM.

GODFREY, Sir Edmund Berry (1621-1678) justice of the peace for Westminster.
P UNKNOWN, c1678, hs, oval, NPG L126.
D UNKNOWN, hs, oval, chalk, NPG 1101.
SC GEORGE BOWER, several medals, BM.
PR UNKNOWN, hl with four vignettes of his murder, line, for broadside *A Poem on the Effigies of Sir E.B.Godfrey*, 1678, BM.

GODOLPHIN, Francis Godolphin, 2nd Earl of (1678-1766) lord privy seal.
P SIR GODFREY KNELLER, c1710, hl, 'Kit-cat Club' portrait, NPG 3209. SIR G.KNELLER, c1710, wl, Blenheim Palace, Oxon, SIR G.KNELLER, 1714, hl, oval, Study Coll of Art, La Salle College, Philadelphia, USA. Perhaps after J.B.VAN LOO, c1740, hl, NPG 889.

GODOLPHIN, Mrs Margaret, née Blagge (1652-1678) friend of John Evelyn, married 1st Earl of Godolphin.
P UNKNOWN, tql seated, Berkeley Castle, Glos.

GODOLPHIN, Sidney (1610-1643) poet.
PR R.CLAMP, hl, stipple, for Harding, *Biographical Mirrour*, 1793, BM, NPG.

GODOLPHIN, Sidney Godolphin, 1st Earl of (1645-1712) statesman and financier.
P After SIR GODFREY KNELLER, (type of c1705), hl with staff, oval, NPG 1800; version, Althorp, Northants. SIR G.KNELLER, wl seated in Garter robes, Blenheim, Oxon. SIR G.KNELLER, tql in Garter robes, on loan to Marlborough House, London.
SC FRANCIS BIRD, bust, Westminster Abbey. J.M.RYSBRACK, marble bust, Althorp.

GODOLPHIN, Sir William (1634?-1696) ambassador.
P UNKNOWN, late 1650s, hl, oval, City Art Gallery, Manchester.

GOLDSALVE, Sir John (d1556) clerk of the signet to Henry VIII.
P HANS HOLBEIN, jun, 1528, hl with his father, Staatliche Gemäldegalerie, Dresden, E Germany. H.HOLBEIN, c1536, hl, John Johnson Coll, Fine Art Museum, Philadelphia, USA.
D H.HOLBEIN, hl, chalks, Royal Coll.

GODWIN, Francis (1562-1633) bishop of Llandaff and Hereford.
P UNKNOWN, 1613, tql in robes, Christ Church, Oxford; version, Balliol College, Oxford.
D UNKNOWN, after portrait of 1613, tql, w/c, NPG 4371.

GODWIN, Thomas (1517-1590) bishop of Bath and Wells.

P UNKNOWN, tql in robes, aged 72, Christ Church, Oxford. UNKNOWN, hl with book, Deanery, Canterbury.

GOLDSMITH, Francis (1613-1655) translator.
PR T.CROSS, hs, oval, line, for Grotius, *Sophomponeas*, 1652, BM.

GOOCH, Sir Thomas, 2nd Bart (1674-1754) bishop of Ely.
P THOMAS HUDSON, tql seated in robes, Lambeth Palace, London, engr J.McArdell, 1749, mezz, BM, NPG. UNKNOWN, before 1737, tql seated, Old Schools, Cambridge. UNKNOWN, Gonville and Caius College, Cambridge.
PR J.T.HEINS, tql when Bishop of Norwich, mezz, BM.

GOODALL, Charles (1642-1712) physician.
P Attrib THOMAS MURRAY, c1690–1700, tql, Royal College of Physicians, London.

GOODERE, Capt Samuel (1687-1741) murderer.
PR R.GRAVE, hl, line, for Caulfield, *Remarkable Persons*, 1819, BM, NPG.

GOODMAN, Gabriel (1529?-1601) dean of Westminster.
D G.P.HARDING, tql seated, w/c, NPG 2414.
SC UNKNOWN, wl relief figure on wall, Westminster Abbey, London. UNKNOWN, bust, Ruthin Church, Clwyd, Wales.

GOODRICH, Thomas (d1554) bishop of Ely and lord chancellor.
SC UNKNOWN, 1554, brass effigy, Ely Cathedral.

GOODRICKE, Sir Henry, Bart (1642-1705) politician.
PR JOHN SMITH, after T.Hill, hl in cuirass, oval, mezz, BM.

GOODWIN, Arthur (1593?-1643) parliamentary commander, friend of John Hampden.
P SIR ANTHONY VANDYCK, 1639, wl, Chatsworth, Derbys.

GOODWIN, John (1594?-1665) republican divine and controversialist.
PR G.GLOVER, hl with book, line, for *Treatise on Justification*, 1642, BM, NPG. UNKNOWN, hl with windmill over head, line, for John Vicar, *Coleman St Conclave visited*, 1648, BM, NPG.

GOODWIN, Thomas (1600-1680) independent divine.
P UNKNOWN, Christ's College, Cambridge.
PR R.WHITE, hs, oval, line, for *Works*, 1681, BM, NPG.

GOODWIN, William (1555?-1620) dean of Christ Church, Oxford.
SC UNKNOWN, bust, Christ Church, Oxford.

GORDON, George (d1649), see 2nd Marquess of Huntly.

GORDON, George (1637-1720), see 1st Earl of Aberdeen.

GORDON, George Gordon, 4th Marquess of Huntly and 1st Duke of (1643-1716) privy councillor and captain of Edinburgh Castle.
PR J.SAUVÉ, hl in armour, when Marquess of Huntly, oval, line, BM.

GORDON, John (1544-1619) dean of Salisbury.
PR UNKNOWN, impression of mural brass formerly in Salisbury cathedral, line, BM.

GORDON, John (1660?-1733), see 16th Earl of Sutherland.

GORDON, Robert (1580-1656) courtier of James I and II, and Charles I, historian of the house of Sutherland.
P UNKNOWN, 1621, hl, SNPG 1513.

GORDON of Gordonstoun, Sir Robert (1647-1704) man of science.
P UNKNOWN, 1692, hl, oval, SNPG 1512.

GORDON of Straloch, Robert (1580-1661) geographer.
P GEORGE JAMESONE, c1625, hl, Robert Gordon College, Aberdeen.

D 11th EARL OF BUCHAN, after G.Jamesone, pencil, SNPG 1632 and 1633.

GORDON, Robert (1665-1732) founder of Gordon's College, Aberdeen.
SC JOHN CHEERE, 1753, statue, Robert Gordon College, Aberdeen.

GORDON, William, see 6th Viscount Kenmure.

GORGES, Sir Arthur (d 1625) poet.
SC UNKNOWN, 1625, brass effigy, All Saints' Church, More Chapel, Chelsea, London.

GORING, George Goring, Baron (1608-1657) royalist.
P Studio of SIR ANTHONY VANDYCK, c1638, hl in armour, Clarendon Coll on loan to Art Gallery, Plymouth. SIR A.VANDYCK, c1635-40, hl with 1st Earl of Newport, Petworth (NT), W Sussex; versions, NPG 762 and Knole (NT), Kent.

GOSTLIN, John (1566?-1626) benefactor of Caius and St Catharine's Colleges, Cambridge.
P UNKNOWN, 1621, bust, Gonville and Caius College, Cambridge. UNKNOWN, hl with book, St Catharine's College, Cambridge.

GOSTLING, William (1696-1777) antiquary.
PR R.GODFREY, after C.Metz, hl, oval, for *Walk in Canterbury*, 1777, line, BM, NPG. C.METZ, hs, etch, BM, NPG.

GOUGE, Thomas (1609-1681) nonconformist divine and philanthropist.
PR R.WHITE, after J.Riley, hs, oval, line, for *Funeral Sermon*, 1682, BM, NPG. M.VAN DER GUCHT, hs, oval, line, NPG.

GOUGE, William (1578-1653) rector of St Anne's, Blackfriars.
PR W.FAITHORNE, hl, oval, line, for W.Jenkyn, *Funeral Sermon*, 1654, BM, NPG. J.DUNSTALL, hl, oval, line, for *Commentary on the Epistle to the Hebrews*, 1655, BM, NPG.

GOUPY, Joseph (d 1763) water-colour painter and etcher.
G GAWEN HAMILTON, 'A Conversation of Virtuosis . . . at the King's Arms', oil, 1735, NPG 1384.
PR R.BEAN, hl with painting, line, NPG.

GOUPY, Lewis (d 1747) miniature painter of French extraction.
PR J.THOMSON, after L.Goupy, hs, stipple, for Walpole, *Anecdotes*, ed 1827, BM, NPG. G.WHITE, after L.Goupy, hs, oval, mezz, BM, NPG.

GOUTER, James, see Gaultier.

GOWER, George (fl 1575-1585) sergeant painter to Queen Elizabeth.
PR J.BASIRE, after G.Gower, hl with palette, line, for Gough, *Hist of Castor*, 1800, BM, NPG.

GOWER, Humphrey (1638-1711) master of St John's College, Cambridge.
P UNKNOWN, tql seated, St John's College, Cambridge.
PR G.VERTUE, after J.Fellowes, 1719, hl in robes, oval, line, BM, NPG.

GOWER, John (1325?-1408?) poet.
SC UNKNOWN, tomb effigy, Southwark Cathedral, London.

GOWER, John Leveson-Gower, 1st Earl of (d 1754) lord privy seal.
PR J.FABER, jun, after 'J.B.Vanloo', tql in robes, mezz, BM, NPG.

GRABE, John Ernest (1666-1711) divine.
SC FRANCIS BIRD, 1711, statue on monument, Westminster Abbey, London.

GRACE, Richard (1620?-1691) Irish colonel, royalist.

PR UNKNOWN, hl in armour, line, facsimile of 1652 print, for Grace, *Memoirs of the Family of Grace*, 1823, BM, NPG.

GRAFTON, Henry Fitzroy, 1st Duke of (1663-1690) second son of Charles II by Barbara Villiers, Duchess of Cleveland.
P Attrib SIR GODFREY KNELLER, tql in Garter robes, Euston Hall, Suffolk. Attrib T.HAWKER, wl in Garter robes, Euston Hall. WILLIAM WISSING, hl as boy in armour, oval, Buccleuch Estates, Selkirk, Scotland. W.WISSING, tql in classical dress, Raby Castle, Durham. UNKNOWN, tql in armour as youth, Ickworth (NT), Suffolk.
PR JOHN SMITH, after Sir G.Kneller, wl as boy, when Lord Euston, mezz, NPG.

GRAFTON, Richard (d 1572?) printer and chronicler.
PR UNKNOWN, hs, oval, woodcut, for Ames, *Typographical Antiquities*, 1749, BM, NPG.

GRAHAM, George (1673-1751) maker of clocks and astronomical instruments.
P THOMAS HUDSON, tql seated, Science Museum, London, engr J.Faber, jun, mezz, BM.

GRAHAM, James (1612-1650), see 1st Marquess of Montrose.

GRAHAM, James (1676-1746) dean of the Faculty of Advocates.
M SIR GEORGE CHALMERS, hs, pencil, V & A.
PR G.CHALMERS, 1739, hl in robes, line, BM.

GRAHAM, John, see 1st Viscount Dundee.

GRAHAM, Richard, see Viscount Preston.

GRAMMONT, Elizabeth, née Hamilton, Countess of (1641-1708) courtier.
P SIR PETER LELY, c1663, tql, one of 'Beauties of Hampton Court', Royal Coll. SIR P.LELY, tql seated, Althorp, Northants. J.G.ECCARDT, after Sir P.Lely, hl, NPG 20.

GRANDISON, Oliver St John, 1st Viscount (1559-1630) lord-deputy of Ireland.
P CORNELIUS JOHNSON, c1622, hl in armour, Lydiard Mansion, Borough of Thamesdown, Wilts.

GRANGE, James Erskine, Lord (1679-1754) judge.
P Attrib WILLIAM AIKMAN, wl in robes, SNPG L236.

GRANT, Sir Francis, see Lord Cullen.

GRANT, Patrick, see Lord Elchies.

GRANTHAM, Thomas Robinson, 1st Baron (1695-1770) diplomat.
D UNKNOWN, early 1740s, hs, chalks, NPG 1586.
PR E.HARDING, hl, stipple, pub 1802, BM, NPG.

GRANVILLE, Sir Bevil, see Grenville.

GRANVILLE, George, see Baron Lansdowne.

GRANVILLE, John (1628-1701), see 7th Earl of Bath.

GRANVILLE, John Carteret, 2nd Earl of (1690-1763) politician.
P Attrib THOMAS HUDSON, 1740s, tql seated in peer's robes, Althorp, Northants. Studio of WILLIAM HOARE, c1750-52, tql with Garter star, NPG 1778. D.VAN DER SMISSEN, 1757, hl in Garter robes, Longleat, Wilts.
M Attrib C.BOIT, Althorp. Attrib C.F.ZINCKE, hs, enamel, Althorp.
SC J.A.DASSIER, copper medal, BM. ISAAC GOSSET, wax medallion, Ham House (NT), London.
PR P.PELHAM, after Sir G.Kneller, c1721-23, hl in robes, when Lord Carteret, mezz, BM.

GRAVELOT or **BOURGUIGNON, Hubert François (1699-1773)** draughtsman and book illustrator.
PR C.E.GAUCHER, after M.de la Tour, hs oval, line, for *Almanachs Iconologiques*, BM. G.MASSARD, after M.de la Tour, hs, oval, line, BM, NPG.

GRAVES, Richard (1677-1729?) antiquary.
PR G.VERTUE, tql, line, BM, NPG.

GRAYDON, John (1660?-1726) vice-admiral.
P SIR GODFREY KNELLER, *c*1703, tql with baton, NMM, Greenwich.

GREATRAKES, Valentine (1629-1683) faith-healer.
PR W.FAITHORNE, tql with boy, line, for *Account*, 1666, BM, NPG.

GREAVES, John (1602-1652) professor of astronomy at Oxford and traveller.
PR E.MASCALL, hs, etch, modern impression, BM, NPG.

GREEN, Thomas (1658-1738) bishop of Norwich and Ely.
P UNKNOWN, tql seated, St Martin-in-the-Fields, London. UNKNOWN, hl, Corpus Christi College, Cambridge.

GREENE, Maurice (1696?-1755) musical composer.
P FRANCIS HAYMAN, 1747, wl seated with Rev John Hoadly, NPG 2106.

GREENHALGH, John (*d*1651) royalist, governor of the Isle of Man,
P UNKNOWN, hl in armour, oval, Bury Library and Museum, Lancs, engr G.E.Madeley, lith, BM, NPG.

GREENHILL, Henry (1646-1708) commissioner of the navy.
PR J.GREENHILL, hl with armillary sphere, etch, BM, NPG.

GREENHILL, John (1644?-1676) portrait-painter.
P Self-portrait, tql with sketch, Dulwich College Gallery, London.
D Self-portrait, hs, chalk, BM. SIR PETER LELY, hs, profile, pastel, BM.

GREGORY, David (1661-1708) astronomer.
SC WILLIAM TOWNESEND, 1708, bust, St Mary's Church, Oxford.

GREGORY, Edmund (fl 1646) author.
PR W.MARSHALL, hl, oval, line, for *Anatomy of Christian Melancholy*, 1646, BM, NPG.

GREGORY, James (1638-1675) mathematician and philosopher.
D 11th EARL OF BUCHAN, after John Scougall, hl, pencil and chalk, SNPG 1637. 11th EARL OF BUCHAN, chalk, SNPG 1640.
PR W.HOLL, hl with globe, stipple, for Chambers, *Dictionary of Eminent Scotsmen*, BM, NPG.

GREGORY, William (*d*1663) composer.
P UNKNOWN, hl, Faculty of Music, Oxford.

GREGORY, Sir William (1624-1696) speaker of House of Commons.
P UNKNOWN, hl in robes, oval, Palace of Westminster, London.

GREENWICH, John Campbell, Duke of (1680-1743), see 2nd Duke of Argyll.

GRENVILLE, Sir Bevil (1596-1643) royalist.
P School of SIR ANTHONY VANDYCK, tql in armour, Petworth (NT), W Sussex.
PR R.COOPER, hl in armour, line and stipple, NPG. W.FAITHORNE, hl in armour, oval, line, for *Verses by the University of Oxford on his death*, 1684, BM, NPG. G.VERTUE, hs, oval, line, with Lord Hopton in set of *Loyalists*, BM.

GRENVILLE, Denis (1637-1703) Jacobite divine, dean of Durham.
PR G.F.EDELINCK, after Beaupoille, hl oval, line, for *Resigned and resolved Christian*, etc, 1689, BM, NPG.

GRENVILLE, John, see Earl of Bath.

GRENVILLE, Sir Richard (1541?-1591) naval commander.
PR WILLEM and MAGDALENA VAN DE PASSE, hs, oval, line, for Holland, *Herwologia*, 1620, BM, NPG.

GRESHAM, Sir Thomas (1519?-1579) founder of the Royal Exchange.
P UNKNOWN, 1544, wl, Mercers' Hall, London. UNKNOWN, *c*1565, tql, NPG 352; version, Mercers' Hall, engr F.Delaram, hl, oval, line, BM, NPG.

GREVILLE, Robert, see 2nd Baron Brooke.

GREW, Nehemiah (1641-1712) physician and botanist.
PR R.WHITE, hs, oval, line, for *Cosmologia Sacra*, 1701, BM, NPG.

GREY de Wilton, Arthur Grey, 14th Baron (1536-1593) lord-deputy of Ireland.
G M.GHEERAERTS, sen, 'Procession of Garter Knights, 1576', etch, BM.

GREY, Elizabeth, see Countess of Kent.

GREY, Forde, see 1st Earl of Tankerville.

GREY, Henry (1594-1651), see 10th Earl of Kent.

GREY, Henry (1599?-1673), see 1st Earl of Stamford.

GREY, Henry (1671-1740), see 1st Duke of Kent.

GREY, Lady Jane, see Dudley.

GREY, Zachary (1688-1766) antiquary.
PR C.KNIGHT, hl, stipple, for harding, *Biographical Mirrour*, 1791, BM, NPG. P.AUDINET, hs, line, for Nichols, *Literary Illustrations*, 1822, BM, NPG.

GRIFFIER, John or **Jan (1656-1718)** painter and etcher.
PR A.BANNERMAN, hl with Gerard Zoust, line, NPG.

GRIFFIN, Benjamin (1680-1740) actor.
P PETER VAN BLEECK, *c*1738, wl with B.Johnson, as Tribulation and Ananias in Jonson's *The Alchemist*, Garrick Club, London, engr van Bleeck, 1748, mezz, BM, NPG.

GRIFFITH, George (1601-1666) bishop of St Asaph.
P UNKNOWN, hl, Christ Church, Oxford, engr E.Harding, 1800, stipple, BM, NPG.

GRIMSTON, Sir Edward (1528?-1599) comptroller of Calais.
P Attrib ROBERT PEAKE, sen, 1590, hl with skull, Gorhambury, Herts. UNKNOWN, 1561, tql as young man, Gorhambury.

GRIMSTON, Sir Harbottle, 2nd Bart (1603-1685) judge, Master of the Rolls.
P UNKNOWN, *c*1650, tql, Gorhambury, Herts. UNKNOWN, *c*1660-70, tql in robes, NPG 381; version, Palace of Westminster, London.

GRIMSTON, Sir Samuel, 3rd Bart (1643-1700) politician.
P Attrib SIR GODFREY KNELLER, tql, 2 types, Gorhambury, Herts.

GRIMSTON, William Luckyn Grimston, 1st Viscount (1683-1756) MP for St Albans.
P MICHAEL DAHL, tql in robes, Gorhambury, Herts, UNKNOWN, tql as young man, Gorhambury.

GRINDAL, Edmund (1519?-1583) archbishop of Canterbury.
P UNKNOWN, *c*1580, tql seated, Lambeth Palace, London; versions, Old Schools, Cambridge; the Deanery, Canterbury.
PR PASSE, hl, line, for Holland, *Herwologia*, 1620, BM, NPG.

GRINDAL, William (*d*1548) hellenist and tutor to Queen Elizabeth I.

PR UNKNOWN, hs, oval, line, for Fuller, *Abel Redevivus*, 1650, BM, NPG.

GROSVENOR, Benjamin (1676-1758) dissenting divine.
P UNKNOWN, tql seated, Dr Williams's Library, London, engr Hopwood, hl, stipple, pub 1808, NPG.

GROSVENOR, Sir Thomas, 3rd Bart (1656-1700) politician.
PR J.YOUNG, after Sir P.Lely, tql, etch, for Young, *Grosvenor Gallery*, 1821, BM.

GROVE, Henry (1684-1738) dissenting tutor.
P By or after JOHN WOLLASTON, hl, oval, Dr Williams's Library, London, engr G.Vertue, 1740, line, for *Sermons and Tracts*, 1741, BM, NPG.

GROVE, Robert (1634-1696) bishop of Chichester.
P UNKNOWN, hl, St John's College, Cambridge.

GUEST, Joshua (1660-1747) lieutenant-general.
SC SIR ROBERT TAYLOR, 1752, bust on monument, Westminster Abbey, London.

GUILDFORD, Sir Henry (1489-1532) master of the horse and comptroller of the household to Henry VIII.
P HANS HOLBEIN, jun, 1527, hl with Garter George, Royal Coll.
D H.HOLBEIN, hs, chalks, Royal Coll.

GUILFORD, Francis North, 1st Baron (1637-1685) lord chancellor.
P Attrib JOHN RILEY, tql seated in robes, NPG 4708.
PR D.LOGGAN, hs in robes, *ad vivum*, oval, line, BM, NPG 632.

GUISE, John (d 1765) general and collector.

P SIR JOSHUA REYNOLDS, hl, Christ Church, Oxford.
SC JOHN BACON, sen, before 1770, marble bust, Christ Church.

GUNNING, Peter (1614-1684) bishop of Ely.
P UNKNOWN, tql seated, St John's College, Cambridge; version Old Schools, Cambridge.
PR D.LOGGAN, hl, oval, line, BM, NPG.

GUTHRIE, James (1612?-1661) Scottish presbyterian divine executed for treason.
PR S.FREEMAN, tql seated, stipple, for Chambers, *Dict of Eminent Scotsmen*, BM, NPG.

GUY, Thomas (1644?-1724) philanthropist and founder of Guy's Hospital.
P JOHN VANDERBANK, 1706, hl, Guy's Hospital, London.
SC DAVID LE MARCHAND, relief bust on ivory tablet, V & A. PETER SCHEEMAKERS, c1734, bronze statue, Guy's Hospital.

GUYSE, John (1680-1761) dissenting minister.
P UNKNOWN, c1630-40, hl, New College, London.
PR J.FABER, jun, after R.van Bleeck, 1734, hl, mezz, BM, NPG.

GWYN, Eleanor or **Nell (1650-1687)** actress and mistress of Charles II.
P Studio of SIR PETER LELY, c1675, tql with lamb, NPG 3976, engr G.Valck, line, BM, NPG.
PR G.VALCK, after S.Cooper, c1670, hl, oval, line, BM. H.GASCAR, c1672-73, wl with two sons as cupids, line, BM, NPG. R.TOMPSON, after Sir P.Lely, c1673-75, tql with two sons, mezz, BM. R.TOMPSON, tql as cupid, mezz, BM.

GYLES, Henry (1640?-1709) glass painter of York.
D Self-portrait, hs, chalk and w/c, BM.
PR F.PLACE, hs, oval, mezz, BM.

H

HAAK, Theodore (1605-1690) translator.
P UNKNOWN, hl, Bodleian Library, Oxford; version, Royal Society, London.

HACKER, Francis (d 1660) regicide.
G UNKNOWN, 'The Regicides Executed in 1660', line engr, for *Rebels no Saints*, 1660, BM.

HACKETT, John (1592-1670) bishop of Lichfield and Coventry.
P Attrib VALENTINE RITZ, before 1679, wl, Trinity College, Cambridge. UNKNOWN, Trinity College.
PR W.FAITHORNE, hs, oval, line, for *Sermons*, 1675, BM, NPG.

HADDINGTON, Thomas Hamilton, 1st Earl of (1563-1637) advocate and statesman.
P After ADAM DE COLONE, tql, SNPG 818. UNKNOWN, hs, Mellerstain, Borders region, Scotland.

HADDINGTON, Thomas Hamilton, 2nd Earl of (1600-1640) covenanter.
P After SIR ANTHONY VANDYCK, hs, Lennoxlove, Lothian region, Scotland.

HADDINGTON, Thomas Hamilton, 6th Earl of (1680-1735) supporter of the Union.
P SIR J.B.MEDINA, SNPG 1610.
PR J.SMITH, after G.Aikman, hl, oval, mezz, BM. UNKNOWN, hs, oval, stipple, pub 1800, NPG.

HADDOCK, Nicholas (1686-1746) admiral.
P UNKNOWN, c1715, tql, NMM, Greenwich. UNKNOWN, c1742-43, tql, NMM.
SC UNKNOWN, copper medal, BM.
PR J.FABER, jun, after T.Gibson, tql with cannon, mezz, BM, NPG.

HADDOCK, Sir Richard (1629-1715) admiral and comptroller of the navy.
P JOHN CLOSTERMAN, hs, oval, Ministry of Defence (DoE), London, engr W.Faithorne, hl, oval, mezz, BM.

HADOW, James (1670?-1747) principal of St Andrew's University.
P UNKNOWN, hl with book, oval, University of St Andrews.

HAKEWILL, George (1578-1649) divine.
P UNKNOWN, c1649, hs, oval, Exeter College Chapel, Oxford. UNKNOWN, hl, Exeter College. UNKNOWN, hl with book, Exeter College.

HALE, Sir Matthew (1609-1676) chief justice of England.
P J.M.WRIGHT, c1670, wl in robes, Guildhall, London. After J.M.WRIGHT, c1670, hs, oval, NPG 465.
PR F.H.VAN HOVE, tql seated, line, for *Origination of Mankind*, 1677, BM, NPG.

HALE, Richard (1670-1728) physician.
P JONATHAN RICHARDSON, c1729-1733, tql seated, Royal College of Physicians, London; version, Bodleian Library, Oxford. J.RICHARDSON, c1729-1733, hl, Royal College of Physicians.

HALES, Sir Edward, 2nd Bart, titular Earl of Tenderden (d 1695) royalist.
G SIR PETER LELY, tql seated with family, oil, c1656, Guildhall, London.

HALES, John (d 1572?) founder of the free school, Coventry.
PR MRS D.TURNER, hs, vignette, etch, BM.

HALES, John (1584-1656) canon of Windsor.
PR UNKNOWN, hl, oval, line, for *Tracts*, 1716, BM, NPG.

HALES, John (d 1679), see Hayls.

HALES, Stephen (1677-1761) physiologist and inventor.
P Studio of THOMAS HUDSON, c1759, hl, oval, NPG 1861.
G WILLIAM VERELST, 'The Georgia Council', oil, c1735-36, Henry Francis du Pont Winterthur Museum, Winterthur, Delaware, USA.
SC JOSEPH WILTON, 1762, relief bust on monument, Westminster Abbey, London.

HALIFAX, Charles Montagu, 1st Earl of (1661-1715) financier.
P SIR GODFREY KNELLER, c1690-95, tql, NPG 800. SIR G.KNELLER, 1699, wl in lord chancellor's robes, Trinity College, Cambridge. SIR G.KNELLER, c1703-10, hl, the 'Kit-cat Club' portrait, NPG 3211. SIR G.KNELLER, (type of c1703-10), tql with Garter ribbon and star, Knole (NT), Kent. Attrib MICHAEL DAHL, (type of c1710), tql with Garter ribbon and star, Bank of England, London.

HALIFAX, Sir George Savile, 1st Marquess of (1633-1695) statesman and writer.
P UNKNOWN, 1660s, tql, Chatsworth, Derbys. Attrib MARY BEALE, c1674-76, tql seated, NPG 2962.
SC UNKNOWN, relief portrait medallion, Westminster Abbey, London.

HALIFAX, William Savile, 2nd Marquess of (1665-1700) statesman.
P By or after SIR GODFREY KNELLER, tql, Chatsworth, Derbys.

HALL, Anthony (1679-1723) antiquary.
PR G.VERTUE, hl, oval, line, BM.

HALL, George (1613-1668) bishop of Chester.
P UNKNOWN, hl, Exeter College, Oxford.

HALL, Jacob (fl 1668) rope-dancer.
P UNKNOWN, hl, Trinity College, Oxford.
PR P.DE BRUNE, after J.van Oost, tql, etch, BM.

HALL, John (1529?-1566?) surgeon and poet.
PR UNKNOWN, hl with flower, woodcut, for *Anatomie*, 1565, BM, NPG.

HALL, John (1627-1656) poet of Durham.
PR W.MARSHALL, hl, oval, line, for *Poems*, 1646, NPG.

HALL, John (1633-1710) bishop of Bristol.
P UNKNOWN, hl, oval, Pembroke College, Oxford.
M THOMAS FORSTER, 1699, hl, oval, Museum and Art Gallery, Bristol.
PR T.TROTTER, hl, line, pub 1796, BM, NPG.

HALL, Joseph (1574-1656) bishop of Exeter and Norwich.
P UNKNOWN, hl with book, oval, Emmanuel College, Cambridge.
PR W.FAITHORNE, hl with medal, oval, line, for J.Whitefoote,

Funeral Sermon, BM, NPG. W.MARSHALL, hl writing in book, line, for *Cases of Conscience*, 1650, BM, NPG. P.D.ZETTER, hl with medal, oval, line, for Boissard, *Bibliotheca Chalcographica*, 1650, BM, NPG.

HALLEY, Edmund (1656-1742) astronomer.
P Attrib THOMAS MURRAY, before 1712, hl with sketch, oval, Royal Society, London. T.MURRAY, *c*1712, tql with globe, Bodleian Library, Oxford. RICHARD PHILLIPS, *c*1721, hl, oval, NPG 4393. Attrib MICHAEL DAHL, *c*1736, tql seated with drawing, Royal Society.
SC J.A.DASSIER, copper medal, BM.
PR G.WHITE, after Sir G.Kneller, *c*1721–23, hl, oval, mezz, BM, NPG.

HALTON, Timothy (1632?-1704) provost of Queen's College, Oxford.
P JAMES MAUBERT, tql seated, Queen's College.
PR M.BURGHERS, hl, oval, line, BM, NPG.

HAMEY, Baldwin, sen (1568-1640) physician.
P UNKNOWN, 1633, hs, Royal College of Physicians, London.

HAMEY, Baldwin, jun (1600-1676) physician.
P MATTHEW? SNELLING, 1674, tql seated with busts of Hippocrates and Aristophanes, Royal College of Physicians, London. UNKNOWN, 1638, hs, oval, Bodleian Library, Oxford.
SC EDWARD PIERCE, *c*1674–75, marble bust, Royal College of Physicians.

HAMILTON, Anne Hamilton, 3rd Duchess of (1636?-1716) married William Douglas, who became on her petition 3rd Duke of Hamilton.
P SIR GODFREY KNELLER, 1679, tql seated, Lennoxlove, Lothian region, Scotland. DAVID SCOUGAL, tql seated, Brodick Castle (NT of Scotland), Isle of Arran.

HAMILTON, Anthony (1646?-1720) author and soldier.
P A.S.BELLE, hl in cuirass, Lennoxlove, Lothian region, Scotland. UNKNOWN, hs in armour, oval, NPG 1467.
PR E.FESSARD, hl in cuirass, oval, line, BM, NPG. W.N.GARDINER, hs in armour, stipple, *Memoirs of Count de Grammont*, 1794, BM, NPG.

HAMILTON, Charles, see Lord Binning.

HAMILTON, Claud, see Baron Paisley.

HAMILTON, Elizabeth, see Countess of Grammont.

HAMILTON, Sir George, 1st Bart (*d*1676) soldier.
P UNKNOWN, hl in armour, oval, NPG 1468.
PR W.N.GARDINER, hl in armour, oval, stipple, for *Memoirs of Count de Grammont*, 1793, NPG.

HAMILTON, George (1666-1737), see 1st Earl of Orkney.

HAMILTON, James (*d*1575), see 2nd Earl of Arran.

HAMILTON, James (1530-1609), see 3rd Earl of Arran.

HAMILTON, James Hamilton, 4th Earl of Arran and 2nd Marquess of (1589-1625) statesman.
P DANIEL MYTENS, 1622, wl, Royal Coll; version, Lennoxlove, Lothian region, Scotland.
PR M.DROESHOUT, 1623, wl, line, BM, V & A. R.VAUGHAN, hl, oval, line, BM, NPG.

HAMILTON, James Hamilton, 3rd Marquess and 1st Duke of (1606-1649) royalist.
P DANIEL MYTENS, 1629, wl, Lennoxlove, Lothian region, Scotland. Attrib SIR ANTHONY VANDYCK, *c*1635, tql, Lennoxlove. SIR A.VANDYCK, before 1649, wl in armour, Lennoxlove.

HAMILTON, James (1656-1734), see 6th Earl of Abercorn.

HAMILTON, James Douglas, 4th Duke of (1658-1712) statesman.
P SIR GODFREY KNELLER, wl in armour, SNPG L12. After SIR G.KNELLER, hs, oval, SNPG 840. After SIR J.B.MEDINA, 1703, tql in armour, Royal College of Surgeons, Edinburgh. Attrib WILLIAM WISSING, tql in armour, Hardwick Hall (NT), Derbys.
M DAVID PATON, 1693, hl, oval, Lennoxlove, Lothian region, Scotland.

HAMILTON, John (*d*1658), see 1st Baron Bargeny.

HAMILTON, John (1656-1708), see 2nd Baron Belhaven.

HAMILTON, Margaret or Mary, Hamilton, née Fielding, 1st Duchess of (1613?-1638) lady of bedchamber to Henrietta Maria.
P DANIEL MYTENS, 1622, hl aged 9, oval, Lennoxlove, Lothian region, Scotland. Studio of SIR ANTHONY VANDYCK, wl, Lennoxlove.

HAMILTON, Thomas (1563-1637), see 1st Earl of Haddington.

HAMILTON, Thomas (1600-1640), see 2nd Earl of Haddington.

HAMILTON, Thomas (1680-1735), see 6th Earl of Haddington.

HAMILTON, William Hamilton, 2nd Duke of (1616-1651) diplomat.
P CORNELIUS JOHNSON, 1649, hl with Earl of Lauderdale, Lennoxlove, Lothian region, Scotland; replica, Ham House (NT), London. After C.JOHNSON, hl, SNPG 859. ADRIAEN HANNEMAN, 1650, tql with Garter star, Royal Coll; copy, NPG 2120.

HAMILTON, William Douglas, 3rd Duke of (1635-1694) statesman.
P SIR GODFREY KNELLER, wl in Garter robes, Lennoxlove, Lothian region, Scotland. SIR G.KNELLER, 1682, tql in armour, Duke of Hamilton, on loan to Holyrood house, Edinburgh.
M DAVID PATON, after S.Cooper, 1693, hs, oval, Lennoxlove.

HAMMOND, Henry (1605-1660) chaplain to Charles I.
P UNKNOWN, tql, Magdalen College, Oxford.

HAMMOND, Robert (1621-1654) parliamentarian.
D G.P.HARDING, after C.Johnson, hl with cuirass, wash, Sutherland Coll, Ashmolean Museum, Oxford.

HAMPDEN, John (1594-1643) statesman.
PR J.HOUBRAKEN, 1740, hs in armour, oval, line, for Birch, *Heads*, BM, NPG (called Hampden but his iconography is obscure and no certain *ad vivum* portrait is yet established).

HAMPDEN, John (1656-1696) politician.
P UNKNOWN, (called Hampden), *c*1690, hs, oval, NPG 3057.

HANBURY, John (1664-1734) politician.
P Attrib JONATHAN RICHARDSON, hl, National Museum of Wales, Cardiff.

HANDEL, George Frederick (1685-1759) musical composer.
P Attrib BALTHASAR DENNER, 1726–28, hs, NPG 1976. UNKNOWN, *c*1739–42, hl, oval, NPG 2151; version, Royal Society of Musicians, London. FRANCIS KYTE, 1742, hs, oval, NPG 2152. THOMAS HUDSON, 1747 or 49, tql seated, Staats und Universitäts-Bibliotek, Hamburg, W Germany; copy, Bodleian Library, Oxford, engr J.Faber, jun, 1748, mezz, BM. T.HUDSON, 1756, wl seated, the 'Gopsall' portrait, NPG 3970.
D JOSEPH GOUPY, *c*1742, pastel, Fitzwilliam Museum, Cambridge.
M G.A.WOLFGANG, *c*1737, tql with book, Royal Coll.
SC L.F.ROUBILIAC, 1738, statue as Apollo, V & A. L.F.ROUBILIAC,

1739, marble bust, Royal Coll. L.F.ROUBILIAC, 1761, monument, Westminster Abbey, London; model, Ashmolean Museum, Oxford. Attrib L.F.ROUBILIAC, terracotta roundel, V & A. Attrib L.F.ROUBILIAC, plaster roundel, profile bust, Sir John Soane's Museum, London. UNKNOWN, terracotta bust, NPG 878.

HANMER, Sir Thomas, 4th Bart (1677-1746) speaker of the House of Commons and editor of Shakespeare.
P Studio of SIR GODFREY KNELLER, hs, oval, Palace of Westminster, London. SIR G.KNELLER, hl in robes, Euston hall, Suffolk.
PR W.BOND, after Sir G.Kneller, hl in speaker's robes, oval, stipple, for Yorke, *Royal Tribes of Wales*, 1798, BM, NPG.

HANNAY, Patrick (d 1629?) poet.
PR T.BERRY, hs, line, small oval in facsimile title for *The Nightingale*, 1622, BM, NPG.

HANNEMAN, Adriaen (1601?-1671) portrait painter.
P Self-portrait, hl, 1647, Koninklijke Academie, 's-Gravenhage, Holland. Self-portrait, hl seated, 1656, Rijksmuseum, Amsterdam, engr A.Bannerman, line, for Walpole, *Anecdotes*, 1762, BM, NPG.
PR R.VAN VOERST, after Sir A.Vandyck, hl, line, BM, NPG.

HANOVER, Sophia, Electress of, see SOPHIA.

HARBIN, George (fl 1713) nonjuror.
P MICHAEL DAHL, hl, Longleat, Wilts.

HARCOURT, Sir Simon (1603?-1642) soldier of fortune.
PR UNKNOWN, hl in armour, line, NPG.

HARCOURT, Simon Harcourt, 1st Viscount (1661?-1727) lord chancellor.
P SIR GODFREY KNELLER, tql in robes, Pembroke College, Oxford.
PR J.SIMON, after Sir G.Kneller, hl in robes, oval, mezz, BM, NPG. UNKNOWN, hs, oval, mezz, NPG.

HARCOURT, Thomas (1618-1679) Jesuit.
PR MARTIN BOUCHE, hs with knife in breast, oval, line, NPG.

HARDINGE, Nicholas (1699-1758) clerk of the House of Commons.
PR H.MEYER, after A.Ramsay, hl seated, stipple, BM, NPG.

HARDWICK, Bess of, see Countess of Shrewsbury.

HARDWICKE, Philip Yorke, 1st Earl of (1690-1764) lord chancellor.
P 'ARNOLD VAN STRAECHEN', c1733-37, wl in robes of chief justice, Middle Temple, London. JAMES WILLS, 1740, tql in lord chancellor's robes, Middle Temple. Studio of MICHAEL DAHL, c1735-43, tql seated in robes, NPG 872. After ALLAN RAMSAY, c1742, tql in robes, Lincoln's Inn, London. WILLIAM HOARE, 1763, tql seated in robes, Antony House (NT), Cornwall.
PR J.FABER, jun, 1737, hl in robes, *ad vivum*, oval, line, BM, NPG. J.FABER, jun, after T.Hudson, tql seated, mezz, BM, NPG.

HARDY, Sir Thomas (1666-1732) admiral.
SC SIR HENRY CHEERE, statue on monument, Westminster Abbey, London.
PR J.FABER, jun, after M.Dahl, 1722, tql with telescope, mezz, BM, NPG.

HARE, Henry (1636-1708), see 2nd Baron Coleraine.

HARE, Henry (1693-1749), see 3rd Baron Coleraine.

HARE, Hugh (1668-1707) translator, son of 2nd Baron Coleraine.
P SIR GODFREY KNELLER, 1685, wl, on loan to DoE, Lancaster House, London.

HARINGTON, John (fl 1550) servant of Henry VIII and friend of Princess Elizabeth.
PR C.WARREN, hs, line, 'drawn by J.Thurston', for *Effigies Poeticae*, pub 1822, BM.

HARINGTON, Sir John (1561-1612) wit and author, translator of *Orlando Furioso*.
P Attrib HIERONIMO CUSTODIS, c1590-95, tql, on loan to Ampleforth College, York. Attrib H.CUSTODIS, hs, NPG 3121.
PR T.COCKSON, hl with chronometer, oval, line, cut from title for trans of Ariosto, *Orlando Furioso*, 1591, BM, NPG.

HARINGTON of Exton, John Harington, 1st Baron (1541-1613) guardian of Princess Elizabeth.
P UNKNOWN, head, Parham, W Sussex.
PR PASSE, hs, oval, line, for Holland, *Herwologia*, 1620, BM, NPG.

HARINGTON of Exton, John Harington, 2nd Baron (1592-1614) friend of Henry, Prince of Wales.
PR R.ELSTRACK, hl, oval, line, BM, NPG. PASSE, hs, oval, line, for Holland, *Herwologia*, 1620, BM, NPG. UNKNOWN, hs, oval, woodcut, for Stock, *Life*, 1614, BM. UNKNOWN, wl on horseback, line, BM.

HARLEY, Sir Edward (1624-1700) governor of Dunkirk.
PR G.VERTUE, after S.Cooper, 1749, hs, oval, line, BM, NPG.

HARLEY, Edward (1664-1735) auditor of the imprest.
PR G.VERTUE, 1751, after J.Richardson, hl, oval, line, BM, NPG.

HARLEY, Edward (1689-1741), see 2nd Earl of Oxford.

HARLEY, Sir Robert (1579-1656) master of the mint.
PR G.VERTUE, 1737, after P.Oliver, hs, oval, line, BM, NPG.

HARLEY, Robert (1661-1724), see 1st Earl of Oxford.

HARMAN, Sir John (1625?-1673) admiral.
P SIR PETER LELY, c1666, tql, NMM, Greenwich; version, NPG 1419.

HAROLD I (d 1040) king of the English.
SC UNKNOWN, silver penny, BM.

HAROLD II (1022?-1066) king of the English.
SC DERMON, after Theodoric, 1066, silver penny, NPG 4050 and BM.
T UNKNOWN, 'Bayeux Tapestry', Bayeux, France

HARPER, John (d 1742) actor.
PR A.MILLER, after G.White, 1739, hl as Jobson in *The Devil to Pay*, oval, mezz, BM, NPG.

HARPER, Sir William (1496?-1573) lord mayor of London.
PR UNKNOWN, hl, line, 'copy from unique print', pub 1793, BM, NPG.

HARRINGTON, James (1611-1677) political theorist.
P Attrib ADRIAN VAN DER VENNE, c1635, hs, oval, NPG 513. After SIR PETER LELY, (type of c1658), hs, NPG 4109, engr W.Hollar, hs, oval, etch, for *Discourses*, 1660, BM.

HARRINGTON, William Stanhope, 1st Earl of (1683?-1756) diplomat and statesman.
P JAMES WORSDALE, c1746-50, hl, NPG 4376.
PR J.FABER, jun, after J.Fayram, tql, mezz, BM, NPG. M.FORD, after B.du Pan, tql in peer's robes, mezz, BM. J.SIMON, after J.Fayram, hl in robes, oval, mezz, BM, NPG.

HARRIS, John (1588?-1658) warden of Winchester College.
P UNKNOWN, hs, oval, Winchester College, Hants; copy, New College, Oxford.

HARRIS, John (1667?-1719) divine and scientific writer.
PR G.WHITE, after R.White, hs, oval, line, for *Lexicon Technicum*, 1704, BM, NPG. G.VERTUE, after A.Russel, hs, oval, line, for *History of Kent*, 1719, BM, NPG.

HARRIS, Joseph (fl 1660-1680) actor.
P UNKNOWN, hl as Cardinal Wolsey, Garrick Club, London.
D JOHN GREENHILL, c1664, hl as Cardinal Wolsey, coloured chalks, Magdalen College, Oxford.

HARRIS, Robert (1581-1658) president of Trinity College.
D THEOPHILUS METCALFE, hs, black w/c, Trinity College, Oxford.
PR M.DROESHOUT, wl with emblems, line, for *Arraignment of the Whole Creature*, 1632, BM.

HARRIS, William (1675?-1740) presbyterian divine.
P UNKNOWN, hl, Dr Williams's Library, London.

HARRISON, John (1579-1656) alderman of Leeds and philanthropist.
P UNKNOWN, hl, St John's Church, Leeds, engr W.Holl, stipple, pub 1816, NPG.
PR UNKNOWN, hl with book, etch, BM, NPG.

HARRISON, John (1693-1776) inventor of the chronometer.
P UNKNOWN, tql seated with watch, Science Museum, London.
SC JAMES TASSIE, paste medallion, profile, NPG 4599.
PR W.HOLL, hl, stipple, NPG. J.R.SMITH, after J.Wright, hl oval, mezz, BM, NPG.

HARRISON, Thomas (1606-1660) parliamentary commander and regicide.
PR M.VAN DER GUCHT, hl in armour, oval, for Ward, *Hist of the rebellion*, 1713, BM, NPG.

HARSNETT, Samuel (1561-1631) archbishop of York.
SC UNKNOWN, 1631, brass effigy, St Mary's Church, Chigwell, Essex.

HART, Aaron (1670-1756) chief rabbi.
PR J.MCARDELL, after B.Dandridge, 1751, hl, mezz, BM, NPG.

HARTGILL, George (fl 1594) astronomer.
PR UNKNOWN, wl with armillary sphere, woodcut, for *Astronomical Tables*, 1594, BM. R.GAYWOOD, wl, etch, for 1656 ed, BM.

HARTOPP, Sir John, 3rd Bart (1637?-1722) nonconformist, friend of Isaac Watts.
P UNKNOWN, hl, Abney Congregational Church, Stoke Newington.
D Attrib SIR GODFREY KNELLER, hl, Pierpont Morgan Library, New York.

HARVEY, Gabriel (1545?-1630) poet.
PR UNKNOWN, hl, oval, etch after a woodcut in Nash, *Have with you to Saffron Walden*, NPG.

HARVEY, Gideon (1640?-1700?) physician to Charles II.
PR P.PHILIPPE, hl with skull, line, for *New Principles of Philosophy*, 1663, BM, NPG. A.HERTOCHS, hl with skeleton, line, for *Great Venus Unmasked*, 1672, BM, NPG.

HARVEY, William (1578-1657) discoverer of the circulation of the blood.
P UNKNOWN, c1627, hl, oval, NPG 5115. UNKNOWN, before 1666, tql seated, Royal College of Physicians, London. UNKNOWN, (perhaps Willian van Bemmel), tql seated, Hunterian Coll, University of Glasgow. UNKNOWN, after etch attrib R.Gaywood, tql seated, NPG 60.
SC EDWARD MARSHALL, 1719, bust on monument, St Andrew's Church, Hempstead, Essex.
PR W.FAITHORNE, bust on pedestal, line, for *De Generatione Animalium*, 1653, BM, NPG. R.GAYWOOD, wl with Lord Bacon, line, for *Eighteen Books of the Secrets of Art and Nature*, 1660, BL. Attrib R.GAYWOOD, c1649, tql seated, etch, BM, libraries of Royal College of Physicians and Royal College of Surgeons, London.

HASELDEN, Thomas (d1740) mathematician.
PR J.FABER, jun, after T.Frye, hl, mezz, BM.

HASELRIG, Sir Arthur, see Hesilrige.

HASTINGS of Loughborough, Edward Hastings, 1st Baron (d1573) lord chamberlain.
P UNKNOWN, hl aged 28, Montacute (NT), Somerset.

HASTINGS, Lady Elizabeth (1682-1739) philanthropist.
PR I.NAYLOR, hs, oval, line, pub 1777, BM, NPG.

HASTINGS, Francis, see 2nd Earl of Huntingdon.

HASTINGS, George, see 1st Earl of Huntingdon.

HASTINGS, Henry (1535-1595), see 3rd Earl of Huntingdon.

HASTINGS, Henry (1551-1650) sportsman.
PR J.BRETHERTON, 1782, wl, etch, BM, NPG.

HASTINGS, Sir Hugh (1307?-1347) soldier.
SC UNKNOWN, brass effigy, St Mary's Church, Elsing, Norfolk.

HASTINGS, Theophilus, see 7th Earl of Huntingdon.

HATFIELD, Martha (b1640) cataleptic.
PR UNKNOWN, aged 11, lying in bed in trance, line, for J.Fisher, *The Wise Virgin*, 1664, BM. UNKNOWN, tql in bed, line, NPG.

HATSELL, Sir Henry (1641-1714) judge and baron of the exchequer.
PR J.GISBORNE, after Sir G.Kneller, tql in robes, mezz, BM, NPG.

HATTON, Sir Christopher (1540-1591) lord chancellor.
P UNKNOWN, c1580, hs, oval, City of Northampton Central Museum and Art Gallery. UNKNOWN, c1585, wl, Inner Temple, London; version, hl, NPG 2162. UNKNOWN, c1588-91, hl, NPG 1518.
M NICHOLAS HILLIARD, c1588-91, wl in chancellor's robes, oval, V & A.

HATTON, Christopher Hatton, 1st Viscount (1632-1706) governor of Guernsey.
P CORNELIUS JOHNSON, 1641, wl as boy, Ankara Embassy (DoE), Turkey.

HAWARDEN, Edward (1662-1735) Roman Catholic controversialist.
PR C.TURNER, tql seated, mezz, pub 1816, BM, NPG.

HAWKINS, Francis (1628-1681) Jesuit.
PR J.PAYNE, hl aged 10, oval, line, for *Youth's Behaviour*, 1654, BM, NPG.

HAWKINS, Sir John (1532-1595) naval commander.
P Attrib FEDERIGO ZUCCARO, 1591, tql, City Art Gallery, Plymouth. UNKNOWN, 1581, hl, NMM, Greenwich.
PR PASSE, hs, oval, line, for Holland, *Herwologia*, 1620, BM, NPG.

HAWKSMOOR, Nicholas (1661-1736) architect.
SC Attrib SIR HENRY CHEERE, c1736, plaster bust, All Souls, Oxford; modern bronze copy, NPG 4261.

HAWKWOOD, Sir John de (d1394) general in the Florentine service.
P PAOLO UCCELLO, wl on horseback, fresco, Duomo, Florence, Italy.

HAWORTH, Samuel (fl 1683) author of 'The True Method of curing Consumption'.
PR R.WHITE, hs, oval, line, for *Method of Curing Consumption*, 1683, BM, NPG.

HAY, George, see 1st Earl of Kinnoull.

HAY, James, see 1st Earl of Carlisle.

HAY, John (1626-1697), see 1st Marquess of Tweeddale.

HAY, John (1645-1713), see 2nd Marquess of Tweeddale.

HAY, John (c1695-1762), see 4th Marquess of Tweeddale.

HAY, Lucy, see Countess of Carlisle.

HAYDOCK, Richard (fl 1600) physician.
PR R.HAYDOCK, hs, oval, line, for trans of Lomazzo, *Artes of Curious Paintinge*, etc, 1598, BM, NPG.

HAYLS or HALES, John (d1679) portrait painter.
D G.VERTUE, after J.Hoskins, painted 1656, hs, oval, pencil and sepia, BM.
PR T.CHAMBARS, hs, small oval with larger oval of Claude le Fevre, line, for Walpole, *Anecdotes*, 1762, BM, NPG.

HAYNE, Thomas (1582-1645) schoolmaster and benefactor.
P UNKNOWN, tql seated, Leicester Museum and Art Gallery.

HAYNES, Hopton (1672?-1749) Unitarian writer.
P UNKNOWN, hl, Dr Williams's Library, London, engr T.Nugent, stipple, for Harding, *Biographical Mirrour*, 1792, BM, NPG.

HAYWARD, Sir John (1564?-1627) historian.
PR J.PAYNE, hs, oval, line, for *Sanctuarie of a troubled Soule*, 1623, copy from engr by W.Hole, 1616, BM. W.PASSE, hl with scroll, line, for *Life of Edward VI*, 1630, BM, NPG.

HAYWOOD, Eliza, née Fowler (1693?-1756) novelist.
PR G.VERTUE, after J.Parmentier, hs, oval, line, BM.

HEAD, Richard (1637?-1686?) author of the *English Rogue*.
PR UNKNOWN, hl with globe, line, BM, NPG.

HEARNE, Thomas (1678-1735) historical antiquary.
PR G.VERTUE, after P.Tillemans, 1723, hl with book, BM, NPG. Repetition with title on book 'Oath of Alleg', for *Vindication of the Oath of Allegiance*, 1731, BM, NPG.

HEATH, Henry (1599-1643) Franciscan friar executed for treason.
PR UNKNOWN, hs knife in breast, oval, line, for Mason, *Certamen Seraphicum*, 1649, BM, NPG.

HEATH, Nicholas (1501?-1578) archbishop of York and lord chancellor.
P HANS EWORTH, 1566, hl, NPG 1388.

HEATH, Sir Robert (1575-1649) chief justice of England.
P CORNELIUS JOHNSON, hs, oval, Inner Temple, London. UNKNOWN, hs in robes, St John's College, Cambridge.
SC UNKNOWN, silver medal, BM.
PR W.HOLLAR, 1664, hs in robes, etch, for Dugdale, *Origines Juridicales*, 1666, BM, NPG.

HEATHCOTE, Sir Gilbert (1651?-1733) lord mayor of London.
P MICHAEL DAHL, tql seated in robes, Bank of England, London.

HEATHER or HEYTHER, William (1563?-1627) musician and founder of professorship at Oxford.
P UNKNOWN, tql in robes, Faculty of Music, Oxford.

HEEMSKERK, Egbert van (1645-1704) painter.
PR J.OLIVER, after E.Heemskerk, hl with caricature and palette, mezz, BM.

HEIDEGGER, John James (1659?-1749) operatic manager.
PR BARLOW, face, death mask?, line, NPG. BARLOW, hs, profile, asleep, oval, line, NPG. J.FABER, jun, after C.Van Loo, hl, mezz, BM, NPG. W.SHARP, face, line, NPG. W.SHARP, hs, profile, oval, line, NPG.

HELWYS, Sir Gervase (1561-1615) lieutenant of the Tower, executed for complicity in murder of Sir T.Overbury.
PR UNKNOWN, wl, copy from woodcut in broadside of his dying speech, line, for Kirby, *Wonderful Museum*, 1813, BM, NPG.

HENCHMAN, Humphrey (1592-1675) bishop of London.
P SIR PETER LELY and studio, c1666, tql seated with book, Clarendon Coll on loan to Plymouth Art Gallery, engr unknown, mezz, BM, NPG.

HENDERSON, Alexander (1583?-1646) presbyterian divine and diplomat.
P Attrib SIR ANTHONY VANDYCK, tql, SNPG 2227. UNKNOWN, hs, SNPG 983.
PR W.HOLLAR, 1641, hl, oval, etch, BM, NPG.

HENEAGE, Sir Thomas (d1595) vice-chamberlain to Queen Elizabeth.
P UNKNOWN, c1580, hs, oval, Ingatestone Hall, Essex.

HENLEY, Anthony (d1711) Whig politician and wit.
PR J.SMITH, after Sir G.Kneller, tql, mezz, BM, NPG.

HENLEY, John (1692-1756) divine, known as 'Orator Henley'.
D WILLIAM HOGARTH, wl christening baby, oil sketch, BM, engr S.Ireland, etch, pub 1786, BM, NPG.
SC UNKNOWN, silver copper medal, BM.
PR E.FINDEN, hl, stipple, NPG. J.STOW, hs, profile, vignette, line, BM, NPG. UNKNOWN, hl, line, pub 1818, NPG.

HENRIETTA Maria (1609-1669) queen of Charles I.
P DANIEL MYTENS, c1630-32, hl with Charles holding wreath, Royal Coll. D.MYTENS, c1630-32, wl with king departing for hunt, Royal Coll. SIR ANTHONY VANDYCK, 1632, tql with crown and rose, Royal Coll. Studio of SIR A.VANDYCK, c1636, wl in white, Royal Coll. SIR A.VANDYCK, c1637-38, wl in scarlet, The Hermitage, Leningrad. SIR A.VANDYCK, c1639, hl to front and hl profile for Bernini, Royal Coll. SIR A.VANDYCK, wl with dwarf, National Gallery of Art, Washington, DC, USA. UNKNOWN, c1635, wl with architectural background, NPG 1247.
G SIR A.VANDYCK, family group, oil, 1632, Royal Coll.
M JOHN HOSKINS, hs with plumed headdress, Royal Coll.
SC HUBERT LE SUEUR, bronze statue, St John's College, Oxford. Various medals, BM.
PR H.DAVID, wl on horseback, line, BM, NPG. W.J.DELFF, after D.Mytens, 1630, hs, oval, line, BM, NPG.

HENRIETTA Anne, Princess, see Duchess of Orleans.

HENRY I (1068-1135) king of England.
SC UNKNOWN, penny, BM. UNKNOWN, wax seals, BM.

HENRY II (1133-1189) king of England.
SC UNKNOWN, 13th cent, tomb effigy, Fontevrault Abbey, France; cast, V & A. UNKNOWN, penny, BM. UNKNOWN, wax seals, BM.

HENRY III (1207-1272) king of England.
SC WILLIAM TOREL, c1291, bronze tomb effigy, Westminster Abbey, London; electrotype, NPG 341. UNKNOWN, various coins, BM. UNKNOWN, wax seals, BM.

HENRY IV (1367-1413) king of England.
SC UNKNOWN, c1408-27, alabaster tomb effigy, Canterbury Cathedral; electrotype, NPG 397. UNKNOWN, coins, BM. UNKNOWN, wax seals, BM.

HENRY V (1387-1422) king of England.
P UNKNOWN, 15th cent, hs, profile, Royal Coll; version, NPG 545.
MS UNKNOWN, wl seated on throne, for John de Galopes trans of Cardinal Bonaventura, *Vita Christi*, 1421?, Ms 213, Corpus Christi College, Cambridge. UNKNOWN, wl, for Thomas Occleve, *De Regimine Principum*, BL Arundel Ms 38, fol 37.
W UNKNOWN, c1440-50, wl in robes, All Souls College, Oxford.

HENRY VI (1421-1471) king of England.
P UNKNOWN, late 15th cent, hs, Royal Coll; versions, NPG 546 and

NPG 2457.

MS Various illuminations: JOHN LYDGATE, *Poems*, BL Harleian Ms 2278; Psalter in BL Cotton Ms Domitian XVII; *Poems and Romances*, *c*1445, BL Ms Royal 15 E VI; drawings in the 'Pageants of Richard Beauchamp, Earl of Warwick', BL Cotton Ms Julius E IV.

SC UNKNOWN, groat, BM. UNKNOWN, wax seal, BM.

W UNKNOWN, *c*1440–50, wl, All Souls College, Oxford.

HENRY VII (1457-1509) king of England.

P UNKNOWN, (type of *c*1500), hs, Society of Antiquaries, London; versions, Christ Church, Oxford; Royal Coll. MICHIEL SITTOW, 1505, hs with rose, arched top frame, NPG 416.

D HANS HOLBEIN, jun, 1536–37, wl with Henry VIII, ink and w/c, NPG 4027. UNKNOWN, hl, Bibliothèque d'Arras, France.

G UNKNOWN, *c*1505–09, wl kneeling with family, votive altar piece, Royal Coll.

SC PIETRO TORRIGIANO, *c*1508–09, polycrome bust, V & A. P.TORRIGIANO, *c*1512–19, bronze effigy, Westminster Abbey, London; electrotype, NPG 290. UNKNOWN, 1509, wax funeral effigy, Westminster Abbey. UNKNOWN, *c*1500, various coins, BM. UNKNOWN, wax seal, BM.

HENRY VIII (1491-1547) king of England.

P UNKNOWN, *c*1520, hs, Anglesey Abbey (NT), Cambs. Attrib JOOS VAN CLEVE, *c*1535, hl with scroll, Royal Coll. HANS HOLBEIN, jun, hl, 1536, Thyssen-Bornemizza Coll, Lugano. HANS EWORTH, after H.Holbein, (type of 1537), 1567, Trinity College, Cambridge; version, Walker Art Gallery, Liverpool. UNKNOWN, *c*1535–47, hl, NPG 1376. UNKNOWN, *c*1535–47, hs, NPG 3638. Attrib H.HOLBEIN, *c*1542, tql with staff, Castle Howard, N Yorks.

D H.HOLBEIN, *c*1536–37, wl with Henry VII, ink and w/c, NPG 4027.

M LUCAS HORNEBOLTE, *c*1526–27, hs, oval, Royal Coll.

G H.HOLBEIN, (heavily restored), 'Henry VIII and the Barber Surgeons', cartoon, 1540–43, Royal College of Surgeons, London. H.HOLBEIN, (heavily restored), 'Henry VIII and the Barber Surgeons', oil, 1540–43, Barbers' Company, London. UNKNOWN, 'Family of Henry VIII', oil, *c*1545, Royal Coll. REMIGIUS VAN LEEMPUT, after H.Holbein, Henry VII, Henry VIII and wives, oil, *c*1669, Royal Coll.

MS UNKNOWN, BL Royal Ms 2A, XVI, fol 63.

SC UNKNOWN, various coins, BM. UNKNOWN, wax seals, BM.

PR G.MATSYS, 1544, hl, line, BM.

HENRY, Frederick (1594-1612) eldest son of James I.

P ROBERT PEAKE, 1604, wl hunting with John Harington, Metropolitan Museum, New York, USA; version, Royal Coll. R.PEAKE, *c*1605, hl, Museum of London; version, wl, NPG 4515. R.PEAKE, *c*1610, wl, Magdalen College, Oxford. Attrib ISAAC OLIVER, wl on horseback, Parham, W Sussex.

M NICHOLAS HILLIARD, 1607, hl in armour, oval, Royal Coll. Studio of I.OLIVER, *c*1610, hs, profile, oval, w/c, NPG 1572. I.OLIVER, *c*1610, hs in armour, Royal Coll.

SC UNKNOWN, various medals, BM.

PR W.HOLE, wl lying in state, line, for Chapman, *Epicede*, 1612, BM. C.PASSE, hl, oval, line, for Passe, *Regiae Angliae . . . Pictura*, 1604, BM. S.PASSE, wl profile with lance, line, pub 1612, BM. W.HOLE, wl profile with lance, line, for Drayton, *Polyolbion*, 1612, BM, NPG.

HENRY, (1640-1660), see Duke of Gloucester

HENRY, Matthew (1662-1714) nonconformist divine and biblical commentator.

PR G.VERTUE, hl, oval, line, for *Sermons*, 1716, BM, NPG.

HENRY, Philip (1631-1696) nonconformist divine.

PR R.WHITE, after R.Holland, hs, oval, line, for M.Henry, *Life*, 1712, BM, NPG.

HEPBURN, James, see 4th Earl of Bothwell.

HERBERT, Arthur, see Earl of Torrington.

HERBERT, George (1593-1633) divine and poet.

D ROBERT WHITE, hs, oval, Houghton Library, Harvard University, Cambridge, Massachusetts, USA, engr R.White, line, for *The Temple*, 1674, BM, NPG.

HERBERT, Henry (1534?-1601), see 2nd Earl of Pembroke.

HERBERT, Henry (1693-1750), see 9th Earl of Pembroke.

HERBERT, Lady Lucy (1669-1744) devotional writer, daughter of 1st Marquis of Powis.

P UNKNOWN, tql, Powis Castle (NT), Powys, Wales.

HERBERT, Mary, see Countess of Pembroke.

HERBERT, Philip (1584-1650), see 4th Earl of Pembroke.

HERBERT, Philip (1619-1669), see 5th Earl of Pembroke.

HERBERT, Sir Thomas, 1st Bart (1606-1682) traveller and author.

P UNKNOWN, 1642, hs, Foreign Office (DoE), London.

PR HALFPENNY, hl in armour, etch, BM, NPG.

HERBERT, Thomas (1656-1733?), see 8th Earl of Pembroke.

HERBERT, William (1507?-1570?), see 1st Earl of Pembroke.

HERBERT, Sir William (d1593) author, of St Julians.

P UNKNOWN, hs, Powis Castle (NT), Powys, Wales.

HERBERT, William (1580-1630), see 3rd Earl of Pembroke.

HERBERT, William (d1696), see 1st Marquess of Powis.

HERBERT, William (d1745), see 2nd Marquess of Powis.

HERBERT of Cherbury, Edward Herbert, 1st Baron (1583-1648) diplomat and author.

P ROBERT PEAKE, 1603, wl in robes of the Bath, Powis Castle (NT), Powys, Wales. UNKNOWN, *c*1600–05, hs, oval, NPG 487. WILLIAM LARKIN, *c*1609–10, hs, oval, Charlecote Park (NT), Warwicks. UNKNOWN, head in clouds, Powis Castle.

M ISAAC OLIVER, wl recumbent, Powis Castle.

PR W.HOLLAR, *c*1635–40, hl, oval, etch, BM.

HERBERT of Cherbury, Richard Herbert, 2nd Baron (1600?-1655) royalist.

P CORNELIUS JOHNSON, 1635, hs in armour, Powis Castle (NT), Powys, Wales.

HERBERT of Cherbury, Edward Herbert, 3rd Baron (d1678) royalist.

P Attrib JOHN RILEY, hs in armour, oval, Powis Castle (NT), Powys, Wales.

HERBERT of Cherbury, Henry Herbert, 4th Baron (d1691) cofferer of the household to William III and Mary.

P GERARD SOEST, hl in armour, oval, Powis Castle (NT), Powys, Wales.

HERICK(E), Sir William (1562-1653) goldsmith and moneylender.

PR J.BASIRE, tql, oval, line, with another of his wife, for Nichols, *Hist of Leicestershire*, 1795, BM, NPG.

HERIOT, George (1563-1624) jeweller to James I and founder of Heriot's Hospital, Edinburgh.

P DAVID SCOUGALL, after P.van Somer, tql, George Heriot Trust, Edinburgh, engr J. and C.Esplens, mezz, BM, NPG.

HERRICK, Robert (1591-1674) poet.
PR W.MARSHALL, bust on pedestal, line, for *Hesperides*, 1648, BM.

HERRING, Thomas (1693-1757) archbishop of Canterbury.
P WILLIAM HOGARTH, 1744, tql seated, TATE T1971. Attrib JOHN WILLS, before 1745, tql seated with college cap, Lambeth Palace, London; version, Bishopthorpe Palace, York. Attrib THOMAS HUDSON, c1748, tql seated, NPG 4895; version, Corpus Christi College, Cambridge. Attrib JOHN SIMON WEBSTER, c1757, tql seated with book, Lambeth, engr J.McArdell, mezz, BM.

HERTFORD, Edward Seymour, Earl of (1539?-1621) courtier who married sister of Lady Jane Grey.
SC UNKNOWN, tomb effigy, Salisbury Cathedral.

HERTFORD, Katherine Seymour, née Grey, Countess of (1540?-1567?) sister of Lady Jane Grey.
P Attrib HANS EWORTH, hl with infant son, Lord Beauchamp, oval, Petworth (NT), W Sussex.
SC UNKNOWN, tomb effigy, Salisbury Cathedral.

HERVEY, John (1616-1679) treasurer of Catherine of Braganza.
P SIR PETER LELY, wl, Ickworth (NT), Suffolk. UNKNOWN, hs, oval, Ickworth.
PR R.TOMPSON, after Sir P.Lely, tql with bust, mezz, BM, NPG.

HERVEY, John (1665-1751), see 1st Earl of Bristol.

HERVEY of Ickworth, John Hervey, Baron (1696-1743) courtier and author.
P UNKNOWN, hs as child, Ickworth (NT), Suffolk. JOHN FAYRAM, c1728–30, tql with key, Ickworth. J.B.VAN LOO, c1740–41, wl seated with purse of privy seal, Ickworth; version, NPG 167. Attrib J.B.VAN LOO, hl, oval, Ickworth.
M UNKNOWN, c1723?, hs as youth, oval, Ickworth.
G WILLIAM HOGARTH, sometimes called 'the Holland House Group', oil, c1738–39, Ickworth.
SC J.L.NATTER, profile medallion, agate, on gold and enamel box, Ickworth.

HERVEY, Thomas (1699-1775) eccentric pamphleteer.
P JOHN FAYRAM, hl, oval, Ickworth (NT), Suffolk.
M UNKNOWN, hs, oval, Ickworth.

HESELTINE, James (1690-1763) composer and organist of Durham Cathedral.
P UNKNOWN, hl, Faculty of Music, Oxford.

HESILRIGE or HASELRIG, Sir Arthur, 2nd Bart (d1661) parliamentarian.
P E.DYER, after R.Walker, tql in armour, Palace of Westminster, London, engr R.Grave, line, BM, NPG.

HETON, Martin (1552-1609) bishop of Ely.
P UNKNOWN, c1609–10, hl, Christ Church, Oxford.

HEWIT, John (1614-1658) royalist divine executed for treason.
PR R.GAYWOOD?, hl, etch, for *Sermons*, 1658, BM, NPG. M.VAN DER GUCHT, hl, oval, line, for Ward, *Hist of the Rebellion*, 1713, BM, NPG. UNKNOWN, hs, oval, line, for Winstanley, *Royal Martyrology*, 1655, BM, NPG.

HEWSON, John (d1662) parliamentary commander and regicide.
PR M.VAN DER GUCHT, hl in cuirass, line, BM, NPG.

HEYDON, John (b1629) astrologer and Rosicrucian.
PR T.CROSS, hl with scroll, line, for *Holy Guide*, 1662, BM, NPG. UNKNOWN, tql oval, line, for *Theomagia*, 1664, BM, NPG. W.SHERWIN, hs in armour, oval, line, NPG.

HEYLIN or HEYLYN, Rowland (1562?-1631) sheriff of London and master of Ironmongers' Company.
P COCKE, 1640, tql, Ironmongers' Hall, London.

HEYLYN, Peter (1600-1662) sub-dean of Westminster and historian.
PR R.WHITE, hl, oval, line, for *Historical Tracts*, 1681, BM, NPG. UNKNOWN, wl seated dictating to secretary, Dutch book illustration, line, BM, NPG.

HEYTHER, William, see Heather.

HEYWOOD, John (1497?-1580?) epigrammatist, singer and player on virginals.
PR UNKNOWN, wl, oval, woodcut, for *The Spider and the Flie*, 1556, BM.

HIBBERT, Henry (1600?-1678) divine.
PR D.LOGGAN, hl, oval, line, BM, NPG.

HICKERINGILL, Edmund (1631-1708) eccentric divine.
PR J.NUTTING, after J.Hull, hs, aged 76, oval, line, for *Miscellaneous Tracts*, 1705, BM.

HICKES, George (1642-1715) nonjuror, Dean of Worcester.
P After ROBERT WHITE, hl, oval, Bodleian Library, Oxford; version, Lincoln College, Oxford.
PR R.WHITE, 1703, hl, oval, line, BM.

HICKES, John (1633-1685) nonconformist divine executed for treason.
PR J.HOPWOOD, hl with book, oval, stipple, for Calamy, *Nonconformists' Memorial*, ed 1802, BM, NPG.

HICKMAN, Charles (1648-1713) bishop of Derry.
P MICHAEL DAHL, hs, oval, Christ Church, Oxford.
PR S.GRIBELIN, after A.Russell, hl, oval, line, for *Sermons*, 1724, BM, NPG.

HICKS, William (1621-1660) puritan.
PR D.LOGGAN, hs, oval, line, for *Exposition of the Revelations*, 1658, BM, NPG.

HIGGINS, Francis (1669-1728) archdeacon of Cashel and prebendary of Christ Church, Dublin.
PR E.LUTTRELL, hs, oval, mezz, BM, NPG.

HIGHMORE, Joseph (1692-1780) portrait painter.
P Self-portrait, c1725, tql with turban, National Gallery of Victoria, Melbourne, Australia.
PR UNKNOWN, hs, oval, line, BM, NPG.

HIGHMORE, Nathaniel (1613-1685) physician.
P UNKNOWN, c1660–65, hs, oval, NPG 4069.
PR A.BLOOTELING, 1677, hs, oval, line, BM, NPG.

HILDERSHAM, Arthur (1563-1632) puritan divine.
P UNKNOWN, 1619, hl with book, NPG 1575.
PR J.PAYNE, hl with book on cushion, line, for *Sermons*, BM, NPG.

HILL, Aaron (1685-1750) dramatist.
PR H.HULSBERGH, hl, oval, line, BM.

HILL, Abraham (1635-1721) treasurer of Royal Society.
P Attrib JOHN HAYLS, hs, Royal Society, London.

HILL, Richard (1655-1727) diplomat.
P UNKNOWN, tql seated, St John's College, Cambridge.
PR M.GAUCI, after Sir G.Kneller, tql, lith, BM.

HILL, Robert (d1623) rector of St Bartholomew Exchange, London.
PR S.PASSE, hl with book, line, BM, NPG.

HILL, Sir Rowland (1492?-1561) lord mayor of London.
P UNKNOWN, 16th cent, hl, Museum of London; version, Tatton Park (NT), Cheshire.

HILLIARD, Nicholas (1547-1619) miniature painter.
M Self-portrait, 1560, hs aged 13, oval, Buccleuch Estates, Selkirk, Scotland. Self-portrait, 1577, hs aged 30, V & A.

HILTON, John (d1657) musician.
P UNKNOWN, 1649, hl with book, Faculty of Music, Oxford.
PR J.CALDWALL, hs, oval, line, for Hawkins, *Hist of Music*, 1776, BM, NPG.

HIND, James (d1652) highwayman and royalist hanged for treason.
PR UNKNOWN, hl, oval, woodcut, for his *Declaration*, 1651, NPG; copy, BM, NPG. UNKNOWN, wl standing by his horse, woodcut, BM, NPG.

HINGSTON, John (d1683) composer and organist.
P UNKNOWN, hs, oval, Faculty of Music, Oxford.

HIPPISLEY, John (fl 1722-1748) actor and dramatist.
P UNKNOWN, hs, Garrick Club, London.
G W.HOGARTH, scene from the *Beggars' Opera*, oil, c1729–31, TATE 2437; version, Yale Center for British Art, New Haven, USA.
PR SYKES, after W.Hogarth, wl as Sir F.Gripe in Mrs Centlivre's *The Busy Body*, etch, BM, NPG. J.H.GREEN, hl as Scapin, etch, BM.

HITCHAM, Sir Robert (1572?-1636) king's sergeant.
P UNKNOWN, (after type of c1620), tql in robes, NPG 467.

HOADLY, Benjamin (1676-1761) bishop and pamphleteer.
P SARAH HOADLY, c1730, tql seated, NPG 31. WILLIAM HOGARTH, 1741, tql seated in Garter robes, TATE 2736. Attrib W.HOGARTH, wl seated in robes, Huntington Library and Art Gallery, San Marino, California, USA.
SC JOSEPH WILTON, relief bust, profile, on monument, Winchester Cathedral.
PR G.VERTUE, hl, when rector of St Peter-le-Poor, oval, line, BM, NPG. J.SIMON, hl, when rector, oval, mezz, BM, NPG. J.BASIRE, after I.Gosset, hs, profile, aged 80, line, for *Works*, 1773, BM, NPG.

HOADLEY, John (1678-1746) archbishop of Dublin and Armagh.
P STEPHEN SLAUGHTER, 1744, tql seated, NGI 317.
SC MARY SLAUGHTER, 1745, wax, hs, profile, V & A.
PR J.FABER, jun, after I.Whood, 1733, hl, oval, mezz, BM, NPG.

HOADLY, Sarah, née Curtis (d1743) portrait painter and first wife of Benjamin Hoadly.
P WILLIAM HOGARTH, wl seated, Huntington Library and Art Gallery, San Marino, California, USA.

HOBART, Sir Henry, 1st Bart (d1625) judge.
P UNKNOWN, (after type of c1615–20), hs in robes, NPG 468. DANIEL MYTENS, c1620, tql in robes, Blickling Hall (NT), Norfolk.
PR S.PASSE, hl in robes, line, BM, NPG.

HOBART, Sir Miles (d1636?) politician.
SC UNKNOWN, c1646–47, marble bust on monument, All Saints' Church, Marlow, Bucks.

HOBART, Sir James (d1507) attorney-general of Henry VII.
P UNKNOWN, wl kneeling with wife, Blickling Hall (NT), Norfolk.

HOBART, John, see 1st Earl of Buckinghamshire.

HOBBES, Thomas (1588-1679) philosopher.
P Attrib DAVID BECK, c1650, hs, SNPG 188. UNKNOWN, c1650, hs, Royal Society, London. J.B.GASPAR, 1663, hs, oval, Royal Society, engr W.Hollar, 1665, hl, line, BM, NPG. J.M.WRIGHT, c1669–70, hl, NPG 225. UNKNOWN, c1677, hl seated with book, aged 89, Hardwick Hall (NT), Derbys.

M SAMUEL COOPER, c1660, hs, oval, w/c, Cleveland Museum of Art, Ohio, USA.
PR W.FAITHORNE, hl, oval, line, BM, NPG. R.VAUGHAN, hs, oval, line, in emblematical title to *Philosophicall Rudiments*, 1651, BM, NPG. UNKNOWN, 1646, hs, line Dutch plate, BM, NPG.

HOBSON, Thomas (1544?-1631) Cambridge carrier.
P UNKNOWN, 1620, wl on horseback, Guildhall, Cambridge. UNKNOWN, (after type of 1629), hl, NPG 1972.
PR J.PAYNE, hl with moneybag, line, BM, NPG.

HOBY, Sir Edward (1560-1617) favourite of James I.
P UNKNOWN, 1578, hs, Bisham Abbey (c/o The Director, The Sports Council), Bucks. UNKNOWN, 1583, tql in armour, NPG 1974.

HOBY, Lady Elizabeth (1528-1609) linguist, wife of Sir Thomas Hoby, afterwards married to Lord John Russell.
P UNKNOWN, c1590, wl, Bisham Abbey (c/o The Director, The Sports Council), Bucks.
SC UNKNOWN, 1609, alabaster tomb effigy, kneeling, All Saints' Church, Bisham, Bucks.

HOBY, Sir Philip (1505-1558) diplomat.
D HANS HOLBEIN, jun, c1538, head, chalks, Royal Coll.
SC UNKNOWN, 1558, alabaster tomb effigy with that of half-brother, Sir Thomas Hoby, All Saints' Church, Bisham, Bucks.

HOBY, Sir Thomas (1530-1566) diplomat.
SC UNKNOWN, 1566, alabaster tomb effigy with half-brother, Sir Philip Hoby, All Saints' Church, Bisham, Bucks.

HOCCLEVE, Thomas, see Occleve.

HODDER, James (fl 1661) writing master and arithmetician.
PR R.GAYWOOD, hs, oval, etch, for *Penman's Recreation*, 1659, BM. R.GAYWOOD, hs, etch, for *Arithmetick*, 1661, BM, NPG.

HODDESDON, John (b1632) poet.
PR 'F', tql aged 18, oval, line, for *Sion and Parnassus*, 1650, BM, NPG.

HODGES, Sir William, 1st Bart (1645?-1714) politician and Spanish merchant.
PR JOHN SMITH, after Sir G.Kneller, hl, oval, mezz, BM.

HODGSON, James (1672-1755) mathematical master at Christ's Hospital.
P UNKNOWN, Christ's Hospital, Horsham, Sussex.
PR G.WHITE, after T.Gibson, tql with sphere, mezz, BM, NPG.

HODSON, William (fl 1640) theological writer.
PR W.MARSHALL, hs, oval, line, for *Tractate on . . . the Apostle's Creed*, 1636, BM, NPG.

HODY, Humphrey (1659-1707) professor of Greek at Oxford.
P Attrib WILLIAM SONMANS, before c1708, hs, Bodleian Library, Oxford. UNKNOWN, before c1708, hs, oval, Wadham College, Oxford.
PR M.VAN DER GUCHT, after T.Forster, hs, oval, line, BM, NPG. KRAUS, hs, oval, line, German book illustration, BM, NPG.

HOGARTH, William (1697-1764) painter and engraver.
P Self-portrait, 1745, hl, oval, with dog, TATE 112. Self-portrait, c1757, wl seated at easel, NPG 289.
D Self-portrait, 1732, wl seated sketching, ink and wash, BM.
G Self-portrait, 'Oh the Roast Beef of Old England', oil, 1748, TATE 1464.
SC L.F.ROUBILIAC, c1741, terracotta bust, NPG 121.

HOLBEIN, Hans, jun (1497-1543) painter.
D Self-portrait, c1523–24, hl with a red beret, chalks, Offentliche Kunstsammlung, Basle, Switzerland. Self-portrait, c1542–43, chalks, Uffizi, Florence.

M Self-portrait, 1543, hs in front of easel, oval, w/c, Wallace Coll, London; versions, Buccleuch Estates, Selkirk, Scotland; and Museum Mayer van den Bergh, Antwerp, The Netherlands.

HOLBROOK, John (d 1437) master of Peterhouse and chancellor of Cambridge University.
P UNKNOWN, wl with book, Peterhouse, Cambridge.

HOLDER, William (1616-1698) canon of St Paul's.
PR D.LOGGAN, hl, oval, line, BM, NPG.

HOLE, Matthew (d 1730) rector of Exeter College.
PR M.VAN DER GUCHT, hs, oval, line, for *Practical Exposition of the Catechism*, 1715, BM, NPG.

HOLGATE, Robert (1481?-1555?) archbishop of York.
P UNKNOWN, hl with book, Holgate Hospital, Hemsworth, Yorks, engr J.Stow, line, pub 1812, BM.

HOLLAND, Sir Henry Rich, 1st Earl of (1590-1649) courtier.
P Studio of DANIEL MYTENS, 1632-33, wl, NPG 3770. Attrib SIR ANTHONY VANDYCK, c1640, wl, Buccleuch Estates, Selkirk, Scotland; copy, hs, oval, NPG 1654.
M Circle of JOHN HOSKINS, c1645, hl, oval, Ham House (NT), London, engr John Godefroy, as after 'Samuel Cooper', line, BM, NPG.
PR W.PASSE, c1625, hl, oval, line, BM, NPG. P.CLOUWET, after Sir A.Vandyck, hl, line, BM, NPG.

HOLLAND, Hezekiah (fl 1638-1661) puritan divine.
PR UNKNOWN, hl with book, line, for *Exposition of the Revelations*, 1650, BM, NPG.

HOLLAND, John (1352?-1400), see Duke of Exeter.

HOLLAND, Philemon (1552-1637) translator.
PR W.MARSHALL, after H.H., hl, oval, line, in title of trans of Xenophon, *Cyropaedia*, 1632, BM, NPG.

HOLLAND, Thomas (d 1612) professor of divinity at Oxford.
PR PASSE, hl, line, for Holland, *Herwologia*, 1620, BM, NPG.

HOLLAR, Wenceslaus (1607-1677) engraver.
PR W.HOLLAR, after J.Meyssens, hl with plate of St Catherine, etch and stipple, for De Bie, *Het Gulden Cabinet*, 1661, BM, NPG. W.HOLLAR, hs, aged 40, etch, BM, NPG.

HOLLES, Denzil Holles, 1st Baron (1599-1680) statesman.
P UNKNOWN, hl, NPG L116.
PR R.WHITE, hs, oval, line, for *Life*, 1699, BM, NPG.

HOLLES, Sir Frescheville (1641-1672) naval captain.
P SIR PETER LELY, before c1672, tql with Sir Robert Holmes, NMM, Greenwich.

HOLLES, John (1564?-1637), see 1st Earl of Clare.

HOLLES, John (1662-1711), see Duke of Newcastle.

HOLMES, George (1662-1749) antiquary, deputy-keeper of the records in the Tower of London.
P UNKNOWN, hs, Society of Antiquaries, London.
PR G.VERTUE, after R.van Bleeck, hl, oval, line, for *Vetusta Monumenta*, vol 2, BM, NPG.

HOLMES, Sir Robert (1622-1692) admiral.
P SIR PETER LELY, before c1672, tql with Sir Frescheville Holles, NMM, Greenwich.
SC UNKNOWN, marble statue, St James' Church, Yarmouth, Isle of Wight.

HOLMES, William (1689-1748) dean of Exeter.
P ENOCH SEEMAN, c1742, tql in robes, St John's College, Oxford.

HOLT, Sir John (1642-1710) lord chief justice of England.
P RICHARD VAN BLEECK, c1700, tql seated in robes, NPG 3101.

SC THOMAS GREEN, statue on monument, Redgrave Church, Suffolk.
PR R.WHITE, after Sir G.Kneller, 1689, hl in robes, oval, line, BM.

HOLTE, Sir Thomas, 1st Bart (1571-1654) royalist, built Aston Hall.
P UNKNOWN, wl, City Art Gallery, Aston Hall, Birmingham.

HOME, Sir George, see Earl of Dunbar.

HOME, Henry, see Lord Kames.

HONDIUS, Abraham (1638?-1691) animal painter.
PR J.SMITH, after A.Hondius, hl with sketch, mezz, BM, NPG. J.HOUBRAKEN after A.Hondius, hs, line, NPG.

HONDIUS, Jodocus (1563-1611) engraver.
PR J.HONDIUS or workshop, hl seated with Gerard Mercator, line, for Mercator, *Atlas*, 1613?, NPG.

HONYWOOD, Mrs Mary, née Waters (1527-1620) celebrated for her longevity, piety and number of lineal descendants.
P UNKNOWN, tql with glass goblet, Oriel College, Oxford.
PR UNKNOWN, hl, stipple, pub 1813, NPG. UNKNOWN, tql, line, NPG.

HONYWOOD, Michael (1597-1681) dean of Lincoln.
P UNKNOWN, Christ's College, Cambridge.
PR W.HOLL, after C.Johnson, hl, stipple, for Dibdin, *Bibliographical Decameron*, 1817, BM.

HOOKE, Nathaniel (d 1763) author.
P BARTHOLOMEW DANDRIDGE, tql with book, NPG 68.

HOOKER, Richard (1554?-1600) theologian.
SC UNKNOWN, 1635, relief bust on monument, St Mary Virgin, Bishopsbourne, Kent.
PR W.HOLLAR?, hs, oval, etch, for Sparrow, *Rationale of the Common Prayer*, 1657, BM, NPG. W.FAITHORNE, hs from mural monument, line, for *Works*, 1662, ed Gauden, BM, NPG. W.HOLLAR, hl with book, aged 50, etch, BM.

HOOPER, George (1640-1727) bishop of Bath and Wells.
P UNKNOWN, c1700-10, tql seated, Royal Coll. THOMAS HILL, 1723, tql seated, Christ Church, Oxford, engr G.White, hl, oval, mezz, BM, NPG.

HOPE, Archibald, see Lord Rankeillor.

HOPE, Charles, see 1st Earl of Hopetoun.

HOPE of Hopetoun, Sir James (1614-1661) lawyer.
P UNKNOWN, hl in robes, oval, SNPG 655; version, Hopetoun House, Lothian region, Scotland.

HOPE, Sir John, see Lord Craighall.

HOPE, Sir Thomas, 1st Bart (d 1646) lord advocate of Scotland.
P GEORGE JAMESONE, 1627, tql seated in robes, SNPG 953.

HOPETOUN, Charles Hope, 1st Earl of (1681-1742) lord high commissioner of church of Scotland.
P WILLIAM AIKMAN, tql in armour, Hopetoun House, Lothian region, Scotland. DAVID ALLAN, wl seated in robes, Hopetoun House.

HOPKINS, Ezechiel (1634-1690) bishop of Derry.
PR J.STURT, hs, oval, line, for *Sermons*, 1691, BM, NPG. M.VAN DER GUCHT, hs, oval, line, for *Death Disarmed*, 1712, BM, NPG.

HOPKINS, John (fl 1700) verse-writer.
PR M.HOVE, hl, oval, line, NPG.

HOPKINS, Matthew (d 1647) witch-finder hanged as sorcerer.
PR UNKNOWN, wl with witches and their familiars, woodcut, from *The Discovery of Witches*, 1647, NPG.

HOPKINS, William (fl 1674) stenographer.
PR UNKNOWN, hl seated, line, for *Flying Penman*, 1674, BM, NPG.

HOPSONN, Sir Thomas (1642-1717) admiral.
P MICHAEL DAHL, *c*1705–08, tql, NMM, Greenwich.

HOPTON of Stratton, Ralph Hopton, 1st Baron (1598-1652) royalist general.
P UNKNOWN, (after type of *c*1637), tql seated, NPG 494.

HORNE, Robert (1519?-1580) bishop of Winchester.
P UNKNOWN, hl, profile, Trinity Hall, Cambridge, engr R.White, after 'Holbein', line, with incorrect title 'Stephen Gardiner', for Burnet, *Hist of the Reformation*, 1681, BM, NPG.
G M.GHEERAERTS, sen, 'Procession of Garter Knights, 1576', etch, BM.

HORNECK, Anthony (1641-1697) prebendary of Westminster.
PR R.WHITE, after M.Beale, hs, oval, line, for *Sermons*, 1706, BM, NPG.

HORSEY, Sir Edward (d 1582?) naval and military commander.
SC UNKNOWN, 1582, alabaster tomb effigy, St Thomas' Church, Newport, Isle of Wight.

HOSKINS, John, sen (d 1664) miniature painter.
M Self-portrait, hs, profile, oval, w/c, Buccleuch Estates, Selkirk, Scotland.

HOSKINS, John, jun (b 1630?) miniature painter.
M Self-portrait, 1656, hs, oval, Buccleuch Estates, Selkirk, Scotland.

HOSKINS, Sir John, 2nd Bart (1634-1705) master in chancery and president of the Royal Society.
PR R.WHITE, bust on pedestal, line, BM.

HOTHAM, Sir John, 1st Bart (d 1645) parliamentarian, governor of Hull.
SC THOMAS SIMON, silver medal, profile bust, BM. Attrib T.SIMON, 1645, silver medal, profile bust, NPG 4364.
PR ROB.WALTON, wl on horseback, etch, NPG.

HOUBLON, Sir James (d 1700) director of the Bank of England.
P SIR GODFREY KNELLER, hl, Bank of England, London.

HOUBLON, Sir John (1630-1712) first governor of the Bank of England.
P ISAAC WHOOD, tql seated in lord mayor's robes, Bank of England, London.
PR R.WILLIAMS, after J.Closterman, tql seated in lord mayor's robes, mezz, BM, NPG.

HOUGH, John (1651-1743) bishop of Worcester.
P SIR GODFREY KNELLER, 1690?, tql seated, Lambeth Palace, London. Attrib JOHN DYER, 1734, tql seated, Magdalen College, Oxford; version, See of Lichfield. UNKNOWN, tql seated, Bodleian Library, Oxford.
M SIMON DIGBY, before 1720, hs, oval, w/c, NPG 3685.
SC THOMAS WHITE, *c*1738–42, bust, All Saints Church, Worcester. L.F.ROUBILIAC, 1746, statue on monument, Worcester Cathedral.
PR R.WILLIAMS, after J.Riley, *c*1690, hs when Bishop of Oxford, oval, mezz, BM. J.FABER, sen, 1715, hl, oval, mezz, BM. J.FABER, jun, after Dyer, *c*1742, tql seated when 91, mezz, BM.

HOVENDEN, Robert (1544-1614) warden of All Souls College, Oxford.
SC UNKNOWN, 1664, stone bust on monument, All Souls College Chapel, Oxford.

HOWARD of Effingham, Charles Howard, 2nd Baron (1536-1624), see 1st Earl of Nottingham.

HOWARD, Charles (1629-1685), see 1st Earl of Carlisle.

HOWARD, Charles (1669-1738), see 3rd Earl of Carlisle.

HOWARD, Elizabeth, see Duchess of Norfolk.

HOWARD, Henrietta, see Countess of Suffolk.

HOWARD, Henry (1517?-1547), see Earl of Surrey.

HOWARD, Henry (1540-1614), see 1st Earl of Northampton.

HOWARD, Henry (1628-1684), see 6th Duke of Norfolk.

HOWARD, Henry (1655-1701), see 7th Duke of Norfolk.

HOWARD, Henry Frederick, see 3rd Earl of Arundel.

HOWARD, Hugh (1675-1737) portrait painter and collector.
PR J.FABER, jun, after M.Dahl, hl, oval, mezz, BM.

HOWARD, John, see 1st Duke of Norfolk.

HOWARD, Leonard (1699?-1767) chaplain to the Princess Dowager of Wales.
PR BELLAMY, hs, etch, BM. J.GOLDAR, hl, line, NPG. PROUD, hl, line, NPG.

HOWARD, Mary, see Duchess of Richmond.

HOWARD, Philip (1557-1595), see 1st Earl of Arundel.

HOWARD, Philip Thomas (1629-1694) grand almoner of Catherine of Braganza and cardinal.
P Attrib CARLO MARATTI, wl in robes, Arundel Castle, W Sussex. UNKNOWN, hs, oval, Bodleian Library, Oxford.
M UNKNOWN, head, oval, oils on copper, NPG 245; version, Arundel Castle.
SC GIOVANNI HAMERANI, bronze medal, BM.
PR H.NOBLIN, hs, oval, line, BM, NPG.

HOWARD, Sir Robert (1626-1698) politician and dramatist.
PR R.WHITE, after Sir G.Kneller, hs, oval, line, for *Plays*, 1692, BM, NPG.

HOWARD, Robert (1683-1740) bishop of Elphin.
PR J.BROOKS, after M.Dahl, tql seated with book, mezz, BM.

HOWARD Thomas (1443-1524), see 2nd Duke of Norfolk.

HOWARD, Thomas (1473-1554), see 3rd Duke of Norfolk.

HOWARD, Thomas (1536-1572), see 4th Duke of Norfolk.

HOWARD, Thomas (1585-1646), see 2nd Earl of Arundel and Surrey.

HOWARD, Lord William (1563-1640) Roman Catholic, Scott's 'Belted Will'.
PR W.K.ASHFORD, after C.Johnson, wl, lith, for *H.Howard, Memorials of the Howard Family*, 1836, BM, NPG.

HOWARD, William (1614-1680), see 1st Viscount Stafford.

HOWARD de Walden, James Howard, 3rd Baron, see 3rd Earl of Suffolk.

HOWARD, de Walden, Theophilus, 2nd Baron, see 2nd Earl of Suffolk

HOWARD de Walden, Thomas Howard, 1st Baron (1561-1626), see 1st Earl of Suffolk.

HOWARD of Effingham, William Howard, 1st Baron (1510?-1573) lord high admiral and lord chamberlain.
PR J.OGBORNE, after HE, tql, line, pub 1774, BM, NPG.

HOWARD of Escrick, William Howard, 3rd Baron (1626-1694) politician.
SC GEORGE BOWER, silver medal, BM.

HOWE, Emmanuel Scrope (d1709) general and diplomat.
PR C.SHERWIN, after Sir P.Lely, hs in armour, oval, stipple, for Sir G.Bromley, *Royal Letters*, 1787, BM, NPG.

HOWE, John (1630-1705) puritan divine.
P After SIR GODFREY KNELLER, c1690–1700, hl, oval, NPG 265. UNKNOWN, c1690–1700, hl, oval, Dr Williams's Library, London.
PR R.WHITE, hs, oval, line, for *Living Temple*, 1702, BM, NPG.

HOWELL, James (1594?-1666) author.
PR C.MELLAN and A.BOSSE, wl, line, for French ed of *Dodona's Grove*, 1641, BM, NPG. W.MARSHALL, hl, oval, line, in title to *Epistolae Ho-Elianae*, 1650, BM, NPG.

HOWELL, Laurence (1664?-1720) nonjuring divine.
PR G.VAN DER GUCHT, hl, oval, line, NPG.

HOWSON, John (1557?-1632) bishop of Durham.
P UNKNOWN, 1631, hl, Christ Church, Oxford, engr Martin Droeshout, hl, oval, line, BM, NPG.

HOY, Thomas (1659-1718?) physician and author.
M THOMAS FORSTER, 1696, hl, oval, plumbago, Royal College of Physicians, London.

HUDDLESTON(E), John (1608-1698) Benedictine, chaplain to Queen Caroline.
P After JACOB HUYSMANS, (type of 1685), hl with crucifix, Ampleforth College, York.

HUDSON, Jeffrey (1619?-1682) dwarf in service of Queen Henrietta Maria.
P DANIEL MYTENS, c1630, wl, Royal Coll. SIR ANTHONY VANDYCK, c1633–35, wl, monkey on shoulder with Henrietta Maria, National Gallery of Art, Washington, USA.
G D.MYTENS, 'Charles I and Henrietta Maria departing for the Chase', oil, c1630–32, Royal Coll.

HUDSON, John (1662-1719) classical scholar and principal of St Mary Hall, Oxford.
P WILLIAM SONMANS, tql, Bodleian Library, Oxford, engr S.Gribelin, hl, oval, line, BM.

HUGGINS, William (1696-1761) translator of Ariosto and Dante.
PR T.MAJOR, after W.Hogarth, hs, oval, line, for trans of Dante (never published), BM.

HUGHES, George (1603-1667) puritan divine.
PR J.CALDWALL, hs, oval, line, NPG.

HUGHES, John (1677-1720) poet.
D JONATHAN RICHARDSON, after a painting, c1714, head, pencil, BM.
PR G.VAN DER GUCHT, after Sir G.Kneller, hs, oval, line, for *Poems*, 1735, BM, NPG.

HUGHES, Margaret (d1719) actress, mistress of Prince Rupert.
PR R.WILLIAMS, after Sir P.Lely, tql seated near fountain, mezz, BM, NPG.

HUGHES, Obadiah (1639-1704) nonconformist divine.
P UNKNOWN, hl, oval, Dr Williams's Library, London.
PR J.CALDWALL, after W.Dobson, hl, oval, line, for Calamy, *Nonconformists' Memorial*, 1775, BM, NPG.

HULLS, Jonathan (fl 1737) inventor of steam navigation.
PR W.T.FRY, hl, stipple, BM, NPG.

HULSE, Edward (1631-1711) court physician to Prince of Orange.
P UNKNOWN, c1690, tql seated, Breamore House, Hants.

HULSE, Sir Edward, 1st Bart (1682-1759) physician to George II.
D FRANCIS COTES, 1757, hs, pastel, Breamore House, Hants, engr J.Watson, oval, mezz, BM.

HUME, Sir David, see Lord Crossrig.

HUME, Patrick, see 1st Earl of Marchmont.

HUMPHREY Plantagenet, Duke of Gloucester (1391-1447) youngest son of Henry IV.
D Attrib JACQUES LE BOUCQ, hs, Library, Arras, France.
MS UNKNOWN, wl in initial letter, Ms Oriel Coll 32, fol 3v, Bodleian Library, Oxford.

HUMPHREY, Laurence (1527?-1590) dean of Winchester.
P UNKNOWN, based on monument?, hl, Christ Church, Oxford; version, Magdalen College, Oxford.
SC UNKNOWN, stone bust on monument, Magdalen College Chapel.
PR PASSE, hl, line, for Holland, *Herwologia*, 1620, BM, NPG. UNKNOWN, hl with book, line, NPG.

HUNGERFORD, Robert Hungerford, 2nd Baron (1409-1459) soldier.
SC UNKNOWN, c1460, alabaster tomb effigy, Salisbury Cathedral.

HUNSDON, George Carey, 2nd Baron (1547-1603) lord chamberlain of the household.
M NICHOLAS HILLIARD, 1601, hs, oval, Berkeley Castle, Glos.

HUNSDON, Henry Carey, 1st Baron (1524?-1596) soldier and statesman.
P Attrib MARCUS GHEERAERTS, hl, Berkeley Castle, Glos.
PR M.GHEERAERTS, sen, 'Procession of Garter Knights, 1576', etch, BM.

HUNT, Arabella (d1705) singer.
PR JOHN SMITH, after Sir G.Kneller, tql seated with lute, mezz, BM, NPG.

HUNT, Roger (fl 1433) speaker of the House of Commons.
SC UNKNOWN, 1473, brass effigy with wife, St Andrew's Church, Great Linford, Bucks.

HUNTER, Robert (d1734) governor of New York.
P Attrib SIR GODFREY KNELLER, c1720, tql with cuirass, New York Historical Society, USA.

HUNTINGDON, Francis Hastings, 2nd Earl of (1514?-1561) lord-lieutenant of Leicestershire.
SC UNKNOWN, alabaster tomb effigy with wife, St Helen's Church, Ashby-de-la-Zouch, Leics.

HUNTINGDON, George Hastings, 3rd Baron Hastings, and 1st Earl of (1488?-1545) favourite of Henry VIII.
P AMBROSIUS BENSON, hl, Musées Royaux de Belgique, Brussels.

HUNTINGDON, Henry Hastings, 3rd Earl of (1535-1595) president of the north.
P UNKNOWN, tql in armour, Tower Armouries, London. UNKNOWN, hs, NPG 1574.
G M.GHEERAERTS, sen, 'Procession of Garter Knights, 1576', etch, BM.

HUNTINGDON, Theophilus Hastings, 7th Earl of (1650-1701) volunteer in French army, and lord-lieutenant of Leicester and Derby.
PR R.WILLIAMS, after Sir G.Kneller, tql, mezz, BM, NPG.

HUNTLY, George Gordon, 2nd Marquess of (d1649) royalist.
P Attrib GEORGE JAMESONE, 1630, hs in armour, oval, Goodwood, W Sussex. SIR ANTHONY VANDYCK, wl in cuirass, Buccleuch Estates, Selkirk, Scotland.

M SAMUEL COOPER, after Sir A.Vandyck, 1640, Mauritshuis, The Hague, Netherlands.

HUTCHESON, Francis (1694–1746) philosopher.
P ALLAN RAMSAY, tql, University of Glasgow.
SC ISAAC GOSSET, copper medal, BM. ANTONIO SELVI, after I.Gosset, 1746, bronze medallion, SNPG 699, engr F.Bartolozzi, stipple, for *Memoirs of Thomas Hollis*, 1780, BM, NPG.

HUTCHESON, Thomas (1589–1641) joint-founder with his brother George, of Hutcheson's Hospital, Glasgow.
P GEORGE JAMESONE, hs, Glasgow Art Gallery.

HUTCHINS, John (1698–1773) historian of Dorset.
PR J.COLLIMORE, after C.Bestland, hs, oval, line, for Bingham, *Memoir*, 1813, BM, NPG.

HUTCHINSON, John (1615–1664) regicide.
PR I.NEAGLE, after 'R.Walker', tql in armour with page, line, pub 1806, BM, NPG.

HUTCHINSON, Lucy, née Apsley (b 1620) wife of John Hutchinson, and author.
PR FREEMAN, after 'R.Walker', tql seated with child, line, for *Memoirs of Col Hutchinson*, pub 1810, BM, NPG.

HUTTON, Matthew (1529–1606) archbishop of York.
P UNKNOWN, hl, Bishopthorpe Palace, York, engr F.Perry, c1760, hs, etch, BM, NPG.
SC UNKNOWN, tomb effigy, York Minster.

HUTTON, Matthew (1693–1758) archbishop of York and Canterbury.
P After THOMAS HUDSON, (type of 1749), tql seated with medallion, Bishopthorpe Palace, York. T.HUDSON, c1754, tql

seated, Lambeth Palace, London, engr J.Faber, jun, mezz, BM, NPG.

HUTTON, Sir Richard (1561?–1639) judge.
PR W.HOLLAR, hs, oval, etch, BM.

HUXHAM, John (1692–1768) physician.
P T.RENNEL, hl, Royal Society, London, engr J.Jenkins, stipple, NPG.

HUYSSING, Hans, see Hysing.

HYDE, Anne, see Duchess of York.

HYDE, Edward, see 1st Earl of Clarendon.

HYDE, Henry, see 2nd Earl of Clarendon.

HYDE, Jane, see Countess of Clarendon.

HYDE, Laurence, see 1st Earl of Rochester.

HYDE, Sir Robert (1595–1665) chief justice of the king's bench.
P CHRISTOPHER GARDINER, tql in robes, Salisbury Corporation, Wilts.
M THOMAS FLATMAN, hs, oval, V & A.
SC PETER BESNIER, marble bust in medallion, Salisbury Cathedral.

HYDE, Thomas (1636–1703) orientalist and Bodley's librarian.
P UNKNOWN, tql with scroll, Bodleian Library, Oxford.
PR F.PERRY, bust in oval frame, line, for *Works*, 1767, BM, NPG.

HYSING or HUYSSING, Hans (1678–1753?) portrait painter.
G GAWEN HAMILTON, 'A Conversation of Virtuosis . . . at the Kinges Armes', oil, 1735, NPG 1384.

I

IBBOT, Benjamin (1680-1725) chaplain to George I.
PR UNKNOWN, hl, oval, mezz, BM, NPG.

INCHIQUIN, Murrough O'Brien, 1st Earl of (1614-1674) royalist.
P J.M.WRIGHT, tql in armour, Manchester City Art Gallery.
SC ABRAHAM SIMON, gold and silver medal, BM.

INGRAM, Sir Arthur (d 1642) courtier.
P GEORG GELDORP, wl, Leeds City Art Gallery, Temple Newsam House, W Yorks.

IRELAND, alias Ironmonger, William (1636-1679) Jesuit executed for treason.
PR UNKNOWN, hs with knife in breast, oval, line, pub 1805, BM, NPG.

IRETON, Henry (1611-1651) parliamentary general, son-in-law of Cromwell.
P Attrib ROBERT WALKER, after S.Cooper, tql in armour, NPG 3301; version, hl, Petworth (NT), W Sussex.
M SAMUEL COOPER, 1649, hs in armour, oval, w/c, Fitzwilliam Museum, Cambridge.

IRONSIDE, Gilbert, sen (1588-1671) bishop of Bristol.
P UNKNOWN, 1662, tql, Trinity College, Oxford.

IRONSIDE, Gilbert, jun (1632-1701) bishop of Bristol and Hereford.

P UNKNOWN, 1691, hl, oval, Wadham College, Oxford.

ISABELLA of Angoulême (d 1246) queen of John, king of England.
SC UNKNOWN, 13th century, wooden tomb effigy, Fontevrault Abbey, France; plaster cast, V & A.

ISABELLA of France (1292-1358) queen of Edward II.
MS UNKNOWN, 'University of Oxford receiving Queen at city gates', Ms 659, Holkham Hall, Norfolk. UNKNOWN, c1470–80, 'Marriage of Edward II', BL Royal Ms 15 E IV, fol 295.

ISHAM, Sir Justinian, 2nd Bart (1610-1674) royalist.
P JAN BAPTIST GASPARS, c1676, tql, Lamport Hall, Northants. Attrib SIR PETER LELY, hs, oval, Lamport Hall.
M SAMUEL COOPER, 1653, hs, oval, w/c, Lamport Hall.

ISHAM, Sir Thomas, 3rd Bart (1657-1681) royalist.
P CARLO MARATTI, c1676, tql seated, Lamport Hall, Northants. SIR PETER LELY, c1679–80, tql, Lamport Hall.
D DAVID LOGGAN, 1681, hs, oval, pencil, Lamport Hall.
PR D.LOGGAN, 1676, hs, ad vivum, oval, line, BM, NPG.

ISLIP, John (d 1532) abbot of Westminster.
MS UNKNOWN, various scenes, *Obituary Roll of John Islip*, Westminster Abbey, London, engr J.Basire, wl, line, 1 of 5 plates for *Vetusta Monumenta*, 1808, BM, NPG. UNKNOWN, 'a book of four indentures', wl seated with judge, ministers of law and monks, BL Harley Ms 1498, fol 76.

J

JACK, Gilbert (1578?-1628) professor of philosophy at Leyden.
PR UNKNOWN, hs, oval, line, BM, NPG.

JACKSON, Arthur (1593?-1666) ejected divine.
PR D.LOGGAN, after Bownest, hs, oval, line, BM, NPG.

JACKSON, John (1686-1763) theological writer.
PR J.MCARDELL, after F.van der Myn, 1757, hl with Bible, mezz, BM, NPG.

JACOB, Hildebrand (1693-1739) poet.
PR J.HOUBRAKEN, after G.Knapton, hl, oval, line, NPG.

JACOMB(E), Thomas (1622-1687) nonconformist divine.
P UNKNOWN, hl with book, Dr Williams's Library, London.
PR J.CALDWALL, after J.Riley, hs, oval, line, NPG.

JAMES I (1394-1437) king of Scotland.
P UNKNOWN, hs, SNPG 682.
PR UNKNOWN, hl, oval, line, for J.Jonston, *Inscriptiones*, 1602, BM.

JAMES II (1430-1460) king of Scotland.
P UNKNOWN, hs, SNPG 683.
PR UNKNOWN, hl, oval, line, for J.Jonston, *Inscriptiones*, 1602, BM.

JAMES III (1451-1488) king of Scotland.
P UNKNOWN, c1474, wl kneeling in robes, with St Andrew and his heir, part of Bonkill altar-piece, Holyroodhouse, Edinburgh.

JAMES IV (1473-1513) king of Scotland.
D Attrib JACQUES LE BOUCQ, hl, Library, Arras, France.
PR UNKNOWN, hl with thistle, oval, line, for J.Jonston, *Inscriptiones*, 1602, BM.

JAMES V (1512-1542) king of Scotland.
P UNKNOWN, c1540, hs, SNPG 686. UNKNOWN, c1540, hl, Royal Coll. UNKNOWN, hl with wife Mary of Guise, Hardwick Hall (NT), Derbys.

JAMES I (1566-1625) of England and VI of Scotland.
P Attrib ARNOLD VAN BROUNCKHORST, 1574, hl as boy with falcon, SNPG 992. Attrib ROWLAND LOCKEY, after A.van Brounckhorst, wl with falcon, NPG 63; version, Hardwick Hall (NT), Derbys. UNKNOWN, c1587, hl, Royal Coll. Attrib ADRIAN VANSON, 1595, hl, SNPG 156, engr, hl, oval, line, for J.Jonston, *Inscriptiones*, 1602, BM. Attrib JOHN DE CRITZ, sen, c1604-07, wl, Losely House, Surrey; versions, wl, Dulwich College Gallery, London; tql, SNPG 561; and hs, NPG 548. PAUL VAN SOMER, 1618, wl, Royal Coll. P.VAN SOMER, c1620, wl in state robes, Royal Coll. DANIEL MYTENS, c1621-23, wl seated in Garter robes, NPG 109.
I NICHOLAS HILLIARD, c1603-08, hs, oval, Royal Coll; version, hl, V & A. N.HILLIARD, c1609-14, hs, oval, 'the Lyte Jewel', BM. N.HILLIARD, c1614, hs, oval, V & A; version, Royal Coll.
G LIVINUS DE VOGELAARE, 'The Memorial of Lord Darnley', oil, c1567-68, Royal Coll, Holyroodhouse, Edinburgh.
SC JOHN BUSHNELL, statue, Temple Bar (Theobald's Park), London. MAXIMILIAN COLTE, statue, Hatfield, Herts. UNKNOWN, bronze bust, Whitehall Banqueting House, London. Various medals and coins, BM.
PR Various engravings, BM.

JAMES II (1633-1701) king of England.
P CORNELIUS JOHNSON, 1639, wl when Duke of York, NPG 5104. WILLIAM DOBSON, c1645-46, hl unfinished, Royal Coll. SIR PETER LELY, 1643, hl, oval, Syon House, Middx. SIR P.LELY, 1647, hl with father, Charles I, Syon House. Attrib CHARLES WAUTIER, c1656-60, tql in armour with Garter ribbon, Royal Coll. SIR P.LELY, c1661-62, wl (marriage portrait?), SNPG 901. SIR P.LELY, c1663, tql seated with 1st wife, Anne Hyde, Petworth (NT), W Sussex; version, NPG 5077. Studio of SIR P.LELY, c1665, tql in armour, Royal Coll. SIR P.LELY, c1665-70, wl in robes of state, Royal Coll. HENRI GASCAR, c1672-73, wl in classical dress, NMM, Greenwich. SIR GODFREY KNELLER, c1684-85, wl in armour with mantle and regalia when king, NPG 666; version, hs, oval, Royal Coll. ANN KILLIGREW, 1685, wl with Garter robes, Royal Coll. Attrib WILLIAM WISSING, c1685-86, wl seated in Garter robes, with crown on table, Royal Hospital, Chelsea, London. NICOLAS DE LARGILLIÈRE, 1686, hs in armour, oval, NMM, engr John Smith, mezz, BM, NPG. UNKNOWN, c1690, tql in armour, NPG 366.
M SAMUEL COOPER, 1661, hs, semi-profile, oval, V & A; version, Badminton House, Avon. S.COOPER, c1665, hs in armour, oval, Royal Coll.
G SIR ANTHONY VANDYCK, the three eldest children of Charles I, oil, 1634?, Galleria Sabauda, Turin. SIR A.VANDYCK, the three eldest children of Charles I, oil, 1635, Royal Coll. SIR A.VANDYCK, the five eldest children of Charles I, oil, 1637, Royal Coll. SIR P.LELY, three children of Charles I, oil, 1647, Petworth. SIR P.LELY and BENEDETTO GENNARI, family group, when Duke of York, oil, c1674, Royal Coll.
SC UNKNOWN, terracotta bust, SNPG 2052. Various medals and coins, BM.
PR W.HOLLAR, after D.Teniers, 1651, hl, aged 18, oval, etch, BM.

JAMES, Francis Edward Stuart, Prince (1688-1766) son of James II and 'the Old Pretender'.
P Attrib NICOLAS DE LARGILLIÈRE, 1691, wl as infant with spaniel, SNPG 2191. BENEDETTO GENNARI, wl as infant with bird, Stonyhurst College, Lancs. N.DE LARGILLIÈRE, 1695, wl with sister, NPG 976. FRANÇOIS DE TROY, 1701, hl, SNPG 909. F.DE TROY, 1704, tql in armour, Magdalene College, Cambridge. Studio of A.S.BELLE, c1712, hl with breastplate, NPG 348. Attrib FRANCISCO TREVISANI, c1712, hl in Garter robes, Holyroodhouse, Edinburgh. Attrib F.TREVISANI, c1718, tql in armour with page, Stanford Hall, Leics. UNKNOWN, c1721, tql in armour, Stanford Hall. UNKNOWN, c1723-30, hs, SNPG 1836. UNKNOWN, c1745, hl with Garter ribbon, NPG 433.
D By or after FRANCESCO PONZONE, c1741, hs, profile, pen and ink, NPG 4535.
SC A.POZZI, ivory profile bust, Brodick Castle (NT for Scotland), Isle of Arran. Various medals, BM and SNPG.
PR J.SMITH, after Sir G.Kneller, wl as infant on cushion, mezz, BM, NPG. GERARD EDELINCK, after N.de Largillière, 1692, hl, oval, line, BM, SNPG. F.CHEREAU, after A.S.Belle, c1712, hl with breastplate, BM. L.HORTHEMELS, after A.S.Belle, c1712, hl in Garter robes, oval, line, BM, NPG, SNPG.

JAMES, Thomas (1573?-1629) Bodley's librarian.
P Attrib GILBERT JACKSON, tql with book, Bodleian Library, Oxford.

JAMES, Thomas (1593?-1635?) arctic navigator.
PR UNKNOWN, hs, oval, line, cut from a map for *Voyage*, 1633, BM, NPG.

JAMES, William (1542-1617) bishop of Durham.
P UNKNOWN, 1617, hl with book, Christ Church, Oxford.

JAMESONE, George (1589?-1644) Scottish portrait painter.
P Self-portrait, *c*1637, hl with miniature, Aberdeen Art Gallery. Self-portrait, *c*1637-40, hl, SNPG 592. Self-portrait, SNPG 2361.
PR A.JAMESONE, after G.Jamesone, hl with wife and child, etch, BM.

JANE Seymour (1509?-1537) third Queen of Henry VIII.
P HANS HOLBEIN, jun, 1536, hl, Mauritshuis, The Hague, Netherlands. H.HOLBEIN, 1536, tql, Kunsthistorisches Museum, Vienna.
D H.HOLBEIN, hl, chalks, Royal Coll.

JANE, William (1645-1707) divine.
P WILLIAM GANDY, 1706, hs, oval, Bodleian Library, Oxford. UNKNOWN, tql seated, Bodleian Library.

JANEWAY, James (1636?-1674) puritan divine.
PR UNKNOWN, hl, oval, line, BM, NPG. UNKNOWN, hl, oval, line, BM, NPG.

JANSSEN VAN CEULEN, see Cornelius Johnson.

JEFFERY, Dorothy, née Pentreath (1685-1777) Cornish fisherwoman.
PR C.ST AUBYN, after J.Opie, tql seated, etch, BM. UNKNOWN, after R.Scadden, hl, oval, line, for *Universal Magazine*, 1781, BM, NPG.

JEFFERY, John (1647-1720) nonconformist divine.
PR A.WALKER, after I.Seeman, hl, oval, line, for *Tracts*, 1751, BM, NPG.

JEFFREYS of Wem, George Jeffreys, 1st Baron (1648-1689) judge.
P Attrib WILLIAM CLARET, *c*1678-80, tql seated, NPG 56. SIR GODFREY KNELLER, 1686, wl in lord chancellor's robes, Erddig (NT), Clwyd, Wales.
PR R.WHITE, after Sir G.Kneller, hs in robes of chief justice, line, BM. R.WHITE, after Sir G.Kneller, hl in lord chancellor's robes, line, BM.

JEGON, John (1550-1618) bishop of Norwich.
P UNKNOWN, hl, Norwich Cathedral.
PR UNKNOWN, 1601, hl, oval, line, pub 1800, BM, NPG.

JEKYLL, Sir Joseph (1663-1738) master of the rolls.
P MICHAEL DAHL, tql in robes, Middle Temple, London; version, hs, oval, Royal Courts of Justice, London, engr G.Vertue, 1731, hs, oval, line, BM, NPG, and tql seated, line, BM.

JENKINS, David (1582-1663) Welsh judge and royalist.
PR W.MARSHALL, hl, line, for *Works*, 1648, BM. UNKNOWN, after W.Marshall, hl, line, for *Works*, 1681, BM, NPG.

JENKINS, Henry (d1670) reputed centenarian.
PR T.WORLIDGE, after Walker, hl, etch, BM, NPG.

JENKINS, Sir Leoline (1623-1685) secretary of state and diplomat.
P HERBERT TUER, 1679, tql seated, NPG 92; version, Jesus College, Oxford, engr G.van der Gucht, line, for Wynne, *Life*, 1724, BM, NPG.

JENKYN, William (1613-1685) ejected minister.
PR G.BURDER, after Gibson, hs, oval, line, NPG.

JENNINGS, David (1691-1762) dissenting minister.
PR J.MCARDELL, after W.Jones, hl, mezz, BM, NPG.

JENNINGS, Frances, see Duchess of Tyrconnel.

JENNINGS, Sir John (1664-1743) admiral.
P SIR GODFREY KNELLER, *c*1708-09, tql, NMM, Greenwich. JONATHAN RICHARDSON, *c*1720, wl, NMM.
SC J.M.RYSBRACK, 1743, bust on monument, parish church, Barkway, Herts.

JENNINGS, Sarah, see Duchess of Marlborough.

JERMYN, Henry (d1684), see Earl of St Albans.

JERMYN, Henry (1636-1708), see 1st Baron Dover.

JERSEY, Edward Villiers, 1st Earl of (1656-1711) statesman.
P HYACINTHE RIGAUD, *c*1698-1701, tql, St John's College, Cambridge. UNKNOWN, hs as young man, oval, St John's College.
D T.ATHOW, wl in robes, wash, Sutherland Coll, Ashmolean Museum, Oxford.

JERSEY, William Villiers, 2nd Earl of (1682?-1721) politician.
PR J.SMITH, after Sir G.Kneller, wl as boy with sister, Mary, mezz, BM, NPG.

JERVAS, Charles (1675?-1739) portrait painter.
PR G.VAN DER GUCHT, profile bust in medallion on a pyramid, etch, for catalogue of his sale 1740, BM, NPG.

JESSEY, Henry (1601-1663) Baptist divine.
PR UNKNOWN, hl with book, line, BM, NPG. J.CALDWALL, hl, oval, line for Palmer ed of Calamy, *Nonconformists' Memorial*, 1775, BM, NPG.

JEWEL, John (1522-1571) bishop of Salisbury.
P UNKNOWN, (after type of *c*1560-70), hs, NPG 242; version, Corpus Christi College, Oxford, engr Passe, hl, line, for Holland, *Herwologia*, 1620, BM, NPG.

JOAN or JOANNA of Navarre (1370?-1437) queen of Henry IV of England.
SC UNKNOWN, tomb effigy, Canterbury Cathedral; electrotype, NPG 398.

JOHN (1167?-1216) king of England.
MS UNKNOWN, 14th century, wl on horseback, BL Cotton Ms Claudius D II, 'De rege Johanne', fol 113. UNKNOWN, wl with monks, BL Cotton Ms Vitellius A XIII, fol 56.
SC UNKNOWN, tomb effigy, Worcester Cathedral.

JOHN of Eltham, Earl of Cornwall (1316-1336) second son of Edward II.
SC UNKNOWN, tomb effigy, Westminster Abbey, London.

JOHN of Gaunt, Duke of Lancaster (1340-1399) fourth son of Edward III.
MS JEAN DE WAURIN, late 15th century, 'John I of Portugal entertains John of Gaunt', Ms of the *Chronique d'Angleterre* executed at Bruges for Edward IV, BL Royal Ms 14 E iv, fol 244b.

JOHN of Lancaster, Duke of Bedford (1389-1435) third son of Henry IV.
MS UNKNOWN, wl, BL Additional Ms 18850, 'The Bedford Hours', fol 256v. UNKNOWN, wl with monks, Ms Douce 305, fol 1, Bodleian Library, Oxford. UNKNOWN, wl being presented with book by Jean Galopes, Lambeth Palace Library Ms 320, fol 1.

JOHNSON, Benjamin (1665?-1742) actor.
P PETER VAN BLEECK, *c*1738, wl with B.Griffin, as Tribulation and Ananias in Jonson's *The Alchemist*, Garrick Club, London, engr van Bleeck, 1748, mezz, BM, NPG.

JOHNSON, Cornelius (1593-1661) portrait painter.
G ADRIAEN HANNEMAN, with his wife Elizabeth and son Cornelis, oil, *c*1637, Rijksmuseum, Amsterdam.

PR W.H.WORTHINGTON, after C.Johnson, hl, line, for Walpole, *Anecdotes*, ed 1862, BM, NPG.

JOHNSON, Esther (1681-1728) Swift's 'Stella'.
P Attrib JAMES LATHAM, hl, oval, NGI 431. UNKNOWN, hl, oval, NGI 599.
PR UNKNOWN, hs, oval, line, 'book illustration', BM.

JOHNSON, Humphrey (fl 1713) writing master.
PR UNKNOWN, hs, oval, line, NPG.

JOHNSON, Maurice (1688-1755) antiquary.
M GEORGE VERTUE, hs, oval, NPG 4684.

JOHNSTON, Arthur (1587-1641) Scottish physician and Latin versifier.
P GEORGE JAMESONE, 1620, hl, King's College, University of Aberdeen. G.JAMESONE, c1629, hl, Marischal College, Aberdeen. JAMES WALES, after G.Jamesone, hs, SNPG 329.
SC J.M.RYSBRACK, 1739, terracotta bust, SNPG 1014.
PR R.COOPER, after G.Jamesone, hs, oval and vignette, line, for *Psalmi Davidici*, 1741, BM, NPG.

JOHNSTON, Sir John, Bart (d1690?) adventurer, hanged for abducting an heiress.
PR UNKNOWN, hl, line, for Caulfield, *Remarkable Persons*, 1819, BM, NPG.

JOHNSTON(E), William, see 1st Marquess of Annandale.

JOLLIE, Timothy (1659?-1714) dissenting minister at Sheffield.
PR W.RIDLEY, hs, oval, stipple, for *Evangelical Mag*, 1805, BM, NPG.

JONES, Henry (1605-1682) bishop of Meath.
P UNKNOWN, hs, Trinity College, Dublin.
M UNKNOWN, tql, Trinity College, Dublin.

JONES, Inigo (1573-1652) architect.
P SIR ANTHONY VANDYCK, c1632–35, hs, oval, The Hermitage, Leningrad; copy, NPG 603. WILLIAM DOBSON, c1644, hs, oval, Chiswick House, London; version, head, NMM, Greenwich.
D SIR A.VANDYCK, hl, black chalk, Chatsworth, Derbys, engr R.van Voerst, hl with sketch, etch, BM, NPG. Self-portrait, hs, pen and ink, Chatsworth.
PR F.VILLAMENA, hl, oval on side of altar, line, BM.

JONES, John (d1660) regicide colonel.
G UNKNOWN, 'The Regicides Executed in 1660', line engr, for *Rebels no Saints*, 1660, BM.
PR UNKNOWN, hs, oval, line, NPG.

JONES, Richard, see 1st Earl of Ranelagh.

JONES, Sir Thomas (1614-1692) chief justice of common pleas.
P WILLIAM CLARET, tql seated in robes, Lincoln's Inn, London, engr R.Tompson, mezz, BM.

JONES, Sir William (1566-1640) justice of the king's bench.
P UNKNOWN, hl in robes, Lincoln's Inn, London.
PR W.SHERWIN, hl in robes with scroll, oval, line, for *Reports*, 1675, BM, NPG.

JONES, Sir William (1631-1682) attorney-general.
P SIMON DUBOIS, 1682, hs, oval, Dulwich College Gallery, London.
SC UNKNOWN, 1682, tomb effigy, Holy Cross Church, Ramsbury, Wilts.

JONSON, Benjamin (1573?-1637) dramatist and poet.
P ABRAHAM BLYENBERCH, c1620, hs, NPG 2752; version, Knole (NT), Kent.
PR R.VAUGHAN, hl with gloves, oval, line, for *Works*, 1640, BM. W.MARSHALL, bust in niche, line, for trans of Horace, *Art of Poetry*, 1640, BM.

JORDAN, Sir Joseph (1603-1685) admiral.
P SIR PETER LELY, c1666, tql, NMM, Greenwich, engr R.Tompson, mezz, BM.

JORTIN, John (1698-1770) ecclesiastical historian.
P UNKNOWN, Jesus College, Cambridge.
PR J.HALL, after E.Penny, hs, oval, line, for *Tracts*, 1790, BM, NPG. A.SMITH, after R.Crosse, hs, oval, line, pub 1805, BM.

JOY, William (1675?-1734) 'the English Samson'.
PR P.VAN DEN BERGE, hs, oval, with 7 vignettes, Dutch inscription, etch, BM. 'J.F.', hl, oval, with 5 vignettes, pub 1699, etch, BM.

JOYCE, George (fl 1647-70) parliamentary officer.
D T.ATHOW, hl in breastplate, wash, Sutherland Coll, Ashmolean Museum, Oxford.

JUNIUS or DUJON, Francis (1589-1677) philologist and antiquary.
P SIR ANTHONY VANDYCK, hl, Bodleian Library, Oxford, engr W.Hollar, etch, BM, NPG, and P.VAN GUNST, hl, line, for *De Pictura Veterum*, 1694, BM.
G After SIR A.VANDYCK, the Madagascar portrait, oil, c1639, Knole (NT), Kent.

JURIN, James (1684-1750) physician.
P Attrib JAMES WORSDALE, tql seated with book, Royal Society, London. UNKNOWN, hl, oval, Trinity College, Cambridge.

JUSTEL, Henri (1620-1693) librarian to Charles II and James II.
PR UNKNOWN, tql seated, profile, oval, line, for *Gent Mag*, 1788, BM, NPG.

JUXON, William (1582-1663) archbishop of Canterbury.
P UNKNOWN, (after type of c1640), tql with staff, NPG 500; version, Longleat, Wilts. UNKNOWN, tql seated, St John's College, Oxford.

K

KAMES, Henry Home, Lord (1696-1782) Scottish judge and author.
P DAVID MARTIN, tql seated in robes, SNPG 822.

KANE, Richard (1666-1736?) brigadier-general.
SC J.M.RYSBRACK, 1736, bust on monument, Westminster Abbey, London.

KEACH, Benjamin (1640-1704) Baptist minister.
PR J.DRAPENTIER, hl, aged 57, oval, line, for *Trumpet blown in Zion*, 1694, BM, NPG. M.VAN DER GUCHT, after I.Surmans, 1701, hl, oval, line, NPG.

KEBLE, Richard (fl 1650) parliamentary judge in Wales.
P ROBERT WALKER, c1652, tql seated, Palace of Westminster, London.

KEELING, Josiah (fl 1691) conspirator.
PR R.WHITE, hl, *ad vivum*, line, BM, NPG.

KEENE, Sir Benjamin (1697-1757) diplomat.
P After L.M.VAN LOO, (type of 1732), tql with ribbon and Bath star, Town Hall, King's Lynn, Norfolk. UNKNOWN, tql, Pembroke College, Cambridge.
SC UNKNOWN, copper medal, BM.

KEITH, George (1553?-1623), see 5th Earl of Marischal.

KEITH, George (1693?-1778), see 10th Earl of Marischal.

KEITH, James Francis Edward (1696-1758) known as 'Marshal Keith', Jacobite and soldier in Russian and Prussian service.
P A.S.BELLE, tql, Marischal College, Aberdeen. ANTOINE PESNE, tql in armour, SNPG 813.
PR A.VAN HAECKEN, after A.Ramsay, hl in armour, oval, mezz, BM, NPG.

KEITH, Robert (1681-1757) bishop of Fife and historian.
PR H.ADLARD, hs, vignette, stipple, BM. T.A.DEAN, hl, stipple, pub 1834, NPG.

KEITH, William, see 7th Earl of Marischal.

KELYNG, Sir John (d1671) lord chief justice of the king's bench.
P SIR PETER LELY, and studio, c1666, tql seated in robes, Clarendon Coll on loan to Plymouth Art Gallery.

KEM(E), Samuel (1604-1670) puritan divine.
PR G.GLOVER, 1638, hl with book, octagonal, line, BM, NPG.

KEMP, John (1380?-1454) cardinal, archbishop of Canterbury and lord chancellor.
PR J.SWAINE, wl in landscape, after altar-piece formerly in Sutherland Coll, line, for *Gent Mag*, 1845, BM, NPG.

KEMP, William (fl 1600) actor and dancer.
PR UNKNOWN, wl dancing, facsimile of woodcut to *Nine Daies Wonder*, 1600, stipple, for Harding, *Shakspeare Illustrated*, 1793, BM, NPG.

KEN, Thomas (1637-1711) bishop of Bath and Wells.
P F.SCHEFFER, 1707, tql, Bishop's Palace, Wells; versions, hl, oval, NPG 1821, and New College, Oxford, engr G.Vertue, hl, oval, line, for Hawkins, *Life*, 1713, BM, NPG.
G UNKNOWN, 'The Seven Bishops Committed to the Tower in 1688', oil, NPG 79. J.DRAPENTIER, 'The Seven Bishops', line engr, c1688, BM.
SC GEORGE BOWER, 1688, silver medal, 'seven bishops', each in medallion, profile, NPG 152A.

KENINGHAM, William, see Cuningham.

KENMURE, William Gordon, 6th Viscount (d1716) Jacobite, beheaded.
PR R.GRAVE, hl with cuirass, line for Caulfield, *Remarkable Persons*, 1819, BM, NPG.

KENNEDY of Dunure, Thomas (d1759) judge of the Scottish exchequer.
P UNKNOWN, tql as young man, Parliament Hall, Edinburgh.

KENNETT, White (1660-1728) bishop of Peterborough and historian.
PR J.FABER, sen, hl, *ad vivum*, oval, mezz, BM, NPG.

KENRICK, Daniel (fl 1685) physician and poet.
PR R.WHITE, hs, oval, line, NPG.

KENT, Elizabeth Grey, née Talbott, Duchess of (1581?-1651) author and wife of 8th Earl of Kent.
P Attrib PAUL VAN SOMER, c1618-20, tql, TATE 398.
PR J.CHANTRY, hs, oval, line, for *Secrets in Physick*, 1656, BM, NPG. W.HOLLAR, after F.Ferdinand, hs, oval, etch, BM, V & A.

KENT, Henry Grey, 10th Earl of (1594-1651) parliamentarian.
SC UNKNOWN, 1658, marble tomb effigy, St John the Baptist Church, Flitton, Beds.

KENT, Henry Grey, 12th Earl and 1st Duke of (1671-1740) lord justice.
P SIR GODFREY KNELLER, 1705, wl with wand, Wrest Park (DoE), Beds.
G PETER ANGELIS, 'Queen Anne and the Knights of the Garter', oil 1713, NPG 624.
SC Attrib J.M.RYSBRACK, statue on monument, St John the Baptist Church, Flitton, Beds.

KENT, William (1685?-1748) architect and landscape gardener.
P BENNEDETTO LUTI, 1718, head, Chatsworth, Derbys. BARTHOLOMEW DANDRIDGE, (perhaps Kent), tql with turban, NPG 1557.
D UNKNOWN, two profile heads, 'Chiswick miscellanies', Chatsworth.
G GAWEN HAMILTON, 'A Conversation of Virtuosis . . . at the Kings Armes', oil, 1735, NPG 1384.
PR A.BANNERMAN, after W.Aikman, hl, oval, line, for Walpole, *Anecdotes*, 1762 ed, BM, NPG. S.F.RAVENET, after W.Aikman, hl, oval, line, BM.

KEPPEL, Arnold Joost van, see 1st Earl of Albemarle.

KER, John (1673-1726) government spy of Kersland.
PR J.VAN DER GUCHT, after Hammond, hl, oval, line, for *Memoirs*, 1726, BM, NPG.

KER, John (1680?-1741), see 1st Duke of Roxburghe.

KER, Robert (1570?-1650), see 1st Earl of Roxburghe.

KER, Robert (*d* 1645), see Earl of Somerset.

KER, Robert (1578-1654), see 1st Earl of Ancram.

KEROUALLE, Louise Renée de, see Duchess of Portsmouth.

KERR, Robert, see 1st Marquess of Lothian.

KERR, William (1605?-1675), see 3rd Earl of Lothian.

KERR, William (1622?-1722), see 2nd Marquess of Lothian.

KERSEY, John (1616-1690?) mathematician.
PR W.FAITHORNE, hl, oval, line, for *Elements of Algebra*, 1673, BM, NPG.

KETEL, Cornelius (1548-1616) portrait painter.
PR H.BARY, after C.Ketel, 1659, hs, line, BM. T.CHAMBERS, after C.Ketel, hs, line, for Walpole, *Anecdotes*, 1762 ed, BM, NPG.

KETTELL, Ralph (1563-1643) third president of Trinity College, Oxford.
P GEORGE BATHURST, hs, Trinity College, Oxford.

KETTLEWELL, John (1653-1695) nonjuror and devotional writer.
PR G.VAN DER GUCHT, after H.Tilson, hs, oval, line, for *Life*, 1718, BM, NPG. G.VAN DER GUCHT, hl, oval, line, NPG. G.VERTUE, hs, oval, line, for *Works*, 1719, BM, NPG.

KIDDER, Richard (1633-1703) bishop of Bath and Wells.
P MARY BEALE, hs, oval, Emmanuel College, Cambridge, engr R.Clamp, stipple, for Harding, *Biographical Mirror*, 1794, BM, NPG.

KIDDERMINSTER, Richard de Beauchamp, Baron (*d* 1388) steward of household to Richard II.
SC UNKNOWN, tomb effigy, Worcester Cathedral.

KIFFIN, William (1616-1701) merchant and Baptist minister.
PR J.HOPWOOD, hs, stipple, for Wilson, *Dissenting Churches*, 1808, BM, NPG.

KILBURNE, Richard (1605-1678) topographer.
PR T.CROSS, hl, oval, for *Survey of Kent*, 1659, BM, NPG.

KILDARE, Gerald Fitzgerald, 9th Earl of (1487-1534) lord high treasurer of Ireland.
P After HANS HOLBEIN?, jun, (type of 1530), hl, Bodleian Library, Oxford.

KILLIGREW, Anne (1660-1685) poetess and painter.
P Self-portrait, wl, Berkeley Castle, Glos.
PR I.BECKET, after A.Killigrew, hs, oval, mezz, BM, NPG. A.BLOOTELING, after A.Killigrew, hs, oval, mezz, BM, NPG.

KILLIGREW, Sir Thomas (1612-1683) dramatist and groom of the bedchamber to Charles II.
P SIR ANTHONY VANDYCK, 1638, tql with dog, Weston Park, Salop; copy, NPG 892. SIR A.VANDYCK, 1638, tql with Lord William Crofts?, Royal Coll. WILLIAM SHEPHERD, *c* 1650, tql seated with dog, NPG 3795, engr W.Faithorne, line, for *Comedies and Tragedies*, 1664, BM, NPG.
PR J.VAN DER VAART, after W.Wissing, hl with sword, oval, mezz, BM. UNKNOWN, tql as pilgrim, mezz, BM.

KILLIGREW, Sir William (1606-1695) dramatist.
D SIR ANTHONY VANDYCK, tql, chalks, BM.
PR M.GAUCI, after Sir A.Vandyck, hl lith, BM. E.HARDING, jun, after Sir A.Vandyck, hl, stipple, with false title 'John Milton', for Harding, *Biographical Mirror*, 1796, BM, NPG.

KILVERT, Richard (*d* 1649) lawyer.
PR UNKNOWN, hl with W.Abell, facsimile of an early woodcut, pub 1798, NPG. UNKNOWN, hl, oval, woodcut with another of W.Abell, facsimile of title to *The Copie of a Letter sent from the*

Roaring Boyes in Elizium, 1641, pub 1810, BM, NPG.

KIMBER, Isaac (1692-1755) Baptist minister and writer.
PR T.KITCHIN, after Smith, hs, oval, line, for *Sermons*, 1756, BM, NPG.

KING, Sir Edmund (1629-1709) physician to Charles II.
P UNKNOWN, tql seated with bust, Royal College of Physicians, London.
D WILLIAM FAITHORNE, bust on pedestal, chalks and w/c, BM.
PR R.WHITE, after Sir G.Kneller, hl, oval, line, BM. R.WILLIAMS, after Sir P.Lely, tql seated with bust, mezz, BM, NPG.

KING, Henry (1592-1669) bishop of Chichester.
P UNKNOWN, tql, Christ Church, Oxford.

KING, John (1559?-1621) bishop of London.
P Attrib NICHOLAS LOCKEY, 1620, hl, oval, NPG 657.
PR F.DELARAM, hl, oval, line, BM, NPG. S.PASSE, after N.Lockey, hl, oval, line, BM, NPG. UNKNOWN, hl, oval, line, for Boissard, *Bibliotheca Chalcographica*, BM, NPG.

KING, Sir John (1639-1677) lawyer.
P UNKNOWN, (probably King), *c* 1674?, tql, NPG 66.
M UNKNOWN, hs, oval, Royal Coll.
PR W.SHERWIN, hs, oval, BM, NPG.

KING of Ockham, Peter King, 1st Baron (1669-1734) lord chancellor.
P DANIEL DE CONING, 1720, wl seated in robes, NPG 470.
PR J.SIMON, after M.Dahl, 1718, tql in chief justice's robes, mezz, BM, NPG. G.VERTUE, 1724, hs in chief justice's robes, oval, line, BM, NPG. J.FABER, jun, 1730, hs in robes, oval, mezz, BM, NPG.

KING, Robert (*d* 1557) bishop of Oxford.
W Attrib RICHARD GREENBURY, 1634, wl in robes, Christ Church Cathedral, Oxford.

KING, William (1650-1729) archbishop of Dublin.
P ROBERT HOME, after C.Jervas, *c* 1783-88, tql seated, Trinity College, Dublin.
PR J.FABER, jun, after C.Jervas, tql seated, mezz, BM. A.MILLER, after C.Jervas, hl, oval, mezz, BM.

KING, William (1663-1712) miscellaneous writer.
PR J.VAN DER GUCHT, after R.Dellow, hs, oval, line, for *Works*, 1734, BM.

KING, William (1685-1763) satirical writer and Jacobite.
P JOHN MICHAEL WILLIAMS, 1750, tql seated, Bodleian Library, Oxford, engr J.Faber, jun, mezz, BM, NPG. THOMAS WORLIDGE, hs, Oriel College, Oxford.
PR J.McARDELL, after T.Hudson, hl, oval, mezz, BM, NPG.

KINGSLEY, William (1698?-1769) general.
PR R.HOUSTON, after J.Reynolds, 1760, hl with breastplate, oval, BM, NPG.

KINGSTON, Sir Evelyn Pierrepoint, 1st Duke of (1665?-1726) magnate and politician.
P SIR GODFREY KNELLER, 1709, hl, the 'Kit-cat Club' portrait, NPG 3213.
G Attrib MICHAEL DAHL?, tql with Earl of Burlington and Lord Berkeley of Stratton, Thoresby Hall, Notts.
M BENJAMIN ARLAUD, 1704, hs, oval, V & A.

KINGSTON, Richard (fl 1700) political pamphleteer.
PR UNKNOWN, hs, line, for *Pillulae Pestilentiales*, 1665, BM.

KINGSTON, Robert Pierrepoint, 1st Earl of (1584-1643) royalist.
P UNKNOWN, hs, Oriel College, Oxford, engr G.Vertue, octagonal, line, for *Loyalists*, BM, NPG.

KINNOULL, George Hay, 1st Earl of (1572-1634) lord high chancellor of Scotland.
P DANIEL MYTENS, 1633, wl in robes, SNPG L189.

KIRBY, John (1690-1753) Suffolk topographer.
P THOMAS GAINSBOROUGH, before 1750, hl, Fitzwilliam Museum, Cambridge.

KIRKE, Percy (1684-1741) general.
SC PETER SCHEEMAKERS, after 1743, bust on monument, Westminster Abbey, London.

KIRKHOVEN, Catherine, see Countess of Chesterfield.

KIRKMAN, Francis (fl 1674) bookseller and author.
PR UNKNOWN, hs, oval, line, for *The Unlucky Citizen*, 1673, BM.

KIRKPATRICK, John (1686?-1728) antiquary.
PR W.C.EDWARDS, after D.Heins, hl, oval, etch, BM.

KNAPTON, George (1698-1778) portrait painter.
G SIR JOSHUA REYNOLDS, 'The Society of Dilettanti', oil, c1777–79, Society of Dilettanti, Brooks's Club, London.

KNATCHBULL, Sir Norton, 1st Bart (1602-1685) scholar and statesman.
P SAMUEL VAN HOOGSTRATEN, 1667, wl, Maidstone County Hall.

KNELLER, Sir Godfrey, 1st Bart (1646-1723) portrait painter.
P Self-portrait, c1680, hs, oval, V & A. Self-portrait, 1685, hl, oval, NPG 3794. Self-portrait, c1688–90, hs with unicorn, oval, Burghley House, Northants. Self-portrait, c1706–11, tql, the 'Kit-cat Club' portrait, NPG 3214.
SC Attrib JEAN CAVALIER, c1690, relief bust, profile, ivory medallion, NPG 1740. J.M.RYSBRACK, bust on monument, Westminster Abbey, London.

KNELLER, John Zacharias (1644-1702) painter.
PR R.COLLIN, after Sir G.Kneller, hs, oval, line, for Sandrart,

Academia Picturae, 1684, BM.

KNIPE, Thomas (1638-1711) headmaster of Westminster school.
PR JOHN SMITH, after M.Dahl, 1712, hl, oval, mezz, BM, NPG.

KNOLLYS, Sir Francis (1514?-1596) statesman.
SC UNKNOWN, alabaster and marble tomb effigy with wife, Rotherfield Greys Church, Oxon.

KNOLLYS, Hanserd (1599?-1691) baptist divine.
PR F.H.VAN HOVE, hs with book, for *Life*, 1692, BM, NPG. UNKNOWN, hl, aged 67, line, NPG.

KNOLLYS, William, see 1st Earl of Banbury.

KNOWLES, Gilbert (fl 1723) botanist and poet.
PR J.FABER, jun, after T.Murray, hl, oval, mezz, for *Materia Medica Botanica*, 1723, BM.

KNOX, John (1505-1572) Scottish reformer and historian.
PR UNKNOWN, hs, oval, woodcut, for French trans by Simon Goulard of Beza, *Icones*, 1581, BL, NPG.

KNOX, Robert (1640?-1720) writer on Ceylon.
P P.TRAMPON, c1708, tql seated, NMM, Greenwich.

KNYVET(T) of Escrick, Thomas Knyvet, Baron (d1622) statesman.
SC NICHOLAS STONE, 1623, marble tomb effigy, kneeling, with wife, St Mary's Church, Stanwell, Middx.

KRATZER, Nicholas (1487-1550?) mathematician and astronomer.
P HANS HOLBEIN, jun, hl, The Louvre, Paris.

KYNASTON, Edward (1640?-1706) actor.
PR R.COOPER, after Sir P.Lely, hl, oval, stipple, pub 1818, NPG.

KYRLE, John (1637-1724) 'the Man of Ross', philanthropist.
P UNKNOWN, hl, Balliol College, Oxford.

L

LACY, Henry de, see 3rd Earl of Lincoln.

LACY, John (1622-1681) playwright and actor.
P J.M.WRIGHT, c1665, triple wl in three of his principal roles, Royal Coll.

LAGUERRE, Louis (1663-1721) painter.
PR A.BANNERMAN, hl, oval with sketches of C.Jervas, and B.Lens, line, for Walpole, *Anecdotes*, 1762, NPG.

LAKE, Arthur (1569-1626) bishop of Bath and Wells.
P RICHARD GREENBURY, 1627, tql, Winchester College, Hants.
PR J.PAYNE, hl, oval, line, for *Works*, 1629, BM, NPG.

LAKE, Edward (1641-1704) archdeacon of Exeter.
PR M.VAN DER GUCHT, hl, oval, line, for *Sermons*, 1705, BM, NPG.

LAKE, John (1624-1689) bishop of Chichester.
G UNKNOWN, 'The Seven Bishops Committed to the Tower in 1688', oil, NPG 79.
SC GEORGE BOWER, 1688, silver medal, 'seven bishops', each in medallion, profile, NPG 152A.
PR D.LOGGAN, 1688, hs, oval, line, BM.

LAMBARDE, William (1536-1601) historian of Kent.
P UNKNOWN, (after type of c1570-75), hs, NPG 4489.
PR G.VERTUE, 1729, hs, oval, line, BM, NPG.

LAMBE, John (d1628) astrologer.
PR UNKNOWN, wl being assaulted by mob, modern copy of woodcut, 1628, woodcut, BM, NPG. UNKNOWN, tql, oval, line, copy of figure in above woodcut, BM, NPG.

LAMBE, William (1495-1580) London merchant and benefactor.
PR UNKNOWN, monument in Lambe's chapel, Monkwell St, line, BM.

LAMBERT, John (1619-1684) soldier.
P After ROBERT WALKER, (type of c1650-55), hl in armour, oval, NPG 252, engr M. van der Gucht, line, for Ward, *Hist of the Rebellion*, 1713, BM, NPG; and J.Houbraken, line, for Birch, *Heads*, 1739, BM, NPG.
SC UNKNOWN, two silver medals, BM.

LA MOTTE, John (1570?-1655) merchant of London.
PR W.FAITHORNE, hl, oval, line, for Bellars, *Funeral Sermon*, 1656, BM, NPG.

LAMPLUGH, Thomas (1615-1691) archbishop of York.
P SIR GODFREY KNELLER, 1689, wl, Bishopthorpe Palace, York; versions, Queen's College, Oxford and York Art Gallery.
SC GRINLING GIBBONS, 1691, standing effigy, York Minster. UNKNOWN, c1694, statue, Queen's College.

LANCASTER, Edmund 'Crouchback', Earl of (1245-1296) son of Henry III.
SC UNKNOWN, tomb effigy, Westminster Abbey, London.

LANCASTER, Sir James (d1618) pioneer of trade with the East Indies.
P UNKNOWN, (copy after type of 1596), tql with globe, Skinners' Hall, London.

LANCASTER, John, Duke of, see JOHN of Gaunt.

LANCASTER, William (1650-1717) provost of Queen's College, Oxford.
P THOMAS MURRAY, tql, Queen's College, Oxford, engr G.VERTUE, 1718, hs, oval, line, BM, NPG.

LANE, Jane, see Lady Fisher.

LANEY, Benjamin (1591-1675) bishop of Peterborough, Lincoln and Ely.
P UNKNOWN, tql seated, Pembroke Hall, Cambridge. UNKNOWN, Usher Art Gallery, Lincoln.

LANGBAINE, Gerard (1609-1658) provost of Queen's College, Oxford.
P UNKNOWN, hs, Queen's College, Oxford.

LANGDALE, Marmaduke Langdale, 1st Baron (1598?-1661) royalist general.
PR W.HUMPHREY, hl in armour, mezz, BM, NPG.

LANGHAM, Simon (1310-1376) archbishop of Canterbury.
SC UNKNOWN, alabaster tomb effigy, Westminster Abbey, London.

LANGHORNE, Richard (d1679) Roman Catholic lawyer executed for complicity in the 'Popish Plot'.
PR UNKNOWN, hs, mezz, copy from print by Luttrell, pub 1802, BM, NPG.

LANGLEY, Batty (1696-1751) architect.
PR J.CARWITHAM, 1741, tql, mezz, BM.

LANGLEY, Edmund de, see EDMUND.

LANGSTON, John (1641?-1704) independent minister at Ipswich.
PR TAYLOR, hs, stipple, for *Evangelical Mag*, 1819, BM, NPG.

LANGWITH, Benjamin (1684?-1743) antiquary and philosopher.
P UNKNOWN, hs, oval, Queen's College, Cambridge.

LANIER, Nicholas (1588-1666) master of the King's music and artist.
P Self-portrait, hs, Faculty of Music, Oxford. SIR ANTHONY VANDYCK, c1630-32, tql, Kunsthistorisches Museum, Vienna.
G WILLIAM DOBSON, hl with the artist and Sir Charles Cotterell, oil, Alnwick Castle, Northd.
PR L.VORSTERMAN, after J.Livens, hl seated, line, BM, NPG.

LANSDOWNE, George Granville, Baron (1667-1735) poet and dramatist, treasurer of the household.
P Attrib JONATHAN RICHARDSON, hl with turban, Longleat, Wilts. UNKNOWN, hs with turban, Bowood, Wilts.
PR G.VERTUE, after 'Sir G.Kneller', hl, line, for *Works*, 1732, BM, NPG. M. VAN DER GUCHT, after 'Sir G.Kneller', hl, line, for *Poems*, 1726, BM, NPG. UNKNOWN, after C.D'Agar, tql in robes with wand, line, BM.

LANT, Thomas (1556?-1600) herald.
PR J.T. DE BRY, after T.Lant, hl, oval, line, for *Funeral Procession of Sir Philip Sidney*, 1587, BM, NPG.

LARDNER, Nathaniel (1684-1768) biblical scholar.
PR J.HOPWOOD, hl, stipple, pub 1817, BM, NPG. T.KITCHIN, hl, oval, line, NPG.

LARKHAM, Thomas (1602-1669) puritan divine.
PR UNKNOWN, 1649, hl, line, NPG.

LAROON, Marcellus (1679-1772) painter.
P Self-portrait, hl, Yale Center for British Art, New Haven, USA.
G Attrib M.LAROON? (formerly attrib W.Hogarth), 'An Assembly of Arts', oil, Ashmolean Museum, Oxford.

LASKI or A LASKO, John (1499-1560) reformer.
PR H.HONDIUS, hl, profile, line, for Verheiden, *Theologorum Effigies*, 1602, BM, NPG. UNKNOWN, hl, line, NPG.

LATEWAR, Richard (1560-1601) scholar.
P UNKNOWN, wl kneeling, St John's College, Oxford.

LATIMER, Hugh (1485?-1555) bishop of Worcester.
P UNKNOWN, hl, NPG 295; versions, Deanery, Canterbury, and Balliol College, Oxford.
PR PASSE, hl, profile, line, for Holland, *Herwologia*, 1620, BM, NPG. G.GYFFORD, hl, line, for *Sermons*, 1635, BM, NPG.

LAUD, William (1573-1645) archbishop of Canterbury.
P SIR ANTHONY VANDYCK, *c*1633-38, tql, Lambeth Palace, London; version, The Hermitage, Leningrad.
SC JOHN ROETTIER, gold and silver medal, BM. Attrib HUBERT LE SUEUR, gilt terracotta bust, Bodleian Library, Oxford. UNKNOWN, 1635, gilt bronze bust, St John's College, Oxford.

LAUDERDALE, Elizabeth Murray, Countess of Dysart and Duchess of (d1698?) court beauty.
P SIR PETER LELY, early 1650s, tql, Ham House (NT), London. SIR P.LELY, tql with black page, Ham House. SIR P.LELY, after *c*1672, tql seated with husband, Ham House. Attrib SIR P.LELY, tql seated, Buccleuch Estates, Selkirk, Scotland.
D UNKNOWN, hs, pastel, Coll of Duke of Hamilton, Holyroodhouse, Edinburgh.
G Attrib JOAN CARLILE, wl with first husband, Sir Lionel Tollemache and her sister, Lady Maynard, oil, *c*1648, Ham House.

LAUDERDALE, John Maitland, 2nd Earl and 1st Duke of (1616-1682) supporter of Charles II and politician.
P CORNELIUS JOHNSON, 1649, hl with Duke of Hamilton, Lennoxlove, Lothian region, Scotland; version, Ham House (NT), London. SIR PETER LELY, *c*1665-70, tql, SNPG 2128. JACOB HUYSMANS, *c*1665-70, tql seated in earl's robes, NPG 2084. SIR P.LELY, *c*1672, tql seated with wife, Ham House. JOHN RILEY, *c*1680, hs with Garter star, Syon House, Brentford, Middx.
D SIR P.LELY, *c*1672-73, head, chalks, BM. EDMUND ASHFIELD, 1674-75, hs, pastels, Ham House.
M SAMUEL COOPER, 1664, hs, oval, w/c, NPG 4198.
SC JOHN ROETTIER, 1672, silver medal, NPG 4362, SNPG 734 and BM. ABRAHAM SIMON, silver medal, BM.
PR G.VALCK, after B.Gennari, tql in Garter robes, line, BM, NPG.

LAUDERDALE, Richard Maitland, 4th Earl of (1653-1695) Jacobite.
PR J.VANDERBANK, after Sir G.Kneller, hs, aged 31, oval, line, BM, NPG.

LAUGHARNE, Rowland (fl 1648) parliamentary commander in Wales.
PR UNKNOWN, hs, oval, line, for Vicars, *England's Worthies*, 1647, BM.

LAURENCE, John (d1732) writer on gardening.
PR G.VERTUE, hs, oval, line, for *Clergyman's Recreation*, 1714, BM, NPG.

LAVINGTON, George (1684-1762) bishop of Exeter.
P THOMAS GAINSBOROUGH, tql seated, Auckland Art Gallery, New Zealand. UNKNOWN, hs, See of Exeter.

LAW of Lauriston, John (1671-1729) financier and speculator.
P Attrib A.S.BELLE, *c*1715-20?, hl, oval, NPG 191.
SC CHRISTIAN WERMUTH, silver and pewter medal, BM. Various medals, BM.
PR E.DESROCHERS, hl with paper, oval, line, BM, NPG. L.SCHENK, wl, line, BM, NPG. G.F.SCHMIDT, after H.Rigaud, hl, oval, line, BM.

LAWES, Henry (1600-1662) musical composer.
P UNKNOWN, *c*1648, hs, Faculty of Music, Oxford.
PR W.FAITHORNE, hl, oval, line, for *Ayres and Dialogues*, 1653, BM, NPG.

LAWES, William (d1645) musical composer.
P UNKNOWN, hl, oval, Faculty of Music, Oxford.

LAWRENCE, Henry (1600-1664) puritan statesman.
PR R.COOPER, hs, oval, stipple, NPG.

LAWRENCE, Stringer (1697-1775) general.
P THOMAS GAINSBOROUGH, hl, oval, NPG 777. SIR JOSHUA REYNOLDS, *c*1760, hl with breastplate, India Office, London. After SIR J.REYNOLDS, *c*1767, tql, Oriental Club, London. Attrib SIR J.REYNOLDS, hs, semi-profile, oval, Victoria Memorial Museum, Calcutta, India.
SC PETER SCHEEMAKERS, 1764, marble statue, India Office, London. WILLIAM TYLER, 1775, bust on monument, Westminster Abbey.

LAWSON, Sir John (d1665) admiral.
P SIR PETER LELY, tql with breastplate, Royal Coll; copy, NMM, Greenwich.

LAYER, Christopher (1683-1723) lawyer and Jacobite conspirator.
PR UNKNOWN, hl, line, pub 1740, BM. UNKNOWN, wl taking leave of family, woodcut, for broadside, 'The Exact Effigies, Life, and Character of C.L. esq.', BM.

LEAKE, Sir John (1656-1720) admiral.
P SIR GODFREY KNELLER, *c*1703-12, tql, NMM, Greenwich.

LEATE, Nicholas (d1631) merchant of London.
P UNKNOWN, before 1631, hl, Ironmongers' Company, London.
PR J.PAYNE, hl, oval, line, BM, NPG.

LE CÈNE, Charles (1647?-1703) Huguenot refugee and author.
PR F.M.LA CAVE, hs, oval, line, NPG.

LECHMERE, Sir Nicholas (1613-1701) judge.
PR V.GREEN, hs in robes, oval, mezz, for Nash, *Worcestershire*, 1781, BM, NPG.

LEDIARD, Thomas (1685-1743) author.
PR C.FRITSCH, after J.S.Wahl, hl, oval, line, for *Grammatica Anglicana*, 1726, BM. UNKNOWN, hl, oval, line, for *Naval Hist of England*, 1735, BM, NPG.

LEE, Fitzroy Henry (1699-1750) vice-admiral.
P UNKNOWN, *c*1725, tql, NMM, Greenwich.

LEE, Sir Henry (1533-1611) master of the ordinance.
P ANTONIO MOR, 1568, hl, NPG 2095. MARCUS GHEERAERTS, 1590, tql with dog, Ditchley Park, Oxon. M.GHEERAERTS, 1602, wl in Garter robes, Armourers and Braziers Company, London.

LEE, Sir James Lockhart, Lord (1595-1674) Scottish judge.
P Attrib ROBERT WALKER, *c*164050, hl in armour, SNPG L291.

LEE, Matthew (1694-1755) benefactor of Christ Church, Oxford.
SC L.F.ROUBILIAC, marble bust, painted, Christ Church, Oxford.

LEE, Nathaniel (1653?-1692) poet.
P UNKNOWN, (called Lee), hl, oval, Garrick Club, London, engr J.Watts, after 'W.Dobson', mezz, pub 1778, BM, NPG.

LEE, Thomas (1552?-1601) captain.
P MARCUS GHEERAERTS, 1594, wl, on loan to TATE.

LEE, Sir Thomas, 1st Bart (1635-1691) politician.
P SIR PETER LELY, hl, semi-profile, Leicester Museum and Art Gallery.

LEE, Sir William (1688-1754) lord chief justice.
P C.F.BARKER, after John Vanderbank, (type of 1738), wl in robes, NPG 471, engr J.Faber, jun, mezz, BM, NPG. ALLAN RAMSAY, 1746, hl in robes, oval, Inner Temple, London.
PR G.JOHNSON, tql in robes, mezz, BM.

LEEDS, Peregrine Osborne, 2nd Duke of (1658-1729) admiral.
PR UNKNOWN, after Petitot, hs with breastplate, oval, stipple, pub 1806, NPG.

LEEDS, Thomas Osborne, 1st Duke of (1631-1712) statesman.
P SIR PETER LELY, c1673, wl in Garter robes with staff of office, on loan from Duke of Leeds to Dover House (DoE), Dover; version, NPG 1472. Probably WILLIAM CLARET, c1682, tql seated in Garter robes, Marlborough House (DoE), London. SIR GODFREY KNELLER, c1680-85, wl in Garter robes with staff, Holkham Hall, Norfolk. SIR G.KNELLER, hl, oval, on loan from Duke of Leeds to Treasury (DoE), London. JOHANN KERSEBOOM and G. VAN DER VAART, 1704, wl in Garter robes with staff, on loan from Duke of Leeds to Lancaster House (DoE), London.

LEGGE, George, see 1st Baron Dartmouth.

LEGGE, Thomas (1535-1607) master of Caius College, Cambridge.
P UNKNOWN, hs, Gonville and Caius College, Cambridge.
SC UNKNOWN, 1607, kneeling effigy on monument, Gonville and Caius College Chapel.

LEGGE, William (1609-1672) soldier and royalist.
P After JACOB HUYSMANS, (type of c1670?), tql, NPG 505.

LEGGE, William (1672-1750), see 1st Earl of Dartmouth.

LE GRAND, Antoine (d1699) Cartesian philosopher.
PR W.FAITHORNE, hs, oval, line, NPG.

LEICESTER, Lettice Dudley, née Knollys, Countess of (1545-1634) wife of Robert Dudley, Earl of Leicester.
P GEORGE GOWER, tql, Longleat, Wilts.

LEICESTER, Philip Sidney, 3rd Earl of (1619-1698) parliamentarian.
P SIR PETER LELY, (probably 3rd Earl of Leicester), c1642-45, hl, oval, Althorp, Northants. UNKNOWN, tql with breastplate as young man, Penshurst, Kent. SIR GODFREY KNELLER, 1685, tql seated, Penshurst.
G UNKNOWN, wl with brothers Algernon and Robert, oil, Penshurst.

LEICESTER, Robert Dudley, Earl of (1532?-1588) favourite of Elizabeth I.
P Attrib STEVEN VAN DER MUELEN, c1560-65, hl, Wallace Coll, London. UNKNOWN, c1570-75, tql, NPG 447. UNKNOWN, c1575-80, tql, NPG 247; version, Hatfield House, Herts. UNKNOWN, c1585-86, wl, Parham Park, W Sussex, engr W.Passe, hs, oval, line, for Holland, *Herwologia*, 1620, BM, NPG. Attrib WILLIAM SEGAR, c1587, tql, Hatfield House; versions, Warwick Castle, Warwicks; and Penshurst, Kent.

D FEDERIGO ZUCCARO, 1575, wl in armour, BM.
M UNKNOWN, c1565, hs, Belvoir Castle, Leics. NICHOLAS HILLIARD, 1576, hs, NPG 4197. N.HILLIARD, c1585-88, wl, Penshurst.
G M.GHEERAERTS, sen, 'Procession of Garter Knights, 1576', etch, BM.
SC JASPER HOLLEMANS, c1588, tomb effigy, St Mary's Church, Beauchamp Chapel, Warwick.
PR R.HOGENBERG, wl, woodcut, for *Bishop's Bible*, 1568, BL.

LEICESTER, Robert Sidney, 1st Earl of (1563-1626) soldier.
P UNKNOWN, c1585-88, tql, NPG 1862. UNKNOWN, c1585-88, hl, New College, Oxford. Attrib ROBERT PEAKE, sen, c1605, wl in peer's robes, Penshurst, Kent. UNKNOWN, c1610, wl, Penshurst. Attrib MARCUS GHEERAERTS, (called 3rd Earl of Leicester), c1615, wl, Longleat, Wilts.
PR S.PASSE, 1617, hl, when Viscount de Lisle, oval, line, BM, NPG.

LEICESTER, Robert Sidney, 2nd Earl of (1595-1677) statesman.
P UNKNOWN, wl as boy with brother William, Penshurst, Kent. CORNELIUS JOHNSON, 1632, hl, Penshurst. UNKNOWN, tql, Althorp, Northants.

LEICESTER, Simon of Montfort, Earl of (1208?-1265) crusader.
SC UNKNOWN, 1258, wl on horseback, wax seal, BL Additional Charter 11296.

LEIGH, Anthony (d1692) actor.
P SIR GODFREY KNELLER, 1689, wl in friar's habit, NPG 1280, engr J.Smith, mezz, BM.

LEIGH, Charles (1662-1701?) physician and naturalist.
PR J.SAVAGE, after W.Faithorne, hl, oval, line, for *Natural Hist of Lancashire*, 1700, BM.

LEIGH, Edward (1602-1671) theological writer and critic.
PR T.CROSS, hl at table, line, for *Critica Sacra*, 1650 ed, BM, NPG. J.CHANTRY, hl, oval, line, for *Critica Sacra*, 1662 ed, BM, NPG.

LEIGH, Samuel (fl 1686) author of a metrical version of the psalms.
PR W.FAITHORNE, hs, oval, line, for *Samuelis Primitiae*, 1661, BM, NPG.

LEIGH, Sir Thomas (1504?-1571) lord mayor of London.
PR UNKNOWN, hl, line, BM, NPG.

LEIGH, Thomas Leigh, 1st Baron (d1671) royalist.
P After HENRY STONE, (type of 1649), hl with skull, Lamport Hall, Northants.

LEIGHTON, Alexander (1568-1649) puritan physician and divine.
PR W.HOLLAR, hs, oval, etch, BM, NPG.

LEIGHTON, Robert (1611-1684) archbishop of Glasgow.
P UNKNOWN, tql, Edinburgh University.
PR R.WHITE, hs, oval, line, BM, NPG.

LELAND, John (1691-1766) dissenting minister.
PR J.BROOKS, after A.Lee, hl, oval, mezz, BM.

LELY, Sir Peter (1618-1680) portrait painter.
P Self-portrait, c1660, tql with statuette, NPG 3897. Self-portrait, c1665-70, hs, Uffizi, Florence. Self-portrait, c1675, tql with Hugh May, Audley End (DoE), Essex.
PR I.BECKETT, after Sir P.Lely, hl, mezz, BM, NPG. A. DE JODE, after Sir P.Lely, hl, line, BM, NPG.

LEMAN, Sir John (1544-1632) lord mayor of London.
P UNKNOWN, 1616, tql in robes, Royal Coll.

LE NEVE, Peter (1661-1729) Norroy king-of-arms and antiquary.
PR J.OGBORNE, after G.Vertue, hl in robes, oval, line, pub 1773, BM, NPG.

LENNARD, Samson (d1633) herald and translator.
PR R.VAUGHAN, hl with scroll, oval, line, for trans of Charron, *On Wisdom*, 1658, BM.

LENNOX, Charles (1672-1723), see 1st Duke of Richmond and Lennox.

LENNOX, Charles Stuart, 6th Duke of (1639-1672), see 3rd Duke of Richmond and Lennox.

LENNOX, Esmé Stuart, 1st Duke of (1542?-1583) courtier.
P UNKNOWN, 1590, hs, SNPG 2213. UNKNOWN, hs, Longleat, Wilts.
D F.QUESNEL?, hs, crayon, Bibliothèque Nationale, Paris.

LENNOX, James Stuart, 4th Duke of, see 1st Duke of Richmond.

LENNOX, Ludovick Stuart, 2nd Duke of, see 1st Duke of Richmond.

LENNOX, Margaret Douglas, Countess of (1515-1578) mother-in-law of Mary Queen of Scots.
P UNKNOWN, 1572, wl, Royal Coll.
G LIVINUS DE VOGELAARE, 'The Memorial of Lord Darnley', oil, 1567-68, Royal Coll; version, Goodwood House, W Sussex.
SC UNKNOWN, marble tomb effigy, Westminster Abbey, London; electrotype, NPG 358.

LENNOX, Matthew Stewart, 4th Earl of (1516-1571) regent of Scotland.
G LIVINUS DE VOGELAARE, 'The Memorial of Lord Darnley', oil, 1567-68, Royal Coll; version, Goodwood House, W Sussex.

LENS, Bernard (1682-1740) miniature painter.
M Self-portrait, 1708, head, oval, Ickworth (NT), Suffolk. Self-portrait, 1721, head, oval, NPG 1624. Self-portrait, 1724, hl with miniature, Ashmolean Museum, Oxford.
PR L.P.BOITARD, after B.Lens, hl, oval, with two Christ's Hospital boys, line, for *Drawing Book*, 1750–51, BM.

LENTHALL, William (1591-1662) speaker of the House of Commons.
P Perhaps by HENRY PAERT, tql in speaker's robes, Palace of Westminster, London. UNKNOWN, tql seated in robes of master of rolls, NPG 12.
M SAMUEL COOPER, 1652, hs, oval, NPG 2766.

LE PIPER, Francis (d1698) painter.
PR E.LUTTRELL, hl, oval, mezz, BM.

LESLIE, Alexander, see 1st Earl of Leven.

LEVEN, Alexander Leslie, 1st Earl of (1580?-1661) general.
P Attrib GEORGE JAMESONE, hl, SNPG 1411.
PR M. VAN DER GUCHT, hl with truncheon, oval, line, for Ward, *Hist of the Rebellion*, 1713, BM, NPG. UNKNOWN, hl in armour, oval, line, for Ricraft, *Survey of England's Champions*, 1647, BM.

LESLIE, Charles (1650-1722) nonjuror and controversialist.
PR F.CHEREAU, after A.S.Belle, hl, oval, line, BM, NPG. UNKNOWN, hl, oval, mezz, BM, NPG.

LESLIE, David, see 1st Baron Newark.

LESLIE, John (1527-1596) bishop of Ross.
P UNKNOWN, SNPG 943.
D 11th EARL OF BUCHAN, after unknown artist, pencil, SNPG 1626.
PR P. VAN GUNST, hs, octagonal, line, for Larrey, *Hist d'Angleterre*, 1697, BM, NPG. BARLOW, hs, line, for Pinkerton, *Iconographia Scotica*, 1795, BM.

LESLIE, John (1630-1681), see 1st Duke of Rothes.

LESLIE, John (1679-1722), see 8th Earl of Rothes.

LESLIE, John (1698?-1767), see 10th Earl of Rothes.

LESLIE, Walter Leslie, Count (1606-1667) soldier of fortune and diplomat.
P UNKNOWN, c1666, tql with order of Golden Fleece, Royal Coll.
PR L.KILIAN, 1637, hl in armour, *ad vivum*, oval, line, BM, NPG.

LESTOCK, Richard (1679?-1746) admiral.
P JOHN WOLLASTON, c1740, hl, NMM, Greenwich, engr J.Faber, jun, 1746, mezz, BM, NPG.

L'ESTRANGE, Sir Roger (1616-1704) royalist journalist and controller of the press.
P Attrib J.M.WRIGHT, c1680?, tql seated, NPG 3771.
PR R.WHITE, after Sir G.Kneller, 1684, hs, oval, line, for *Fables of Aesop*, 1692, BM, NPG.

LE STRANGE, Sir Thomas (1494-1545) high sheriff of Norfolk.
D HANS HOLBEIN, jun, c1536, hs, chalks, Royal Coll.

LESUEUR, Robert (1580?-1670) sculptor.
SC Attrib CLAUDE WAURIN, 1635, medal, BM; electrotype, NPG 939.

LEVEN, David Melville, 2nd Earl of Melville and 3rd Earl of (1660-1728) statesman and soldier.
P SIR J.B.MEDINA, 1691, tql in armour, SNPG 1528.

LEVENS, Peter (fl 1587) scholar and medical writer.
PR I.CHANTREY, hl with flask, line, for *The Path-way to Health*, 1664 ed, NPG.

LEVERIDGE, Richard (1670?-1758) singer and composer.
P THOMAS FRYE, hl, Warwick Castle, Warwicks. FRANCIS VAN DER MYN, hl with letter, Garrick Club, London, engr A. van der Myn, hl, oval, mezz, pub 1753, BM.
PR W.PETHER, after T.Frye, hl with sheet music, mezz, BM, NPG.

LEVESON, Sir Richard (1570-1605) admiral.
P UNKNOWN, wl, Arbury Hall, Warwicks.
SC HUBERT LE SUEUR, c1634, bronze statue, St Peter's Church, Wolverhampton, Staffs.

LEVESON-GOWER, John, see 1st Earl of Gower.

LEVINZ, Sir Cresswell (1627-1701) judge.
P JONATHAN RICHARDSON, tql seated in robes, Gray's Inn, London.
PR R.WHITE, after Sir G.Kneller, hs, oval, line, for *Reports*, 1702, BM, NPG.

LEWIS, David, pseudonym Charles Baker (1617-1679) Jesuit.
G UNKNOWN, 'Titus Oates and Jesuits', lith, 1685, pub J.Bormeester, Amsterdam, BM.
PR ALEX VOET, hs with knife in breast, oval, line, NPG.

LEWIS, John (1675-1747) historian and antiquary.
PR G.WHITE, hl, oval, mezz, *Hist of Thanet*, 1736, BM, NPG.

LEWIS, William (1592-1667) provost of Oriel College, Oxford.
P UNKNOWN, hl, oval, Oriel College, Oxford.

LEXINGTON, Robert Sutton, 2nd Baron (1661-1723) lord of the bedchamber to William III.
SC WILLIAM PALMER, tomb effigy with wife, St Wilfrid's Church, Kelham, Notts.

LEY, James, see 1st Earl of Marlborough.

LEYBOURN, William (1626-1700?) mathematician.
PR R.GAYWOOD, hs, aged 30, etch, for *Arithmetick*, BM, NPG.

R. WHITE, hs, oval, line, for *Compleat Surveyor*, 1674, BM, NPG. R. WHITE, hs, oval, line, for *Cursus Mathematicus*, 1690, BM, NPG. UNKNOWN, hs, aged 27, oval, etch, for *Compleat Surveyor*, 1653, BM, NPG. UNKNOWN, tql seated, line, for *Dialling*, 1669, BM, NPG.

LEYCESTER, Sir Peter, 1st Bart (1614-1678) antiquary.
PR UNKNOWN, hs, oval, stipple, NPG.

LHUYD, Edward (1660-1709) Celtic scholar and naturalist.
PR UNKNOWN, hs in initial letter 'E', engr, for *The Donation Book* of The Ashmolean Museum, Oxford.

LICHFIELD, Lord Bernard Stuart, titular Earl of (1623?-1645) royalist.
P THOMAS GAINSBOROUGH, after Sir Anthony Vandyck, (type of *c*1638), wl with brother, John, Art Museum, St Louis, Missouri, USA.

LIGHTFOOT, John (1602-1675) biblical scholar.
P UNKNOWN, hl with book, St Catherine's College, Cambridge.
PR R. WHITE, hs, oval, line, for *Works*, 1684, BM, NPG.

LIGONIER, John or **Jean Louis, 1st Earl of (1680-1770)** field marshal.
P PHILIP MERCIER, 1738, hl, French Protestant Hospital, Rochester. BARTHOLOMEW DANDRIDGE, 1752, wl on horseback, French Protestant Hospital. DAVID MORIER, *c*1759-62, wl on horseback, Anglesey Abbey (NT), Cambs. D. MORIER, *c*1759-62, wl on horseback, Royal Coll. Attrib D. MORIER, 1758?, wl with Richard Cox, Lloyds Bank, Cox and King's Branch, London. SIR JOSHUA REYNOLDS, *c*1760, wl on horseback, Ligonier Society, Pittsburgh, USA; version, life size, TATE 143. Attrib HENRY MORLAND, 1757-70, hl, oval, Officers' House, Hyde Park Barracks, London. UNKNOWN, tql, National Army Museum, London.
G D. MORIER, wl on horseback with Duke of Cumberland, oil, *c*1749, Royal Coll. D. MORIER, wl on horseback with George III, oil, *c*1760-65, Royal Coll.
SC L. F. ROUBILIAC, *c*1761?, terracotta bust, NPG 2013. L. F. ROUBILIAC, *c*1761-62, marble bust, Royal Coll. J. F. MOORE, 1773, portrait medallion on monument, Westminster Abbey, London.
PR G. BOCKMAN, after J. Worsdale, 1756, hl with Bath star and ribbon, mezz, BM. J. BROOKS, after J. Latham, tql with breastplate and Bath insignia, mezz, BM.

LILBURNE, John (1614?-1657) political agitator.
PR G. GLOVER, hs, oval, line, for *Christian Man's Trial*, 1641, BM, NPG. W. HOLLAR, hs, oval, etch, BM, NPG. UNKNOWN, wl with book, for *Trial*, 1649, BM, NPG. UNKNOWN, hs, oval, with bars over portrait, line, for broadsheet, pub 1659, NPG.

LILBURNE, Robert (1613-1665) regicide.
M SAMUEL COOPER, 1650, hs in armour, oval, V & A. S. COOPER, 1650, hs in armour, w/c, The Fitzwilliam Museum, Cambridge.

LILLY, William (1602-1681) astrologer.
P UNKNOWN, 1646, hl, Ashmolean Museum, Oxford, engr W. Marshall, line, for *Christian Astrology*, 1647, BM, NPG.
PR T. CROSS, hs, oval, line, for *Almanack*, 1678, NPG. UNKNOWN, hs, line, for *Merlini Anglici Ephemeris*, 1667, BM. UNKNOWN, hs with two other men, oval, line, NPG.

LILY, William (1468?-1522) grammarian and first highmaster of St Paul's School.
PR UNKNOWN, hl with book, line, modern impression, BM, NPG.

LINACRE, Thomas (1460?-1524) physician to Henry VIII.
P UNKNOWN, (called Linacre), hs with letter, Royal Coll.

LINCOLN, Edward Fiennes de Clinton, 1st Earl of (1512-1585) lord high admiral.
P UNKNOWN, *c*1560-65, hs with Garter insignia, NPG 2918. Attrib HANS EWORTH, 1562, hl with compass, Ashmolean Museum, Oxford. UNKNOWN, *c*1570-75, hs, NMM, Greenwich. UNKNOWN, 1584, tql seated, NPG 900.
D HANS HOLBEIN, jun, *c*1534-35, hs, chalks, Royal Coll.
G M. GHEERAERTS, sen, 'Procession of Knights of Garter 1576', etch, BM.

LINCOLN, Henry de Lacy, 3rd Earl of (1249?-1311) soldier and statesman.
PR W. HOLLAR, monument with effigy formerly in St Paul's Cathedral, etch, for Dugdale, *St Pauls*, 1658, BM.

LINDSAY, Colin, see 3rd Earl of Balcarres.

LINDSAY, John, see 17th Earl of Crawford.

LINDSEY, Montague Bertie, 2nd Earl of (1608?-1666) royalist.
M SAMUEL COOPER, 1649, hs with armour, oval, w/c, The Fitzwilliam Museum, Cambridge; version, 1657, hs, oval, Fitzwilliam Museum.
PR W. FAITHORNE, after Sir A. Vandyck, hl in armour, oval, line, BM, NPG. R. COOPER, after Vandyck, tql with truncheon, stipple, BM, NPG.

LINDSEY, Robert Bertie, 1st Earl of (1582-1642) admiral.
P CORNELIUS JOHNSON, hs, Warwick Castle, Warwicks.
D J. HOUBRAKEN, after C. Johnson, hs, oval, wash, Sutherland Coll, Ashmolean Museum, Oxford.
PR R. VON VOERST, after G. Geldorp, hs, oval, line, BM, NPG.

LINFORD, Thomas, see Lynford.

LIONEL of Antwerp, Duke of Clarence (1338-1368) third son of Edward III.
SC UNKNOWN, *c*1377-88, effigy on tomb chest of Edward III, Westminster Abbey, London.

LISLE, Sir George (*d*1648) royalist.
PR M. VAN DER GUCHT, hl, oval, line, for Ward, *Hist of the Rebellion*, 1713, BM, NPG. G. VERTUE, hs, oval, with Sir C. Lucas, line, for *Loyalists*, BM, NPG.

LISLE, John (1610?-1664) regicide.
PR UNKNOWN, hs, oval, mezz, BM, NPG.

LISLE, Samuel (1683?-1749) bishop of St Asaph.
P UNKNOWN, hs, Wadham College, Oxford.

LISTER, Sir Matthew (1571?-1656) physician.
PR P. VAN SOMER, hl, oval, line, BM, NPG.

LITHGOW, William (1582-1645?) traveller.
PR UNKNOWN, wl in oriental dress, woodcut, for *Adventures*, 1632, BM, NPG. UNKNOWN, wl with servant, copy from woodcut for *Pilgrim's Farewell*, 1618, BM, NPG.

LITTLETON or **LYTTELTON, Edward Littleton, 1st Baron (1589-1645)** lord keeper.
P Possibly after SIR ANTHONY VANDYCK, (type of *c*1640), tql in robes, NPG 473.
PR W. FAITHORNE, after Sir A. Vandyck?, hl with purse of great seal, oval, line, BM, NPG. R. WILLIAMS, tql in robes, mezz, BM, NPG.

LITTLETON or **LYTTELTON, Sir Thomas (1422?-1481)** judge.
PR UNKNOWN, wl kneeling, line, copy from a plate by R. Vaughan, for Coke, *Institutes*, 1684, BM, NPG.

LITTLETON or **LYTTELTON, Sir Thomas (1647?-1710)** speaker of the House of Commons.
PR J. SIMON, after T. Forster, 1700, hl in robes, oval, mezz, BM.

LIVESEY, Sir Michael, 1st Bart (1611-1663?) regicide.
P UNKNOWN, *c*1650, wl in armour, seated, NMM, Greenwich.

LIVINGSTONE, Sir James (d1670), see 1st Earl of Newburgh.

LIVINGSTONE, James (d1674), see 1st Earl of Callander.

LLOYD, Sir Nathaniel (1669-1745) master of Trinity Hall, Cambridge.
P THOMAS GIBSON, 1734, wl seated, All Souls College, Oxford; version, tql, Lincoln College, Oxford. UNKNOWN, wl seated, Trinity Hall, Cambridge.

LLOYD, Richard (1595-1659) royalist divine.
PR UNKNOWN, hl, line, facsimile copy of rare print, pub 1793, BM, NPG.

LLOYD, William (1627-1717) bishop of St Asaph, Lichfield and Worcester.
P UNKNOWN, tql seated, Lambeth Palace, London. UNKNOWN, hs, oval, Corpus Christi College, Oxford.
G UNKNOWN, 'The Seven Bishops Committed to the Tower in 1688', oil, NPG 79.
SC GEORGE BOWER, 1688, silver medal, 'seven bishops', each in medallion, profile, NPG 152A.
PR D.LOGGAN, hl, ad vivum, oval, line, BM, NPG. G.VERTUE, after T.Forster, hl, oval, line, BM, NPG. G.VERTUE, after F.Weideman, 1714, tql seated, line, BM, NPG.

LLOYD, William (1637-1710) nonjuring bishop of Norwich.
P UNKNOWN, tql seated, Bishop's Palace, Peterborough.

LLWYD, Humphrey (1527-1568) Welsh antiquary.
PR R.CLAMP, hl, oval, stipple, for Harding, Biographical Mirrour, 1795, BM, NPG. J.FABER, sen, hl, oval, mezz, BM.

LOBB, Theophilus (1678-1763) medical and religious writer.
PR J.HULETT, after N.Brown, tql seated, line, for J.Greene, Memoirs, 1767, BM, NPG.

LOCKE, John (1632-1704) philosopher.
P JOHN GREENHILL, c1672-76, hs, oval, NPG 3912, engr P. van Gunst, line, BM, NPG. SYLVESTER or SYLVANUS BROUNOWER, c1685, hs, Christ Church, Oxford. HERMAN VERELST, 1689, hl, oval, NPG 3846. MICHAEL DAHL, c1696, hs, oval, NPG 114. After SIR GODFREY KNELLER, 1697, tql seated, Christ Church. By or after SIR G.KNELLER, 1704, hl, oval, Virginia Museum of Fine Arts, Richmond, USA; version, NPG 550.
D S.BROUNOWER, c1685, hs, oval, plumbago, NPG 4061. SIR G.KNELLER, head, chalks, Yale Center for British Art, New Haven, USA.
SC J.M.RYSBRACK, c1733, marble bust, Royal Coll.

LOCKE, Matthew (1630?-1677) musical composer.
P UNKNOWN, hs, Faculty of Music, Oxford.

LOCKEY, Thomas (1602-1679) librarian of the Bodleian Library, Oxford.
P UNKNOWN, tql with book, Bodleian Library, Oxford.

LOCKHART, Sir James, see Lord Lee.

LOCKHART, Philip (1690?-1715) Jacobite.
PR A.JOHNSTON, tql in armour, mezz, BM, NPG. R.GRAVE, hl in armour, line, for Caulfield, Remarkable Persons, 1819, BM, NPG.

LOCKHART of Carnwath, Sir George (1630?-1689) lord president of the court of session.
P Attrib SIR J.B.MEDINA, hl in robes, oval, SNPG L292. UNKNOWN, tql in robes, Parliament Hall, Edinburgh.

LOCKHART of Carnwath, George (1673-1731) Jacobite and author.
P SIR J.B.MEDINA, 1707, tql in armour, SNPG L293.

LOCKHART of Lee, Sir William (1621-1676) soldier and diplomat.

P Attrib SIR J.B.MEDINA, hl in armour, oval, SNPG L290. UNKNOWN, hl in classical dress, Haddo House, Grampian region, Scotland. UNKNOWN, hl in armour, SNPG 941.

LOCKYER, Nicholas (1611-1685) puritan divine.
PR W.HOLLAR, hl, oval, etch, for Baulme for bleeding England and Ireland, 1643, BM, NPG.

LODGE, William (1649-1689) amateur artist and engraver.
P ALEXANDER COMER, c1685, tql with dog, Patrick Allan-Fraser College of Art, on loan to York Art Gallery.
D GEORGE VERTUE, after A.Comer, 1727, hl, sketch, York Art Gallery.
PR A.BANNERMAN, hl, vignette, line, for Walpole, Catalogue of Engravers, 1765, BM, NPG.

LOFTUS, Adam (1533-1605) archbishop of Armagh and Dublin and lord chancellor of Ireland.
P UNKNOWN, tql seated with purse of great seal, Trinity College, Dublin. UNKNOWN, wl in robes, Trinity College.
PR UNKNOWN, tql seated with purse, stipple, BM.

LOFTUS of Ely, Adam Loftus, 1st Viscount (1568?-1643) lord chancellor of Ireland.
P UNKNOWN, 1619, wl in robes, NGI 410.

LOGAN, James (1674-1751) man of science and Penn's agent in America.
P GUSTAVUS HESSELIUS, hl, Historical Society of Pennsylvania, Philadelphia, USA.

LOMBART, Peter (1620?-1681) engraver and portrait painter.
G J.W.COOK, 'Early Masters', 8 medallions of engravers working in England in early 17th century, line, for Walpole, Anecdotes, ed 1828, BM, NPG.

LONG, Sir James (1617-1692) royalist, soldier and antiquary.
P UNKNOWN, hs in armour, oval, NPG 4638.

LONG, Sir Robert (d1673) auditor of the exchequer.
P After SIR PETER LELY, hs, oval, NPG 4637.

LONG, Roger (1680-1770) divine and astronomer.
P BENJAMIN WILSON, 1769, hl, Pembroke College, Cambridge, engr E.Fisher, 1769, mezz, BM, NPG.

LONGESPÉE or LUNGESPÉE, William, see Earl of Salisbury.

LONSDALE, John Lowther, 1st Viscount (1655-1700) first lord of treasury.
P MARY BEALE, 1677?, tql with breastplate, Longleat, Wilts. HYACINTHE RIGAUD, hs, oval, 10 Downing Street (DoE), London.

LOTHIAN, Robert Kerr, 1st Marquess of (1636-1703?) statesman.
P Attrib DAVID SCOUGALL, 1654, hs in armour, SNPG 1414. Attrib SEBASTIANO BOMBELLI, hl in armour, oval, SNPG L211. SIMON VERELST, NPG 1410. UNKNOWN, hs, oval, Edinburgh University.

LOTHIAN, William Kerr, 3rd Earl of (1605?-1675) soldier and statesman.
D W.N.GARDINER, hl in armour, wash, Sutherland Coll, Ashmolean Museum, Oxford. H.MEYER, tql in armour, wash, Sutherland Coll, Ashmolean Museum.
PR H.MEYER, after G.Jamesone, tql in armour, stipple, for Lodge, Portraits, 1819, BM.

LOTHIAN, William Kerr, 2nd Marquess of (1662?-1722) soldier and statesman.
D W.N.GARDINER, after Sir J.B.Medina, hl in armour, wash, Sutherland Coll, Ashmolean Museum, Oxford.

LOUDON, John Campbell, 1st Earl of (1598-1663) lord chancellor of Scotland.
SC ABRAHAM SIMON, silver medal, profile, BM.
PR UNKNOWN, after G.Jamesone, hl, stipple, BM, NPG.

LOVAT, Simon Fraser, 11th Baron (1667?-1747) Jacobite.
P After WILLIAM HOGARTH, 1746, wl seated, NPG 216.
D Attrib W.HOGARTH, 1746, wl seated, Harris Museum and Art Gallery, Preston.
PR W.HOGARTH, 1746, wl seated, etch, BM. J.SIMON, after Le Clare, hl in armour, oval, mezz, BM.

LOVE, Christopher (1618-1651) puritan divine executed for treason.
PR A.CONRADUS, 1651, hl in pulpit, line, BM, NPG. T.CROSS, hl aged 35, oval, for Grace, 1652, BM, NPG. UNKNOWN, hl with book, oval, woodcut, for Christian's Combat, 1664, BM.

LOVE, Nicholas (1608-1682) regicide.
P UNKNOWN, tql with book, Winchester College, Hants.

LOVE, Richard (1596-1661) dean of Ely.
P UNKNOWN, hl, Corpus Christi College, Cambridge, engr M.Tyson, etch, BM, NPG.

LOVEDAY, Robert (fl 1655) translator.
PR W.FAITHORNE, hs, octagonal, line, for Letters, 1659, BM, NPG.

LOVELACE of Hurley, John Lovelace, 3rd Baron (1638?-1693) statesman.
P MARCELLUS LAROON, sen, 1689, wl in peer's robes, Wadham College, Oxford.

LOVELACE, Richard (1618-1658) cavalier and poet.
P UNKNOWN, hs in armour, Dulwich College Gallery, London.
PR W.HOLLAR, hs, oval, etch, BM. R.GAYWOOD, as Orpheus, etch, BM.

LOVELL, Sir Thomas (d1524) speaker of the House of Commons.
SC PIETRO TORRIGIANO, c1518, bronze relief medallion, profile, Westminster Abbey, London; plaster cast, NPG 1565.

LOVETT, Richard (1692-1780) lay clerk of Worcester Cathedral and writer on electricity.
P After JOSEPH WRIGHT, tql seated with instruments, NMM, Greenwich, engr R.Hancock, mezz, BM, NPG.

LOWE, Peter (1550?-1612?) founder of the Faculty of Physicians and Surgeons of Glasgow.
P UNKNOWN, hl, Royal College of Physicians and Surgeons, Glasgow.

LOWER, Sir William (1600?-1662) dramatist.
PR UNKNOWN, hl, oval, for Noble Gratitude, 1659, BM.

LOWIN, John (1576-1659) actor.
P UNKNOWN, 1640, hl, Ashmolean Museum, Oxford.

LOWNDES, William (1652-1724) secretary to the treasury.
P By or after SIR GODFREY KNELLER, hs, oval, HM Treasury, London. RICHARD PHILIPS, wl, Bank of England, London.

LOWTHER, Sir John, see 1st Viscount Lonsdale.

LUCAN, Patrick Sarsfield, titular Earl of (d1693) Jacobite.
P UNKNOWN, (called Earl of Lucan), hs in breastplate, NGI.
PR M.TILLIARD, hs in armour, oval, line, BM, NPG.

LUCAS, Richard (1648-1715) prebendary of Westminster.
PR G. VAN DER GUCHT, hl, oval, line, BM, NPG.

LUCKYN, William, see 1st Viscount Grimston.

LUCY, Sir Thomas (1532-1600) politician.

SC UNKNOWN, c1600, alabaster tomb effigy with wife, St Leonard's Church, Charlecote, Warwicks.

LUCY, Sir Thomas (1585?-1640) statesman.
M WILLIAM LARKIN, hs, oval, Charlecote Park (NT), Warwicks.
G UNKNOWN, family group, c1615-20, Charlecote Park.
SC UNKNOWN, c1640, marble tomb effigy with wife, St Leonard's Church, Charlecote.

LUDLOW, Edmund (1617?-1692) regicide.
PR R.WHITE, hs in armour, oval, line, for Memoirs, 1698, BM, NPG. M. VAN DER GUCHT, hl in armour, oval, line, for Ward, Hist of the Rebellion, 1713, BM, NPG.

LUKE, Sir Samuel (d1670) parliamentarian.
P UNKNOWN, hs, oval, Woburn Abbey, Beds. UNKNOWN, hs, oval, Bedford Town Hall.

LUMLEY, John Lumley, 1st Baron (1533?-1609) collector, genealogist and antiquary.
PR J.FITTLER, hs, oval, pub 1789, line, BM. UNKNOWN, hl from picture at Lumley Castle, lith, BM, NPG. UNKNOWN, head, oval, line, pub 1791, BM.

LUMLEY, Richard, see 2nd Earl of Scarborough.

LUNSFORD, Sir Thomas (1610?-1653?) royalist commander.
PR W.N.GARDINER, hl with breastplate, oval, for Harding, Biographical Mirrour, 1794, BM, NPG.

LUPTON, William (1676-1726) divine.
PR G.VERTUE, 1727, hl, oval, line, for Sermons, 1729, BM, NPG.

LUTWYCHE, Sir Edward (d1709) judge.
PR R.WHITE, after T.Murray, 1703, hl in robes, oval, line, for Reports, 1704, BM, NPG.

LYDGATE, John (1370?-1451) poet.
MS Miniatures appear in various illuminated Ms including: BL Harley Ms 2278, fol 9, Life of St Edmund; BL Harley Ms 4826, Secreta Secretorum; BL Arundel Ms 119, fol 1, Thebes; BL Cotton Augustus A IV, Troy-book; BL Harley Ms 1766, fol 3, Fall of Princes; Bodleian Library Ms Digby 232, Troy Book.

LYE, Edward (1694-1767) Anglo-Saxon and Gothic scholar.
P FRANCES REYNOLDS, tql seated, Bodleian Library, Oxford, engr T.Burke, stiple, pub 1784, NPG.

LYE, Thomas (1621-1684) nonconformist divine.
PR UNKNOWN, hs, octagon, copy from head for Farewell Sermons of Ejected Ministers, 1662, line, pub 1814, BM, NPG.

LYNFORD or LINFORD, Thomas (1650-1724) divine.
P UNKNOWN, Christ's College, Cambridge.

LYON of Carse, Sir Patrick (d1695?) Scottish judge.
PR R.WHITE, hs, oval, line, BM, NPG.

LYON, Patrick, see 1st Earl of Strathmore.

LYSTER, Sir Richard (d1554) chief justice of the court of king's bench.
SC UNKNOWN, tomb effigy, St Michael's Church, Southampton.

LYTE, Thomas (1568?-1638) genealogist.
P UNKNOWN, hs wearing 'Lyte Jewel', Taunton Museum, Somerset.

LYTTELTON, Sir Charles, 3rd Bart (1629-1716) royalist and governor of Jamaica.
PR P.W.TOMKINS, hl in armour, stipple, for Memoirs of Count Grammont, BM, NPG.

LYTTELTON, see LITTLETON.

M

MACCLESFIELD, Charles Gerard, 1st Earl of (1620?-1694) royalist commander.
P WILLIAM DOBSON, hs, Dunedin Public Art Gallery, New Zealand. UNKNOWN, hl, oval, Longleat, Wilts.

MACCLESFIELD, George Parker, 2nd Earl of (1697?-1764) astronomer.
P THOMAS HUDSON, c1753–54, tql seated in peer's robes, Royal Society, London, engr J.Faber, jun, 1754, mezz, BM. BENJAMIN WILSON, 1760, wl seated in robes, Thomas Coram Foundation for Children, London.

MACCLESFIELD, Sir Thomas Parker, 1st Earl of (1667?-1732) lord chancellor.
P After SIR G.KNELLER, tql seated in robes of chief justice, NPG 799, engr G.Vertue, 1712, line, BM, NPG. Studio of SIR G.KNELLER, wl in robes with purse, Royal Courts of Justice (DoE), London. After SIR G.KNELLER, c1718, tql seated in lord chancellor's robes, Althorp, Northants.
G BENJAMIN FERRERS, 'The Court of Chancery', oil, c1725, NPG 798.

MACDOWELL, William (1590-1666) diplomat and professor of philosophy.
PR UNKNOWN, hl, oval, line, BM.

MACE, Thomas (1619?-1709?) musician.
PR W.FAITHORNE, after H.Cooke, hl seated, oval, line, for *Musick's Monument*, 1676, BM, NPG.

MACFARLAN of Macfarlan, Walter (d1767) antiquary.
P J.T.SETON, 1757, hl, oval, SNPG L34.

MACHEN, Thomas (1568-1614) politician.
SC UNKNOWN, c1615, kneeling effigy with wife, Gloucester Cathedral.

MACKENZIE, George (1630-1714), see 1st Earl of Cromartie.

MACKENZIE, Kenneth, see 4th Earl of Seaforth.

MACKENZIE of Rosehaugh, Sir George (1636-1691) king's advocate for Scotland and author.
P SIR GODFREY KNELLER, hl, oval, Parliament Hall, Edinburgh, engr R.White, 1686, line, BM; version, Bodleian Library, Oxford.
PR P.VANDERBANK, hs, oval, line, BM, NPG.

MACKLIN, Charles (1699?-1797) actor and dramatist.
P Attrib JOHAN ZOFFANY, c1775, wl as 'Shylock', National Theatre Coll, London. SAMUEL DE WILDE, c1781, wl as 'McSycophant', NGI 307; version, Garrick Club, London. Attrib JOHN OPIE, c1792, hl, NPG 1319.
D JAMES ROBERTS, 1778, wl as 'Sir Gilbert Wrangle' in Cibber, *The Refusal*, BM, engr Cooke, line, for Bell, *British Theatre*, 1779, BM. J.H.RAMBERG, 1784, wl as 'Shylock', oval, indian-ink wash and pen, BM, engr T.Cook, line, BM.
G J.ZOFFANY, scene from *Merchant of Venice*, oil, c1768–1775, TATE 6005.
SC J.C.LOCHÉE, 1784, Wedgwood medallion, profile, Wedgwood Museum, Barlaston, Stoke-on-Trent, engr J.Corner, line, for *European Mag*, 1787, BM, NPG.

MACLAURIN, Colin (1698-1746) mathematician and scientist.
PR S.FREEMAN, after Percey, hl, oval, stipple, NPG. PAGE, hs, oval, stipple, NPG. TROTTER, hl, stipple, NPG.

MACSPARRAN, James (d1757) divine and writer on America.
P JOHN SMIBERT, 1735, hl, oval, Bowdoin College Museum of Art, Brunswick, Maine, USA.

MACWARD, Robert (1633?-1687) covenanting minister.
PR UNKNOWN, hl with book, stipple, NPG.

MADDEN, Samuel (1686-1765) miscellaneous writer and philanthropist.
P THOMAS HICKEY, hs, NGI 397.
SC JOHN VAN NOST, 1751?, marble bust, Royal Dublin Society.
PR J.BROOKS, tql, mezz, BM, NPG. S.HARDING, after R.Hunter, hl, stipple, for *European Mag*, 1802, BM, NPG. R.PURCELL, after R.Hunter, tql seated, mezz, BM.

MAINWARING, Arthur, see Maynwaring.

MAINWARING, Sir Philip (1589-1661) secretary for Ireland.
P After SIR ANTHONY VANDYCK, c1636, tql seated with 1st Earl of Strafford, Weston Park, Salop.

MAITLAND, John (1616-1682), see 1st Duke of Lauderdale.

MAITLAND, Richard, see 4th Earl of Lauderdale.

MAITLAND of Lethington, William (1528?-1573) secretary to Mary Queen of Scots.
PR C.PICART, after picture at Thirlestane, hs, stipple, for Lodge, *Portraits*, 1818 ed, BM, NPG.

MAITLAND of Thirlestane, John Maitland, 1st Baron (1545?-1595) lord high chancellor of Scotland.
M UNKNOWN, c1590, head, w/c, NPG 2769.
PR R.COOPER, after picture at Thirlestane, hs, stipple, for Lodge, *Portraits*, 1819, BM, NPG.

MAITTAIRE, Michael (1668-1747) schoolmaster and philologist.
PR J.FABER, jun, after B.Dandridge, hl, oval, mezz, BM, NPG. UNKNOWN, hs, oval, line, BM, NPG.

MAKIN, Bathusa (fl 1673) learned lady, tutor to Princess Elizabeth.
PR W.MARSHALL, hl, oval, line, BM, NPG.

MALARD, Michael (fl 1717-1720) French protestant divine in London.
PR UNKNOWN, hl, oval, line, for *French and Protestant Companion*, 1719, BM, NPG.

MALDEN, Daniel (d1736) criminal who escaped twice from Newgate.
PR R.GRAVE, hl with handcuffs, line, for Caulfield, *Remarkable Persons*, 1820, BM, NPG.

MALET, Sir Thomas (1582-1665) judge.
P UNKNOWN, (after type of 1661), hl in robes, NPG 784.

MANCHESTER, Charles Montagu, 1st Duke of (1660?-1722) diplomat.

P SIR GODFREY KNELLER, c1710, hl, the 'Kit-cat Club' portrait, NPG 3216.
PR UNKNOWN, wl in peer's robes, stipple and line, pub 1864, NPG.

MANCHESTER, Edward Montagu, 2nd Earl of (1602-1671) soldier and lord chamberlain.
P SIR PETER LELY, c1661-65, tql with Garter star and key and wand of office, NPG 3678. Studio? of SIR P.LELY, c1661-65, wl in Garter robes, NPG 1838; version, tql, Woburn Abbey, Beds.
SC UNKNOWN, c1643, silver medal, NPG 4359.

MANCHESTER, Sir Henry Montagu, 1st Earl (1563?-1642) judge and statesman.
P UNKNOWN, tql in robes, Middle Temple, London.
PR F.DELARAM, hl in robes, oval, line, BM, NPG. W.FAITHORNE, hs, oval, line, BM, NPG. F.H. VAN HOVE, hs, oval, line, for *Contemplatio Mortis*, ed 1656, BM, NPG.

MANLEY, Thomas (1628-1690) author.
PR T.CROSS, hl aged 21, line, for *Temporis Augustiae*, 1649, BM. T.CROSS, hl, aged 24, line, NPG.

MANLOVE, Timothy (d1699) presbyterian divine and physician.
PR M. VAN DER GUCHT, hl, oval, line, NPG.

MANNERS, Edward, see 3rd Earl of Rutland.

MANNERS, Francis, see 6th Earl of Rutland.

MANNERS, Henry, see 2nd Earl of Rutland.

MANNERS, John (1604-1679), see 8th Earl of Rutland.

MANNERS, John (1638-1711), see 1st Duke of Rutland.

MANNERS, Roger, see 5th Earl of Rutland.

MANNERS, Thomas, see 1st Earl of Rutland.

MANSEL, Sir Robert (1573-1656) admiral.
P Studio of DANIEL MYTENS, c1615, tql, Penrice Castle, Gower, Wales.

MANTON, Thomas (1620-1677) presbyterian divine.
PR R.WHITE, hs, oval, line, for *Sermons*, 1678, BM, NPG. R.WHITE, hs, oval, line, for *Sermons*, 1681, BM, NPG.

MANWOOD, Sir Roger (1525-1592) judge.
D Manner of G.P.HARDING, hs in robes, profile, w/c, NPG 475.
SC UNKNOWN, bust on monument, St Stephen's Church, Hackington, Kent.

MAR, John Erskine, 1st Earl of (d1572) regent of Scotland.
P UNKNOWN, hl, oval, SNPG 653.

MAR, John Erskine, 2nd Earl of (1562?-1634) lord high treasurer of Scotland.
P Attrib ADAM DE COLONE, 1626, hl with Garter George, SNPG 2211.
D 11th EARL OF BUCHAN, pencil and chalk, SNPG 1628.

MAR, John Erskine, 6th Earl of (1675-1732) leader of Jacobite rising of 1715.
P SIR GODFREY KNELLER, 1714, wl in robes of Thistle Knight, with son, SNPG L237.
D Studio of SIR G.KNELLER, pen and wash, SNPG 110.
PR J.SMITH, 1703, hs in armour, oval, mezz, SNPG; 1707 reprint, NPG.

MARCH, John (1640-1692) vicar of Newcastle.
PR J.STURT, hs, oval, line, for *Sermons*, 1693, BM, NPG.

MARCHMONT, Alexander Hume Campbell, 2nd Earl of (1675-1740) statesman.
P UNKNOWN, hl, oval, SNPG 819.

MARCHMONT, Patrick Hume, 1st Earl of (1641-1724) lord chancellor of Scotland.

P WILLIAM AIKMAN, c1720, hl, oval, SNPG L22.
PR JOHN SMITH, after Sir G.Kneller, hl, oval, mezz, BM. R.WHITE, after Sir G.Kneller, 1698, hs, oval, line, BM, NPG.

MARGARET (1282?-1318) queen of Edward I.
SC UNKNOWN, (called Margaret), statue, Lincoln Cathedral.

MARGARET of Anjou (1430-1482) queen consort of Henry VI.
MS UNKNOWN, 15th century, wl seated with king, BL Royal Ms II, 15 EVI, fol 2b. Various scenes in Georges Chastellain, 'Chronicle of the Dukes of Burgundy', Bibliothèque Nationale, Paris.
SC PIETRO DI MARTINO, 1463, gilt bronze medal, profile, V & A.

MARGARET of Denmark (1457?-1486) queen of James III of Scotland.
P UNKNOWN, c1476, wl kneeling with man in armour behind her, part of Bonkill altar-piece, Holyroodhouse, Edinburgh.

MARGARET Tudor (1489-1541) queen of James IV of Scotland.
P DANIEL MYTENS, (after type of c1515-16), wl, Royal Coll, Holyroodhouse, Edinburgh.
MS UNKNOWN, c1503-13 in Bruges, wl kneeling in front of altar, for the *Hours of James IV*, National Library, Vienna.
W UNKNOWN, c1518-28, (called Margaret), wl kneeling, The Vyne (NT), Hants.

MARGARET of York, Duchess of Burgundy (1446-1503) sister of Edward IV.
P Attrib HUGO VAN DER GOES, c1467-68, hl, The Louvre, Paris. UNKNOWN, c1520-30, hs, Society of Antiquaries, London.
D UNKNOWN, hl, Bibliothèque d'Arras, France.
MS UNKNOWN, 15th century, wl with Christ, BL Add Ms 7970, fol iv. Master of Mary of Burgundy, 1477, wl kneeling, register of Guild of St Anne, Royal Coll. Master of Mary of Burgundy, wl, kneeling at prayer, Oxford, Bodleian Library, Ms Douce 365.

MARISCHAL, George Keith, 5th Earl of (1553?-1623) founder of Marischal College, Aberdeen.
P UNKNOWN, hl, oval, Marischal College, Aberdeen.

MARISCHAL, George Keith, 10th Earl of (1693?-1778) Jacobite and favourite of Frederick the Great.
P PIERRE PARROCEL, c1715-20, wl in armour, Marischal College, Aberdeen; version, tql, SNPG 311, engr J.Simon, mezz, BM. Attrib PLACIDO COSTANZI, wl in armour with black page, NPG 552.
SC UNKNOWN, hl, relief ivory medallion, BM.

MARISCHAL, William Keith, 7th Earl of (1614?-1661) leader of the Covenanters.
P GEORGE JAMESONE, 1636, hl, SNPG 994.

MARKHAM, Gervase (1568?-1637) author.
PR UNKNOWN, hl, oval, line, in title of *Perfect Horseman*, 1655, BM, NPG. B.READING, hl, enlarged from above, line, BM, NPG.

MARKLAND, Jeremiah (1693-1776) classical scholar.
PR J.CALDWALL, hs, oval, stipple, for Nichols, *Literary Anecdotes*, vol 4, BM, NPG.

MARLBOROUGH, James Ley, 1st Earl of (1550-1629) judge.
P UNKNOWN, (after type of c1615), hs in robes, NPG 1258. DANIEL MYTENS, 1627, wl with wand of office, Harvard University Law School, Cambridge, Mass, USA.
SC UNKNOWN, 1629, tomb effigy with wife, All Saints' Church, Westbury, Wilts.

MARLBOROUGH, John Churchill, 1st Duke of (1650-1722) soldier.
P Attrib JOHN CLOSTERMAN, after J.Riley, c1685-90, hl in armour, oval, NPG 501; versions, hl, Althorp, Northants; tql,

Blenheim, Oxon. Attrib SIR GODFREY KNELLER, 1690, hl in armour, Althorp; version, c1701, tql with ribbon and Garter star, NPG 553. J.CLOSTERMAN, c1705, wl on horseback with angels, Chelsea Hospital, London. ADRIAN VAN DER WERFF, c1705, tql in armour, Pitti Palace, Florence. SIR G.KNELLER, c1706, wl on horseback with cherubs, NPG 902. ISAAC WHOOD, c1711, wl seated with General Armstrong, Blenheim. SIR G.KNELLER, 1712, wl in armour, Althorp. LOUIS LAGUERRE, murals of victories, Blenheim.

M CHRISTIAN RICHTER, hs, oval, Buccleuch Estates, Selkirk, Scotland. C.F.ZINCKE, hs, oval, Althorp.

SC Studio of J.M.RYSBRACK, c1730, marble bust, NPG 2005; version, Bodleian Library, Oxford. J.M.RYSBRACK, 1732, monumental statue with wife, Blenheim Chapel. Various medals, BM.

MARLBOROUGH, Sarah Churchill, née Jennings, Duchess of (1660-1744) friend of Queen Anne.

P Attrib SIMON VERELST, c1680, hl with bouquet, Althorp, Northants. SIR GODFREY KNELLER, 1691, tql seated with Lady Fitzhardinge, Blenheim, Oxon. SIR G.KNELLER, c1700, tql seated with key, Althorp; version, NPG 3634. SIR G.KNELLER, 1705, tql, Petworth (NT), W Sussex. Attrib SIR G.KNELLER, after 1722, tql in black as widow, Blenheim.

M CHARLES BOIT, hs, oval, enamel, Althorp. BERNARD LENS, 1720, wl, V & A. C.F.ZINCKE, hs, oval, Althorp.

SC J.M.RYSBRACK, 1732, monumental statue with Duke, Blenheim Chapel.

MARSH, Narcissus (1638-1713) archbishop of Armagh.

P UNKNOWN, 1704, wl seated with book, Exeter College, Oxford. UNKNOWN, tql seated, Trinity College, Dublin.

MARSHALL, William (d1219), see 1st Earl of Pembroke.

MARSHALL, William (d1231), see 2nd Earl of Pembroke.

MARSHALL, Thomas (1621-1685) dean of Gloucester.

P UNKNOWN, hs, Lincoln College, Oxford.

MARSHALL, William (fl 1640) engraver.

G J.W.COOK, 'Early Masters', 8 medallions of engravers working in England in early 17th century, line, for Walpole, *Anecdotes*, ed 1828, BM, NPG.

MARSHAM, Sir John, 1st Bart (1602-1685) writer on chronology.

PR R.WHITE, hs, oval, line, for *Chronicus Canon*, 1672, BM.

MARSTON, Charles Boyle, 1st Baron, see 4th Earl of Orrery.

MARTEN, Sir Henry (1562?-1641) judge of the admiralty and prerogative courts.

P UNKNOWN, hs, oval, Trinity Hall, Cambridge, engr J.J. van der Berghe, 1798, stipple, for Adolphus, *British Cabinet*, BM, NPG.

MARTEN, Henry (1602-1680) regicide.

P SIR PETER LELY, c1647-50, hs, oval, NPG 5176.

MARTIN, Gregory (d1582) biblical translator and tutor to sons of 4th Duke of Norfolk.

P UNKNOWN, 1573, hs, Arundel Castle, W Sussex. UNKNOWN, St John's College, Oxford.

MARTIN, Sir Richard (1534-1617) master of the mint and lord mayor of London.

SC STEPHEN OF HOLLAND, 1562, silver medal, profile, BM.

PR B.WRIGHT, wl in niche, line, cut from sheet titled 'The armes of all the Cheife corporations of England', 1600, BM.

MARTIN, Richard (1570-1618) recorder of London.

PR S.PASSE, 1620, hl, oval, line, BM.

MARTIN, Thomas (1697-1771) antiquary.

PR P.S.LAMBORN, after T.Bardwell, hl with vase, etch, for *Hist of Thetford*, 1779, BM, NPG. T.COOK, after J.Fenn, head, profile, etch, BM, NPG.

MARVELL, Andrew (1621-1678) poet and political satirist.

P UNKNOWN, 1655-60, hs, oval, NPG 554. UNKNOWN, c1660, hs, Hull Museums.

PR UNKNOWN, hl, octagonal, line, for *Poems*, 1681, BM, NPG.

MARY I (1516-1558) queen of England and Ireland.

P MASTER JOHN, 1544, tql, NPG 428. ANTONIO MOR, 1554, tql seated, Prado, Madrid; versions, Isabella Stewart Gardner Museum, Boston, USA; Castle Ashby, Northants. HANS EWORTH, 1554, tql, Society of Antiquaries, London. H.EWORTH, 1554, hl with flower, NPG 4861. UNKNOWN, 1557, wl with Philip, Woburn Abbey, Beds.

D HANS HOLBEIN, jun, c1536, (called Princess Mary), hl, chalks, Royal Coll.

M H.EWORTH, hl, oval, Buccleuch Estates, Selkirk, Scotland.

G UNKNOWN, 'The Family of Henry VIII', oil, c1545, Royal Coll.

SC JACOPO DA TREZZO, c1555, medal, hl profile, BM; electrotype, NPG 446.

MARY II (1662-1694) queen of England, Scotland and Ireland.

P SIR PETER LELY, c1672, tql as Diana as child, Royal Coll. SIR P.LELY, c1677, tql seated when Princess of Orange, Royal Coll. GASPAR NETSCHER, before 1684, hs, oval, Althorp, Northants; version, wl seated with parrot, Rijksmuseum, Amsterdam. WILLEM WISSING, c1685, tql seated in landscape, Royal Coll. W.WISSING, c1685, tql seated with palace in background, Royal Coll; copy, NPG 606. JAN VAN DER VAART, 1688, hl with Fontagne head-dress, Audley End (DoE), Essex. J. VAN DER VAART, c1689, hs with ermine cape, Petworth (NT), W Sussex. By or after J. VAN DER VAART, c1689, tql seated with crown and sceptre on table, NPG 197. SIR GODFREY KNELLER, 1690, wl in state robes, Royal Coll.

G SIR PETER LELY and BENEDETTO GENNARI, James II and family, oil, c1670-80, Royal Coll.

SC R. VER HULST, 1683, bust, Mauritshuis, The Hague. UNKNOWN, c1690, medal, profile bust, BM. UNKNOWN, 1694, funeral effigy, Westminster Abbey, London.

PR W.FAITHORNE, jun, after J. van der Vaart, 1698, tql seated, mezz, BM, NPG. P. VAN GUNST, after J.H.Brandon, hl, life-size, oval, line, BM, NPG.

MARY of Guise (1515-1560) queen of James V of Scotland.

P UNKNOWN, 16th century, hl with husband, Hardwick Hall (NT), Derbys.

D JANET (FRANCOIS CLOUET), head, chalks, BM, Cracherode G.g. 1-420.

MARY of Modena (1658-1718) queen of James II of England.

P SIR PETER LELY, tql seated with spaniel, Althorp, Northants; version, c1675-80, with lamb, Royal Coll. Attrib SIR P.LELY, c1677, wl with orange tree in vase, Royal Coll. SIMON VERELST, c1675, tql in male riding habit, Royal Coll. WILLEM WISSING, c1685, tql seated with dog, NPG 214; version, 1687, with cockatoo, SNPG 976. BENEDETTO GENNARI, c1692, tql, The Prado, Madrid.

SC Various medals, BM.

PR J.SMITH, after Sir Godfrey Kneller, hl, oval, mezz, BM, NPG. J.SMITH, after N. de Largillière, hl, oval, mezz, BM, NPG.

MARY, Princess of Orange (1631-1660) daughter of Charles I.

P CORNELIUS JOHNSON, 1639, wl, NPG 5105. Studio of VANDYCK, c1641, wl, DoE, Embassy, The Hague, Netherlands. SIR ANTHONY VANDYCK, 1641, wl with William II, The

Rijksmuseum, Amsterdam. GERARD HONTHORST, *c*1647, hl, oval, Ashdown House (NT), Oxon. G.HONTHORST, *c*1647, wl with flower, Rijksmuseum. G.HONTHORST, 1652, wl with infant William III, Raadhuis, Breda, The Netherlands. ADRIAN HANNEMAN, *c*1650–55, tql, Syon House, Brentford, Middx. A.HANNEMAN, *c*1655, tql with feathered turban, Royal Coll; version, *c*1664, tql with black page, Mauritshuis, The Hague. A.HANNEMAN, 1659, hl, SNPG 1308; version, tql oval, Holkham Hall, Norfolk. A.HANNEMAN, 1660, tql with pearls, Royal Coll. BARTHOLOMEW VAN DER HELST, *c*1655–60, wl seated, Rijksmuseum.

G SIR A.VANDYCK, the three eldest children of Charles I, oil, 1634?, Galleria Sabauda, Turin. SIR A.VANDYCK, the three eldest children of Charles I, oil, 1635, Royal Coll. SIR A.VANDYCK, the five eldest children of Charles I, oil, 1637, Royal Coll.

MARY, Queen of Scots (1542-1587) third child of James V of Scotland and Mary of Guise.

P UNKNOWN, (after miniature type of *c*1660–65), tql with Darnley, Hardwick Hall (NT), Derbys. UNKNOWN, 1583, hl with James I as boy, Blair Castle, Tayside region, Scotland. After NICHOLAS HILLIARD, *c*1610, wl, so-called 'Sheffield' or 'Oudry' type, Hatfield House, Herts; versions, wl, Hardwick Hall; tql, NPG 429. UNKNOWN, *c*1604–20, wl with crucifix, 'Memorial Portrait', The Trustees of St Mary's College, Blairs, Aberdeen.

D UNKNOWN, 1552, hl, crayon, Musée Condé, Chantilly, France. FRANCOIS CLOUET, *c*1560, hl, Bibliothèque Nationale, Paris. F.CLOUET, *c*1560, hl with white mourning robes, Bibliothèque Nationale.

M UNKNOWN, *c*1560–65, hs, oval, Uffizi, Florence. UNKNOWN, *c*1575–80, head, oval, St Mary's College. NICHOLAS HILLIARD, *c*1578, hs, oval, so-called 'Sheffield' or 'Oudry' type, Royal Coll.

SC CORNELIUS and WILLIAM CURE, *c*1606–16, alabaster tomb effigy, Westminster Abbey, London. JACOPO PRIMAVERA, medal, hs, profile, BM; electrotype, NPG 1918.

MARY Tudor (1496-1533) queen of Louis XII of France and daughter of Henry VII and Elizabeth of York.

P UNKNOWN, (called Mary), hl with 2nd husband, 1st Duke of Suffolk, Woburn Abbey, Beds.

D SCHOOL OF THE CLOUETS, hs, chalks, Bibliothèque Méjanes, Aix-en-Provence, France. UNKNOWN, hs, chalks, Album of the Medicis, Uffizi, Florence. UNKNOWN, hs, chalks, Album Destailleur, Château de Chantilly, France.

MS UNKNOWN, 'her reception and entry into Paris 1514', *Codex Membran*, BL Cotton Ms Vespasian B II, fol 15. Master of Mary of Burgundy, seated at prayer, Vienna, National Library, Cod 1857.

MASCALL, Leonard (*d*1589) author and translator.

PR R.GAYWOOD, head, etch, for *Government of Cattle*, ed 1662, BM.

MASON, John (1503-1566) statesman and chancellor of Oxford University.

SC SIR HENRY CHEERE, *c*1756, bronze bust, All Souls College, Oxford.

MASON, William (fl 1672-1709) stenographer.

PR UNKNOWN, hl, oval, woodcut, for *La Plume Volante*, BM.

MASSEREENE, John Clotworthy, 1st Viscount (*d*1665) Irish presbyterian and landowner.

P UNKNOWN, hl, NPG 2110.

MASSEREENE, Sir John Skeffington, 2nd Viscount (*d*1695) supporter of William of Orange.

P SIR PETER LELY, wl, Arbury Hall, Warwicks.

MASSEY, Sir Edward (1619?-1674?) parliamentary general.

P SIR PETER LELY, *c*1650, wl with breastplate, National Gallery of Canada, Ottawa. UNKNOWN, *c*1648–51, hl, NPG 2107.

PR UNKNOWN, hl in armour, line, for Ricraft, *Survey of England's Champions*, 1647, BM, NPG.

MASSINGER, Philip (1583-1640) dramatist.

PR T.CROSS, hl with oval wreath above head, etch, for *Three New Plays*, 1655, BM, NPG.

MASSUE, Henri de, see 1st Earl of Galway.

MASTER, Sir William (*d*1662) high sheriff of Gloucestershire.

SC Possibly by JASPER LATHAM, tomb effigy, St John the Baptist Church, Cirencester, Glos.

MATHER, Cotton (1663-1728) minister of Boston, New England.

PR P.PELHAM, after P.Pelham, hl, oval, mezz, BM.

MATHER, Increase (1639-1723) president of Harvard College, USA.

P JOHN VANDERSPRIET, 1688, tql seated, Massachusetts Historical Society, Boston, USA, engr R.White, hs, oval, line, NPG.

MATHER, Richard (1596-1669) New England congregational divine.

PR J.FOSTER, *c*1670, hl, woodcut, Massachusetts Historical Society, Boston, USA.

MATILDA (1102-1167) empress, daughter of Henry I.

SC UNKNOWN, *c*1142, impression of her Great Seal affixed to charter relating to lands granted to the Cluniac Priory of St James by Exeter, King's College, Cambridge.

MATILDA, Duchess of Saxony (1156-1189) daughter of Henry II of England.

SC UNKNOWN, tomb effigy, St Blassius Cathedral, Braunschweig, W Germany.

MATON, Robert (1607-1653?) divine.

PR T.CROSS, hs, line, for *Fifth Monarchy*, 1655, BM.

MATTHEW, Tobias or Tobie (1546-1628) archbishop of York.

P UNKNOWN, *c*1610–11, tql with book, Christ Church, Oxford; version, 1616, NPG 1048.

PR R.ELSTRACK, hl with book, oval, line, BM, NPG. UNKNOWN, hl, oval, line, for Boissard, *Bibliotecha Chalcographica*, 1650, BM, NPG.

MATTHEW, Sir Tobias or Tobie (1577-1655) diplomat and writer.

PR J.GAMMON, hs, oval, line, for *Collection of Letters*, 1660, BM, NPG.

MAULE, James, see 4th Earl of Panmure.

MAURICE, Prince (1620-1652) son of Frederick V elector of the Palatine and Elizabeth of Bohemia, daughter of James I.

D T.ATHOW, after William Dobson, hs in breastplate, wash, Sutherland Coll, Ashmolean Museum, Oxford.

MAWSON, Mathias (1683-1770) bishop of Ely.

P UNKNOWN, Corpus Christi College, Cambridge.

MAXWELL, William, see 5th Earl of Nithsdale.

MAXWELL, Winifred, see Countess of Nithsdale.

MAY, Baptist (1629-1698) keeper of the privy purse to Charles II.

P UNKNOWN, *c*1650, hs, oval, Ickworth (NT), Suffolk. SIR PETER LELY, 1662, hs, oval, Ickworth. Studio of LELY, *c*1672, tql, Royal Coll.

MAY, Hugh (1622-1684) architect and controller of the works at Windsor Castle.

P SIR PETER LELY, c1675, tql with Lely, Audley End (DoE), Essex.
M SAMUEL COOPER, 1653, hs, oval, w/c, Royal Coll.

MAY, Sir Humphrey (1573-1630) statesman.
P UNKNOWN, wl, Magdalene College, Cambridge; version, tql, Ickworth (NT), Suffolk.

MAY, Thomas (1595-1650) poet and historian.
PR UNKNOWN, hl, with wreath above head, line, for *History of the Parliament*, 1655, BM, NPG.

MAYERNE, Sir Theodore Turquet de (1573-1655) physician and chemist.
P SIR P.P.RUBENS, c1630, tql seated with statue of Aesculapius, The North Carolina Museum of Art, Raleigh, USA; copy, NPG 1652. After SIR PETER LELY, c1650, hs, Royal Coll. UNKNOWN, tql with skull, Royal College of Physicians, London.
D SIR P.P.RUBENS, c1629-30, hl, chalk and wash with oils, BM.
M UNKNOWN, hs, oval, enamel, NPG 3066.
SC NICHOLAS BRIOT, 1625, cast of medal, BM.
PR W.ELDER, hl with skull, aged 82, oval, line, BM. NPG. UNKNOWN, 1636, hl with skull, oval, etch, BM.

MAYNARD, Sir John (1602-1690) lawyer.
P UNKNOWN, c1680, wl in robes, Blickling Hall (NT), Norfolk; versions, tql, Inner Temple, London; hs, oval, NPG 476.

MAYNE, Cuthbert (d1577) priest.
PR D.FOURNIER, hs, 12-sided frame, mezz, NPG.

MAYNWARING or Mainwaring, Arthur (1668-1712) politician and journalist.
P SIR GODFREY KNELLER, c1705-10, hl, the 'Kit-cat Club' portrait, NPG 3217, engr J.Simon, before 1715, mezz, BM, NPG.

MAYNWARING, Everard (1628-1699?) medical writer.
PR R.WHITE, hs, aged 38, oval, line, NPG.

MAYO, Richard (1631?-1695) ejected divine.
P UNKNOWN, hs, oval, Dr Williams's Library, London.

MAYOW, John (1640-1679) physiologist and chemist.
PR W.FAITHORNE?, hl, oval, line, for *Tractatus quinque*, 1674, BM, NPG.

MEAD, Matthew (1630?-1699) independent divine.
PR R.WHITE, 1683, hs, oval, line, BM, NPG. J.NUTTING, 1699, hs, oval, line, NPG.

MEAD, Richard (1673-1754) physician.
P JONATHAN RICHARDSON, c1738, hl, NPG 4157. Attrib WILLIAM HOARE, c1740, tql seated, Royal College of Physicians, London. Studio? of ALLAN RAMSAY, 1740, hl, NPG 15. ARTHUR POND, 1743, hs, profile, Royal College of Physicians. A.RAMSAY, 1747, wl seated, Thomas Coram Foundation for Children, London.
D WILLIAM STUKELEY, hs, Royal College of Physicians. J.RICHARDSON, 1738, head, BM. J.RICHARDSON, 1739, profile head, Ashmolean Museum, Oxford.
M BERNARD LENS, 1726, hl, oval, Royal College of Physicians.
SC PETER SCHEEMAKERS, 1754, marble bust on monument, Westminster Abbey, London. L.F.ROUBILIAC, c1756, marble bust, Royal College of Physicians; terracotta model, BM.

MEARS, John (1695?-1767) Irish presbyterian divine.
PR UNKNOWN, after R.Hunter, hl, oval, mezz, BM, NPG.

MEDINA, Sir John Baptist (1659-1710) portrait painter.
P Self-portrait, c1690-1700, hl, Rhode Island School of Design, Providence, USA. Self-portrait, c1695-1700, hs, Uffizi, Florence. Self-portrait, 1708, hl, oval, Royal College of Surgeons, Edinburgh. Self-portrait, hl, oval, SNPG 1555.

MEDLEY, Henry (d1747) vice-admiral.
SC SIR HENRY CHEERE, 1747, bust on monument, York Minster.
PR J.FABER, jun, after J.Ellys, 1745, tql, mezz, BM, NPG. UNKNOWN, hl, oval, line, NPG.

MEGGOT, Richard (d1692) dean of Winchester.
PR R.WHITE, after Sir G.Kneller, hs, oval, line, BM, NPG. R.WHITE, after Sir G.Kneller, hs, oval on pedestal, line, BM, NPG.

MELCOMBE, George Bubb Dodington, Baron (1691-1762) politician.
PR UNKNOWN, hs, oval, line, for *European Mag*, 1784, BM, NPG.
C GEORGE TOWNSHEND, pencil and ink, 1751–58, wl, NPG 4855/21 and /22.

MELDRUM, Sir John (d1645) parliamentary general.
PR UNKNOWN, hl in armour, line, copy from print in Ricraft, *Survey of England's Champions*, 1647, BM, NPG.

MELFORT, John Drummond, 1st Earl and titular Duke of (1649-1714) secretary of state for Scotland and Jacobite.
P SIR GODFREY KNELLER, wl in robes of Thistle Knight, SNPG 1083.
PR I.BECKETT, after Sir G.Kneller, hl, oval, mezz, BM, NPG. P.VANDERBANK, after Sir G.Kneller, hl in armour, oval, line, BM, NPG.

MELMOTH, William (1666-1743) bencher of Lincoln's Inn and religious writer.
PR N.SCHIAVONETTI, hs, oval, stipple, for *Memoirs of a late Eminent Advocate*, pub 1796, BM, NPG.

MELVILLE, David, see 3rd Earl of Leven.

MELVILLE, George Melville, 1st Earl of (1634?-1707) secretary of state for Scotland.
P SIR J.B.MEDINA, tql in armour, SNPG 1532.
PR R.WHITE, after Sir J.B.Medina, hs, oval, line, BM, NPG.

MENNES, Sir John (1599-1671) admiral.
P SIR ANTHONY VANDYCK, c1640, tql with breastplate, Clarendon Coll on loan to Plymouth Art Gallery; copies, NPG 4097, and NMM, Greenwich.

MENTEITH, Robert (d1660?) Scottish Catholic priest.
PR B.LOCHON, after P.Mignard, hl, oval, line, for *Hist des Troubles de la Grand Bretagne*, 1661, BM, NPG, V & A.

MERCIER, Philip (1689-1760) portrait painter.
PR J.FABER, jun, after P.Mercier, 1735, hl with easel and palette, mezz, BM, NPG. P.MERCIER, wl with family, etch, BM.

MERKE, Thomas (d1409) bishop of Carlisle.
MS UNKNOWN, 15th century French, meeting of Richard II and Henry IV at Flint Castle, 'Histoire du Roy d'Angleterre Richard II', BL Harley Ms 1319, fol 50.

MERRET(T), Christopher (1614-1695) physician.
D G.P.HARDING, hs, oval, w/c, Royal College of Physicians, London.

METCALFE, Theophilus (fl 1650) stenographer.
PR UNKNOWN, hl with book, line, for *Short Writing*, BM, NPG.

METHUEN, John (1650?-1706) lord chancellor of Ireland.
P ADRIEN CARPENTIERS, tql seated in robes, Corsham Court, Wilts. UNKNOWN, hl, oval, Corsham Court.
PR W.HUMPHREY, hl, oval, mezz, pub 1774, BM, NPG.

METHUEN, Sir Paul (1672-1757) diplomat.
P ADRIEN CARPENTIERS, after c1725, tql in Bath robes, Corsham Court, Wilts. JOSEPH HIGHMORE, c1725, hl with Bath star, Corsham. Attrib JOHN RILEY, hl as boy, Corsham. UNKNOWN, hs, oval, Corsham.

M BERNARD LENS, 1723, hs, oval, Corsham. UNKNOWN, hs, oval, Corsham.
SC PETER SCHEEMAKERS, marble bust, Corsham.

MEWS, Peter (1619-1706) bishop of Winchester.
P Attrib MICHAEL DAHL, tql seated with robes of Garter Prelate, St John's College, Oxford. UNKNOWN, tql with Garter robes and hand on helmet, Bishop's Palace, Wells.
M DAVID LOGGAN, c1680, hs, oval, plumbago, NPG 1872. D.LOGGAN, c1680, hs, oval, BM, engr Loggan, line, BM, NPG.

MICHELBURN(E), John (1647-1721) governor of Londonderry.
PR UNKNOWN, hs, oval, line, BM.

MICKLETHWAITE, Sir John (1612-1682) physician.
P UNKNOWN, tql, Royal College of Physicians, London.

MIDDLESEX, Charles Sackville, 1st Earl of, see 6th Earl of Dorset.

MIDDLESEX, Lionel Cranfield, 1st Earl of (1575-1645) lord treasurer.
P DANIEL MYTENS, c1620-25, wl in robes, Knole (NT), Kent.
SC NICHOLAS STONE, 1645, tomb effigy with wife, Chapel of St Benedict, Westminster Abbey, London.
PR W.HOLLAR, hs, oval, etch, BM.

MIDDLETON, Conyers (1683-1750) divine.
P J.G.ECCARDT, 1746, hl, NPG 626. UNKNOWN, c1730-35, hl with book, University Library, Cambridge.
SC GIOVANNI POZZO, 1724, medal, profile bust, BM.

MIDDLETON, Sir Hugh, see Myddelton.

MIDDLETON or MYDDELTON, Jane, née Needham (1645-1692) court beauty.
P SIR PETER LELY, c1663-65, tql with cornucopia, Royal Coll. SIR P.LELY, c1665, tql with glass jar, Althorp, Northants. SIR P.LELY, c1670, wl, Goodwood House, W Sussex.
PR R.TOMPSON, after Sir P.Lely, tql seated on ground, mezz, BM, NPG.

MIDDLETON, John Middleton, 1st Earl of (1608-1673) soldier.
P SIR GODFREY KNELLER, tql in armour, Castle Ward (NT), Co Down, N Ireland.

MIDDLETON, Richard (d1641) divine.
PR R.ELSTRACK, head, oval, line, for Heavenly Progress, 1617, BM, NPG.

MIDDLETON, Sir Thomas (1550-1631), see Myddelton.

MIDDLETON, Thomas (1570?-1627) dramatist.
PR UNKNOWN, hl crowned with laurel, oval, line, for Two New Playes, 1657, BM.

MILBOURNE, Luke (1649-1720) poet.
P UNKNOWN, hs, oval, Exeter College, Oxford.

MILDMAY, Sir Anthony (d1617) ambassador.
P UNKNOWN, c1615, wl, Emmanuel College, Cambridge.
M Attrib NICHOLAS HILLIARD, c1585, wl with breastplate, w/c, Cleveland Museum of Art, Ohio, USA.

MILDMAY, Sir Walter (1520?-1589) chancellor of the exchequer and founder of Emmanuel College, Cambridge.
P UNKNOWN, 1574, hl, Emmanuel College, Cambridge. UNKNOWN, 1579, hl, Emmanuel. UNKNOWN, 1588, wl, Emmanuel.

MILL, Humphrey (fl 1646) verse-writer.
PR UNKNOWN, hs, oval, etch, for Second part of the Night Search, 1646, BM, NPG.

MILL, John (1645-1707) principal of St Edmund Hall, Oxford.
P UNKNOWN, hs, oval, Queen's College, Oxford; copy, St Edmund Hall, Oxford.

MILLER, Joseph (1684-1738) actor.
PR A.MILLER, after C.Stoppelaer, 1739, hl as Teague in Howard, The Committee, mezz, BM.

MILLER, Philip (1691-1771) gardener.
PR C.F.MAILLET, 1787, hl, profile, oval, NPG.

MILLINGTON, Sir Thomas (1628-1704) physician.
P UNKNOWN, hl, Royal College of Physicians, London.

MILLS, John (1670-1736) actor.
P Attrib PETER VAN BLEECK, hs, Garrick Club, London, engr R.Clamp, stipple, for Harding, Biographical Mirror, 1798, BM, NPG.

MILTON, Andrew Fletcher, Lord (1692-1766) lord justice clerk.
P ALLAN RAMSAY, 1748, hl in robes, oval, SNPG L263; version, Edinburgh University.

MILTON, John (1608-1674) poet.
P Attrib CORNELIUS JOHNSON, 1618, hl, oval, Pierpont Morgan Library, New York, USA. UNKNOWN, c1629, hs, oval, the 'Onslow' portrait, NPG 4222.
SC Attrib EDWARD PIERCE, c1660, clay bust, Christ's College, Cambridge; plaster cast, NPG 2102.
PR W.MARSHALL, hl, oval, line, for Poems, 1645, BM, NPG. W.FAITHORNE, 1670, hs, oval, line, for History of England, 1670, BM, NPG 610.

MISAUBIN, John (d1734) physician.
D WILLIAM HOGARTH, hl with Dr Ward, Royal Coll.
PR A.POND, after A.Watteau, wl with syringe, etch, BM.

MOCKET, Thomas (1602-1670?) puritan divine.
PR T.CROSS, hl with book, line, for Christian Advice, 1671, BM, NPG.

MODENA, Mary of, see MARY.

MOFFET, Thomas (1553-1604) physician and author.
MS WILLIAM ROGERS, hl, oval, line, for Insectorum Theatrum, BL Ms Sloane 4014, fol 3.

MOHUN, Charles Mohun, 5th Baron (1677-1712) duellist.
P SIR GODFREY KNELLER, 1707, hl, the 'Kit-cat Club' portrait, NPG 3218.

MOHUN, Michael (1620?-1684) actor.
P UNKNOWN, hl with sword, Knole (NT), Kent, engr E.Harding, jun, for Harding, Biographical Mirror, 1793, BM, NPG.

MOIVRE, Abraham de (1667-1754) mathematician.
P JOSEPH HIGHMORE, 1736, hl, oval, Royal Society, London.
SC J.A.DASSIER, copper medal, BM.

MOLESWORTH, John Molesworth, 2nd Viscount (1679-1726) ambassador.
P ANTHONY LEE, after Rosalba Carriera, tql, Pencarrow House, Cornwall.
SC ANTONIO SELVI, copper and lead medal, BM.

MOLESWORTH, Richard Molesworth, 3rd Viscount (1680-1758) field-marshal.
P ANTHONY LEE, tql in uniform, Pencarrow House, Cornwall, engr J.Brooks, mezz, BM.
SC ANTONIO SELVI, copper medal, BM.

MOLESWORTH, Robert Molesworth, 1st Viscount (1656-1725) statesman.
PR P.PELHAM, after T.Gibson, 1721, hl, oval, mezz, BM, NPG.

MOLYNEUX of Maryborough, Caryll, 3rd Viscount (1621?-1699) royalist.
P GARRETT MORPHEY, hl in armour, NGI.

MOLYNEUX, Sir Thomas, 1st Bart (1661-1733) physician.
SC L.F.ROUBILIAC, 1752, statue on monument, Armagh Cathedral, N Ireland.

MOLYNEUX, William (1656-1698) philosopher.
P ROBERT HOME, c1782, wl seated, Trinity College, Dublin, engr H.Brocas, 1803, hs, stipple, NGI.
PR P.SIMMS, hs, oval, line, for *Treatise on Ireland*, 1725, NPG.

MOMPESSON, Sir Giles (1584-1651?) politician.
SC UNKNOWN, seated effigy with wife, St Mary's Church, Lydiard Tregoze, Wilts.
PR UNKNOWN, satirical print titled 'The description of Giles Mompesson late Knight censured by Parliament the 17th March, 1620', 3 vignettes, line, NPG.

MOMPESSON, William (1639-1709) divine, hero of the plague of Eyam.
P UNKNOWN, hs, Graves Art Gallery, Sheffield.

MONAMY, Peter (1670?-1749) marine painter.
P Attrib WILLIAM HOGARTH and P.MONAMY, wl with Thomas Walker, The Art Institute of Chicago, USA.
PR J.FABER, jun, after T.Stubly, 1731, hl with seascape, mezz, BM, NPG.

MONCK, Christopher, see 2nd Duke of Albemarle.

MONCK, George, see 1st Duke of Albemarle.

MONCK, Nicholas (1610-1661) bishop of Hereford.
P UNKNOWN, hl with book, Bishop's Palace, Hereford.
PR R.DUNKARTON, after D.Loggan, hl, mezz, NPG.

MONMOUTH, Henry Carey, 2nd Earl (1596-1661) translator.
M SAMUEL COOPER, hs, oval, Metropolitan Museum of Art, New York, USA, engr W.Faithorne, line, for *I Ragguagli di Parnasso*, 1656, BM, NPG.
G Attrib PAUL VAN SOMER, family group, oil, c1617, NPG 5246.
PR W.MARSHALL, bust on pedestal, line, for trans of Lenault, *Use of the Passions*, 1649, BM, NPG.

MONMOUTH, Robert Carey, 1st Earl (1560?-1639) soldier and statesman.
G Attrib PAUL VAN SOMER, family group, oil, c1617, NPG 5246.

MONMOUTH and BUCCLEUCH, Ann Scott, Duchess of, see Countess of Buccleuch.

MONMOUTH and BUCCLEUCH, James Scott, Duke of (1649-1685) pretender.
P JACOB HUYSMANS, tql in teens seated as John the Baptist, Buccleuch Estates, Selkirk, Scotland. SIR PETER LELY, c1665–75, wl in Garter robes, Buccleuch Estates. SIR P.LELY, c1665–75, hs in armour, oval, Buccleuch Estates. SIR GODFREY KNELLER, 1678, tql in armour, Buccleuch Estates. SIR G.KNELLER, 1679, wl in Garter robes, Buccleuch Estates. WILLIAM WISSING, 1680s, tql in armour, Palace House, Hants; version, hs, NPG 151, engr J. van der Vaart, hs, oval, mezz, BM, NPG. W.WISSING, c1683, wl in armour with servant? and globe, Clarendon Coll on loan to Palace of Westminster, London. Attrib SIR G.KNELLER, 1680s, wl in Garter robes, Goodwood, W Sussex.
D SAMUEL COOPER, c1660, hs, Royal Coll.
M NICHOLAS DIXON, c1663 or after, hl in armour with Garter ribbon, oval, Buccleuch Estates.

MONNOYER, Jean Baptiste (1634-1699) flower painter.
D SIR GODFREY KNELLER, c1697–99, head, chalks, Witt Coll,

Courtauld Institute of Art, London.
PR G.WHITE, after Sir G.Kneller, 1715, hl, oval, mezz, BM, NPG.

MONRO, Alexander (1697-1767) physician.
PR J.BASIRE, after A.Ramsay, hl, oval, line, for *Works*, 1781, BM, NPG.

MONRO, James (1680-1752) physician.
P J.M.WILLIAMS, 1747, hl, oval, Royal College of Physicians, London.

MONSEY, Messenger (1693-1788) physician.
P MARY and THOMAS BLACK, 1764, tql seated, Royal College of Physicians, London.
D JOHN WOLCOT (PETER PINDAR), crayon, Sir John Soane Museum, London.
PR W.BROMLEY, hl when old, line, for *European Mag*, 1789, BM, NPG.

MONTAGU, Charles (1661-1715), see 1st Earl of Halifax.

MONTAGU, Charles (1660?-1722), see 1st Duke of Manchester.

MONTAGU, Sir Edward (d1557) judge.
P UNKNOWN, tql in robes, Boughton House, Northants (Buccleuch Estates, Selkirk, Scotland). UNKNOWN, wl with book, Boughton. UNKNOWN, wl seated writing, Boughton.

MONTAGU, Edward (1602-1671), see 2nd Earl of Manchester.

MONTAGU, Edward (1625-1672), see 1st Earl of Sandwich.

MONTAGU, Edward (1635-1655) politician.
P UNKNOWN, hl with breastplate, Boughton House, Northants (Buccleuch Estates, Selkirk, Scotland).

MONTAGU, Sir Henry, see 1st Earl of Manchester.

MONTAGU, Sir James (1666-1723) judge and baron of the exchequer.
PR G.VERTUE, after Sir G.Kneller, 1722, hs in robes, oval, line, BM, NPG.

MONTAGU, John (1655?-1728) divine, son of 1st Earl of Sandwich.
P UNKNOWN, hl, oval, Trinity College, Cambridge.

MONTAGU, John Montagu, 2nd Duke of (1690-1749) courtier.
P SIR GODFREY KNELLER, 1699, hl as boy, oval, Boughton House, Northants (Buccleuch Estates, Selkirk, Scotland). Attrib JOHN VERELST, hs in teens, oval, Boughton. UNKNOWN, tql as young man with dog, Boughton. SIR G.KNELLER, 1709, hl, the 'Kit-cat Club' portrait, NPG 3219. SIR G.KNELLER, 1715, tql in breastplate, Petworth (NT), W Sussex. MICHAEL DAHL, 1716, tql in breastplate, Beaulieu Abbey, Hants. Attrib CHARLES JERVAS, 1720s, wl in Garter robes, Boughton; version, hl, Beaulieu. UNKNOWN, 1740s, tql with Garter George, Boughton, engr J.McArdell as after T.Hudson, mezz, BM, NPG; version, Beaulieu. 'Shalk', 1747, wl with cannon, Buccleuch Estates. UNKNOWN, 1740s, wl on horseback, Beaulieu.
G Attrib J.VERELST, tql seated with James O'Hara, 2nd Baron Tyrawley, 1712, oil, NPG 2034. MARCELLUS LAROON, 'Concert at Montagu House, 1736', pen and ink, BM.
SC J.A.DASSIER, medal, BM. L.F.ROUBILIAC, 1752, portrait medallion on monument, St Edmund's Church, Warkton, Northants; terracotta models for monument, Westminster Abbey and V & A.

MONTAGU, Lady Mary Wortley, née Pierrepont (1689-1762) author of the *Letters*.
P After SIR GODFREY KNELLER, (type of c1712–15), hl, Stratfield Saye, Hants. CARLO DELLA RUSCA, 1739, hl with book and skull,

Ankara Embassy (DoE), Turkey.

G J.B.VANMOUR, wl in oriental dress with son and attendants, oil, c1717, NPG 3924.

PR C.WATSON, after Sir G.Kneller, hl seated in turban, oval, stipple, for *Works*, 1803, BM. C.WATSON, hl, oval, stipple, *Works*, 1803, BM, NPG. C.WATSON, after J.Richardson, 1817, hl, oval, stipple, NPG.

MONTAGU, Ralph Montagu, 1st Duke of (1638?-1709) statesman.

P BENEDETTO GENNARI, hl, oval, Boughton House, Northants (Buccleuch Estates, Selkirk, Scotland). Attrib JOHN RILEY, hs, oval, Boughton. Attrib JOHN CLOSTERMAN, hl, Boughton. UNKNOWN, tql seated, Beaulieu Abbey, Hants.

MONTAGU, Sir William (1619?-1706?) judge.

P SIR GODFREY KNELLER, 1680, wl in robes, Law Courts (DoE), London.

MONTAGU of Boughton, Edward Montagu, 1st Baron (1562-1644) royalist.

P JEREMIAH VAN DER EYDEN, wl in robes, Boughton House, Northants (Buccleuch Estates, Selkirk, Scotland); version, tql, Boughton. UNKNOWN, c1615-20, tql as Knight of Bath, Boughton. UNKNOWN, tql as older man, Boughton.

MONTAGU of Boughton, Edward Montagu, 2nd Baron (1616-1684) royalist.

P Attrib ROBERT WALKER, (called 2nd Baron), tql, Boughton House, Northants (Buccleuch Estates, Selkirk, Scotland).

MONTAGUE, Anthony Browne, 1st Viscount (1526-1592) statesman.

P HANS EWORTH, 1569, tql with Garter collar, NPG 842. Attrib LUCAS DE HEERE, wl with Garter collar, Burghley House, Northants.

D G.P.HARDING, after Lucas de Heere, 1848, hs, w/c, NPG 2398.

PR M.GHEERAERTS, sen, 'Procession of Garter Knights, 1576', etch, BM.

MONTAGU(E), James (1568?-1618) bishop of Winchester.

P UNKNOWN, hs, oval, Sidney Sussex College, Cambridge; copy, Bishop's Palace, Wells.

PR S.PASSE, 1617, hl, oval, line, BM, NPG. PASSE, hl, line, for Holland, *Herωologia*, 1620, BM, NPG. UNKNOWN, after Passe, hl, oval, line, for Boissard, *Bibliotheca Chalcographica*, 1650, BM, NPG.

MONTAGU(E), Walter (1603?-1677) royalist and abbot of St Martin near Pontoise, France.

PR W.MARSHALL, wl, line, for *Devout Essays*, 1648, NPG.

MONTAIGNE or **MOUNTAIN, George (1569-1628)** archbishop of York.

P UNKNOWN, 19th century copy of contemporary portrait, hs, Bishopthorpe, York.

SC UNKNOWN, bust on monument, All Saints' Church, Cawood, Yorks.

PR G.YEATS or YATE, c1622, hl with book, oval, line, BM, NPG.

MONTEAGE, Stephen (1623?-1687) merchant and accountant.

PR E. LE DAVIS, hs, oval, line, for *Debtor and Creditor*, 1675, BM, NPG.

MONTFORT, Simon of, see Earl of Leicester.

MONTROSE, James Graham, 1st Marquess and 5th Earl of (1612-1650) royalist.

P Attrib GERARD HONTHORST, tql in armour, SNPG 998. After G.HONTHORST, hl in armour, NPG 4406.

D After W.DOBSON, hl, wash, SNPG 1773.

SC UNKNOWN, medal, BM.

PR R.C.BELL, after G.Jamesone, 1629, hl, line, for Napier, *Memorials of Montrose*, vol ii, 1850, BM. R.COOPER, after

W.Dobson, hl in armour, stipple, for Lodge, *Portraits*, 1819, BM, NPG. J.HOUBRAKEN, hs, oval, line, for Birch, *Heads*, 1740, BM, NPG.

MOORE, Sir Francis (1558-1621) sergeant-at-law.

PR W.FAITHORNE, hl, oval, line, for *Reports*, 1663, BM, NPG.

MOORE, Francis (1657-1715?) astrologer.

PR J.DRAPENTIER, hl, oval, BM.

MOORE, John (1595?-1657) divine.

PR J.DRAPENTIER, hs with book, oval, line, NPG.

MOORE, Sir John (1620-1702) lord mayor of London.

P UNKNOWN, Christ's Hospital, Horsham, Sussex.

SC GRINLING GIBBONS, 1695, statue, Christ's Hospital. SIR WILLIAM WILSON, 1701, statue, Appleby School, Leics.

PR J.MCARDELL, after 'Sir P.Lely', tql seated in lord mayor's robes, mezz, BM, NPG.

MOORE, John (1646-1714) bishop of Norwich and Ely.

P SIR GODFREY KNELLER, 1705, tql seated, Clare College, Cambridge, engr W.Faithorne, mezz, BM, NPG.

MOORE, Sir Jonas (1617-1679) mathematician.

PR T.CROSS, after H.Stone, hl, aged 35, line, for *Arithmetick*, 1650, BM, V & A. UNKNOWN, hs, aged 45, line, for *Arithmetick*, ed 1660, BM, NPG.

MOR or MORE, Sir Anthony (1512?-1576?) portrait painter.

P Self-portrait, tql seated at easel, Uffizi, Florence.

PR UNKNOWN, tql profile at easel, line, NPG.

MORAY, Alexander Stewart, 5th Earl of (1634-1700) secretary of state for Scotland.

PR P.VANDERBANK, after Sir G.Kneller, hs in peer's robes, oval, line, BM, NPG.

MORAY, James Stewart, Earl of (1531?-1570) regent of Scotland.

P UNKNOWN, hs, Hamilton Coll, Holyroodhouse, Edinburgh.

MORDAUNT, Charles, see 3rd Earl of Peterborough.

MORDAUNT, John (d1506?) speaker of the House of Commons.

SC UNKNOWN, c1506, alabaster, tomb effigy with wife, All Saints' Church, Turvey, Beds.

MORDAUNT, John (d1642), see 1st Earl of Peterborough.

MORDAUNT, Sir John (1698-1780) general.

P BARTHOLOMEW DANDRIDGE, 1735, tql with dog, Althorp, Northants.

MORDAUNT of Avalon, John Mordaunt, 1st Viscount (1627-1675) cavalier and conspirator.

SC JOHN BUSHNELL, statue on monument, All Saints' Church, Fulham, London.

PR W.FAITHORNE, hs in armour, oval, line, BM, NPG.

MORDAUNT of Turvey, John Mordaunt, 1st Baron (1490?-1560?) courtier.

SC T.KIRBY, c1560, alabaster effigy, All Saints' Church, Turvey, Beds.

MORDEN, Sir John, 1st Bart (1623-1708) founder of Morden College, Blackheath.

PR Attrib SIR PETER LELY, tql, Morden College, Blackheath, London.

MORE, Alexander (1616-1670) Protestant minister and opponent of Milton.

P UNKNOWN, hl with book, St John's College, Cambridge.

PR L.VISSCHER, after W.Vaillant, hl, oval, line, BM, NPG. UNKNOWN, after C.Passe, hl, line, BM, NPG.

MORE, Anne, née Cresacre (1511-1577) wife of John, only son of Sir Thomas More.
D HANS HOLBEIN, jun, c1526–27, hl, semi-profile, chalks, Royal Coll.
G H.HOLBEIN, 'Thomas More, his father and his household', pen and ink, c1527–28, Kunstmuseum, Basel, Switzerland. ROWLAND LOCKEY, partly after H.Holbein, 'Sir Thomas More and his descendants', oil, c1595–1600, NPG 2765.

MORE, Sir Anthony, see Mor.

MORE, Cresacre (1572-1649) great-grandson and biographer of Sir Thomas More.
G ROWLAND LOCKEY, partly after H.Holbein, 'Sir Thomas More and his descendants', oil, c1595–1600, NPG 2765.

MORE, Sir George (1553-1632) lieutenant of the Tower of London.
P UNKNOWN, 1608, tql, Loseley Park, Surrey.

MORE, Gertrude, real name Helen, (1606-1633) Benedictine nun and great-granddaughter of Sir Thomas More.
PR R.LOCHON, hl in robes, line, for Spiritual Exercises, 1658, BM.

MORE, Henry (1614-1687) Platonist and theologian.
P School of SIR PETER LELY, hs, oval, Royal Society, London.
PR W.FAITHORNE, tql, ad vivum, line, for Opera Theologica, 1675, BM, NPG. D.LOGGAN, hs, ad vivum, oval, line, for Works, 1679, BM, NPG.

MORE, Sir John (1453?-1530) judge and father of Sir Thomas More.
D HANS HOLBEIN, jun, c1526–27, hs, chalks, Royal Coll.
G H.HOLBEIN, 'Thomas More, his father and his household', pen and ink, 1527–28, Kunstmuseum, Basel, Switzerland. ROWLAND LOCKEY, partly after H.Holbein, 'Sir Thomas More and his descendants', oil, c1595–1600, NPG 2765.

MORE, John (1510-1547) son of Sir Thomas More.
D HANS HOLBEIN, jun, c1526–27, hl, chalks, Royal Coll.
G H.HOLBEIN, 'Thomas More, his father and his household', pen and ink, c1527–28, Kunstmuseum, Basel, Switzerland. ROWLAND LOCKEY, partly after H.Holbein, 'Sir Thomas More and his descendants', oil, c1595–1600, NPG 2765.

MORE, John (d1592) divine known as 'Apostle of Norwich'.
PR PASSE, hl, line, for Holland, Herwologia, 1620, BM, NPG. C.AMMON, hs, oval, line, for Boissard, Bibliotheca Chalcographica, 1652, BM, NPG.

MORE, John (1557-1599?) eldest son of Thomas More II.
G ROWLAND LOCKEY, partly after H.Holbein, 'Sir Thomas More and his descendants', oil, c1595–1600, NPG 2765.

MORE, Margaret, see Roper.

MORE, Maria, née Scrope (1534-1607) wife of Thomas More II.
G ROWLAND LOCKEY, partly after H.Holbein, 'Sir Thomas More and his descendants', oil, c1595–1600, NPG 2765.

MORE, Robert (1671-1727?) writing master.
PR W.SHERWIN, hl, oval, line, for General Penman, 1725, BM.

MORE, Sir Thomas (1478-1535) lord chancellor and author.
P HANS HOLBEIN, jun, 1527, hl, Frick Coll, New York; copy, NPG 4358.
D H.HOLBEIN, c1526–27, hs, chalks, Royal Coll (two drawings).
G H.HOLBEIN, 'Thomas More, his father and his household', pen and ink, c1527–28, Kunstmuseum, Basel, Switzerland. ROWLAND LOCKEY, partly after H.Holbein, 'Sir Thomas More and his descendants', oil, c1595–1600, NPG 2765.
SC UNKNOWN, various medals, BM.

MORE, Thomas II (1531-1606) grandson of Sir Thomas More.
G ROWLAND LOCKEY, partly after H.Holbein, jun, 'Sir Thomas More and his descendants', oil, c1595–1600, NPG 2765.

MORETON, William (1641-1715) bishop of Kildare and Meath.
P MICHAEL DAHL, tql with book, Christ Church, Oxford.

MORGAN, Sir Charles (1575?-1642) soldier.
P M.J. VAN MIEREVELDT, 1623, hs in armour, Ashdown House (NT), Oxon.

MORGAN, Sir Henry (1635?-1688) buccaneer and lieutenant-governor of Jamaica.
PR UNKNOWN, hl, line, for Esquemelin, Hist of the Bucaniers, 1684, BM, NPG.

MORGAN, Sylvanus (1620-1693) arms painter and genealogist.
PR R.GAYWOOD, hs, aged 41, oval, etch, for Sphere of Gentry, 1661, BM, NPG.

MORGAN, Sir Thomas (d1679?) parliamentary commander and governor of Jersey.
D C.W.BAMPFYLDE, after Sir A.Vandyck, wl, wash, Sutherland Coll, Ashmolean Museum, Oxford, engr E.Gulston, etch, BM, NPG.

MORICE, Humphrey (1671?-1731) governor of the Bank of England.
P SIR GODFREY KNELLER, hl, oval, Bank of England, London.

MORICE, Sir William (1602-1676) secretary of state to Charles II and theologian.
P Attrib JACOB HUYSMANS, c1666, tql, Antony House (NT), Cornwall. UNKNOWN, hl, oval, Antony House. UNKNOWN, hs, oval, Exeter College, Oxford, engr J.Houbraken, line, for Birch, Heads, 1747, BM, NPG.

MORISON, Robert (1620-1683) professor of botany at Oxford.
P WILLIAM SONMANS, hs, oval, Library of Botanic Gardens, Oxford, engr R.White, line, for Plantarum Historia, 1680, BM, NPG.

MORLAND, Sir Samuel, 1st Bart (1625-1695) diplomat and inventor.
M SAMUEL COOPER, hs, oval, w/c, V & A.
SC GEORGE BOWER, silver medal, BM. JAN ROETTIER, silver medal, BM.
PR W.HOLLAR, after Conzal, 1650, hs, oval, etch, BM. P.LOMBART, after Sir Peter Lely, hl, oval, line, for Hist of the Evangelical Churches of Piemont, 1658, BM, NPG. UNKNOWN, hs, oval, line, for Description of two Arithmetical Instruments, 1673, BM, NPG.

MORLEY, George (1597-1684) bishop of Winchester.
P SIR PETER LELY, c1660, tql seated with book, Christ Church, Oxford; version, hl, Rousham House, Oxon. Studio of SIR P.LELY, c1662, tql with robes of prelate of the Order of the Garter, NPG 2951.
D After SIR P.LELY, (type of c1660), hs, chalks, NPG 491.

MORLEY, Henry Parker, 10th Baron (1476-1556) courtier and author.
D ALBRECHT DÜRER, 1523, hl, pencil, BM.

MORLEY, John (1656-1732) butcher and estate agent.
PR J.SIMON, after Sir G.Kneller, tql with book, mezz, BM, NPG. G.VERTUE, after J.Richardson, 1726, hs, oval, line, BM, NPG.

MORNINGTON, Richard Colley Wellesley, 1st Baron (1690?-1758) politician.
P Attrib JAMES LATHAM, hl, oval, Stratfield Saye House, Hants.

Attrib JONATHAN RICHARDSON, hl, oval, Stratfield Saye.
UNKNOWN, tql seated with book, Stratfield Saye.
M H.P.BONE, hl in peer's robes, oval, Stratfield Saye.
G WILLIAM HOGARTH, family group, oil, *c*1731, Stratfield Saye.

MORRIS, John (1617?-1649) royalist commander.
PR J.STOW, hl in armour, line, BM, NPG.

MORSE, Henry (1595-1645) Jesuit, known as Claxton and Warde.
PR UNKNOWN, *c*1645, hl with dagger in breast, line, NPG.

MORTIMER, Cromwell (d1752) physician.
PR RIGOU, after W.Hogarth, wl seated, satirical print, line, BM.

MORTON, James Douglas, 4th Earl of (d1581) regent of Scotland.
P Attrib ARNOLD VAN BROUNCKHORST, *c*1575, tql, SNPG 1857.
UNKNOWN, 1577, hl, SNPG 839.

MORTON, John (1420?-1500) archbishop of Canterbury and cardinal.
SC UNKNOWN, tomb effigy, Canterbury Cathedral, engr, line, NPG.

MORTON, Richard (1637-1698) physician.
P UNKNOWN, *c*1692, hs, oval, Royal College of Physicians, London.
PR R.WHITE, hs, oval, line, for *Phthisiologia*, 1689, BM, NPG.
W.ELDER, after B.Orchard, hs, oval, line, for *Exercitationes*, 1692, BM, NPG.

MORTON, Thomas (1564?-1659) bishop of Durham.
P UNKNOWN, 1637, wl, St John's College, Cambridge.
UNKNOWN, 1637, hl, St John's College.
PR W.FAITHORNE, hs, oval, line, for J.Barwick, *Funeral Sermon*, 1660, BM, NPG.

MORTON, William Douglas, 7th Earl of (1582?-1648?) lord high treasurer of Scotland.
P UNKNOWN, hl in robes, SNPG 1858.

MORTON, Sir William (d1672) judge.
P Attrib GERARD SOEST, hl in robes, Inner Temple, London.

MOSS, Robert (1666-1729) dean of Ely.
PR G.VERTUE, hs, oval, line, for *Sermons*, 1736, BM, NPG.

MOTTERSHEAD, Joseph (1688-1771) dissenting minister.
PR W.PETHER, after H.Pickering, tql seated, mezz, BM.

MOTTEUX, Peter Anthony (1660-1718) translator and dramatist.
G G.A.PELLEGRINI, wl with his family, pen and ink and wash, BM.

MOUNTAIN, George, see Montaigne.

MOUNTGARRET, Richard Butler, 1st Viscount (d1571) statesman.
SC UNKNOWN, tomb effigy, St Canice's Cathedral, Kilkenny, Eire.

MOUNTNORRIS, Francis Annesley, 1st Viscount Valentia and Baron (1585-1660) statesman.
D UNKNOWN, hl, wash Sutherland Coll, Ashmolean Museum, Oxford.
PR UNKNOWN, hl, stipple, pub 1809, BM, NPG.

MOXON, John (1627-1700) mathematician and printer.
PR F.H. VAN HOVE, hs, oval, line, for *Mathematicks made Easie*, 1692, BM, NPG. UNKNOWN, hs, oval, line, for *Tutor to Astronomy*, 1699, BM, NPG.

MOYLE, Walter (1672-1721) political writer.
PR G.VERTUE, hl, oval, line, for *Works*, 1726, BM, NPG.

MUDGE, Zachariah (1694-1769) divine.
PR J.WATSON, after Sir J.Reynolds, hl, mezz, BM. S.W.REYNOLDS, after Sir J.Reynolds, hl, mezz, BM, NPG.

MUGGLETON, Lodowicke (1609-1698) founder of Muggletonian sect.
P By or after WILLIAM WOOD, *c*1674, hl, NPG 4939 and NPG 557.
SC UNKNOWN, *c*1698, plaster cast of death mask, NPG 1847.
PR G. VAN CASSEEL, hs, oval, line, BM, NPG. UNKNOWN, hl, oval, mezz, BM, NPG.

MULGRAVE, Sir Edmund Sheffield, 1st Earl of (1564?-1646) statesman.
PR R.ELSTRACK, hl, when Lord Sheffield, oval, line, BM, NPG, V & A.

MULGRAVE, Edmund Sheffield, 2nd Earl of (1611?-1658) vice-admiral of Yorkshire and member of Cromwell's council.
PR R.GRAVE, hl, line, NPG.

MUNDEN, Sir John (d1719) admiral.
P MICHAEL DAHL, 1705, tql with breastplate, NMM, Greenwich.

MURCOT, John (1625-1654) puritan divine.
PR W.FAITHORNE, hl with book, oval, line, for *Works*, 1657, BM, NPG.

MURRAY, Andrew, see 1st Baron Balvaird.

MURRAY, Elizabeth, see Duchess of Lauderdale.

MURRAY, Sir James (1655-1708), see Lord Philiphaugh.

MURRAY, James (1690?-1764), see 2nd Duke of Atholl.

MURRAY, John (1635?-1703), see 1st Marquess of Atholl.

MURRAY, John (1659/60-1724), see 1st Duke of Atholl.

MURRAY, Thomas (1663-1734) portrait painter.
P Self-portrait, hs, Uffizi, Florence, engr, mezz, for C.Lasinio, *Ritratti de Pittori nella Galleria di Firenze*, BM, NPG.
PR J.SMITH, after T.Murray, hl, oval, mezz, BM, NPG.

MURRAY, William, see 1st Earl of Dysart.

MURRAY of Gorthy, Sir David (1567-1629) poet.
P UNKNOWN, 1603, hl, SNPG L20.

MYDDELTON or MIDDLETON, Sir Hugh, 1st Bart (1560?-1631) projector of the New River.
P CORNELIUS JOHNSON, 1628, tql, The Baltimore Museum of Art, Maryland, USA; version, Goldsmiths' Company, London.

MYDDELTON, Jane, see Middleton.

MYDDELTON or MIDDLETON, Sir Thomas (1550-1631) lord mayor of London.
P UNKNOWN, tql, Chirk Castle, Clwyd, Wales.

MYDDELTON, Sir Thomas (1586-1666) parliamentarian.
P UNKNOWN, tql in armour, Chirk Castle, Clwyd, Wales, engr W.Bond, stipple, for Yorke, *Royal Tribes of Wales*, 1799, BM.
PR UNKNOWN, hs in armour, oval, line, for Vicar, *England's Worthies*, 1647, BM, NPG.

MYLNE, John (1611-1667) master mason.
P UNKNOWN, hl with bust, SNPG 1536.
D UNKNOWN, tql, pencil, SNPG 105.

MYNGS, Sir Christopher (1625-1666) admiral.
P SIR PETER LELY, tql, NMM, Greenwich.

MYTENS, Daniel (1590?-1647?) portrait-painter.
P Self-portrait, *c*1625, hs, Brukenthal Museum, Sibiu, Romania. Self-portrait, *c*1630, hs, Royal Coll. Self-portrait, *c*1630, hs, Kilkerran House, Strathclyde region, Scotland.

MYTTON, Thomas (1597?-1656) parliamentary commander.
PR UNKNOWN, hs, oval, line, for Vicar, *England's Worthies*, 1647, BM, NPG.

NAGLE, Sir Richard (fl 1689-1691) attorney-general for Ireland.
P WILLIAM DOBSON, NGI 1150.

NALTON, James (1600?-1662) puritan divine.
PR J.CHANTRY, hl with book, oval, line, for *Sermons*, 1677, BM, NPG.

NAPIER, Sir Archibald Napier, 1st Baron (1576-1645) treasurer-depute of Scotland.
P GEORGE JAMESONE, 1637, hl, part of diptych, SNPG 1833. After G.JAMESONE, hl, Parliament Hall, Edinburgh.

NAPIER of Merchiston, John (1550-1617) discoverer of logarithms.
P UNKNOWN, 1616, tql seated, SNPG L147.
PR F.DELARAM, 1620, hl, oval, line, BM.

NAPIER, Richard (1559-1634) astrologer.
P UNKNOWN, hl with book, Ashmolean Museum, Oxford.

NARY, Cornelius (1660-1738) Irish Catholic priest.
PR J.BROOKS, hl with book, mezz, BM. A.MILLER?, tql seated, mezz, BM.

NASH, Richard, 'Beau Nash' (1674-1762) gambler and dandy.
P ADRIEN CARPENTIERS, 1745, hl, oval, Guildhall, Bath. Ascribed to WILLIAM HOARE, hl, oval, Guildhall, Bath. W.HOARE, c1761, hl, Pump Room, Bath; copy, NPG 1537. UNKNOWN, tql with architectural plan, Borough of Royal Tunbridge Wells.
D THOMAS WORLIDGE, 1736, wl, Royal Coll. BENJAMIN MORRIS, c1742, hs, pastel, Royal National Hospital for Rheumatic Diseases, Bath.
M NATHANIEL HONE, 1750, hs, oval, enamel, Holburne Menstrie Museum, Bath.
SC PRINCE HOARE, marble bust, Victoria Art Gallery, Bath. JOSEPH PLURA, 1752, statue, Pump Room. UNKNOWN, plaster bust, Guildhall, Bath.
PR J.FABER, jun, after T.Hudson, 1740, hl, oval, mezz, BM, NPG.

NASH(E), Thomas (1567-1601) author.
PR UNKNOWN, wl in fetters, line, facsimile of rough woodcut in G.Harvey, *Trimming of Thomas Nash*, 1597, BM, NPG.

NASSAU, Henry, see Count of Auverquerque.

NAUNTON, Sir Robert (1563-1635) secretary of state.
PR S.PASSE, tql, line, BM, NPG. R.COOPER, hl, aged 52, stipple, for *Memoirs*, ed Caulfield, 1814, BM, NPG.

NAYLER, James (1617?-1660) Quaker.
PR UNKNOWN, hs with letter B on forehead, line, for Pagit, *Heresiography*, 1654, BM, NPG. UNKNOWN, hl, etch, German satirical plate, BM, NPG. UNKNOWN, wl, two vignettes, etch, NPG.

NEAL, Daniel (1678-1743) dissenting minister and historian.
PR J. VAN DEN BERGHE, after J.Wollaston, hs, oval, stipple, for *Hist of the Puritans*, 1793, BM, NPG. S.F.RAVENET, after J.Wollaston, hl, oval, line, NPG.

NEALE, Thomas (d1699?) master of the royal mint.
SC UNKNOWN, silver-copper medal, profile, BM.

NEILE, Richard (1562-1640) archbishop of York.
P UNKNOWN, hs, St John's College, Cambridge; copy, 19th century, Bishopthorpe Palace, York.

NELSON, Robert (1656?-1715) religious writer.
P SIR GODFREY KNELLER, wl seated, Examination Schools, Oxford, engr G.Vertue, hs, oval, line, for *Address to Persons of Quality*, 1715, BM, NPG.

NESBITT, John (1661-1727) nonconformist divine.
PR G.WHITE, after J.Wollaston, hl, oval, mezz, BM, NPG. J.FABER, sen, 1709, hl, oval, mezz, BM.

NESSE, Christopher (1621-1705) nonconformist minister and author.
PR UNKNOWN, hs, aged 56, oval, line, for *Works*, BM, NPG.

NETHERSOLE, Sir Francis (1587-1659) secretary to Elizabeth of Bohemia.
M PETER OLIVER, 1619, hs, oval, V & A.

NEVE, Cornelius (fl 1637-1664) portrait painter.
P Self-portrait, hl, oval, Ashmolean Museum, Oxford.
G Self-portrait, family group, Petworth (NT), W Sussex.

NEVILLE, Edmund (1605-1647) Jesuit.
G J.G.HEINSCH, after W.P.Kilian, vignette, attacked by men in an open boat, line, NPG.

NEVILL(E), George (1461?-1535?), see 5th Baron Abergavenny.

NEVILL(E), Grey (1681-1723) politician.
PR G.WHITE, after M.Dahl, 1720, hl seated with letter, mezz, BM, NPG.

NEVILL(E), Henry (1525?-1563?), see 5th Earl of Westmorland.

NEVILLE, Sir Henry (1564?-1615) diplomat.
P Attrib BIAGIO REBECCA, tql, Audley End (DoE), Essex. UNKNOWN, c1600, hs, oval, Audley End, engr W.N.Gardiner, stipple, for Harding, *Biographical Mirrour*, 1794, BM, NPG.

NEVILL, Ralph (1364-1425), see 1st Earl of Westmorland.

NEVILL(E), Richard (1428-1471), see Earl of Warwick.

NEVILL(E), Sir Thomas (d1542) speaker of the House of Commons.
SC UNKNOWN, kneeling brass effigy, St Lawrence Church, Mereworth, Kent.

NEVILLE, Thomas (1547?-1614) dean of Canterbury.
P UNKNOWN, wl with architectural background, Trinity College, Cambridge. UNKNOWN, tql, Trinity College. UNKNOWN, hs, Trinity College. UNKNOWN, hl, The Deanery, Canterbury.
SC UNKNOWN, monument, Canterbury Cathedral.

NEWARK, David Leslie, 1st Baron (d1682) royalist general.
P By or after GEORGE JAMESONE, hl, SNPG L267.
D 11th EARL OF BUCHAN, after unknown artist, pencil and chalk, SNPG 1638.
PR C.TIEBOUT, hs in armour, stipple, for Pinkerton, *Iconographia Scotica*, 1795, BM, NPG.

NEWBURGH, James Livingstone, 1st Earl of (d1670) gentleman of the bedchamber to Charles I.

D W.N.GARDINER, hs in armour, oval, wash, Sutherland Coll, Ashmolean Museum, Oxford.

NEWBURY, Jack of, see John Winchcombe.

NEWCASTLE, John Holles, Duke of (1662-1711) statesman.

P Attrib SIR GODFREY KNELLER, wl in Garter robes, Malmö Museum, Sweden.

SC FRANCIS BIRD, after James Gibbs, 1723, marble reclining effigy on monument, Westminster Abbey, London.

NEWCASTLE, Margaret Cavendish, Duchess of (1624?-1674) writer, 2nd wife of 1st Duke of Newcastle.

SC UNKNOWN, c1676, marble tomb effigy, with husband, Westminster Abbey, London.

PR W.GREATBACH, after A.Diepenbeke, wl, line, pub 1846, BM, NPG.

NEWCASTLE, Sir Thomas Pelham-Holles, 1st Duke of (1693-1768) statesman.

P WILLIAM HOARE, c1752, tql seated in Garter robes, Palace of Westminster, London.

D W.HOARE, c1752, hs with Garter ribbon and star, chalks, NPG 757.

G SIR GODFREY KNELLER, tql seated with 7th Earl of Lincoln, the 'Kit-cat Club' portrait, oil, c1721, NPG 3215.

PR J.FABER, jun, after Sir G.Kneller, wl in peer's robes with staff of office, mezz, BM, NPG.

NEWCASTLE, William Cavendish, 1st Duke of (1592-1676) statesman.

P After SIR ANTHONY VANDYCK, wl, Althorp, Northants.

M SAMUEL COOPER, after Sir A.Vandyck, wl, w/c, Buccleuch Estates, Selkirk, Scotland.

SC UNKNOWN, c1676, marble tomb effigy, wl with wife, Westminster Abbey, London.

NEWCOMB, Thomas (1682?-1765?) divine and poet.

PR J.FABER, jun, after H.Hawkins, hl, oval, mezz, for *Poem on the Last Judgment*, 1723, BM.

NEWCOME, Henry (1627-1695) nonconformist minister.

PR R.WHITE, hs, oval, line, BM, NPG. JOHN BULL, hl, line, NPG.

NEWCOME, Peter (1656-1738) divine.

PR G.VERTUE, hs, oval, line, BM, NPG.

NEWCOMEN, Elias (1550?-1614) schoolmaster.

SC UNKNOWN, brass, Stoke Fleming Church, Devon.

NEWCOURT, Richard (d1716) author.

M BERNARD LENS, sen, hs, oval, indian ink, V & A, engr J.Sturt, line, NPG.

NEWDIGATE, Sir Richard, 1st Bart (1602-1678) barrister.

P GERARD SOEST, wl in robes, Arbury Hall, Warwicks.

M UNKNOWN, hs, oval, Arbury.

NEWHALL, Sir Walter Pringle, Lord (1664?-1736) Scottish judge.

P Attrib ANDREW ALLAN, hl in robes, oval, SNPG 2174, engr R.Cooper, as after A.Allan, line, BM. SIR J.B.MEDINA, hs, oval, Parliament Hall, Edinburgh.

NEWHAVEN, William Cheyne, 2nd Viscount (1657-1728) lord-lieutenant of Bucks.

SC WILLIAM WOODMAN, c1728-32, monumental effigy, reclining, Drayton Beauchamp Church, Bucks.

NEWMAN, John (1677?-1741) presbyterian minister.

P UNKNOWN, hl, oval, Dr Williams's Library, London, engr J.Hopwood, stipple, for Wilson, *Dissenting Churches*, BM, NPG.

NEWMAN, Thomas (1692-1758) dissenting minister.

PR J.MCARDELL, after S.Webster, hl, oval, mezz, BM.

NEWPORT, Andrew (1623-1699) royalist.

P School of SIR PETER LELY, hs with breastplate, Weston Park, Salop.

NEWPORT, Francis, see 1st Earl of Bradford.

NEWPORT, Mountjoy Blount, Baron Mountjoy and Earl of (1597?-1666) royalist.

P SIR ANTHONY VANDYCK, wl with breastplate, Yale Center for British Art, New Haven, USA; copy, Weston Park, Salop. After DANIEL MYTENS, wl with stick, Lennoxlove, Lothian region, Scotland.

G SIR A.VANDYCK, c1635-40, hl with Lord Goring and a page, Petworth (NT), W Sussex; copies with minor variations, NPG 762; Knole (NT), Kent.

NEWTE, John (1655?-1716) divine.

PR M. VAN DER GUCHT, after Thomas Foster, hs, oval, line, NPG.

NEWTON, Benjamin (1677-1735) divine.

PR G. VAN DER GUCHT, hl, oval, line, for *Sermons*, 1736, BM, NPG.

NEWTON, Sir Henry (1618-1701), see Puckering.

NEWTON, Sir Henry (1651-1715) British envoy in Tuscany.

SC MASSIMILIANO SOLDANI-BENZI, copper medal, BM, engr B.Fariat, line, NPG.

NEWTON. Sir Isaac (1642-1727) scientist.

P Studio of SIR GODFREY KNELLER, 1689, tql, Royal Coll. G.KNELLER, 1702, hs, oval, NPG 2881. CHARLES JERVAS, c1703, tql seated, Royal Society, London. SIR JAMES THORNHILL, 1710, tql, Trinity College, Cambridge. THOMAS MURRAY, 1718, tql, Trinity College. SIR G.KNELLER, 1720, tql seated, Petworth (NT), W Sussex. JOHN VANDERBANK, 1725, tql seated, Trinity College; version, Royal Society. J.VANDERBANK, 1726, tql seated, Royal Society. UNKNOWN, c1726, tql seated, NPG 558.

SC DAVID LE MARCHAND, c1718, ivory bust, BM. J.M.RYSBRACK?, 1727, plaster death mask, Royal Society and Trinity College; iron cast, NPG 2081. J.M.RYSBRACK, 1731, reclining statue on monument, Westminster Abbey, London. J.M.RYSBRACK, 1733, marble bust, Royal Coll. L.F.ROUBILIAC, 1751, marble bust, Trinity College. L.F.ROUBILIAC, 1755, marble statue, Trinity College.

PR G.B.BLACK, after W.Gandy, jun, hl, aged 64, lith, BM, NPG.

NEWTON, James (1670?-1750) botanist and M.D.

PR UNKNOWN, hs, oval, line, NPG.

NEWTON, John (1622-1678) mathematician and astrologer.

PR UNKNOWN, hl, aged 39, oval, line, NPG.

NEWTON, Richard (1676-1753) educational reformer and divine.

P UNKNOWN (called Newton), hl, oval, Bodleian Library, Oxford.

NICHOLAS, Abraham (1692-1744?) writing-master.

PR G.BICKHAM, hs, oval, line, for *Compleat Writing Master*, 1722, BM. UNKNOWN, hl, line, NPG.

NICHOLAS, Sir Edward (1593-1669) secretary of state to Charles I and Charles II.

P ADRIAEN HANNEMAN, c1652-53, hl, Wilton House, Wilts, engr A.Hertochs, oval, line, BM, NPG. SIR PETER LELY, c1662, tql seated, NPG 1519.

NICHOLLS, Sir Augustine, see Nicolls.

NICHOLS, William (1664-1712) theological writer.

PR M. VAN DER GUCHT, after J.Richardson, hs, oval, line, for *Discourses on the Common Prayer*, 1710, BM, NPG. J.BASIRE, after J.Richardson, hl, oval, line, NPG.

NICOLLS or **NICHOLLS, Sir Augustine (1559-1616)** judge.

SC UNKNOWN, *c*1616, alabaster kneeling effigy, V & A.

NICOLSON, William (1655-1727) divine and antiquary.
P UNKNOWN, hs, Queen's College, Oxford.

NISBET of Dirleton, Sir John (1609?-1687) Scottish judge.
M UNKNOWN, w/c, SNPG L25.
PR R.WHITE, after D.Paton, hs in robes, oval, line, BM, NPG.

NITHSDALE, William Maxwell, 5th Earl of (1676-1744) Jacobite.
P SIR J.B.MEDINA, *c*1699, tql in armour, Traquair House, Borders region, Scotland.

NITHSDALE, Winifred Maxwell, née Herbert, Countess of (d1749) Jacobite and wife of 5th Earl.
P SIR J.B.MEDINA, *c*1699, tql seated with dog, Traquair House, Borders region, Scotland, engr Cook, line, NPG.

NOEL, William (1695-1762) judge.
PR W.GAUCI, after portrait belonging to Lord Berwick, tql in robes, lith, BM, NPG.

NORFOLK, Elizabeth Howard, née Stafford, Duchess of (1494-1558) second wife of 3rd Duke of Norfolk.
SC UNKNOWN, tomb effigy with husband, Framlingham Church, Suffolk.

NORFOLK, Henry Howard, 6th Duke of (1628-1684) courtier.
P ADRIAEN HANNEMAN, 1660, hl with bust, Arundel Castle, W Sussex. SIR GODFREY KNELLER, tql seated in peer's robes, Arundel Castle. SIR PETER LELY, 1677, wl in peer's robes, Arundel Castle. J.M.WRIGHT, tql, Powis Castle (NT), Powys, Wales. THOMAS WYCK, wl on horseback, Arundel Castle. UNKNOWN, tql in armour, Arundel.

NORFOLK, Henry Howard, 7th Duke of (1655-1701) lord-lieutenant of Norfolk, Berkshire and Surrey.
P SIMON VERELST, wl, Arundel Castle, W Sussex. UNKNOWN, tql in armour, Arundel Castle.

NORFOLK, John Howard, 1st Duke of (1430?-1485) admiral of England.
P UNKNOWN, late 16th century, hl with Garter George, Arundel Castle, W Sussex; version, Royal Coll.

NORFOLK, Thomas Howard, 2nd Duke of (1443-1524) warrior.
P UNKNOWN, 16th century, hl profile, Arundel Castle, W Sussex.

NORFOLK, Thomas Howard, 3rd Duke of (1473-1554) soldier and statesman.
P HANS HOLBEIN, jun, *c*1538–39, hl with staff of office, Royal Coll; version, Arundel Castle, W Sussex.
SC UNKNOWN, tomb effigy with wife, Framlingham Church, Suffolk.

NORFOLK, Thomas Howard, 4th Duke of (1536-1572) formed project of marriage with Mary Queen of Scots and executed for treason.
P Attrib JOHN BELKAMP, (after type of *c*1563), hl with Garter George, oval, Knole (NT), Kent. BIAGIO REBECCA, after Steven van der Meulen?, (type of *c*1565), hs, Audley End (DoE), Essex. UNKNOWN, (posthumous), wl, Arundel Castle, W Sussex.
PR R.ELSTRACK, tql under arch, line, BM.

NORMANDY, Robert, Duke of, see ROBERT.

NORRIS, Sir John (1547?-1597) general in Ireland.
P Attrib JOHN BELKAMP, hl, oval, Knole (NT), Kent.
PR UNKNOWN, after 'F.Zuccaro', hs, oval, line, for Thane *Autography*, BM, NPG.

NORRIS, John (1657-1711) divine.
SC SIR HENRY CHEERE, *c*1756, bronze bust, All Souls College, Oxford.

NORRIS, Sir John (1660?-1749) admiral.
P SIR GODFREY KNELLER, 1711, tql, NMM, Greenwich. THOMAS HUDSON, tql, Stockholm Embassy (DoE), Sweden. GEORGE KNAPTON, tql, NMM.
PR T.BURFORD, 1741, tql, *ad vivum*, mezz, BM.

NORTH, Dudley North, 3rd Baron (1581-1666) statesman.
P UNKNOWN, (called 3rd Baron but possibly 4th Baron), hs, The Vyne (NT), Hants, engr, line, pub 1783, BM, NPG.

NORTH, Dudley North, 4th Baron (1602-1677) courtier and essayist.
M JOHN HOSKINS, hs, oval, NPG L152 (41).

NORTH, Sir Dudley (1641-1691) financier and economist.
P UNKNOWN, *c*1680, tql seated, NPG 4709, engr G.Vertue, 1743, hl, oval, line, for R.North, *Lives of the Norths*, 1742–44, BM, NPG.

NORTH, Edward North, 1st Baron (1496?-1564) chancellor of the court of augmentations.
P UNKNOWN, hl with flower, Peterhouse College, Cambridge, engr, stipple, for Harding, *Biographical Mirror*, 1802, BM, NPG.
PR H.MEYER, after Lord Guilford's portrait, tql, stipple, for Lodge, *Portraits*, 1817, BM, NPG.

NORTH, Francis, see 1st Baron Guilford.

NORTH, Sir John (1551?-1597) scholar and soldier.
P UNKNOWN, hs, The Vyne (NT), Hants.

NORTH, John (1645-1683) professor of Greek and master of Trinity College, Cambridge.
P MISS NORTH, after Blenwell, hl, Trinity College, Cambridge.

NORTH, Roger (1653-1734) lawyer and author.
P After SIR PETER LELY, 1680, hl, NPG 766, engr G.Vertue, line, for *Examen*, 1740, BM, NPG.

NORTH, William North, 6th Baron (1678-1734) general.
P SIR GODFREY KNELLER, tql, Phillimore Ives Memorial Gallery, Stellenbosch, S Africa, engr J.Simon, mezz, BM.

NORTHAMPTON, Henry Howard, 1st Earl of (1540-1614) warden of the Cinque ports.
P Unknown follower of H.CUSTODIS, 1594, hl with sphere, Mercers' Company, London. Attrib JOHN BELKAMP, before *c*1605, hs, oval, Knole (NT), Kent. UNKNOWN, after *c*1605, hs with Garter George, Petworth (NT), W Sussex.
G UNKNOWN, 'The Somerset House Conference 1604', oil, 1604, NPG 665.
SC NICHOLAS STONE, kneeling effigy, Trinity Hospital, Greenwich.

NORTHAMPTON, Spencer Compton, 2nd Earl of (1601-1643) courtier.
P CORNELIUS JOHNSON, 1633, hs, Castle Ashby, Northants. C.JOHNSON, 1634, hl, Knole (NT), Kent. HENRY PAERT, after C.Johnson and Sir A.Vandyck, tql in armour, NPG 1521.

NORTHAMPTON, Sir William Parr, Marquess of (1513-1571) brother of Catherine Parr.
D HANS HOLBEIN, jun, hl, chalks, Royal Coll.
SC STEPHEN OF HOLLAND, silver medal, profile bust, BM.

NORTHCOTE, Sir John, 1st Bart (1599-1676) politician.
D ABRAHAM WIVELL, hl, wash, Sutherland Coll, Ashmolean Museum, Oxford, engr A.Wivell, stipple, pub 1817, BM, NPG.

NORTHUMBERLAND, Sir Algernon Percy, 10th Earl of (1602-1668) soldier and statesman.
P SIR ANTHONY VANDYCK, *c*1636-38, wl, Alnwick Castle, Northd. SIR A.VANDYCK, *c*1636-38, hl in armour with anchor

Alnwick Castle.

G SIR A.VANDYCK, tql with 1st wife, Lady Ann Cecil, and daughter, oil, Petworth (NT), W Sussex.

PR W.HOLLAR, wl in armour on horseback, line, BM, NPG.

NORTHUMBERLAND, George Fitzroy, 2nd Duke of (1665-1716) youngest son of Charles II by Barbara Villiers, Duchess of Cleveland.

P School of SIR GODFREY KNELLER, 1714, tql in armour with Garter ribbon and George, Euston Hall, Suffolk.

PR H.GASCAR, wl in Roman dress as boy, mezz, BM, NPG. R.WILLIAMS, after W.Wissing, hl in Garter robes, oval, mezz, BM, NPG.

NORTHUMBERLAND, Sir Henry Percy, 1st Earl of (1342-1408) soldier and statesman.

MS UNKNOWN, early 15th century French, 'The Earl of Northumberland received by Richard II at Conway', BL Harley Ms 1319, fol 37b.

NORTHUMBERLAND, Sir Henry Percy, 9th Earl of (1564-1632) soldier and statesman.

P SIR ANTHONY VANDYCK, tql seated, Petworth (NT), W Sussex. UNKNOWN, wl with Garter George, Petworth; version, Alnwick Castle, Northd.

PR F.DELARAM, hl with hat, oval, line, BM, NPG. F.DELARAM, 1619, hl, oval, line, BM, NPG.

NORTHUMBERLAND, Sir Thomas Percy, 7th Earl of (1528-1572) follower of Mary Queen of Scots beheaded for treason.

P UNKNOWN, 1566, wl kneeling, Petworth (NT), W Sussex. UNKNOWN, wl, Alnwick Castle, Northd.

NORTON, John (b1662) youthful prodigy.

PR W.SHERWIN, hl, line, for *The Scholar's Vade Mecum*, 1674, BM, NPG.

NOTT, Sir Thomas (1606-1681) gentleman usher to Charles II.

PR R.WHITE, 1678, hs, *ad vivum*, line, BM, NPG.

NOTTINGHAM, Charles Howard, 1st Earl of (1536-1624) lord high admiral.

P UNKNOWN, c1600, hl with Garter ribbon, oval, Knole (NT), Kent; version, Royal Coll, engr S.Passe, hl with globe, oval, line, BM, NPG. UNKNOWN, (after type of c1602), wl in Garter robes, NPG 4434, engr William Rogers, wl, line, for Segar, *Honor Military and Civil*, 1602, BM, NPG. DANIEL MYTENS, c1620, wl in Garter robes, NMM, Greenwich.

M NICHOLAS HILLIARD, 1605, hs, oval, NMM.

G M.GHEERAERTS, sen, 'Procession of Garter Knights, 1576', etch, BM. UNKNOWN, 'The Somerset House Conference, 1604', oil, 1604, NPG 665.

PR THOMAS COCKSON, c1596-1603, wl on horseback, line, BM.

NOTTINGHAM, Daniel Finch, 2nd Earl of, see 7th Earl of Winchilsea.

NOTTINGHAM, Heneage Finch, 1st Earl of (1621-1682) lord chancellor.

P After SIR GODFREY KNELLER, (type of c1680?), tql in robes, NPG 1430. J.M.WRIGHT, hl in robes, Longleat, Wilts. Attrib SIR PETER LELY, tql in robes, Gorhambury, Herts.

SC UNKNOWN, 1682, marble tomb effigy, All Saints' Church, Ravenstone, Bucks.

PR R.WHITE, after Sir G.Kneller, hl in robes, oval line, BM, NPG. UNKNOWN, wl in robes, line, for Guillim, *Heraldry*, 1679, BM, NPG.

NOWELL, Alexander (1507?-1602) dean of St Paul's.

P UNKNOWN, tql, Brasenose College, Oxford; version, hl, Bodleian Library, Oxford.

PR PASSE, hl, line, for Holland, *Herwologia*, 1620, BM, NPG. W.HOLLAR, after monument in old St Paul's Cathedral, etch, for Dugdale, *Hist of St Paul's*, 1658, BM, NPG.

NOY(E), Sir William (1577-1634) attorney-general.

P UNKNOWN, after C.Johnson, hs, oval, Exeter College, Oxford.

PR W.FAITHORNE, hs, oval, line, for *Compleat Lawyer*, 1674, BM, NPG. UNKNOWN, after 'C.Johnson', hs, oval, line, for Ward, *Hist of the Rebellion*, 1713, BM, NPG.

NUGENT, Christopher (d1742) Irish general.

P PIETRO LONGHI, wl in uniform, NGI 261.

NYE, Nathaniel (b1624) writer on gunnery.

PR W.HOLLAR, hs, aged 20, oval, etch, for *Art of Gunnery*, 1647, BM, NPG.

O

OATES, Titus (1649-1705) informer.
M LAWRENCE CROSSE, hs, oval, Buccleuch Estates, Selkirk, Scotland.
SC GEORGE BOWER, medal, BM. UNKNOWN, medal, BM.
PR R.TOMPSON, after T.Hawker, hl, oval, mezz, BM, NPG. R.WHITE, hl, *ad vivum*, oval, line for broadside *A Poem Upon Mr Tytus Oates*, 1679, BM, NPG 634. UNKNOWN, wl in pillory, line, pub 1685, BM. UNKNOWN, wl in pillory surrounded by soldiers, woodcut, for broadside, *The Doctor Degraded, or the Reward of Deceit*, pub 1685, BM.

O'BRIEN, Barnabas, see 6th Earl of Thomond.

O'BRIEN, Murrough, see 1st Earl of Inchiquin.

OCCLEVE or **HOCCLEVE, Thomas (1370?-1450?)** poet.
MS UNKNOWN, 15th cent, wl kneeling presenting his book to Henry V, for *De Regimine Principum*, BL Arundel Ms 38, fol 37.

OFFALEY, Lettice Digby, Baroness (1588?-1658) held Geashill Castle against Irish rebels.
P UNKNOWN, hl in mourning, Sherborne Castle, Dorset.

OGILBY or **OGILVIE, John (1580?-1615)** Jesuit.
PR 'M.K.', wl hanging from gibbet being disembowelled, line, NPG.

OGILBY, John (1600-1676) author and printer.
P Attrib SIR PETER LELY, hs, Bodleian Library, Oxford.
PR W.MARSHALL, hl with medallion, oval, line, for trans of *Virgil*, 1649, BM, NPG. W.FAITHORNE, after Sir P.Lely, hl, oval, line, for *Virgil*, 1654, BM, NPG. R.GAYWOOD, sculptured bust, etch, for *Fables of Aesop*, 1672, BM, NPG. P.LOMBART, after Sir P.Lely, hl, octagonal, line, BM, NPG.

OGILVIE, John, see Ogilby.

OGILVY, James (1586-1664), see 1st Earl of Airlie.

OGILVY, James (1615?-1703?), see 2nd Earl of Airlie.

OGILVY, James (1664-1730), see 1st Earl of Seafield.

OGLANDER, Sir John (1585-1655) deputy-governor of the Isle of Wight.
P CORNELIUS JOHNSON, hl, Nunwell House, Isle of Wight.
SC UNKNOWN, oak tomb effigy, St Mary's Church, Brading, Isle of Wight.

OGLE, Sir Chaloner (1681-1750) admiral.
P THOMAS HUDSON, wl, Bowes Museum, Barnard Castle, on loan to St Mary's College, University of Durham. UNKNOWN, c1718, tql, NMM, Greenwich.
SC UNKNOWN, medal, wl, BM.
PR J.BERNIGEROTH, after C.Zincke, hl, oval, line, BM. VAN WERDLEN, after G.Hansson, tql, mezz, BM.

OGLE, Sir John (1569-1640) military commander.
PR W.FAITHORNE, hl, oval, line, for *Commentaries of Sir F.Vere*, 1657, BM, NPG.

OGLE, John (1647?-1685) gamester and buffoon.
PR UNKNOWN, hl, line, BM, NPG. UNKNOWN, hl, line, NPG.

OGLETHORPE, James Edward (1696-1785) general and founder of colony at Georgia.
P UNKNOWN, (called Oglethorpe), hs in armour, oval, Oglethorpe University, Georgia, USA.
G WILLIAM HOGARTH, 'The Comitty of the house of Commons', oil, c1729, NPG 926. Copy after W.VERELST, the Georgia Council, oil, 1734, Rhodes Memorial, Atlanta, Georgia.
SC Attrib JEAN DASSIER, medal, BM.
PR T.BURFORD, tql in armour, mezz, BM. S.IRELAND, wl seated profile, etch, pub 1785, BM, NPG.

O'HARA, James, see 2nd Baron Tyrawley.

OKEY, John (d1662) parliamentary commander and regicide.
PR UNKNOWN, wl on horseback, line, BM. Copy, etch, pub 1812, BM, NPG. UNKNOWN, hs, oval, line, NPG.

OLDCORNE, Edward (1561-1606) Jesuit.
PR G.BOUTTATS, two Jesuits undergoing torture, line, NPG. UNKNOWN, hl with angel above, line, BM, NPG.

OLDENBURG, Henry (1615?-1677) first secretary of the Royal Society.
P JOHN VAN CLEEF, hl with watch, Royal Society, London.

OLDFIELD, Anne (1683-1730) actress.
P Attrib SIR GODFREY KNELLER, hl, Garrick Club, London. Attrib JONATHAN RICHARDSON, tql seated with book in lap, Garrick Club, engr J.Simon, as after J.Richardson, mezz, BM, NPG. UNKNOWN, hs, Garrick Club. UNKNOWN, hl, NPG 431.
PR E.FISHER, after J.Richardson, tql with book, mezz, BM, NPG.

OLDFIELD, Joshua (1656-1729) presbyterian minister.
P UNKNOWN, tql seated, Dr Williams's Library, London, engr, hl, stipple, pub 1814, NPG.

OLDHAM, Hugh (d1519) bishop of Exeter and founder of Manchester grammar school.
P UNKNOWN, tql in robes, Corpus Christi College, Oxford.

OLDHAM, John (1653-1683) poet.
PR M. VAN DER GUCHT, hs, oval, line, for *Works*, 1704, BM, NPG.

OLDHAM, Nathaniel (fl 1740) extravagant collector of curiosities.
G JOSEPH HIGHMORE, 'Mr. Oldham and his guests', oil, c1750, TATE 5864.
PR J.FABER, jun, after J.Highmore, wl with gun and dog, mezz, BM.

OLDYS, William (1696-1761) herald and antiquary.
PR E.BALSTON, hl, oval, stipple, for *European Mag*, pub 1795, BM, NPG.

OLIVER, Isaac (1556-1617) miniature painter.
M Self-portrait, c1590, hl, oval, NPG 4852. Self-portrait, hl with hat, Royal Coll.
PR H.HONDIUS, after I.Oliver, tql with miniature, line, BM, NPG.

OLIVER, Peter (1594-1648) miniature painter.
P ADRIAEN HANNEMAN, c1632-35, hs, Royal Coll.
M Self-portrait, c1625-30, hs, profile, NPG 4853.

OLIVER, William (1695-1764) physician.
P THOMAS HUDSON, hl, National Hospital for Rheumatic Diseases, Bath.
G WILLIAM HOARE, Dr Oliver examining patients, 1742, National Hospital for Rheumatic Diseases.

O'NEILL, Hugh, see 2nd Earl of Tyrone.

O'NEILL, Sir Phelim (1604?-1653) Irish rebel.
PR UNKNOWN, tql, facs of contemporary print, line, BM, NPG.

ONSLOW, Arthur (1691-1768) speaker of the House of Commons.

P HANS HYSING, c1728, wl in robes, Palace of Westminster, London; versions, hl, oval, NPG 1940; and Clandon Park (NT), Surrey. JOSEPH HIGHMORE, 1735, tql in robes, Palace of Westminster.

G SIR JAMES THORNHILL and WILLIAM HOGARTH, House of Commons group, oil, 1730, Clandon Park.

SC Possibly PETER SCHEEMAKERS, tomb effigy, Holy Trinity Church, Guildford, Surrey.

C GEORGE TOWNSHEND, 1st Marquess Townshend, wl, *Townshend Album*, NPG 4855.

ONSLOW, Richard (1528-1571) speaker of the House of Commons.

P UNKNOWN, wl in robes, Clandon Park (NT), Surrey; copy, tql, Palace of Westminster, London.

ONSLOW, Richard Onslow, 1st Baron (1654-1717) speaker of the House of Commons.

P Attrib SIR GODFREY KNELLER, wl in robes, Clandon Park (NT), Surrey. Attrib SIR G.KNELLER, hs, Clandon Park. UNKNOWN, hs in robes, Palace of Westminster, London.

ORFORD, Edward Russell, Earl of (1653-1727) admiral.

P SIR GODFREY KNELLER, c1693-97, wl with breastplate, NMM, Greenwich. SIR G.KNELLER, c1710, tql with globe, NMM. Attrib THOMAS GIBSON, tql, NMM, engr G.Vertue, as after Gibson, 1716, line, BM, NPG.

PR W.ELDER, after W.Wissing, hl in armour, when Admiral Russell, oval, line, NPG. R.WHITE, hl in armour, oval, line, BM. UNKNOWN, hl in armour, oval, mezz, BM, NPG.

ORFORD, Sir Robert Walpole, 1st Earl of (1676-1745) statesman.

P CHARLES JERVAS, c1708-10, tql seated, Houghton Hall, Norfolk. SIR GODFREY KNELLER, c1710-15, hl, the 'Kit-cat Club' portrait, NPG 3220. Attrib JOHN WOOTTON, c1727, tql with dog, Althorp, Northants. J.WOOTTON and JONATHAN RICHARDSON, c1727, wl with hunt, Houghton. HANS HYSING, c1734, wl in robes, King's College, Cambridge. Studio of J.B.VANLOO, 1740, tql in robes, NPG 70; tql seated, Royal Coll. Attrib STEPHEN SLAUGHTER, tql seated with secretary, Henry Legge, The Treasury (DoE), London.

SC J.M.RYSBRACK, c1726-30, marble bust, Houghton. J.M.RYSBRACK, 1738, terracotta bust, NPG 2126. J.A.DASSIER, 1744, copper medal, profile bust, Fitzwilliam Museum, Cambridge.

PR G.BOCKMAN, after T.Gibson, tql with Garter ribbon and George, mezz, BM, NPG. J.HOUBRAKEN, after A.Pond, hl, oval, line, for Birch, *Heads*, 1746, BM, NPG.

ORKNEY, George Hamilton, 1st Earl of (1666-1737) general.

P UNKNOWN, tql in armour with Thistle star, National Army Museum, Camberley, Surrey. UNKNOWN, wl in robes, SNPG 1017.

PR J.HOUBRAKEN, after Maingaud, hs in armour, oval, line, for Birch, *Heads*, 1746, BM.

ORLEANS, Henrietta Anne Stuart, Duchess of (1644-1670) fifth daughter of Charles I, married Philippe, Duke of Orleans.

P SIR PETER LELY, c1660, tql seated, Goodwood, W Sussex. PIERRE MIGNARD, after 1661, hl with spaniel, oval, Versailles; version, NPG 228. P.MIGNARD, wl seated, SNPG 899. HENRI GASCAR, c1661-70, wl as Minerva, Goodwood. ANTOINE MATHIEU, c1661-70, wl with portrait of husband, Versailles. J.M.WRIGHT, c1660-70, tql, Royal Coll. UNKNOWN, wl as Minerva, Royal Coll.

M Attrib JEAN PETITOT, hs, set in agate snuff-box, NPG 1606.

PR C.MELLAN, c1655, hs, line, BM. Copy of MELLAN, hs, oval, line, pub Paris, BM, NPG.

ORMONDE, James Butler, 1st Duke of (1610-1688) lord steward of the household.

P JUSTUS VAN EGMONT, 1648, hl with armour, Claydon House (NT), Bucks. After SIR PETER LELY, c1665, tql in Garter robes, NPG 370; version, hs, oval, Buccleuch Estates, Selkirk, Scotland. J.M.WRIGHT, c1670, wl in Garter robes, Hardwick Hall (NT), Derbys. SIR P.LELY, c1680, wl in armour, Euston Hall, Suffolk; version, tql, Chatsworth, Derbys.

ORMONDE, James Butler, 2nd Duke of (1665-1745) Jacobite leader and statesman.

P SIR GODFREY KNELLER, c1701-2, wl in Garter robes, Examination Schools, Oxford. SIR G.KNELLER, 1713, tql in armour, NGI 485. Attrib MICHAEL DAHL, 1714, hl in armour, NPG 78; version, hl, Deene Park, Northants. Attrib M.DAHL, hs in armour, oval, Badminton House, Avon.

ORMONDE, Piers Butler, 8th Earl of (d1539) statesman and soldier.

SC UNKNOWN, tomb effigy, St Canice's Cathedral, Kilkenny, Eire.

ORMONDE, Thomas Boleyn, Earl of (1477-1539), see Earl of Wiltshire.

ORRERY, Charles Boyle, 4th Earl of (1674-1731) statesman and antagonist of Bentley.

P After CHARLES JERVAS, 1707, tql, NPG 894; version, Christ Church, Oxford, engr B.Baron, 1732, hs, line, BM, NPG.

D THOMAS FORSTER, hs, as boy, plumbago, Christ Church.

ORRERY, Roger Boyle, 1st Earl of (1621-1679) statesman, soldier and dramatist.

PR J.MYNDE, hl in armour, oval, line, BM, NPG.

ORTELIUS, Abraham (1527-1598) map-maker of Antwerp.

SC UNKNOWN, 1578, silver medal, Koninglijk Penningkabinet, The Hague.

PR UNKNOWN, hs, profile, oval, line, for *Theatrum Orbis*, 1603, NPG.

OSBALDESTON, Richard (1690-1764) bishop of Carlisle and London.

P THOMAS HUDSON, 1752, tql seated, Jesus College, Cambridge; version, Fulham Palace, London, engr J.McArdell, mezz, BM.

OSBORN(E), Henry (1698?-1771) admiral.

P Attrib CLAUDE ARNULPHY, c1744, hl with compass, NMM, Greenwich.

OSBORNE, Peregrine, see 2nd Duke of Leeds.

OSBORNE, Thomas, see 1st Duke of Leeds.

OSSORY, Thomas Butler, Earl of (1634-1680) courtier and man of action.

P SIR PETER LELY, c1675-76, tql in armour, Uffizi, Florence; version, c1678, tql in armour with dog, NPG 371.

OTWAY, Thomas (1652-1685) dramatist.

P Attrib JOHN RILEY, (called Otway), hs, Christ Church, Oxford. UNKNOWN, (called Otway), hs, oval, Knole (NT), Kent. UNKNOWN, (called Otway), hl, oval, Winchester College, Hants; similar to J.Houbraken engr, after M.Beale, line, for Birch, *Heads*, 1741, BM.

PR L. DU GUERNIER, hs, oval, line, for *Works*, 1712.

OUGHTRED, William (1575-1660) mathematician.

D WENCESLAUS HOLLAR, hs, profile, BM. G.P.HARDING, after W.Hollar engr, hl, w/c, NPG 2906a.

PR W.HOLLAR, 1644, hl, 'aged 73', *ad vivum*, etch, pub 1646, NPG. Same engr. for *Clavis Mathematicae*, 1647, BM.

OVERALL, John (1560-1619) bishop of Norwich.
PR W.HOLLAR, hs, oval, etch, for Sparrow, *Rationale*, 1657, BM,
NPG. R.WHITE, same picture, line, for *Convocation Book*, 1690,
BM, NPG.

OVERBURY, Sir Thomas (1581-1613) poet and victim of
court intrigue.
P Attrib MARCUS GHEERAERTS, *c*1613, hs, oval, Bodleian Library,
Oxford.
PR R.ELSTRACK, *c*1615, hl writing, line, BM. S.PASSE, hl, oval, line,
BM, NPG.

OVERTON, John (1640-1708?) printseller.
PR UNKNOWN, hl, aged 68, mezz, BM, NPG.

OWEN, Alice (*d*1613) philanthropist.
P CHARLES CRIPPS, after contemporary portrait, tql, The Dame
Alice Owen Foundation, The Worshipful Company of Brewers,
London.

OWEN, James (1654-1706) presbyterian.
PR S.NICHOLLS, hl, aged 51, oval, line, NPG.

OWEN, John (1560?-1622) epigrammist.
PR UNKNOWN, hs, line, for *Epigrams*, 1633, BM. UNKNOWN, hs with
laurel wreath on head, oval, line, for *Epigrams*, 1668, BM, NPG.
UNKNOWN, hs, oval, line, for *Epigrams*, 1669, BM, NPG.

OWEN, Sir John (1600-1666) Welsh royalist.
PR J.CALDWALL, hl in armour, line, for Pennant, *Tour in Wales*, BM,
NPG.

OWEN, John (1616-1683) theologian.
P Attrib JOHN GREENHILL, 1668, hl, National Museum of Wales,
Cardiff; version, unknown artist, NPG 115. UNKNOWN, hs,
Baptist College, Bristol.
PR R.WHITE, hs, oval, line, for *Life*, 1709, BM, NPG. R.WHITE, hl,
oval, line, BM, NPG. UNKNOWN, hs, line, for J.Thane,
Autography, 1788, NPG.

OWEN, Thomas (*d*1598) judge.
SC UNKNOWN, marble tomb effigy, Westminster Abbey, London.

OWTRAM, William (1626-1679) divine and Hebraist.
PR R.WHITE, hs, oval, line, for *Twenty Sermons*, 1697, BM.

OXENDEN, Henry (1609-1670) poet.
PR G.GLOVER, hs, oval, line, for *Religionis Funus*, 1647, BM.

OXFORD, Aubrey de Vere, 10th Earl of (1340?-1400)
statesman.

MS UNKNOWN, wl with wife, in *Codex membran*, BL Ms Nero D VII,
fol 109.

OXFORD, Aubrey de Vere, 20th Earl of (1626-1703)
soldier and statesman.
P SIR GODFREY KNELLER, hl in armour, Antony House (NT),
Cornwall. SIR G.KNELLER, *c*1690, wl in Garter robes, NPG 4941.
Attrib GERARD SOEST, hl in armour, Dulwich College Gallery,
London.

OXFORD, Edward de Vere, 17th Earl of (1550-1604)
courtier, soldier and poet.
P UNKNOWN, (after type of 1575), hl, NPG LIII.

OXFORD, Edward Harley, 2nd Earl of (1689-1741) patron
of the arts and collector.
P MICHAEL DAHL, hl with turban, Society of Antiquaries, London.
M.DAHL, tql in peer's robes, BM. SIR GODFREY KNELLER, *c*1716,
tql, Christ Church, Oxford. Attrib JONATHAN RICHARDSON,
*c*1725?, hl in turban, NPG 1808.
D M.DAHL, head, black chalk, BM.
PR G.VERTUE, after M.Dahl, 1745, wl in peer's robes, line, BM, NPG.
G.VERTUE, after M.Dahl, 1746, hl with medal of Queen Anne,
line, BM, NPG.

OXFORD, Henry de Vere, 18th Earl of (1593-1625) soldier
and statesman.
P UNKNOWN, (after type of *c*1620–25); hs, oval, NPG 950.
UNKNOWN, wl with wand of office, Wilton House, Wilts.
PR J.PAYNE, hl, line, BM. R.VAUGHAN, hl, oval, line, BM, NPG.
UNKNOWN, wl on horseback with Henry, 3rd Earl of
Southampton, line, BM, NPG.

OXFORD, John de Vere, 15th Earl of (1490?-1540)
courtier.
SC Attrib CORNELIUS HARMAN, marble tomb effigy with wife, St
Nicholas Church, Castle Hedingham, Essex.

OXFORD, Robert Harley, 1st Earl of (1661-1724)
politician.
P SIR GODFREY KNELLER, 1714, wl in Garter robes, NPG 4011.
After SIR G.KNELLER, tql in Garter robes, NPG 16. JONATHAN
RICHARDSON, *c*1718, tql, in Garter robes, Christ Church,
Oxford. Attrib J.RICHARDSON, wl seated with Garter star,
Longleat, Wilts.
G PETER ANGELIS, 'Queen Anne and the Knights of the Garter,
1713', oil, *c*1713, NPG 624.

P

PACKE, Sir Christopher (1593?-1682) lord mayor of London.
PR J.BASIRE, hl, oval, line, for J.Nichols, *Leicestershire*, 1795, BM, NPG.

PACKINGTON or PAKINGTON, Sir John (1549-1625) courtier.
P UNKNOWN, *c*1580-90, wl, Kentchurch Court, Hereford.
PR R.CLAMP, from a painting, wl, stipple, for Harding, *Biographical Mirror*, 1794, BM, NPG.

PADDY, Sir William (1554-1634) physician to James I.
P MARCUS GHEERAERTS, *c*1600, wl, St John's College, Oxford.
UNKNOWN, tql seated, St John's College.
SC UNKNOWN, marble bust on monument, St John's College.

PAGE, Sir Francis (1661?-1741) judge.
P UNKNOWN, tql in robes, Inner Temple, London.
SC HENRY SCHEEMAKERS, *c*1730-41, tomb effigy with wife, St Peter's Church, Steeple Aston, Oxon.
PR G.VERTUE, after J.D'Agar, 1720, hl, oval, line, BM, NPG.
G.VERTUE, after J.Richardson, 1733, hl, oval, line, BM, NPG.

PAGET, Charles (1560-1612) Roman Catholic conspirator.
P UNKNOWN, *c*1595, tql, Parham Park, W Sussex.

PAGET, Thomas Catesby Paget, Baron (*d*1742) statesman and author.
PR E.HARDING, hl, oval, stipple, for Adolphus, *British Cabinet*, 1799, BM, NPG.

PAGET, William Paget, 1st Baron (1505-1563) secretary of state and lord privy seal.
P Attrib MASTER OF THE STATTHALTERIN MADONNA, *c*1549?, hl with Garter George, NPG 961. UNKNOWN, *c*1549-54, tql with Garter George, Plàs Newydd (NT), Isle of Anglesey, Gwynedd.

PAISLEY, Claud Hamilton, Baron (1543?-1622) partisan of Mary Queen of Scots.
PR E.HARDING, hs, stipple, for Adolphus, *British Cabinet*, 1800, BM, NPG.

PAKINGTON, Dorothy, Lady (*d*1679) reputed author of 'The Whole Duty of Man'.
PR V.GREEN, hl, mezz, for Nash, *Hist of Worcestershire*, 1781, BM, NPG.

PAKINGTON, John (1549-1625), see Packington.

PAKINGTON, Sir John, 4th Bart (1671-1727) politician.
P THOMAS SHUTER, *c*1723-24, wl, Guildhall, Worcester.
SC JOSEPH ROSE, sen, 1727, tomb effigy on monument, Hampton Lovett Church, Worcs.

PALMER, Barbara, née Villiers, see Duchess of Cleveland.

PALMER, Sir Geoffrey (1598-1670) attorney-general.
P SIR PETER LELY, *c*1660-63, tql seated, Rockingham Castle, Northants; version, NPG 4622. Studio of SIR P.LELY, *c*1660-63, tql in robes, Clarendon Coll on loan to Plymouth Art Gallery, engr R.White, hs, oval, line, BM, NPG.

PALMER, Herbert (1601-1647) puritan divine.
PR UNKNOWN, hl, line, for Clarke, *Lives of Puritan Divines*, NPG.

PALMER, James (1585-1660) divine.
PR T.TROTTER, hs, oval, line, pub 1794, BM, NPG.

PALMER, Roger, see Earl of Castlemaine.

PANMURE, James Maule, 4th Earl of (1659?-1723) Jacobite.
P Attrib JOHN SCOUGALL, SNPG L233.
M DAVID PATON, hl in armour, oval, Lennoxlove, Lothian region, Scotland.

PANTON, Thomas (*d*1685) gambler.
PR UNKNOWN, hl, etch, with incorrect title 'Captain Edward Panton', pub 1813, BM, NPG.

PAPILLON, David (1581-1655?) architect and military engineer.
PR T.CROSS, head, oval, line, for *Arts of Fortification and Assailing*, 1645, BM, NPG.

PAPILLON, Thomas (1623-1702) merchant and politician.
P SIR GODFREY KNELLER, 1698, hl, oval, NPG 5188.

PARKE, Daniel (1669-1710) governor of the Leeward Islands.
PR G.VERTUE, after Sir G.Kneller, hs in armour, oval, line, for French, *Account of Col Parke's Administration*, 1717, BM.

PARKER, George (1651-1743) almanac maker.
PR W.ELDER, hs, oval, line, for *Ephemeris*, 1694, BM, NPG and V & A.
J.NUTTING, hs, oval, line, BM, NPG.

PARKER, George (1697?-1764), see 2nd Earl of Macclesfield.

PARKER, Henry, see 10th Baron Morley.

PARKER, Matthew (1504-1575) archbishop of Canterbury.
P UNKNOWN, hl seated with book, Lambeth Palace, London, engr R.Hogenberg, line, for *De Antiquitate Britannicae Ecclesiae*, 1572, BM, NPG. UNKNOWN, *c*1572, hl with book, Corpus Christi College, Cambridge.

PARKER, Sir Philip (fl 1578-80) country gentleman.
PR J.FABER, jun, 1747, hl, oval, mezz, for *Hist of the House of Yvery*, BM, NPG.

PARKER, Samuel (1681-1730) nonjuror and theological writer.
PR G.VERTUE, after H.Green, hl, oval, line, BM, NPG.

PARKER, Sir Thomas (1667?-1732), see 1st Earl of Macclesfield.

PARKER, Sir Thomas (1695?-1784) chief baron of the exchequer.
PR J.TINNEY, tql seated in robes, mezz, BM, NPG.

PARKHURST, John (1512?-1575) bishop of Norwich.
P UNKNOWN, hs, 'aged 64', Bishop's Palace, Norwich.

PARKINSON, John (1567-1650) apothecary and herbalist.
PR CHRISTOPHER SWITZER, hl with flower, oval, woodcut, for *Paradisus Terrestris*, 1629, BM, NPG. W.MARSHALL, hs with flower, oval, line, for *Theatrum Botanicum*, 1640, BM, NPG.

PARKYNS, Sir Thomas, 2nd Bart (1664-1741) country gentleman and author of a work on wrestling.
PR UNKNOWN, wl, etch, for *The Inn-Play or Cornish Hugg Wrestler*, 1713, NPG.

PARNELL, Thomas (1679-1718) poet.
SC EDWARD SMYTH, marble bust, Trinity College, Dublin.
PR J.HOPWOOD, after Sir G.Kneller, hs, oval, stipple, for *Poems*, BM, NPG. J.DIXON, hl, oval, mezz, pub 1771, BM, NPG.

PARR, Thomas (1483?-1635) centenarian.
P SIR P.P.RUBENS, *c*1620, hs, Atkins Museum of Fine Arts, Kansas City, USA, engr as 'Old Parr' by J.Condé, line for *European Mag*, 1793, BM, NPG. UNKNOWN, *c*1635, tql Ashmolean Museum, Oxford; copy, NPG 385.
PR C. VAN DALEN, *c*1635, hl seated, line, BM, NPG.

PARR, Sir William, see Marquess of Northampton.

PARRY, Edward (d1650) bishop of Killaloe.
PR J.DICKSON, hl with book, line, for *David Restored*, 1660, BM, NPG.

PARRY, Sir Thomas (d1560) controller of the household to Queen Elizabeth.
D HANS HOLBEIN, jun, hs, chalks, Royal Coll.

PARSONS, Humphrey (1676?-1741) lord mayor of London.
PR J.FABER, jun, tql, mezz, BM. 'W.P.', hs, oval, in emblematical plate, BM. UNKNOWN, bust on pedestal with a funeral verse, line, NPG.

PARSONS or **Persons, Robert (1546-1610)** Jesuit missionary.
PR C.GREGORI, hs, oval, line, BM. J.NEEFFS, hl, line, NPG. J.VALDOR, hs, aged 64, line, BM.

PARSONS, Sir William, 1st Bart (1570?-1650) lord justice of Ireland.
PR S.PAUL (S. de Wilde), hs in armour, oval, mezz, pub 1777, BM, NPG.

PARSONS, William (1658-1725?) chronologer.
PR S.GRIBELIN, profile bust, oval, line, BM, NPG. S.GRIBELIN, after P.Berchet, 1696, hs, oval, line, NPG.

PARTRIDGE, John (1644-1715) astrologer and almanack-maker.
PR R.WHITE, hs, oval, line, for *Astrological Vade Mecum*, 1679, BM, NPG. R.WHITE, hs, oval, line, for *Treasury of Physick*, 1682, BM.

PASOR, Mathias (1599-1658) mathematician.
PR 'SaL', 1645, hs, oval, line, NPG.

PASTON, Robert, see 1st Earl of Yarmouth.

PASTON, Sir William (1528-1610) founder of North Walsham grammar school.
P UNKNOWN, tql, Paston Grammar School, N Walsham, Norfolk, engr W.C.Edwards, etch, BM, NPG.

PATE, Richard (1516-1588) educational benefactor.
P UNKNOWN, 1550, hl with book, Corpus Christi College, Cambridge. UNKNOWN, hl, Folk Museum, Gloucester.

PATERSON, William (1658-1719) founder of the Bank of England.
D UNKNOWN, hs, pen and ink, BM, engr, woodcut, BM.

PATON, David (fl 1650-1700) painter.
M Self-portrait, 1683, hs, oval, Uffizi, Florence.

PATRICK, Simon (1626-1707) bishop of Ely.
P SIR PETER LELY, *c*1668, hs, oval, NPG 1500. UNKNOWN, *c*1691, tql seated, Lambeth Palace, London. UNKNOWN, Ely Cathedral; copy, Queen's College, Cambridge.
PR R.WHITE, 1700, hs, *ad vivum*, oval, line, BM, NPG. G. VAN DER GUCHT, 1727, after Sir G.Kneller, hs, oval, line, NPG.

PAUL, William (1678-1716) Jacobite.
PR R.GRAVE, hs, line, for Caulfield, *Remarkable Persons*, 1819, BM, NPG. UNKNOWN, hl, oval, line, NPG.

PAULET or **POULET, Sir Amias (d1538)** soldier.
SC UNKNOWN, tomb effigy with wife, St George's Church, Hinton St George, Somerset.

PAULET or **POULET, Sir Amias (1536?-1588)** keeper of Mary Queen of Scots.
D G.P.HARDING, (after type of *c*1575), hs with Garter George, w/c, NPG 2399.
SC UNKNOWN, alabaster tomb effigy, St George's Church, Hinton St George, Somerset (formerly in St Martin-in-the-Fields, London).

PAULET, Charles, see 1st Duke of Bolton.

PAULET or **POULET, Sir Hugh (d1572?)** military commander and governor of Jersey.
SC UNKNOWN, tomb effigy, with wife, St George's Church, Hinton St George, Somerset.

PAULET, John, see 5th Marquess of Winchester.

PAULET, Sir William, see 1st Marquess of Winchester.

PEAKE, Sir Robert (1592?-1667) printseller and royalist.
PR E.HARDING, hs, stipple, for Harding, *Biographical Mirrour*, 1796, BM, NPG.

PEARCE, Zachary (1690-1774) bishop of Bangor and dean of Westminster.
P THOMAS HUDSON, 1754, hl seated, Lambeth Palace, London. EDWARD PENNY, tql, Trinity College, Cambridge. UNKNOWN, tql seated with book, St Martin-in-the-Fields Church, London.
SC WILLIAM TYLER, 1774, bust, Westminster Abbey, London.
PR T.CHAMBARS, after E.Penny, 1768, hs, oval, line, NPG.

PEARSALL, Richard (1698-1762) dissenting divine.
PR W.RIDLEY, hl, oval, stipple, for *Evangelical Mag*, BM.

PEARSE, Edward (1633?-1674?) nonconformist divine.
PR R.WHITE, 1673, hs, oval, line, NPG.

PEARSON, John (1613-1686) bishop of Chester.
P ISAAC WHOOD, 1737, wl in robes, Trinity College, Cambridge.
PR D.LOGGAN, 1682, hs, *ad vivum*, oval, line, BM, NPG, V & A. H. VAN HOVE, 1675, hl, oval, line, NPG.

PECK, Francis (1692-1743) antiquary.
PR J.FABER, jun, after J.Highmore, hl, mezz, BM. UNKNOWN, after B.Collins, jun, tql, profile, etch, for *Desiderata Curiosa*, 1732, BM, NPG.

PECKE, Thomas (fl 1655-1664) verse-writer.
PR 'P.F.', hs, line, for *Parnassi Puerperium*, 1659, BM, NPG.

PECKHAM, John (d1292) archbishop of Canterbury.
SC UNKNOWN, oak tomb effigy, Canterbury Cathedral.

PEECKE or **PEEKE, Richard (fl 1620-1626)** adventurer.
PR UNKNOWN, wl in combat, line, facs of woodcut for *Three to One, being an English Spanish Combat*, BM, NPG.

PELHAM, Henry (1695?-1754) prime minister.
P WILLIAM HOARE, 1751?, tql seated in robes, NPG 221. JOHN SHACKLETON, *c*1752, tql seated in robes, NPG 871.
PR E.HARDING, hl in armour, stipple, for Coxe, *Memoirs of Lord Walpole*, 1802, BM, NPG. R.HOUSTON, after J.Shackleton, tql seated with secretary John Roberts, mezz, BM, NPG.

PELHAM-HOLLES, Sir Thomas, see 1st Duke of Newcastle.

PELLETT, Thomas (1671?-1744) physician.
P MICHAEL DAHL, 1737, tql seated, Royal College of Physicians, London. WILLIAM HOGARTH, *c*1735-39, hs, oval, TATE T1570.

PEMBERTON, Sir Francis (1625-1697) chief justice of the king's bench.
P UNKNOWN, hs in robes, Emmanuel College, Cambridge.

G R.WHITE, 'Counsel for the Seven Bishops', hl, oval, mezz, 1688, BM, NPG.

SC UNKNOWN, monument, St Mary and St Michael's Church, Trumpington, Cambs.

PEMBERTON, Henry (1694-1771) physician and writer.

SC After SILVANUS BEVAN, 1778, Wedgwood medallion, profile bust, The Emily Winthrop Miles Coll, Brooklyn Museum, New York, USA.

PEMBLE, William (1592?-1623) puritan divine.

G G.VERTUE, 3 wl figures, line, cut out of *Oxford Almanack*, 1745, NPG.

PR J.STOW, hs, oval, line, pub 1817, NPG.

PEMBROKE, Aymer de Valence, 2nd Earl of (d1324) soldier and diplomat.

SC UNKNOWN, tomb effigy on monument, Westminster Abbey, London, engr J.Cole, for Dart, *Westmonasterium*, BM, NPG.

PEMBROKE, Henry Herbert, 2nd Earl of (1534?-1601) courtier and statesman.

P UNKNOWN, c1590, tql, National Museum of Wales, Cardiff.

PR PASSE, hl, oval, line, for Holland, *Herwologia*, 1620, BM, NPG.

PEMBROKE, Henry Herbert, 9th Earl of (1693-1750) statesman known as 'architect earl'.

P JONATHAN RICHARDSON, c1709-10, tql, Wilton House, Wilts. CHARLES JERVAS, c1714, hs, Wilton.

D WILLIAM HOARE, 1744, head, chalks, Wilton. SIR JOSHUA REYNOLDS, c1749-50, hl with wife, red chalk, Wilton.

SC L.F.ROUBILIAC, 1750, marble bust, Wilton; replica, Birmingham City Art Gallery.

PEMBROKE, Mary Herbert, née Sidney, Countess of (1555?-1621) sister of Sir Philip Sidney, wife of 2nd Earl of Pembroke, and patron of the arts.

PR S.PASSE, 1618, hl with book, oval, line, BM, NPG.

PEMBROKE, Philip Herbert, Earl of Montgomery and 4th Earl of (1584-1650) courtier.

P Attrib WILLIAM LARKIN, c1615, wl in Garter robes, Audley End (DoE), Essex. UNKNOWN, c1615-25, wl in garter robes, NPG 5187. DANIEL MYTENS, 1624, wl in peer's robes with key and wand of office, Hardwick Hall, (NT), Derbys. D.MYTENS, c1625, wl with wand, Wilton House, Wilts. Attrib D.MYTENS, tql seated, Hatfield House, Herts. SIR ANTHONY VANDYCK, c1635-40, wl with Garter star and wand, Wilton. SIR A.VANDYCK, c1635-40, tql with wand, Longleat, Wilts; version, hs, NPG 1489.

M Attrib ALEXANDER COOPER, hs, oval, NPG 4614.

G SIR A.VANDYCK, family group, oil, c1634-35, Wilton.

PR S.PASSE, hl when Earl of Montgomery, oval, line, BM, NPG. R. VAN VOERST, after D.Mytens, 1630, hs, oval, line, BM, NPG.

PEMBROKE, Philip Herbert, 5th Earl of (1619-1669) courtier.

P SIR ANTHONY VANDYCK, c1635-39, tql, Wilton House, Wilts. Style of SIR A.VANDYCK, tql with sister, Countess of Carnarvon, Chatsworth, Derbys.

G SIR A.VANDYCK, family group, oil, c1634-35, Wilton.

PEMBROKE, Thomas Herbert, 8th Earl of (1656-1733?) lord high admiral.

P JOHN GREENHILL, c1676, hs in armour, oval, Wilton House, Wilts. WILLEM WISSING, c1685, tql in armour, Garter insignia added later, Wilton.

SC UNKNOWN, marble bust, Trinity College, Dublin.

PEMBROKE, William Marshall, 1st Earl of (d1219) crusader and statesman.

SC UNKNOWN, 13th century, marble tomb effigy, Temple Church, London.

PEMBROKE, William Marshall, 2nd Earl of (d1231) soldier and statesman.

SC UNKNOWN, 13th century, marble tomb effigy, Temple Church, London.

PEMBROKE, William de Valence, titular Earl of (d1296) half-brother of Henry III.

SC UNKNOWN, tomb effigy, Westminster Abbey, London.

PEMBROKE, William Herbert, 1st Earl of (1507?-1570?) esquire of the body to Henry VIII.

P UNKNOWN, 1557, tql in armour, Duke of Hamilton on loan to Holyrood house, Edinburgh. Attrib HANS EWORTH, 1567, wl with wand of office and dog, Wilton House, Wilts; version, tql, Wilton.

G UNKNOWN, 'Edward VI granting Bridewell Charter', oil, 17th century, Bridewell Royal Hospital, Witley, Surrey.

SC STEPHEN OF HOLLAND, silver medal, BM.

PR PASSE, hl, oval, line, for Holland, *Herwologia*, 1620, BM.

PEMBROKE, William Herbert, 3rd Earl of (1580-1630) lord chamberlain.

P ABRAHAM BLYENBERCH, 1617, tql with wand of office, Powis Castle (NT), Powys, Wales. PAUL VAN SOMER, 1617, tql with wand, Royal Coll. DANIEL MYTENS, c1625, tql with wand, Wilton House, Wilts; version, tql, on loan to Audley End (DoE), Essex. SIR ANTHONY VANDYCK, after D.Mytens, posthumous, wl with wand, Wilton.

SC HUBERT LE SUEUR, bronze statue, Bodleian Library, Oxford.

PEMBROKE and MONTGOMERY, Anne, née Clifford, Countess of (1590-1676) aristocrat and landowner.

P UNKNOWN, (type of c1603), wl as girl, part of Appleby Castle triptych, Record Office, The Castle, Carlisle. Attrib WILLIAM LARKIN, c1610, wl with feather fan when Countess of Dorset, Knole (NT), Kent. Attrib W.LARKIN, c1615-20, hs, Knole. UNKNOWN, c1646, wl part of Appleby Castle triptych, The Castle, Carlisle; version, hl, oval, NPG 402.

G SIR ANTHONY VANDYCK, 4th Earl of Pembroke, family group, oil, c1634-35, Wilton House, Wilts.

PR R.WHITE, hs, aged 13, oval, line, BM.

PENDEREL, Richard (d1672) royalist.

P ISAAC FULLER, c1660-70, 'Charles II at Whiteladies', NPG 5247. I.FULLER, c1660-70, 'Charles II on Humphrey Penderel's Mill Horse', NPG 5251.

PR R.HOUSTON, after G.Soest, hl, oval, mezz, BM, NPG.

PENGELLY, Sir Thomas (1675-1730) chief baron of the exchequer.

G BENJAMIN FERRERS, 'The Court of Chancery', oil, c1725, NPG 798.

PR J.FABER, jun, after J.Worsdale, 1730, tql in robes, mezz, NPG.

PENINGTON or PENNINGTON, Sir John (1568?-1646) admiral.

PR C. VAN DALEN, hl in armour, oval, line, BM, NPG.

PENN, Sir William (1621-1670) admiral.

P SIR PETER LELY, c1666, tql, NMM, Greenwich.

PENNINGTON, Sir Isaac (1587? 1661) lord mayor of London.

PR UNKNOWN, hl, line, facsimile of rare woodcut, pub 1800, BM, NPG.

PENNINGTON, Sir John, see Penington.

PENNY, Thomas (d1589) botanist and entomologist.

PR W.ROGERS, hs, profile, line, for T.Moffet, *Insectorum Theatrum*, BL Ms Sloane 4014, fol 3.

PENRUDDOCK, John (1619-1655) royalist colonel.
PR G.VERTUE, hl in armour, for Ward, *Hist of the Rebellion*, 1713, BM, NPG. G.VERTUE, 1735, hl, octagonal, line, for *Loyalists*, BM, NPG. R.EARLOM, hl in armour, oval, mezz, pub 1810, BM, NPG.

PEPLOE, Samuel (1668-1752) bishop of Chester.
PR J.FABER, jun, after H.Winstanley, 1733, tql seated, mezz, BM, NPG.

PEPUSCH, John Christopher (1667-1752) musician.
P UNKNOWN, *c*1710, hl, oval, Faculty of Music, Oxford. THOMAS HUDSON, 1730s, tql in robes, NPG 2063.
M BENJAMIN ARLAUD, hs, oval, Royal Coll.

PEPYS, Elizabeth, née St Michel (1640-1669) wife of the diarist.
SC Attrib JOHN BUSHNELL, *c*1672, bust on monument, St Olave's, Hart Street, London; plaster cast, NPG 4824.
PR T.THOMSON, after J.Hayls, hl as St Catherine, stipple, for Pepys, *Diary*, pub 1828, BM, NPG.

PEPYS, Samuel (1633-1703) secretary to the admiralty and diarist.
P JOHN HAYLS, 1666, hl with sheet of music, NPG 211. After SIR PETER LELY or by JOHN GREENHILL, *c*1670, tql, Magdalene College, Cambridge. SIR GODFREY KNELLER, *c*1682-06, hs, oval, NMM, Greenwich; version, Royal Society, London. Attrib JOHN CLOSTERMAN, *c*1695, hl, oval, NPG 2100. UNKNOWN, perhaps posthumous, tql with book, Magdalene College.
G ANTONIO VERRIO, 'James II and his Court', fresco, 1682, Christ's Hospital, Horsham, Sussex.
SC JEAN CAVALIER, 1688, ivory medallion, profile bust, The Clothworkers' Company, London.

PERCEVAL, Sir John, see 1st Earl of Egmont.

PERCEVAL, Sir Philip (1605-1647) politician.
PR J.FABER, jun, 1743, hs, oval, mezz, for *Hist of House of Yvery*, BM, NPG.

PERCEVAL, Sir Richard (1550-1620) colonist and politician.
PR J.FABER, jun, 1743, hs, oval, mezz, for *Hist of House of Yvery*, BM, NPG.

PERCY, Alan (*d*1560) master of St John's College, Cambridge.
P UNKNOWN, 1549, tql, Guildhall, Norwich; copy, St John's College, Cambridge.

PERCY, Sir Algernon, see 10th Earl of Northumberland.

PERCY, Elizabeth, see Duchess of Somerset.

PERCY, George (1580-1632) author and colonist.
P UNKNOWN, hl, Syon House, Brentford, Middx.

PERCY, Sir Henry (1342-1408), see 1st Earl of Northumberland.

PERCY, Sir Henry (1564-1632), see 9th Earl of Northumberland.

PERCY, Sir Thomas (1528-1572), see 7th Earl of Northumberland.

PERCY, Thomas (1560-1605) organiser of the 'Gunpowder plot'.
G CRISPIN VAN DE PASSE, 'Gunpowder Plot Conspirators, 1605', line engr, BM, NPG 334A.
PR C.PASSE, hs, oval, line, BM, NPG.

PERCY of Alnwick, Henry Percy, Baron (*d*1659) royalist.
P SIR ANTHONY VANDYCK, *c*1638, hl, Petworth (NT), W Sussex.

PERKINS, Joseph (fl 1675-1711) poet.
PR R.WHITE, hs, oval, line, NPG.

PERKINS, William (1558-1602) puritan divine.
P UNKNOWN, hl, Christ's College, Cambridge, engr R.Elstrack, oval, line, BM, NPG. UNKNOWN, hs, Dr Williams's Library, London.

PERNE, Andrew (1519?-1589) dean of Ely.
P UNKNOWN, Peterhouse, Cambridge.

PERRONET, Vincent (1693-1785) vicar of Shoreham, Kent.
PR J.SPILSBURY, 1787, hl, mezz, BM, NPG.

PERROT, Sir John (1527?-1592) lord deputy of Ireland.
PR V.GREEN, hl, oval, mezz, pub 1776, BM, NPG. W.TRINGHAM, wl, line, NPG.

PERSE, Stephen (1548-1615) founder of the Perse grammar school at Cambridge.
SC Attrib MAXIMILIAN COLTE, tomb effigy on monument, Gonville and Caius College Chapel, Cambridge.

PERSONS, Robert, see Parsons.

PERTH, James Drummond, 4th Earl and 1st titular Duke of (1648-1716) lord chancellor of Scotland.
P Attrib ALEXIS SIMON BELLE, SNPG L223. After NICHOLAS DE LARGILLIÈRE, (type of *c*1714), hl with Garter star, Public Library, Neuchâtel, Switzerland. JOHN RILEY, *c*1680-84, hs, oval, SNPG 1850, engr R.White, 1686, hs in chancellor's robes, oval, line, BM, NPG.
M After J.RILEY, hs, oval, NPG 2153.
PR W.FAITHORNE, 1769, hl, oval, line, BM, NPG. R.WHITE, after Sir G.Kneller, 1682, hs, oval, line, BM, NPG.

PERTH, James Drummond, 5th Earl and 2nd titular Duke of (1675-1720) Jacobite.
P SIR J.B.MEDINA, hl, SNPG 1531.

PERYAM, Sir William (1534-1604) judge.
D UNKNOWN, (after type of 1600), hs, oval, w/c, NPG 477.
SC UNKNOWN, tomb effigy, Holy Cross Church, Crediton, Devon.

PETERBOROUGH, Anastasia Robinson, Countess of (*d*1755) singer and second wife of 3rd Earl.
PR J.FABER, jun, after J.Vanderbank, 1723, tql seated at piano, mezz, pub 1727, BM, NPG.

PETERBOROUGH, Charles Mordaunt, 3rd Earl of (1658-1735) admiral, general and diplomat.
P SIR GODFREY KNELLER, *c*1689-1697, hs, oval, Ranger's House (GLC), Blackheath, London. SIR G.KNELLER, tql in armour, Ministry of Defence (DoE), London. UNKNOWN, wl, Burghley House, Northants.
G PETER ANGELIS, 'Queen Anne and the Knights of the Garter', oil, *c*1713, NPG 624.
PR P.VAN GUNST, after Sir G.Kneller, hl in armour, oval, mezz, BM, NPG. J.SIMON, after Sir G.Kneller, 1705, hl, oval, mezz, BM, NPG. J.SIMON, after M.Dahl, hs in armour, oval, mezz, BM, NPG.

PETERBOROUGH, John Mordaunt, 1st Earl of (*d*1642) general.
D S.HARDING, wl, wash, Sutherland Coll, Ashmolean Museum, Oxford.

PETERS, Hugh (1598-1660) puritan divine and parliamentarian.
P UNKNOWN, hl, Queen's College, Cambridge.
PR UNKNOWN, 1660, hl, aged 61, oval, etch, NPG. UNKNOWN, hl with book, oval, line, for *Dying Father's last Legacy*, 1660, NPG. UNKNOWN, tql with windmill on head and a devil, line, for broadside *Don Pedro de Quixot*, 1660, BM, NPG. UNKNOWN, wl in

pulpit, preaching, with title 'No Life to Lechery', for W.Yonge, *Life*, 1663, facsimile, BM, NPG.

PETRE, Edward (1631-1699) Jesuit confessor of James II.
SC Various medals, by several artists, BM.
PR UNKNOWN, tql, profile, line, copied from satirical broadside *La Belle Constance dragonée Arlequin déodat*, pub 1820, BM, NPG.

PETRE, Sir William (1505?-1572) secretary of state.
P UNKNOWN, hl, aged 40, Ingatestone Hall, Essex. Attrib STEVEN VAN DER MEULEN, 1567, tql with staff of office, Ingatestone Hall; version, NPG 3816. Attrib S. VAN DER MEULEN, 1567, tql seated, Exeter College, Oxford.
SC Perhaps by CORNELIUS CURE, tomb effigy with wife, St Edmund and St Mary, Ingatestone, Essex.

PETRE, William Petre, 4th Baron (c1626-1684) royalist accused of complicity in 'Popish plot'.
P UNKNOWN, c1663, tql seated, Ingatestone Hall, Essex.

PETRUCCI, Ludovico (fl 1603-1619) poet and soldier of fortune.
PR UNKNOWN, hl, oval, line, NPG.

PETT, Peter (1610-1670) shipbuilder.
P Attrib SIR PETER LELY, c1645, hl with the 'Sovereign of the Seas', NMM, Greenwich; copy, NPG 1270.

PETT, Phineas (1570-1647) first master of the Shipwrights' Company.
P UNKNOWN, 1612, tql, NPG 2035.

PETTUS, Sir John (1613-1690) deputy-governor of the royal mines.
PR W.SHERWIN, hl, aged 57, octagonal, line, for *Fodinae Regales*, 1670, BM, NPG. R.WHITE, 1683, hs, aged 70, oval, line, NPG.

PETTY, Sir William (1623-1687) political economist.
P ISAAC FULLER, c1649-51, tql with skull, NPG 2924. JOHN CLOSTERMAN, tql seated, Bowood, Wilts.
PR E.SANDYS, 1683, hs, oval, line, for set of maps of Ireland, BM, NPG.

PETYT, Sylvester (d1719) lawyer.
P RICHARD VAN BLEECK, c1700, tql seated, NPG 719.

PETYT, William (1636-1707) archivist and antiquary.
P RICHARD VAN BLEECK, tql seated, Public Record Office (DoE), London. R. VAN BLEECK, hl with book, Inner Temple, London.
PR R.WHITE, hs, *ad vivum*, oval, line, BM, NPG.

PEYTON, Sir Henry (d1622?) adventurer.
P DANIEL MYTENS, 1621, wl, Courteenhall, Northants.

PHELIPS, Sir Edward (1560?-1614) speaker of the House of Commons.
P UNKNOWN, tql, Montacute (NT), Somerset. UNKNOWN, hs, Palace of Westminster, London.

PHELIPS, Sir Robert (1586?-1638) parliamentarian.
P Attrib H.G.POT, 1632, hl, NPG 3790.

PHILIP II of Spain (1527-1598) king of Spain and husband of Mary I.
P SIR ANTHONY MOR, c1549, tql, Althorp, Northants; version, Royal Coll. Attrib A.MOR, hs, Prado, Madrid. TITIAN, 1551, wl in armour, Prado; version by Sir P.P.Rubens, Chatsworth, Derbys. Attrib LUCAS DE HEERE, c1553, hs, Prado. UNKNOWN, c1580, wl in armour, NPG 347.
G UNKNOWN, 1557, wl with Mary, Woburn Abbey, Beds.
SC Attrib LEONE LEONI, bust, Royal Coll. After JACOPO DA TREZZO, 1555, medal, profile, bust, electrotype, NPG 446.

PHILIPHAUGH, Sir James Murray, Lord (1655-1708) lord register of Scotland.
P UNKNOWN, hl, SNPG 948.

PHILIPPA of Hainault (1314?-1369) queen of Edward III.
MS UNKNOWN, her marriage ceremony, Bibliothèque Nationale, Ms Français 2675, fol 27.
SC JEAN DE LIÈGE, c1367, marble tomb effigy, Westminster Abbey, London; electrotype, hs, NPG 346.

PHILIPPS, Sir Erasmus, 5th Bart (d1743) economic writer.
P THOMAS HUDSON, c1740, tql, Picton Castle, Haverfordwest, Dyfed.

PHILIPPS, Fabian (1601-1690) lawyer and author.
PR G.P.HARDING, hs, oval, stipple, pub 1814, BM, NPG.

PHILIPS, Ambrose (1675?-1749) poet.
PR T.COOK, after M.Ashton, hs, profile, oval, line, pub 1782, BM, NPG. P.AUDINET, after M.Ashton, hs, oval, line, for *Biographical Mag*, 1795, BM, NPG.

PHILIPS, John (1676-1709) poet.
P UNKNOWN, c1700, hs, oval, NPG 1763.
SC UNKNOWN, portrait medallion, profile, Westminster Abbey, London.
PR M. VAN DER GUCHT, after 'Sir G.Kneller', hl, oval, line, BM, NPG.

PHILIPS, Katherine, née Fowler (1631-1664) poet known as 'the matchless Orinda'.
P UNKNOWN, hl, Knole (NT), Kent, engr W.Finden, line, for *Effigies Poeticae*, 1822, BM, NPG.
PR W.FAITHORNE, bust in niche, line, for *Poems*, 1667, BM, NPG.

PHILIPS or PHILLIPS, Robert (d1650?) confessor to Queen Henrietta Maria.
PR UNKNOWN, hl, oval, etch, BM, NPG.

PHILPOT, John (1516-1555) protestant martyr.
G UNKNOWN, wl about to be burned at stake, woodcut, for J.Foxe, *Actes and Monuments*, 1563, NPG.

PHIPPS, Sir Constantine (1656-1723) lord chancellor of Ireland.
PR J.SIMON, hl in robes, oval, mezz, BM, NGI (Chaloner Smith Coll). UNKNOWN, German copy, line, BM, NPG.

PICKERING, Sir William (1516-1575) courtier and diplomat.
SC UNKNOWN, tomb effigy, Church of St Helen, Bishopsgate, London.

PIERCE, Edward (d1698) sculptor and mason.
PR A.BANNERMAN, hs, with father, line, for Walpole, *Anecdotes*, NPG.

PIERREPOINT, Sir Evelyn, see 1st Duke of Kingston.

PIERREPOINT, Henry, see 1st Marquess of Dorchester.

PIERREPOINT, Robert, see 1st Earl of Kingston.

PIERS, John (1523?-1594) archbishop of York.
P UNKNOWN, after c1588, hl with book, Christ Church, Oxford.

PILKINGTON, Sir Thomas (d1691) lord mayor of London.
PR R.WHITE, after J.Linton, 1691, hl in robes, oval, line, BM, NPG. R.DUNKARTON, hl, oval, mezz, pub 1812, BM, NPG.

PINCHBECK, Christopher (1670?-1732) clock and watch-maker.
PR J.FABER, jun, after I.Whood, hl with watch, oval, mezz, BM, NPG.

PINCK(E), Robert, see Pinke.

PINDAR, Sir Paul (1565?-1650) diplomat.
PR T.TROTTER, hl, aged 48, oval, line, pub 1794, BM, NPG. T.COOK, hl, oval, from sign in Bishopsgate street, line, for *Gent Mag*, June 1787, BM, NPG.

PINE, John (1690-1756) engraver and herald.
P WILLIAM HOGARTH, hs, oval, Beaverbrook Art Gallery, Fredericton, New Brunswick, Canada, engr J.McArdell, mezz, BM, NPG.

PINGO, Thomas (1692-1776) medallist and engraver to the Mint.
PR J.CARWITHAM, 1741, hl, mezz, BM, NPG.

PINKE or **PINCK(E), Robert (1572?-1647)** warden of New College, Oxford.
P UNKNOWN, hs, oval, New College.
SC UNKNOWN, marble bust, New College.

PINKETHMAN, William (d1725) actor.
D GEORGE VERTUE, tql as Don Lewis in *Fop's Fortune*, pen, ink and chalk, BM.
PR J.SMITH, after R.Schmutz, hl with paper, mezz, BM, NPG.

PITCAIRNE, Archibald (1652-1713) physician and poet.
P SIR J.B.MEDINA, hl, oval, Royal College of Surgeons, Edinburgh, engr R.Strange, line, BM, NPG.

PITT, Christopher (1699-1748) poet.
PR G. VAN DER GUCHT, hl, oval, line, BM, NPG.

PIX, Mary, née Griffith (1666-1720?) dramatist.
P UNKNOWN, hl, NPG 4554.

PLACE, Francis (1647-1728) amateur artist.
P Self-portrait, *c*1680, hl, Patrick Allan-Fraser Art College, Arbroath, Tayside region, Scotland. THOMAS MURRAY, *c*1693, hs, oval, Patrick Allan-Fraser Art College.
PR G.BARRETT, hs, vignette, line, for Walpole, *Catalogue of Engravers*, 1794, BM, NPG.

PLAYFORD, John (1623-1686?) musician and music publisher.
PR R.GAYWOOD, hl, aged 38, etch, for *Intro to Musick*, 1660, BM; plate reworked, 1663 ed, BM, NPG. F.H. VAN HOVE, hl, aged 57, oval, line, BM, NPG. D.LOGGAN, hs, oval, line, for same work, 1680, BM, NPG.

PLOT, Robert (1640-1696) antiquary and keeper of the Ashmolean Museum.
P WILLIAM RIEDER, hs, oval, Ashmolean Museum, Oxford. UNKNOWN, tql seated, Bodleian Library, Oxford, engr E.Harding, line, for *Biographical Mirrour*, 1796, NPG.

PLOWDEN, Edmund (1518-1585) jurist.
SC UNKNOWN, tomb effigy, Temple Church, London.
PR T.STAYNER, hl, oval, with monument at Temple Church below, line, BM, NPG.

PLUKENET, Leonard (1642-1706) botanist.
PR J.COLLINS, hl with flower, oval, line, for *Phytographia*, 1691, BM, NPG.

PLUMPTRE, Henry (d1746) president of the Royal College of Physicians.
P UNKNOWN, *c*1740-44, tql seated in robes, Royal College of Physicians, London.

PLUNKET, Oliver (1629-1681) Roman Catholic archbishop of Armagh.
P By or after GARRETT MORPHEY, hl with crucifix, NPG 262 on loan to NGI; version, Bodleian Library, Oxford.
M UNKNOWN, hs, oval, pencil, Sutherland Coll, Ashmolean Museum, Oxford.
PR R.LAURIE, hs, mezz, BM, NPG. J. VAN DER VAART, after G.Morphey, hs, oval, mezz, BM, NGI.

PLYMOUTH, Thomas Windsor, 1st Earl of (1627?-1687) royalist.
D G.P.HARDING, after Sir P.Lely, hs in armour, oval, wash, Sutherland Coll, Ashmolean Museum, Oxford.

POCAHONTAS (1595-1617) American Indian princess.
P UNKNOWN, (called Pocahontas), hl with fan, oval, national Gallery of Art, Washington, DC, USA.
PR S.PASSE, 1616, hl, oval, line, BM.

POCOCKE, Edward (1604-1691) orientalist.
P Attrib WILLIAM SONMANS, hs, oval, Bodleian Library, Oxford. UNKNOWN, hl seated with book, Bodleian.
SC UNKNOWN, 1691, stone bust, Christ Church Cathedral, Oxford.
PR F.MORRELLON LA CAVE, after 'W.Greene', hl, oval, line, for *Works*, 1740, BM, NPG.

POLE, John de la, see 2nd Duke of Suffolk.

POLE, Margaret, see Countess of Salisbury.

POLE, Michael de la, see 2nd Earl of Suffolk.

POLE, Reginald (1500-1558) cardinal and archbishop of Canterbury.
P UNKNOWN, after *c*1536, tql seated in cardinal's robes, Lambeth Palace, London, engr Passe, line for Holland, *Herwologia*, 1620, BM. UNKNOWN, after *c*1556, hl in robes, NPG 220; version, Lambeth.

POLLEXFEN, Sir Henry (1632?-1691) chief justice of common pleas.
G R.WHITE, 'Counsel for the Seven Bishops', line engr, 1688, BM, NPG.
PR T.BERRY, after R.White, hs, oval, line, pub 1821, BM, NPG.

POLTON, Sir William Calderwood, Lord (1660?-1733) Scottish advocate.
P Attrib SIR J.B.MEDINA, hs, oval, Arniston House, Midlothian region, Scotland.

POMFRET, Samuel (1650-1722) nonconformist divine.
PR UNKNOWN, hl, mezz, BM, NPG. UNKNOWN, hl, oval, mezz, NPG.

PONSONBY, Henry (d1745) major-general.
G JAMES WORSDALE, 'The Hell-Fire Club', oil, *c*1735, NGI 134.

POOLE, Matthew (1624-1679) biblical commentator.
PR J. VAN MONTALEGRE, hl, oval, line, pub Nuremberg, BM. R.WHITE, 1680, hs, oval, line, BM, NPG.

POPE, Alexander (1688-1744) poet.
P UNKNOWN, *c*1695, hl, oval, Yale University, New Haven, USA. CHARLES JERVAS, *c*1714, hl, oval, Bodleian Library, Oxford. Attrib C.JERVAS, *c*1714, wl seated, NPG 112. SIR GODFREY KNELLER, 1719, hl with book, Raby Castle, Co Durham. Attrib JONATHAN RICHARDSON, (after Sir G.Kneller type of 1721), hs profile with laurel wreath, Walker Art Gallery, Liverpool. Studio of MICHAEL DAHL, *c*1727, hl, NPG 4132. J.RICHARDSON, 1736 or before, hl, Museum of Fine Arts, Boston, USA. Attrib J.RICHARDSON, *c*1737, hs profile with wreath, NPG 1179. Attrib J.RICHARDSON, *c*1738, head, profile, NPG 561. J.RICHARDSON, 1742, hs, Fitzwilliam Museum, Cambridge. J.B.VANLOO, 1742, hl seated with letter, Scone Palace, Tayside region, Scotland.
D WILLIAM HOARE, *c*1739-43, hl, pastel, NPG 299. W.HOARE, *c*1739-43, wl profile, red chalk, NPG 873.
SC J.M.RYSBRACK, 1730, marble bust, Athenaeum Club, London. L.F.ROUBILIAC, 1738, marble bust, Temple Newsam, Leeds. L.F.ROUBILIAC, *c*1738, terracotta bust, Barber Institute of Fine Arts, Birmingham.
PR J.SMITH, after Sir G.Kneller, 1717, hl with book, mezz, BM, NPG. G.WHITE, after Sir G.Kneller (type of *c*1722), hl, mezz, BM, NPG.

POPE, Sir Thomas (1507?-1559) founder of Trinity College, Oxford.
P UNKNOWN, (after type of *c*1559), *c*1596, tql with mermaid whistle pendant, Trinity College, Oxford.

POPHAM, Edward (1610?-1651) admiral and general at sea.
SC UNKNOWN, tomb effigy, with wife, standing figures, Westminster Abbey, London.
PR S. DE WILDE, hs, oval, stipple, BM, NPG.

POPHAM, Sir John (1531?-1607) chief justice of the king's bench.
P UNKNOWN, before 1592, hl in robes, Littlecote House, Wilts.
D G.P.HARDING, (after type of after c1592), tql in robes, w/c, NPG 2405.
SC UNKNOWN, tomb effigy with wife, St John Baptist, Wellington, Somerset.

PORDAGE, John (1607-1681) astrologer and mystic.
PR W.FAITHORNE, hs, oval, line, for *Theologia Mystica*, 1683, BM. W.FAITHORNE, hs, oval, line, BM, NPG.

PORTER, Endymion (1587-1649) royalist.
P WILLIAM DOBSON, c1643-45, tql with page, TATE 1249. SIR ANTHONY VANDYCK, hl with artist, oval, Prado, Madrid.
G After SIR A.VANDYCK, family group, oil, Mount Holyoke College, Mass, USA.
SC JEAN VARIN or WARIN, 1635, bronze medal, profile head, BM.

PORTLAND, Sir Richard Weston, 1st Earl of (1577-1635) statesman.
P Attrib DANIEL MYTENS, c1633, wl with staff of office, Woburn Abbey, Beds. After SIR ANTHONY VANDYCK, (type of c1633), wl with staff of office, Clarendon Coll on loan to Council House, Plymouth; version, tql, Gorhambury, Herts, engr W.Hollar, hl, etch, for Vandyck, *Iconographie*, BM, NPG.
SC Attrib HUBERT LE SUEUR, c1635, bronze tomb effigy, Winchester Cathedral. CLAUDE WARIN, 1633, medal, profile bust, BM.

PORTLAND, William Bentinck, 1st Earl of (1649-1709) friend and agent of William III.
P Studio of HYACYNTHE RIGAUD, c1698-9, tql in armour, NPG 1968.
G W.FAITHORNE, 'The Impeached Lords', oval, mezz, BM.

PORTLESTER, Roland Fitzeustace, Baron (d1496) lord-treasurer of Ireland.
SC UNKNOWN, c1496, tomb effigy with wife, New Abbey, Kilcullen, County Kildare, Eire.

PORTMAN, Sir William, 6th Bart (1641?-1695?) soldier and politician.
PR UNKNOWN, hl in Roman dress, oval, mezz, BM. E.HARDING copy from last, stipple, for Adolphus, *British Cabinet*, pub 1800, BM, NPG.

PORTSMOUTH, Louise Renée de Keroualle, Duchess of (1649-1734) mistress of Charles II.
P SIMON VERELST, c1670-72, tql seated, Parham Park, W Sussex. S.VERELST, c1670-80, tql seated with rose, Royal Coll. HENRI GASCAR, c1672-78, tql sitting with cupid, Goodwood, W Sussex, engr St Baudet, oval, line, BM. SIR PETER LELY, c1670-78, wl seated as shepherdess, Althorp, Northants, engr G.Valck, 1678, tql mezz, BM, NPG. PIERRE MIGNARD, 1682, tql seated with black page, NPG 497. PHILIPPE VIGNON, c1682, tql seated with flower wreath, Royal Coll. UNKNOWN, c1682, tql with pearls and coral, Goodwood. SIR GODFREY KNELLER, 1684, wl, Goodwood. SIR G.KNELLER, 1687, wl, Sherborne Castle, Dorset.
M UNKNOWN, hs, oval, Berkeley Castle, Glos.
SC GEORGE BOWER, 1673, silver medal, profile, BM. JOHN ROETTIER, silver and copper medal, profile, BM.
PR E. LE DAVIS, tql seated with flower, line, BM, NPG. P. VAN SOMER, after Sir P.Lely, tql seated holding tress of hair, mezz, BM, NPG.

POTTER, Barnaby (1577-1642) provost of Queen's College, Oxford, and bishop of Carlisle.
P UNKNOWN, hl with book, Queen's College.

POTTER, Christopher (1591-1646) provost of Queen's College, Oxford.
P Attrib GILBERT JACKSON, 1634, hl with book, Queen's College.

POTTER, John (1674?-1747) archbishop of Canterbury.
P THOMAS HUDSON, c1746, wl, Bodleian Library, Oxford. T.HUDSON, 1746, tql seated, Lambeth Palace, London. By or after THOMAS GIBSON, c1737-47, tql seated, Lambeth Palace, engr G.Vertue, as after T.Gibson, line, BM, NPG.
PR G.VERTUE, after M.Dahl, 1727, hs, oval, line, BM, NPG.

POULETT, John Poulett, 1st Baron (1586-1649) royalist commander.
PR E.HARDING, hl, stipple, for Adolphus, *British Cabinet*, 1799, BM, NPG.

POULETT, Sir John Poulett, 1st Earl (1663-1743) politician.
P J.B.CLOSTERMAN, wl as youth with dog, Yale Center for British Art, New Haven, USA.
G PETER ANGELIS, 'Queen Anne and the Knights of the Garter, 1713', oil, c1713, NPG 624.
SC J.M.RYSBRACK, 1745, bust on monument, St George's Church, Hinton St George, Somerset.

POULET(T), see Paulet.

POWELL, Sir John (1633-1696) judge.
P UNKNOWN, (after type of c1690-95), hl in robes, NPG 479.

POWELL, Sir John (1645-1713) judge.
SC THOMAS GREEN, statue on monument, Gloucester Cathedral.
PR W.SHERWIN, hs in robes, oval, line, BM, NPG.

POWIS, William Herbert, 1st Marquess and titular Duke of (d1696) statesman and Roman Catholic aristocrat.
P UNKNOWN, c1675, hl in robes, Powis Castle (NT), Powys, Wales.

POWIS, William Herbert, 2nd Marquess and titular Duke of (d1745) Roman Catholic aristocrat.
P UNKNOWN, hl in armour, Powis Castle (NT), Powys, Wales.

POWLE, Henry (1630-1692) speaker of the House of Commons.
PR G.VERTUE, after Sir G.Kneller, 1737, hs, oval, line, BM, NPG.

POWYS, Sir Thomas (1649-1719) judge.
SC ROBERT HARTSHORNE, 1720, statue on monument, St John Baptist Church, Thorpe Achurch, Northants.

POYNTZ, Stephen (1685-1750) diplomat.
P Attrib J.B.VANLOO, 1732, tql, Althorp, Northants, engr J.Faber, jun, mezz, BM, NPG.
PR J.FABER, jun, after J.Fayram, hl, oval, mezz, BM, NPG.

POYNTZ, Sir Sydenham (fl 1645-1650) soldier.
P UNKNOWN, hs in armour, oval, Althorp, Northants. UNKNOWN, hs in armour with gold chain, Althorp.
PR UNKNOWN, hs in armour, oval, line, for Vicar, *England's Worthies*, 1647, BM, NPG. UNKNOWN, hs in armour, line, copy from plate for Ricraft, *Survey of England's Champions*, 1647, BM, NPG.

PRANCE, Miles (fl 1680) perjurer and accomplice of Titus Oates.
PR R.WHITE, hs, oval, line, BM, NPG.

PRATT, Sir John (1657-1725) lawyer.
P After MICHAEL DAHL?, (type of c1718), hl in robes, NPG 480.

PRESTON, John (1587-1628) master of Emmanuel College, Cambridge.
P UNKNOWN, Emmanuel College, Cambridge.
PR W.MARSHALL, hl, oval, line, for *Doctrine of the Saints' Infirmities*,

1637, BM, NPG. UNKNOWN, hs, oval, line, for *New Covenant*, 1629, BM, NPG. UNKNOWN, hl with book, line, NPG. UNKNOWN, hl, line, BM, NPG.

PRESTON, Richard Graham, Viscount (1648-1695) Jacobite.

PR UNKNOWN, hl, stipple, pub 1813, NPG.

PRICE, Arthur (*d*1752) archbishop of Cashel.

P BENJAMIN WILSON, 1749, wl in vice-chancellor's robes, Trinity College, Dublin.

PRICE, Hugh (1495?-1574) founder of Jesus College, Oxford.

P School of HANS HOLBEIN, hs, Jesus College, Oxford.

PRICE, John (1600-1676?) scholar and professor of Greek at Pisa.

PR W.HOLLAR, 1644, hl, etch, BM, NPG. W.HOLLAR, after J.Danckert, tql seated with book, etch, BM, NPG. R. DE PERSYN, after L. de Jong, hl, line, for ed of Apuleius, *Metamorphoses*, 1650, BM, NPG.

PRICE, Robert (1655-1733) judge.

PR G.VERTUE, after Sir G.Kneller, 1714, hl when baron of exchequer, oval, line, BM, NPG.

PRIDEAUX, Humphrey (1648-1724) dean of Norwich and orientalist.

P ENOCH SEEMAN, hs, oval, Christ Church, Oxford.

PR G.VERTUE, after E.Seeman jun, hl with book, oval, line, for *Old and New Testaments Connected*, 1716, BM, NPG.

PRIDEAUX, John (1578-1650) bishop of Worcester.

P J.SMITH, (after type of *c*1612), tql seated, Christ Church, Oxford; another copy, Exeter College, Oxford.

PR W.FAITHORNE, hs, oval, line, for *Doctrine of practical Praying*, 1655, BM, NPG.

PRIMROSE, Sir Archibald, 1st Bart (1616-1679), see Lord Carrington.

PRIMROSE, Archibald (1661-1723), see 1st Earl of Rosebery.

PRINGLE, Sir Walter, see Lord Newhall.

PRIOR, Matthew (1664-1721) poet, politician and diplomat.

P After HYACINTHE RIGAUD, 1699, hl with book, Mapledurham House, Oxon. SIR GODFREY KNELLER, 1700, tql seated, Trinity College, Cambridge. Attrib MICHAEL DAHL, 1713, NPG 3682. A.S.BELLE, *c*1713–14, tql seated, St John's College, Cambridge. THOMAS WRIGHT, after Jonathan Richardson, (type of *c*1718), tql seated, NPG 91. M.DAHL, 1718?, tql with book, Knole (NT), Kent.

SC ANTOINE COYSEVOX, 1714, bust on monument, Westminster Abbey, London. After A.COYSEVOX, late 18th century, Staffordshire plaque, profile bust, NPG L152(10).

PRIOR, Thomas (1682?-1751) founder of the Dublin Society and philanthropist.

SC JOHN VAN NOST, 1751, marble bust, Royal Dublin Society. J. VAN NOST, bust? on monument, Christ Church Cathedral, Dublin.

PR C.SPOONER, after J. van Nost, 1752, tql mezz, Chaloner Smith Coll, NGI. J.HALL, hs, profile, oval, line, for Maty, *Memoirs of Chesterfield*, 1777, BM, NPG.

PRITCHARD, Sir William (1632?-1705) lord mayor of London.

D T.ATHOW, wl in robes, wash, Sutherland Coll, Ashmolean Museum, Oxford.

PROBYN, Sir Edmund (1678-1742) judge.

PR J.FABER, jun, tql seated in robes, *ad vivum*, mezz, BM, NPG.

PRUJEAN, Sir Francis (1593-1666) physician.

P Attrib ROBERT STREATER, 1662?, hl, Royal College of Physicians, London.

PRYNNE, William (1600-1669) puritan lawyer and pamphleteer.

PR W.HOLLAR, hs, oval, etch, BM, NPG. UNKNOWN, hs, aged 40, oval, line, for *Prelate's Tyranny*, 1641, BM, NPG. UNKNOWN, hl with glove, oval, line, BM, NPG.

PSALMANAZAR, George (1679?-1763) literary impostor and Hebrew scholar.

PR UNKNOWN, hl, line, BM, NPG.

PUCKERING, Sir Henry, formerly Newton, 3rd Bart (1618-1701) royalist.

P UNKNOWN, wl seated, Trinity College, Cambridge.

PUCKERING, Sir John (1544-1596) lord keeper of the great seal.

SC UNKNOWN, tomb effigy with wife, Westminster Abbey, London.

PUCKLE, James (1667?-1724) author of *The Club*.

PR G.VERTUE, after J.Closterman, hs, oval, line, for *Club*, 1713, BM, NPG.

PULLEN, Josiah (1631-1714) vice-principal of Magdalen Hall, Oxford.

P ROBERT BYNG, hl, oval, Bodleian Library, Oxford.

PR UNKNOWN, hl, oval, mezz, BM, NPG.

PULTENEY, Sir William, see 1st Earl of Bath.

PURBECK, John Villiers, Viscount (1591?-1657) courtier.

G UNKNOWN, 'The Family of the Duke of Buckingham', oil, 1628, Royal Coll.

PURCELL, Henry (1659-1695) composer.

P By or after J.B.CLOSTERMAN, 1695, hl, oval, NPG 1352, engr R.White, line, for *Orpheus Britannicus*, 1698, BM, NPG. UNKNOWN, hs, NPG 2150.

D J.B.CLOSTERMAN, 1680s, head, black chalk, NPG 4994.

PR Attrib R.WHITE, hs, oval, line, for *Sonnatas of Three Parts*, 1683, BM, NPG.

PURCHAS, Samuel (1575?-1626) editor of Hakluyt's *Voyages*.

PR UNKNOWN, hl with books, line, for *Hakluytus Posthumus*, 1625, BL. UNKNOWN, copy of above, printed in Amsterdam by Jacob Benjamin, NPG. UNKNOWN, hl with books, oval, line, NPG.

PURSGLOVE, Robert (1500?-1579) suffragan bishop of Hull.

SC UNKNOWN, brass effigy, Tideswell Church, Derbys.

PYM, John (1584-1643) parliamentary leader.

PR UNKNOWN, after E.Bower, hs, woodcut, for pamphlet 'Master Pym his Speech in Parliament', 1641, NPG 1425. G.GLOVER, after E.Bower, hs, line, for S.Marshall, *Funeral Sermon*, 1644, BM, NPG.

PYNSON, Richard (*d*1530) printer in London.

PR UNKNOWN, hs, profile, oval, woodcut, NPG.

Q

QUARLES, Francis (1592-1644) poet.
P WILLIAM DOBSON, (called Quarles), *c*1642–44, hl seated, NPG 288.
PR W.MARSHALL, hl with pen and emblems, line, for *Solomon's Recantation entitled Ecclesiastes*, 1645, BM, NPG. T.CROSS, copy, hs, oval, line, for *Boanergest Barnabas*, 1646, BM.

QUARLES, John (1624-1665) poet son of Francis.
PR W.FAITHORNE, hs, octagonal, line, BM, NPG. W.MARSHALL, hl, oval, line, for *Fons Lachrymarum*, 1649, BM.

QUICK, John (1636-1706) nonconformist divine.
PR J.STURT, hs, aged 55, oval, line, for *Synodicon in Gallia Reformata*, 1692, BM, NPG.

QUEENSBERRY, Charles Douglas, 3rd Duke of (1698-1778) lord justice-general and keeper of great seal of Scotland.
P NATHANIEL DANCE, hl, Buccleuch Estates, Selkirk, Scotland. ANNE FORBES, 1772, hl in robes, Penicuik House, Midlothian region, Scotland. Attrib THOMAS HUDSON, tql seated, Buccleuch Estates. Attrib T.HUDSON, hl in robes, SNPG 2166.
G Attrib T.HUDSON, wl seated with duchess and two sons, oil, Buccleuch Estates. JOHN WOOTTON, 'The Shooting Party', oil, 1740, Royal Coll.
PR V.GREEN, after G.Willison, 1773, hl, oval, mezz, BM, NPG.

QUEENSBERRY, James Douglas, 2nd Duke of (1662-1711) lord privy seal.

P SIR GODFREY KNELLER, *c*1692, hs in armour, oval, Buccleuch Estates, Selkirk, Scotland. Attrib SIR G.KNELLER, tql in armour, Buccleuch Estates. Studio of SIR G.KNELLER, *c*1703, tql in armour, Clarendon Coll on loan to Plymouth Art Gallery. Attrib SIR J.B.MEDINA, SNPG 2045. UNKNOWN, tql with Garter sash, SNPG 1171.
SC JOHN VAN NOST, 1711, marble effigy, Durisdeen Church, Dumfries.
PR L. DU GUERRIER, after Sir G.Kneller, hl in Garter robes, oval, line, BM.

QUEENSBERRY, William Douglas, 1st Duke of (1637-1695) lord justice-general of Scotland.
P SIR GODFREY KNELLER, tql seated in robes, Buccleuch Estates, Selkirk, Scotland.

QUIN, James (1693-1766) actor.
P Attrib WILLIAM HOGARTH, *c*1730, wl, Garrick Club, London. W.HOGARTH, *c*1740–45, hs, oval, TATE 1935. FRANCIS HAYMAN, 1754, wl as Falstaff, NGI 295. THOMAS GAINSBOROUGH, 1763, wl seated, NGI 565; version, hs, Royal Coll.
SC THOMAS KING, relief portrait medallion, Bath Abbey, Somerset.
PR J.FABER, jun, after T.Hudson, 1744, hl, mezz, BM, NPG. J.MCARDELL, wl as Falstaff, mezz, BM and Chaloner Smith Coll, NGI.

R

RADCLIFFE or **RADCLYFFE, Charles (1693-1746)** Jacobite and titular Earl of Derwentwater.
PR J.BASIRE, hl, line, BM, NPG. UNKNOWN, hl, oval, mezz, BM.

RADCLIFFE or **RADCLYFFE, Sir James, Bart,** see 3rd Earl of Derwentwater.

RADCLIFFE, John (1650?-1714) physician.
P SIR GODFREY KNELLER, c1710-12, tql seated, Radcliffe Camera, Oxford; version, Royal College of Physicians, London.
SC FRANCIS BIRD, c1719, statue, University College, Oxford. J.M.RYSBRACK, statue, Radcliffe Camera.

RADCLIFFE, Robert, see 5th Earl of Sussex.

RADCLIFFE, Sir Thomas, see 3rd Earl of Sussex.

RADNOR, John Robartes, 1st Earl of (1606-1685) lord president of the Council.
P SIR GODFREY KNELLER, 1683, tql seated in robes, Antony House (NT), Cornwall.
PR UNKNOWN, after S.Cooper, hl in armour, oval, stipple, pub 1806, BM, NPG.

RAINBOWE, Edward (1608-1684) bishop of Carlisle.
P J.FREEMAN, after unknown artist, Magdalene College, Cambridge.
PR J.STURT, hs, aged 74, oval, line, for J.Banks, *Life*, 1688, BM, NPG.

RAINOLDS or **REYNOLDS, John (1549-1607)** president of Corpus Christi College, Oxford.
P UNKNOWN, hl with book, Corpus Christi College, engr Passe, line, for Holland, *Herwologia*, 1620, BM, NPG.
SC UNKNOWN, painted stone bust, Corpus Christi College Chapel.

RAINSFORD, Sir Richard (1605-1680) judge.
P W.P.CLARET, c1668, tql seated in robes, Audley End (DoE), Essex. GERARD SOEST, 1678, tql seated in robes, Lincoln's Inn, London; copy, hl, oval, NPG 643.

RAINTON, Sir Nicholas (1569-1646) lord mayor of London.
P Attrib WILLIAM DOBSON, 1643, tql, St Bartholomew's Hospital, London.

RALEIGH, Sir Walter (1552?-1618) military and naval commander and author.
P Attrib to monogrammist H, 1588, tql, NPG 7. UNKNOWN, (after type of c1590), tql in armour, Colonial Williamsburg, Virginia, USA. UNKNOWN, 1602, wl with son, NPG 3914.
M NICHOLAS HILLIARD, c1585, hs, oval, w/c, NPG 4106.
PR S.PASSE, hl with globe, oval, line, for *Hist of the World*, 1617, BM, NPG.

RAMSAY, Allan (1686-1758) Scottish poet.
P WILLIAM AIKMAN, 1723, hl, oval, SNPG 973. UNKNOWN, hl, oval, SNPG 316.
D ALLAN RAMSAY, 1729, hs, profile, chalks, SNPG 2023. A.RAMSAY, 1745, hs, chalk, SNPG 3.
PR R.COOPER, hl with book, *ad vivum*, line, NPG. G.VERTUE, after J.Smibert, hl, oval, line, for *Poems*, 1721, BM, NPG.

RAMSAY, Sir James (1589?-1638) Scottish soldier of fortune.
PR S.FÜRCK, hs in armour, aged 47, *ad vivum*, oval, line, BM, NPG. S.FÜRCK, hl in armour, oval, line, BM, NPG.

RAMSAY or **RAMESEY, William (fl 1645-1676)** physician and astrologer.
PR T.CROSS, bust on pedestal, line, for *Astrology Vindicated*, 1651, BM. T.CROSS, hl with emblems, line, for *Astrologia Restaurata*, 1653, BM. W.SHERWIN, hs, aged 42, line, for *Treatise on Worms*, 1668, BM, NPG. W.SHERWIN, tql seated, line, for *Character of True Nobility and Gentility*, 1672, BM, NPG.

RAND, Isaac (d1743) apothecary and director of Chelsea Physic Garden.
P UNKNOWN, (probably Rand), 1732, hl, oval, Apothecaries' Hall, London.

RANDOLPH, Thomas (1605-1635) poet.
PR W.MARSHALL, bust on pedestal, line, for *Poems*, 1640, BM, NPG.

RANELAGH, Richard Jones, 1st Earl of (1641?-1712) paymaster-general.
P SIR PETER LELY, tql, Royal Hospital, Chelsea, London. UNKNOWN, tql in armour, Ranelagh School, Bracknell, Berks.

RANKEILLOR, Archibald Hope, Lord (1639-1706) judge.
P UNKNOWN, hl in robes, oval, Hopetoun House, Lothian region, Scotland.

RAPIN or **RAPIN de THOYRAS, Paul (1661-1725)** historian.
PR J.HOUBRAKEN, after J.Brandon, 1725?, hl in armour, oval, line, NPG. G.KING, after J.Brandon, 1732, hl in armour, oval, line, NPG. G.VERTUE, 1734, hl in armour with book, line, NPG.

RAVIS, Thomas (1560?-1609) bishop of Gloucester and London.
P UNKNOWN, hl, aged 49, Christ Church, Oxford; copy, Fulham Palace, London.

RAVIUS, Christian (1613-1677) orientalist and theologian.
PR UNKNOWN, hl, aged 32, oval, line, for *Grammar of Oriental Languages*, 1649, NPG.

RAWDON, Sir George, 1st Bart (1604-1684) general in Ireland.
PR R.WHITE, hl in armour, aged 63, oval, line, BM, NPG.

RAWDON, Marmaduke (1610-1669) traveller and antiquary.
PR R.WHITE, hs, oval, line, BM, NPG.

RAWLET, John (1642-1686) divine and author.
PR R.WHITE, hs, oval, line, for *Poetick Miscellanies*, 1687, BM, NPG.

RAWLINSON, Christopher (1677-1733) antiquary.
PR J.SMITH, after A.Grace, 1701, hs, oval, mezz, BM, NPG.

RAWLINSON, Richard (1690-1755) antiquary and Jacobite.
P UNKNOWN, hl, Bodleian Library, Oxford, engr, stipple, for Harding, *Biographical Mirrour*, 1803, NPG.
D UNKNOWN, hl, oval, pencil, St John's College, Oxford.
PR M. VAN DER GUCHT, hl, oval, line, BM, NPG. W.SMITH, after G.Vertue, hl, oval, mezz, BM, NPG.

RAWLINSON, Sir Thomas (1647-1708) lord mayor of London.
P SIR GODFREY KNELLER, wl in robes, Bridewell Royal Hospital, Witley, Surrey, engr G.Vertue, 1719, line, BM, NPG.

RAY, John (1627-1705) naturalist.
P UNKNOWN, after 1680, hs, oval, NPG 563.
D WILLIAM FAITHORNE, after 1680, hs, oval, pastel, BM, engr W.Elder, line, for *Stirpium Europaearum*, 1694, BM, NPG.

RAYMOND, Sir Robert Raymond, 1st Baron (1673-1733) lord chief justice.
P Attrib JOHN VANDERBANK, wl in robes, Bodleian Library, Oxford. UNKNOWN, tql in robes, Gray's Inn, London.
SC SIR HENRY CHEERE, c1732, marble bust, V & A. SIR H.CHEERE, c1732, tomb effigy on monument, St Lawrence Church, Abbots Langley, Herts.
PR G.VERTUE, after J.Richardson, tql seated in robes, line, BM, NPG. J.SIMON, after I.Maubert, hl in robes, mezz, BM, NPG.

RAYMOND, Sir Thomas (1627-1683) judge.
P UNKNOWN, tql seated in robes, Gray's Inn, London.

READ, Sir William (d1715) quack oculist.
PR W.FAITHORNE, hl, oval, mezz, BM.

READING, John (1677-1764) organist.
P UNKNOWN, hl, oval, Dulwich College Gallery, London.

REEDE, John de Reede, Baron (1593-1683) diplomat.
PR W.HOLLAR, 1650, hs, profile, oval, etch, NPG.

REEVE, Sir Thomas (d1737) chief justice.
P JACOPO AMICONI, Graves Art Gallery, Sheffield.
PR B.BARON, after J.Amiconi, tql seated in robes, line, BM, NPG. G.BOCKMAN, after J.Amiconi, hl in robes, oval, mezz, BM, NPG.

REISEN, Charles Christian (1680-1725) seal engraver.
PR G.WHITE, after J.Vanderbank, hl, mezz, BM, NPG.

REYNARDSON, Sir Abraham (1590-1661) lord mayor of London.
P After CORNELIUS JOHNSON, tql, Merchant Taylors' Company, London.

REYNELL, Carew (1636-1690) economic writer.
PR W.FAITHORNE, hl, oval, line, BM, NPG.

REYNOLDS, Edward (1599-1676) bishop of Norwich.
PR D.LOGGAN, hl, aged 58, oval, line, for *Works*, 1658, BM, NPG.

REYNOLDS, James (1686-1739) chief baron of the exchequer.
P WILLIAM PARKER, wl seated in robes, Guildhall, Bury St Edmunds, engr G.Vertue, tql, line, BM, NPG.
SC UNKNOWN, seated effigy on monument, Cathedral, Bury St Edmunds, Suffolk.

REYNOLDS, Sir James (1684-1747) judge.
PR J.FABER, jun, after J.Parmentier, tql seated in robes, mezz, pub 1748, BM.

REYNOLDS, John, see Rainolds.

REYNOLDS, Thomas (1667?-1727) minister.
PR G.WHITE, after T.Murray, hl, oval, mezz, BM.

RICH, Sir Henry, see 1st Earl of Holland.

RICH, Jeremiah (d1660?) stenographer.
PR T.CROSS, hl, line, NPG, V & A. UNKNOWN, tql, aged 24, line, BM. UNKNOWN, hs, oval, line, for *Pen's Dexterity*, 1659, BM, NPG.

RICH, John (1682?-1761) pantomimist and theatrical manager.
D UNKNOWN, 1753, wl as Harlequin, w/c, Garrick Club, London.
G Attrib JOSEPH HIGHMORE, (called Rich family), oil, unfinished, Garrick Club, London. WILLIAM HOGARTH, scene from 'The Beggar's Opera', oil, c1729-31, Yale Center for British Art, New Haven, USA; version, TATE 2437.

RICH, Mary, see Countess of Warwick.

RICH, Sir Richard Rich, 1st Baron (1496?-1567) lord chancellor.
D HANS HOLBEIN, jun, 1536, head, chalks, Royal Coll.
SC Attrib EPIPHANIUS EVESHAM, 1620, reclining effigy on monument, Holy Cross Church, Essex.

RICH, Sir Robert, see 2nd Earl of Warwick.

RICHARD I, called Richard Coeur-de-Lion (1157-1199) king of England.
SC UNKNOWN, wax seal, BM and Public Record Office. UNKNOWN, tomb effigy, Fontevrault Abbey, France. UNKNOWN, tomb effigy, Rouen Cathedral, France.

RICHARD II (1367-1400) king of England.
P UNKNOWN, c1388, wl seated in robes, Westminster Abbey, London.
G UNKNOWN, 'The Wilton Diptych', oil, c1395 or later, NG 4451.
MS The Ipswich Charter, 1380, wl seated, Suffolk County Record Office, Ipswich. The Shrewsbury Charter, 1389, wl seated, Guildhall, Shrewsbury, Salop. UNKNOWN, c1389, wl seated being presented with book, *Book of Statutes*, Ms A7, fol 133, St John's College, Cambridge. ROGER DYMMOK, 1395, wl seated, *Liber contra XII Errores et Hereses Lolladorum*, Ms 17, fol 1a, Trinity Hall, Cambridge. Probably by PHILIPPE DE MAZIÈRES, 1395-96, wl seated with courtiers, BL Royal Ms 20B VI, fol 2.
SC NICHOLAS BROKER and GODFREY PREST, c1395-97, tomb effigy, gilt copper, Westminster Abbey, London; electrotype, NPG 330. UNKNOWN, silver half-groat, BM.
W Attrib HEREBRIGHT OF COLOGNE, end of 14th century, Richard kneeling before John the Baptist, Winchester College Chapel, Hants.

RICHARD III (1452-1485) king of England.
P UNKNOWN, 15th century, hs, Royal Coll; version, NPG 148. UNKNOWN, c1516, hs, Society of Antiquaries, London.
MS UNKNOWN, 1483-85, 'The Rous Roll', wl with wife and son, English version, BL Add Ms 48976, Latin version, College of Arms, London. UNKNOWN, 'The Salisbury Roll', wl with wife, Buccleuch Estates, Selkirk, Scotland.
SC UNKNOWN, silver halfpenny, BM.

RICHARDS, Michael (1673-1721) brigadier-general.
SC UNKNOWN, 1721, statue in armour on monument, St Luke's Church, Charlton village, Greenwich.
PR J.FABER, jun, after Sir G.Kneller, 1719, hl in armour, oval, mezz, pub 1735, BM, NPG.

RICHARDS, Nathaniel (d1652) dramatist.
PR UNKNOWN, hl with book, oval, line, for *Tragedy of Messalina*, 1640, BM, NPG.

RICHARDS, William (1643-1705) divine and author.
PR J.SMITH, after Sir G.Kneller, hl, mezz, BM, NPG.

RICHARDSON, John (d1625) biblical scholar.
P UNKNOWN, Peterhouse College, Cambridge.

RICHARDSON, John (1580-1654) bishop of Ardagh.
PR T.CROSS, hl, aged 74, oval, line, for *Annotations*, 1655, BM, NPG.

RICHARDSON, Jonathan, sen (1665-1745) portrait painter and connoisseur.
P Self-portrait, c1728, hl, Polesden Lacey (NT), Surrey. Self-portrait, c1729, hl, NPG 706.
D Self-portrait, various, pencil and/or chalk, Ashmolean Museum, Bodleian Library, BM, Fitzwilliam Museum, and NPG 1831, 1693, 3779 and 3023.
G Attrib self-portrait, hl of Richardson sen and jun, with Milton, oil, Capesthorne, Cheshire.

RICHARDSON, Jonathan, jun (1694-1771) portrait painter.
D JONATHAN RICHARDSON, sen, 1729, head, BM.
G Attrib J.RICHARDSON, sen, hl of Richardson sen and jun, with Milton, oil, Capesthorne, Cheshire.

RICHARDSON, Richard (1663-1741) botanist and antiquary.
PR J.BASIRE, hl, oval, line, for Nichols, *Illustrations of Literary History*, 1817, BM, NPG.

RICHARDSON, Samuel (1689-1761) novelist.
P JOSEPH HIGHMORE, 1747, tql, Stationers' and Newspaper Makers' Company, London; version, hl, NPG 161. J.HIGHMORE, 1750, wl, NPG 1036.
G Attrib FRANCIS HAYMAN, family group, oil, on loan to The Holburne of Menstrie Museum, Bath. SUSANNA HIGHMORE, family group, sketch, Pierpont Morgan Library, New York.

RICHARDSON, Sir Thomas (1569-1635) judge.
P UNKNOWN, hs in robes, Lincoln's Inn, London.
SC HUBERT LE SUEUR, bust on monument, Westminster Abbey, London.

RICHARDSON, William (1698-1775) antiquary.
P By or after HERMAN VAN DER MYN, tql seated, Emmanuel College, Cambridge.

RICHMOND, Henry Fitzroy, 1st Duke of (1519-1536) natural son of Henry VIII by Elizabeth Blount, after Talboys.
M Attrib LUCAS HORENBOUT, c1534, hs, Royal Coll.

RICHMOND, James Stuart, 4th Duke of Lennox and 1st Duke of, (1612-1655) courtier.
P SIR ANTHONY VANDYCK, c1633-37, wl with Garter star, Buccleuch Estates, Selkirk, Scotland; version, Clarendon Coll on loan to Plymouth Art Gallery. SIR A.VANDYCK, c1633-37, wl with dog, Metropolitan Museum of Art, New York. SIR A.VANDYCK, c1633-37, hl with apple, The Louvre, Paris. SIR A.VANDYCK, c1633-37, tql seated with dog, Kenwood (GLC), London. Attrib THEODORE RUSSEL, hl in armour with Garter George, NPG 4518.

RICHMOND, Ludovick Stuart, 2nd Duke of Lennox and 1st Duke of (1574-1624) statesman.
P Attrib PAUL VAN SOMER, c1620, wl in Garter robes, Corporation of York. UNKNOWN, c1620, hl in Garter robes with wife, Parham Park, W Sussex. DANIEL MYTENS, c1618-23, wl with rod of office, Petworth (NT), W Sussex; version Arundel Castle, W Sussex.
M ISAAC OLIVER, c1605, hs, heart-shaped, w/c, NPG 3063.
SC UNKNOWN, tomb effigy, Westminster Abbey, London.
PR S.PASSE, 1616, hl in Garter robes, oval, line, BM, NPG.

RICHMOND, Mary, née Howard, Duchess of (d1557) married Henry Fitzroy, Duke of Richmond.
D HANS HOLBEIN, jun, hs, chalks, Royal Coll.

RICHMOND and DERBY, Margaret Beaufort, Countess of (1443-1509) mother of Henry VII.
P MAYNARD?, c1511-12, wl, Christ's College, Cambridge; versions, hl, NPG 551; Royal Coll; Hatfield House, Herts. ROWLAND LOCKEY, c1598, wl at prayer, St John's College, Cambridge.
SC PIETRO TORRIGIANO, 1513, gilt bronze effigy, Westminster Abbey, London; electrotype NPG 356.

RICHMOND and LENNOX, Charles Lennox, 1st Duke of (1672-1723) son of Charles II and Duchess of Portsmouth.
P SIR PETER LELY, wl as infant St John the Baptist, Goodwood House, W Sussex. Attrib SIR G.KNELLER, hl as child with staff, oval, Goodwood. WILLEM WISSING, c1681, wl seated in Garter robes as boy, Goodwood. Attrib THOMAS HUDSON, tql as boy

with spaniel, Goodwood. Attrib HENRI GASCAR, tql as boy in Roman dress, oval, Goodwood. Attrib SIR G.KNELLER, hs as youth, oval, Goodwood. SIR G.KNELLER, tql as young man, Goodwood. SIR G.KNELLER, c1710, hl, the 'Kit-cat Club' portrait, NPG 3221.

RICHMOND and LENNOX, Charles Stuart, 3rd Duke of (1639-1672) royalist.
P SIR PETER LELY, after c1661, wl in Garter robes, Lennoxlove, Lothian region, Scotland.
PR E.SCRIVEN, hs in armour, octagonal, stipple, pub 1810, NPG.

RICHMOND and LENNOX, Frances Theresa Stuart Duchess of (1647-1702) courtier.
P SIR PETER LELY, c1662, tql with bow as Diana, Royal Coll. JACOB HUYSMANS, 1664, tql in man's dress, Royal Coll. SIR P.LELY?, c1678-80, wl, Museum of Fine Arts, Budapest. Similar type, SIR GODFREY KNELLER?, Goodwood House, W Sussex and Royal Coll. HENRI GASCAR, c1678, wl as Minerva, Goodwood. WILLIAM WISSING and JAN VAN DER VAART, 1687, wl, NPG 4996.
M SAMUEL COOPER, c1663-64, hs, oval, w/c, unfinished, Royal Coll. S.COOPER, c1664, hl as cavalier, oval, Mauritshuis, The Hague, Netherlands.
SC JOHN ROETTIER, c1667, silver medal, BM; modern strike from die, NPG 1681. UNKNOWN, funeral effigy, Westminster Abbey, London.

RICRAFT, Josiah (fl 1645-1679) author and merchant.
PR W.FAITHORNE, hl, line, for *Characters of the Oriental Languages*, 1645, BM, NPG.

RIDGLEY, Thomas (1667?-1734) independent theologian.
P UNKNOWN, hs, oval, Dr Williams's Library, London.
PR J. VAN DER GUCHT, after B.Dandridge, hl, oval, line, for *Body of Divinity*, 1731, BM, NPG.

RIDLEY, Mark (1560-1624) physician and mathematician.
PR UNKNOWN, hl, oval, line, for *Treatise of Magneticall Bodies*, 1613, BM, NPG.

RIDLEY, Nicholas (1500?-1555) bishop of Rochester and London.
P UNKNOWN, 1555, hl with book, NPG 296.
PR W. and M.PASSE, hl with book, line, for Holland, *Herwologia*, 1620, BM, NPG.

RILEY, John (1646-1691) portrait painter.
D JONATHAN RICHARDSON, jun, after lost self-portrait, head, BM.

RIVERS, Anthony Woodville, 2nd earl (1442?-1483) soldier and author.
MS UNKNOWN, wl presenting book to Edward IV, for *The Dictes and Sayings of the Philosophers*, Ms 265, Lambeth Palace, London.

RIVINGTON, Charles (1688-1742) publisher.
PR F.C.LEWIS, after J.Slater, hl aged 76, chalk manner, BM. UNKNOWN, hl, oval, photogravure, NPG.

ROBARTES, Sir John, see 1st Earl of Radnor.

ROBERT, Duke of Normandy (1054?-1134) eldest son of William the Conqueror.
SC UNKNOWN, (called Robert), c1280, painted wood tomb effigy, Gloucester Cathedral; electrotype, NPG 440.

ROBERTS, Francis (1609-1675) puritan divine.
PR T.CROSS, hl, line, for *Clavis Bibliorum*, 1648, BM, NPG, V & A.

ROBERTS, Lewis (1596-1640) merchant and author.
PR G.GLOVER, hl, octagonal, line, for *Marchants Mapp of Commerce*, 1638, BM, NPG.

ROBERTSON of Struan, Alexander Robertson, 13th Baron (1670?-1749) Jacobite, poet and clan chieftain.
P UNKNOWN, hl in armour, oval, SNPG 438.

ROBINSON, Anastasia, see Countess of Peterborough.

ROBINSON, Benjamin (1666-1724) presbyterian divine.
P UNKNOWN, hs, oval, Dr Williams's Library, London, engr J.Hopwood, stipple, pub 1808, NPG.

ROBINSON, Bryan (1680-1754) physician.
P BENJAMIN WILSON, c1748-50, tql seated, Trinity College, Dublin, etch, B.Wilson, BM, NPG.

ROBINSON, Henry (1553?-1616) bishop of Carlisle.
P UNKNOWN, hs, Queen's College, Oxford.
SC UNKNOWN, brass effigy, Queen's College Chapel.

ROBINSON, John (1650-1723) bishop of London.
PR M. VAN DER GUCHT, tql seated, line, BM, NPG. G.VERTUE, after M.Dahl, hl, oval, line, BM, NPG.

ROBINSON, John (1682-1762) organist of Westminster Abbey.
PR G.VERTUE, after T.Johnson, tql playing on a spinet, line, BM.

ROBINSON, Thomas, see 1st Baron Grantham.

ROCHESTER, Henry Wilmot, 1st Earl (1612?-1658) royalist.
D W.N.GARDINER, hs in armour, wash, Sutherland Coll, Ashmolean Museum, Oxford.
PR UNKNOWN, hs in armour, oval, line and stipple, pub 1816, NPG.

ROCHESTER, John Wilmot, 2nd Earl of (1647-1680) poet and courtier.
P After JACOB HUYSMANS?, c1665-70, tql with monkey, NPG 804. Attrib SIR PETER LELY, c1677?, tql, Jones Coll, V & A, engr R.White, 1681, hs, oval, line, BM, NPG. UNKNOWN, tql seated, Knole (NT), Kent.

ROCHESTER, Laurence Hyde, Earl of (1641-1711) politician.
P SIR GODFREY KNELLER, 1685, wl in peer's robes, NPG 4033. After WILLEM WISSING, (type of c1685-87), tql in Garter robes, NPG 819; version, Hardwick Hall (NT), Derbys.

ROCHFORD, Frederick Nassau Zuylestein, 3rd Earl of (1682?-1738) statesman.
P BARTHOLOMEW DANDRIDGE, (probably 3rd Earl), 1735?, tql in peer's robes, Brodick Castle (NT for Scotland), Isle of Arran.

ROCHFORD, William Henry Zuylestein, 1st Earl of (1645?-1709) master of robes to William III.
P UNKNOWN, tql in armour, Castle Amerongen, The Netherlands.

ROCHFORD, William Nassau Zuylestein, 2nd Earl of (1681-1710) soldier.
P SIR GODFREY KNELLER, (probably 2nd Earl), tql in peer's robes, Brodick Castle (NT for Scotland), Isle of Arran.

ROCKINGHAM, Sir Lewis Watson, 1st Baron (1584-1653) royalist.
P WILLIAM DOBSON, c1644-45, hl, oval, Rockingham Castle, Northants. UNKNOWN, hl, oval, Rockingham.

ROE, Sir Thomas (1581?-1644) diplomat.
P After M.J. VAN MIEREVELDT?, (type of c1640), hs, oval, NPG 1354, engr G.Vertue, line, for *Negociations*, 1740, BM, NPG.

ROESTRATEN, Pieter van (1627-1700) painter.
PR J.SMITH, after P.Roestraten, hl with glass and pipe, mezz, BM. UNKNOWN, hl with flask, glass and lobster, mezz, BM.

ROETTIERS, Norbert (1665?-1727) medallist.
P NICOLAS DE LARGILLIÈRE, c1708, hl with medal, Fogg Art Museum, Harvard University, Cambridge, Mass, USA.

ROGER of Salisbury (d1139) bishop of Salisbury.
SC UNKNOWN, marble relief effigy on tomb, Salisbury Cathedral.

ROGERS, Daniel (1573-1652) divine.
P UNKNOWN, hl with book, Dr Williams's Library, London.

ROGERS, Sir Edward (1498?-1567?) esquire of the body to Henry VIII.
P UNKNOWN, 1567, hl with staff of office, NPG 3792.

ROGERS, John (1500?-1555) Protestant martyr.
PR PASSE, hl with book, line, for Holland, *Herwologia*, 1620, BM, NPG.

ROGERS, John (1572?-1636) puritan vicar of Dedham, Essex.
SC UNKNOWN, bust on monument, St Mary the Virgin, Dedham, Essex.
PR UNKNOWN, hl with book, line, BM, NPG.

ROGERS, John (1627-1665?) fifth-monarchy man and minister of Purleigh, Essex.
PR W.HOLLAR, after D.Saville, tql, line, for *Bethshemesh*, 1653, BM.

ROGERS, Nehemiah (1593-1660) divine.
PR M.BERNIGEROTH, hs, oval, line, BM, NPG.

ROGERS, Richard (1532?-1597) dean of Canterbury.
P UNKNOWN, hl seated with book, The Deanery, Canterbury.

ROGERS, Richard (1550?-1618) puritan divine of Wethersfield, Essex.
PR UNKNOWN, hl with book, oval, line, for Boissard, *Bibliotheca Chalcographica*, 1650, BM, NPG. UNKNOWN, hl with book, oval, line, NPG.

ROGERS, Thomas (d1616) Protestant divine.
PR J.JUNE, hl, oval, line, BM.

ROGERS, Timothy (1658-1728) nonconformist minister.
P UNKNOWN, hl, oval, Dr Williams's Library, London.
PR R.WILLIAMS, after R.Byng, hl with quill pen, mezz, BM, NPG.

ROGERS, Woodes (1679-1732) governor of the Bahamas.
G W.HOGARTH, family group, oil, 1729, NMM, Greenwich.

ROKEBY, Sir Thomas (1631?-1699) judge.
P UNKNOWN, tql seated in robes, Gray's Inn, London.

ROLLE, Henry (1589?-1656) judge.
P UNKNOWN, 1656, wl seated in robes, Inner Temple, London.
PR A.HERTOCKS, hl, oval, line, for *Abridgment of the Law*, 1668, BM, NPG.

ROLLOCK or ROLLOK, Robert (1555?-1599) divine and principal of Edinburgh University.
P UNKNOWN, 1599, hl with book, oval, SNPG 635. UNKNOWN, Edinburgh University.

ROMNEY, Henry Sidney, 1st Earl of (1641-1704) politician.
P SIR PETER LELY, early 1650s, wl with two whippets, Althorp, Northants. SIR P.LELY, early 1650s, wl with dog, Penshurst, Kent. SIR GODFREY KNELLER, tql in armour, Penshurst. Attrib SIR J.B.MEDINA, tql in armour, British Embassy (DoE), The Hague, Netherlands.

ROOKE, Sir George (1650-1709) admiral.
P MICHAEL DAHL, c1700-05, tql, NMM, Greenwich. M.DAHL, c1700-05, tql on loan to Maidstone County Hall, Kent. Studio of M.DAHL, c1700-05, hs, oval, NPG 1992.
SC BENGT RICHTER, silver medal, BM. UNKNOWN, 1708, bust on monument, Canterbury Cathedral.

PR R.WILLIAMS, after M.Dahl, 1704, hl in armour, oval, mezz, BM, NPG.

ROOKWOOD, Ambrose (1578?-1606) conspirator.
PR UNKNOWN, tql, oval, stipple, for Caulfield, *Hist of the Gunpowder Plot*, 1804, BM, NPG.

ROPER, Abel (1665-1726) bookseller and Tory journalist.
PR G.WHITE, after H.Hysing, hl, oval, mezz, BM, NPG.

ROPER, Margaret, née More (1505-1544) daughter of Sir Thomas More.
M HANS HOLBEIN, jun, *c*1536–40, hl, oval, w/c, Metropolitan Museum of Art, New York.
G H.HOLBEIN, 'Thomas More, his father and his household', pen and ink, 1527–28, Kunstmuseum, Basel, Switzerland. ROWLAND LOCKEY, partly after H.Holbein, 'Sir Thomas More and his descendants', oil, *c*1595–1600, NPG 2765.

ROPER, William (1493/8-1578) son-in-law and biographer of Sir Thomas More.
M HANS HOLBEIN, jun, *c*1536–40, hl, oval, w/c, Metropolitan Museum of Art, New York.

ROS, Robert de (*d*1227) knight Templar.
SC UNKNOWN, marble tomb effigy, Temple Church, London.

ROSCOMMON, Wentworth Dillon, 4th Earl of (1633?-1685) poet and critic.
P CARLO MARATTA, wl in classical dress, Althorp, Northants.

ROSEBERY, Archibald Primrose, 1st Earl of (1661?-1723) privy councillor.
P SIR J.B.MEDINA, hl in armour, oval, SNPG L264.
PR P.VANDERBANK, after J.Riley, hl in armour, oval, line, BM.

ROSEWELL, Samuel (1679-1722) nonconformist minister.
PR J.FABER, sen, after J.Wollaston, hl, oval, mezz, BM.

ROSS, Alexander (1591-1654) chaplain to Charles I.
PR J.GODDARD, 1652, hl with two emblematical figures either side, line, NPG. P.LOMBART, hl, aged 63, line, for *Pansebeia*, 1653, BM, NPG.

ROTHERAM, Thomas (1423-1500) archbishop of York.
P UNKNOWN, hl in robes, Lincoln College, Oxford.
SC UNKNOWN, wooden funeral effigy, York Minster.

ROTHES, John Leslie, 7th Earl and 1st Duke of (1630-1681) lord chancellor.
P L.SCHUNEMAN, 1667, tql in robes, SNPG 860.
PR C.PICART, after Sir P.Lely, tql with armour, stipple, for Lodge, *Portraits*, 1819, BM, NPG.

ROTHES, John Leslie, 8th Earl of (1679-1722) vice-admiral of Scotland.
P UNKNOWN, hl in armour, oval, SNPG 896.

ROTHES, John Leslie, 10th Earl of (1698?-1767) general.
PR J.McARDELL, after J.Reynolds, tql in uniform, mezz, BM, NPG.

ROUBILIAC, Louis François (1705?-1762) sculptor.
P ANDREA SOLDI, 1751, hl with sculpture, Dulwich College Gallery, London; version, *c*1757–58, Garrick Club, London. ADRIEN CARPENTIERS, 1761?, tql with statuette of Shakespeare, NPG 303; version, Yale Center for British Art, New Haven, USA.
SC Attrib JOSEPH WILTON, *c*1761, marble bust, NPG 2145.
PR D.MARTIN, after A.Carpentiers, tql with statuette, mezz, pub 1765, BM, NPG.

ROUS, Francis (1579-1659) puritan speaker of the Little Parliament.
P UNKNOWN, 1653, hl seated in robes, Eton College, Berks. UNKNOWN, hl, oval, Pembroke College, Oxford, engr

W.Faithorne, 1656, line, for *Treatises and Meditations*, 1657, BM, NPG.

ROUS, John (1411?-1491) antiquary of Warwick.
MS UNKNOWN, 1483–85, 'The Rous Roll', wl seated, Latin version, College of Arms, London, engr W.Hollar, with two other vignettes, etch, BM, NPG.

ROWE, Elizabeth, née Singer (1674-1737) author.
PR G.VERTUE, hl, oval, line, for *Works*, 1739, BM, NPG.

ROWE, Nicholas (1674-1718) poet laureate and dramatist.
P After SIR GODFREY KNELLER, (type of *c*1710), hs, oval, Knole (NT), Kent. UNKNOWN, (after type of *c*1718?), hl, NPG 1512.
PR J.FABER, sen, 1715, tql, mezz, BM. M. VAN DER GUCHT, hl, line, for *Works*, 1715, BM, NPG.

ROWLEY, Sir William (1690?-1768) admiral.
P UNKNOWN, *c*1762, tql, NMM, Greenwich.
PR J.FABER, jun, after C.Arnulphy, 1743, tql, mezz, pub 1745, BM, NPG. J.BROOKS, 1745, tql, mezz, BM, NPG.

ROXBURGHE, John Ker, 1st Duke of (1680?-1741) statesman.
P JONATHAN RICHARDSON, 1723, wl in Garter robes, Floors Castle, Borders region, Scotland. JOHN VANDERBANK, 1738, tql, Inveraray Castle, Strathclyde region, Scotland. UNKNOWN, tql in Garter robes, SNPG 1021; version, Floors Castle. UNKNOWN, hs, oval, Floors Castle.

ROXBURGHE, Robert Ker, 1st Earl of (1570?-1650) lord privy seal of Scotland.
P UNKNOWN, tql in robes, Floors Castle, Borders region, Scotland.

RUDDIMAN, Thomas (1674-1757) philologist and publisher.
P WILLIAM DENUNE, 1749, hl, oval, SNPG 2013, engr F.Bartolozzi, hs, oval, stipple, pub 1793, NPG.

RUDYERD, Sir Benjamin (1572-1658) politician and poet.
P DANIEL MYTENS, 1627, tql, Audley End (DoE), Essex, engr W.Hollar, hs, oval, etch, BM, NPG and J.Payne, hl, line, BM, NPG.

RUGGLE, George (1575-1622) author of *Ignoramus*.
PR UNKNOWN, wl holding paper inscribed 'Ignoramus', line, NPG.

RUNDLE, Thomas (1688?-1743) bishop of Derry.
P UNKNOWN, tql seated, Durham Cathedral. UNKNOWN, tql, Lambeth Palace, London.

RUPERT, Prince, Count Palatine (1619-1682) soldier and patron of science.
P M.J. VAN MIEREVELDT, 1625, wl, Royal Coll. SIR ANTHONY VANDYCK, *c*1630, wl with dog, Kunsthistoriches Museum, Vienna. GERARD HONTHORST, *c*1632–34, hs in armour, oval, The Louvre, Paris. SIR A.VANDYCK, *c*1635–40, tql in armour with brother Prince Charles Louis, The Louvre. Studio of SIR A.VANDYCK, *c*1637, wl, oval, Royal Coll. Attrib G.HONTHORST, *c*1641–42, hs in armour, oval, NPG 4519. SIR PETER LELY, 1665, tql with breastplate, Royal Coll. SIR P.LELY, *c*1670, wl in Garter robes, Euston Hall, Suffolk; version, tql, NPG 608. J.M.WRIGHT, 1672, wl in armour, Magdalen College, Oxford. JACQUES D'AGAR, *c*1678, tql in classical dress, Corporation of New Windsor. UNKNOWN, *c*1670+, tql with page, Knebworth House, Herts.
M After SIR P.LELY, (type of *c*1665–70), hs, NPG 233. SAMUEL COOPER, *c*1670, hs, oval, Buccleuch Estates, Selkirk, Scotland.
G After WILLIAM DOBSON, drinking group, oil, *c*1642–46, Ashdown House (NT), Oxon.
SC C.P.DIEUSSART, bust as young man, Ashmolean Museum, Oxford. JOHN DWIGHT, *c*1680, stoneware bust, BM.

RUSHOUT, Sir John, 4th Bart (1684-1775) politician.
SC J.F.MOORE, 1769, bust, Worcester Infirmary. J.M.RYSBRACK, c1775, bust on monument, St Peter and St Paul Church, Blockley, Glos.

RUSHWORTH, John (1612?-1690) historian.
PR R.WHITE, hs, oval, line, for *Historical Collections*, part iii, 1692, BM, NPG.

RUSSELL, Lord Edward (d1551) eldest son of 2nd Earl of Bedford.
P UNKNOWN, 1573, hl, Woburn Abbey, Beds; w/c drawing by G.P.Harding, NPG 2410.

RUSSELL, Edward (1653-1727), see Earl of Orford.

RUSSELL, Francis (1527?-1585), see 2nd Earl of Bedford.

RUSSELL, Lord Francis (d1585) soldier and father of 3rd Earl of Bedford.
P UNKNOWN, c1573, hl, Woburn Abbey, Beds; w/c drawing by G.P.Harding, NPG 2411.

RUSSELL, Francis (1593-1641), see 4th Earl of Bedford.

RUSSELL, John, see 1st Earl of Bedford.

RUSSELL, Lucy, see Countess of Bedford.

RUSSELL, Rachel, née Wriothesley, Lady (1636?-1723) wife of Lord William Russell who acted as his 'writer' during his trial.
P Attrib SIR GODFREY KNELLER, wl with white cap, Woburn Abbey, Beds. UNKNOWN, (called Lady Russell), tql seated with lace head-covering, Woburn Abbey.

RUSSELL, Sir William, 1st Bart (d1654) treasurer of the navy.
P MARCUS GHEERAERTS, 1625, wl, Woburn Abbey, Beds.

RUSSELL, William (1613-1700), see 1st Duke of Bedford.

RUSSELL, William Russell, Lord (1639-1683) politician.
P CLAUDE LEFEVRE, c1659, hl in armour, oval, Woburn Abbey, Beds. SIR GODFREY KNELLER, c1680, hs, oval, Woburn Abbey, engr P.Vanderbank, c1683, line, BM, NPG.
M Attrib THOMAS FLATMAN, hs, oval, NPG L152 (16).
SC GEORGE BOWER, 1683, silver medal, one of 'seven-headed hydra' symbolizing the Rye House Plot, BM.

RUSSELL of Thornhaugh, Sir William Russell, 1st Baron (1558?-1613) soldier.
P Attrib GEORGE GOWER, c1580, hs, Woburn Abbey, Beds. UNKNOWN, c1588, wl with small dog, Woburn Abbey.

RUSTAT, Tobias (1606?-1694) yeoman of the robes to Charles II and philanthropist.
P School of SIR PETER LELY, tql seated, Jesus College, Cambridge, engr W.N.Gardiner, stipple, NPG.
SC Attrib ARNOLD QUELLIN, c1685, relief portrait medallion, Jesus College.

RUTHERFORD, John (1695-1779) physician and grandfather of Sir Walter Scott.
P UNKNOWN, hl, Abbotsford, Borders region, Scotland.

RUTHERFORD, Samuel (1600-1661) Scottish divine and rector of University of St Andrews.
P UNKNOWN, University of St Andrews, Fife, Scotland.

RUTHVEN, Patrick, see Earl of Brentford.

RUTLAND, Edward Manners, 3rd Earl of (1549-1587) statesman.
P UNKNOWN, Belvoir Castle, Leics.
SC GERARD JOHNSON, 1591, alabaster tomb effigy with wife, St Mary's Church, Bottesford, Leics.

RUTLAND, Francis Manners, 6th Earl of (1578-1632) statesman.
P UNKNOWN, wl in Garter robes, Belvoir Castle, Leics.
SC UNKNOWN, c1632, alabaster tomb effigy with two wives, St Mary's Church, Bottesford, Leics.
PR UNKNOWN, hl in Garter robes, oval, line, BM, NPG.

RUTLAND, Henry Manners, 2nd Earl of (d1563) soldier and statesman.
P UNKNOWN, Belvoir Castle, Leics.
SC UNKNOWN, c1563, alabaster tomb effigy with wife, St Mary's Church, Bottesford, Leics.

RUTLAND, John Manners, 8th Earl of (1604-1679) statesman.
P UNKNOWN, wl in peer's robes, Belvoir Castle, Leics.
M SAMUEL COOPER, 1656, hs, oval, Belvoir Castle. JOHN HOSKINS, jun, 1656, hs, oval, Belvoir.
SC GRINLING GIBBONS, c1684, marble standing tomb effigy with wife, St Mary's Church, Bottesford, Leics.

RUTLAND, John Manners, 9th Earl and 1st Duke of (1638-1711) soldier and statesman.
P J.B.CLOSTERMAN, wl in coronation robes, Hardwick Hall (NT), Derbys. UNKNOWN, wl in robes with bust, Belvoir Castle, Leics.

RUTLAND, Roger Manners, 5th Earl of (1576-1612) statesman who took part in Essex's conspiracy.
P UNKNOWN, Belvoir Castle, Leics.
SC NICHOLAS JOHNSON, c1612, alabaster tomb effigy with wife, St Mary's Church, Bottesford, Leics.

RUTLAND, Thomas Manners, 1st Earl of (d1543) soldier and statesman.
SC RICHARD PARKER, c1543, alabaster tomb effigy with wife, St Mary's Church, Bottesford, Leics.

RUVIGNY, Henri de Massue, 2nd Marquess of, see 1st Earl of Galway.

RYCAUT, Sir Paul (1628-1700) diplomat and author.
P After SIR PETER LELY, c1679-80?, hl, NPG 1874, engr R.White, oval, line, for *Hist of the Turkish Empire*, 1679, BM, NPG. JOHANN RUNDT, c1690?, tql, Royal Society, London.

RYDER, Sir Dudley (1691-1756) judge.
P JAMES CRANKE, wl in robes, Lincoln's Inn, London, engr J.Faber, jun, mezz, BM.
SC SIR HENRY CHEERE, relief portrait medallion, St Wulfram Church, Grantham, Lincs.

RYDER, John (1697?-1775) archbishop of Tuam.
P UNKNOWN, tql, Queen's College, Cambridge.

RYMER, Thomas (1641-1713) author and antiquary.
PR UNKNOWN, wl with dog, from a contemporary caricature, line, for Caulfield, *Remarkable Persons*, 1819, BM, NPG.

RYSBRACK, John Michael (1693?-1770) sculptor.
P Attrib JOHN VANDERBANK, c1728, tql with bust, NPG 1802. ANDREA SOLDI, 1753, tql with statuette of Hercules, Yale Center for British Art, New Haven USA.
D Attrib JONATHAN RICHARDSON, sen, profile head, V & A.
G GAWEN HAMILTON, 'A Conversation of Virtuosis . . . at the Kings Armes', oil, 1735, NPG 1384.
PR J.FABER, jun, after John Vanderbank, tql with bust of a woman, mezz, pub 1734, BM, NPG.

RYVES, Bruno (1596-1677) dean of Windsor.
P UNKNOWN, hl, Woburn Abbey, Beds.
PR R.EARLOM, hs, oval, mezz, BM, NPG.

S

SABINE, Joseph (1662?-1739) general and governor of Gibraltar.
PR J.FABER, jun, after Sir G.Kneller, 1711, tql, mezz, pub 1742, BM, NPG.

SACHEVERELL, Henry (1674?-1724) political preacher.
P THOMAS GIBSON, c1710, hl, Magdalen College, Oxford, engr A.Johnson, oval, mezz, BM, NPG, and P.SCHENCK, BM, NPG.
SC UNKNOWN, 1710, silver medal, BM.
PR J.SMITH, after A.Russell, 1710, hl, oval, mezz, BM, NPG. G.VERTUE, after A.Russell, hl, line, pub 1714, BM, NPG.

SACKVILLE, Charles, see 6th Earl of Dorset.

SACKVILLE, Sir Edward, see 4th Earl of Dorset.

SACKVILLE, Lionel Cranfield, see 1st Duke of Dorset.

SACKVILLE, Richard (1589-1624), see 3rd Earl of Dorset.

SACKVILLE, Richard (1622-1677), see 5th Earl of Dorset.

SACKVILLE, Robert, see 2nd Earl of Dorset.

SACKVILLE, Thomas, see 1st Earl of Dorset.

SADLEIR or SADLER, Sir Ralph (1507-1587) diplomat.
SC UNKNOWN, tomb effigy, St Mary's Church, Standon, Herts.

ST ALBAN, Francis Bacon, First Baron Verulam and Viscount (1561-1626) lord chancellor and philosopher.
P Attrib WILLIAM LARKIN, (type of c1617), tql, Trinity College, Cambridge; versions, hs, Hardwick Hall (NT), Derbys; University of London Library. Attrib ABRAHAM BLYENBERCH, c1618, tql in chancellor's robes, The Royal Society, London; version, wl, NPG 1288. JOHN VANDERBANK, after A.Blyenberch, 1731, tql, NPG 1904.
M NICHOLAS HILLIARD, 1578, hs, Belvoir Castle, Leics.
SC UNKNOWN, seated tomb effigy, St Michael's Church, St Albans; electrotype, NPG 408. L.F.ROUBILIAC, 1751, marble bust, Trinity College, Cambridge.
PR S.PASSE, after W.Larkin, hl, line, for *Sylva Sylvarum*, 1627, BL, NPG. W.MARSHALL, after S.Passe, tql seated at desk, line, for *History of Henry VII*, 1641, BM, NPG.

ST ALBANS, Charles Beauclerk, 1st Duke of (1670-1726) son of Charles II by Nell Gwynn.
P UNKNOWN, tql, Berkeley Castle, Glos.
M UNKNOWN, c1680, hs, oval, Royal Coll.
'R R.WHITE, wl in peer's robes with brother Lord James Beauclerk, line, for Guillim *Heraldry*, 1679, BM, NPG.

ST ALBANS, Diana de Vere, Duchess of (d1741) wife of Charles Beauclerk, 1st Duke of St Albans.
P SIR GODFREY KNELLER, wl, one of Hampton Court Beauties, Royal Coll.

ST ALBANS, Henry Jermyn, Earl of (d1684) courtier.
P UNKNOWN, tql, Ickworth (NT), Suffolk.
PR R.GODFREY, after Sir P.Lely, hs in Garter robes, stipple, for Harding, *Biographical Mirrour*, 1793, BM, NPG.

ST ANDRE, Nathaniel (1680-1776) anatomist.
PR R.GRAVE, hl, line, for Caulfield, *Remarkable Characters*, 1819, NPG.

SAINT-ÉVREMOND, Charles de Marguetel de (1613?-1703) wit and courtier.
P SIR GODFREY KNELLER, hl, Althorp, Northants, engr R.White, hl, oval, line, for *Works*, 1700, BM, NPG. Attrib JAMES PARMENTIER, c1701, hl, oval, NPG 566, engr P. van Gunst, line, for *Oeuvres Meslées*, 1709, BM, NPG.

ST JOHN, Henry, see 1st Viscount Bolingbroke.

ST JOHN, Oliver (1559-1630), see 1st Viscount Grandison.

ST JOHN, Oliver (1580?-1646), see 1st Earl of Bolingbroke.

ST JOHN, Oliver (1598?-1673) chief-justice.
P PIETER NASON, 1651, wl, NPG 4978; version, Lydiard Mansion, Borough of Thamesdown, Wilts.

ST JOHN of Bletso, Oliver St John, 1st Baron (d1582) courtier.
D G.P.HARDING, after Arnold van Brounckhorst, (type of 1578), hs, w/c, NPG 2408.

ST LO, George (d1718) naval commander.
M ROBERT WHITE, hs, oval, BM.
PR J.NUTTING, hl, oval, line, BM, NPG.

SALISBURY, James Cecil, 3rd Earl (d1683) courtier.
P SIR GODFREY KNELLER, c1680-81, wl in Garter Robes, Hatfield House, Herts.

SALISBURY, James Cecil, 4th Earl of (d1693) Jacobite.
P WILLIAM WISSING, c1687, wl painted over earlier portrait of James, Duke of Monmouth, Hatfield House, Herts. W.WISSING, hs, oval, Hatfield House.
G J.M.WRIGHT, wl seated with sister, oil, c1668-69, Hatfield House.

SALISBURY, Margaret Pole, Countess of (1473-1541) daughter of George Plantagenet, Duke of Clarence.
P UNKNOWN, (called Margaret), 1530s, hl with barrel-shaped jewel, NPG 2607.
MS UNKNOWN, 1477-85, wl with pet animals, Rous Roll, BL Add Ms 48976.

SALISBURY, Robert Cecil, 1st Viscount Cranbourne and 1st Earl of (1563?-1612) statesman.
P JOHN DE CRITZ, 1599, tql with seal bag, Ingatestone Hall, Essex; version, 1602, NPG 107. J. DE CRITZ, c1606, wl with seal bag, Hatfield House, Herts. J. DE CRITZ, 1608, tql in Garter robes, Hatfield House.
G UNKNOWN, 'The Somerset House Conference, 1604', oil, NPG 665.
SC MAXIMILIAN COLT, tomb effigy, Salisbury Chapel, Hatfield Church.

SALISBURY, William Longespée, Earl of (d1226) crusader.
SC UNKNOWN, tomb effigy, Salisbury Cathedral.

SALMON, William (1644-1712) scientist.
PR W.SHERWIN, 1671, hs, oval, line, BM, NPG. BURNFORD, hl, oval, line, for *Synopsis Medicinae*, 1681, BM. UNKNOWN, 1686, hs, oval, line, NPG. R.WHITE, 1687, hs, oval, line, BM, NPG.

SALTER, Samuel (d1756?) divine.
PR VIVARES, hs, etch, NPG.

SALTONSTALL, Charles (fl 1642) writer on navigation.
PR W.MARSHALL, hl, aged 29, oval, line, for *Art of Navigation*, 1642, BM, NPG.

SALTONSTALL, Richard (1586-1661?) colonist.
P UNKNOWN, hl, Peabody Museum, Salem, Mass, USA.

SANCROFT, William (1617-1693) archbishop of Canterbury.
P UNKNOWN, 1650, hl with book, oval, Emmanuel College, Cambridge. P.P.LENS, after David Loggan, (type of 1680), wl seated, Emmanuel College; version, hl, Lambeth Palace, London.
D EDWARD LUTTEREL, c1688?, hl, chalks, NPG 301.
G UNKNOWN, 'The Seven Bishops Committed to the Tower in 1688', oil, NPG 79.
SC GEORGE BOWER, 1688, obverse side of silver medal, NPG 152A. UNKNOWN, tomb effigy, St Peter and St Paul Church, Fressingfield, Suffolk, engr F.H. van Hove, line, NPG.
PR D.LOGGAN, 1680, hs, *ad vivum*, oval, line, BM, NPG 636. R.WHITE, after E.Lutterel?, hs, oval, line, BM, NPG.

SANDERSON, Nicholas, see Saunderson.

SANDERSON, Robert (1587-1663) bishop of Lincoln.
P Attrib JOHN RILEY, 1662, hl, oval, Christ Church, Oxford, engr W.Dolle, line, for *Sermons*, 1662, BM, NPG, V & A.

SANDERSON, Sir William (1586?-1676) historian.
PR W.FAITHORNE, after G.Soest, hs, oval, line, for *Graphice*, 1658, BM, NPG.

SANDFORD, Francis (1630-1694) herald.
D GEORGE VERTUE, hl, pencil, NPG 4311.

SANDILANDS, James, see 7th Baron Torphicen.

SANDWICH, Edward Montagu, 1st Earl of (1625-1672) admiral.
P SIR PETER LELY, c1658-59, tql with breastplate, NMM, Greenwich. Studio of SIR P.LELY, (type of c1660), hs with Garter star, NPG 609. SIR P.LELY, c1667-68, tql, with breastplate and cannon, NMM. 'FELICIANO', tql with Garter star, Lisbon Embassy (DoE), Portugal.

SANDYS, Edwin (1516?-1588) archbishop of York.
P UNKNOWN, (after type of 1571), hs with wife, NPG 1268; version, Bishopthorpe, York, engr Passe, hl, line, for Holland, *Herwologia*, 1620, BM, NPG.
SC UNKNOWN, alabaster tomb effigy, Southwell Cathedral, Notts.

SANDYS, Sir Edwin (1561-1629) statesman.
PR V.GREEN, hl, oval, mezz, for Nash, *Hist of Worcestershire*, 1781, BM.

SANDYS, George (1578-1644) traveller and poet.
PR G.POWLE, after C.Johnson, hl, oval, etch, for Nash, *Hist of Worcestershire*, 1781, BM. W.RADDON, after C.Johnson, hl, line, for *Effigies Poeticae*, pub 1824, BM, NPG.

SARMENTO, Jacob de Castro (1692-1762) Portuguese physician of Jewish descent.
PR R.HOUSTON, after R.E.Pine, tql seated, mezz, BM, NPG.

SARSFIELD, Patrick, see titular Earl of Lucan.

SAUNDERS, Sir Edward (d1576) judge.
SC UNKNOWN, 1573, sandstone and marble kneeling effigy with wife, St Michael's Church, Weston-under-Wetherly, Warwicks.

SAUNDERS, Laurence (d1555) Protestant martyr.
PR UNKNOWN, wl being burned at stake, woodcut for Foxe, *Book of Martyrs*, 1563, NPG. PASSE, hl, line, for Holland, *Herwologia*, 1620, BM, NPG.

SAUNDERS, Richard (1613-1687?) astrologer.
PR T.CROSS, tql, line, for *Physiognomy and Chiromancie*, 1653, BM,

NPG. UNKNOWN, hl, oval, line, for *Astrological Judgment of Physick*, 1677, BM, NPG. UNKNOWN, hl, oval, line, BM, NPG.

SAUNDERSON or SANDERSON, Nicholas (1682-1739) mathematician.
P JOHN VANDERBANK, c1718–19, hl with armillary sphere, Old Schools, Cambridge. UNKNOWN, Christ's College, Cambridge.

SAVAGE, Sir Arnold (d1410) speaker of the House of Commons.
SC UNKNOWN, brass effigy with wife, St Bartholomew Church, Bobbing, Kent.

SAVAGE, Henry (1604?-1672) divine.
P Attrib JOHN TAYLOR, hl with book, Balliol College, Oxford.

SAVAGE, Sir John (d1492?) politician and soldier.
SC UNKNOWN, alabaster tomb effigy with wife, St Michael's Church, Macclesfield, Cheshire.

SAVAGE, John (1673-1747) divine and historian.
PR M. VAN DER GUCHT, after T.Forster, hs, oval, line, for *Hist of Germany*, 1702, BM, NPG.

SAVILE, Sir George, see 1st Marquess of Halifax.

SAVILE or SAVILLE, Sir Henry (1549-1622) scholar.
P MARCUS GHEERAERTS, 1621, wl, Bodleian Library, Oxford; version, Eton College, Berks.

SAVILE or SAVILLE, Sir John (1545-1607) judge.
P UNKNOWN, tql in robes, Harvard Law School, Cambridge, Mass, USA.

SAVILE or SAVILLE, William, see 2nd Marquess of Halifax.

SAWYER, Sir Robert (1633-1692) attorney-general.
G R.WHITE, 'Counsel for the Seven Bishops', line engr, 1688, BM, NPG.

SAXONY, Matilda, Duchess of, see Matilda.

SAY, Sir John (d1478?) speaker of the House of Commons.
SC UNKNOWN, brass effigy with wife, St Augustine Church, Broxbourne, Herts.

SAY, Samuel (1676-1743) dissenting minister.
P UNKNOWN, hl, oval, Dr Williams's Library, London.
PR C.HALL, after J.Richardson, hs, line, BM, NPG. J.HOPWOOD, hl, stipple, for Wilson, *Dissenting Churches*, 1809, BM, NPG.

SAYE and SELE, William Fiennes, 1st Viscount (1582-1662) parliamentarian and lord privy seal.
PR W.FAITHORNE?, hs, oval, line, BM, NPG. W.HOLLAR, hs, oval, etch, BM, NPG. UNKNOWN, wl on horseback, line, sold by J.Hinde, BM, NPG.

SCALEITS or SCARLETT, Robert (1499?-1594) sexton of Peterborough Cathedral.
P UNKNOWN, wl with spade, Peterborough Cathedral, engr W.Williams, etch, BM, NPG.

SCAMBLER, Edmund (1510?-1594) bishop of Norwich.
PR W.C.EDWARDS, from a painting, tql, line, pub 1844, BM, NPG.

SCARBOROUGH or SCARBURGH, Sir Charles (1616-1694) physician.
P RICHARD GREENBURY, 1651, tql with Edward Arris, Barbers' Company, London. Attrib JEAN DEMETRIUS, c1660?, tql seated with book, Royal College of Physicians, London.

SCARBOROUGH, Richard Lumley, 2nd Earl of (1688?-1740) soldier.
P SIR GODFREY KNELLER, 1717, hl, the 'Kit-cat Club' portrait, NPG 3222.
PR J.HALL, after J.B.Vanloo, hs in Garter robes, oval, line, for Maty,

Memoirs of Lord Chesterfield, 1777, BM, NPG. UNKNOWN, after picture at Lumley Castle, hl in Garter robes, lith, NPG.

SCARLETT, Robert, see Scaleits.

SCHEEMAKERS, Peter (1691-1781) sculptor.
P A.B. DE QUERTENMONT, 1776, hl, NPG 2675.
PR 'W.HOARE', hs, profile, etch, BM.

SCHEVEZ or **SCHIVES, William (d1497)** archbishop of St Andrews.
SC Attrib QUENTIN METSYS, 1491, bronze medallion, BM, and Musée des Antiquités, Rouen, France; plaster cast, SNPG 48.

SCHMIDT, Bernard, see Smith.

SCHOMBERG or **SCHONBERG, Frederick Armand de Schomberg, 1st Duke of (1615-1690)** general.
PR S.GRIBELIN, after M.Dahl, 1689, hl in armour, oval, line, BM, NPG. J.SMITH, after Sir G.Kneller, c1689, wl on horseback, mezz, BM, NPG. J.HOUBRAKEN, after Sir G.Kneller, hl in armour, oval, line, pub 1739, BM, NPG.

SCHOMBERG, Meinhard Schomberg, 3rd Duke of (1641-1719) general.
PR J.SMITH, after Sir G.Kneller, tql in armour, mezz, BM, NPG.

SCOBELL, Henry (d1660) clerk of the Parliament.
SC THOMAS SIMON, 1649, gold medal, profile head, NPG 4363.

SCOTT, Anne, see Countess of Buccleuch.

SCOTT, Henry, see 1st Earl of Deloraine.

SCOTT, James, see Duke of Monmouth and Buccleuch.

SCOTT, John (1639-1695) divine.
PR M. VAN DER GUCHT, hs, oval, line, NPG. R.WHITE, hs, oval, line, BM, NPG.

SCOTT, Sir Thomas (1535-1594?) high sheriff of Kent.
PR S. DE WILDE, from a painting, hl in armour, etch, pub 1803, BM, NPG.

SCOTT, Thomas (1580?-1626) political writer.
PR C.PASSE, 1624, hl, line, BM, NPG. W.MARSHALL, after C.Passe, hs, oval, line, BM, NPG.

SCOTT, Thomas (d1660) regicide.
G UNKNOWN, 'The regicides executed in 1660', line engr, for *Rebels no Saints*, 1660, BM.
PR G.P.HARDING, hs, oval, line, pub 1809, NPG. UNKNOWN, hs, oval, with vignettes, line, NPG.

SCOTT, Sir William (1459-1524) soldier and statesman.
SC UNKNOWN, brass effigy, St Mary's Church, Brabourne, Kent.

SCOUGALL, Henry (1650-1678) Scottish divine.
PR T.TROTTER, hl, line, for Pinkerton, *Iconographia Scotica*, 1796, BM, NPG.

SCOUGALL, John (1645?-1730?) portrait painter.
P Self-portrait, (called Scougall), hl, NGS 2032.

SCOUGALL, Patrick (1607?-1682) bishop of Aberdeen.
PR T.TROTTER, hl, line, for Pinkerton, *Iconographia Scotica*, 1796, BM, NPG.

SCROGGS, Sir William (1623-1683) judge.
P After J.M.WRIGHT, tql seated in robes, NPG 1850.

SCROPE, Adrian (1601-1660) regicide.
P By or after ROBERT WALKER, tql in armour, NPG 4435, engr C.Townley, hs, etch, pub 1801, BM, NPG.

SCROPE, John (1662?-1752) judge and recorder of Bristol.
P Attrib SIR GODFREY KNELLER, tql, City of Bristol Museum and Art Gallery.

SCROPE, Richard (1350?-1405) archbishop of York.
W UNKNOWN, wl in robes, York Minster.

SCUDAMORE, John Scudamore, 1st Viscount (1601-1671) soldier and statesman.
P EDWARD BOWER, 1642, hs in armour, oval, Kentchurch Court, Hereford.

SCUDDER, Henry (d1659?) divine.
PR W.SHERWIN, hl, line, for *Christian's Daily Walke*, 1674, BM, NPG.

SEAFIELD, James Ogilvy, 1st Earl of (1664-1730) lord chancellor of Scotland.
P SIR J.B.MEDINA, 1695, tql, SNPG 1064. SIR GODFREY KNELLER, c1704, tql seated in robes, Royal College of Surgeons, Edinburgh. UNKNOWN, tql, Hopetoun House, Lothian region, Scotland.

SEAFORTH, Kenneth Mackenzie, 4th Earl of (d1701) royalist.
D ROBERT WHITE, hs, pencil on vellum, BM, engr R.White, oval, line, BM, NPG.

SECKER, Thomas (1693-1768) archbishop of Canterbury.
P CHARLES PHILLIPS, 1740, tql seated, Diocese of Oxford. Attrib THOMAS HUDSON, c1747-58, hl, St James's Church, Piccadilly, London. Attrib ALLAN RAMSAY, tql seated, Lambeth Palace, London. Attrib SIR JOSHUA REYNOLDS, c1758, tql, Lambeth Palace, London; versions, St Edmund Hall, Oxford; NPG 850.
PR J.McARDELL, after T.?Willes, 1747, hl, oval, mezz, BM, NPG.

SEDDON, John (1644-1700) writing-master.
PR J.STURT, after W.Faithorne, hl, oval, line, for *Penman's Paradise*, 1695, BM, NPG.

SEDGWICK, Obadiah (1600?-1658) puritan divine.
D T.ATHOW, after unknown artist, hl, NPG 2452, line engr, pub 1792, BM, NPG.

SEDLEY, Catherine, see Countess of Dorchester.

SEDLEY, Sir Charles (1639?-1701) wit and dramatist.
P Attrib JOHN RILEY, hs, oval, Knole (NT), Kent.
PR M. VAN DER GUCHT, hs, oval, line, for *Works*, 1722, BM, NPG.

SEEMAN, Enoch (1694-1744) portrait painter.
PR J.FABER, jun, after E.Seeman, tql aged 19, mezz, BM, NPG.

SEGAR, Sir William (d1633) Garter king-of-arms.
PR F.DELARAM, hl in robes, oval, line, BM, NPG, V & A.

SELDEN, John (1584-1654) jurist and antiquary.
P Studio of SIR PETER LELY, (after type of c1650), tql, Clarendon Coll on loan to Plymouth Art Gallery; version, hl, NPG 76.
PR J.CHANTRY, hl, oval, line, for *God Made Man*, 1661, BM, NPG. R.WHITE, hs, oval, line, for *Jani Anglorum Facies altera*, 1683, BM, NPG.

SERGISON, Charles (1654-1732) commissoner of navy.
SC THOMAS ADY(E), 1732, relief portrait medallion on monument, Cuckfield Church, Sussex.

SERMON, William (1629?-1679) physician.
PR T.CROSS, hl, aged 42, oval, line, BM. T.CROSS, hl, line, BM, NPG. W.SHERWIN, hs, oval, line, for *Ladies' Companion*, 1671, BM, NPG.

SETON, Sir Alexander, see 1st Earl of Dunfermline.

SETON, Charles, see 2nd Earl of Dunfermline.

SETON, George Seton, 5th Baron (1531-1585) supporter of Mary Queen of Scots.
P UNKNOWN, 157?, tql, NGS on loan to SNPG L309.
G FRANS POURBUS, sen, 1572, family group, NGS on loan to SNPG L312.

SETON, George (1584-1650), see 3rd Earl of Winton.

SEVER, Henry (d1471) divine.
SC UNKNOWN, brass effigy, Merton College Chapel, Oxford.

SEWALL, Samuel (1652-1730) colonist and judge.
P NATHANIEL EMMONS, 1728, tql seated, Massachusetts Historical Society, Boston, USA. JOHN SMIBERT, 1729, hs, Museum of Fine Arts, Boston, USA.

SEYMOUR, Algernon, see 7th Duke of Somerset.

SEYMOUR, Lady Arabella, née Stuart (1575-1615) wife of William Seymour and cousin of James I.
P UNKNOWN, 1577, tql as infant, Hardwick Hall (NT), Derbys. UNKNOWN, 1589, wl at thirteen, Hardwick Hall. UNKNOWN, c1605, wl, DoE.
PR J.WHITTAKERS, sen, 1619, hl, oval, line, BM, NPG.

SEYMOUR, Charles, see 6th Duke of Somerset.

SEYMOUR, Edward (1506?-1552), see 1st Duke of Somerset.

SEYMOUR, Edward (1539?-1621), see Earl of Hertford.

SEYMOUR, Edward (1561-1612), see Baron Beauchamp.

SEYMOUR, Sir Edward, 4th Bart (1633-1708) speaker of the House of Commons.
P JAMES LONSDALE, after unknown artist, c1803, wl seated in robes, Palace of Westminster, London.
SC J.M.RYSBRACK, 1728, tomb effigy, All Saints' Church, Maiden Bradley, Wilts.
PR W.WORTHINGTON, tql seated in robes, line, pub 1821, BM, NPG.

SEYMOUR, Jane, see JANE Seymour.

SEYMOUR, Lady Katherine, see Countess of Hertford.

SEYMOUR, William, see 2nd Duke of Somerset.

SEYMOUR of Sudeley, Thomas Seymour, Baron (1508?-1549) lord high admiral.
P UNKNOWN, (after a contemporary type), hs, NPG 4571; version, Longleat, Wilts.

SEYMOUR of Trowbridge, Francis Seymour, 1st Baron (1590?-1664) royalist.
P Attrib PAUL VAN SOMER, wl, Petworth (NT), W Sussex.

SHADWELL, Thomas (1642?-1692) dramatist and poet laureate.
P UNKNOWN, 1690, hl, NPG 4143.
SC FRANCIS BIRD, 1692, marble bust on monument, Westminster Abbey, London.

SHAFTESBURY, Anthony Ashley-Cooper, 1st Earl of (1621-1683) politician.
P After JOHN GREENHILL, c1672-3, tql seated in robes, NPG 3893, engr A.Blooteling, 1673, line, BM. Attrib J.GREENHILL, tql in breastplate, Althorp, Northants.
SC GEORGE BOWER, silver medal, BM.
PR R.WHITE, 1680, hl, oval, line, BM, NPG.

SHAFTESBURY, Anthony Ashley-Cooper, 3rd Earl of (1671-1713) moral philosopher.
PR S.GRIBELIN, after J.Closterman, wl, line, for *Characteristics*, 1723, BM, NPG. J.HOPWOOD, hl, oval, stipple, NPG.

SHAKESPEARE, William (1564-1616) dramatist and poet.
P UNKNOWN, hs, oval, 'the Chandos portrait', NPG 1.
SC GERARD JOHNSON or JANSSEN, c1620, bust on monument, Holy Trinity Church, Stratford-upon-Avon; plaster cast, NPG 1735.
PR MARTIN DROESHOUT, hs, line, 1st state, First Folio, BL. M.DROESHOUT, hs, line, 3rd state, NPG 185.

SHANNON, Henry Boyle, 1st Earl of (1682-1764) Whig politician.
P STEPHEN SLAUGHTER, 1744, tql seated in Speaker's gown, Palace of Westminster, London; version, unknown artist, NGI 394.
SC JOHN VAN NOST, 1754, marble bust, Rotunda Hospital, Dublin. UNKNOWN, 1753, brass medal, BM.

SHARINGTON, Sir William (1495?-1553) vice-treasurer of the mint at Bristol.
D HANS HOLBEIN, jun, hs, chalks, Royal Coll.

SHARP, James (1613-1679) archbishop of St Andrews.
P After SIR PETER LELY?, tql seated, SNPG 1529, engr G.Vertue, 1710, line, BM, NPG.
PR D.LOGGAN, hl, *ad vivum*, oval, line, BM, NPG.

SHARP, John (1645-1714) archbishop of York.
P After ROBERT WHITE, tql, Bishopthorpe Palace, York; version, The Deanery, Canterbury.
D R.WHITE, hs?, pencil sketch, Christ's College, Cambridge.
SC FRANCIS BIRD, 1714, tomb effigy, York Minster.
PR R.WHITE, 1691?, hs, *ad vivum*, oval, line, BM, NPG.

SHARP, Thomas (1693-1758) divine.
PR UNKNOWN, hl, stipple, pub 1825, NPG.

SHAW, Peter (1694-1763) physician.
P UNKNOWN, c1740?, hs in turban, Royal College of Physicians, London. UNKNOWN, c1740–50, hl, Royal College of Physicians.

SHAW, Thomas (1694-1751) divine and African traveller.
P UNKNOWN, hs, St Edmund Hall, Oxford. UNKNOWN, hs, Queen's College, Oxford.
PR J.GREEN, hl, oval, line, BM, NPG.

SHEFFIELD, Sir Edmund (1564?-1646), see 1st Earl of Mulgrave.

SHEFFIELD, Edmund (1611?-1658), see 2nd Earl of Mulgrave.

SHEFFIELD, John, see 1st Duke of Buckingham and Normanby.

SHELDON, Gilbert (1598-1677) archbishop of Canterbury.
P Studio of SIR PETER LELY, c1665, tql, NPG 1837; versions, Lambeth Palace, London; Bodleian Library, Oxford. Attrib SIR P.LELY, wl seated, Sheldonian Theatre, Oxford. UNKNOWN, hs, oval, All Souls College, Oxford.
M SAMUEL COOPER, 1667, hl, w/c, Walters Art Gallery, Baltimore, Maryland, USA.
PR D.LOGGAN, hl, *ad vivum*, oval, line, BM.

SHELLEY, George (1666?-1736?) writing master at Christ's Hospital
PR G.BICKHAM, hl, oval, line, for *Natural Writing*, 1709, BM, NPG, V & A. G.BICKHAM, after B.Lens, hs, oval, line, for 1714 ed of previous work, BM, NPG.

SHELLEY, Sir Richard (1513?-1589?) last grand prior of the Knights of St John in England.
SC UNKNOWN, two medals, BM.

SHELTON, Thomas (1601-1650?) stenographer.
PR T.CROSS, hl, oval, line, for *Book of Psalms*, 1660, BM. UNKNOWN, hl, aged 46, line, NPG; same engr 'aged 49', 1650, NPG.

SHEPHERD or SHEPPARD, Sir Fleetwood (1634-1698) courtier and poet.
P Attrib SIR GODFREY KNELLER, tql with rod of office, Knole (NT), Kent.

SHERIDAN, Thomas (1687-1738) schoolmaster and writer.
PR T.COOK, hs, oval, line, for *Life of Swift*, 1784, BM, NPG.

SHERIDAN, William (1636-1711) bishop of Kilmore.
PR W.SHERWIN, hs, oval, line, for *Sermons*, 1704, BM, NPG.

SHERLOCK, Richard (1612-1689) divine.
PR M. VAN DER GUCHT, hs, oval, line, BM, NPG.

SHERLOCK, Thomas (1678-1761) bishop of London.
P JOHN VANDERBANK, tql seated with book as young man, St Catherine's College (wrongly called Benjamin Hoadly). seated, Fulham Palace, London, engr S.F.Ravenet, 1756, line, BM, NPG. 'JONES', tql seated as prelate of Order of Garter, St Catherine's College (wrongly catalogued as Benjamin Hoadly).
PR LELIUS, after Jones, 1737, tql seated in robes of chancellor of the Garter, mezz, BM, NPG.

SHERLOCK, William (1641?-1707) dean of St Paul's.
PR R.WHITE, hs, oval, line, for *Discourse on the Divine Providence*, 1694, BM, NPG.

SHERWIN, William (1607-1687?) divine.
PR W.SHERWIN, hs, aged 65, oval, line, for *Clavis*, 1672, BM, NPG.

SHIPPEN, Robert (1675-1745) principal of Brasenose College, Oxford.
SC SIR ROBERT TAYLOR, 1745, bust on monument, Brasenose College.

SHIPPEN, William (1673-1743) parliamentary Jacobite.
P THOMAS HUDSON, hl, Badminton House, Avon.

SHIRLEY, Sir Anthony (1565-1635?) traveller and ambassador to Persia.
PR D.CUSTOS, hs in armour, oval, line, for Custos, *Atrium Heroicum Caesarum*, 1600–02, BM, NPG. 'IOANNES ORLANDI', 1601, hl, line, NPG. G.SADELER, hs in armour, oval, line, BM, NPG.

SHIRLEY, James (1596-1666) dramatic poet.
P UNKNOWN, tql seated, Bodleian Library, Oxford.
PR W.MARSHALL, 1646, hl, oval, line, NPG. R.GAYWOOD, after 'G.Phenik', bust, etch, for *Six Plays*, 1653, BM, NPG.

SHIRLEY, Sir Robert (1581?-1628) envoy in service of Shah of Persia.
P SIR ANTHONY VANDYCK, 1622, wl in Persian dress, Petworth (NT), W Sussex. UNKNOWN, wl in Persian dress, Berkeley Castle, Glos.
M PETER OLIVER, hs, oval, Buccleuch Estates, Selkirk, Scotland.
PR M.GREUTER, hl, oval, with vignette of papal audience, line, BM.

SHIRLEY, Sir Robert, Bart (1629-1656) royalist.
PR J.BASIRE, hl in armour, oval, line, for Nichols, *Hist of Leicestershire*, 1800, BM, NPG.

SHIRLEY, William (1694-1771) colonial governor.
PR J.McARDELL, after T.Hudson, tql, mezz, Chaloner Smith Coll, NGI.

SHORE, Jane (d1527?) mistress of Edward IV.
P Fontainebleu School, (called Shore), hs, Eton College, Berks.

SHORTON, Robert (d1535) archdeacon of Bath and first master of St John's College, Cambridge.
P UNKNOWN, hl, oval, St John's College; version, Pembroke College, Cambridge.

SHOVELL, Sir Clowdisley (1650-1707) admiral.
P UNKNOWN, c1692–94, tql in armour, on loan to NMM, Greenwich. MICHAEL DAHL, 1702, wl in armour, NMM; version, NPG 797. M.DAHL, c1702–5, tql, NMM.
SC Attrib GRINLING GIBBONS, tomb effigy on monument, Westminster Abbey, London.
PR J.SMITH, after W. de Ryck, tql with globe, mezz, BM, NPG.

SHOWER, Sir Bartholomew (1658-1701) recorder of London.
PR J.NUTTING, hl, oval, line, for *Reports*, 1708, BM, NPG.

SHOWER, John (1657-1715) nonconformist divine.
P UNKNOWN, hs, oval, Dr Williams's Library, London.
PR M. VAN DER GUCHT, hs, oval, line, for *Reflections on the late Earthquake*, 1693, BM, NPG. R.WHITE, hs, oval, line, for W.Pong, *Memoirs*, 1716, BM, NPG.

SHREWSBURY, Charles Talbot, 1st Duke of (1660-1718) politician.
P SIR GODFREY KNELLER, c1685, hs, oval, Boughton House, Northants (Buccleuch Estates, Selkirk, Scotland). After SIR G.KNELLER, (type of c1685), hl with Garter ribbon and star, oval, NPG 1424. SIR G.KNELLER, c1685–90, wl in peer's robes, Eastnor Castle, Herefords. SIR G.KNELLER, c1685–94, wl in Garter robes, Charterhouse School, Godalming, Surrey.
G PETER ANGELIS, 'Queen Anne and the Knights of the Garter', oil, 1713, NPG 624.

SHREWSBURY, Elizabeth Talbot, née Hardwick, Countess of (1518-1608) heiress known as 'Bess of Hardwick'.
P UNKNOWN, c1580, hl, Hardwick Hall (NT), Derbys. UNKNOWN, c1590, tql, Hardwick Hall; version, NPG 203.
SC UNKNOWN, tomb effigy, All Saints Church, Derby.

SHREWSBURY, George Talbot, 4th Earl (1468-1538) soldier and statesman.
SC UNKNOWN, tomb effigy with two wives, Cathedral of St Peter and St Paul, Sheffield.

SHREWSBURY, George Talbot, 6th Earl of (1528?-1590) keeper of Mary Queen of Scots.
P UNKNOWN, c1580, hs with Garter George, Hardwick Hall (NT), Derbys; copy, head, w/c, NPG 2822.
SC UNKNOWN, tomb effigy, Cathedral of St Peter and St Paul, Sheffield.
PR M.GHEERAERTS, sen, 'Procession of Garter Knights, 1576', etch, BM.

SHREWSBURY, Gilbert Talbot, 7th Earl of (1553-1616) son of Bess of Hardwick.
D G.P.HARDING, tql, wash, Sutherland Coll, Ashmolean Museum, Oxford.

SHREWSBURY, John Talbot, 1st Earl of (1388?-1453) soldier and statesman.
P UNKNOWN, hl with surcoat of arms, Compton Wynyates, Warwicks.
MS UNKNOWN, c1445, wl presenting book to Margaret of Anjou, 'Poems and Romances', BL Royal Ms 15 E VI; and wl being presented with sword by Henry VI, BL Royal Ms 15 E VI, fol 405.
SC UNKNOWN, tomb effigy, St Alkmund's Church, Whitchurch, Salop.

SHUCKBURGH, Sir Richard (1596-1656) royalist.
SC PETER BENNIER, bust on monument, St John Baptist Church, Upper Shuckburgh, Warwicks.

SHUTE, Josiah (1588-1643) archdeacon of Colchester.
PR W.MARSHALL, hl with book, oval, line, for *19 Sermons on Genesis XVI*, 1649, BM, NPG.

SIBBALD, Sir Robert (1641-1722) Scottish physician and antiquary.
P UNKNOWN, hl, Royal College of Physicians, Edinburgh, engr Lizars, line, for Jardine, *Naturalist Library*, BM, NPG.

SIBBES, Richard (1577-1635) puritan divine.
P UNKNOWN, hl with book, oval, Bodleian Library, Oxford.
PR W.MARSHALL, hl, aged 58, oval, line, for *Fountaine Sealed*, 1637,

BM; copy, for *Precious Promises*, 1638, BM, NPG. J.PAYNE, hs, oval, line, BM, NPG.

SIDNEY, Algernon (1622-1683) republican and patriot.
P JUSTUS VAN EGMONT, 1663, hl with breastplate, Penshurst, Kent; copy, NPG 568.
M JOHN HOSKINS, (called Sidney), hs, oval, Buccleuch Estates, Selkirk, Scotland.
SC GEORGE BOWER, silver medal, BM.

SIDNEY, Sir Henry (1529-1586) lord deputy of Ireland and president of Wales.
P UNKNOWN, 1573, wl, Petworth (NT), W Sussex; versions, NPG 1092, and Penshurst, Kent.
PR PASSE, hl, oval, line, for Holland, *Herwologia*, 1620, BM, NPG.

SIDNEY, Henry (1641-1704), see 1st Earl of Romney.

SIDNEY, Sir Philip (1544-1586) soldier, statesman and poet.
P UNKNOWN, *c*1577, tql, Longleat, Wilts; version, Warwick Castle, Warwicks and copy, NPG 2096. Attrib JOHN DE CRITZ, *c*1585, hs, Penshurst, Kent. After J. DE CRITZ, tql in armour, Blickling Hall (NT), Norfolk.
PR PASSE, hl, oval, line, for Holland, *Herwologia*, 1620, BM, NPG.

SIDNEY, Philip (1619-1698), see 3rd Earl of Leicester.

SIDNEY, Robert (1563-1626), see 1st Earl of Leicester.

SIDNEY, Robert (1595-1677), see 2nd Earl of Leicester.

SIMON, Abraham (1617-1692) medallist and modeller in wax.
P Attrib self-portrait, *c*1670–80, head, NPG 1642.
D GEORGE VERTUE, after Sir Godfrey Kneller, hl seated with wax portrait, red chalk and indian ink, BM.
SC A.SIMON, profile head, wax model, BM.
PR A.BLOOTELING, after Sir P.Lely, hs, mezz, BM, NPG. A.SIMON, 3 heads borne on wings of an eagle, etch, BM. G.VERTUE, profile bust, oval, line, for Vertue, *Medals, Coins, etc of T.Simon*, 1753, BM, NPG.

SIMON, Thomas (1623?-1665) medallist and seal engraver.
PR G.VERTUE, hl, oval, line, for Vertue, *Medals, Coins, etc of T.Simon*, 1753, BM, NPG.

SIMPSON, Christopher (1605?-1669) violist and writer on music.
P Attrib JOHN CARWARDEN, hs, oval, Faculty of Music, Oxford.
PR W.FAITHORNE, after J.Carwarden, hs, oval, line, for *Division Viol*, 1659, BM, NPG. UNKNOWN, wl playing viola da gamba, portrait?, line, for *Division Viol*, NPG. W.FAITHORNE, hl, oval, line, for *Compendium of Practical Musick*, 1667, BM, NPG.

SIMPSON or SIMSON, Edward (1578-1651) divine and historian.
PR UNKNOWN, hl aged 73 with book, oval, line, for *Chronicon*, 1652, BM, NPG. UNKNOWN, hl, oval, line, NPG.

SIMPSON, Sidrach or Sydrach (1600?-1655) divine and master of Pembroke Hall, Cambridge.
PR UNKNOWN, hl with book, line, NPG.

SIMSON, Edward, see Simpson.

SIMSON, Robert (1687-1768) mathematician.
P DE NUNE, hl, The Royal Technical College, Glasgow, engr, hl, oval, line, for Trail, *Life and Writings of R.Simpson*, 1812, NPG.

SINCLAIR, James (*d*1762) general.
P FRANCIS COTES, 1762, hl, Dunrobin Castle, Highland region, Scotland.

SKEFFINGTON, Sir John, see 2nd Viscount Massereene.

SKELTON, Bevil (fl 1661-1692) diplomat.
PR M. VAN SOMER, 1678, tql in armour, *ad vivum*, line, NPG.

SKINNER, Matthew (1689-1749) sergeant-at-law.
P UNKNOWN, tql in robes with seal, Christ Church, Oxford.

SKIPPON, Philip (*d*1660) parliamentary commander.
PR UNKNOWN, hs in breastplate, oval, line, for Vicars, *England's Worthies*, 1647, BM. UNKNOWN, hl in armour, line, copy from print in Ricraft, *Survey of England's Champions*, BM, NPG. UNKNOWN, hl with breastplate, stipple, NPG.

SLANNING, Sir Nicholas (1606-1643) royalist.
PR R.COOPER, hl in armour, oval, stipple, NPG. UNKNOWN, hs in armour, oval, line, NPG.

SLATER, Samuel (*d*1704) nonconformist divine.
PR R.WHITE, 1692, hl, *ad vivum*, oval, line, BM, NPG.

SLATER or SLAYTER, William (1587-1647) chaplain to Queen Anne of Denmark.
PR UNKNOWN, hs, line, for *The Psalms*, BM, NPG.

SLINGSBY, Sir Henry (1602-1658) royalist.
SC Attrib THOMAS RAWLINS, silver medal, BM.
PR G.VERTUE, hs, octagonal, line, for *Loyalists*, BM, NPG.

SLOANE, Sir Hans (1660-1753) physician and collector.
P SIR GODFREY KNELLER, 1716, hl, oval, Royal Society, London. THOMAS MURRAY, *c*1725, hl, Royal College of Physicians, London, engr J.Faber, jun, 1728, hs, oval, mezz, BM, NPG. JONATHAN RICHARDSON, 1730, wl seated in robes, Examination Schools, Oxford. STEPHEN SLAUGHTER, 1736, tql seated, NPG 569. Attrib JOHN VANDERBANK, wl seated, BM.
SC J.A.DASSIER, medal, BM. J.M.RYSBRACK, 1737, statue, Chelsea Physic Garden, London. J.M.RYSBRACK, terracotta bust, BM.

SMALBROKE or SMALLBROKE, Richard (1672-1749) bishop of Lichfield and Coventry.
P UNKNOWN, hs, Magdalen College, Oxford.
PR G.VERTUE, after T.Murray, 1733, hl, oval, line, BM, NPG.

SMALLWOOD, John, see Winchcombe.

SMALRIDGE, George (1663-1719) bishop of Bristol and dean of Christ Church, Oxford.
P SIR GODFREY KNELLER, tql seated, Christ Church, engr G.Vertue, hs, oval, line, for *Sermons*, 1724, BM, NPG. H.RODD, tql seated, City Art Gallery, Bristol. UNKNOWN, tql, Christ Church.

SMART, Peter (1569-1652?) puritan divine.
PR W.HOLLAR, 1641, hl with book, etch, BM, NPG.

SMEDLEY, Jonathan (fl 1689-1729) dean of Clogher.
PR J.FABER, jun, after R.Dellon, 1723, hl, oval, mezz, BM.

SMELLIE, William (1697-1763) teacher of midwifery.
P Self-portrait, hl, Royal College of Surgeons, Edinburgh.

SMIBERT, John (1684-1751) portrait painter.
P Self-portrait, *c*1728, tql seated, Montclair Art Museum, Montclair, New Jersey, USA.
G JOHN SMIBERT, 'the Bermuda Group', oil, *c*1729–30, Yale University Art Gallery, New Haven, USA.

SMITH or SCHMIDT, Bernard (1630?-1708) organ builder.
P UNKNOWN, hl, oval, Faculty of Music, Oxford, engr J.Caldwall, hs, oval, line, NPG.

SMITH, Erasmus (1611-1691) educational benefactor.
P UNKNOWN, 1666, Christ's Hospital, Horsham, Sussex.
PR G.WHITE, hl, oval, mezz, BM, NPG.

SMITH, Henry (1550?-1591) puritan divine.
PR T.CROSS, hl with book, line, for *Sermons*, 1657, V & A. UNKNOWN, hl, line, for *Sermons*, 1660?, BM, NPG.

SMITH, James (1645-1711) Roman Catholic priest.
PR UNKNOWN, hs, oval, stipple, NPG.

SMITH, Sir Jeremiah (1615-1675) admiral.
P SIR PETER LELY, *c*1666-67, tql, NMM, Greenwich.

SMITH, John (1580?-1631) soldier and colonist.
PR S.PASSE, 1616, hl, oval, line, BM, NPG 4594.

SMITH, John (1652-1742) engraver.
P SIR GODFREY KNELLER, 1696, hl with engraved portrait, TATE 273, engr J.Smith, 1716, mezz, BM, NPG.

SMITH, John (1655-1723) speaker of the House of Commons.
P After SIR GODFREY KNELLER, wl in robes, Palace of Westminster, London.

SMITH, John (1657-1726) judge and chief baron of the exchequer.
P UNKNOWN, hl in robes, oval, Parliament Hall, Edinburgh.
PR J.BASIRE, tql in robes, line, for Nichols, *Hist of Leicestershire*, 1795, BM, NPG.

SMITH, Joseph (1670-1756) provost of Queen's College, Oxford.
P J.MAUBERT, hl, oval, Queen's College, engr B.Baron, line, NPG.

SMITH, Miles or Milo (1552?-1624) bishop of Gloucester.
P UNKNOWN, tql with book, Christ Church, Oxford.

SMITH, Robert (1689-1768) mathematician and founder of prize at Cambridge.
P JOHN VANDERBANK, 1730, hs, Trinity College, Cambridge. J.FREEMAN, 1783, (posthumous), wl seated, Trinity College.
SC PETER SCHEEMAKERS, 1758, marble bust, Trinity College.

SMITH, Sir Thomas (1513-1577) secretary of state and diplomat.
P UNKNOWN, hl with globe, Eton College, Berks.
G M.GHEERAERTS, sen, 'Procession of Garter Knights, 1576', etch, BM.
SC UNKNOWN, tomb effigy, St Michael's Church, Theydon Mount, Essex.
PR UNKNOWN, tql, oval, woodcut, for Gabriel Harvey, *Lachrymae pro Obitu*, 1578, BL.

SMITH or SMYTHE, Sir Thomas (1558?-1625) governor of the East India Company and diplomat.
PR S.PASSE, 1616, hl, oval, line, BM, NPG.

SMITH, Thomas (1615-1702) bishop of Carlisle.
PR J.SMITH, after T.Stephenson, hl, oval, mezz, BM, NPG.

SMITH, Thomas (1706?-1762) admiral.
P RICHARD WILSON, *c*1744-46, tql with telescope, NMM, Greenwich, engr J.Faber, jun, 1746, mezz, BM, NPG.

SMITH or SMYTHE, William (1460?-1514) bishop of Lincoln and founder of Brasenose College, Oxford.
SC UNKNOWN, brass effigy, Lincoln Cathedral.

SMITH, William (1651?-1735) antiquary.
P UNKNOWN, hs, oval, University College, Oxford.

SMYTHE, Sir Thomas, see Smith.

SMYTHE, William, see Smith.

SNAGGE, Thomas (1536-1592) speaker of the House of Commons.
SC UNKNOWN, alabaster tomb effigy with wife, St Mary's Church, Marston Moretaine, Beds.

SNAPE, Andrew (1675-1742) provost of King's College, Cambridge.
PR J.FABER, sen, hl, oval, mezz, BM.

SOEST, Gerard (*d*1681) portrait painter.
P Self-portrait, (called Soest), hs, NGI 605, engr A.Bannerman, hs with Edema and Griffier, line, for Walpole, *Anecdotes*, 1762, BM, NPG.

SOMERS, John Somers, Baron (1651-1716) lord chancellor.
P SIR PETER LELY?, hs as young man, Eastnor Castle, Herefordshire. Attrib JOHN RILEY, hs, oval, as young man, Dulwich College Gallery, London. SIR GODFREY KNELLER, *c*1690, hs, Eastnor Castle, engr J.Houbraken, hs, oval, line, for Birch, *Heads*, 1745, BM, NPG. SIR G.KNELLER, *c*1700-10, hl, NPG 490. SIR G.KNELLER, *c*1700-10, hl with book, the 'Kit-cat Club' portrait, NPG 3223. SIR G.KNELLER, *c*1700-10, wl in Chancellor's robes, Knole (NT), Kent.
M UNKNOWN, *c*1690-1700, hl, w/c, NPG 3658.
PR J.SMITH, after J.Richardson, 1713, hl, oval, mezz, BM, NPG.

SOMERSET, Algernon Seymour, 7th Duke of (1684-1750) colonel and governor of Minorca.
P Attrib JOHN VANDERBANK, tql as young man, Petworth (NT), W Sussex. Attrib GEORGE KNAPTON, tql seated as old man, Syon House, Brentford, Middx.

SOMERSET, Charles (1460?-1526), see 1st Earl of Worcester.

SOMERSET, Charles Seymour, 6th Duke of (1662-1748) courtier.
P JOHN RILEY, *c*1682, hs in armour, oval, Petworth (NT), W Sussex. J.RILEY and J.B.CLOSTERMAN, after *c*1684-88, wl in Garter robes, Petworth. SIR GODFREY KNELLER, *c*1703, hl, the 'Kit-cat Club' portrait, NPG 3224. SIR G.KNELLER, 1713, tql in Garter robes, Petworth.
SC GRINLING GIBBONS, 1691, statue, Trinity College, Cambridge. J.M.RYSBRACK, 1756, marble statue, Senate House, University of Cambridge.

SOMERSET, Edward Seymour, 1st Duke of (1506?-1552) the Protector.
P UNKNOWN, hl with Garter George, Longleat, Wilts.
M NICHOLAS HILLIARD, 1560, hs, oval, Buccleuch Estates, Selkirk, Scotland.
G UNKNOWN, 'Edward VI and the Pope', oil, *c*1548-49, NPG 4165.
PR PASSE, hl with Garter George, oval, line, for Holland, *Herwologia*, 1620, BM, NPG.

SOMERSET, Edward (1553-1628), see 4th Earl of Worcester.

SOMERSET, Edward (1601-1667), see 2nd Marquess of Worcester.

SOMERSET, Elizabeth Percy, Duchess of (1667-1722) heiress, wife of 6th Duke of Somerset.
P SIR PETER LELY, *c*1669-70, wl with spaniel as child, Syon House, Brentford, Middx. Studio of SIR P.LELY, *c*1679-80, tql with flower garland, Syon House. Attrib JOHANN KERSEBOOM, tql seated with flower, Petworth (NT), W Sussex. JOHN RILEY and J.B.CLOSTERMAN, *c*1687-88, wl with son, Petworth. SIR GODFREY KNELLER, 1713, tql seated in robes, Petworth. MICHAEL DAHL, *c*1711-14, tql seated in robes, Petworth.
D After SIR P.LELY, *c*1679-80, hs, chalks, NPG 1753.
PR J. VAN DER VAART, after Sir P.Lely, wl seated on ground, mezz, BM, NPG.

SOMERSET, Henry (1577?-1646), see 1st Marquess of Worcester.

SOMERSET, Henry (1629-1700), see 1st Duke of Beaufort.

SOMERSET, Henry (1684-1714), see 2nd Duke of Beaufort.

SOMERSET, John Beaufort, 1st Earl of (1373?-1410) deputy constable of England.

MS UNKNOWN, wl kneeling, Latin *Book of Hours*, BL Royal Ms 2A, XVIII, fol 23v.

SC UNKNOWN, alabaster tomb effigy, St Michael-the-Warrior's Chapel, Canterbury Cathedral.

SOMERSET, John Beaufort, 1st Duke of (1403-1444) captain-general in Aquitaine and Normandy.

SC UNKNOWN, tomb effigy with wife, Wimborne Minster, Dorset, engr J.Basire, line, for Gough, *Sepulchral Monuments*, 1786, BM, NPG.

SOMERSET, Robert Carr or Ker, Earl of (d 1645) favourite of James I.

P After a miniature by JOHN HOSKINS, (type of c1620-30), hs with earring, NPG 1114.

M UNKNOWN, c1611, hs, w/c, NPG 4260. JOHN HOSKINS, c1620-30, hs with earring, Royal Coll; version, Buccleuch Estates, Selkirk, Scotland.

PR R.ELSTRACK, c1610, wl with countess, line, for *Truth brought to Light*, 1651, BM, NPG, V & A. S.PASSE, c1615, hs in Garter robes, oval, line, BM.

SOMERSET, William (1526-1589), see 3rd Earl of Worcester.

SOMERSET, William Seymour, 2nd Duke of (1588-1660) royalist.

P ROBERT WALKER, 1656, tql in armour, Syon House, Brentford, Middx.

SOMERVILLE, William (1675-1742) poet.

P UNKNOWN, hl, oval, NPG 1308.

PR R.RHODES, hs, line, pub 1815, NPG.

SOMMERS, William (d 1560) Henry VIII's jester.

MS UNKNOWN, wl with the King, Henry VIII *Psalter*, BL Royal Ms 2A. XVI, fol 63v.

PR F.DELARAM, wl, line, BM.

SOMNER, William (1598-1669) Anglo-Saxon scholar and antiquary.

PR M.BURGHERS, hl, oval, line, for *Treatise of the Roman Ports*, 1693, BM, NPG, V & A.

SOPHIA, Princess, Electress of Hanover (1630-1714) mother of George I.

P GERARD HONTHORST, c1643, hs with rose, Wilton House, Wilts. G.HONTHORST, c1645, hl, oval, Staatlichen Schlösser und Gärten, Schloss Charlottenburg, W Berlin. G.HONTHORST, 1650, hl, Ashdown House (NT), Oxon. UNKNOWN, hs with hood, oval, Royal Coll.

M UNKNOWN, hl in old age, oval, Royal Coll.

SC UNKNOWN, 1648, marble bust, NPG 4520. Various medals, BM.

PR W.FAITHORNE, jun, hl in widow's dress, oval, mezz, BM, NPG. J.SMITH, after F.Weideman, hl with veil, oval, mezz, BM, NPG. W.VAILLANT, hl, profile, etch, BM. UNKNOWN, hl, oval, line, German inscription, BM.

SOPHIA DOROTHEA of Zell(e) (1666-1726) wife of George I.

P UNKNOWN, hs, oval, Gripsholm Castle, Sweden.

G UNKNOWN, tql seated with children, oil, c1691, Bomann Museum, Celle, W Germany.

PR W.FAITHORNE, jun, after F.Kerseboom, hl, oval, mezz, BM. A.BIRELL, after F.Kerseboom, hl, oval, stipple, pub 1802, BM, NPG. UNKNOWN, hl in straw hat, stipple, pub 1845, BM.

SOPHIA DOROTHEA, Queen of Prussia (1685-1757) daughter of George I.

P UNKNOWN, (called Queen of Prussia), tql seated as young woman, Blenheim, Oxon. ANTOINE PESNE, c1732, tql with dog, Drottningholm Castle, Stockholm. A.PESNE, c1732, tql seated, Drottningholm, variant engr J.G.Wolffgang, 1732, line and stipple, BM. A.PESNE, 1748, tql seated in mourning dress with dog, Gripsholm Castle, Sweden. A.PESNE, tql seated in mourning, Drottningholm.

M After J.L.HIRSCHMANN, c1706, hl, oval, NPG 489, engr J.Smith, 1706, mezz, BM, NPG.

PR J.SMITH, after F.Weideman, 1715, hl, oval, mezz, BM, NPG.

SOUTH, Robert (1634-1716) divine and prebendary of Westminster.

P UNKNOWN, hl, Bodleian Library, Oxford; version, Christ Church, Oxford.

SC Attrib FRANCIS BIRD, tomb effigy on monument, Westminster Abbey, London.

PR R.WHITE, hs, *ad vivum*, oval, line, NPG. G.VERTUE, after R.White, hs, oval, line, BM, NPG.

SOUTHAMPTON, Charles Fitzroy, 1st Duke of, see 1st Duke of Cleveland.

SOUTHAMPTON, Elizabeth Wriothesley, née Vernon, Countess of (1572?-1648?) courtier.

P UNKNOWN, c1595-1600, wl with dog, Buccleuch Estates, Selkirk, Scotland. UNKNOWN, c1610, hl, oval, Buccleuch Estates. UNKNOWN, c1615, hl, oval, Woburn Abbey, Beds. UNKNOWN, c1620, hl, NPG 570.

SOUTHAMPTON, Henry Wriothesley, 2nd Earl of (1545-1581) courtier.

SC GERARD JOHNSON, c1594, tomb effigy with father, 1st Earl, and mother, St Peter's Church, Titchfield, Hants.

SOUTHAMPTON, Henry Wriothesley, 3rd Earl of (1573-1624) Shakespeare's patron.

P UNKNOWN, c1595-1600, wl, NPG L114. Attrib JOHN DE CRITZ, sen, c1601-03, tql with cat, Buccleuch Estates, Selkirk, Scotland. DANIEL MYTENS, c1618?, hl in armour, Althorp, Northants; version, NPG 52.

M NICHOLAS HILLIARD, 1594, hs, oval, Fitzwilliam Museum, Cambridge.

PR S.PASSE, 1617, hl, oval, line, BM.

SOUTHAMPTON, Thomas Wriothesley, 1st Earl of (1505-1550) lord chancellor of England.

P After HANS HOLBEIN, jun, (type of 1538), hs, Woburn Abbey, Beds.

D H.HOLBEIN, 1538?, hs, chalks, The Louvre, Paris.

M H.HOLBEIN, 1538, head, oval, Metropolitan Museum of Art, New York.

SOUTHAMPTON, Thomas Wriothesley, 4th Earl of (1607-1667) royalist.

P After SIR PETER LELY, (type of c1661), hs with Garter star, NPG 681.

M SAMUEL COOPER, 1661, hs, oval, Woburn Abbey, Beds.

SC THOMAS SIMON, 1664, silver medal, profile bust, NPG 4360.

SOUTHAMPTON, William Fitzwilliam, Earl of (1490-1542) lord high admiral.

P School of HANS HOLBEIN, jun, wl, Fitzwilliam Museum, Cambridge. After H.HOLBEIN, hs, Hardwick Hall (NT), Derbys.

D H.HOLBEIN, c1540, hs, chalks, Royal Coll.

SOUTHCOTE, John (1511-1585) judge.

P UNKNOWN, (probably Southcote), tql in robes, Ingatestone Hall, Essex.

SOUTHERNE, Thomas (1660-1746) poet and dramatist.

PR J.SIMON, after J.Worsdale, hl, oval, mezz, BM, NPG.

SOUTHWELL, Edward (1671-1731?) secretary of state for Ireland.
PR J.SMITH, after Sir G.Kneller, 1708, hl, mezz, BM, NGI (Chaloner Smith Coll).

SOUTHWELL, Sir Richard (1504-1564) courtier and official.
P HANS HOLBEIN, jun, 1536, hl, Uffizi, Florence; copy, NPG 4912.
D H.HOLBEIN, 1536, hs, chalks, Royal Coll.

SOUTHWELL, Robert (1561?-1595) Jesuit and poet.
PR W.J.ALAIS, hs, oval, stipple, for Grossart ed of *Poems*, 1872, BM, NPG. UNKNOWN, hl with knife in breast, line, BM, NPG.

SOUTHWELL, Sir Robert (1635-1702) secretary of state for Ireland.
P SIR GODFREY KNELLER, tql seated, Royal Society, London.
PR J.SMITH, after Sir G.Kneller, hs, oval, mezz, BM, NPG.

SPARKE, Edward (d1692) divine.
PR A.HERTOCHS, 1662, hs, oval, line, for *Scintilla Altaris*, 1663, BM, NPG. UNKNOWN, hs, oval, line, for 1866 ed, BM, NPG.

SPARKE, Thomas (1548-1616) puritan divine.
SC Attrib R.HAYDOCK, brass effigy, hs with emblems, St Mary's Church, Bletchley, Bucks, engr, line, BM, NPG.

SPARROW, Anthony (1612-1685) bishop of Exeter and Norwich.
P UNKNOWN, hl, oval, Queen's College, Cambridge; version, Bishop's Palace, Exeter, engr, line, pub 1798, BM, NPG.

SPARROW, John (1615-1665?) mystic.
PR D.LOGGAN, 1659, hl, line, BM, NPG.

SPEED, John (1552?-1629) historian and cartographer.
P After SOLOMON SAVERY, hs, Bodleian Library, Oxford.
SC UNKNOWN, marble bust, St Giles, Cripplegate, London. UNKNOWN, brass effigy, Burrell Coll, Glasgow Art Gallery and Museum.
PR S.SAVERY, tql seated, line, for *Chronicle of England*, 1632, BM, NPG.

SPELMAN, Sir Henry (1564?-1641) antiquary and historian.
P After CORNELIUS JOHNSON, (type of c1628?), hs, NPG 962; version, tql, Clarendon Coll on loan to Plymouth Art Gallery.
PR W.FAITHORNE, hs, oval, line, BM, NPG.

SPENCE, Joseph (1699-1768) critic and friend of Pope.
PR G.VERTUE, after I.Whood, hl, oval, line, for *Polymetis*, 1747, BM, NPG.

SPENCER, Charles, see 3rd Earl of Sunderland.

SPENCER, Dorothy, see Countess of Sunderland.

SPENCER, Henry, see 1st Earl of Sunderland.

SPENCER, John (1630-1693) master of Corpus Christi College, Cambridge, and dean of Ely.
P UNKNOWN, Corpus Christi College.
PR G.VERTUE, 1727, hl, oval, line, for *De Legibus Hebraeorum*, 1727, BM, NPG.

SPENCER, Robert (1640-1702) see 2nd Earl of Sunderland.

SPENCER of Wormleighton, Robert Spencer, 1st Baron (1570-1627) wealthy follower of James I.
P MARCUS GHEERAERTS, wl in peer's robes, Althorp, Northants.
M UNKNOWN, hs, oval, Althorp.

SPENSER, John (1559-1614) president of Corpus Christi College, Oxford.
SC UNKNOWN, bust on monument, Corpus Christi College Chapel.

SPINCKES, Nathaniel (1653-1727) nonjuror.
PR G.VERTUE, after J.Wollaston, hl with book, line, for *Sick Man Visited*, 1731, BM, NPG.

SPOTSWOOD or SPOTTISWOOD, Alexander (1676-1740) colonial governor.
P CHARLES BRIDGES, tql, Commonwealth of Virginia, Richmond, USA.

SPOTTISWOOD(E), John (1565-1637?) archbishop of St Andrews and lord chancellor of Scotland.
P UNKNOWN, hs with book, Parliament Hall, Edinburgh.
PR W.HOLLAR, hs, oval, etch, for *Hist of the Church of Scotland*, 1655, BM, NPG.

SPOTTISWOOD(E), Sir Robert (1596-1646) Scottish judge.
P UNKNOWN, 1636, hl in robes, SNPG 1288.

SPRAGGE, Sir Edward (d1673) admiral.
P SIR PETER LELY, hs in breastplate, oval, Inveraray Castle, Strathclyde region, Scotland. UNKNOWN, c1672, hl, NMM, Greenwich.
PR UNKNOWN, hl in breastplate, oval, mezz, BM, NPG.

SPRAT, Thomas (1635-1713) bishop of Rochester and dean of Westminster.
P Attrib JOHN CLOSTERMAN, wl, Walker Art Gallery, Liverpool. MICHAEL DAHL, tql seated with son, Bodleian Library, Oxford, engr J.Smith, 1712, mezz, BM, NPG. SIR GODFREY KNELLER, hs, oval, Christ Church, Oxford. UNKNOWN, hl, oval, The Deanery, Westminster.
PR M. VAN DER GUCHT, after 'Sir P.Lely', hs, oval, line, for *Life of Cowley*, 1710, BM, NPG.

STACKHOUSE, Thomas (1677-1752) theologian.
PR G.VERTUE, after J.Wollaston, 1743, hl, oval, line, for *Hist of the Bible*, 1752, BM, NPG.

STAFFORD, Edward, see 3rd Duke of Buckingham.

STAFFORD, William Howard, 1st Viscount (1614-1680) magnate, executed for treason.
P After SIR ANTHONY VANDYCK, tql, Arundel Castle, W Sussex.
M UNKNOWN, (after type of c1670), hs, oval, w/c, NPG 2015.
PR E.LUTTRELL, hl, oval, mezz, BM.

STAIR, James Dalrymple, 1st Viscount (1619-1695) Scottish lawyer and statesman.
P After SIR J.B.MEDINA, tql in peer's robes, Parliament Hall, Edinburgh.

STAIR, John Dalrymple, 2nd Earl of (1673-1747) general and diplomat.
P WILLIAM AIKMAN, c1727, tql in robes of Knight of Thistle, Glasgow City Art Gallery. UNKNOWN, SNPG 324.
M UNKNOWN, hs in armour, oval, SNPG 2195.
PR J.FABER, after A.Ramsay, 1703, tql in breastplate, mezz, BM, NPG.

STAMFORD, Henry Grey, 1st Earl of (1599?-1673) parliamentary general.
PR W.HOLLAR, hl, oval, etch, BM, NPG.

STANBRIDGE, John (1463-1510) grammarian.
PR UNKNOWN, wl seated with scholars, woodcut for *Accidentia*, 1529?, BM, NPG.

STANHOPE, George (1660-1728) dean of Canterbury.
P Attrib SIR GODFREY KNELLER, tql with book, The Deanery, Canterbury.
PR M. VAN DER GUCHT, hs, oval, line, for *Explanations of the Epistles and Gospels*, 1706, BM, NPG. J.FABER, jun, after J.Ellys, 1729, tql seated, mezz, BM.

STANHOPE, James Stanhope, 1st Earl of (1673-1721) soldier and statesman.
P SIR GODFREY KNELLER, c1705-10, hl, the 'Kit-cat Club' portrait, NPG 3225. Attrib JOHAN VAN DIEST, c1718, tql with breastplate, NPG 6. Attrib J. VAN DIEST, c1718, tql seated, Madrid Embassy (DoE), Spain. Attrib J. VAN DIEST, tql in peer's robes, DoE, London.
SC J.M.RYSBRACK, 1733, statue on monument, Westminster Abbey, London.

STANHOPE, Philip (1633-1713), see 2nd Earl of Chesterfield.

STANHOPE, Philip (1694-1773), see 4th Earl of Chesterfield.

STANHOPE, William, see 1st Earl of Harrington.

STANLEY, Charlotte, see Countess of Derby.

STANLEY, Edward, see 3rd Earl of Derby.

STANLEY, Henry, see 4th Earl of Derby.

STANLEY, James, see 7th Earl of Derby.

STANLEY, Thomas (1625-1678) scholar and humanist.
P GERARD SOEST, c1660, hl, NPG 166.
PR W.FAITHORNE, after Sir P.Lely, hs, octagonal, line, for *Hist of Philosophy*, 1655, BM, NPG. W.H.WORTHINGTON, after Sir P.Lely, hl, line, pub 1821, NPG.

STANLEY, William (1647-1731) dean of St Asaph.
P UNKNOWN, Corpus Christi College, Cambridge.

STANYAN, Abraham (1669?-1732) diplomat.
P SIR GODFREY KNELLER, c1710?, hl, the 'Kit-cat Club' portrait NPG 3226, engr J.Faber, jun, 1733, mezz, BM, NPG.

STAPLETON, Sir Philip (1603-1647) parliamentarian.
D JOHN BULLFINCH, tql in armour, wash, Sutherland Coll, Ashmolean Museum, Oxford. G.P.HARDING, hl in breastplate, w/c, NPG 2397.

STAPLETON or STAPYLTON, Sir Robert (d1669) dramatist and translator.
PR W.MARSHALL, hl, oval, line, for trans of Juvenal, *Satires*, 1647, BM, NPG. P.LOMBART, hl, oval, line, for 1660 ed of *Satires*, BM, NPG.

STAPLETON, Thomas (1535-1598) professor of theology at Louvain.
PR L.GAULTIER, hs, aged 63, oval, line, BM, NPG.

STAPYLTON, Sir Robert, see Stapleton.

STAVELY, Thomas (1626-1684) lawyer and antiquary.
PR UNKNOWN, hl seated, oval, line, for Nichols, *Hist of Leicestershire*, 1795, BM, NPG.

STAWELL, Sir John (1599-1662) royalist.
D T.ATHOW, tql, wash, Sutherland Coll, Ashmolean Museum, Oxford.

STAYNER, Sir Richard (d1662) admiral.
PR C.TURNER, hl in armour, oval, mezz, pub 1810, BM, NPG.

STEARNE, see Sterne.

STEBBING, Henry (1687-1763) divine.
P JOSEPH HIGHMORE, 1757, tql seated, NPG 572.
PR J.ROBERTS, after J.Weller, hs, oval, line, for *Tracts*, 1766, BM, NPG. UNKNOWN, after N.Dance, hs, oval, stipple, NPG.

STEEL(E), Richard (1629-1692) non-conformist divine.
P UNKNOWN, hs, oval, Dr Williams's Library, London, engr J.Hopwood, line and stipple, pub 1809, BM, NPG.

STEELE, Sir Richard (1672-1729) dramatist and essayist.
P SIR GODFREY KNELLER, 1711, hl, the 'Kit-cat Club' portrait,

NPG 3227. JONATHAN RICHARDSON, 1712, tql, NPG 5067; version, hs, NPG 160. UNKNOWN, tql in turban, DoE, London, same type as engr G.Vertue, after J.Thornhill, 1713, hl, oval, line, BM, NPG.
M Attrib CHRISTIAN RICHTER, c1720, hs, oval, one of group of 4, NPG 1506.

STEELE, William (d1680) lord chancellor of Ireland.
P UNKNOWN, Harvard Law School, Cambridge, Mass, USA.

STEPHEN (1097?-1154) king of England.
MS UNKNOWN, wl with bird, *Codex Membran*, BL Cotton Ms Vitellius A XIII, fol 4b. UNKNOWN, wl seated with eagle, Peter of Langtoft, 'Chronicle of England', BL Royal Ms 20 A II, fol 7.
SC UNKNOWN, impression of Great Seal, King's College, Cambridge.

STENNETT, Joseph (1663-1713) Baptist minister.
PR G.VERTUE, hl, oval, line, for *Works*, 1732, BM, NPG.

STENNETT, Joseph (1692-1758) Baptist minister.
P ANDREA SOLDI, 1744, hl with book, Baptist College, Bristol, engr W.Walker, line, NPG.

STEPNEY, George (1663-1707) poet and diplomat.
P SIR GODFREY KNELLER, c1705, hl, the 'Kit-cat Club' portrait, NPG 3228.

STERNE or STEARNE, John (1624-1669) founder of Irish College of Physicians.
P UNKNOWN, tql seated with bust of Hippocrates, Trinity College, Dublin.

STERNE or STEARNE, John (1660-1745) bishop of Clogher.
P J.B.YEATS, after Thomas Carlton, 1717, hl, Trinity College, Dublin, engr T.Beard, oval, mezz, BM, NPG.

STERNE, Richard (1597-1683) archbishop of York.
P UNKNOWN, hl, Jesus College, Cambridge, engr F.Place, mezz, BM, NPG. UNKNOWN, tql seated, Bishopthorpe Palace, York; version, Jesus College.
SC UNKNOWN, tomb effigy, York Minster.

STEUART of Goodtrees, Sir James (1635-1713) lord advocate of Scotland.
P Attrib SIR J.B.MEDINA, hs in robes, oval, SNPG 776.
PR G.VERTUE, after Sir J.B.Medina, hs in robes, oval, line, BM, NPG.

STEVENSON, Matthew (fl 1660-80) poet.
PR R.GAYWOOD, hl, oval, etch, for *Poems*, 1664, BM.

STEWARD or STEWART, Richard (1593?-1651) provost of Eton.
P Attrib CORNELIUS DE NEVE, hl, Eton College, Berks, engr J.Stow, line, pub 1822, BM, NPG.

STEWART, Alexander (1634-1700), see 5th Earl of Moray.

STEWART, Alexander (d1704), see 5th Lord Blantyre.

STEWART, Frances Theresa, see Duchess of Richmond and Lennox.

STEWART, Henry, see Lord Darnley.

STEWART, James, see Earl of Moray.

STEWART, James Francis Edward (1688-1766), see JAMES Francis Edward Stewart.

STEWART, John (1481-1536), see Duke of Albany.

STEWART, Sir John (1600?-1659), see 1st Earl of Traquair.

STEWART, Matthew, see 4th Earl of Lennox.

STEWART, Richard, see Steward.

STEWART, see Stuart.

STILL, John (1543?-1608) bishop of Bath and Wells.
P UNKNOWN, 1607, hs with book, Trinity College, Cambridge, engr J.Jones, mezz, pub 1789, BM.

STILLINGFLEET, Edward (1635-1699) bishop of Worcester.
P Attrib MARY BEALE, c1690, tql seated, NPG 1389.
D UNKNOWN, c1670, hs, oval, chalks, NPG 2516.
PR A.BLOOTELING, after Sir P.Lely, hs, oval, line, BM, NPG. R.WHITE, after M.Beale, hs, oval, line, for *Sermons*, 1696, BM, NPG.

STIRLING, William Alexander, 1st Earl of (1567-1640) poet and statesman.
P UNKNOWN, hl, SNPG L141.
PR UNKNOWN, tql, line for *the Monarchicke Tragedie*, 1616, BM, NPG. UNKNOWN, hs, line, for *Recreation of the Muses*, 1637, BM.

STOCK, Richard (1569?-1626) puritan divine.
PR T.RAWLINS, hs under arch, line, for *Commentary on Malachy*, 1641, BM, NPG. UNKNOWN, hs, oval, line, for Boissard, *Bibliotheca Chalcographica*, 1650, BM, NPG. UNKNOWN, hs, oval, line, BM, NPG.

STONE, Henry, 'Old Stone' (d1653) painter.
PR A.BANNERMAN, after Sir P.Lely, hl with drawing, line, for Walpole, *Anecdotes*, 1762, BM, NPG.

STONE, Nicholas, sen (1586-1647) sculptor and architect.
PR T.CHAMBARS, profile portrait medallion with another of his son, Nicholas, line, for Walpole, *Anecdotes*, 1762, BM, NPG.

STONE, Nicholas, jun (d1647) mason and statuary.
PR T.CHAMBARS, portrait medallion with another of his father, line, for Walpole, *Anecdotes*, 1762, BM, NPG.

STOW(E), John (1525?-1605) antiquary and chronicler.
SC Attrib NICHOLAS JOHNSON, alabaster seated effigy on monument, St Andrew Undershaft, London.
PR J.SWAINE, profile bust, oval, line, facs copy of engr for *Survey*, 1603, pub 1837, BM, NPG.

STRADLING, Sir Edward, 2nd Bart (1601-1644) royalist.
D T.ATHOW, hl, wash, Sutherland Coll, Ashmolean Museum, Oxford.

STRAFFORD, Sir Thomas Wentworth, 1st Earl of (1593-1641) statesman.
P After SIR ANTHONY VANDYCK, (type of c1632-33), tql in armour, Rockingham Castle, Northants, and NPG 2960; version, with wolfhound, NPG 1077. SIR A.VANDYCK, c1636, tql in armour, Petworth (NT), W Sussex; version, NPG 4531. After SIR A.VANDYCK, (type of c1636), tql seated with Sir Philip Mainwaring, Weston Park, Salop. After SIR A.VANDYCK, (type of c1636), hl in armour, Euston Hall, Suffolk.
M Attrib JOHN HOSKINS, hs, oval, NPG L152 (9).
SC THOMAS RAWLINS, gold medal, BM.

STRAFFORD, Thomas Wentworth, 3rd Earl of (1672-1739) diplomat.
P P.C.LEYGEBE, 1711, wl on horseback, Foreign Office (DoE), London. CHARLES D'AGAR, c1712, tql in Garter robes, Palace of Westminster, London.
G GAWEN HAMILTON, family group, oil, 1732, National Gallery of Canada, Ottawa.
SC J.M.RYSBRACK, c1740, terracotta statuette, model for statue, V & A.
PR G.VERTUE, after Sir G.Kneller, 1714, hs in Garter robes, oval, line, for Knowler, *Strafford Letters*, 1739, BM, NPG.

STRANGE, Sir John (1696-1754) master of the rolls.
P UNKNOWN, hs in robes, Harvard Law School, Cambridge, Mass, USA.
PR J.HOUBRAKEN, hs in robes, oval, line, for *Reports*, 1755, BM, NPG.

STRATFORD, Nicholas (1633-1707) bishop of Chester.
P UNKNOWN, hl, Bishop's House, Chester.

STRATHALLAN, William Drummond, 1st Viscount (1617?-1688) royalist general.
P Attrib L.SCHUNEMAN, tql in armour, SNPG 1433.

STRATHMORE, Patrick Lyon, 3rd Earl of Kinghorne and 1st Earl of (1643?-1695) privy councillor.
P Attrib L.SCHUNEMAN, tql in robes, SNPG 1609.
PR R.WHITE, after Sir G.Kneller, hl in robes, oval, line, BM, NPG.

STREATER, Robert (1624-1680) painter.
PR A.BANNERMAN, after R.Streater, hl, line, for Walpole, *Anecdotes*, BM, NPG.

STREET, Sir Thomas (1626-1696) judge.
P After ROBERT WHITE, wl in robes, Inner Temple, London. UNKNOWN, hl in robes, Harvard Law School, Cambridge, Mass, USA.
PR R.WHITE, 1688, hs in robes, *ad vivum*, oval, line, BM, NPG.

STRICKLAND, Thomas John Francis (1679?-1740) bishop of Namur.
P A.S.BELLE, tql as a young man, Sizergh Castle (NT), Cumbria. JOHN VANDERBANK, hl, oval, Sizergh Castle, engr J.Faber, jun, mezz, BM, NPG.

STRICKLAND, Walter (fl 1642-1657) politician.
P PIETER NASON, c1651, wl, NPG 5235.

STRODE, Sir George (1583-1663) royalist.
PR G.GLOVER, hs in armour, oval, line, for trans of Fonseca, *Discours of Love*, 1652, BM, NPG.

STRYPE, John (1643-1737) historian and antiquary.
PR G.VERTUE, tql seated, line, for *Ecclesiastical Memoirs*, 1733, BM, NPG.

STUART, Arabella, see Seymour.

STUART, Bernard, see titular Earl of Lichfield.

STUART, Charles, see 3rd Duke of Richmond and Lennox.

STUART, Esmé, see 1st Duke of Lennox.

STUART, Frances Theresa, see Duchess of Richmond and Lennox.

STUART, Henrietta, see Duchess of Orleans.

STUART, Henry, see Lord Darnley.

STUART, James, see 1st Duke of Richmond.

STUART, Ludovick, see 1st Duke of Richmond.

STUART, see Stewart.

STUBBS or STUBBES, Henry (1606?-1678) ejected minister.
PR UNKNOWN, hs, oval, line, NPG.

STUBBS, Philip (1665-1738) archdeacon of St Albans.
PR J.FABER, sen, 1708, hl, oval, mezz, BM. J.FABER, jun, after T.Murray, hl, oval, mezz, BM.

STUKELEY, William (1687-1765) antiquary.
P Attrib RICHARD COLLINS, c1726, wl, Society of Antiquaries, London. UNKNOWN, hs, Lydiard Mansion, Borough of Thamesdown, Wilts.
D SIR GODFREY KNELLER, 1720, profile head, NPG 4266. GERARD VAN DER GUCHT, 1722, hs, profile, asleep, Bodleian Library, Oxford. Self-portrait, 1726, hs, oval, Bodleian Library. Self-portrait, profile head, BM.
PR J.SMITH, after Sir G.Kneller, 1721, hl, oval, mezz, BM, NPG.

STURT, John (1658-1730) engraver.
PR W.HUMPHREY, after W.FAITHORNE, hl, with drawing, oval, mezz, BM, NPG. BARRETT, hl, vignette, line, for Walpole, *Cat of Engravers*, 1794, BM, NPG.

SUCKLING, Sir John (1609-1642) poet.
P SIR ANTHONY VANDYCK, c1638, wl, Frick Coll, New York; copy, hs, NPG 448.

SUFFOLK, Charles Brandon, 1st Duke of (d1545) soldier and statesman.
P UNKNOWN, hl with wife, Mary, Queen of France, Woburn Abbey, Beds; version, Montacute (NT), Somerset. UNKNOWN, tql seated, NPG 516.

SUFFOLK, Charles Brandon, 3rd Duke of (1537?-1551) died young of 'sweating sickness'.
M HANS HOLBEIN, jun, hl as child, oval, Royal Coll.

SUFFOLK, Henrietta Howard, née Hobart, Countess of (1681-1767) mistress of George II.
P Attrib MICHAEL DAHL, c1715–25, wl, Blickling Hall (NT), Norfolk. Attrib CHARLES JERVAS, c1725?, tql seated, on loan to NPG 3891.
PR J.HEATH, hl, stipple, for *Works of Lord Orford*, pub 1798, BM, NPG.

SUFFOLK, Henry Brandon, 2nd Duke of (1535-1551) son of 1st Duke of Suffolk, died of 'sweating sickness'.
M HANS HOLBEIN, jun, hl as child, oval, Royal Coll.

SUFFOLK, James Howard, 3rd Baron Howard de Walden and 3rd Earl of (1619-1688) courtier.
P ENOCH SEEMAN, after unknown original, wl in armour, Audley End (DoE), Essex.

SUFFOLK, John de la Pole, 2nd Duke of (1442-1491) soldier and statesman.
SC UNKNOWN, alabaster tomb effigy with wife, St Andrew's Church, Wingfield, Suffolk.

SUFFOLK, Michael de la Pole, 2nd Earl of (1361?-1415) soldier.
SC UNKNOWN, wooden tomb effigy with wife, St Andrew's Church, Wingfield, Suffolk.

SUFFOLK, Theophilus Howard, 2nd Baron Howard de Walden and 2nd Earl of (1584-1640) warden of the Cinque ports.
P BIAGIO REBECCA, after a drawing, wl, Audley End (DoE), Essex. UNKNOWN, 19th cent copy, hl, Ranger's House (GLC), London.

SUFFOLK, Thomas Howard, 1st Baron Howard de Walden and 1st Earl of (1561-1620) lord high treasurer.
P UNKNOWN, (after type of c1605), hl with Lesser George, oval, NPG 4572. Attrib JOHN BELKAMP, c1614, hl with Garter George, oval, Knole (NT), Kent. UNKNOWN, 1617, wl in Garter robes, NMM, Greenwich.
PR T.BLOOD, after F.Zuccaro, hl, stipple, for Lodge, *Portraits*, BM, NPG. R.ELSTRACK, hl, oval, line, BM, NPG.

SUNDERLAND, Anne, née Churchill, Countess of (1683-1716) celebrated beauty.
P SIR GODFREY KNELLER, 1688, wl as child with sister Henrietta, Althorp, Northants. Attrib SIR G.KNELLER, c1709–10, wl with son Robert, later 4th Earl of Sunderland, Althorp. Studio of SIR G.KNELLER, c1710, tql seated, NPG 803. CHARLES JERVAS, c1715, wl with daughter, Diana, Althorp. Attrib C.JERVAS, wl with flower basket, Althorp; version, Blenheim, Oxon. C.JERVAS. wl seated as madonna, Palace House, Hants.
SC DAVID LE MARCHAND, ivory bust, V & A.

SUNDERLAND, Charles Spencer, 3rd Earl of (1674-1722) statesman and bibliophile.
P SIR GODFREY KNELLER, 1720, wl in Garter robes, Blenheim, Oxon. STEPHEN SLAUGHTER, after Sir G.Kneller, (type of 1720), wl with Garter ribbon and star, Althorp, Northants.

SUNDERLAND, Dorothy, née Sidney, Countess of, (1617-1684) Waller's 'Sacharissa'.
P SIR ANTHONY VANDYCK, c1640, tql with flower basket, Chatsworth, Derbys. SIR A.VANDYCK, c1640, tql, Petworth (NT), W Sussex. SIR ANTHONY VANDYCK, hl as shepherdess, c1640, Penshurst, Kent; version, Althorp, Northants. Studio of SIR A.VANDYCK, c1643, hl with flowers, Althorp.

SUNDERLAND, Henry Spencer, 1st Earl of (1620-1643) royalist.
P UNKNOWN, (probably Sunderland), hl as young man, Penshurst, Kent. UNKNOWN, tql in armour, Althorp, Northants.

SUNDERLAND, Robert Spencer, 2nd Earl of (1640-1702) secretary of state.
P SIR PETER LELY, tql seated as young man, Knole (NT), Kent. SIR P.LELY, .166(6)?, tql with bust of Diana, Althorp, Northants. CARLO MARATTI, wl in classical dress, Althorp. UNKNOWN, tql, Penshurst, Kent.

SUNDON, Charlotte Clayton, Lady (d1742) woman of the bedchamber to Queen Caroline.
PR E.HARDING, hl, stipple, for Adolphus, *British Cabinet*, 1799, BM, NPG.

SURREY, Henry Howard, Earl of (1517?-1547) poet.
P HANS HOLBEIN, jun, c1540, hl, Museu de Arte, Sao Paulo, Brazil. UNKNOWN, (after type of c1646), wl, Arundel Castle, W.Sussex; versions, Knole (NT), Kent.
D UNKNOWN, c1540, head, profile, Pierpont Morgan Library, New York. Three further drawings, inscribed 'Thomas Earl of Surry' in the Royal Coll, two by H.Holbein, could be the sitter.

SUSSEX, Robert Radcliffe, 5th Earl of (1569?-1629) earl marshal.
P Attrib MARCUS GHEERAERTS, c1593, wl in armour, Tower of London Armouries. Attrib M.GHEERAERTS, c1599, wl in Garter robes, Woburn Abbey, Beds.

SUSSEX, Sir Thomas Radcliffe, 3rd Earl of (1526?-1583) soldier and statesman.
P UNKNOWN, (after type of c1565), hs with Garter George and staff of office, NPG 105 and NPG 312.
G M.GHEERAERTS, sen, 'Procession of Garter Knights, 1576', etch, BM.
SC RICHARD STEVENS, 1589, alabaster tomb effigy, St Andrew's Church, Boreham, Essex.

SUTHERLAND, John Gordon, 16th Earl of (1660?-1733) privy councillor to Queen Anne.
P UNKNOWN, tql seated with Thistle star, Dunrobin Castle, Highland region, Scotland. UNKNOWN, hl with Thistle star, oval, Dunrobin Castle.

SUTTON, Sir Richard (d1524) co-founder of Brasenose College, Oxford.
P UNKNOWN, tql with surcoat of arms, Brasenose College.
MS UNKNOWN, 1520, wl kneeling, Brasenose College.
W UNKNOWN, hs, oval, Brasenose College.

SUTTON, Robert, see 2nd Baron Lexington.

SUTTON, Thomas (1532-1611) founder of the Charterhouse, London.
P UNKNOWN, wl seated, Charterhouse, London.
SC NICHOLAS STONE and NICHOLAS JOHNSON, 1615, tomb effigy,

Charterhouse Chapel.
PR R.ELSTRACK, hl, oval, line, BM, NPG. PASSE, hs, oval, line, for *Herwologia*, 1620, BM, NPG.

SWIFT, Jonathan (1667-1745) satirist.
P CHARLES JERVAS, *c*1709–10, hl, oval, Bodleian Library, Oxford; version, NPG 4407. C.JERVAS, *c*1718, tql seated NPG 278. FRANCIS BINDON, *c*1724, wl with cherub, NGI 598. Attrib F.BINDON, hl, with turban, oval, NGI.
D ISAAC WHOOD, 1730, hs, profile, NGI 2614.
SC L.F.ROUBILIAC, marble bust, Trinity College, Dublin. JOHN VAN NOST, marble bust, National Museum of Ireland.
PR A. VAN HAECKEN, after Markham, 1740, tql seated, mezz, BM. B.WILSON, after T.Barber, profile bust, etch, for Lord Orrery, *Remarks on Life and Writings of Swift*, 1752, BM, NPG.

SWINNY, Owen Mac (*d*1754) theatrical manager.
PR P. VAN BLEECK, 1749, hl, mezz, BM. J.FABER, jun, after J.B.Vanloo, tql seated, mezz, BM.

SYDENHAM, Cuthbert (1622-1654) puritan divine.
PR R.GAYWOOD, hl, etch, for *Mysterie of Godliness*, 1654, BM, NPG.

SYDENHAM, Thomas (1624-1689) physician.
P MARY BEALE, 1688, hl, NPG 3901. After M.BEALE?, hl, oval, Royal College of Physicians, London. EBENEZER SADLER?, hl, Hatfield House, Herts. UNKNOWN, *c*1680?, hl, oval, Royal College of Physicians.
PR A.BLOOTELING, after M.Beale, hl, oval, line, for *Observationes Medicae*, 1676, BM, NPG. J.HOUBRAKEN, after Sir P.Lely, hl, oval, line, for Birch, *Heads*, 1747, BM, NPG.
SC JOSEPH WILTON, 1757, marble bust, Royal College of Physicians.

SYLVESTER, Josuah (1563-1618) poet.
PR C. VAN DALEN, hs, oval, line, BM, NPG.

SYLVESTER, Matthew (1636?-1708) nonconformist divine.
P UNKNOWN, hl, oval, Dr Williams's Library, London.
PR M. VAN DER GUCHT, after I.Schivermans, hs, oval, line, NPG.

T

TAFFE, Nicholas Taafe, 6th Viscount (1677-1769) general in the Austrian army.
PR J.DIXON, after R.Hunter, hl in robes, mezz, BM. E.BOCQUET, hs in robes, oval, stipple, pub 1806, NPG.

TALBOT, Charles, see 1st Duke of Shrewsbury.

TALBOT, Elizabeth, see Countess of Shrewsbury.

TALBOT, George (1468-1538), see 4th Earl of Shrewsbury.

TALBOT, George (1528?-1590), see 6th Earl of Shrewsbury.

TALBOT, Gilbert, see 7th Earl of Shrewsbury.

TALBOT, John, see 1st Earl of Shrewsbury.

TALBOT, Peter (1620-1680) titular archbishop of Dublin.
P UNKNOWN, c1660, hl, NGI.

TALBOT, Richard, see titular Duke of Tyrconnell.

TALBOT, William (1659?-1730) bishop of Durham.
P After SIR GODFREY KNELLER, tql seated, Bishop Auckland Palace, Durham, engr hl, oval, mezz, NPG. After SIR G.KNELLER, tql seated in robes of Garter prelate, Raby Castle, Durham, engr G.Vertue, 1720, line, BM, NPG.
PR J.FABER, jun, after Sir G.Kneller, tql in Garter robes, mezz, BM, NPG.

TALBOT of Hensal, Charles Talbot, 1st Baron (1685-1737) lord chancellor.
P After JOHN VANDERBANK, (type of c1733-39), tql in robes, NPG 42; version, Inner Temple, London.
SC JOHN CHEERE, after J.Vanderbank, c1749, bronze bust, All Souls College, Oxford.

TALLENTS, Francis (1619-1708) ejected divine.
PR J.CALDWALL, hs, oval, line, NPG. J.HOPWOOD, hs, oval, stipple, BM, NPG.

TALLIS, Thomas (1510?-1585) musical composer.
PR UNKNOWN, hl, oval, with another of William Byrd, from a rare Italian engr, reproduction, BM.

TALMASH, Thomas, see Tollemache.

TANCRED, Christopher (1689-1754) educational benefactor.
P UNKNOWN, wl, Christ's College, Cambridge.

TANFIELD, Sir Lawrence (d1625) judge.
D T.ATHOW, wl in robes, wash, Sutherland Coll, Ashmolean Museum, Oxford.
SC Attrib GERARD CHRISTMAS, 1628, tomb effigy with wife, St John Baptist, Burford, Oxon.

TANKERVILLE, Forde Grey, 1st Earl of (1654-1701) Whig politician.
P SIR PETER LELY, c1672, tql seated, Audley End (DoE), Essex.
PR A.BROWNE, after Sir P.Lely, tql, mezz, BM, NPG. C.N.SCHURTZ, after Sir P.Lely, 1689, hl, oval, line, BM, NPG.

TANNER, Thomas (1674-1735) bishop of St Asaph and antiquary.
P UNKNOWN, tql seated, Christ Church, Oxford; copy, All Souls College, Oxford.

SC SIR HENRY CHEERE, c1756, bronze head, All Souls.
PR G.VERTUE, hl, oval, line, pub 1736, BM, NPG.

TARLTON, Richard (1530-1588) comic actor.
MS JOHN SCOTTOWE, wl with pipe and tabor, in ornamented letter, BL Harleian Ms 3885, fol 19.
PR UNKNOWN, wl with pipe and tabor, line, facs of woodcut for *Jests*, 1611, BM.

TATHAM, John (fl 1632-1664) dramatist and poet.
PR R.VAUGHAN, hl, oval, line, NPG. UNKNOWN, hl, oval, line, BM, NPG.

TAYLOR, Brook (1685-1731) mathematician.
P UNKNOWN, c1715, hl, oval, Royal Society, London, engr R.Earlom, mezz, for *Contemplatio Philosophica*, 1793, BM.
M LOUIS? GOUPY, c1720, tql with book, gouache, NPG 1920.

TAYLOR, Jeremy (1613-1667) bishop of Down, Connor and Dromore.
P UNKNOWN, tql seated, All Souls College, Oxford, engr P.Lombart, hl with book, oval, line, for *Ductor Dubitantium*, 1660, BM, NPG.
PR P.LOMBART, wl with a family and skeleton in a mirror, line, for *Holy Dying*, 1650, BM, NPG. W.FAITHORNE, wl on pedestal with visions of heaven and hell, line, for *Holy Living*, 1663, BM, NPG.

TAYLOR, John (1580-1653) the 'water-poet'.
P JOHN TAYLOR, 1655, hl, Bodleian Library, Oxford. UNKNOWN, hl, Watermen's Company, London.
PR UNKNOWN, wl as king's waterman, line, for *Memorial of All the English Monarchs*, 1622, NPG. T.COCKSON, hl, oval, in title for *Works*, 1630, BM, NPG.

TAYLOR, John (1694-1761) unitarian minister at Norwich.
PR J.HOUBRAKEN, after D.Heins, 1746, hl, oval, line, for *Concordance*, 1754, BM, NPG.

TAYLOR, Thomas (1576-1633) puritan divine.
PR W.MARSHALL, c1632, hl, aged 56, oval, line, BM, NPG. UNKNOWN, wl in pulpit, vignette, line, for *The Parable of the Sower and the Seed*, 1634, NPG.

TEMPEST, Pierce (1653-1717) print publisher.
PR F.PLACE, after E.Heemskerk, profile bust, mezz, BM, NPG.

TEMPLE, Dorothy, née Osborne, Lady (1627-1695) letter writer.
P CASPAR NETSCHER, 1671, tql seated, NPG 3813.

TEMPLE, Sir John (1600-1677) master of the rolls in Ireland.
P CORNELIUS JOHNSON, hl, Berkeley Castle, Glos.

TEMPLE, Sir Richard, see 1st Viscount Cobham.

TEMPLE, Sir William (1628-1699) diplomat and author.
P After SIR PETER LELY, (type of c1660), hl, NPG 152. CASPAR NETSCHER, 1675, tql seated, NPG 3812.

TENISON, Edward (1673-1735) bishop of Ossory.
P SIR GODFREY KNELLER, 1720, tql, Corpus Christi College, Cambridge, engr G.Vertue, 1731, line, BM, NPG.

TENISON, Thomas (1636-1715) archbishop of Canterbury.
P Attrib SIMON DU BOIS, tql seated, Lambeth Palace, London. After ROBERT WHITE, (type of c1695-1702), tql seated, NPG

1525. UNKNOWN, tql seated, Knole (NT), Kent.
PR R.WHITE, c1695–1702, hs, *ad vivum*, oval, line, BM, NPG.

TERRY, Edward (1590-1660) writer of travels.
PR R.VAUGHAN, hl, aged 64, oval, line, for *Voyage to East India*, 1655, BM, NPG.

TESDALE, Thomas (1547-1610) co-founder of Pembroke College, Oxford.
P UNKNOWN, tql, Pembroke College; version, Bodleian Library, Oxford.

THELWALL, Sir Eubule (1562-1630) principal and benefactor of Jesus College, Oxford.
P UNKNOWN, tql seated, Jesus College.

THIRLBY, Thomas (1506?-1570) bishop of Westminster, Norwich and Ely.
P UNKNOWN, Trinity Hall, Cambridge.

THOMAS, Duke of Clarence (1388?-1421) second son of Henry IV by Mary de Bohun.
SC UNKNOWN, alabaster tomb effigy with wife and her first husband, John Beaufort, Marquess of Somerset, Canterbury Cathedral.

THOMAS, Elizabeth (1677-1731) poet.
PR G.KING, hl, aged 30, oval, line, for *Pylades and Corinna*, 1731, NPG. UNKNOWN, hs, oval, line, BM, NPG.

THOMAS, John (1696-1781) bishop of Peterborough, Salisbury and Winchester.
P GEORGE HAYTER, after B.Wilson, (type of c1771), tql in robes of prelate of the Garter, All Souls College, Oxford. NATHANIEL DANCE, 1773, tql seated in Garter robes, Lambeth Palace, London.
PR R.HOUSTON, after B.Wilson, 1771, tql in Garter robes, mezz, BM, NPG.

THOMAS, William (1613-1689) bishop of St David's and Worcester.
P UNKNOWN, tql seated, Jesus College, Oxford. UNKNOWN, tql seated, Hurd Episcopal Library, Hartlebury Castle, Worcs.

THOMAS, William (1670-1738) antiquary.
PR V.GREEN, hl, mezz, for Nash, *Worcestershire*, 1776, BM, NPG.

THOMOND, Barnabas O'Brien, 6th Earl of (d1657) royalist.
P CORNELIUS JOHNSON, 1643, hs, Petworth (NT), W Sussex.

THOMPSON or THOMSON, Sir William (1678-1739) baron of the exchequer.
P UNKNOWN, tql seated in robes, Wallington Hall (NT), Northd.
PR J.FABER, jun, after I.Seeman, 1739, tql seated in robes, mezz, BM, NPG.

THORESBY, Ralph (1658-1725) antiquary and topographer.
P UNKNOWN, hs, Society of Antiquaries, London, engr G.Vertue, hs, oval, line, for *Ducatus Leodiensis*, 1712, BM, NPG.

THORNBOROUGH, John (1551-1641) bishop of Worcester.
P UNKNOWN, wl, NPG 5234.

THORNE, Robert (1492-1532) merchant and geographer.
D UNKNOWN, after portrait, w/c, Bristol Corporation.

THORNHILL, Sir James (1675-1734) decorative painter.
P Self-portrait, c1707, hs, oval, NPG 4688. Attrib WILLIAM HOGARTH, hs, oval, Uffizi, Florence. JONATHAN RICHARDSON, c1730–34, hs, NPG 3962. Self-portrait, wl, mural, the Painted Hall, Greenwich.
D J.RICHARDSON, 1733, head, pencil, BM.
PR J.FABER, jun, after J.Highmore, 1732, hl, oval, mezz, BM, NPG.

J.HIGHMORE, 1723, profile bust, etch, NPG. S.IRELAND, after W.Hogarth, hs, etch, BM, NPG.

THOROTON, Robert (1623-1678) antiquary.
PR W.G.WALKER, hs, oval, line, for J.Throsby, *History of Nottinghamshire*, 1791, NPG.

THORPE, John (1682-1750) antiquary.
PR J.BAYLY, after J.Wollaston, tql seated, line, for *Registrum Roffense*, 1769, BM, NPG.

THROCKMORTON, Sir Nicholas (1515-1571) diplomat.
P UNKNOWN, c1562, tql, NPG 3800.
SC UNKNOWN, tomb effigy, St Katherine Cree, Aldgate, London.

THURLOE, John (1616-1668) secretary of state.
P UNKNOWN, tql, NPG 1033.
D JOHN BULLFINCH, tql, w/c, NPG 4248.
M SAMUEL COOPER, (called Thurloe), hs, oval, Buccleuch Estates, Selkirk, Scotland.
C ABRAHAM and THOMAS SIMON, c1653, medallion, profile head, BM.
PR G.VERTUE, tql seated, line, for *State Papers*, 1742, BM, NPG.

THYNNE, Sir John (d1580) courtier and builder of Longleat.
UNKNOWN, 1566, tql, Longleat, Wilts.

THYNNE, Sir Thomas (1640-1714), see 1st Viscount Weymouth.

THYNNE, Thomas (1648-1682) courtier and husband of Elizabeth Percy.
P SIR GODFREY KNELLER, tql, Longleat, Wilts, engr R.White, hs, oval, line, BM, NPG. SIR PETER LELY, tql, Longleat, engr A.Browne, mezz, BM, NPG.
SC ARNOLD QUELLIN, c1682–84, effigy on monument, Westminster Abbey, London.

TICHBORNE, Sir Henry (1581?-1667) governor of Drogheda.
D T.ATHOW, hs in armour, wash, Sutherland Coll, Ashmolean Museum, Oxford.

TICHBORNE, Robert (d1682) lord mayor of London and regicide.
PR UNKNOWN, 1657, wl on horseback, line, BM, NPG.

TICKELL, Thomas (1686-1740) poet.
P Attrib SIR GODFREY KNELLER, tql, Queen's College, Oxford, engr Clamp, hl, oval, stipple, for Harding, *Biographical Mirrour*, 1796, NPG.

TIDCOMB, John (1642-1713) general.
P SIR GODFREY KNELLER, c1710, hl with turban, the 'Kit-cat Club' portrait, NPG 3229, engr J.Faber, jun, 1735, mezz, BM, NPG.

TILLEMANS, Pieter (1684-1734) painter.
SC J.M.RYSBRACK, (probably Tillemans but called Rysbrack), 1727, terracotta bust, Yale Center for British Art, New Haven, USA.
PR T.CHAMBARS, after H.Hysing, hl, line, for Walpole, *Anecdotes*, 1762, BM, NPG.

TILLOTSON, John (1630-1694) archbishop of Canterbury.
P MARY BEALE, c1672, tql seated, The Deanery, Canterbury. After SIR GODFREY KNELLER, (type of c1691–94), hl, NPG 94; version, tql seated, Lambeth Palace, London.
PR A.BLOOTELING, after Sir P.Lely, hs, oval, line, BM, NPG. P.VANDERBANK, after M.Beale, hs, oval, line, BM, NPG. R.WHITE, hs, *ad vivum*, oval, line, for *Sermons*, 1688, BM, NPG. UNKNOWN, after portrait medallion on monument at St Lawrence Jewry, London, hl, oval, line, for Hutchinson, *Life*, 1717, BM.

TILSON, Henry (1659-1695) portrait painter.
PR T.CHAMBARS, after H.Tilson, hl, line, for Walpole, *Anecdotes*, 1762, NPG.

TINDAL, Matthew (1653?-1733) deist.
SC UNKNOWN, copper and silver medal, BM.
PR J.FABER, jun, after B.Dandridge, 1733, hl, aged 78, mezz, BM, NPG.

TINDAL, Nicholas (1687-1774) historian.
PR B.PICART, after G.Knapton, hl, oval, line, for trans of Rapin, *Hist of England*, 1733, BM, NPG.

TIPTOFT, John, see Earl of Worcester.

TOLLEMACHE or **TALMASH, Thomas (1651?-1694)** general.
P SIR GODFREY KNELLER, 1688, tql, Buccleuch Estates, Selkirk, Scotland. SIR G.KNELLER, hl in armour, Ham House (NT), London.
SC UNKNOWN, bust on monument, St Mary's Church, Helmingham, Suffolk.

TOMPION, Thomas (1639-1713) father of English watchmaking.
P SIR GODFREY KNELLER, c1685-90, hs with watch, British Horological Institute, Newark, Notts, engr J.Smith, hs, oval, mezz, BM, NPG.

TOMPSON, Richard (d1693?) printseller.
PR F.PLACE, after G.Soest, hs, oval, mezz, BM.

TONG, William (1662-1727) presbyterian divine.
P UNKNOWN, hl, oval, Dr Williams's Library, London.
PR J.SIMON, after J.Wollaston, hl, oval, mezz, BM, NPG.

TONSON, Jacob, sen (1656?-1736) publisher.
P SIR GODFREY KNELLER, 1717, hl with book, the 'Kit-cat Club' portrait, NPG 3230.

TONSON, Jacob (d1735) nephew and successor of Jacob, sen.
P SIR GODFREY KNELLER, c1720?, hl, NPG 4091.

TONSTALL, Cuthbert, see Tunstall.

TOOKE, George (1595-1675) soldier and writer.
D JOHN BRAND, after E.Marmion engr, hs, oval, pen and ink, NPG.

TORPHICEN, James Sandilands, 7th Baron (d1753) lieutenant-colonel.
P ANDREW HAY, 1710, hl in armour, oval, Mellerstain, Borders region, Scotland.

TORRINGTON, Arthur Herbert, Earl of (1647-1716) admiral.
PR R.WHITE, after J.Riley, hs in armour, oval, line, BM.

TOTNES, George Carew, Earl of (1555-1629) statesman.
P UNKNOWN, (after type of c1615-20), tql, NPG 409; version, Gorhambury House, Herts.

TOTTENHAM, Charles (1685-1758) Irish politician.
P Attrib JAMES LATHAM, 1731, wl, NGI 411.

TOWNELEY, John (1697-1782) soldier and translator of *Hudibras* into French.
PR W.SKELTON, hs, oval, line, NPG.

TOWNSEND, Isaac (d1765) admiral.
P UNKNOWN, c1706-07, wl, NMM, Greenwich.

TOWNSHEND, Charles Townshend, 2nd Viscount (1674-1738) statesman.
P Studio of SIR GODFREY KNELLER, tql as young man, NPG 1363. SIR G.KNELLER, 1704?, wl in peer's robes, NPG 3623. After SIR G.KNELLER, (type of c1715-20), tql in Garter robes, NPG 1755; version, wl in coronation robes, Audley End (DoE), Essex.

PR J.SIMON, after Sir G.Kneller, hs in peer's robes, oval, mezz, BM, NPG.

TOWNSHEND, Horatio Townshend, 2nd Viscount (1630?-1687) statesman.
P SIR PETER LELY, wl, National Museum of Wales, Cardiff. UNKNOWN, tql, Felbrigg Hall (NT), Norfolk.
PR W.C.EDWARDS, tql, line, BM, NPG.

TRADESCANT, John (d1638?) traveller, botanist and collector.
P Attrib EMANUEL DE CRITZ, hs, oval, Ashmolean Museum, Oxford. UNKNOWN, hs, Ashmolean Museum. UNKNOWN, hl lying dead, Ashmolean Museum. UNKNOWN, hs, double-portrait with wife, oval, Ashmolean Museum.
PR W.HOLLAR, hs, oval, etch, for *Museum Tradescantianum*, 1656, BM, NPG.

TRADESCANT, John (1608-1662) gardener and collector.
P Attrib EMANUEL DE CRITZ, 1652, hs with skull, NPG 1089. Attrib E. DE CRITZ, hl with his friend Zythepsa, Ashmolean Museum, Oxford. Attrib E. DE CRITZ, tql with spade, Ashmolean Museum. UNKNOWN, hl with second wife Hester, Ashmolean Museum.
PR W.HOLLAR, hs, *ad vivum*, oval, etch, for *Museum Tradescantianum*, 1656, BM, NPG.

TRAPP, John (1601-1669) biblical commentator.
PR R.GAYWOOD, hl with book, oval, etch, for *Commentary on the Minor Prophets*, 1654, BM, NPG.

TRAPP, Joseph (1679-1747) professor of poetry at Oxford.
P UNKNOWN, hl, Bodleian Library, Oxford, engr R.Clamp, stipple, for Harding, *Biographical Mirrour*, 1796, BM, NPG.

TRAQUAIR, Sir John Stewart, 1st Earl of (1600?-1659) lord high treasurer of Scotland.
P UNKNOWN, tql in robes with rod of office, Traquair House, Borders region, Scotland; version, Buccleuch Estates, Selkirk, Scotland.

TREBY, Sir George (1644?-1700) chief justice of common pleas.
PR ROBERT WHITE, hs in robes, *ad vivum*, oval, line, BM, NPG 638.

TREGONWELL, Sir John (d1565) Henry VIII's agent in the dissolution of the monasteries.
PR H.MEYER, after 'H.Holbein', hl, stipple, for C.S.Gilbert, *Survey of Cornwall*, 1821, BM, NPG.

TREGURY, Michael (d1471) archbishop of Dublin.
SC UNKNOWN, tomb effigy, St Patrick's Cathedral, Dublin.

TRELAWNY, Charles (1654-1731) major-general.
M THOMAS FORSTER, hl in armour, pencil, Holburne of Menstrie Museum, Bath.

TRELAWNY, Sir Jonathan, 3rd Bart (1650-1721) bishop of Bristol, Exeter and Winchester.
P SIR GODFREY KNELLER, 1708, tql seated in robes of prelate of the Garter, Christ Church, Oxford. UNKNOWN, hs, oval, Corpus Christi College, Oxford.
G UNKNOWN, 'The Seven Bishops Committed to the Tower in 1688', oil, NPG 79.
SC GEORGE BOWER, 1688, silver medal, one of seven bishops each in a medallion, profile, NPG 152A.

TRENCHARD, Sir John (1640-1695) secretary of state.
PR C.BESTLAND, hs in armour, oval, from a miniature by O.Humphry after a picture, stipple, pub 1789, BM, NPG. J.WATSON, tql in robes, mezz, BM, NPG.

TRESHAM, Francis (1567?-1605) betrayer of the 'Gunpowder plot'.

PR UNKNOWN, hl, oval, stipple and line, for Caulfield, *Hist of the Gunpowder Plot*, NPG.

TRESHAM, Sir Thomas (*d* 1559) grand prior of the order of St John in England.
SC Attrib GABRIEL and THOMAS ROILEY, 1562, alabaster tomb effigy, All Saints' Church, Rushton, Northants.

TRESHAM, Sir Thomas (*d* 1605) Roman Catholic recusant.
P UNKNOWN, tql in armour, Buccleuch Estates, Selkirk, Scotland.

TREVOR, Sir John (1626-1672) secretary of state.
P SIR PETER LELY, tql seated, Glynde Place, Sussex.
G UNKNOWN, family group, wl as boy, oil, Glynde Place.

TREVOR, Sir John (1637-1717) judge and speaker of the House of Commons.
P After JOHN CLOSTERMAN, (type of *c* 1690-92), tql seated in robes, Palace of Westminster, London.

TREVOR, Sir Sackville (1567-1635) naval commander.
P Attrib CORNELIUS JOHNSON, tql in armour, Glynde Place, Sussex.

TREVOR, Sir Thomas (1573-1656) chief baron of the exchequer.
P CORNELIUS JOHNSON, tql in robes, Glynde Place, Sussex.

TREVOR of Bromham, Thomas Trevor, Baron (1658-1730) judge.
P Attrib THOMAS MURRAY, *c* 1702, tql in robes, National Museum of Wales, Cardiff, engr R.White, 1702, as after T.Murray, hs, oval, line, BM, NPG.
PR J.SYMPSON, tql in peer's robes, line, NPG.

TRIMNELL, Charles (1663-1723) bishop of Norwich and Winchester.
P UNKNOWN, tql seated with badge of Garter prelate, New College, Oxford, engr J.Faber, sen, 1719, and 1721 with Garter badge added, mezz, BM. Attrib MICHAEL DAHL?, tql, Nostell Priory (NT), W Yorks.

TROSSE, George (1631-1713) nonconformist minister.
PR G.VERTUE, after J.Mortimer, hl, oval, line for Hallet, *Life*, 1714, BM, NPG.

TRUMBULL, William (*d* 1635) diplomat.
PR S.GRIBELIN, hs, oval, line, BM, NPG. G.VERTUE, after O.Venius, 1726, tql, line, BM, NPG.

TRUMBULL, Sir William (1639?-1716) secretary of state.
P SIR PETER LELY, *c* 1670s, hs, oval, Althorp, Northants.
SC SIR HENRY CHEERE, *c* 1756, bronze bust, All Souls College, Oxford.
PR G.VERTUE, after Sir G.Kneller, 1724, hl, oval, line, BM, NPG.

TRYON, Thomas (1634-1703) religious eccentric, vegetarian and mystic.
PR R.WHITE, hl, oval, line, for *Knowledge of Man's Life*, 1703, BM.

TUCKNEY, Anthony (1599-1670) puritan divine and master of St John's College, Cambridge.
PR R.WHITE, hs, oval, line, for *Sermons*, 1676, BM, NPG.

TUDOR, Margaret, see MARGARET.

TUDOR, Mary, see MARY.

TUDWAY, Thomas (1645?-1726) musician.
P THOMAS HILL, *c* 1705, hl with sheet music, Faculty of Music, Oxford.

TUKE, Sir Bryan (*d* 1545) secretary to Henry VIII.
P HANS HOLBEIN, jun, *c* 1527, hl, National Gallery of Art, Washington, DC, USA; version, Cleveland Museum of Art, Ohio, USA.

TULL, Jethro (1674-1741) agricultural writer and inventor.
P UNKNOWN, tql, Agricultural Society of England, London.

TUNSTALL or TONSTALL, Cuthbert (1474-1559) master of the rolls and bishop of London and Durham.
P UNKNOWN, 16th? century, hl, Burton Constable, Humberside.

TURNER, Anne, née Norton (1576-1615) murderess.
PR UNKNOWN, wl, copy from a woodcut in broadsheet of her dying speech, line, BM, NPG.

TURNER, Daniel (1667-1741) physician.
PR J.FABER, jun, 1734, hl seated, *ad vivum*, mezz, BM, NPG. G.VERTUE, after J.Richardson, hl, oval, line, BM, NPG. G.VERTUE, after J.Richardson, hl, oval, with motto, line, BM, NPG.

TURNER, Francis (1638?-1700) bishop of Ely.
P Attrib MARY BEALE, *c* 1683-88, hl, oval, NPG 573. UNKNOWN, 1670, hl, St John's College, Cambridge. UNKNOWN, hs, oval, Corpus Christi College, Oxford.
G UNKNOWN, 'The Seven Bishops Committed to the Tower in 1688', oil, NPG 79.
SC GEORGE BOWER, 1688, silver medal, one of seven bishops each in a medallion, profile, NPG 152A.

TURNER, James (1608?-1664) parliamentary colonel hanged for burglary.
PR UNKNOWN, tql, line, copy from *Life and Death*, 1664, for Caulfield, *Remarkable Persons*, 1793, BM, NPG.

TURNER, Sir James (1615-1686?) soldier and author.
PR R.WHITE, hl in armour, oval, line, for *Pallas Armata*, 1683, BM, NPG.

TURNER, Robert (fl 1640-1664) astrologer and herbalist.
PR UNKNOWN, hs, oval, with man digging below, line, for *British or English Physitian*, 1664, BM, NPG. UNKNOWN, hs, aged 39, oval, with 3 men below, line, for trans of Friar Moultron, *Complete Bonesetter*, NPG.

TURNER, Thomas (1591-1672) dean of Canterbury.
P UNKNOWN, tql with book, The Deanery, Canterbury.

TURNER, Thomas (1645-1714) president of Corpus Christi College, Oxford.
SC THOMAS STAYNER, 1714, statue on monument, St Michael's Church, Stowe-Nine-Churches, Northants.

TURNOR, Sir Christopher (1607-1675) baron of the exchequer.
PR S.HARDING, after J.M.Wright, hl in robes, stipple, for Harding, *Biographical Mirrour*, 1792, BM, NPG.

TURNOR, Sir Edward (1617-1676) judge and speaker of the House of Commons.
P Probably by J.M.WRIGHT, hl with mace, Palace of Westminster, London. By or after J.M.WRIGHT, hl with robes, Harvard Law School, Cambridge, Mass, USA.

TUTCHIN, John (1661?-1707) Whig pamphleteer.
PR M. VAN DER GUCHT, hs, oval, line, BM, NPG.

TWEEDDALE, John Hay, 2nd Earl and 1st Marquess of (1626-1697) lord chancellor of Scotland.
P Attrib SIR GODFREY KNELLER, 1678, tql seated, Floors Castle, Borders region, Scotland. SIR G.KNELLER, *c* 1695, hs, TATE 3272. SIR PETER LELY, tql seated, SNPG 2225.
PR J.SMITH, after Sir G.Kneller, hl in peer's robes, oval, mezz, BM. J.SMITH, after Sir G.Kneller, hl in chancellor's robes, oval, mezz, BM.

TWEEDDALE, John Hay, 2nd Marquess of (1645-1713) lord chancellor.

P GERARD SOEST, tql in robes, Glasgow City Art Gallery. Attrib FERDINAND VOET, hs, oval, SNPG 2224.

TWEEDDALE, John Hay, 4th Marquess of (c1695-1762) lord justice-general for Scotland.
P WILLIAM AIKMAN, hl, SNPG 2226.

TWISDEN or TWYSDEN of Bradbourne, Sir Thomas, 1st Bart (1602-1683) judge.
P After J.M.WRIGHT, hl in robes, Kent Archaeological Society on loan to East Malling Research Station, Bradbourne House, Kent. UNKNOWN, c1660, wl seated in robes, Inner Temple, London. UNKNOWN, c1670, tql seated in robes, Bradbourne House.
PR UNKNOWN, hs in robes, mezz, BM.

TWISSE, William (1578?-1646) puritan divine.
PR T.TROTTER, hs, oval, line, pub 1783, NPG.

TWYSDEN, John (1607-1688) physician.
P UNKNOWN, c1650, hs, oval, Kent Archaeological Society on loan to East Malling Research Station, Bradbourne House, Kent.

TWYSDEN, Sir Thomas, see Twisden.

TWYSDEN of Roydon, Sir Roger, 2nd Bart (1597-1672) historical antiquary.
P UNKNOWN, 1648, hl, Kent Archaeological Society on loan to East Malling Research Station, Bradbourne House, Kent.

TYERS, Jonathan (d1767) proprietor of Vauxhall Gardens.
G FRANCIS HAYMAN, called Tyers with his daughter and son-in-law, oil, c1740–45, Yale Center for British Art, New Haven, USA.
SC L.F.ROUBILIAC, terracotta bust, V & A; marble bust, City Art Gallery, Birmingham.

TYLDESLEY, Sir Thomas (1596-1651) royalist.
PR J.COCHRAN, tql with breastplate, stipple, Baines, *Lancashire*, 1838, BM, NPG.

TYRAWLEY, James O'Hara, 2nd Baron (1682?-1773) soldier and diplomat.
P Attrib JOHN VERELST, 1712, tql seated with 2nd Duke of Montagu, NPG 2034.

TYRCONNEL, Frances, née Jennings, Duchess of (1647?-1730) famous beauty.
P MARY BEALE, hl, oval, Althorp, Northants; version, Beaulieu, Hants.
M SAMUEL COOPER, c1665, hl, oval, NPG 5095.

TYRCONNELL, Richard Talbot, titular Duke of (1630-1691) soldier and Jacobite.
P UNKNOWN, c1690, tql with breastplate and Garter star, NPG 1466.
PR W.N.GARDINER, hl in armour, oval, stipple, for Harding, *Biographical Mirrour*, 1794, BM, NPG.

TYRONE, Hugh O'Neill, 2nd Earl of (1550?-1616) soldier.
P UNKNOWN, hs in armour, Harbour Commissioners, Belfast.

TYRRELL, Sir Thomas (1594-1672) judge.
P J.M.WRIGHT, c1650-60, wl in robes, Inner Temple, London.

TYSON, Edward (1650-1708) physician.
P EDMUND LILL(E)Y, c1695?, tql seated, Royal College of Physicians, London.
SC EDWARD STANTON, bust on monument, All Hallows Church, Twickenham, Middx.

TYSON, Richard (1680-1750) physician.
P UNKNOWN, (called Richard Tyson), c1710–20, tql seated, Royal College of Physicians, London.

U

UNDERHILL, Cane (1634-1710?) actor.
P By or after ROBERT BING, tql as Obadiah in Howard, *The Committee*, Garrick Club, London, engr J.Faber, jun, 1712, mezz, BM, NPG.

UNTON, Sir Henry (1557?-1596) diplomat and soldier.
P UNKNOWN, hl, Arundel Castle, W Sussex. UNKNOWN, c1596, hl, surrounded by scenes from his life, NPG 710.

URQUHART, Sir Thomas (1611-1660) author and translator.
PR G.GLOVER, 1641, wl, *ad vivum*, line, BM, NPG. G.GLOVER, wl seated surrounded by Apollo and Muses, line, BM.

URRY, John (1666-1715) editor of Chaucer.
PR N.PIGNÉ, hl, oval, line, BM, NPG.

URSWICK, Christopher (1448-1522) diplomat and churchman.
SC UNKNOWN, brass effigy, St John's Church, Hackney, London.

URSWICK, Sir Thomas (d1479) chief baron of the exchequer.
SC UNKNOWN, brass effigy, St Peter and St Paul Church, Dagenham, Essex.

USSHER, James (1581-1656) archbishop of Armagh.
P UNKNOWN, 1641, hl, Jesus College, Oxford. WILLIAM FLETCHER, 1644, hl, Bodleian Library, Oxford. After SIR PETER LELY, (type of 1654), tql seated, Chatsworth, Derbys; version, hs, NPG 574.
PR W.MARSHALL, hl, line, for *Body of Divinity*, 1647, BM, NPG.

V

VALENTIA, Francis Annesley, 1st Viscount, see Baron Mountnorris.

VANBRUGH or **VANBURGH, Sir John (1664-1726)** architect and dramatist.
P SIR GODFREY KNELLER, c1704-10, hl, the 'Kit-cat Club' portrait, NPG 3231. Attrib THOMAS MURRAY, c1718, hl, NPG 1568. JONATHAN RICHARDSON, 1625, tql, College of Arms, London.

VANDERBANK or **VANDREBANC, John (1694?-1739)** portrait painter.
D Self-portrait, 1738, hs, pen and ink, NPG 3647.

VANDERBANK or **VANDREBANC, Peter (1649-1697)** engraver.
D SIR GODFREY KNELLER, head, chalks, BM.
PR G.WHITE, after Sir G.Kneller, hl, oval, mezz, BM, NPG.

VAN DER DOORT, Abraham (d1640) medallist and keeper of Charles I's collections.
P Attrib WILLIAM DOBSON, head, The Hermitage, Leningrad. After W.DOBSON?, head, NPG 1569.
PR V.GREEN, after W.Dobson, (wrongly as 'Dobson's Father'), head, mezz, pub 1776, NPG.

VAN DER GUCHT, Gerard (1696-1776) engraver.
D WILLIAM STUKELY, 1721, profile head, indian ink, BM.
PR J.CALDWALL, after B. van der Gucht, hs, oval, etch, NPG.

VAN DE VELDE, Willem (1610-1693) marine painter.
P Self-portrait?, (called Willem, sen), hl, NMM, Greenwich.
PR G.SIBELIUS, after Sir G.Kneller, hl, oval, line, BM, NPG.

VAN DE VELDE, Willem (1633-1707) painter.
P LODEWIJK VAN DER HELST, c1672, hl with sketch, Rijksmuseum, Amsterdam.
PR J.SMITH, 1707, after Sir G.Kneller, 1680, hl, mezz, BM, NPG.

VAN DIEST, Adriaen (1656-1704) landscape painter.
PR A.BANNERMAN, after A. van Diest, hl, oval with another of J. van der Does (falsely identified as F. le Piper), line, for Walpole, *Anecdotes*, 1762, BM.

VANDREBANC, see Vanderbank.

VANDYCK, Sir Anthony (1599-1641) painter.
P Self-portrait, c1614-15, head, Gemäldegalerie der Akademie, Vienna. Self-portrait, c1621, tql, The Hermitage, Leningrad; version, Alte Pinakothek, Munich. After SIR A.VANDYCK, c1621, hs, NPG 1291. Self-portrait, c1633, tql with Endymion Porter, oval, Prado, Madrid. After SIR A.VANDYCK, (type of c1633-34), hs with sunflower, Berkeley Castle, Glos. Self-portrait, hs, oval, The Louvre, Paris.
PR J.NEEFS, after Sir A.Vandyck, bust on pedestal, etch, for *Centum Icones*, 1645, BM, NPG.

VANE, Sir Henry (1589-1655) secretary of state.
P After M.J. VAN MIEREVELDT, (type of late 1630s), hl, NPG 1118; version, Raby Castle, Durham.

VANE, Sir Henry (1613-1662) revolutionary.
P SIR PETER LELY, c1650, hs, Raby Castle, Durham.
PR W.FAITHORNE, hs, oval, line, for Sikes, *Life*, 1662, BM, NPG.

VAN HAECKEN, Joseph (1699?-1749) painter.
PR J.FABER, jun, after T.Hudson, hl seated, mezz, BM, NPG.

VAN HOMRIGH, Esther (1690-1723) Swift's 'Vanessa'.
P Attrib CHARLES JERVAS, NGI.

VAN HUYSUM, Jacob or **James (1687?-1746)** flower painter.
P Self-portrait, c1739, hl, Ashmolean Museum, Oxford.

VAN SOMER, Paul (1576-1621) portrait painter.
PR S.PASSE, 1622, hs, oval, line, BM.

VAN SON, Jan Francis (1658-1718?) painter.
PR A.BANNERMAN, hl, oval, line, for Walpole, *Anecdotes*, 1762, BM, NPG.

VAN VOERST, Robert (1596-1636) engraver.
PR R. VAN VOERST, after Sir A.Vandyck, tql, line, for *Centum Icones*, 1645, BM.

VAUGHAN, Sir John (1603-1674) judge.
P J.M.WRIGHT, 1671, wl in robes, Inner Temple, London.
PR R.WHITE, hs in robes, oval, line, for *Reports*, 1677, BM, NPG.

VAUGHAN, John (1640?-1713), see 3rd Earl of Carbery.

VAUGHAN, Richard (1550?-1607) bishop of London.
P UNKNOWN, hs, with book, Bodleian Library, Oxford.
PR PASSE, hs, line, for Holland, *Herwologia*, 1620, BM, NPG.

VAUX of Harrowden, Thomas Vaux, 2nd Baron (1510-1556) poet.
D HANS HOLBEIN, jun, hs, chalks, Royal Coll. H.HOLBEIN, hs, slightly older, chalks, Royal Coll.

VENNER, Tobias (1577-1660) medical writer.
PR W.FAITHORNE, hs, oval, line, for *Via Recta ad Vitam Longam*, 1660, BM, NPG.

VENNING, Ralph (1621?-1674) nonconformist divine.
PR W.HOLLAR, 1674, hl, oval, etch, BM, NPG, V & A.

VENTRIS, Sir Peyton (1645-1691) judge.
P JOHN RILEY, tql seated in robes, Middle Temple, London, engr R.White, hs, oval, line, for *Reports*, 1696, BM, NPG.

VERE, Aubrey de (1340?-1400), see 10th Earl of Oxford.

VERE, Aubrey de (1626-1703), see 20th Earl of Oxford.

VERE, Diana de, see Duchess of St Albans.

VERE, Edward de, see 17th Earl of Oxford.

VERE, Sir Francis (1560-1609) soldier.
P UNKNOWN, hs, profile, oval, NPG L112.
SC UNKNOWN, tomb effigy, Westminster Abbey, London, engr R.Gaywood, 1657, etch, BM, NPG.

VERE, Henry de, see 18th Earl of Oxford.

VERE, John de, see 15th Earl of Oxford.

VERE of Tilbury, Horace Vere, Baron (1565-1635) soldier.
P J.A. VAN RAVESTEYN, (probably Vere of Tilbury), 1611, tql in armour, no 139, Mauritshuis, The Hague, Netherlands. M.J. VAN MIEREVELDT, 1629, hs in armour, Ashdown House (NT), Oxon; version, NPG 818.
PR F.DELARAM, hl in armour, oval, line, BM, V & A.

VERMIGLI, Pietro Martire (1500-1562) reformer.
P UNKNOWN, (after type of 1560), hl with book, NPG 195.
PR H.HONDIUS, hl, line, for Verheiden, *Praestantium Theologorum Effigies*, 1602, BM, NPG.

VERNEY, Sir Edmund (1590-1642) soldier.
P UNKNOWN, hs in breastplate, oval, Stanford Hall, Leics.
SC EDWARD MARSHALL, 1653, bust on family monument, All Saints Church, Middle Claydon, Bucks.
PR RIVERS, hs in armour, stipple, NPG.

VERNEY, John (1699-1741) judge.
P UNKNOWN, tql in robes, Middle Temple, London.
PR G.VERTUE, after A.Ramsay, tql seated in robes, line, BM, NPG.

VERNEY, Sir Ralph, 1st Bart (1613-1696) politician.
P CORNELIUS JOHNSON, 1634, hl, Claydon House (NT), Bucks. SIR PETER LELY, c1680, tql, Claydon House.
SC EDWARD MARSHALL, 1653, bust on family monument, All Saints Church, Middle Claydon, Bucks.

VERNON, Edward (1684-1757) admiral.
P CHARLES PHILIPS, 1743, tql, NMM, Greenwich. THOMAS GAINSBOROUGH, c1753, tql, NPG 881.
SC Attrib J.M.RYSBRACK, marble bust, NMM. Attrib J.M.RYSBRACK, marble bust, Sudbury Hall (NT), Suffolk. J.M.RYSBRACK, c1753, bust on monument, Westminster Abbey, London. UNKNOWN, various medals, BM.
PR J.FABER, jun, after T.Bardwell, 1740, tql, mezz, BM, NPG. G.BOCKMAN, after G.Hansoon, tql, mezz, BM.

VERNON, James (1646-1727) secretary of state.
P SIR GODFREY KNELLER, 1677, hs, oval, NPG 2963. FRANCIS HAYMAN, hl with book, Phoenix Art Museum, Arizona, USA.

VERNON, Sir Richard (d1451) speaker of the House of Commons.
SC UNKNOWN, tomb effigy with wife, St Bartholomew's Church, Tong, Salop.

VERNON, Thomas (1654-1721) law reporter.
SC CHRISTOPHER HORSNAILE, 1721, effigy on monument, Hanbury Church, Worcs.
PR G.VERTUE, after Sir G.Kneller, hs, oval, line, for *Reports*, 1726, BM, NPG.

VERRIO, Antonio (1639?-1707) decorative painter.
P SIR GODFREY KNELLER, c1690, hs, oval, Burghley House, Northants. Self-portrait, c1700?, hl, oval, NPG 2890.
PR A.BANNERMAN, hl, oval, line, for Walpole, *Anecdotes*, 1762, BM, NPG.

VERTUE, George (1683-1756) engraver and antiquary.
P THOMAS GIBSON, 1723, hl, Society of Antiquaries, London. JONATHAN RICHARDSON, 1733, hl, oval, NPG 576.
D J.RICHARDSON, 1735, hs, profile, Society of Antiquaries. Attrib self-portrait, 1741, hl seated, pencil and chalk, NPG 4876.
G GAWEN HAMILTON, 'A Conversation of Virtuosis . . . at the Kings Armes', oil, 1735, NPG 1384.
SC SYLVANUS BEVAN, ivory statuette, tql, BM.
PR W.HUMPHREY, after G.Vertue, wl with wife, etch, BM, NPG.

VERULAM, Baron, see Viscount St Alban.

VESEY or **VOYSEY, John (1465?-1554)** bishop of Exeter.
SC UNKNOWN, painted tomb effigy, Holy Trinity Church, Sutton Coldfield, Warwicks.

VETCH, Samuel (1668-1732) colonist.
P UNKNOWN, c1705, tql, New York City Museum, USA.

VICARY, Thomas (d1561) surgeon.
G HANS HOLBEIN, jun, (heavily restored), 'Henry VIII and the Barber Surgeons', cartoon, 1540-43, Royal College of Surgeons, London. H.HOLBEIN, (heavily restored), 'Henry VIII and the Barber Surgeons', oil, 1540-43, Barbers' Company, London.

VILLIERS, Barbara, see Duchess of Cleveland.

VILLIERS, Christopher, see 1st Earl of Anglesey.

VILLIERS, Edward, see 1st Earl of Jersey.

VILLIERS, Sir George (1544?-1606) sheriff of Leicestershire.
SC NICHOLAS STONE, 1631, tomb effigy, Westminster Abbey, London.

VILLIERS, George (1592-1628), see 1st Duke of Buckingham.

VILLIERS, George (1628-1687), see 2nd Duke of Buckingham.

VILLIERS, John, see Viscount Purbeck.

VILLIERS, William, see 2nd Earl of Jersey.

VINCENT, Nathaniel (1639?-1697) nonconformist divine.
P UNKNOWN, hs, oval, Dr Williams's Library, London.
PR R.WHITE, hs, oval, line, for *True Touchstone of Grace and Nature*, 1681, BM, NPG.

VINER or **VYNER, Sir Robert, 1st Bart (1631-1688)** lord mayor of London.
P UNKNOWN, hl, Goldsmiths' Company, London.
G After J.M.WRIGHT, family group, oil, 1673, Newby Hall, N Yorks.
PR W.FAITHORNE, hl, oval, line, BM, NPG.

VINER, Sir Thomas, Bart (1588-1665) lord mayor of London.
P UNKNOWN, tql in robes, Goldsmiths' Company, London; version, NPG 4509.

VIVES, Johannes Ludovicus (1492-1540) scholar.
PR E. DE BOULONOIS, hl, line, for Boissard, *Bibliotheca Chalcographica*, 1650, NPG.

VOS or **VOSSIUS, Gerard John (1577-1649)** scholar.
PR A.BLOOTELING, after Sandra(rt), hl, line, V & A. T.MATHAM?, hl, line, NPG. G.VERTUE?, hl, oval, line, NPG.

VOYSEY, John, see Vesey.

VYNER, see Viner.

W

WAAD or **WADD, Sir William (1546-1623)** diplomat and lieutenant of the Tower.
PR UNKNOWN, hl, line, BM, NPG.

WADDING, Luke (1588-1657) Irish Franciscan and author.
P Attrib JUSÈPE DE RIBERA, hl, NGI 298.
PR G.VALET, after C.Maratti, tql seated, line, BM.

WADDINGTON, Edward (1670?-1731) bishop of Chichester.
P HAMLET WINSTANLEY, 1730, tql, King's College, Cambridge, engr J.Faber, jun, mezz, BM, NPG.

WADE, George (1673-1748) field-marshal.
P Attrib JOHANN VAN DIEST, c1731?, wl in breastplate, SNPG L28. Attrib J. VAN DIEST, c1731?, hl in breastplate, oval, NPG 1594. Attrib J. VAN DIEST, c1732-36, tql, SNPG 2416, engr J.Faber, jun, 1736, hl, oval, mezz, BM, NPG. Attrib J.B.VANLOO, c1737-42, tql, formerly United Service Club, London (c/o Crown Commissioners).
D ALEXANDER VAN HAECKEN, after J.Vanderbank, tql, pencil and chalk, SNPG 353.
SC L.F.ROUBILIAC, 1746, relief portrait medallion on monument, profile, Westminster Abbey, London.

WADHAM, Nicholas (1532-1609) founder of Wadham College, Oxford.
P UNKNOWN, 1595, hl, Petworth (NT), W Sussex; version, Wadham College.
SC UNKNOWN, 1613, stone statue, Wadham College. UNKNOWN, 1618, brass effigy with wife, St Mary's Church, Ilminster, Somerset. UNKNOWN, silver medal, BM.

WADSWORTH, Thomas (1630-1676) nonconformist divine.
P UNKNOWN, hs, oval, Dr Williams's Library, London. UNKNOWN, Christ's College, Cambridge.
PR R.WHITE, hs, oval, line, for *Remains*, 1680, BM, NPG.

WAGER, Sir Charles (1666-1743) admiral.
P SIR GODFREY KNELLER, 1710, hl, NMM, Greenwich. THOMAS GIBSON, c1731, hl in breastplate, oval, NMM, engr J.Faber, jun, 1732, mezz, BM, NPG.
SC PETER SCHEEMAKERS, 1743, relief portrait medallion on monument, Westminster Abbey, London.

WAINFLEET, William of, see Waynflete.

WAKE, William (1657-1737) archbishop of Canterbury.
P THOMAS GIBSON, tql seated, Christ Church, Oxford. ISAAC WHOOD, 1736, tql seated, Lambeth Palace, London. UNKNOWN, c1730, tql seated, NPG 22.
SC JEAN DASSIER, silver and copper medal, BM.
PR J.FABER, jun, after J.Ellys, tql seated, mezz, BM, NPG.

WALDBY, Robert (d1398) archbishop of York.
SC UNKNOWN, brass effigy, Westminster Abbey, London.

WALDEGRAVE, James Waldegrave, 1st Earl of (1685-1741) diplomat.
D UNKNOWN, hs with Garter ribbon and star, pastel, NPG 1875.

WALKER, Sir Edward (1612-1677) Garter King at Arms.
P WILLIAM DOBSON, c1645, tql seated with bust, The Shakespeare Centre, Stratford-upon-Avon. Attrib W.DOBSON, tql in robes, College of Arms, London. UNKNOWN, tql seated with Charles I, NPG 1961.

WALKER, George (1645?-1690) soldier and divine.
P UNKNOWN, tql in armour, NPG 2038.
PR P.VANDERBANK, after Sir G.Kneller, 1689, hs, oval, line, BM, NPG.

WALKER, Richard (1679-1764) founder of Botanic Garden, Cambridge.
P J.T. or D.HEINS, 1751, hs, Trinity College, Cambridge, engr P.S.Lamborn, line, for *Cat of Plants in the Botanic Garden*, 1771, BM, NPG.

WALKER, Robert (d1658?) portrait painter.
P Self-portrait, c1640-55, hs with sketch, NPG 753; version, with statuette of Mercury, Ashmolean Museum, Oxford, engr P.Lombart, before c1663, line, BM, NPG.

WALKER, Thomas (1698-1744) actor and dramatist.
P UNKNOWN, (called Walker), hs, NPG 2202.
G WILLIAM HOGARTH, 'A Scene from *The Beggar's Opera*', oil, c1729-31, TATE 2437; version, Yale Center for British Art, New Haven, USA.
PR J.FABER, jun, after J.Ellys, 1728, hl as Captain Macheath in *Beggar's Opera*, oval, mezz, BM, NPG.

WALL, John (1588-1666) divine.
P JOHN TAYLOR, tql, Oxford Town Hall.

WALLER, Edmund (1606-1687) poet.
P Attrib ISAAC FULLER, c1640-50, hl, Rousham House, Oxon. SIR PETER LELY, c1665, tql seated, Clarendon Coll on loan to Plymouth Art Gallery. SIR GODFREY KNELLER, 1684, tql seated, Rousham, engr G.Vertue, hs, oval, line, BM, NPG. After JOHN RILEY, c1685, hs, oval, line, NPG 144.
M DAVID LOGGAN, (called Waller), 1685, hs, oval, pencil, NPG 4494.
PR P.VANDERBANK, hs, aged 23, oval, line, BM, NPG. W.BROMLEY, after C.Johnson, hs, aged 23, oval, line, for *Effigies Poeticae*, 1824, BM, NPG. P.VANDERBANK, after Sir P.Lely, hs, aged 76, oval, line, for *Poems*, 1711, BM, NPG.

WALLER, Sir William (1597?-1668) parliamentary general.
P SIR PETER LELY, c1645, hs in armour, oval, Goodwood, W Sussex, engr N.Yeates, line, for *Meditations*, 1680, BM, NPG. UNKNOWN, hs, NPG 2108.
SC UNKNOWN, silver badge, BM.
PR RODTTERMONDT, after C.Johnson, 1643, hl in armour, oval, etch, BM, NPG.

WALLIS, John (1616-1703) mathematician and divine.
P GERARD SOEST, before c1681, hl, Royal Society, London. SIR GODFREY KNELLER, 1701, wl, Bodleian Library, Oxford; version, hl, oval, NPG 578.
SC WILLIAM TOWNESEND, 1703, bust, St Mary's Church, Oxford.
PR W.FAITHORNE, hl, oval, line, for *Mechanica*, 1670, BM, NPG. D.LOGGAN, 1678, hs, *ad vivum*, oval, line, BM, NPG. M.BURGHERS, after W.Sonmans, hl, oval, line for *Opera Mathematica*, 1699, BM, NPG, V & A.

WALMESLEY, Sir Thomas (1537-1612) judge.
P UNKNOWN, tql seated in robes, Lincoln's Inn, London.

WALPOLE, Robert (1650-1700) Whig supporter and father of 1st Earl of Orford.
PR UNKNOWN, hs, octagonal, stipple, pub 1801, NPG, and for W.Cox, *Memoirs of Lord Walpole*, 1802, BM.

WALPOLE, Sir Robert (1676-1745), see 1st Earl of Orford.

WALPOLE of Wolterton, Horatio Walpole, 1st Baron (1678-1757) diplomat.
P JONATHAN RICHARDSON, c1722, tql, Houghton Hall, Norfolk. After J.B.VANLOO, (type of 1739), hs, oval, Hardwick Hall (NT), Derbys. D.HEINS, 1740, wl, Blackfriars' Hall, Norwich. UNKNOWN, 1747, hl, St Mary's College, Strawberry Hill, Middx.
PR J.SIMON, 1741, after J.B.Vanloo, 1739, tql seated, mezz, BM, NPG.

WALSH, William (1663-1708) critic and poet.
P Begun by SIR GODFREY KNELLER, c1708, hl, the 'Kit-cat Club' portrait, NPG 3232.

WALSINGHAM, Sir Francis (1530-1590) statesman.
P Attrib JOHN DE CRITZ, sen, c1585–89, hl, NPG 1807; version, King's College, Cambridge.
PR PASSE, hs, oval, line, for Holland, *Herwologia*, 1620, BM, NPG.

WALTER, Hubert (d1205) archbishop of Canterbury and statesman.
SC UNKNOWN, tomb effigy, Canterbury Cathedral.

WALTER, Sir John (1566-1630) judge.
P UNKNOWN, tql in robes, Inner Temple, London.

WALTHAM, John de (d1395) bishop of Salisbury and treasurer of England.
SC UNKNOWN, late 14th century, brass effigy, Westminster Abbey.

WALTON, Brian or Bryan (1600?-1661) bishop of Chester.
P UNKNOWN, (called Walton), Peterhouse College, Cambridge.
PR P.LOMBART, tql seated, line, for *Biblia Polyglotta*, 1657, BM, NPG.

WALTON, Sir George (1665-1739) admiral.
P BARTHOLOMEW DANDRIDGE, c1734–39, tql, NMM, Greenwich.

WALTON, Izaak (1593-1683) miscellaneous writer.
P JACOB HUYSMANS, c1675?, hl, NPG 1168.

WANDESFORD, Christopher (1592-1640) lord deputy of Ireland.
D G.P.HARDING, (after type of 1630), hs, oval, w/c, NPG 2407.

WANLEY, Humfrey or Humphrey (1672-1726) librarian and antiquary.
P THOMAS HILL, 1711, tql seated, Society of Antiquaries, London; version, 1716, Bodleian Library, Oxford. T.HILL, 1717, hs, oval, Bodleian Library; version, NPG 579. T.HILL, c1722?, tql seated with bust, BM.

WANLEY, Nathaniel (1634-1680) divine and compiler of 'The Wonders of the Little World'.
P UNKNOWN, hs, Bodleian Library, Oxford.

WARBECK, Perkin (1474-1499).
D UNKNOWN, hs, Bibliothèque d'Arras, France.

WARBURTON, John (1682-1759) herald and antiquary.
PR A.MILLER, after G. van der Gucht, 1740, wl in tabard, mezz, BM, NPG.

WARBURTON, William (1698-1779) bishop of Gloucester and editor of Pope.
P CHARLES PHILIPS, c1737, tql seated, NPG 23, engr T.Burford, mezz, BM, NPG. WILLIAM HOARE, c1757, tql with book, Episcopal Palace, Gloucester. W.HOARE, 1765, hs, oval, Hurd Episcopal Library, Hartlebury Castle, Worcs.
D W.HOARE, c1765, profile head, Hartlebury Castle.
SC Attrib THOMAS KING, 1779, relief portrait medallion, Gloucester Cathedral.
PR H.GRAVELOT, portrait medallion, profile, etch, BM, NPG. J.HOUBRAKEN, hs, oval, line, BM, NPG.
C J.LODGE, after T.Worlidge, head, etch, NPG.

WARD, Sir Edward (1638-1714) judge.
SC J.M.RYSBRACK, c1720, marble tomb effigy, St Rumbald's Church, Stoke Doyle, Northants.
PR R.WHITE, after Sir G.Kneller, 1702, hs in robes, oval, line, NPG.

WARD, Edward (1667-1731) burlesque poet.
PR M. VAN DER GUCHT, hs, oval, line, for *Nuptial Dialogues*, 1710, BM, NPG. W.SHERWIN, hs, oval, line, for *Hudibras Redevivus*, 1715, BM. T.JOHNSON, c1721, hl, aged 54, oval, mezz, BM.

WARD, John (1679?-1758) antiquary and biographer.
P ALLAN RAMSAY, 1749, hl with turban, oval, County Museum, Warwick. UNKNOWN, hl, NPG 590.

WARD, Joshua (1685-1761) quack doctor.
G UNKNOWN, after T.Bardwell, wl in crowd, line engr, pub 1749, BM.
SC AGOSTINO CARLINI, c1760, statue, Royal Society of Arts, London.
PR J.FABER, jun, after E.Loving, hl, mezz, BM.

WARD, Mary (1585-1645) founder of a female order modelled on the Jesuits.
PR J.MOERL, hl with sacred emblems, oval, line, BM.

WARD or WARDE, Sir Patience (1629-1696) lord mayor of London.
P JOHN RILEY, wl, Squerryes Court, Kent. UNKNOWN, tql, Squerryes Court.
D T.ATHOW, wl in robes, wash, Sutherland Coll, Ashmolean Museum, Oxford. UNKNOWN, wl in robes, w/c, NPG.

WARD, Samuel (d1643) master of Sidney Sussex College, Cambridge.
P UNKNOWN, Sidney Sussex College.

WARD, Seth (1617-1689) bishop of Salisbury.
P JOHN GREENHILL, c1673, tql in robes of Garter prelate, Guildhall, Salisbury, Wilts; version, Trinity College, Oxford.
SC UNKNOWN, bust, Salisbury Cathedral.
PR D.LOGGAN, 1678, hl in robes, *ad vivum*, oval, line, BM, NPG 644.

WARDE, Sir Patience, see Ward.

WARDER, Joseph (fl 1688-1718) physician.
PR H.HULSBERGH, hl, aged 58, oval, line, NPG.

WARE, Isaac (d1766) architect.
P ANDREA SOLDI, c1754, hl with his daughter, pointing to plans of Wrotham Park, RIBA, London.
SC L.F.ROUBILIAC, c1741, marble bust, NPG 4982.

WARE, Sir James (1594-1666) Irish historian and antiquary.
PR G.VERTUE, 1738, hs, oval, line, for *Works*, 1739, BM, NPG.

WARHAM, William (1450?-1532) archbishop of Canterbury.
P HANS HOLBEIN, jun, c1527, hl, The Louvre, Paris; copy, NPG 2094.
D H.HOLBEIN, c1527, hs, chalks, Royal Coll.
MS UNKNOWN, Henry VIII in procession with lords and clergy, Parliament Roll of 1512, Trinity College, Cambridge.
SC UNKNOWN, tomb effigy, Canterbury Cathedral.

WARING, William (1610-1679) Jesuit.
G UNKNOWN, 'Titus Oates and Jesuits', line engr, BM.
PR M.BOUCHE, hs with dagger in breast, oval, line, NPG.

WARKWORTH, John (d1500) historian.
P UNKNOWN, mid-16th century, hl with book, Peterhouse College, Cambridge.

WARNER, Sir Edward (1511-1565) lieutenant of the Tower.
SC UNKNOWN, c1565, brass effigy, St Protase and St Gervase Church, Little Plumstead, Norfolk.

WARNER, John (1581-1666) bishop of Rochester.
P JOHN TAYLOR, c1670, tql, Magdalen College, Oxford.
SC JOSHUA MARSHALL, 1666, effigy? on monument, Rochester Cathedral.

WARREN, Thomas (1617?-1694) nonconformist divine.
PR J.CALDWALL, hs, oval, line, NPG.

WARRINGTON, George Booth, 2nd Earl of (1675-1758) lord-lieutenant of Chester.
P Attrib SIR GODFREY KNELLER, hl, Lanhydrock House (NT), Cornwall. MICHAEL DAHL, tql in peer's robes, Tatton Park (NT), Cheshire.

WARRINGTON, Henry Booth, 2nd Baron Delamere and 1st Earl of (1652-1694) chancellor of exchequer.
P SIR GODFREY KNELLER, hs with armour, oval, DoE, 10 Downing Street, London.

WARWICK, Ambrose Dudley, Earl of (1528?-1590) soldier and statesman.
P UNKNOWN, wl with Garter George and page, Longleat, Wilts.
G M.GHEERAERTS, sen, 'Procession of Garter Knights, 1576', etch, BM.
SC UNKNOWN, alabaster tomb effigy, St Mary's Church, Beauchamp Chapel, Warwicks.
PR PASSE, hs, oval, line, for Holland, *Herwologia*, 1620, BM, NPG.

WARWICK, Mary Rich, née Boyle, Countess of (1625-1678) religious writer.
P Attrib EDMUND ASHFIELD, tql, Burghley House, Northants.
PR R.WHITE, hl, oval, line, for Walker, *Life*, 1678, BM, NPG.

WARWICK, Sir Philip (1609-1683) historian.
PR R.WHITE, after Sir P.Lely, hs, oval, line, for *Memoirs*, 1701, BM, NPG.

WARWICK, Richard de Beauchamp, 13th Earl of (1381/2-1439) lieutenant of France and Normandy.
MS UNKNOWN, wl in armour with infant Henry VI, English version of Rous Roll, BL Ms 48976. Various scenes drawn by John Ross of Warwick, 'The History of the life and acts of Richard Beauchamp, E. of Warwick', BL Cotton Ms Julius EIV.
SC UNKNOWN, c1453-56, tomb effigy, gilt-bronze, Beauchamp Chapel, St Mary's, Warwicks.

WARWICK, Richard Nevill(e), Earl of (1428-1471) the 'king-maker'.
MS UNKNOWN, wl on horseback in battle, Ghent Ms 236, University of Ghent, Belgium.

WARWICK, Sir Robert Rich, 2nd Earl of (1587-1658) lord high admiral.
P DANIEL MYTENS, 1632, wl, NMM, Greenwich. DANIEL MYTENS, (called Warwick), wl, Hardwick Hall (NT), Derbys. SIR ANTHONY VANDYCK, c1632-35, wl, Metropolitan Museum of Art, New York. SIR A.VANDYCK, wl in armour, Buccleuch Estates, Selkirk, Scotland.
SC UNKNOWN, silver medal, BM.
PR W.HOLLAR, wl in armour, etch, BM, NPG.

WARWICK, Thomas de Beauchamp, 12th Earl of (d1401) statesman.
SC UNKNOWN, alabaster tomb effigy, Collegiate Church of St Mary, Warwicks.

WASSE, Joseph (1672-1738) divine and classical scholar.
M JONATHAN RICHARDSON, jun, 1734-35, pencil, V & A.

WATERHOUSE, Edward (1619-1670) antiquary and author.
PR D.LOGGAN, hl, *ad vivum*, oval, line, for *Fortescutus Illustratus*, 1663, BM, NPG, V & A. A.HERTOCHS, hs, oval, line, for *Gentleman's Monitor*, 1665, BM, NPG.

WATERLAND, Daniel (1683-1740) theologian.
P UNKNOWN, Magdalene College, Cambridge.
PR J.FABER, after R.Philips, hl, oval, mezz, NPG. J.FITTLER, hl, oval, line, BM, NPG.

WATSON, Sir Lewis, see 1st Baron Rockingham.

WATSON, Thomas (d1686) puritan divine.
P UNKNOWN, hl with book, Dr Williams's Library, London.
PR F. VAN HOVE, hs, oval, line, for *Art of Divine Contentment*, 1662, BM, NPG. H.SCHATEN, tql seated, oval, line for German trans of *Works*, BM, NPG. J.STURT, hs, oval, line, NPG.

WATSON, Thomas (1637-1717) bishop of St David's.
P UNKNOWN, (perhaps Watson), hl with book, St John's College, Cambridge.

WATTS, Isaac (1674-1748) hymn-writer.
P UNKNOWN, hl, oval, Dr Williams's Library, London; version, NPG 264.
PR G.VERTUE, after I.Whood, 1710?, hl, oval, line, BM, NPG. G.VERTUE, hs, oval, line, pub 1722, BM, NPG. G.WHITE, 1727, hl with book, oval, mezz, BM, NPG. G.VERTUE, hl with book, line, for *Horae Lyricae*, 1742, BM, NPG.

WATTS, Richard (1529-1579) founder of almshouses at Rochester.
SC CHARLES EASTON, after contemporary bust, 1730, bust on monument, Rochester Cathedral.

WAYNFLEET or **WAINFLEET, William of (1395?-1486)** bishop of Winchester and founder of Magdalen College, Oxford.
P RICHARD GREENBURY, 1638, tql in robes, Magdalen College; version, New College, Oxford. UNKNOWN, hs, Magdalen College; version, New College.
SC UNKNOWN, tomb effigy, Winchester Cathedral.
W UNKNOWN, hs, Magdalen College.

WEBB or **WEBBE, George (1581-1642)** bishop of Limerick.
PR T.CROSS, tql, line, BM, V & A. T.SLATER, after T.Cross, tql, line, for *Practice of Quietness*, ed 1705, BM, NPG.

WEBB, John Richmond (1667?-1724) general.
PR J.FABER, sen, after M.Dahl, hl in armour, oval, mezz, BM, NPG.

WEBBE, George, see Webb.

WECKHERLIN, Georg Rudolph (1584-1653) under-secretary of state and poet.
PR W.FAITHORNE, after D.Mytens, hs, oval, line, NPG.

WEEVER, John (1576-1632) antiquary and poet.
PR T.CECILL, hl with skull, oval, line, for *Funeral Monuments*, 1631, BM, NPG.

WELBY, Henry (1552-1636) eccentric recluse.
PR W.MARSHALL, wl seated, aged 84, line, for *Life*, 1637, BM.

WELDON, Sir Anthony (d1649?) historical writer and courtier.
PR UNKNOWN, after Bullfinch, hl, oval, line, pub 1779, NPG.

WELDON, John (1676-1736) musician.
P UNKNOWN, (called Weldon), hs, Faculty of Music, Oxford.

WELLES, Lionel de Welles, 6th Baron (1405?-1461) soldier.
SC UNKNOWN, alabaster tomb effigy with wife, St Oswald's Church, Methley, Yorks.

WELLESLEY, Richard Colley, see 1st Baron Mornington.

WELTON, Richard (1671?-1726) nonjuring divine.
PR UNKNOWN, hs, oval, line, BM, NPG.

WENTWORTH, Henrietta Maria Wentworth, Baroness (1657?-1686) mistress of the Duke of Monmouth.
PR R.WILLIAMS, after Sir G.Kneller, wl in robes, mezz, BM, NPG.

WENTWORTH, Sir Thomas (1593-1641), see 1st Earl of Strafford.

WENTWORTH, Thomas (1672-1739), see 3rd Earl of Strafford.

WENTWORTH of Nettlestead, Thomas Wentworth, 1st Baron (1501-1555) lord chamberlain.
P Attrib JOHN BETTES, 1549, hl with staff of office, NPG 1851.
D Attrib HANS HOLBEIN, jun, before c1543, hs, chalks, Royal Coll.

WENTWORTH of Nettlestead, Thomas Wentworth, 2nd Baron (1525-1584) soldier and statesman.
P Attrib STEVEN VAN DER MEULEN, 1568, hl, NPG 1852.

WENTWORTH of Nettlestead, Sir Thomas, 4th Baron (1591-1667), see 1st Earl of Cleveland.

WESLEY, Richard Colley, see 1st Baron Mornington.

WESLEY, Samuel (1662-1735) divine and author.
PR N.PARR, hs, oval, line, BM, NPG. G.VERTUE, wl seated, line, for *Job*, 1736, NPG. UNKNOWN, tql, line, for *Maggots, or Poems on Several Subjects*, 1685, BM, NPG.

WEST, John, see 1st Earl De La Warr.

WEST, Richard (d1726) lawyer and playwright.
P Attrib JONATHAN RICHARDSON, c1725, tql in lord chancellor's robes, NPG 17.

WEST, Thomas, see 3rd Baron De La Warr.

WEST, William, see 1st Baron De La Warr.

WESTFALING, Herbert, see Westphaling.

WESTMORLAND, Henry Nevill(e), 5th Earl of (1525?-1563?) lieutenant-general of the north.
SC UNKNOWN, monumental effigy with two wives, Staindrop Church, Durham.

WESTMORLAND, John Fane, 7th Earl of (1682?-1762) soldier and statesman.
SC THOMAS ADY or ADYE, 1742, marble bust, V & A.

WESTMORLAND, Mildmay Fane, 2nd Earl of (1602-1665) lord-lieutenant of Northamptonshire.
P UNKNOWN, 1640, Emmanuel College, Cambridge.
PR W.HOLLAR, hl, oval, etch, BM, NPG. P.WILLIAMSON, after J.B.N., 1662, hl with map, oval, line, BM, NPG.

WESTMORLAND, Ralph Nevill(e), 1st Earl of (1364-1425) soldier and statesman.
MS UNKNOWN, wl kneeling with family, for *Neville Hours*, Latin, 1158, fol 27V, Bibliothèque Nationale, Paris.
SC UNKNOWN, alabaster tomb effigy with two wives, Staindrop Church, Durham, etch, B.Howlett, after C.A.Stothard, jun, NPG.

WESTFIELD, Thomas (1573-1644) bishop of Bristol.
SC UNKNOWN, effigy? on monument, Bristol Cathedral.

WESTON, Sir Richard, see 1st Earl of Portland.

WESTON, Sir Robert (1515?-1573) lord chancellor of Ireland.
SC SIR HENRY CHEERE, after contemporary portrait?, c1756, bronze bust, All Souls College, Oxford.

WESTON, Stephen (1665-1742) bishop of Exeter.
P THOMAS HUDSON, c1731, tql seated, Episcopal Palace, Exeter, engr G.White, 1731, mezz, BM, NPG.

WESTPHALING or **WESTFALING, Herbert (1533?-1602)** bishop of Hereford.
P UNKNOWN, 1601, tql with book, Christ Church, Oxford; versions, hl, Jesus College, Oxford, and Bishop's Palace, Hereford.
SC UNKNOWN, tomb effigy, Hereford Cathedral.

WETENHALL, Edward (1636-1713) bishop of Kilmore and Ardagh.
PR I.BECKETT, after J. van der Vaart, hs, oval, mezz, BM.

WEYMOUTH, Sir Thomas Thynne, 1st Viscount (1640-1714) statesman.
P SIR PETER LELY, tql, Lee Coll, Courtauld Institute, London. School of JOHN RILEY, hs, oval, Longleat, Wilts. WILLEM WISSING, c1682, tql in peer's robes, Longleat.
M Attrib NICHOLAS DIXON, after Sir Peter Lely, hs, oval, NPG L152 (17).

WHARTON, Anne, née Lee, Lady (1632?-1685) poet.
PR R.EARLOM, after Sir P.Lely, tql seated, with incorrect title 'Marchioness of Wharton', for *Houghton Gallery*, 1776, BM, NPG. NPG.

WHARTON, Sir George, 1st Bart (1617-1681) royalist and astrologer.
PR R.VAUGHAN, bust on pedestal, oval, line, for *Hemeroscopeion*, 1654, BM, NPG. T.CROSS, hs, oval, line, for *Calendarium Ecclesiasticum*, 1657, BM, NPG. D.LOGGAN, 1663, hs, aged 46, oval, line, BM, NPG. W.FAITHORNE, hs, oval, line, BM, NPG.

WHARTON, Henry (1664-1695) divine and author.
PR R.WHITE, after H.Tilson, hs, oval, line, for *Sermons*, 1698, BM, NPG.

WHARTON, Philip Wharton, 4th Baron (1613-1696) soldier and statesman.
P SIR ANTHONY VANDYCK, 1632, tql as shepherd, National Gallery of Art, Washington.
PR W.HOLLAR, hs, oval, etch, BM, NPG.

WHARTON, Philip Wharton, Duke of, (1698-1731) follower of the 'Old Pretender'.
D ROSALBA CARRIERA, hs, pastel, Royal Coll.
PR J.SIMON, after C.Jervas, hl in peer's robes, mezz, BM. G.VERTUE, after C.Jervas, hl in robes, line, for *Life*, 1732, BM, NPG.

WHARTON, Thomas (1614-1673) physician.
P UNKNOWN, c1650, hs, Royal College of Physicians, London.

WHARTON, Thomas Wharton, 1st Marquess (1648-1715) statesman.
P SIR GODFREY KNELLER, c1710, hl, the 'Kit-cat Club' portrait, NPG 3233. School of KNELLER, tql, NGI 474.

WHATELEY, William (1583-1639) puritan divine.
PR UNKNOWN, hs, oval, line, for *Prototypes*, 1647, BM, NPG.

WHELER, Sir George (1650-1723?) prebendary of Durham and traveller.
P UNKNOWN, hl, Library, Durham Cathedral.
PR W.BROMLEY, tql seated, line, for Surtees, *Hist of Durham*, 1816, BM, NPG.

WHETSTONE, Sir William (d1711) admiral.
P MICHAEL DAHL, c1707, tql, NMM, Greenwich.

WHICHCOTE, Benjamin (1609-1683) provost of King's College, Cambridge.
P MARY BEALE, 1682, hs, oval, Emmanuel College, Cambridge; version, Lambeth Palace, London.
PR R.WHITE, hs, oval, line, for *Discourses*, 1701, BM, NPG.

WHISTLER, Daniel (1619-1684) physician.
P UNKNOWN, c1660-70, hs, oval, Royal College of Physicians, London.

WHISTON, William (1667-1752) divine.
P After SARAH HOADLY, c1720?, hs, NPG 243.
SC UNKNOWN, (called Whiston), carved wooden head, NPG 733.
PR G.VERTUE, 1720, hl with book, line, BM, NPG. B.WILSON, hs, etch, for *Memoirs*, 1753, BM, NPG.

WHITAKER, Tobias (d1666) physician.
PR J.CHANTREY?, hs, etch, for *Elenchus . . . concerning Smallpox*, 1661, NPG.

WHITAKER, William (1548-1595) master of St John's College, Cambridge.
P UNKNOWN, hs with book, St John's College.
PR J.PAYNE, 1620, hl with book, oval, line, BM. PASSE, hl with book, line, for Holland, *Herwologia*, 1620, BM, NPG.

WHITBY, Daniel (1638-1726) prebendary of Salisbury.
PR M. VAN DER GUCHT, after E.Knight, hs, oval, line, for *Commentary on the New Testament*, 1700, BM, NPG.

WHITE, Francis (1564?-1638) bishop of Ely.
PR T.COCKSON, hl with book, oval, line, for *Reply to Jesuit Fisher*, 1624, BM, NPG, V & A. G.MOUNTIN, hl with book, oval, line, BM, NPG.

WHITE, Jeremiah (1629-1707) chaplain to Oliver Cromwell.
PR UNKNOWN, hl, line, for *Persuasive to Moderation*, 1708, BM, NPG.

WHITE, John (1570-1615) divine.
PR UNKNOWN, hl with book, oval, line, for *Works*, 1624, BM, NPG.

WHITE, Richard (1539-1611) jurist and historian.
SC LODOVICO LEONI, bronze medal, BM.

WHITE, Robert (1645-1703) draughtsman and engraver.
PR A.BANNERMAN, hs, oval with four others, line, for Walpole, *Catalogue of Engravers*, 1763, NPG.

WHITE, Sir Thomas (1492-1567) lord mayor of London and founder of St John's College, Oxford.
P UNKNOWN, tql, Merchant Taylors' Company, London; version, St John's College.

WHITE, Thomas (1550?-1624) founder of Sion College, London.
P UNKNOWN, hs, Sion College; version or copy, Bodleian Library, Oxford.

WHITE, Thomas (1593-1676) philosopher and friend of Thomas Hobbes.
PR G.VERTUE, 1713, hs, oval, line, with wrong birth and death dates, BM, NPG.

WHITE, Thomas (1628-1698) bishop of Peterborough.
P UNKNOWN, hs, oval, Magdalen College, Oxford. UNKNOWN, hs, Bishop's Palace, Peterborough.
G UNKNOWN, 'The Seven Bishops Committed to the Tower in 1688', oil, NPG 79.
SC GEORGE BOWER, 1688, silver medal, one of seven bishops each in a medallion profile, NPG 152A.

WHITEHEAD, David (1492?-1571) chaplain to Queen Anne Boleyn.
PR PASSE, hl, line, for Holland, *Herwologia*, 1620, BM, NPG.

WHITELOCKE, Bulstrode (1605-1675) lawyer and diplomat.
P UNKNOWN, 1634, hl, NPG 4499. UNKNOWN, c1650?, hs, oval, NPG 254.
SC ABRAHAM and THOMAS SIMON, 1653, silver medal, BM.
PR W.FAITHORNE, hl in armour, oval, line, for *Piscatoris Poemata*, 1656, BM, NPG. R.GAYWOOD, hs, oval, etch, BM, NPG.

WHITELOCKE, Sir James (1570-1632) judge.
P UNKNOWN, c1632, hs in robes, NPG 4498.
SC UNKNOWN, alabaster tomb effigy with wife, St Mary's Church, Fawley, Bucks.

WHITGIFT, John (1530?-1604) archbishop of Canterbury.
P UNKNOWN, c1583, hl, Lambeth Palace, London; version, Trinity College, Cambridge. UNKNOWN, c1598, tql, University Library, Cambridge; copy, hs, NPG 660.
SC UNKNOWN, alabaster tomb effigy, St John the Baptist Church, Croydon, Surrey.

WHITHORNE, Thomas (fl 1571-1590) musical amateur.
PR UNKNOWN, hs, aged 40, oval, woodcut, for *Duos*, 1590, BM, NPG.

WHIMORE, Sir George (d1654) lord mayor of London.
P UNKNOWN, tql, Haberdashers' Company, London.

WHITSON, John (1557-1629) merchant and adventurer.
P UNKNOWN, tql?, Trustees of the Bristol Municipal Charities.
SC UNKNOWN, tomb effigy, St Nicholas' Church, Bristol.
PR E.McINNES, tql, mezz, NPG.

WHITTINGTON, Richard (d1423) mayor of London.
MS UNKNOWN, c1445-50, death-bed scene, for 'Almshouse Ordinances', The Mercers' Company, London.

WHITWORTH, Charles Whitworth, Baron (1675-1725) diplomat.
P JACK ELLYS, c1722, tql seated with young boy, Knole (NT), Kent.
SC L.F.ROUBILIAC, 1757, marble bust, Trinity College, Cambridge.

WIDDRINGTON, Sir Thomas (d1664) speaker of the House of Commons.
D T.ATHOW, hl in robes, wash, Sutherland Coll, Ashmolean Museum, Oxford.

WIGAN, John (1696-1739) physician and author.
P UNKNOWN, tql, NPG 4588.

WILCOCKS, Joseph (1673-1756) bishop of Gloucester and Rochester.
P JOHN VANDERBANK, 1737, tql, Magdalen College, Oxford.
PR R.GRAVES, hl with badge of the Bath, line, BM, NPG. J.SIMON, after E.Seeman, tql seated, mezz, BM, NPG.

WILDE or WYLDE, Sir William, 1st Bart (1611?-1679) judge.
D T.ATHOW, after J.M.Wright, wl in robes, wash, Sutherland Coll, Ashmolean Museum, Oxford.

WILDMAN, Sir John (1621-1693) politician.
M JOHN HOSKINS, (called Wildman), 1647, hs, oval, V & A.
PR W.HOLLAR, (called Wildman), 1653, hs, oval, etch, BM.

WILFORD, Sir James (1516?-1550) defender of Haddington.
P UNKNOWN, 1547, tql in armour, Coughton Court (NT), Warwicks; copy? attrib John Belkamp, hs in armour, oval, Knole (NT), Kent.

WILKINS, David (1685?-1745) scholar.
P J.COLE, hl with book, Society of Antiquaries, London. UNKNOWN, hs, as young man, oval, Lambeth Palace, London.

WILKINS, John (1614-1672) bishop of Chester.
P MARY BEALE, hs, oval, Wadham College, Oxford, engr A.Blooteling, line, BM, NPG. M.BEALE, tql seated, Bodleian Library, Oxford; version, Royal Society, London.

WILKS, Robert (1665?-1732) actor.
PR J.FABER, jun, after J.Ellys, tql, mezz, BM, NPG. UNKNOWN, tql with snuff-box, oval, mezz, BM, NPG.

WILLES, Sir John (1685-1761) chief justice of common pleas.
P Studio of THOMAS HUDSON, c1744, tql seated in robes, NPG 484.
PR J.FABER, jun, after T.Hudson, 1742, tql in robes, mezz, BM, NPG. G.VERTUE, 1744, after J.B.Vanloo, tql seated in robes, line, BM, NPG.

WILLETT, Andrew (1562-1621) prebendary of Ely.
PR UNKNOWN, hl, oval, line, for *Synopsis Papismi*, ed 1630, BM, NPG.

WILLIAM I (1027-1087) 'the Conqueror', king of England.
SC Attrib THEODORIC, 1068, silver penny, profile head, NPG 4051. Attrib THEODORIC, c1068–71, silver penny, head, NPG 4052. Various coins, BM. Wax seal, BL.
T UNKNOWN, 'Bayeux Tapestry', Bayeux, France.

WILLIAM II (d1100) king of England, called Rufus.
SC Various coins, BM. Wax seal, BL.

WILLIAM of Nassau (1626-1650) Prince of Orange and father of William III.
P SIR ANTHONY VANDYCK, c1641, wl with wife, Princess Mary, Rijksmuseum, Amsterdam; copy of William alone, hl, NPG 964. GERARD HONTHORST, c1647, wl in armour, Rijksmuseum.
SC ROMBOUT VERHULST, marble bust, Mauritshuis, The Hague.

WILLIAM III (1650-1702) king of England, Scotland and Ireland.
P GERARD HONTHORST, 1652, wl as infant with his mother, Raadhuis, Breda, The Netherlands. G.HONTHORST, 1653, wl with his Aunt Maria, Mauritshuis, The Hague. CORNELIUS JOHNSON, 1657, tql, Knole (NT), Kent. ABRAHAM RAGUINEAU, 1661, hl in armour, oval, Mauritshuis. ADRIAEN HANNEMAN, 1664, tql in armour, Royal Coll. JAN DE BAEN, c1668, wl in classical dress, NPG L152 (7). CASPAR NETSCHER, c1677?, wl in armour, Rijksmuseum, Amsterdam. SIR PETER LELY, 1677, tql in armour, Syon House, Brentford, Middx; copy, NPG 1902. WILLEM WISSING, 1685, tql in armour, Royal Coll. SIR GODFREY KNELLER, c1690, wl in state robes, Royal Coll. SIR G.KNELLER, c1695-1700, hl in Garter robes, Royal Coll. UNKNOWN, c1690-1700, wl in armour on horseback, NPG 1026. SIR G.KNELLER, 1701, wl in armour on horseback, Royal Coll. UNKNOWN, c1690 foll, wl seated in robes, NPG 4153.
M CHARLES BOIT, c1690-99, hs, oval, NPG 1737.
SC JAN BLOMMENDAEL, 1676, statue, Mauritshuis. ROMBOUT VERHULST, 1683, bust, Mauritshuis. J.CAVALIER, 1690, medallion, profile bust, V & A. J.BLOMMENDAEL, 1699, bust, Mauritshuis. Attrib MRS GOLDSMITH, death mask, Westminster Abbey, London. Various medals, BM.

WILLIAM, Duke of Gloucester, see Gloucester.

WILLIAM de Valence, see titular Earl of Pembroke.

WILLIAMS, Daniel (1643?-1716) nonconformist divine and benefactor.
P UNKNOWN, hs, oval, Dr Williams's Library, London, engr J.Caldwall, line, NPG.

WILLIAMS, John (1582-1650) archbishop of York and lord keeper.
P GILBERT JACKSON, 1625, wl in robes, St John's College, Cambridge. UNKNOWN, wl in robes, Westminster Abbey Library, London.
SC UNKNOWN, kneeling tomb effigy, Llandegai Church, Gwynedd, Wales.
PR F.DELARAM, c1621, hl, oval, line, BM, V & A. W.HOLLAR, wl, etch, BM. UNKNOWN, pre c1625, hl, oval, line, BM, NPG.

WILLIAMS, John (1636?-1709) bishop of Chichester.
P SIMON? VERELST, tql seated, Lambeth Palace, London.

WILLIAMS, Thomas (1513?-1566) speaker of the House of Commons.
SC UNKNOWN, brass effigy, Harford Church, Devon.

WILLIAMS, Sir William, 1st Bart (1634-1700) speaker of the House of Commons.
P UNKNOWN, (after type of c1680–81), hl in robes, Palace of Westminster, London.

WILLIAMS, William Peere (1664-1736) law reporter.
PR G.VERTUE, after Sir G.Kneller, hs, oval, line, for *Reports*, 1740, BM, NPG.

WILLIAMSON, Sir Joseph (1633-1701) statesman and diplomat.
P Attrib SIR PETER LELY?, c1660-70, tql, Queen's College, Oxford. Style of LELY, c1660-70, hs, oval, NPG 1100. SIR GODFREY KNELLER, tql, Royal Society, London.

WILLIS, Browne (1682-1760) antiquary.
PR M.TYSON, after M.Dahl, hs, etch, for Nichols, *Literary Anecdotes*, vol 8, 1814, BM, NPG.

WILLIS, Richard (1664-1734) bishop of Winchester.
P MICHAEL DAHL, tql seated, Bishop's Palace, Salisbury, engr J.Simon, mezz, BM, NPG.
SC SIR HENRY CHEERE, 1734, tomb effigy, Winchester Cathedral.

WILLIS, Thomas (1621-1675) physician.
P UNKNOWN, hl, oval, Bodleian Library, Oxford. UNKNOWN, hl, Royal College of Physicians, London.
PR D.LOGGAN, hs, oval, line, for *Pharmaceutice Rationalis*, 1674, BM, NPG.

WILLOUGHBY, Francis (1635-1672) naturalist.
SC L.F.ROUBILIAC, 1751, marble bust, Trinity College, Cambridge; terracotta model, BM.
PR LIZARS, hs with book, line, for William Jardine, *The Naturalist's Library*.

WILLOUGHBY DE ERESBY, Peregrine Bertie, Lord (1555-1601) soldier.
P UNKNOWN, wl, Drummond Castle, Tayside region, Scotland; version, attrib Hieronimo Custodis, hl, Rockingham Castle, Northants. UNKNOWN, wl in armour, DoE, The Armouries, Tower of London.
M NICHOLAS HILLIARD, c1600, oval, V & A.

WILLOUGHBY of Parham, Francis Willoughby, 5th Baron (1613?-1666) parliamentary general.
PR UNKNOWN, hl, line, for Ricraft, *Survey of England's Champions*, 1647, BM, NPG.

WILLS, Sir Charles (1666-1741) general.
PR J.SIMON, after M.Dahl, hs in breastplate, oval, mezz, BM, NPG.

WILMINGTON, Spencer Compton, 1st Earl of (1673?-1743) statesman.
P SIR GODFREY KNELLER, c1710, hl, 'Kit-cat Club' portrait, NPG 3234. SIR G.KNELLER, c1725, tql with ribbon and star of Bath, Castle Ashby, Northants.

WILMOT, Henry, see 1st Earl of Rochester.

WILMOT, John, see 2nd Earl of Rochester.

WILSON, Edward (d1694) dandy.
PR UNKNOWN, wl, stipple, BM, NPG.

WILSON, John (1595-1674) lutenist and professor of music at Oxford.
P ROBERT FISHER, 1655, hs in robes, Faculty of Music, Oxford.

WILSON, Thomas (1525?-1581) secretary of state and scholar.
P UNKNOWN, c1575, tql, NPG 3799.

WILSON, Thomas (1563-1622) divine.
PR T.CROSS, hl, oval, line, for *Christian Dictionary*, 1655, BM, NPG, V & A.

WILSON, Thomas (1663-1755) bishop of Sodor and Man.
PR G.VERTUE, 1726, after J.Fellows, hl, oval, line, BM, NPG. T.NOVAL, after van der Mühlen, tql seated, line, pub 1752, BM. J.SIMON, after C.Philips, tql seated with map, mezz, BM.

WILTSHIRE, Thomas Boleyn, Earl of (1477-1539) lord privy seal.
SC UNKNOWN, brass monumental effigy, wl, Hever Church, Kent, line engr, NPG.

WIMBLEDON, Sir Edward Cecil, Viscount (1572-1638) general.
P M.J.VAN MIEREVELDT, 1610, hs in armour, NPG L164. M.J.VAN MIEREVELDT, 1631, hs, NPG 4514. M.J.VAN MIEREVELDT, tql, Walker Art Gallery, Liverpool.
PR S.PASSE, 1618, hs, oval, line, BM, NPG.

WINCH, Sir Humphrey (1555?-1625) judge.
SC UNKNOWN, bust on monument, St Mary's Church, Everton, Beds.

WINCHCOMBE or SMALLWOOD or NEWBURY, John (d1520) clothier.
SC UNKNOWN, brass effigy with wife, St Nicholas Church, Newbury, Berks.

WINCHESTER, John (d1460?) bishop of Moray.
SC UNKNOWN, tomb effigy, Elgin Cathedral, Morayshire, Scotland.

WINCHESTER, John Paulet, 5th Marquess of (1598-1675) royalist.
PR W.HOLLAR, hs, oval, etch, BM, NPG. UNKNOWN, tql in armour, etch, BM, NPG.

WINCHESTER, Sir William Paulet or Poulet, 1st Marquess of (1485?-1572) statesman.
P UNKNOWN, tql with Garter George and staff of office, NPG 65.

WINCHILSEA, Anne Finch, Countess of (d1720) poet.
M LAWRENCE CROSSE, hs, oval, NPG 4692.

WINCHILSEA, Daniel Finch, 7th Earl of (1647-1730) statesman.
P SIR GODFREY KNELLER, c1720?, head in three poses, NPG 3910. Attrib JONATHAN RICHARDSON, 1726, tql in earl's robes, NPG 3622. Attrib JOHN RILEY, tql Gorhambury, Herts.
PR J.HOUBRAKEN, after Sir G.Kneller, hl in peer's robes as Earl of Nottingham, oval, line, BM, NPG.

WINDEBANK, Sir Francis (1582-1646) secretary of state.
PR R.COOPER, tql, stipple, NPG. G.GLOVER, hl, oval, satiric print with another of Baron Finch of Fordwich, line, 1641, BM. P.PAUL, hl, etch, NPG.

WINDSOR, Thomas, see 1st Earl of Plymouth.

WING, Tycho (1696-1750) astrologer.
P JOHN VANDERBANK, c1727-1731, hl with globe, Stationers' Hall, London, engr G.White, mezz, NPG.

WING, Vincent (1619-1668) astronomer.
PR T.CROSS, hl with compass, oval, line, for *Astronomia Britannica*, 1652, BM, NPG, V & A.

WINGFIELD, Sir Anthony (1485?-1552) comptroller of the household.
PR MRS D.TURNER, hs, etch, BM, NPG.

WINNINGTON, Sir Francis (1634-1700) lawyer.
M UNKNOWN, c1670, hs, oval, NPG 305.

WINNINGTON, Thomas (1696-1746) politician.
P J.B.VANLOO, wl, Worcester Corporation.
M C.F.ZINCKE, hs, oval, NPG 85.
G WILLIAM HOGARTH, 'The Holland House Group', oil, c1738-39, Ickworth (NT), Suffolk.
SC L.F.ROUBILIAC, marble bust, Stanford Church, Worcs.
PR UNKNOWN, hs, oval, stipple, for Coxe, *Memoirs of Lord Walpole*, 1802, BM, NPG.

WINSTANLEY, Hamlet (1698-1756) painter and engraver.
PR J.FABER, jun, 1731, after H.Winstanley, tql seated at easel, mezz, BM, NPG.

WINSTANLEY, William (1628?-1698) poet and compiler.
PR UNKNOWN, tql with books, oval, line, for *Royal Martyrology*, 1662, BM. F.H. VAN HOVE, bust on pedestal, line, for *Lives of the Poets*, 1687, BM, V & A.

WINTER, Sir Edward (1622?-1686) agent of East India Company at Madras.
SC UNKNOWN, 1686, bust on monument, St Mary's Church, Battersea, London.

WINTER, Robert (d1606) Gunpowder Plot conspirator.
G CRISPIN VAN DE PASSE, 'Gunpowder Plot Conspirators, 1605', line engr, NPG 334A.

WINTER, Thomas (1572-1606) Gunpowder Plot conspirator.
G CRISPIN VAN DE PASSE, 'Gunpowder Plot Conspirators, 1605', line engr, NPG 334A.

WINTHROP, John (1587?-1649) governor of Massachusetts.
P UNKNOWN, hs, oval, The American Antiquarian Society, Worcester, USA; version, State House, Boston, USA.
M UNKNOWN, hs, Massachusetts Historical Society, Boston, USA.

WINTON, George Seton, 3rd Earl (1584-1650) royalist.
P UNKNOWN, 1628, tql, Traquair House, Borders region, Scotland.

WINWOOD, Sir Ralph (1563-1617) secretary of state and diplomat.
P Attrib ABRAHAM BLYENBERCH, 1613, tql, Buccleuch Estates, Selkirk, Scotland.
PR H.HONDIUS, c1606-10, hs, oval, line, BM, NPG, V & A.

WISE, Henry (1653-1738) gardener.
P SIR GODFREY KNELLER, c1715, hl, oval, Royal Coll.

WISEMAN, Richard (1622?-1676) surgeon.
P UNKNOWN, hl, oval, Royal College of Surgeons, London.
M SAMUEL COOPER, 1660, hs, oval, Belvoir Castle, Leics.

WISHART, George (1513?-1546) Scottish reformer.
P UNKNOWN, 1543, hl, SNPG 580.

WISHART, Sir James (d1723) admiral.
P MICHAEL DAHL, before c1704, tql, NMM, Greenwich.
M J.FABER, jun, 1704, hs?, pen and ink, V & A.
PR J.FABER, jun, 1722, after M.Dahl, tql, mezz, NPG.

WISHART, Robert (d1316) bishop of Glasgow.
SC UNKNOWN, tomb effigy, Glasgow Cathedral.

WISSING. Willem or **William (1656-1687)** portrait painter.
PR J.SMITH, after W.Wissing, hs, oval, mezz, BM, NPG.

WITHER(S), George **(1588-1667)** poet and pamphleteer.
PR R.COOPER, tql, aged 21, oval, copy from W.Hole, for *Abuses Stript and Wipt*, 1613, stipple, BM, NPG. F.DELARAM, hl, oval, line, BM, V & A. J.PAYNE, hs, oval, line, for *Emblemes*, 1635, BM, NPG. UNKNOWN, hl in armour, profile, oval, line, BM.

WOGAN, Sir Charles **(1698?-1752?)** Jacobite soldier of fortune.
P UNKNOWN, hl, NGI 395.

WOLLASTON, William **(1660-1724)** moral philosopher.
P After MICHAEL DAHL?, tql seated with book, Royal Coll. UNKNOWN, Sidney Sussex College, Cambridge.
SC J.M.RYSBRACK, *c*1733, marble bust, Royal Coll.
PR G.VERTUE, hs, oval, line, for *Religion of Nature*, 1731, BM, NPG.

WOLSEY, Thomas **(1475?-1530)** cardinal and statesman.
P UNKNOWN, 16th century, tql in robes, profile, NPG 32; version, Sampson Strong, Christ Church, Oxford.
D JACQUES LE BOUCQ, (after type of *c*1515-20), hs, Bibliothèque d'Arras, France.

WOLSTENHOLME, Sir John **(1562-1639)** merchant adventurer.
SC NICHOLAS STONE, 1641, tomb effigy, St John the Evangelist, Stanmore, Middx.

WOOD, Anthony **(1632-1695)** antiquary and historian.
D ROSE, 1677, bust on pedestal, w/c and wash, Bodleian Library, Oxford.
PR M.BURGHERS, tql in architectural frame, line, for *Athenae Oxonienses*, BM, NPG, V & A.

WOOD, Thomas **(1661-1722)** legal writer.
PR M. VAN DER GUCHT, hs, oval, line, for *Institutes of the Laws of England*, 1724, BM, NPG.

WOOD, Sir William **(1609-1691)** archer and author.
PR R.CLAMP, tql with shield, oval, stipple, for Harding, *Biographical Mirror*, 1793, BM, NPG.

WOODALL, John **(1556?-1643)** surgeon.
PR G.GLOVER, hs, oval, line, for *Surgeon's Mate*, 1639, BM, NPG.

WOODFORD, Samuel **(1636-1700)** divine and poet.
M THOMAS FLATMAN, 1661, hs, oval, Fitzwilliam Museum, Cambridge.

WOODROFFE, Benjamin **(1638-1711)** divine.
P UNKNOWN, hs, Worcester College, Oxford.
PR R.WHITE, hs, *ad vivum*, oval, line, for *Examinis et examinantis Examen*, 1700, BM.

WOODVILLE, Anthony, see 2nd Earl Rivers.

WOODWARD, John **(1665-1728)** geologist and physician.
P UNKNOWN, hs as older man, oval, Department of Geology, Cambridge University.
SC After SILVANUS BEVAN, Wedgwood medallion, profile, Wedgwood Museum, Barlaston, Staffs.
PR W.HUMPHREY, hs, oval, mezz, pub 1774, BM, NPG.

WOOLSTON, Thomas **(1676-1733)** freethinker.
PR J. VAN DER GUCHT, after B.Dandridge, hl, oval, line, BM, NPG.

WOOTTON, John **(1686?-1765)** painter of sporting subjects and landscapes.
D Self-portrait, head, chalk, BM.
G GAWEN HAMILTON, 'A Conversation of Virtuosis . . . at the King Arms', oil, 1735, NPG 1384.

WORCESTER, Charles Somerset, 1st Earl of **(1460?-1526)** soldier and diplomat.

P UNKNOWN, (posthumous), tql with staff of office, Badminton House, Avon.
SC UNKNOWN, tomb effigy with wife, St George's Chapel, Windsor, Berks.

WORCESTER, Edward Somerset, 4th Earl of **(1553-1628)** statesman.
P FREDERICK ZUCCARO, tql with Garter George, Gorhambury, Herts, version, Badminton House, Avon, engr S.Passe, 1618, hl, oval, line, BM, NPG.

WORCESTER, Edward Somerset, 2nd Marquess of **(1601-1667)** royalist and scientist.
P UNKNOWN, tql in armour, Badminton House, Avon.
G UNKNOWN, tql in classical dress with wife and child, oil, Badminton.

WORCESTER, Henry Somerset, 1st Marquess of **(1577?-1646)** royalist.
P CORNELIUS JOHNSON, tql, Badminton House, Avon. UNKNOWN, tql, Badminton, engr T.A.Dean, as after C.Jonson, stipple, for Lodge, *Portraits*, 1827, BM, NPG.

WORCESTER, John Tiptoft, Earl of **(1427?-1470)** soldier and statesman.
SC UNKNOWN, tomb effigy with wives, Ely Cathedral.

WORCESTER, William Somerset, 3rd Earl of **(1526-1589)** statesman and soldier.
P UNKNOWN, 1569, tql in armour, Badminton House, Avon. UNKNOWN, 1581, tql in armour, Badminton.
M Attrib NICHOLAS HILLIARD, *c*1575, hs in armour, oval, Badminton.
PR M.GHEERAERTS, sen, 'Procession of Garter Knights, 1576', etch, BM.

WORSDALE, James **(1692?-1767)** portrait painter.
PR W.DICKINSON, after R.E.Pine, tql with beehive, mezz, pub 1769, BM, NPG.

WORTLEY, Sir Francis, 1st Bart **(1591-1652)** poet.
P UNKNOWN, tql in armour, Tower of London.
PR A.HERTOCHS, hl in armour, oval, line, BM, NPG.

WOTTON, Sir Henry **(1568-1639)** diplomat and poet.
P UNKNOWN, tql seated, Eton College, Berks; copy, NPG 1482.
PR UNKNOWN, tql seated, aged 72, line, for *State of Christendom*, 1657, BM, NPG.

WOTTON, Nicholas **(1497?-1567)** secretary of state and dean of Canterbury.
P UNKNOWN, tql, The Deanery, Canterbury.
SC UNKNOWN, kneeling effigy, Canterbury Cathedral.

WRAY, Sir Christopher **(1524-1592)** judge.
P UNKNOWN, (after type of 1582), hs in robes, NPG 1484.

WREN, Christopher **(1591-1658)** dean of Windsor.
P UNKNOWN, tql in robes, Lambeth Palace, London, engr G. van der Gucht, hs oval, line, for *Parentalia*, 1750, BM, NPG.

WREN, Sir Christopher **(1632-1723)** architect and scientist.
P Attrib JOHN CLOSTERMAN, *c*1695, tql seated, Royal Society, London, engr E.Kirkhall, as after J.Closterman, hs, oval, line, BM. SIR GODFREY KNELLER, 1711, tql seated with plans of St Paul's, NPG 113. ANTONIO VERRIO, SIR G.KNELLER and SIR JAMES THORNHILL, wl seated, Sheldonian theatre, Oxford.
SC EDWARD PIERCE, 1673, marble bust, Ashmolean Museum, Oxford. DAVID LE MARCHAND, *c*1723, relief ivory portrait medallion, profile, NPG 4500. UNKNOWN, 1723, plaster death mask, All Souls College, Oxford. G.C.GAAB, copper medal, profile bust, BM.

WREN, Christopher (1675-1747) son of Sir Christopher and biographer.
PR J.FABER, jun, 1750, hs, oval, mezz, for *Parentalia*, 1750, BM, NPG.

WREN, Matthew (1585-1667) bishop of Ely.
P UNKNOWN, hs, oval, Pembroke College, Cambridge, engr G. van der Gucht, line, for *Parentalia*, 1750, BM, NPG.

WRIGHT, Christopher (1570?-1605) conspirator in the Gunpowder Plot.
G CRISPIN VAN DE PASSE, 'Gunpowder Plot Conspirators, 1605', line engr, NPG 334A.

WRIGHT, John (1568?-1605) conspirator in the Gunpowder Plot.
G CRISPIN VAN DE PASSE, 'Gunpowder Plot Conspirators, 1605', line engr, NPG 334A.

WRIGHT, Sir Nathan (1654-1721) lord keeper.
P UNKNOWN, hs in robes, oval, Inner Temple, London. UNKNOWN, wl in robes, on loan to Royal Courts of Justice, London.
SC UNKNOWN, c1728, statue with son on monument, Gayhurst Church, Bucks.
PR R.WHITE, hl in robes, *ad vivum*, oval, line, BM.

WRIGHT, Peter (1603-1651) Jesuit.
PR C.GALLE, hl with knife in breast, line, BM.

WRIGHT, Robert (1560-1643) bishop of Lichfield and Coventry.
P UNKNOWN, c1632, hl, Trinity College, Oxford; version, Wadham College, Oxford.

WRIGHT, Sir Robert (d1689) judge.
PR R.WHITE, after J.Riley, hs in robes, oval, line, BM, NPG.

WRIGHT, Samuel (1683-1746) dissenting divine.
P UNKNOWN, hl, oval, Dr Williams's Library, London.

WRIOTHESLEY, Elizabeth, see Countess of Southampton.

WRIOTHESLEY, Henry (1545-1581), see 2nd Earl of Southampton.

WRIOTHESLEY, Henry (1573-1624), see 3rd Earl of Southampton.

WRIOTHESLEY, Thomas (1505-1550), see 1st Earl of Southampton.

WRIOTHESLEY, Thomas (1607-1667), see 4th Earl of Southampton.

WROTH, Mary, née Sidney, Lady (fl 1621) author of *Urania*.
P Attrib JOHN DE CRITZ, sen, (called Lady Mary), c1620, wl with stringed musical instrument, Penshurst, Kent.

WYAT or WYATT, Sir Henry (d1537) courtier.
P HANS HOLBEIN, jun, c1527-28, hl, The Louvre, Paris; copy, NGI 370.

WYATT, Sir Thomas (1503?-1542) poet.
P After HANS HOLBEIN, jun (type of c1640), hs, profile, oval, NPG 2809; version, Bodleian Library, Oxford. After H.HOLBEIN, (type of c1648), hs, profile, oval, NPG 1035.
D H.HOLBEIN, c1535, hs, chalks, Royal Coll.
PR Attrib H.HOLBEIN, hs, profile, oval, woodcut, for Leland, *Naeniae*, 1542, BL.

WYATT, Sir Thomas (1521?-1554) conspirator.
P UNKNOWN, (after type of c1545-50), head, profile, oval, NPG 3331.

WYCHE, Sir Cyril (1632?-1707) statesman and scientist.
P UNKNOWN, c1693, tql NPG 1422.

WYCHERLEY, William (1640-1716) dramatist.
P After SIR PETER LELY?, c1668, hs, NPG 880. THOMAS MURRAY, c1700, hs, University of London Library. UNKNOWN, hl, oval, Knole (NT), Kent.
M Attrib LAWRENCE CROSSE, hs, oval, NPG L152(18).

WYCK, John (1652-1700) painter.
PR J.FABER, jun, 1730, after Sir G.Kneller, 1685, hl, oval, mezz, BM.

WYKEHAM, William of (1324-1404) bishop of Winchester and founder of New College, Oxford.
MS UNKNOWN, late 14th century, wl with eleven other benefactors, Ms, New College, Oxford.
SC UNKNOWN, alabaster tomb effigy, Winchester Cathedral.
W After attrib HEREBRIGHT OF COLOGNE, c1393, wl with Virgin and child, modern copy, Winchester College, Hants.

WYLDE, Sir William, see Wilde.

WYNDHAM, Sir Hugh (1603?-1684) judge.
P J.M.WRIGHT, c1670-74, wl in robes, Guildhall Library, London.
SC JOHN VAN NOST, c1684-92, statue, St Nicholas Church, Silton, Dorset.

WYNDHAM, Sir Wadham (1610-1688) judge.
P J.M.WRIGHT, c1670-74, wl in robes, Lincoln's Inn, London.

WYNDHAM, Sir William, 3rd Bart (1687-1740) politician and chancellor of the exchequer.
P SIR GODFREY KNELLER, 1714, tql in robes, Petworth House (NT), W Sussex. Attrib JONATHAN RICHARDSON, c1713-14, tql seated in robes, NPG 4447. SIR G.KNELLER and JOHN WOOTTON, 1715, wl on horseback, Petworth.
G SIR G.KNELLER, family group, c1714?, Petworth.

WYNDHAM of Finglass, Thomas Wyndham, Baron (1681-1745) lord chancellor of Ireland.
P ISAAC SEEMAN, 1739, tql in robes with wand of office, on loan to Maidstone County Hall. UNKNOWN, tql in peer's robes, Wadham College, Oxford.

WYNN of Gwydir, Sir John, 1st Bart (1553-1626) antiquary.
PR R.VAUGHAN, hl, oval, line, BM. W.SHARP, tql, line, for D.Barrington, *Miscellanies*, 1781, BM, NPG.

WYNN of Gwydir, Sir Richard, 2nd Bart (1588-1649) groom of the bedchamber to Charles I.
PR F.BARTOLOZZI, after C.Johnson, hl, line, for Pennant, *Tour in Wales*, 1784, BM, NPG.

WYNN, Sir Watkin Williams, 3rd Bart (1693?-1749) Jacobite.
P After MICHAEL DAHL, (type of c1729), tql, NPG 2614. Attrib THOMAS HUDSON, c1734-40, tql, Jesus College, Oxford, engr J.Faber, mezz, NPG.
G JOHN WOOTTON, wl with Duke of Beaufort and grooms, Badminton House, Avon.
SC J.M.RYSBRACK, 1754, effigy on monument, Ruabon Church, Wrexham, Clwyd.
PR J.ABERRY, 1753, after T.Hudson, tql, etch, NPG.

WYNNE, John (1667-1743) bishop of St Asaph and Bath and Wells.
P UNKNOWN, hl with book, Jesus College, Oxford. UNKNOWN, hl, National Museum of Wales, Cardiff. UNKNOWN, Bishop's Palace, Wells.

Y

YALE, Elihu (1648-1721) governor of East India Company at Madras and benefactor of Yale University.

P ENOCH SEEMAN, wl, Yale University Art Gallery, New Haven, USA.

YARMOUTH, Robert Paston, 1st Earl of (1631-1683) friend of Charles II.

PR P. VAN DER BANK, hl in armour, oval, line, BM, NPG. B.READING, hl in armour, oval, line, NPG.

YELVERTON, Sir Christopher (1536-1612) judge.

P UNKNOWN, 1602, hs in robes, Gray's Inn, London.

YELVERTON, Sir William (1400?-1472?) judge.

SC UNKNOWN, brass effigy with wife, St Mary's Church, Rougham, Norfolk.

YONGE, John (1463-1526) bishop of Callipoli.

SC UNKNOWN, brass effigy, New College Chapel, Oxford.

YONGE, John (1467-1516) master of the rolls and diplomat.

SC PIETRO TORRIGIANO, c1516, tomb effigy, Public Record Office, London; plaster cast of head, NPG 1585.

YONGE, Thomas, see Young.

YONGE, Sir William, 4th Bart (d1755) politician.

P JOHN VANDERBANK, wl in robes of Order of the Bath, Sudbury Hall (NT), Derbys.

YORK, Anne Hyde, Duchess of (1637-1671) wife of James, Duke of York, later James II, and mother of Mary II and Queen Anne.

P SIR PETER LELY, c1661–62, wl seated (marriage portrait?), SNPG 1179. SIR P.LELY, c1662, tql seated, Royal Coll. SIR P.LELY, c1663, tql seated with husband, Petworth (NT), W Sussex;

version, NPG 5077. SIR P.LELY, c1662–66, wl seated, Royal Coll. After SIR P.LELY, c1670, hl, oval, NPG 241; version, tql seated, Knole (NT), Kent.

G SIR P.LELY and BENEDETTO GENNARI, family group, oil, c1674, Royal Coll.

YORK, Edmund de Langley, 1st Duke of, see EDMUND.

YORK, Margaret, see MARGARET.

YORK and ALBANY, Ernest Augustus, Duke of (1674-1728) fifth son of Ernest Augustus, elector of Hanover, and brother of George I.

P UNKNOWN, after J.Simon?, hs in armour, Royal Coll.

G UNKNOWN, 'Royal Hunting Party at Göhrde, oil, 1725, Royal Coll.

PR J.SIMON, 1718, hl in armour, oval, mezz, BM.

YORKE, James (fl 1640) heraldic writer.

PR T.RAWLYNS, hl, oval, line, for *Union of Honour*, 1641, BM, NPG.

YORKE, Philip, see 1st Earl of Hardwicke.

YOUNG, Edward (1683-1765) poet.

P JOSEPH HIGHMORE, 1754, hl, oval, All Souls College, Oxford.

YOUNG, John (1514-1580) master of Pembroke Hall, Cambridge.

P UNKNOWN, 1579, hl, Old Schools, Cambridge.

YOUNG, Sir Peter (1544-1628) tutor to James I and Charles I.

P UNKNOWN, 1622, tql, SNPG 627.

YOUNG or YONGE, Thomas (1507-1568) archbishop of York.

SC UNKNOWN, effigy? on monument, York Minster.

Z

ZINCKE, Christian Frederick (1684?-1767) miniature painter.
D WILLIAM HOARE, 1752, hl, chalks, BM.
PR J.FABER, jun, after H.Hysing, tql with wife, mezz, BM, NPG.

ZOUCHE of Harringworth, Edward la Zouche, 11th Baron (1556?-1625) statesman.
P UNKNOWN, c1612, tql, Parham Park, W Sussex. Attrib DANIEL MYTENS, c1618, wl seated, Royal Coll.

ZOUCHE, Richard (1590?-1661) judge.
P Attrib CORNELIUS JOHNSON, 1620, hs, NPG 5056.

ZUCCARO, ZUCHARO or **ZUCCHERO, Federigo (d1609)** painter.
P Attrib FRANCESCO POURBUS, hs?, Uffizi, Florence.

ZUYLESTEIN, Frederick Nassau, see 3rd Earl of Rochford.

ZUYLESTEIN, William Henry, see 1st Earl of Rochford.

ZUYLESTEIN, William Nassau, see 2nd Earl of Rochford.